New Practical Dictionary
for Crossword Puzzles

NEW PRACTICAL
DICTIONARY
FOR CROSSWORD
PUZZLES

Compiled by Frank Eaton Newman

COMPLETELY REVISED,
UPDATED EDITION
MORE THAN 75,000 ANSWERS
TO DEFINITIONS

DOUBLEDAY & COMPANY, INC.
Garden City, New York

Library of Congress Cataloging in Publication Data

Newman, Frank Eaton.
  New practical dictionary for crossword puzzles.

  1. Crossword puzzles—Glossaries, vocabularies, etc.
I. Title.
GV1507.C7N4 1975   793.73′2′03
ISBN 0-385-05280-4
Library of Congress Catalog Card Number 74–5608

Preface to the Completely Revised Edition

THE WELCOME accorded the previous editions of this dictionary, as evidenced by the sale of the book, encouraged me to compile and publish this new edition, *completely* revised from A to Z. It has been brought into tune with the language of the 1970s, new definitions and answer words have been added throughout, and errors have been corrected. The revision has been planned so as to be of maximum usefulness to the crossword-puzzle solver.

The clear listing of words in this revised and enlarged *New Practical Dictionary for Crossword Puzzles* enables the novice as well as the expert to apply this short-cut method in locating the word desired.

Definitions are listed in light type and answers in bold capital letters.

The purpose of this book, as conceived by the compiler, is not to attempt to explain the meaning of the words included, but to present them in an easy-to-find manner for use in solving problems.

While the primary aim of the work is to aid the puzzle solver, the fund of facts concerning various subjects and other research information make it a useful addition to any library as a reference book.

To those who have so generously contributed to the book, and to the memory of my beloved wife, and to the devotees of this fascinating and educational pastime, this book is dedicated.

FRANK EATON NEWMAN

Abbreviations

abb(r).	abbreviated	geomet.	geometrical
Abys.	Abyssinian	Ger.	Germany
Af.	Africa	Gr.	Greece, Greek
Afr.	African	Hawai.	Hawaiian
A., Am.	America	Heb.	Hebrew
Amer.	American	her.	heraldry
anc.	ancient	Hung.	Hungarian
Ang.-Sax.	Anglo-Saxon	Ind.	Indian
Ar.	Arabia	inflam.	inflammation
Arab.	Arabian	inst(r).	instrument
arc.	archaic	isl.	island(s)
arch.	architecture	It., Ital.	Italian
assoc.	associated	Jap.	Japanese
Assyr.	Assyrian	lang.	language
astron.	astronomy	Lat.	Latin
Aus.	Austria(n)	leg.	legendary
Austral.	Australia(n)	math.	mathematical
Babyl.	Babylonia(n)	meas.	measure
Ber.	Bermuda	med.	medicinal
bib.	biblical	Medit.	Mediterranean
biol.	biology	memb.	member
bot.	botany	Mex.	Mexican
Braz.	Brazilian	miscel.	miscellaneous
Cal.	California	mix.	mixture
Can.	Canadian	Moham.	Mohammedan
Cen.	Central	mon.	monetary
char.	character	mus.	musical
charac.	characteristic	myth.	mythology
Chin.	Chinese	naut.	nautical
col.	colloquial	N.Z.	New Zealand
collec.	collective	N., No.	north, number
comb.	combining	obs.	obsolete
comp.	compound	per(t).	pertaining
compo.	composition	penin.	peninsula
Const.	Constantinople	peren.	perennial
deriv.	derivative	Peruv.	Peruvian
dial.	dialect	Phil. I.	Philippine Is.
E., Ea.	east	pl.	plural
eccl.	ecclesiastical	poet.	poetical
Egypt.	Egyptian	Poly.	Polynesian
Eng.	England	prov.	provincial
Ethiop.	Ethiopian	Rom.	Roman
Eur.	European	Rus(s).	Russian
exclam.	exclamation	Scand.	Scandinavian
fig.	figuratively	Scot.	Scottish
Fr.	France, French	Script.	Scripture

Shak.	Shakespeare	Test.	Testament
Skr.	Sanskrit	Teu(t).	Teutonic
S., So.	south	trop.	tropical
Sp., Span.	Spanish	U.S.	United States
sub.	substance	var.	variable, variant
Tag.	Tagalog	W.	west
ter.	territorial	zool.	zoological

New Practical Dictionary
for Crossword Puzzles

A

A.F.L. head .... MEANY
A.R.C. first pres. .... BARTON
aardvark ...... ANTEATER, EDENTATE,
      TAMANDUA
Aaron's death mount .... HOR
abaca .... HEMP, LUPIS
Abaddon ... HELL, SATAN, APOLLYON
abalone .... SEA EAR, ORMER, AWABI,
      NACRE
abandon ABDICATE, WAIVE, MAROON,
      DESERT, FORSAKE, FREEDOM, DROP
abandoned .... DERELICT, LORN, LOST
abase ...... AVALE, LOWER, HUMBLE,
      SHAME, LESSEN
abash .... SHAME, CONFUSE
abate ..... EBB, LOW, OMIT, LESSEN,
      ALLAY, SUBSIDE
abatement .... LETUP, DECREASE
abatis .... SLASHING
abbé .... MONK
abbess .... AMMA, VICARESS
abbey NUNNERY, PRIORY, FLY, ABADIA
abbot .... ABBAS, COARB
abbot, dignity of an ...... ABBACY
Abbott hero .... ROLLO
abbreviate .... REDUCE, CURTAIL,
      SHORTEN, CONDENSE
Abderite, the .... DEMOCRITUS
abdicate .... DEMIT, RESIGN, RETIRE,
      RENOUNCE
abdominal ..... HA(E)MAL, VENTRAL
abduct .... KIDNAP
Abélard's ladylove .... HELOISE
abelmosk .... MUSK, MALLOW
abet .... EGG, FOMENT, INSTIGATE,
      INCITE, BACK, PROMOTE, UPHOLD
abhor .... HATE, DETEST, LOATHE
abhorrence ...... AVERSION, ODIUM
abide .... STAY, TARRY, DWELL, LIVE,
      BEAR, REMAIN, (A)WAIT
abies .... FIR, CONIFER
abigail .... MAID
Abijah's son .... ASA
ability .. CAN, POWER, SKILL, CALIBER,
      MIGHT, TALENT
abject .... LOW, VILE, BASE
abjure .... RECANT, REPUDIATE,
      RETRACT, DENY

able ... ADEPT, FIT, SMART, BASTANT,
      CLEVER, FERE
ablution ..... WIDU, WASH, BATHING,
      WUDU, WUZU
_____ Abner LIL
abnormal .... ERRATIC, QUEER
abode .. DAR, HABITAT, INN, RESET,
      LODGE, WON, SITTING, TENT,
      WOON, WONE
abode of bliss ..... EDEN, GOSHEN,
      ARCADIA
abode of dead ... ARALU, AARU, AALU
abode of human beings; myth. .....
      MIDGARD
abode of gods .... ASGARD, OLYMPUS
abolish .... ANNUL, CANCEL, REPEAL,
      END, KILL
abolitionist .... STEVENS, LUNDY,
      GARRISON
Abominable Snowman .... YETI
abomination ...... HATE, AVERSION
aboriginal ..... YAO, NATIVE, FIRST,
      INERI, WARRAGAL
aborigines .... SAVAGES, NATIVES
abound .. SWARM, FLEET, TEEM, SNEE,
      EXUBERATE
abounding .. COPIOUS, RIFE, REPLETE
about .... ANENT, CIRCA, (IN)RE,
      CONCERNING, NEAR, SOME, UMBE
above .... OVER, ATOP, ABUNE, OER,
      PAST, ALOFT
abrade ..... RUB, FRET, SCRAPE, RASP,
      CHAFE
Abraham's birthplace .... UR
Abraham's brother .. HARAN, NAHOR
Abraham's father .... TEHAR
Abraham's grandfather ..... NAHOR
Abraham's nephew .... LOT
Abraham's son .... MEDAN, SHUAH,
      ISAAC
Abraham's wife ...... SARAH, SARAI,
      KETURAH
abrasive .... SAND, EMERY, GARNET,
      PUMICE, CORUNDUM
abridge ... RASEE, SHORTEN, CURTAIL,
      DIMINISH
abridgment .... DIGEST, EPITOME,
      COMPEND

1

abroad .... AWAY, OFF, DISTANT, OVERSEAS
abrogate ... ANNUL, REPEAL, CANCEL
abrupt ... STEEP, RUDE, HASTY, CURT, CRAGGY, BRUSQUE, ICTIC
Absalom's captain .... AMASA
Absalom's slayer .... JOAB
abscond ..... FLEE, DECAMP, DESERT, ELOPE
absence .... AWOL, WANT
absence of blood poison ... ASEPSIS
absence of hair .... ACOMIA
absence of taste .... AGEUSIA
absent .... OFF, GONE, LOST, AWOL, AWAY
absinthe .... AJENJO
absolute .... DEAD, VERY, PLENARY, UTTER, MERE, TOTAL, TAT
_____ absolute .... CAPTAIN
absolve .... ACQUIT, REMIT, PARDON, SHRIFT, SHRIVE
absolved .. FREED, CLEARED, SHROVE
absorb .. ENGULF, SUCK, SOAK, DRINK
absorbed ... LOST, RAPT, ENGROSSED
absorption .... MERGER
abstain . CEASE, DENY, DISUSE, SPARE, WAIVE
abstract ..... STEAL, EPITOME, BRIEF, COMPEND, SUMMARY, VIDIMUS
abstruse ... ACROAMATIC, ESOTERIC, RECONDITE
abundance . GALORE, PLENTY, UBERTY, BOUNTY, PLETHORA, ROUTH, MORT
abundant . AMPLE, FLUSH, RIFE, OPIME
abuse .... REVILE, RAIL, SNASH, GALI, GALEE, MISTREAT
abut .... ADJOIN, BORDER
abyss GULF, PIT, CHASM, APSU, VOID, VORAGE, SWALLOW
Abyssinia .... AKSUM, AXUM, ETHIOPIA
Abyssinian (see "Ethiopian")
acacia ...... BABUL, LOCUST, ARABIC, MYALL, WATTLE, YARRAN
academic ...... SCHOLASTIC, CLASSIC
Acadian .... CAJUN
acarus .... MITE
accelerate ...... REV, SPEED, HASTEN
accent . MARK, ICTUS, STRESS, GRAVE, ARSIS, BROGUE
accenting syllable .... ARSIS, UPBEAT
accept .. ADMIT, ALLOW, FANG, TAKE, TAE
accepted standard .. PAR, NORM, TYPE
access .... ENTRY, ENTREE, FIT, DOOR
accessory ... ABETTOR, APPURTENANT, ADJUNCT
accident .... CHANCE, EVENT, MISHAP
acclaim .... ECLAT, LAUD, PRAISE, OVATION, SHOUT

acclamation .... SHOUT, PLAUDIT, APPLAUSE
acclivity ...... SLOPE, SLANT, TALUS
accolade .... OSCAR, EMMY, AWARD, HONOR
accommodate .... FIT, LEND, FAVOR, LODGE, SUIT
accomplice ... ABETTOR, PAL, LOUKE, ALLY, BUDDY, CHUM, SHILL
accomplish ... WIN, ATTAIN, ENACT, EFFECT, PERFORM
accomplished .... DID, DONE, TERSE, BESEEN
accord .... CONCERT, UNITY, UNISON
accordingly .... ALLA, AUX, ALA, PURSUANT, THEN, THUS
accost .... HAIL, GREET, ADDRESS
account ...... TAB, SAKE, TALE, TAIL, JUDGE, ANSWER, SCORE, RECITAL, PROCESS
accountant .... CPA, CLERK, AUDITOR
accouter .... ARRAY, EQUIP, GEAR
accredit .... DEPUTE, ALLOT, APPOINT
accrue ..... ISSUE, RESULT, REDOUND
accumulate . COLLECT, FUND, HOARD, STORE, AMASS
accuracy .... FIDELITY
accurate .. JUST, TRUE, CLOSE, EXACT, CORRECT
accuse .... BLAME, IMPLEAD, DELATE, INDICT, CENSURE, ARRAIGN
accustom . ENURE, INURE, HABIT, USE, WONT
ace . ONE, TIB, UNIT, JOT, PIP, BASTO, PILOT, TOPS
ace-queen comb. .... TENACE
acerb ... BITTER, HARSH, SHARP, TART
acetaldehyde .... ETHANAL
acetic acid ... VINEGAR, ESTER, SOUR
acetone .... KETONE
acetylene deriv. .... TOLAN, TOLANE
ache .. PAIN, PANG, THROE, STOUND
Acheson .... DEAN
achieve . ATTAIN, REALIZE, WIN, GET, REACH
Achilles' parents .... PELEUS, THETIS
Achilles' slayer .... PARIS
acid ... NITRIC, OLEATE, TART, AMIC, AMIDE, AMINO, BORIC, TARTAR, VALINE, PROLINE, HARD
acidity .... ACERBITY, ACOR
acknowledge .. OWN, SIGN, THANK, AVOW, NOD, ADMIT
acme .. HEYDAY, CLIMAX, APEX, TOPS, CAP
acolyte ...... HELPER, PATENER, BOY
acomia .... BALDNESS
aconite .... BIKH, BISH, BIK
acorn(s) ... CAMATA, OVEST, MAST, BELOTE, PANNAGE

acorn-shaped .... BALANOID
acquaint ..... APPRISE, TELL, POSSESS
acquiesce .... ACCEDE, AGREE, CHIME
acquire .... EARN, LEARN, GET, REAP,
                       WIN, ATTAIN
acquit .... EXCULPATE, FREE, EXCUSE,
                           CLEAR
acre, one fourth of .... ROOD
acre; one half plot .... ERVEN
acrid ..... SHARP, BASK, SOUR, TART,
                        PUNGENT
acrimonious .. CAUSTIC, ACID, SNELL,
                     HARSH, SHARP
acropolis .... CADMEA, LARISSA
acrobat ...... TUMBLER, NAT, TOPPLER
across .... OVER, OER, TRAVERSE,
                   ATHWART, TRAN, DIA
acrostic .... AGLA, PUZZLE
act . DEED, FEAT, PLAY, WORK, EMOTE,
                   LAW, BEHAVE, BILL
action .... DEED, FACT, GEST(E),
                   PRAXIS, AGENCY
action, field of ..... VENUE, ARENA,
                STAGE, STADIUM
action to recover .... TROVER
active .... AGILE, BRISK, SPRY, SPRIG,
           NIMBLE, LISH, YARE, YEP
activity ... STIR, WORK, MOVEMENT,
                       ACTION
actor .. MIME, MUM, THESPIAN, SERIO,
       MIMIC, STAR, MUMMER, PLAYER,
     EXTRA, HEAVY, SUPER, HISTRIO(N)
actor, poor ..... HAM, BARNSTORMER
actors .... CAST, TROOP
actor's part .... ROLE, FUNCTION
actress .... INGENUE, STAR, DIVA,
                     HEROINE
actual ...... REAL, VERITABLE, TRUE,
               GENUINE, BEING
actuate .. ROUSE, MOVE, EGG, INCITE,
             INSTIGATE, SHARPEN
acute .... KEEN, TART, SHARP
adage . PROVERB, DICT, MAXIM, SAW,
                       SAYING
Adam; Norse .... ASK
Adam-and-Eve .... CRAWFOOT,
                   PUTTYROOT
"Adam Bede," author of ...... ELIOT
adamant .... HARD, STONY
Adam's grandson .... ENOS
Adam's needle .... YUCCA
Adam's other wife .... LILITH
Adam's rib .... EVE
Adam's son ...... ABEL, CAIN, SETH
adapt ...... FIT, SORT, SUIT, ADJUST,
              CONFORM, COMPLY
add (up) ..... SUM, TOT, TOTE, FOOT,
    TOTAL, APPEND, JOIN, AUGMENT,
                    INCREASE
adda .... LIZARD, SKINK

Addams; social worker .... JANE
addax .... PYGRAG
adder .... SNAKE, VIPER, NEDDER,
                    HAGWORM
addict .... FAN, FIEND, DEVOTEE,
                 BUFF, VOTARY
addiction ...... HABIT, WAY, WONT
Addison; Brit. poet ... JOSEPH, CLIO,
                    ATTICUS
addition . ADDEND, AUGEND, EKE, ELL,
    ALSO, AND, ELSE, TOO, CODICIL,
            APPENDIX, PARAGOG
addition, contract .... RIDER
addled .... ASEA, MUDDLED
address . GREET, CALL, ACCOST, TACT,
    TULK, TALK, SKILL, SERMON, SPEECH
adduce .... ADVANCE, ASSIGN, CITE,
                       QUOTE
adept .. DAB(STER), DEACON, EXPERT,
                     VERSED
adequate ...... EQUAL, DUE, DIGNE,
                   ENOUGH
Adhem, ben .... ABOU
adhere GLUE, CLING, ACCRETE, STICK,
                     CLEAVE
adherent .... IST, DISCIPLE, VOTARY,
          SEQUEL(A), FOLLOWER
adhesive .... GUM, GLUE, PASTE,
    GLUTEN, STICKUM, MUCILAGE
adipose .... FAT, FATTY, PURSY
adit ..... ENTRANCE, ACCESS, STULM
adjacent . CONTIGUOUS, NIGH, NEAR
adjective .... ADNOUN
adjourn .... DEFER, PROROGUE, RISE,
                 POSTPONE
adjudge . DEEM, AWARD, TRY, DECREE,
                 CONDEMN
adjudicate .... ACT, TRY, HEAR
adjust .. TRIM, SQUARE, ATTUNE, FIT,
    ALIGN, ALINE, REGULATE, TRUE,
                   SET(TLE)
adjutant ...... HELPER, STORK, ALLY,
    MARABOU, ARGALA, HURGILLA
ad lib .... IMPROVISE, OFFHAND
adman .... HUCKSTER
Admetus' wife .... ALCESTIS
administer ..... HUSBAND, MANAGE,
           DISPENSE, EXECUTE
administration .... SWAY, REGIMEN
admiral ..... SPEE, NELSON, HALSEY,
             NIMITZ, TIRPITZ
admission ... ADIT, ACCESS, ENTREE
admit ... ALLOW, PROFESS, RECEIVE,
              ADHIBIT, OWN
admixture .... ALLOY, BLEND
admonish .... CHIDE, ADVISE, WARN,
           REPROVE, MONITOR
ado ..... FUSS, STIR, POTHER, BUSTLE
adobe .... BRICK, CLAY
adolescence . NONAGE, YOUTH, TEENS

adopt . PASS, TAKE, ASSUME, BORROW, ARROGATE
adore ..... LOVE, REVERE, WORSHIP, WURTH
adorn .. DRESS, GARNISH, DECORATE, DIGHT, GRACE, PINK, ENRICH, TRIM
Adriatic island .. LAGOSTA, LASTOVO
adrift .... LOST, ASEA, AFLOAT
adroit .. CLEVER, DEFT, NEAT, HABILE, SMART, SKILLFUL, ADEPT
adulterate .. DEFILE, DEBASE, DEACON, SOPHISTICATE
adult insect .... IMAGO
advance . MARCH, NOSE, RISE, GAIN, CREEP, FORWARD, FURTHER, ADDUCE, PASS
advantage ...... BOTE, START, STEAD, SAKE, PROFIT, USE, GAIN, BENEFIT, KINCH
adventitious ... CASUAL, ACCIDENTAL
adventure ..... GEST, GESTE, QUEST, SEEK, EXPLOIT
adventuress .. DEMIREP, GOLDDIGGER
adventurous .... DARING, RASH
advice . AVISO, LORE, REDE, COUNSEL
advise .... ACQUAINT, TELL
"Advise and Consent" author . DRURY
adviser . MENTOR, MONITOR, NESTOR, ASSESSOR
advocate ...... ABET, ABETTOR, PRO, PARACLETE, APOLOGIST, URGE, PLEAD(ER), CHAMPION, DEFENDER
adytum .... SANCTUARY, SHRINE
Aegean island inhabitant .. SAMIOTE
Aegean Sea arm .... SAROS
Aegean Sea island .. IOS, NIO, SAMOS
Aegeon, wife of .... AEMILIA
Aegir, wife of .... RAN
Aeneas' father .... ANCHISES
Aeneas' great-grandson ...... BRUT
Aeneas' wife .... CREUSA
Aeneid author .... VERGIL, VIRGIL
Aeolus' daughter .... HALCYONE
aeonian .... ETERNAL, INFINITE
aerial .... AIRY, ANTENNA
aeroplane (see "airplane")
aerostat .... BALLOON
Aether, father of .... EREBUS
Aetolian prince .... TYDEUS
afar .... AWAY, OFF, DISTANT
Afara, one of the ... SAHO, HAMITE
affair . GEAR, AMOUR, PARTY, THING, MATTERS, LOVE _____
affect ..... ASSUME, MINCE, IMPRESS, INSPIRE
affected .... FEIGNED, POSEY, FALLAL
affectionate . FOND, LOVING, TENDER
afferent .... ESODIC
affiance ... BETROTH, PLEDGE, PLIGHT
affiliate ...... JOIN, ADOPT, CONNECT

affinity .... RELATION, RAPPORT
affirm .... ASSERT, AVER, SWEAR, VOUCH, STATE, AFFY
affirmative ..... VOW, AMEN, OATH, YES, YEA, AYE
affix .... PIN, SEAL, STAMP, SUBJOIN, ADD, FASTEN, APPEND, ATTACH
affliction . TRY, WOE, SCOURGE, PAIN, STOUR, DISTRESS
afford . GIVE, GRANT, LEND, FURNISH, SUPPLY
affray ...... MELEE, BATTLE, COMBAT, FEUD, FIGHT
affright ... CONFUSE, ALARM, DAUNT, AGRISE
affront ... INSULT, OFFEND, OFFENCE
affy .... BETROTH, ESPOUSE
Afghan . DURANI, CARPET, DOG, WRAP
Afghan city .... KABUL
Afghan coin .... AMANIA, PUL
Afghan lang. ...... PASHTO, PUSHTO
Afghan prince .... AMIR, AMEER
afire .... FERVID, FERVENT, BURNING
afloat ...... BUOYED, AWASH, ASEA, ADRIFT
aforesaid . DITTO, PRIOR, ANTECEDENT
aforethought . PREPENSE, DELIBERATE
afraid .... ADRAD, SCARED, RADE, SCAIRT, FEARFUL
afreet; Arab. myth. ... JINNEE, JINNI
Africa, anc. name .... LIBYA
African boss .... BAAS
    "   cape .... RAS
    "   capital ...... LAGOS, ACCRA, DAKAR
    "   coin .... RIAL, DINAR, TALARI
    "   colonist .... BOER
    "   council .... RAAD
    "   country ..... CHAD, CONGO, GABON, DAHOMEY, TANZANIA, MALI, GUINEA, NIGER, SOMALI, RWANDA, TOGO, SENEGAL, SUDAN, GHANA
    "   desert .... SAHARA, ERG
    "   dialect .... TAAL
    "   fetish .... JUJU, GRIGRI
    "   garment .... KAROSS
    "   general in Boer War . BOTHA
    "   giant; Gr. myth ... ANTAEUS
    "   grassy country .. VELD, VELDT
    "   gulf .... GUINEA
    "   headland .... RAS
    "   hill .... KOP
    "   horse disease .... SURRA
    "   hunt .... SAFARI
    "   hut .... KRAAL
    "   kingdom .. BURUNDI, NUMIDIA
    "   lake .... NYASA
    "   language .... TAAL, BANTU
    "   mount. range .... ATLAS

4

" native ASHA, ASHANTI, FULA, DAMARA, ZULU, JUR, TIBU, HOTTENTOT, IBO
" plateau .... KAROO
" rawhide strap .... RIEM
" religious sect .... ABELITE
" river .. CONGO, NIGER, UELE, BENIN, VAAL, RIET, ZAMBEZI, NILE, PIBOR
" soldier .... SPAHI, ASKARI, ZOUAVE, TURKO, TURCO
" sorcery . OBI, OBIISM, OBEAH
" stockade ...... BOMA, KRAAL
" town . ORAN, BONE, DURBAN, TUNIS, GABES, FES, FEZ, TRIPOLI, KENYA, NAIROBI
" tree .. ARTAR, BAOBAB, BITO, SHEA, OLAX, COLA, ASSAGAI
" tribe .... EWE, FAN, FON, BENI, BONI, GALA, BANTU, BERBER, EDO, EBOE, KAFFIR, WATUSI, SENUSI
" valley .... WADI, LAAGTE
" village .... STAD, KRAAL
" wheat .... SORGHUM, IMPHEE
" worm .... LOA
Afrikaans .... TAAL
aft .... ABAFT, ASTERN
afterbirth .... PLACENTA
aftermath .. ARRISH, EDDISH, ROWEN, EDGREW
afterpiece .... EPODE, EXODE
afterthought .... REGRET, RUE
afterward .... LATER, THEN
Agag, slayer of .... SAMUEL
again .... ANEW, EFT, ENCORE, MORE, ITERUM, NEWLY
against ... ANTI, VERSUS, CON, GAIN, GIN
Aga's son .... ALI, KARIM
agalite .... TALC
agalloch .... AGAL, AGAR, ALOE, GAROO, GARROO, TAMBAC
agama .... LIZARD
Agamemnon's brother .... MENELAUS
" daughter ... IPHIGENIA, ELECTRA
" father .... ATREUS
" son .... ORESTES
" wife .... CLYTEMNESTRA
agar-agar, found in .... GELOSE
agate ...... MARBLE, ONYX, QUARTZ, RUBY
agave .... CANTALA, DATIL, KARATTO, MAGUEY, MESCAL
agave fiber .... ISTLE, PITA, SISAL
age .. RIPEN, AEON, EON, ERA, YEARS, SENESCE
" ; abbr., Lat. .... AET
" , an .... DAY, TIME, OLAM

" , at the same .... COEVAL
" of moon on June first .... EPACT
" , parentage .... ELD, PARAGE
" , per. to an .... ERAL, EVAL
" , per. to old .... GERATIC, SENILE
aged ..... OLDEN, NESTORIAN, ANILE, ANCIENT, GRAY, HOARY, ELDERLY
agency .... HAND, MEANS, OPA, TASS
Agenor's daughter .... EUROPA
Agenor's father .... ANTENOR
agent ... DOER, GENE, PROCTOR, SPY, ENVOY, FACTOR, SCALPER, COMPRADOR
aggrandize .... ADVANCE, EXALT
aggravate ..... ENHANCE, NAG, TWIT
agile .. LISH, LISSOME, SPRINGE, SPRY, FAST, QUICK, NIMBLE, LITHER
agitate ... ALARM, CHURN, STIR, WEY, FRET, ROUSE, FLURRY, PERTURB, DISTURB
aglet ..... LACE, SPANGLE, STUD, TAG
agnall ...... HANGNAIL, WHITLOW
agnate .... AKIN, COGNATE, KINDRED
agnomen .... EPITHET, NICKNAME, SURNAME, ALIAS, NAME
agnus .... LAMB
ago .... ERST, GONE, PAST, SINCE, SYNE, BACK
agog .... EAGER, EXPECTANT
agonize ...... RACK, STRAIN, TORTURE
agony .... GRIPE, PAIN, PANIC, THROE, TORMENT, TORTURE
agouti .... PACA, RODENT
agree .... CONCUR, GRANT, JIBE, MATCH, TALLY, TAIL, CHIME, TOADY
agreeable ... DULCET, SUAVE, AMENE, CONSONANT, LIEF, COMELY
agreement .... TREATY, CARTEL, MISE, ACCORD, DEAL, FIT, PACT, UNISON, SORTANCE, COVENANT, LEAGUE
agricultural overseer ... AGRONOME
Agrippina's son .... NERO
agua .... TOAD
Ahab's daughter .. ATHALIE, ATHALIA
Ahab's wife .... JEZEBEL
Aherne .... BRIAN
Ahira, father of .... ENAN
ai .... SLOTH
aid .... ABET, HELP, SUCCOR, ASSIST, BACK
Aïda, lover of .... RADAMES
Aïda's rival .... AMNERIS
aide .... SUBALTERN, ASSISTANT
ailment ..... PAIN, MALADY, DISEASE, DISORDER, TROUBLE
aim .... INTENT, BUTT, GOAL, SCOPE, END, POINT, ETTLE, VISIE, PURPOSE
air ... MIEN, TUNE, ASPECT, BEARING, MELODY, (A)ETHER, OZONE, AERATE

5

air; comb. form .... AER, AERI
air component ..... HELIUM, ARGON,
             OXYGEN, NITROGEN
" gauge .... AEROMETER
", in the open .... ALFRESCO
", per. to the .... AURAL, AERIAL
" -port, part of ....APRON
" race marker .... PYLON
", spirit of the .... ARIEL
aircraft . AVION, PLANE, HELICOPTER,
   GIRO, BOMBER, FIGHTER, GLIDER,
     SPAD, JET, MIG, KITE, STUKA,
   TAUBE, COPTER, FIGHTER, CLIPPER,
   KAMIKAZE, ZERO, ZEPPELIN, BLIMP
" : air driven back by prop....
                       SLIPSTREAM
" : angle made by wing ......
                       DIHEDRAL
" carrier .... FLATTOP
" control surfaces ... ELEVONS
" designer .... SIKORSKY
" : fairing over propeller hub..
                       SPINNER
" : fairing over radar aerial...
                       RADOME
" : flapping of aerofoil ....
                       FLUTTER
" , flapping-wing . ORNITHOPTER
" : high-efficiency glider .....
                       SAILPLANE
" instrument ..... BAROGRAPH
" : landing overstalled ......
                       PANCAKING
". : main member of fuselage..
                       LONGERON
" : movable flaps .... GILLS
" navigational aid .... GEE
" : notice to airmen ... NOTAM
" radar navigational aid ......
                       LORAN
" rate-of-climb indicator .....
                       VARIOMETER
" : rearward aerodynamic force
                       DRAG
" : recovery from a dive ......
                       PULLOUT
" : simple form of parachute..
                       PARASHEET
" : small airscrew .. WINDMILL
" : structure for nacelles ......
                       MONOCOQUE
" : towed target ..... DROGUE
" : trainer .... LINK
" : tube with open end PITOT
" : twisting force .... TORQUE
" : unit of pressure .. MILLIBAR
airplane, bombing .... SUPERFORT
airplane
" cockpit .... CABIN
" engine .... RAMJET

" engine covering . COWLING
" , high-pressured .... JET
" instrument ...... BOMBSIGHT
" part .. LONGERON, AILERON,
     AIRFOIL, ELEVON, FLAP,
     HOOD, KEEL, NOSE, WING,
     TAIL, EMPENNAGE, SKEW,
                       GUN
" propeller .... AIRSCREW
Air defense command .... SAC
airman, non-flying .... KIWI
airport ... KENNEDY, IDLEWILD, ORLY,
   SCUTTLE, SHANNON, OHARE,
   CROYDON, TEMPELHOF, DROME,
                       LAGUARDIA
airport part .... APRON, HANGAR,
             RUNWAY, TARMAC
airtight ...... HERMETICAL, HERMETIC
Air Force girl .... WASP
air maneuvers .... AEROBATICS
air navigation system ..... SHORAN,
                       TELERAN
airy .... AERIAL, JAUNTY, GAY
aisle .... NAVE, ALLEY, LANE
ait .... EYOT, HOLM, ISLET
Ajax, father of .... TELAMON
akin .... AGNATE, GERMANE, SIB
Alabama, city in .... ANNISTON,
             SELMA, EUFAULA
" county ...... BIBB, LAMAR,
                       BLOUNT
alameda .... PROMENADE, WALK
alamo .... MISSION, POPLAR
alar ...... WINGED, PTERIC, AXILLARY
alarm ...... TOCSIN, DISMAY, FEAR,
   PANIC, FRIGHTEN, STARTLE, SOS
alas ...... OHONE, OIME, HEU, OCH,
             OTOTOTOI, VAE
Alaska, capital of .... JUNEAU
Alaska, former capital of ...... SITKA
Alaskan city ... NOME, ANCHORAGE,
                       FAIRBANKS
Alaskan garment .... PARKA
Albania, capital of .... TIRANA
Albanian dialect .... TOSK
" king .... ZOG
" river ... ARTA, DRIN, MATIA
" seaport .... SCUTARI
albatross .. GONEY, GOONEY, NELLY,
             NELLIE, MALMUCK
Albéniz, composer .... ISAAC
albite, variety of .... PERICLINE
alburnum ... BLEA, SPLINT, SAPWOOD
Alcinoüs' daughter .... NAUSICAA
alcohol ...... TALITOL, IDITOL, IDITE,
   NEROL, AMYL, ETHAL, STERIN,
                       STEROL
alcoholic .... BEERY, VINY, WINO,
             SOT, DRUNKARD

alcoholic beverage .... MEAD, NEGUS
    PUNCH, GROG, FIZZ, TODDY,
    COCKTAIL
alcoholic content, increase in ......
    NEEDLE
alcine bird .... AUK
alcove .... BAY, NOOK, ORIEL,
    RECESS, RETREAT, STALL
aldehyde deriv. .... ACETAL
alder .... SAGEROSE, ARN, OLER
ale, a kind of .... FLIP, PURL, ALEGAR,
    MUM, DARBY, NAPPY, STINGO, YILL
alembic .... CUP, RETORT, STILL,
    LIMBEC(K)
Alençon product .... LACE
Aleppo, ancient name of ..... BEREA
alert .... PEART, AWARE, GLEG,
    WARN, SPRACK
Aleutian isle .... ATTU, ATKA
alewife .... WALLEYE, HERRING,
    POMPANO, BANG, SAWBELLY
Alex. Hamilton's birthplace ... NEVIS
Alexander's birthplace .... PELLA
Alexandrian patriarch .... PAPA
    "   theologian ...... ARIUS
alfalfa .... LUCERNE, GRASS,
    COCHLEA, MEDIC
alfresco .... OUTSIDE
alga .... DIATOM, DESMID,
    FUCUS, DASYA, NORI
algae genus .... ALARIA, DASYA
algaroba .... CAROB
Algeria, Roman name for .. POMARIA
Algerian ruler .... BEY, DEY
Algerian half bushel .... TARRI
Algerian seaport ...... BONE, ORAN
algesis .... ACHE, PAIN
Algonquian Ind. .... OTTAWA, ALGIC
Ali Baba's brother .... CASSIM
alias .... EPITHET, (PEN)NAME,
    OTHER, TITLE, ELSE
alidade .... DIOPTER
alien .... FOREIGN, REMOTE,
    ADVERSE, METIC, PEREGRINE
alien resident; Heb. .... GER
alienate .... ESTRANGE, WEAN
alight .... DESCEND, LATCH, LAND
alike; comb. form .... ISO
aliment ... FOOD, MANNA, PABULUM
alined .... AROW, JOINED
alkali .... SODA, LYE, SALT,
    REH, ANTACID
alkaline .... LIME, OXIDE
alkaloid .... ARABINE, ARICIN(E),
    SOLANINE, EMETINE, ESERINE,
    CERIN(E), CODEIN(E), KAIRIN(E),
    ARICINE, THEIN(E), CAFFEIN(E)
alkaloid in mustard seed . SINAPIN(E)
alkaloid poison .... CURARE
alkaloid in poison hemlock .. CONIN

all .... EVERY, TOTAL, WHOLE
all; comb. form .... PAN
all; mus. .... TUTTI
all; prefix .... OMNI
allan .... GULL
Allasch .... KUMMEL
allay .... COOL, AGATE, EASE
allege .... INFER, PLEAD, ADDUCE,
    ASSERT, AVER
alleged force .... OD, ODYLE
allegory .... PARABLE, EMBLEM,
    FABLE, APOLOG(UE)
Allen .... ETHAN, STEVE, FRED
allergy .... SENSITIVENESS, ATOPY
alleviate .... ALLAY, EASE,
    CALM, LESSEN, LIGHTEN, MITIGATE
alley .... LANE, LOKE, TRANCE,
    VENNEL, WEENT
_____ alley .... BLIND
alliance ..... NATO, SEATO, LEAGUE,
    AXIS, UNION, ENTENTE
allied ...... KINDRED, AGNATE, AKIN,
    SIMILAR, KIN, COGNATE
alligator .... CAYMAN, JACARE,
    LAGARTO, LIZARD, YACARE
alligator pear .... AVOCADO
allium .... GARLIC, ONION
allot .... CAVEL, CAST, METE,
    SORT, RATION, PORTION
allow .... ENDURE, LET, GRANT,
    YIELD, CONCEDE
allowance ...... LEAVE, ARRAS, TARE,
    TRET, STINT, SUTTLE, STIPEND,
    TANTUM
allowing that .... IF, PROVIDED
alloy .... ASEM, LAY, AMALGAM
alloy, black metal .... NIELLO
alloy, Chinese .... PAKTONG
alloy: copper and zinc ..... BRASS
alloy in cheap jewelry ..... OROIDE
alloy: iron and carbon ...... STEEL
alloy like German silver .... ALBATA
  " : nickel and steel .... INVAR
  " , pewter-like .... BIDRI
  " rich in zinc .... TUTENAG
  " : tin and copper .... PEWTER
  " : tin and lead ... PEWTER, TERNE
alloyed .... SPURIOUS, BASE
allspice .... PIMENTO
allure .... BAIT, SEDUCE, DECOY,
    CHARM, ALLECT, ENTICE,
    TEMPT, WIN
allusion ... INSTANCE, INKLING, HINT,
    INNUENDO
allusive .... METAPHORICAL, PUNNING
alluvial clay .... ADOBE
alluvial deposit ... MUD, SILT, PLACER
alluvial fan .... DELTA
alluvial matter .... GEEST
ally ..... LEAGUE, UNION, PAL, JOIN

7

allylene .... PROPINE
almain .... (GERMAN) DANCE
almandine .... SPINEL
almandite .... GARNET
almond .. AMYGDALA, BADAM, CANARI
almond-flavored liqueur .... RATAFIA
almond oil; Fr. .... AMARIN
almost .... ANEAR, NIGH, NEARLY
alms ..... HANDOUT, DOLE, CHARITY,
PASSADE
alms chest ... ARCA, ALMOIN, TRONC
alms distributor .... ALMONER
aloe .... AGAVE, TAMBAC
alone .... SOLO, SINGLE, SOLITARY,
SINGLY
alone; stage direction .... SOLUS
aloof .... ABACK, FROSTY, REMOTE
alpaca .... (L)LAMA, PACO
alpaca-like animal ...... GUANACO,
VICUNA
Alpha .... CHIEF, DENEB, FIRST
alphabet .... CROSSROW, PRIMER
"   character .. OGAM, OGHAM,
RUNE
"   , Kashmir .... SARADA
"   , teacher of ... ABECEDARIAN
Alpine dress .... DIRNDL
Alpine dwelling .... CHALET
Alpine herdsman .... SENN
Alpine primrose .... AURICULA
Alpine wild goat .... STEINBOK, IBEX
Alpine wind .... FOEHN
Alps, Italian .... DOLOMITES
Alps, peak of . EIGER, MATTERHORN,
MONTBLANC MOENCH, BERNINA
Alps pass ..... CENIS, COL, SIMPLON,
GOTTHARD, BRENNER
alsike .... CLOVER
also ... AND, EKE, TOO, BESIDES, ITEM
altar .... ARA, CHANCEL, BOMOS,
HAIKAL, HESTIA,
CHANTRY, ESCHARA
altar carpet .... PEDALE
altar cloth . DOSSAL, HAPLOMA, PALLA
altar, part of an .... APSE, PREDELLA,
SEPTUM, PISCINA, PYX, REREDOS,
GRADIN, RETABLE, MENSA, FRONTAL
alter .... VARY, MUTATE, WEND,
MODIFY, QUALIFY
alter ego .... FRIEND, SELF
alterant .... REMEDY, AID, HELP
alternate .. ELSE, OTHER, VARY, ROTATE
althorn .... ALTO, SAXHORN
although .. EEN, EVEN, THAT, ALBE(IT)
altitude barometer ...... OROMETER
aluminous pyroxene .... AUGITE
aluminum comp. .... WAVELLITE,
THERMITE
aluminum hydroxide ...... BAUXITE
aluminum pistachio color .. EPIDOTE

always .... AY, AYE, EER, EVER,
ALGATE, EVERMORE
Aly's father .... AGA
amadou .... PUNK, TINDER
amalgamate ... BLEND, MERGE, UNITE,
COMBINE
amalgamating pan .... TINA
amanuensis .... SCRIVENER
amaryllis .... MISTRESS, AGAVE,
SWEETHEART
amass .... GATHER, HEAP
amateur .... DABBLER, TYRO, NOVICE,
DILETTANTE, HAM
amateur, non- .... PRO, SKILLED
amative . AMOROUS, EROTIC, LOVING
amaze ... STAGGER, STUN, ASTONISH,
ASTOUND, SHOCK
amazed ..... AGHAST, AGOG, AGAPE
Amazon estuary .... PARA
"   rise, site of .... ANDES
ambassador ...... ENVOY, MINISTER,
AGENT, DIPLOMAT, LEGATE,
ELCHI, ELCHEE, VAKIL
amber .... YELLOW, ELECTRUM,
AUMER, LAMMER, SUCCIN
ambiguity ..... PARADOX, OBSCURITY
ambiguous .... FORKED, VAGUE
ambitious .... EMULOUS
ambry .. CUPBOARD, CLOSET, PANTRY
ambulate ... MOVE, WALK, GAD, HIKE
ambush .... TRAP, COVER, LURK,
BLIND, (A)WAIT
"Amelia," char. in Fielding's ... BATH
ameliorate .. BETTER, REFORM, AMEND
amend .... BETTER, BEET(E),
CORRECT, IMPROVE, RECTIFY
amends, make .... EXPIATE, REDRESS,
ATONE
ament ...... CATTAIL, CATKIN, JULUS,
IULUS, GOSLING, CHAT
amerce .... TREAT, FINE, MULCT
America, myth. discoverer of ....
VOTAN
America, reputed discov. of ....
LEIF ERICSSON
American cartoonist .... NASH
ARNO, CAPP
"   chemist .... UREY
"   composer .... NEVIN
"   engineer .... EADS
"   educator .... KERR
"   humorist .. ADE, COBB, NYE
"   Indian . AMERIND, PAMPERO,
REDSKIN, HOSTILE, BRAVE,
TAWNEY, BUCK, ROJO, INJUN
"   inventor .... IVES, OTIS,
EDISON
"   jurist .... COOLEY, HOLMES
"   naturalist ... BAIRD, SETON,
AUDUBON

8

" nature writer .... BEEBE
" painter .. SARGENT, HOMER,
　　　　RYDER, SLOANE, INNESS
" patriot ..... REVERE, ALLEN,
　　　　　　　HALE, OTIS
" philanthropist .... BARTON
" physician .... MINOT
" pioneer .... BOONE
" poet ..... LANIER, TOWNE,
　　　　AGEE, BENET, AIKEN
" socialist .... DEBS
" suffrage leader ...... CATT
Amerind .... UTE, CREE, REDSKIN
Amerind symbol .... XAT
amice ... CAPE, HOOD, EPHOD, EFOD
amide, an .... ANILIDE
amidic .... AMIC
amidine .... STARCH
Amina's mother .... TERESA
amino acid ...... LEUCINE, ALANIN(E),
　　CYSTINE, GLYCINE, SERIN(E),
　　　　PROLINE, VALIN(E)
aminobenzene .... ANILIN
ammonia component ...... DIAMINE,
　　　　AMIDE, AMINE
ammoniac plant .... OSHAC
ammunition carrier ...... CAISSON,
　　　　　FOURGON
ammunition holder .... TRAY
amoeba, an .... PROTEUS
among .... AMID(ST), IN, MID, IMELLE
Amon's wife .... MUT
amor ...... LOVER, EROS, AMOROSO,
　　　　　　CUPID
AMORC, one of ...... ROSICRUCIAN
amorous .... LOVING, EROTIC, JOLLY
amorphous .... CHAOTIC, FORMLESS
amount PRICE, RATAL, SLUMP, INTAKE,
　EFFECT, FLOW, SUM, NICK, FECK
ampersand .... AND, ALSO
amphibia; genus .... RANA
amphibian ...... ANURA, FROG, OLM,
　　　　TOAD, CAUDATE
" , immature ...... TADPOLE
amphibian tank .... ALLIGATOR
amphibian tractor .... AMTRAC, DUCK
amphibole .... EDENITE, URALITE
amphitheater .... ARENA, CAVEA,
　　　　CIRCUS, CIRQUE
amphora .. URN, VASE, DIOTA, PELIKE
ample .... ENOUGH, FULL, ENOW,
　　COPIOUS, ABUNDANT, PLENTY
amplify .... DILATE, EXTEND, PAD,
　　　　WIDEN, INCREASE
amulet .. CHARM, PERIAPT, TALISMAN,
　MOJO, SAFFI, SAFIE, SAPHIE,
　　　　HAGSTONE
amusing .... DIVERTING, DROLL,
　　　　FARCICAL, RISIBLE
amygdala .... ALMOND, TONSIL

Amy's sisters .... MEG, BETH, JO
ana .... MEMORABILIA, EVENTS
anaconda .... ABOMA, BOA,
　　　　PYTHON, SUCURI
Anacreon's birthplace .... TEOS
anesthetic ... GAS, SEDATIVE, OPIATE
analgesic .... CODEINE, OPIUM,
　　　　ANODYNE, ASPIRIN
analogy ..... SIMILARITY, AGREEMENT
analyze .... DISSECT, DECOMPOUND,
　　　　ASSAY, PARSE
Ananias' wife .... SAPPHIRA
anarchist ... NIHILIST, TERRORIST, RED
anarchy .... DISORDER, LICENSE, RIOT
anathematize .... CURSE, BAN
anatomy ..... SKELETON, STRUCTURE,
　　　　　　BODY
Anaximander's principle ... APEIRON
ancestor .... ELDER, FORBEAR, FAMILY,
　　STOCK, SIRE, ATAVIC, ATAVUS
ancestral .... AVAL, AVITAL
ancestry .... RACE, LINEAGE
anchor ...... KEDGE, KILLICK, MOOR
anchor, bill of .... PEE
" lift .... CAT
" -lifting apparatus .. CAPSTAN
" , part of .. PALM, ARM, FLUKE,
　　　　PEAK, PEE, CATFALL
" , small .... GRAPNEL
" , timber .... GROUSER
anchorage ... MOORAGE, ROADSTEAD,
　　　　STAY, RIDING
anchoret .... ASCETIC, EREMITE
anchorite .... MONK, STYLITE
anchovy .... SPRAT, SARDINE,
　　　　WHITEBAIT
ancient .... ELD, OLD, AGED,
　PRIMEVAL, FERN, HOARY, NOACHIC
" country .... ELIS, ELON,
　　ARCADIA, LACONIA, PHRYGIA
and .... AMPERSAND, ALSO
and; Fr. .... ET
" not .... NOR, NEITHER
" so forth .... (ETC)ETERA
Andalusia, province in .... JAEN
Andean tableland .... PUNA
" tribe .... ANTI
Anderson .... MARIAN
"Andersonville" author ..... KANTOR
andiron .... FIREDOG, HESSIAN
android .... ROBOT
anemone .... ADAMSIA, BOWBELLS
anent .... ABOUT, WITH, ON, RE
anesthetic . NUPERCAINE, TETRACAINE,
　　PROCAINE, PENTOTHAL,
　　PHENACAINE, ETHYLENE,
　NOVOCAIN, ETHER, GAS, CHLORAL
angel(s) .... CHERUB(IM), DULIA,
　POWER, MIGHT, MAH, SERAPH(IM)

angel, apostate .... EBLIS
" in "Paradise Lost" ...... URIEL
" of death .... AZRAEL
" of the planet Jupiter . ZADKIEL
" of music; Koran ...... ISRAFIL
" ; Sp. .... SERAF
angelfish .... MONK, QUOTT,
SQUAT(INA)
Angeli .... PIER
anger .... BILE, RILE, FUME, IRE,
TEEN, TIFF, RAGE, CRAB, HUFF, ARR,
SPLEEN, CHOLER, GRAME, IRISH
angle ...... RAVELIN, ANCON, ARRIS,
HADE, STEEVE, CORNEL, ELBOW,
INGLE
angle of a trench .... ZIG
" of pipe .... TEE
" of ramification ....AXIL
" , to .... FISH, SCHEME
Anglian kingdom .... DEIRA
Anglo-Ind. empire, founder of ......
CLIVE
" " gatehouse .... CERAME
" " pageant .... TAMASHA
" " weight .... TOLA, SER
Anglo-Saxon assembly ...... GEMOT,
MOOT
" " epic poem ...... BEOWULF
" " fine for manslaughter ....
WEREGILD
Anglo-Saxon freeman .... THANE
" " god .... WODEN
" " goddess .... EOSTRE
" " infantry .... FYRD
" " king .... EDGAR, INE
" " king's council, one of ...
WITAN
Anglo-Saxon letter .. EDH, ETH, WEN,
WYN, YOK, YOGH
" " sheriff .... REEVE
" " writer .... AELFRIC
angry .... IRATE, CROSS, RACUND,
IREFUL, MAD, SORE, WRAW,
CROUSE
anguish ..... AGONY, DOLOR, PANG,
MISERY, REMORSE, THROE
angular .... SCRAWNY, BONY, GAUNT
angular meas., unit of .... MIL
anhydrous .... DRY
aniline dye ..... BENZOLE, MAGENTA
animal .... BEAST, CRITTER,
MAMMAL, CREATURE
" and plant life .... BIOTA, BIOS
" , coat of .... PELAGE
" food, caused by .... CREATIC
" , footless .... APOD
" , imaginary .... SNARK
" life, simple form of .... AMEBA
" life, study of .... ZOOLOGY
" , ten-footed .... DECAPOD

" with long body ...... ANNELID
animal's body .... SOMA
animals carrying young . MARSUPIALS
animals; Scot. .... MERES
" with no nervous system ....
ACRITA
animate .... ACT, ENSOUL, FIRE,
VIVIFY, ENLIVEN
animated .... ALIVE, BRISK, GAY
anion, opposed to .... CATION
anise .... DILL, ANET
ankle ... CUIT, TARSUS, COOT, TALUS,
SHACKLE, HOCK
ankle iron .... FETTER, BASIL
ankles, per. to .... TARSAL, TALARIC
anlage .... PROTON
anna, one fourth of an .... PICE
Annam tribes .... MOIS
Annamese boat .... GAYYOU
Annamese measure ...... GON, MAU
annatto .... ACHIOTE, ORLEAN(S)
Anne, wife of Henry VIII .. BOLEYN
anneal .... FUSE, TEMPER, SMELT
annealing chamber .... LEER
annex .... ADD, JOIN, AFFIX,
APPEND, ATTACH
Annie Oakley .... PASS
annotation .... GLOSS, APOSTIL,
COMMENT, NOTE, REFERENCE
announce .... BID, DEEM,
BLARE, HERALD, VOICE
announcement .... BLURB
annoy .. IRK, BAIT, BORE, DEVIL, NAG,
HARASS, VEX, BOTHER, PEEVE,
MOLEST, FESH, HOX, ARR, PEEVE,
HARRY, NETTLE, PESTER
annoyance, expression of .... TUT
annoyer .... TRIER, HARRIER
annual .... ETESIAN, YEARLY
annuity .... RENTE, INCOME,
TONTINE, PENSION, STIPEND
annul .. BLANK, CASS, CANCEL, UNDO,
REPEAL, REVOKE, ABROGATE
annular piece ..... SPUT, DOD, HOOP
anodyne .... SEDATIVE, OPIATE
anoint .... ANELE, FAT, OIL,
SMEAR, CHRISM
anoint, as a priest .... ENOIL, SHRIVE
anomalous .... ODD, ABNORMAL
another .... FURTHER, SECOND, ALIAS
answer .... SOLVE, REPARTEE,
COMEBACK, REACT
ant .... PISMIRE, ANAY, EMMET,
MYRMICID, TERMITE, MIRE,
ERGATES, NEUTER
" genus .... FORMICA, ECITON,
TERMES
" nest .... FORMICARY
antagonist ..... RIVAL, FOE, FOEMAN
antagonistic .... INIMICAL

antarctic explorer .... BYRD, ROSS
antarctic sea .... WEDDEL
anteater .... PANGOLIN, MANIS,
    AARDVARK, TAMANDU, ECHIDNA
antelope .... GAZEL, GAZELLE, TAKIN,
                  YAKIN
   " , African .. HARTEBEEST, KOB,
    KUDU, ORIBI, ORYX, WANTO,
  STEINBOK, TORA, ADDAX, BONGO,
  BLESBOK, ELAND, GEMSBOK, GNU,
  PALLAH, SPRINGBOK, BONTEBOK
antelope, African, striped ....
              KOODOO, KUDU
   " , ancient .... PYGARG
   " , Chinese .... DZEREN
   " , E. Indian .... NILGAI,
                  NYLGAU
antelope, Egyptian .... BUBALIS
   " , European .... CHAMOIS
   " ; genus ...... BUBAL, BUBALIS
   " , goat ....SERAU, SEROW
   " , Himalayan .... GORAL
antelope, Indian CHICARA, NYL, SASIN
   " , red buck .... PALLAH
   " , reddish-brown ... NAGOR
   " , Siberian .... SAIGA
antelope, Somali .... BEIRA
   " , So. African ...... BLESBOK,
               SASSABY
   " , Tibetan .... GOA
   " -like .... BOVID
antenna ..... FEELER, AERIAL, HORN,
    LOOP, DOUBLET, CERCUS, DIPOLE
antenna, insect, end of ...... CLAVA
anterior ... PRIOR, BEFORE, PREVIOUS
anthelion .... HALO, AUREOLE,
          NIMBUS, ANTISUN
anthem .... SONG, MOTET
anthocyanin .... OENIN, ENIN
anthologize .... COMPILE
anthology ...... ANA, POSY, CORPUS,
              GARLAND
anthropoid .... APE, LAR
antiaircraft ...... FLAK, SKYSWEEPER,
              ACKACK
antibiotic .... ACTINOMYCIN,
   AUREOMYCIN, STREPTOMYCIN,
          CAPREOMYCIN
antic .... DIDO, PRANK, CAPER, DROLL
anticlimax ...... BATHOS, DECREASE,
          COMEDOWN
antidote .. CACOON, CEDRIC, EMETIC,
    GUACO, SODA, ANTACID
Antigone's sister .... ISMENE
antimalarial drug .... ATEBRIN
antimissile missile .... ABM
antimony .... KOHL, STIBIUM, SURMA
antiquity ...... AGO, ELD, ANCIENT,
            PAST, YORE

antiseptic .... EUSOL, IATROL, EGOL,
   IODIN, IODOL, SALOL, IODINE,
    LYSOL, CRESOL, BISMUTH
   " acid ...... BORIC, TEREBENE
   " surgery, father of .. LISTER
antitoxin lymph .... SERUM
antler, branch of .. PRONG, BAY, BEZ,
              BROW
   " .... SPIKE, DAG, HORN, DAGUE
"Antony and Cleopatra" char. .. IRAS
Anu's consort .... ANAT
anvil .... STITHY, TEEST, JAW
   " bone .... INCUS
anxiety ...... CARE, CONCERN, PANIC,
    ANGOR, ANGST, NEUROSIS
any .... ONI, ALL, ARY, SOME
anything .... AUGHT
aorist ___ .... TENSE
aoudad .... ARUI, CHAMOIS
Apache chief .... GERONIMO
apart ... ASIDE, SOLUS, SPLIT, ALOOF,
    ALONE, ENISLED, AROOM,
            ASUNDER
apartment .... SUITE, FLAT,
    STEW, WON, DINGLE
ape .... CHIMPANZEE, GIBBON,
   GORILLA, PRIMATE, KRA, ORANG,
    OURANG, LAR, SIAMANG
ape, to ..... PORTRAY, COPY, PARROT,
         SIMULATE, MIME
apeman .... ALALUS
aperture ..... VENT, ORIFICE, RIMA,
    STOMA, SLOT, BORE, PORE,
        FORAMEN, GAP
ape genus .... SIMIA
apex ...... HALO, ACME, NOON, ZENITH,
   APOGEE, CLIMAX, CUSP, VERTEX
   " covering .... EPI
   " , having a rounded ..... RETUSE
   " of elbow .... ANCON
aphis .... APHID, LOUSE, PUCERON
aphorism ... ADAGE, AXIOM, DICTUM,
    MAXIM, PROVERB, SAW
aphoristic .... GNOMIC
Aphrodite .... URANIA, VENUS
Aphrodite's mother .... DIONE
   " sweetheart .... ARES
   " temple site ..... PAPHOS
apiece .... EACH, PER
aplomb ... ASSURANCE, POISE, SURETY
apocryphal book .... TOBIT, ESDRAS
Apollo, birthplace of .... DELOS
   " , mother of ... LATONA, LETO
   " , priest of .... ABARIS
   " , seat of .... ABAE
Apollo's festival .... DELIA
   " son .... ION, HYMEN
   " twin .... ARTEMIS, DIANA
apoplexy, plant .... ESCA

11

apostate .... DISLOYAL, DESERTER, RAT, RENEGADE, SECEDER, TURNCOAT, RECREANT
Apostle .... JOHN, JUDE, LEVI, JAMES, JUDAS, PATER, SIMON, ANDREW, CEPHAS, PHILIP, THOMAS, MATTHEW, MATTHIAS, REMI, ULFILA(S), DISCIPLE
apostle of Rome .... NERI
    " of the Franks .... REMI
    " of the Goths .... ULFILAS
apothegm .. AXIOM, ADAGE, DICTUM, APHORISM, SAYING
apparatus .... GEAR, RIGGING, TOOL, TACKLE, TIPPLE
apparent .... OVERT, PATENT, VISIBLE, MANIFEST, EVIDENT, PLAIN
apparition .... GHOST, REVENANT, PHANTOM, SPECTER, SHADE, EIDOLON, WRAITH, THURSE, SWARTH
appeal .... PLEAD, PRAYER, REQUEST, ENTREAT(Y)
appealing ...... BESEECHING, CATCHY
appear ...... EMERGE, LOOM, ARRIVE, SEEM, OCCUR, ARISE
appearance .... AIR, GUISE, MIEN, RESEMBLANCE, OSTENT, PHASE, LEER, ROE, PHASM, ASPECT
appease .... CALM, PLACATE, PACIFY, MEASE, MITIGATE
appellation .... EPITHET, TITLE, NAME
append .... ADD, ADJOIN, AFFIX, HANG, ANNEX
appendage .... TAB, AWN, PENDICLE, ADNEXA, ADDENDUM, CODICIL, STIPEL, STIPULE
appetite ... APPETENCE, ZEST, OREXIS, PICA, BULIMIA, ASITIA
appetizer .... CANAPE, ZEST, APERITIF, ANTIPASTO
applaud .... EXTOL, LAUD, PRAISE
applauders .... CLAQUE, CLAPPERS
applause .... BRAVO, ECLAT, ENCORE, OVATION, PLAUDIT
apple .... GOLDEN, ROSE, SORB, COSTARD, GREENING, CRAB, RUSSET, SPY
    " blight .... APHID
    " , crushed .... POMACE
    " disease .... STIPPEN
    " , emu; (Austral.) ..... COLANE
apple, immature .... CODLiNG
    " , love .... TOMATO
    " , Persian .... PEACH
    " seed .... PIP
    " seller; Eng. .... COSTER
    " -shaped .... POMIFORM
apples, per. to .... MALIC
applied decoration, form of .. GESSO

apply .... EMPLOY, UTILIZE, USE, DEVOTE, ADDRESS
appointment ...... SET, TRYST, DATE
apportion .... ALLOT, METE, DEAL, DOLE, LOT, DISPOSE
appraise ...... ASSAY, EVALUE, LOVE, GAUGE, ASSESS, ESTIMATE
apprehend .... DREAD, FEAR, ARREST, NAB, SEIZE, GRIPE, INTUE
apprehension ...... CAPTURE, ALARM
apprentice .... TRAINEE, DEVIL, NOVICE, WAISTER
approach .... ADIT, COME, STALK, NEAR, COAST, ACCESS
approbation .... FAVOR, PLAUDIT
appropriate .... PROPER, FIT, USURP, DUE, APT, BORROW, ASSELF, MEET
approve .... FAVOR, ENDORSE, OKAY, OK, RATIFY
apricot .... UME, ANSU, MEBOS
apron .... BRAT, BOOT, HOOVER, TOUSER, DICKY, BARVEL, PINAFORE
apt .... CLEVER, DEFT, FIT, PAT, FAIN, LIABLE, DEXTROUS
apteryx .... MOA, KIWI, RATITE
aptitude .... FLAIR, TALENT, SKILL, KNACK, GIFT, VERVE, FACULTY
aqua .... WATER
aquamarine .... BERYL, BLUE, PIGMENT
aquarium ...... GLOBE, POND, TANK
aqueduct .... CONDUIT, CANAL, ITER
Ara, constellation .... ALTAR
Arab .... SARACEN, GAMIN, SEMITE
Arab faction in Medina .... AUS
———— Arabia .... SAUDI
Arabian beverage .... LEBAN
    " chieftain .. AMIR, EMIR, REIS, SHEIK
    " city ...... DAMAR, MEDINA, SANA
    " demon .... EBLIS, GENIE
    " desert .... DAHNA, DAHANA
    " district .... ASIR, HEJAZ
    " garment .... ABA, HAIK
    " headkerchief cord .... AGAL
    " judge .... CADI
    " kingdom .... HIRA
    " letter............ ALIF, KAF
"Arabian Nights," char. in .... AGIB, AMINA, SINBAD, DERRID, DERRIS, HARUN
    " illustrator .... DULAC
    " romance, an .... ANTAR
    " "Sacred Territory" .. HARAM
    " seaport ...... ADEN, MOCHA
    " seashore .... TEHAMA
    " shrub .... KAT
    " spirit; myth. .. AFREET, JINN
    " state .... OMAN, MUSKAT
    " tent village .... DOUAR

```
"        town, extinct ........ MAREB          areca palm ................. BETEL
"        tribe .......... AUS, KEDAR           arena .... FIELD, RING, HIPPODROME,
"        wagon .............. ARABA                    SPACE, SPHERE, RINK, OVAL,
"        weight ...... NEVAT, CHEKI,                                    STADIUM
                  DIRHEM, KELLA           arenose .................... SANDY
Arabic acid ............... ARABIN            Ares ....................... MARS
"        letter .... BA, THA, JIM, KHA,       "  , parents of ... HERA, ZEUS, ENYO
         DAL, LAM, MIM, NUN, DAD, YA          "  , sister of .................. ERIS
"        scripture .......... ALCORAN         argali, bearded ............ AOUDAD
araceous ................... AROID            Argentine city ......... SALTA, RIO,
araceous plant ...... CABBAGE, LILY,                              LANUS, ROSARIO
                    TARO, ARUM               "        first lady .......... EVITA
arachnid ... SPIDER, MITE, SCORPION,          "        plain ..... PAMPAS, PAMPA
                              TICK           "        president ... PERON, ROSAS
Arafura Sea islands ........... ARU          Argolis, vale of ............ NEMEA
Arakanese .................. MAGHI            Argonaut ......... JASON, OCTOPUS,
Aramaic dialect ............ SYRIAC                                    AGASTUS
Aramean deity ............ RIMMON            Argos, princess of ......... DANAE
Arawakan Ind. tribe; Brazil . GUANA          argot ......... CANT, FLASH, SLANG,
arbiter ...... REFEREE, JUDGE, UMPIRE,                          LINGO, JARGON
              OVERMAN, STICKLER              argue ......... MOOT, RATIOCINATE,
arbitrary ......... DESPOTIC, THETIC              CONTEND, DISCUSS, REASON,
"        dictum .. DOGMA, FIGMENT                                    PLEA(D)
arbor ...... BOWER, PERGOLA, TRELLIS,         argument ......... DEBATE, POLEMIC,
              HERBER, RAMADA, SPINDLE                    HASSLE, CON, PRO, TOPIC
arboreal animal .. DASYURE, SLOTH,           argumentative .... ERISTIC, FORENSIC
                              UNAU           arid ............ LEAN, DRY, JEJUNE,
arcade .... ARCATURE, PORTICO, ORB                     STERILE, PARCHED, SERE
Arcadian ......... BUCOLIC, RUSTIC,           Aries .................... RAM, SIGN
                          SHEPHERD           arikara ...................... REE
"        princess ............ AUGE           arista ..... BEARD, APPENDAGE, AWN
arcanum ........... SECRET, MYSTERY           arise ........ WAX, APPEAR, ASCEND,
arch .... FORNIX, ARC, CHIEF, HANCE,                                ISSUE, REVOLT
OGIVE, PEND, BOW, COPE, COVE,                Aristotle's birthplace ....... STAGIRA
OGEE, VAULT, ROGUISH                         "        work ... ETHICS, ORGANON
archangel ... SATAN, MICHAEL, URIEL          Arius, disciple of ........... ARIAN
archbishop ........ HATTO, ANSELM,            Arizona city ... PHOENIX, KINGMAN,
BECKET, PRIMATE, CRANMER,                                              MESA
CUSHING, SPELLMAN, COOKE,                    "        county .. PINAL, PIMA, YUMA
METROPOLITAN, ABP                            "        river ................. GILA
archbishopric ................. SEE           "        state flower ...... SAGUARO
arched ............ VAULTED, COPED            arm .... BAY, GIB, JIB, INLET, BRANCH
archery target, center of ..... CLOUT         arm bone ... HUMERUS, ULNA, RADIUS
archetypal ........ ORIGINAL, IDEAL           arm, per. to ...... BRACHIAL, ELBOW
archetype .... IDEA, EXAMPLE, MODEL           arm, to walk arm in ........ OXTER
archfiend ............. DEVIL, SATAN          armadillo ....... TATU, PELUDO, TATOU,
architect ...... SURVEYOR, SAARINEN,          POYOU, PEBA, TATOUAY, APAR,
ADAM, WREN, BREUER, EIFFEL,                              MATACO, LORICATE
WRIGHT, GROPIUS, BRAMANTE                     armament works .... SKODA, KRUPP
arctic ............ NORTHERN, POLAR           Armenian mountain ........ ARARAT
arctic exploration base ....... ETAH          "        capital .......... ERIVAN
"        explorer ... ERIC, KANE, PEARY       armhole, garment ............ SCYE
Arden, Miss ................. EVE             armistice ............. PEACE, TRUCE
ardent .. EAGER, RETHE, WARM, FIERY,          armor ... MAIL, PLATE, EGIS, GRAITH,
FERVID, AMOROUS                                              AVENTAIL, TACE
ardor .......... ZEAL, ELAN, SPLEEN,          "  , arm ... REREBRACE, BRASSART
VERVE, FOUGUE                                 "  for a horse .......... BARDES
area .......... CLOSE, AREOLA, TREF,          "  for horse's head ..... TESTIERE
RANGE, SCOPE, SPACE,                          armor for the thigh ......... CUISH
SECTION, SITE, EXTENT                         "   "   " throat ...... GORGET
```

" , parts of .... CUIRASS, GREAVE,
TASSE, JERYNE, TASSET
armor, protective .. PANOPLY, AEGIS
" , shoulder .... AILETTE
" , thigh .... CUISSE
armored vehicle ...... TANK, PANZER
armpit .... CHELIDON, AXILLA
arms, having eight ...... OCTOPOD
Armstrong, Louis .... SATCHMO
army ... HORDE, HOST, MILITIA, FERD,
HERE, IMPI, LEGION, TROOPS
" follower .... SUTLER
Army proving ground .... ABERDEEN
aroma . NIDOR, SAVOR, SCENT, SMELL,
FLAVOR, BOUQUET
aromatic ... PUNGENT, BALMY, SPICY,
SAVORY, REDOLENT
aromatic herb ...... CLARY, NONDO,
MINT
" med. leaves .... BUCHU
" seed .... ANISE
" spice .... CLOVE, MACE
" tree .... BALSAM
arose .... SPRANG, STOOD
arouse .... ACCITE, SUMMON, EVOKE,
ANIMATE, EXCITE, REVIVE,
STIR, PIQUE, PROVOKE
arracacha .... APIO
arraign .... CITE, INDITE, PEACH
arrange .... ALINE, ETTLE, PLAT, RAIL,
SERIATE, DAIKER, TIER,
PERMUTE, STOW
arrange a ballet .... CHOREOGRAPH
arrange in battle formation ....
DEPLOY
arrange side by side .... APPOSE
arranged in threes .... TERNATE
arrangement .... TAXIS, FILE, INDEX,
SETUP, GIG, POSTURE
arrangement, per. to .... TACTIC
arras .... TAPESTRY, DRAPERY
array .... DECK, MUSTER, ADORN,
DRESS, PAREL, ROBE,
ADIGHT, FIG
arrest .... DWARF, STUNT, NAB, HALT,
RESTRAIN, STOP, SIST
arrish .... STUBBLE
arrive .... FLOW, COME, LIGHT,
REACH
arrogant ... CAVALIER, JOLLY, PROUD,
HIGH
arrow .... DART, REED, SHAFT
" , feathered .... VIRE
" , fit, to string of bow ... NOCK
" handle .... STELE
" maker .... BOWYER, FLETCHER
" poison; S. Afr. ...... ECHUGIN
" poisoned .... SUMPIT
" poisons ...... ANTIAR, CURARE,
INEE, UPAS, URALI, WOORALI

arrow, short .... SPRITE
arrowroot .... CANNA, ARARAO,
TAPIOCA, MARANTA, TACCA,
ARARU, MUSA, PIA
arrow-shaped .... BELOID
" -worm .... SAGITTA
arroyo .... HONDO
arsenic mixture ... ERINITE, REALGAR,
SPEISS
arsis .... ICTUS
arson ...... BURNING, CAUTERY, FIRE
arsonist .... PYRO
art .... ARS, SCELE, WIT,
TECHNIC, SKILL
" style .... GENRE, DADA(ISM),
POP, CUBISM, BAROQUE
Artemis .... UPIS, DELIA, PHOEBE
artery, large .... STREET, AORTA
artery of neck .... CAROTID
artery, pulse of .... ICTUS
artful ...... POLITIC, PRACTIC, WILY,
SHREWD, CRAFTY, CUNNING
" _____ .... DODGER
arthritis .... GOUT
Arthur, Chester _____ .... ALAN
Arthur, King, lance of .... RON
Arthurian king .... BORS
" lady .... ENID, ELAINE
" resting place ..... AVALON
" town .... ASTOLAT
artichoke .... CANADA, CYNARA,
CHOROGI
" , leafstalk of .... CHARD
article; Fr. ..... LA, LE, LES, UN, UNE
article; Ger. ... DER, DIE, DAS, EIN(E)
article; Sp. .... LOS, LAS
artifice ... TRICK, CRAFT, GUILE, RUSE,
WILE, FINESSE, STRATAGEM
artificial language .. ESPERANTO, RO,
IDO, VOLAPUK, ARULO
artillery discharge ... RAFALE, SALVO
artisan .... CRAFTSMAN
artist .... RAPIN, BRUSH, FICTOR,
DAB(STER), ARTISAN, MUSICIAN,
SKETCHER
artist's utensil ...... EASEL, CRAYON,
DIPPER, PALETTE, OIL, TEMPERA,
VARNISH
artless .... NAIF, NAIVE, CANDID
artlessness .... NAIVETE, INNOCENCE
arts, the three liberal .... TRIVIUM
arum .... ARAD, CALLA, TARO,
ARIODES, MANDRAKE
Aryan .... MEDE, SLAV
Aryan deity .... ORMUZD
Aryan god of fire .... AGNI
Aryan of India .... HINDU
as .... WHILE, SIMILAR, SUPPOSE,
SINCE, THUS, QUA
as; Sp. .... COMO

14

as it is written; mus. ....STA
as usual; mus. .... ALSOLITO
asafetida ...... LASER, FERULA, HING,
NARTHEX
asbestos .... AMIANTH, XYLITE
ascend ..... ARISE, UPGO, STAIR, STY,
FLY, CLIMB, MOUNT
ascendency .... MASTERY, SWAY
ascending ..... MOUNTING, ANODAL,
ANODIC
ascent, steep ....STIPE, INCLINE, SLOPE
ascetic .... ESSENE, HERMIT, STOIC,
RECLUSE, SOLITARY, AUSTERE,
YOGI(N), FAKIR
aseptic .... STERILE
Asgard, bridge to; myth .... BIFROST
ash .... EMBER, ASE, AXAN,
VAREC, CINDERS
ash, fruit of .... KEY, SAMARA
" , mountain; Am. .... ROWAN
" , prickly; Afr. .... ARTAR
" tree .... ROWAN, SORB
" tree, the mighty .... YGGDRASILL
Ash Wednesday is first day of _____
.... LENT
ashen ...... PALE, LIVID, GRAY, WAN
Asher, daughter of ... SERAH, BERIAH
" , son of .... ISUI, JIMNAH
Asherite, an .... AMAL
ashy .... WAXEN
Asia Minor, city of .... MYRA, TROY,
USHAK, ISSUS
" " ; Green term ..... ANATOLIA
" " , mountain in .... IDA
Asia Minor province; Rom. . GALATIA
" " , river in ...... HALYS, IRIS
Asian mountains .... ALAI, URAL,
ALTAI, HIMALAYA, EVEREST
Asian open grassy tract .... MAIDAN
Asian plain ....CHOL
Asian tableland .... PAMIR
Asian tongue .... PAMIR, PALI,
SHAN, TAMIL
Asian tree .... ASOK(A), BANYAN,
NARRA
Asiatic country .... KOREA, IRAK,
IRAN, SIAM
" lake .... BAIKAL, BALKASH
" mammal .... PANDA
" mountain .... ALTA, KALKA,
URAL
" native .... INNUIT, YUIT
" nomad, per. to ...... TATARIC
" people .... HUNS, SERES, SERIC
" plague .... CHOLERA
" plant .... SESAME, RAMIE
" revolving storm .... TYPHOON
" river ..... MEKONG, AMUR, ILI,
OB, YALU
" sea .... ARAL, AZOV

" snowstorm .... BURAN
Asiatic trade wind ..... MONSOON
" tree .... ASAK, MEDLAR
" tribe ...... TAI, TURKI, UZBEG,
LOLO, USUN, MORO, SULU
aside ..... AWAY, GONE, OFF, HENCE,
APART, WHISPER
asinine .... IDIOTIC, SILLY, STUPID
ask .... SPER, BEG, BID,
DUN, THIG, FRAIST, INVITE, SOLICIT,
ENTREAT, FRAYN
askew .. ASKANT, AGEE, AMISS, AWRY
asleep .... DORMANT
asp .... URAEUS, VIPER, HAJE
aspect .... PHASE, SHAPE, AIR, GUISE,
MIEN, STATE, FACIES
aspect of two planets .... DECIL
aspen .... QUAKING, POPLAR, TREMBLE
asperse .... VILIFY, LIBEL, REVILE, SLUR
asphyxia, asphyxiant .... APNOEA(L),
APNEA
aspic .... GALANTINE
aspiration .... DESIRE, HOPE
ass . DONKEY, JACKASS, DOLT, CHUMP,
CUDDY, EQUID, JENNET
ass, wild .... ONAGER, QUAGGA
assa .... CAAMA
Assam mongoloid .... GARO
Assam shrub .... TEA
" silk worm .... ERIA, ERI
Assamese dialect .... LHOTA
Assamese hill tribesman . AHOM, AKA
Assam's capital .... SHILLONG
assart .... CLEARING, GRUB
assassin ..... SICARIAN, CAIN, THUG,
BOOTH, GUITEAU
assault ..... CHARGE, ONSET, THRUST,
FRAY, ASSAIL
assay .... TRY, ANALYSIS
assayer .... TESTER, TRIER
assaying vessel .... CUPEL, CUP
assemble .... MASS, POD, MUSTER,
COLLECT, MEET, CONVENE
assembly .. BEVY, DIET, SYNOD, KIVA,
HUI, GEMOT(E), PLENUM
" place .... AGORA, FORUM
assent . ACCEDE, AMEN, GRANT, NOD,
CONCUR
assert ..... ALLEGE, AVER, POSE, SAY,
STATE, VOICE, POSIT, THREAP,
THREEP, AVOUCH
assess EXTENT, LEVY, MISE, RATE, BOTE,
SCOT, ASK, CESS
assessment; Old Eng. law .. SCUTAGE
assessment, rate of ... RATAL, WORTH
assessor .... JUDGE, RATER, JURAT
asseverate ...... VOW, OATH, SWEAR
assign ALLOT, FIX, SEAL, SET, APPOINT,
REFER

15

assist ...... ABET, AVAIL, SPEED, HELP, LOGROLL, COMFORT, SUBSIDY, SUCCOR
assistance .... ALMS, DOLE, GIFT
assistant AIDE, ALLY, HELPER, ACOLYTE, SECOND, SIDEKICK
assistants ...... AIDES, STAFF, MATES
associate ... CHUM, CRONY, HOBNOB, ALLY, BUDDY, HERD, JOIN, MOOP, FELLOW, MINGLE, SOCIUS
association ... HONG, HANSE, CARTEL, BUND, ARTEL, COMPANY
association football .... SOCCER
assonance .... PUN
assuasive .... LENITIVE, LENIENT
assume ... PREMISE, INFER, ARROGATE, USURP, DON, FEIGN, SUPPOSE, SHAM
assurance ...... FAY, FAITH, APLOMB, PLEVIN, BRASS
assuredly .... CERTES, SURE(LY)
Assyria .... ASSHUR, ASSUR
Assyria, anc. capital of ... ANTIOCH, NINEVEH
Assyrian .... AMORITE, SHEMITE
" city ... ARBELA, HARA, OPIS, AKKAD
" god .... ASHUR, ASUR, NABO, NUSKU, SIN, APSU
" goddess .... ALLATU, ISHTAR, ISTAR, NAMA
" mountain .... ZAGROS
" queen .... SEMIRAMIS
" royalty .... PHUL
" sun god .... HADAD
Astaire .... FRED, ADELE
aster ... COCASH, BEEWEED, YARROW
asterisk mark .... STAR
astern .... ABAFT, AFT, REAR
asteroid, first-discovered ...... CERES
" nearest Earth .... EROS
asthmatic .... PURSY, PUFFY
astir ...... EAGER, VIGILANT, AGOG
Astolat's lily maid .... ELAIN(E)
astound ..... AMAZE, STAGGER, STUN
astral ..... STARRY, STELLAR, SIDEREAL
astral fluid .... OD, ODYL(E)
astray, go .ERR, MANG, DEVIATE, SIN, WRY
astringent ..... COTO, HARSH, ALUM, CUTCH, KATH(A), STYPTIC
" gum .... KINO
astrologer ...... JOSHI, JOTI, JOTISI, CHALDEAN, STARGAZER
astrological belief .... SIDERISM
astronaut ALDRIN, CARPENTER, TITOV, BORMAN, WHITE, GLENN, CERNAN, CONRAD, COOPER, GAGARIN, ARMSTRONG, LOVELL
astronomer .... BRAHE, GALILEO, HERSCHEL, KEPLER, SHAPLEY, MITCHELL
astronomical ...... URANIC, URANIAN
astronomical cycle .... SAROS
" inst. ABA, ARMIL, ORRERY
" meas. .... APSIS
astronomy, muse of .... URANIA
astute .... KEEN, SHREWD, CANNY
asunder .... ATWAIN, APART
asylum . RETREAT, ALTAR, JAIL, HOME, HAVEN, BEDLAM, SHELTER
at all ... EVER, ANYWAY, ANY, AUGHT, AVA
at home .... HERE, IN
at last .... ULTIMATELY, FINALLY
at right angles to the keel ... ABEAM
at the same time .... COEVAL
ataman .... HETMAN, COSSACK
atap .... NIPA
Athena, form of ... ERGANE, PALLAS, ALEA, HIPPIA, ITONIA
Athenian .... METIC, ATTIC
" astronomer .... METON
" clan .... OBE
" courtesan ... ASPASIA, THAIS
" general ... NICIAS, PHOCION
" juryman .... DICAST
" lawgiver .... SOLON
" magistrate .... ARCHON
" market place .... AGORA
" room ADYTUM, ATRIUM, CELLA
" ruler .... CLEON, ARCHON, DRACO, CODRUS
" sculptor .... PHIDIAS
athletic event ... AGON, BOUT, GAME, MEET, PLAY, MATCH, TRACK, GYMKHANA, OLYMPIAD, TOURNEY
Atlantic flier . CORRIGAN, LINDBERGH
atlas .... MAPS, SATIN, TITAN
Atlas' daughter .... CALYPSO
" mother .... CLYMENE
Atli's wife .... GUDRUN
atmosphere ... AURA, CLIME, CLIMATE
atmospheric gas .... ARGON, XENON
atoll .... BIKINI
atom . BIT, ION, IOTA, MONAD, DYAD, OCTAD, TRIAD, ISOBAR, HENAD
atom-bomb test site ..... ENIWETOK
atomic particle ... LEPTON, HYPERON, MUMESON, NEUTRINO, PROTON, ELECTRON, PION
atomy .... MOTE, PIGMY, PYGMY
atone for .... AMEND, EXPIATE
atonic sound .... SURD
Atreus, brother of .... THYESTES
Atridae, father of the ...... ATREUS
attach . SEIZE, ANNEX, APPEND, JOIN, LOVE, INSET
attached ... ADNATE, AFFIXED, SESSILE

16

attack ..... ICTUS, AFFRET, FIT, BESET, BLITZ, OFFENSE, AGGRESS, OPPUGN, YOKE, THUG, ASSAULT, ONSET
attain .. WIN, EARN, END, GAIN, GET, ACHIEVE, REACH, PROVE
attainment .... SKILL, SUCCESS
attar .... OIL, PERFUME
attempt .... EFFORT, SEEK, ESSAY, TRY, SAY, MIRD, OSSE, STAB, TRIAL, ETTLE, FRAIST, STRIVE
attend ... SERVE, HARK, AID, FOLLOW, TEND, HEED, STAY, NURSE, MINISTER, (A)WAIT
attendants .... SUITE, RETINUE, TRAIN
attended .... MINDED
attending ones .... ENTOURAGE
attention .... EAR, LISTEN, HIST
attentive ALERT, EARED, WARY, INTENT
attenuate ...... THIN, RAREFY, DILUTE
attest SEAL, ADJURE, AFFIRM, WITTEN, WITNESS, VOUCH, CERTIFY
attic LOFT, GARRET, GRENIER, SOLAR, SOLLAR, TALLET
Attica, subdivision of .... DEME
attire ... ARRAY, GARB, GUISE, LIVERY, REGALIA
attired in armor .... PANOPLIED
attorney .... LAWYER, VAKIL, VAKEEL, COUNSEL, ADVOCATE
attract ... ALLURE, BAIT, DRAW, PULL, TOLE, ENTICE
attribute .... QUALITY, ASCRIBE, OWE, PLACE, POWER, ASSIGN, IMPUTE
attrition ABRASION, FRICTION, WEAR
Auber, opera by .... LEMACON
auction ...... PORTSALE, ROUP, SALE, VENDUE, BRIDGE, HAMMER
audacious ..... BRAZEN, SAUCY, BOLD
audacity .. TEMERITY, CRUST, COURAGE, CHEEK, NERVE
Auden; poet .... WYSTAN
audience ...... EAR, ASSEMBLY, PUBLIC
audition .... HEARING, TRYOUT
auditor ... HEARER, APPOSER, CENSOR, LISTENER
auditory ... OTIC, AURAL, AURICULAR
auditory hallucination ... PHONEME
auger ..... GIMLET, BORER, WIMBLE
auger's cutting edge .... LIP
augment ... SWELL, ADD, EKE, EXPAND
augur .... PORTEND, BODE, OMEN, PRESAGE, DIVINER, FORETELL
August, first day of .... LAMMAS
auk .... ALCA, MURRE, ARRIE, NODDY, URIA, FALK, ROTCH(E)
auk family, per. to ALCIDINE, ALCINE
auks; genus .... ALLE, ALCA
aunt .... TANTE, TIA

aureola GLORIA, LIGHT, HALO, NIMBUS
au revoir .... GOODBYE, ADIEU
auricle .... PINNA, TRUMPET, EAR
Auriga, star in .... CAPELLA
aural .... AURICULAR, OTIC
aurochs . BISON, TUR, URUS, WISENT, BONASUS
aurora .... EOS, DAWN
auroral .... EASTERN, ROSEATE, EOAN
aurum .... GOLD
auspices .... OMEN, SIGN, EGIS, AID, FAVOR
Austen, J.; novel by .... EMMA
austere ...... ASCETIC, HARSH, STERN
Australia, settlers of .... BASS, COOK
Australia, native of ... MYALL, MAORI, AUSSIE
Australian acacia .... MYALL
"   bee .... KARBI
"   beefwood .... BELAR
"   bird COOEY, KOEL, LOWAN, MALLEE
"   boomerang .... KILEY
"   cape .... HONE, YORK
"   city MANLY, PERTH, HOBART, DARWIN
"   cockatoo .... GALAH
"   conversation ...... YABBER
"   cry .... COOEE, COOEY
"   foodfish .... MADO
"   gum tree .... TUART, KARRI
"   hawk .... KAHU
"   horse .... WALER
"   hut .... MIAMIA, MIMI
"   lake .... EYRE, FROME
"   lizard .... GOANNA
"   mahogany ..... GUNNUNG
"   manna .... LAAP
"   marsupial WOMBAT, KOALA, TAIT
"   parakeet .... ROSELLA
"   parrot .... LORY
"   peninsula .... EYRE
"   pepper .... KAVA
"   petrel .... TITI
"   prime minister ... MENZIES
"   seaport .... SYDNEY
"   shield .... MULGA
"   shrub .... CORREA, OLEARIA
"   soldier .... ANZAC
"   tribal group .... KOKO
"   water mole ...... PLATYPUS
"   wild dog .... DINGO
"   zone (arid), per. to .... SONORAN
Austrian coin .... HELLER, DUCAT, SCHILLING
"   measure .... SEIDEL
"   psychiatrist .. FREUD, ADLER, JUNG

17

"   rifleman .... JAGER, JAEGER
"   river ... DRAVE, DRAU, MUR,
                ENNS, ISER, DANUBE
"   ruler, former ...... KAISER
"   town .... GRAZ, LINZ, WIEN,
                SALZBURG, KREMS
author .... PARENT, DOER, MAKER,
                WRITER, CREATOR
auto, type of . BERLIN(E), LIMOUSINE,
                SEDAN, ROADSTER
"   court .... MOTEL
"   shelter .... CARPORT
autocrat .... DESPOT, MOGUL, TORSE,
                TSAR, CZAR
automaton .... ANDROID, GOLEM,
                PUPPET, ROBOT
automobile part .... STATOR, CHOKE,
    HOOD, BRAKE, BONNET, PISTON,
   WIPER, CHASSIS, STARTER, MUFFLER
autumn flower .... ASTER
auxiliary .... SUB, ALLY, HELPER
avarice .... GREED, CUPIDITY, AVIDITY
ave .... HAIL
avellane .... FILBERT, HAZEL
avenger .. NEMESIS, GOEL, WREAKER
avenging spirit ...... FURY, KER, ATE,
                MEGAERA, ERINYS
avens .... GEUM
avenue ... GATE, ARTERY, PIKE, ROAD,
                WAY, AVENIDA
aver . ASSERT, STATE, ALLEGE, AFFIRM,
                VERIFY
average PAR, MEAN, MEDIAL, NORMAL,
                MEDIOCRE, SOSO
averse .... LOATH, RELUCTANT
aversion ..... PHOBIA, HATE, ENMITY,
                DISTASTE, DISLIKE
avert . DETER, THWART, PARRY, CHECK,
                SHIELD
Avesta part YASNA, GATHAS, YASHT,
                VENDIDAD
aviator .... ACE, ICARUS, PILOT, FLIER,
                MANBIRD, AERONAUT
avid ...... EAGER, GREEDY, DESIROUS
avifauna .... ORNIS
avocado .... PEAR, COYO, CHININ,
                AHUACA, PERSEA
avocet ..... BARKER, SCOOPER, TILTER
avoid . ELUDE, ESCHEW, AVERT, EVITE,
                SHUN, SHIRK, EVITATE
avow .... DEPONE, SWEAR
avowal ....OATH
await .... BIDE
avoidance SHIRKING, GOBY, EVASION
award ACCOLADE, ALLOT, MEED, PRIZE,
    MEDAL(LION), OSCAR, EMMY, TONY,
                CONFER, TROPHY, CUP
aware ... HEP, CONSCIOUS, MINDFUL,
                RECK

away .... OUT, ASIDE, FRO, OFF, VIA,
                APART, ABSENT, GONE
away from the mouth ...... ABORAL
aweather, opposed to .... ALEE
aweigh .... ATRIP
awkward LOUTISH, GALOOT, GAUCHE,
    INEPT, UNCOUTH, UNGAINLY
awl .... BROACH, TAP, BROD, BROG,
    ELSIN, ELSON, ELSHIN, FIBULA
awn . AVEL, ARISTA, BARB, BEARD, PILE
awning ..... SHELTER, TILT, CANOPY,
    VELARIUM, TENTOTY, SEMIAN(NA)
awry ... ASQUINT, AGEE, AMISS, EVIL,
                ASKEW, GLEED, GLEYD
ax .... ADZ(E), AXE, HACHE, POLEAX,
    FASCES, TWIBIL, LABRYS, BOUCHER,
                MATAX, MACANA, BESAGUE
axilla ....ARMPIT
axis . AXON, SKENE, ARBOR, BAR, PIN,
                SPINDLE
axis deer ... CHITAL, CHEETAL, CHITRA,
                CHITTRA
aye-aye .... LEMUR(OID)
Ayres .... LEW
Azores island ... FAYAL, FLORES, PICO
"   , port of .... HORTA
"   volcano .... PICO
azote .... NITROGEN
Aztec hero .... NATA
Aztec myth. figure .... NANA, NATA,
                COXCOX
Aztec language .... NAHUATL
Aztec temple ..... TEOCALLI, TEOPAN
azure ..... CERULEAN, BICE, CELESTE
azym, opposed to .... ENZYME

B

baa .... BLEAT
Baba .... ALI
babble . PRATTLE, BLAT, PRATE, PALTER,
    RABBLE, HAVERAL, HAVERIL, GLAVER
babel .... CONFUSION
Babel site .... SHINAR
Babism, creed of .... BAHAISM
baboon ..... PAPA, CHACMA, BAVIAN,
                MANDRILL, SPHINX
babul; Afr. ...... ATTALEH, BABLAH,
                BABOOT, GARAD, GARRAT
baby ..... CHRISM, CHRISOM, INFANT,
                MOPPET, TOTO, WEAN
baby carriage .... PERAMBULATOR,
                GOCART, PRAM, STROLLER,
                WAGON
baby food .... PAP
Babylon .... SHINA
"   , anc. kingdom near ... ELAM

18

Babylonian abode of the dead ARALU
"   city .... AKKAD, CUNAXA
"   chaos .... APSU
"   dead language ... ACCAD
"   Earth Mother .... ISHTAR
"   god .. BEL, OANNES, BAAL
"   hell .... ALALU
"   hero .... ETANA
"   numeral .... SAROS
"   people .... SUMERIAN(S)
"   priestess .... ENTUM
"   river .... TIGRIS
"   tower .... ZIGGURAT,
                   ZIKURAT
baby's complete outfit ...... LAYETTE
bacalao .... ABADEJO, SCAMP
baccarat term .... BANCO
baccate .... PULPY
Bacchanal cry .. EVOE
bagpipe music .... PIBROCH
bacchante .... MAENAD
bachelor .... AGAMIST, CELIBATE,
                   COELEBS
bachelor's button .... KNAPWEED
back ...... SUPPORT, FRO, REAR, AFT,
         AID, ABET, ASSIST, BEHIND,
         DORSUM, HELP, TERGUM,
         POSTIC, STERN, SPONSOR
back, go .... RETURN, REGRESS
back, per. to .... DORSAL, TERGAL
back country .... STICKS, BUSH
backbite .... MALIGN, VILIFY, ASPERSE
backbone .... LADDER, RIGBANE
    GRATE, VERTEBER, VERTEBRA, SPINE,
                   CHINE
backgammon term ...... BLOT, IRISH,
         FALLES, LURCH, TABLES
background .... FOND
backward ...... SLACK, TARDY, HIND,
                   FRO
backwater .... BAYOU
bacon .... BARD(E), JAMON, LARD,
         FLITCH, GAMMON, RASHER,
               SOWBELLY
Bacon work ..... NOVUM ORGANUM
bacteria dissolver .... ASEPTIC, LYSIN
bacteria .... SARCINA, BACILLI,
         FUNGUS, GERM, COCCI,
         VIBRO, AEROBE, SPIRILLA
bad .... BASE, WANTON, EVIL, ILL,
         SAD, LITHER, WICKED, VICIOUS
bad luck .... AMBSACE, DEUCE, EVIL,
              JINX, HOODOO
bad-mannered person .. GOOP, BOOR
bad; Sp. .... MALO
badderlocks .... MURLIN
badge ... EMBLEM, ENSIGN, PIN, STAR,
    MON, PATCH, PLAQUE, INSIGNE
badger .. PATE, BAUSON, HYRAX, DAS,

BROCK, MELES, RATEL, TELEDU,
    HURON, CHEVY, MUSTELID,
               MUSTELINE
Badger State .... WISCONSIN
badger, to ...... FRET, HARRY, HECKLE,
                TEASE, BAIT
baffle .... DEFEAT, FOIL, HINDER,
         BALK, EVADE, ELUDE, MATE,
              POSE, THWART
baffling ..... ELUSIVE, EVASIVE
bag .. ASCUS, ETUI, POKE, STEAL, CYST,
    SACHET, JAG(G), POUCH, POUGH,
         POUGE, POAK(E), SWAG,
      PAGGLE, KAREETA, MUSETTE,
               SAC(KET)
bagatelle .... GAME, TRIFLE, CANNON
baggage ...... SWAG, STUFF, SAMAN,
    DUNNAGE, FARDAGE, PLUNDER
bagpipe .... BIGNOUDRONE, BINIOU,
    CHORUS, GEWGAW, MUSETTE,
    SAMBUKE, DULCIMER, DUDELSACK
bagpipe part .... LILL, CHANTER
bah .... ROT, PAH
Bahama island ...... ABADO, BIMINI,
                ANDROS
Bahama Is. capital .... NASSAU
bail .... LADE, REPLEVY, REPLEVIN
bailer .... SPOUCHER
bailey .... PRISON
bailiff .... REEVE, FACTOR, SAFFO,
    SCHOUT, VARLET, BUMTRAP,
               TIPSTAFF
bait .... DECOY, LURE, BRIBE, TRAP,
    HANK, SHRAP(E), BERLEY,
         CAPELIN, GUDGEON
bait, to drop .... DAB, DIB, DAP
baker ...... ROASTER, OVEN, FURNER,
             BAXTER, SOAK
baker's dozen .... THIRTEEN
baker's itch .... PSORIASIS
baker's utensil .. BRAKE, PEEL, ROOKER
baking dish .... RAMEKIN
baking pit .... IMU, UMU
Balaam's beast .... ASS
balance .. OFFSET, POISE, EVEN, REST,
       PEISE, OUNCEL, STEELYARD
balance of sails .... ATRY
balance weight ...... RIDER, BALLAST
balcony .... POY, ORIEL, GALLERY,
                PERGOLA
bald .... BARE, MERE, POLLED,
       PLAIN, CALLOW, ACOMOUS
Balder, giant slayer of .... LOKI
balderdash .... ROT, NONSENSE
Balder's wife .... NANNA
baldicoot .... MONK, COOT
baldness .... ALOPECIA, ACOMIA
bale .... LADE, DIP, SEROON, SERON,
                SARPLER

Balearic is. .... MINORCA, MAJORCA,
    " is. town .... PALMA
    " " language ...... CATALAN
balk ...... COND, FOIL, GIB, HUE, JIB,
    STAY, REEST
Balkis was queen of .... SHEBA
ball .... PELLET, ORB, IVORY,
    GLOBE, SPHERE, DANCE, BAW,
    CLEW, (K)NUR, GOLI, TICE,
    PALLE, PINDA, GLOME
ball, hit .... BOWL, BUNT, LOB, SWAT
ball, low .... LINER
ballad .. SONNET, DERRY, LAY, SONG
ball game .... BOWL, CRICKET, RUGBY,
    PELOTA, BOCCIE, POOL, GOLF,
    SOCCER, SQUASH, JAIALAI,
    LACROSSE
ballerina .... FONTEYN, SHEARER,
    TALLCHIEF, MARKOVA,
    PAVLOVA, ULANOVA
balloon .... MONTGOLFIER, AEROSTAT,
    SAUSAGE
balloon framework .... NACELLE
ballot .... SUFFRAGE, ELECT, VOTE,
    PROXY, TICKET
balm .... ANODYNE, BALSAM,
    UNGUENT, CANADA
balsam .... BALM, STORAX, SAPIN,
    TOLU, COPAIBA, BENJAMIN
Baltic island .. SAREMA, ALSEN, OSEL
Baltic seaport .... REVAL, RIGA
Baluch tribesman .... MARI
Baluchistan, capital of ...... QUETTA,
    KALAT
    " , dominant race of ....
    BRAHOES
    " mountain ... BOLAN, HALA
    " ruler .... KHAN, SIRDAR
balustrade ..... BALCONET, BANISTER,
    RAILING
Balzac .... HONORE
Balzac hero .... GORIOT
Bambi .... DEER
    " author .... SALTEN
bamboo ..... NANDIN, REED, GLUMAL,
    BATAK(AN), WHANGEE
ban .... TABU, TABOO, CURSE,
    EXCLUDE, ANATHEMA
banal .... CORNY, CLICHE, FLAT,
    STALE, TRITE, HACKNEYED
banana .... ENSETE, FEI, MUSA,
    LACATAN, SAGUING
banana bunch .... STEM, HAND
band(s) .... TENIA, LIGULA, TAPE,
    RADULA, PATTE, BAUN, FERD, FESS,
    GARLAND, COMBO, SWATH(E),
    SWADDLE, STRIA(E)
band wheel .... RIGGER
bandage ...... TRUSS, FILLET, LIGATE,
    SPICA, GALEA, CRAVAT,

CAPELINE, STUPE
bandicoot .... BADGER, MARSUPIAL
bandit ... FOOTPAD, THIEF, LADRONE,
    CACO, BRAVO, TORY, BRIGAND
band leader ...... LOMBARDO, WELK,
    VALLEE, WARING, WHITEMAN,
    SOUSA, GOODMAN, MILLER,
    CHORAGUS, STRAUSS, MAESTRO
bane .... PEST, POISON, VENOM
baneful, something .... UPAS, VILE
bang ...... CUDGEL, RAP, SLAM, CLAP,
    BEAT, IMPEL, SOUND
Bani, son of .... UEL
banish .... DEPORT, DISPEL, EXILE,
    EJECT, WREAK, RELEGATE
banjo, Japanese .... SAMISEN
bank .... BRAE, DUN, SAND, RIPA,
    CAJA, BINK, BANCO,
    RIVAGE, LOMBARD
banker .... BANYA, FUGGER, MELLON,
    MORGAN, SHROFF, SOUCAR, SARAF
banknote ... BILL, BUCK, CRISP, FIVER,
    GRAND, CENTURY, SAWBUCK,
    TENNER, GREENBACK
bankrupt . INSOLVENT, BREAK, QUISBY,
    FAILURE, CRASH, RUIN
banquet ...... DIFFA, FEAST, JUNKET,
    MANGERY, SYMPOSIUM
banteng .... TSINE, BANTINE
banter ... JOSH, BORAK, CHAFF, JEST,
    QUEER, RALLY, QUIZ, BADINAGE
Bantu family, one of .. DUALA, ZULU,
    VIRA, YAKA, BAKALAI
Bantu language ..... SUTO, VILI, ILA,
    RONGA
baobab tree .... LALO, MOWANA,
    IMBONDO, TEBELDI
baptism term .... FONT, LAVER,
    PISCINA
bar .... FID, ROD, DETER, MOIL, RACK,
    RISP, FESS, SKEY, SLIP, BLOCK,
    EASER, HUMET, STANG, ANCONY,
    BULLION, UPLONG
Bara, Miss .... THEDA
barb .... FLUE, JAG, SPINE, NAG
barbarians who pay tribute .. LAETAE
Barbados native .... BIM
barbarian ..... VANDAL, GOTH, HUN,
    SAVAGE
bard .... POET, RUNER, SCOP, OVATE,
    VATES, MINSTREL
barbarity .... FERITY, CRUELTY,
    SAVAGERY
barbarous .... CRUEL, FELL
Barbary States .. MOROCCO, ALGERIA,
    TUNISIA, TRIPOLITANIA
barbed-wire obstacle .... ABATIS,
    ABATTIS, HEDGEHOG
barber .... FIGARO, TONSOR, POLLER,
    SHAVER, SHAVESTER

Bard's river .... AVON
bare ..... MERE, NUDE, STRIP, SCARRY,
        PLAIN, JIMP, CALLOW, HISTIE
bargain .. PACT, PACTION, PRIG, DEAL,
        TROG, PALTER, NIFFER
barge .. HOY, PRAAM, TENDER, BARCA,
        CASCO, DUMMY, GABBARD
bark .... CORTEX, RIND
  " , kind of .... BARGE, PINNACE
  " , animal's .... BAY, YAP, YELP
  " , inner .... BAST, LIBER
  " , of a tree .... NIEPA
  " , strip of .... ROSS
  " , tonic .... CANELLA
  " yielding yercum .... MUDAR
barker .... PISTOL, TOUT, SPIELER,
        ROSSER, SPRUIKER
barley .... BIGG, TSAMBA, BERE,
        MALT, TISANE, PTISAN
barn .... BYRE, MEW, SKIPPER,
        AMBER, LATHE
barnacle .... CIRRIPED, BREY, ACORN,
        ANATIFA, BALANID
barometer .... GLASS, ANEROID
barometer gauge .... MANOMETER
barometric line .... ISOBAR
baron .... FREEMAN, PEER, NOBLE,
        FREIHERR
barony .... HAN, FIEF
barrack .... CASERN, CAMP
barracuda ...... SENNET, SPET, BARRY,
        BECUNA, PICUDA, SNOOK
barrel .... KNAG, KEG, TIERCE, BUTT,
        FESSEL, RUMBLE, HOGSHEAD,
        BANGEE, KILDERKIN, CADE
barrel maker .... COOPER
barrel part ...... HOOP, LAG, STAVE
barren ... DULL, STERILE, EFFETE, ARID
barricade .... ABATIS, BAR, OBSTACLE
barrier .. SCREEN, DAM, FENCE, PALE,
        TREBLE
barrister ..... ATTORNEY, COUNSELOR
barrow .... TUMULUS, BIER, GURRY,
        HURLY, KURGAN
Barrymore .... LIONEL, ETHEL, JOHN
bartender ... TAPSTER, MIXER, SKINKER
barter ...... PERMUTE, SWAP, TRAFFIC,
        CHOP, COMMERCE, MONG, TROG
Baruch .... BERNARD
base .... MEAN, LOW, SITE, BAD, BED
  " of column ...... DADO, PATTEN,
        PLINTH, SOCLE, PEDIMENT
  " ; root .... RADIX
baseball club .... SOX, DODGERS,
        GIANTS, YANKEES, INDIANS,
        ORIOLES, PIRATES, CUBS, METS,
        REDS, ASTROS, BRAVES, PHILLIES,
        CARDINALS, TWINS, ANGELS,
        TIGERS, SENATORS
baseball coach ...... DUROCHER, LEO,

DYKES, LIP, STENGEL, LOPEZ
baseball-field dispute ...... RHUBARB
baseball hero .... RUTH, GEHRIG,
        COBB, DEAN, MAYS, AARON,
        MANTLE, MARIS, KOUFAX,
        REESE, LEFTY, SANDY
baseball team .... NINE
baseball term .... BAG, BUNT, FRAME,
        SACK, SLAP, STICK,
        INNING, DIAMOND
Bashan, king of .... OG
bashful .... SHEEPISH, MODEST,
        TIMID, COY, SHY, VERECUND
Bashkir capital .... UFA
basil .... OCYME, TULSI, TOOLSI
basilica .... CANOPY, LATERAN
basin ... LAVER, CHAFER, FONT, PAN,
        STOUP, DOCK, HOLLOW, CAVITY,
        CUVETTE, TANK, RECEIPT, PISCINA
bask .... APRICATE, SUN, BEEK
basket .... SCUTTLE, DOSSER, BIN,
        HAMPER, MAUND, GABION,
        HOBBET, HOBBIT
  " , fish ..... CAWL, KRAIL, CREEL,
        KREEL, CAUL
  " for figs ...... CABAS, TAPNET
  " for fruit ..... POTTLE, PUNNET
  " of balloon .... NACELLE
  " to carry coal .... CORF
  " used in pelota .... CESTA
  " weaving .... SLEWING
  " , wicker .. BASSINET, HANAPER
  " willow .... OSIER
basket work .... SLARTH, SLATH,
        STAKE, STROKE, WALE
basketball player(s) .... CAGER, FIVE,
        GUARD, CENTER,
        HOOPMAN, CAGESTER
basking shark .... SUNFISH, SAILFISH
Basque ancestor .... IBERIAN
Basque cap .... BERET
Basque game .... PELOTA
Basque province ...... BISCAY, ALAVA
bass .... CHUB, ROCK, CHERNA,
        ACHIGAN, GROWLER,
        TALLIWAG, BACHELOR
bassoon .... FAGOT, CURTAL,
        DOLCIAN, DULCIAN
bast .... BARK, RAMIE, PHLOEM, FIBER
basta .... ENOUGH, STOP
baste .... SEW, LARD
bat ...... CLUB, CHUCK, HARPY, STICK,
        CUDGEL, POMMEL, RACKET, DRIVER,
        BACKIE, BAUKIE, NOCTULE,
        VAMPIRE, SEROTINE, REREMOUSE
  " , wing-footed as the ...... ALIPED
Bataan bay .... SUBIC
  " capital .... BALANGA
bate .... GRAINS, GRAINER
batfish .... ANGLER, DIABLO, LOPHIID

bath(s) .... BAIN, TUB, THERM(E), HAMMAM, BALNEUM, THERMAE, PISCINE
bathhouse .... BAGNIO, CABANA
bathe .... LAVE, TOSH, STEW, SUFFUSE, BASK
bathing suit .... BIKINI, TRUNKS, MAILLOT
baton .... WAND, SCEPTRE, SCEPTER, STICK, BOURDON, CROSSBAR
baton race .... RELAY
batter .... FRUSH, PASTE, RAM, BRUISE, BOMBARD, SLUGGER
batter cake .... WAFFLE
battery .... CELL, PILE, LEYDEN
battery term ... GRID, POLE, CHARGER
battle .... FIGHT, MART, TILT, WAR, COMBAT, CONFLICT, HOSTING
battle area .... ARENA, TERRAIN, ETO, CHAMP, TAHUA, SECTOR
battle array .... ACIES, HERSE, PHALANX
battle cry ...... ABOO, BANZAI, ABU
battlement .... CRENEL, PINION, EMBRASURE, RAMPART, MERLON
battle site .... ALAMO, ANZIO, ISSUS, MARNE, SEDAN, SOMME, BATAAN, CANNAE, VERDUN, BULLRUN, DUNKIRK, MARENGO, SALAMIS, BORODINO, MARATHON, WATERLOO
batty .... CRAZY, SILLY
bauble .... GEWGAW, TOY, MAROTTE
Bavarian city .... MUNICH, HOF
″ lake .... WURM
″ river .... ISAR, INN, LECH, ILLER, NAB, REGEN
bawl .... BARK, YELL, BELLOW, GOLLY
bay . BIGHT, VOE, GULF, HOPE, LOCH, INLET, BAHIA, SINUS, WICK
bay color .... ROAN
Bay State .... MASS.
Bayard's master .... RINALDO
Baylor University site .... WACO
bazaar .... AGORA, EXPOSITION, FAIR
be .... ARE, EXIST, LIE
beach .... PRAYA, PLAYA, SANDS, COAST, STRAND, SHILLA, SLIP, SHINGLE, SHORE
beach flea .. SCUD, SCROW, SANDBOY
beacon .... SIGN, FANAL, PHAROS, FLAG, VANE, SEAMARK, NEEDFIRE
beacon light ...... LANTERN, CRESSET
Beaconsfield .... DISRAELI
bead(s) ..... BUGLE, GRAIN, ARANGO, ROSARY, RONDEL, CHAPLET, GLOBULE

beadle .... OFFICER, POKER, MACER, BEDRAL
beady .... GLOBULAR
beak .... LORA, NEB, TUTEL, BILL, RAM, ROSTEL, SPERON
beak, trim with .... PREEN
beaker .... POCAL, CUP, GLASS, BIKER, HORN
beam .... RAY, SILE, SHINE, CABER
beaming ..... BRIGHT, RADIANT, ROSY
bean . URD, LENTIL, ADSUKI, CALABAR, SOY(A), TONKA, ESERINE, LIMA, HARICOT, HABA, FREJOL, FRIJOL, KAMAS, ESERE
″ , per. to eye of .... HILAR
″ weevil .... HARIA
bear ... CARRY, ENDURE, TOTE, WEAR, YIELD, DUB, DREE, SUPPORT
″ ; animal .. KOALA, URSUS, BHALU, DUBB, GRIZZLY, KODIAK, MUSQUAW, POLAR
″ ; astron. .... URSA
bear's ear .... PRIMULA, AURICULA
beard .... AWN, ARISTA, GOATEE, CRINITE, ANE, IMPERIAL, VANDYKE, BURNSIDE, BARB, DOWN, TUFT, PAPPUS, ZIFFS, STILETTO
bearded ... ARISTATE, AWNY, BARBATE
bearer .... SAKI, TOTER, CARRIER, ESQUIRE
bearing ...... AIM, AIR, PORT, MIEN, GEST(E), ORLE, HABIT
beast .... ANIMAL, BRUTE, BURRO, HOOF, FERIN(E), VACHE, JUMENT, OUTLAW, ROTHER
″ , colossal .. MONSTER, BEHEMOTH
beat .... PULSE, DRUB, LACE, WHIP, POMMEL, LARRUP, SLAP, TAN, BEST, FLOG, DRASH, FLAIL, HAMMER,
″ into plate .... MALLEATE
″ ; naut. .... TACK
″ , to; Scot. .... TOWEN
beater .... RAB, STOCK, TRIMMER, PULSATOR, HOLLANDER
beau .... BLADE, FLAME, SWAIN, DANDY, SPARK, BRUMMEL
beaut .... LULU
beautifier .... MOUCHE, MASCARA
beautiful .... BONNY, FAIR, TEMPEAN, SHEEN, WLONK, COMELY, LOVELY, HANDSOME
beauty .... NINON, VENUS, BELLE, WLITE
beautify .... ADORN, GRACE, QUAINT, EMBELLISH
beaver .... CASTOR, HAT, RODENT, BAVIERE
beaver skin .... PLEW, WOOM
because .. INASMUCH, SINCE, FOR, AS
″ ; Sp. .... PORQUE

22

bêche-de-mer ...... PIDGIN, TREPANG
becloud .... DIM, OBSCURE, HIDE
bed ...... BUNK, LAIR, LITTER, STEAD,
    DOSS, SLEEP, BASSINET, COT,
    COUCH, FLASK, LIBKIN, LIBKEN,
    THORE, REPOSAL, PLANCHER
bedbug ...... CHINCH, CIMEX, PUNEE,
    PUNIE, PUNICE, COREID, PUNAISE
bedeck .. PRINK, ADORN, TRAP, TRIM
Bedouin .... ARAB, NOMAD, RIFF
bedroom ... CABIN, CUBICLE, DORMER
bed stone in porcelain mill ... PAVER
beet sugar ...... SUCROSE
bee .... APIS, DOR, KARBI, MASON,
    NURSE, DINGAR, DRONE,
    DRONER, STINGER
" family .... APIDAE
" , girl named for .... MELISSA
" , part of a .... LORUM
" , per. to .... APIAN
" , pollen brush of .... SCOPA
beebread .... CERAGO
beech nuts ... MAST, BUCK, PANNAGE
beef ...... JUNK, MART, STEER, CATTLE
" , dried .... BUCCAN, VIFDA
" in onion .... MIROTON
" , lean .... LIRE
beehive ...... APIARY, ALVEARY, SKEP,
    GUM(E), PYCHE, SWARM(ER)
Beehive State .... UTAH
beekeeper .... APIARIST, SKEPPIST
beer ...... PORTER, ALE, BOCK, MUM,
    SUDS, HUFF, LAGER, STOUT,
    STINGO
beer, moistening wood with ....
    CISSING
beer shop .... FARO, JERRY,
    MUGHOUSE
beery .... MAUDLIN
beeswax ...... CAPPING, CEROSIN(E)
beet .... CHARD, ASA, BETA, MANGEL,
    MANGOLD
Beethoven work ... FIDELIO, EROICA,
    MISSA, NINTH,
    CONCERTO, SONATA
beetle . AMARA, MELOE, WEEVIL, DOR,
    ELATER, GOGA, IPID, FIDIA,
    GOGGA, HISPA, CHAFER, LAMIID,
    LARIID, LADYBUG
beetle, early stage .... LARVA
" , horny substance of ... CHITIN
beetle-like talisman .... SCARAB
beetle's wing cover .... SHARD
beetle's wings, upper .... ELYTRA
befall .... COME, HAP, OCCUR, BETIDE
before .. CORAM, AVANT, ERE, FORNE,
    SAID, PRIOR, ANTE, SOONER
before; prefix .... PRE, PRAE
before this time .... GONE, OVER,
    ERENOW, FORMER

beg .... BESEECH, IMPLORE, SUE,
    CADGE, ASK, CRAVE, ENTREAT,
    MAUND, PLEAD, PRAY, SORN,
    SOLICIT, SCHOOL, THIG
beget .... PROCREATE, KIND, SIRE,
    FATHER, ENGENDER, GENERATE
beggar .... MENDICANT, LAZAR, BAUL,
    RANDY, THRUM, ARMINE, MUMPER,
    SORNER, SCAFFER
begin .... OPEN, START, ENTER,
    FANG, TEE, COMMENCE
beginner .... DEBUTANT, ENTRANT,
    BOOT, TYRO, ROOKIE, FRESHMAN
beginning .... ONSET, ALPHA, ORIGIN,
    FRONT, INITIAL, NASCENT
begone .... OUT, SCAT, AROINT,
    AVAUNT
" ; arc. Ital. .... VIA
beguile ... COZEN, LURE, WISE, VAMP,
    WILE
Behan .... BRENDAN
behest .... BID, MANDATE, ORDER
behind ...... (AB)AFT, LATE, TARDY,
    HIDDEN, AFTER, AREAR,
    ASTERN, SLOW
behold .... ECCE, LO, VOILA,
    ESPY, VISE
beige .... ECRU, HOPI, GREGE
being(s) .... ESSE, ENTITY, ENS,
    ENTIA, LIFE, HUMAN, ANTEAL
Beja .... HAMITE
Beja's son .... IRI
beldam ...... FURY, ALECTO, CRONE,
    HAG, VIXEN
Belgian .... FLEMING, WALLOON
" block layer .... PAVER
" commune .... JETTE, ATH,
    TAMINES, ANS, MOLL, NAMUR,
    VORST, ZELE
" currency unit .... BELGA
" dialect .... WALLOON
" king .... ALBERT, LEOPOLD,
    BAUDOUIN
" river ...... LESSE, MEUSE, YSER,
    DYLE, LEIE, SCHELDE,
    LYS, SAMBRE
" statesman .... SPAAK
" town .... ALOST, ATH, GHENT,
    NAMUR, OSTENDE, MONS, YPRES
" violinist .... YSAYE
Belial .... DEVIL
belief .. CREDO, CREED, FAY, DOGMA,
    MIND, VIEW, TENET, TROTH
believer .... IST, OMNIST, DEIST,
    THEIST
bell(s) .... CODON, CAMPANA, KNELL,
    CARILLON, GONG, TOCSIN,
    SIGNAL
" tower .... CAMPANILE
bell town .... ADANO

belladonna .. MANICON, ATROPIN(E)
bellicose .... WARLIKE, MILITANT
Bellini, opera by .... NORMA
bellowing ... AROAR, YAWPING, WAIL
belly .... BULGE, PAUNCH, RIFF,
　　　　　　　　　　　　　THARM
belly-god ..... SYBARITE, CORMORANT
belong .... APPERTAIN, INHERE, OWN
belonging to a particular people ....
　　　　　　　　　　　　ENDEMIC
belongings .... CHATTEL, TRAPS
beloved one ..... DEAR, INAMORATA,
　　　　　　　IDOL, LOVE, DARLING
below .... NEATH, SOTTO
belt .... CINGLE, BALDRIC, CESTUS,
　　　CORDON, RING, ZONE, GIRDLE,
　　　　　LACE, CIRCUIT, ZONAR
belt, conveyor .... APRON
bemoan .... DEPLORE, WAIL, SOB
bemuse .... DISTRACT, ADDLE
bench ..... EXEDRA, PEW, BAR, BANC,
　　　SETTEE, ZYGA, ZYGON, THWART
bend .... CROOK, (IN)FLEX, KINK,
　　　SAG, CROUCH, NID, WARP,
　　　BOW, BULGE, SUBMIT, CURVE
bend in timber .... SNY
bending ...... LITHE, PLIANT, SUPPLE
benedict .... BRIDEGROOM
benefactor ...... PROMOTER, DONOR,
　　　PATRON, SPONSOR, ANGEL
benefice .... GLEBE, ANNAT
benefit .... HELP, AVAIL, BEHOOF,
　　　INTEREST, SAKE, BOON, BOOT,
　　　　　　　　　　　　　PROFIT
beneficiary .... HEIR, USER,
　　　　　　LEGATEE, DONEE
Benét; Amer. poet .... STEPHEN
Bengal city .... DACCA, PATNA
　　"　　district .... NADIA
　　"　　native .... KOL, BANIAN
　　"　　singer .... BAUL
benign ..... SUAVE, GENIAL, GENTLE
Benin Negro .... EBO(E)
benne seeds .... SESAMES
bent ... SWAYED, CRANK, BIAS, TASTE,
　　　FLAIR, KNACK, PRONATE
benthos .... FAUNA
berry-like .... BACCATE
benzoin, gum .... BENJAMIN
bequest .... LEGACY, GIFT, WILL
berate .... SCOLD, CENSURE, UPBRAID,
　　　　　　　CHIDE, REVILE
Berber ...... TUAREG, DAZA, TIB(B)U,
　　RIFF, HAMATIN, HAMITE, KABYLE
bereave ...... DEPRIVE, DIVEST, STRIP
bereft .... LOST, POOR
beret .... BIRETTA, TAM
berg .... FLOE, BARROW, MOUNTAIN
———— berg .... ICE
Berkshire racecourse .... ASCOT

Bermuda grass .... DOOB
Bernard De .... VOTO
Berra .... YOGI
berry .... CURRANT, BACCA, HAW,
　　　　ALLSPICE, SALAL, PASA
berry smoked in cigarette .... CUBEB
berserk ...... MAD, AMOK, ENRAGED,
　　　　　　　　　　FRENZIED
Bert .... LAHR, PARKS
berth .... BED, JOB, BUNK, DOCK,
　　　　　　　　SLIP, BILLET
bertha ...... CAPE, CANNON, COLLAR
beseech ..... OBTEST, BEG, SUE, PRAY,
　　　ADJURE, APPEAL, ENTREAT
best; comb. form .... ARISTO
beset .... HARRY, OBSESS, SIT,
　　　　　　ATTACK, INFEST
besides ..... THEN, ALSO, OVER, TOO,
　　　　YET, INBY, EXCEPT
besiege .... BESET, GIRD, OBSIDE,
　　　　　PESTER, PLAGUE
besmear ..... SLAKE, SMOTTER, DAUB,
　　　　　　　SOIL, TAINT
besom .... BROOM, MOP, HEATHER
bespangle ...... STUD, STAR, ADORN
bespoil ...... FLEECE, STRIP, PLUNDER
best ... UTMOST, VANQUISH, OUTWIT,
　　　AONE, BEAT, ELITE, CHOICE
bestow .. GRANT, ADD, GIVE, RENDER,
　　　AWARD, CONFER, DONATE
bet ...... HEDGE, GO, STAKE, WAGER,
　　　　　ANTE, BAS, POT
bet, fail to pay ...... WELCH, WELSH
betake oneself ..... REPAIR, JOURNEY
betel-nut extract .... CATECHU
betel-nut tree .... ARECA
Bethlemite, rich .... BOAZ
betoken ... DENOTE, PRESAGE, AUGUR
betray ...... BEGUILE, PEACH, SELL,
　　BLAB, TRAP, SNARE, TRICK, REVEAL
betrayer ... SEDUCER, TRAITOR, JUDAS
betroth .... AFFY, TOKEN, PLEDGE,
　　　　　　　　　PLIGHT
better .... EMEND, TOP, IMPROVE,
　　　REFORM, CORRECT, AMEND
betting system .... PARLAY
between ...... AMELL, MESNE, AMONG
bevel .. EDGE, ASLANT, SNAPE, CANT,
　　　REAM, MITER, MITRE, CHAMFER
beveled edge .... BEARD, WANY
bewail .... GRIEVE, LAMENT,
　　　　　CRY, WEY, WEEP
beverage .. ADE, ALE, POP, TEA, BEER,
　　　CIDER, MORAT, NEGUS, NECTAR
　　　　　POTABLE, GROG, POP
　　"　, oriental ...... LEBAN, RAKI,
　　　　　　RAKEE, ARRACK
　　"　, Poly. .... KAVA
　　"　, S. Am. .... MATE
　　"　　stand .... CELLARET

24

bevy .... COVEY, FLOCK, HERD, PACK, DROVE, SWARM
bewildered ...... ASEA, WILL, DAZED, ADDLED, AMAZED, CONFUSED
bewitch .... CHARM, ENAMOR, ENSORCEL, HEX, TAKE, THRILL, ENCHANT
beyond .... BY, PAST, YONDER, ULTRA
beyond; prefix .... META
bezel .... TEMPLATE, FACET, RIM, EDGE, SEAL
bhang .... HEMP
bhang, product of .... MAJOON
Bhutan pine .... KAIL
bias .... CLINAMEN, PARTIAL, PLY, SLOPE, TENDENCY, SLANT, BENT, SWAY
Bible, books of the .... GENESIS, EXODUS, RUTH, ESTHER, EZRA, JOB, JUDGES, PSALMS, MACCABEES
Bible version ...... PESHITO, DOUAY, VULGATE
biblical city ..... UR, DAN, LUZ, NOB, ONO, CANA, ETAM, GATH, GAZA, MYRA, TYRE
biblical coin .... MITE, TALENT
biblical country .. CANAAN, CHALDEA, SEIR, EDOM, ELAM
biblical desert .... PARAN
biblical giant .. ANAK, ENIM, GOLIATH
biblical hunter .... NIMROD
biblical king .. AGAG, OG, GOG, PUL, TOU, AHAB, AMON, BERA, DOEG, ELAH, JEHU, OMRI, REBA, SAUL
biblical language .... ARAMAIC
biblical measure ...... BEKA, CUBIT, EPHAH, GERAH, SHEKEL, OMER
biblical merchant .... TUBAL
biblical mountain .. ARARAT, HOR(EB), SINAI, NEBO, ZION
biblical name .. ANANI, ARAM, AROD, AROM, EBAL, EBED, ER, EZEL, GADDI, HELI, IRA, IRAD, ISHMAEL, IVAH, JAEL, MAGOG, MERAB, MESHECH, NER, NOB, OSEE, REBA, SEMEL, UCAL
biblical instruments . URIM, THUMMIM
biblical priest ..... ELI, IRA, AARON, EZRA, ANNAS, URIAH
biblical prophet ..... DANIEL, ISAIAH, AMOS, JOEL, HOSEA, MOSES, JONAH, MICAH, NAHUM, ELIJA ELISHA
biblical queen .... ESTHER, SHEBA, VASHTI
biblical shepherd .... ABEL, DAVID
biblical tower .... BABEL, EDAR
biblical valley . BACA, ELAH, SHAVEH, SIDDIM
biblical well .... ESEC, ESEK

biblical: worthless .... RACA
bicker .... ARGUE, DISPUTE, PETTIFOG, SPAT, TIFF, CAVIL, WRANGLE
bicycle .... TANDEM, ORDINARY, JIGGER, BIKE, BONESHAKER
bid ..... ENJOIN, OVERTURE, TENDER, INVITE
biddy .... CHICKEN
bier .... PYRE, LITTER, COFFIN
bifurcation ... BRANCHED, WYE, FORK
big shot; slang .... VIP
bighorn .... ARGALI, CIMARRON
bight .... LOOP, BAY, NOOSE, GULF, COVE
bigot .... ZEALOT, FANATIC
bile .... GALL, VENOM, CHOLER, BILK
bilk ...... GYP, HOAX, TRICK, CHEAT, SWINDLE
bill .... BEAK, LIST, TICKET, TAB, NEB, CERE, LAW, DUN, ACT, CARD, MENU, NOTE, POSTER, PLACARD
" of an anchor .... PEE
billhook .... KNIFE, SNAGGER
billiards .... POOL
billiards term ... CUE, CAROM, MASSE
billow .... EAGRE, BORE, WAVE, SEA, SURGE, SWELL, ROLLER
billy .... CAN, CUDGEL, CLUB, COMRADE
bin .... KENCH, CANCH, ARK
binate .... DOUBLE, TWOFOLD
bind .... GIRD, ROPE, WAP, LINK, TAPE, TRUSS, UNITE, OOP, COHERE, SECURE
bind to secrecy .... FRAP, TILE
bind with fetters ... GYVE, TIE, IRON
binding .... YAPP
binding machine .... BALER
binge ...... HIT, SOAK, SPREE, PARTY
bingo .... KENO, LOTTO, BEANO
binnacle ...... PYX, COMPASS, NEEDLE
biography ...... LIFE, MEMOIR, VITA, PROFILE
biological term .... GENE, BIOTIC, BIOTICAL, RIMA
biology .... GENETICS
bion, opposed to .... MORPHON
birch .... BETULA, FLOG, STICK, TREE, ALNUS
bird: adjutant ...... STORK, ARGALA, MARABOU
" , African .... COLY, LORY, LOURI
" , arctic .... LONGSPUR
" ; genus Ajaja .... SPOONBILL
" : albatross .... NELLY
" , Andean .... CONDOR
" : apteryx .... KIWI
" , area from bill to eye of . LORE
" , Asian .... MYNA(H), PITTA
" ; auk family ...... PUFFIN, ALCA

25

" , Austral. .... EMEU, EMU, LEIPOA
" beak .... CERAL, LORA, NEB
" : blackbird . RAVEN, ANI, MERL(E),
        AMSEL, OUSEL, OUZEL
" : bluebird .... IRENA
" : bobolink .... ORTOLAN
" : bob-white ..... COLIN, QUAIL
" , Braz. ...... CARIAMA, SERIEMA,
        TOUCAN
" brood .... COVEY
" : butcher .... SHRIKE
" : carrion crow .. URUBU, VULTURE
" catcher .... FOWLER
" : chatterer .... JAY
" , class of .... AVES
" : cockatoo .... ARARA
" , corvine .. CROW, DAW, RAVEN
" : crow, cry of .... CAW
" , crowlike .. CORVINE, PIE, ROOK
" , Cuban ... TOCORORO, TROGON
" : dabchick ... GREBE, GALLINULE
" , diving .... GREBE, LOON, AUK
" dog .... POINTER, SETTER
" : duck family ...... MERGANSER,
        SMEW
" : eagle; bib. .... GIER
" : eagle, nest of ..... AERIE, EYRIE
" : eagle, sea .... ERN(E)
" , Egypt. sacred .... IBIS
" , emulike ....CASSOWARY
" , extinct .... DODO, MOA
" , fable .... ROC
" : falcon .... MERLIN, SAKER,
        TERCEL, BESRA, SHAHEEN,
        SHAHIN, PEREGRINE
" : finch ... TOWHEE, MORO, SERIN
" , finchlike .... GROSBEAK,
        CHEWINK
" : fish hawk .... OSPREY
" , flightless ... DODO, EMU, MOA,
        RHEA, OSTRICH, PENGUIN
" , flightless; genus ...... APTERYX
" : flycatcher ..... OSCINE, PEWEE,
        PEEWEE
" : frigate .... IWA
" : fulmar, giant .... NELLY
" , gallinaceous, order of ....
        RASORES
" , game .. PTARMIGAN, PHEASANT,
        GROUSE, QUAIL
" , gluttonous .... CORMORANT
" : guan; genus .... ORTALIS
" : gull, per. to .... LARINE
" , gull, sea .... MEW, TERN
" , gull-like .... JAEGER, SKUA
" , Hawaiian ... MAMO, IWA, IIWI,
        OOAA
" ; heron family ... IBIS, BITTERN,
        EGRET
" , honey-eating .... TUI, MANUAO

" house .... NEST, AVIARY, COTE
" , humming ...... COLIBRI, SYLPH,
        AVE, TROCHILUS
" : iao .... MANUAO
" : ibis .... STORK, GUARA
" , Ind. .... AMADAVAT, SHAMA
" , insectivorous .... VIREO
" : jackdaw ...... COE, KAE, DAW
" jaw, part of .... MALA
" , jay-like .... PIET
" , killing of .... AVICIDE
" : kite .... GLEDE, ELANET,
        CHILLA, PUTTOCK
" , Latin for .... AVIS, AVES
" life .... ORNIS
" , limicoline .... AVOCET
" , long-legged .... WADER
" , long-neck .... SWAN
" , loon-like .... GREBE
" : lyre .... MENURA
" : macaw .... ARA, ARARA
" : magpie .... MAG, PIET
" , marsh, long-leg .... STILT
" , mound ..... LEIPOA, MEGAPOD
" , myth. .... ROC, PHOENIX,
        PHENIX, SIMURG
" , New Zeal. ...... LOWAN, KIWI,
        MOA, TUA
" , non-passerine .. HOOPOE, TODY
" of petrel family .... FULMAR
" of prey .. BUZZARD (GOS)HAWK,
        EAGLE, OWL, ELANET,
        KITE, KESTREL
" , one-year-old .... ANNOTINE
" : oriole .... PIROL
" , oscine ...... CROW, TANAGER,
        VIREO
" : osprey .... ERN, ERNE
" , ostrich-like .... EMU
" : owl .... LULU, UTUM,
        RAPTOR
" : parrot .... KAKA(POS), KEA,
        LORY, LORILET
" : parson .... POE, TUI
" : partridge .. SEESEE, TINAMOU,
        TINAMIDA
" , passerine ..... SPARROW, PITTA,
        STARLING
" , pelican-like .... SOLAN
" , per. to ...... AVIAN, ORNITHIC,
        AVINE
" : petrel .... TITI, TEETEE, PRION
" : pewee .... PHOEBE
" ; pheasant's nest .... NIDE
" : pigeon .... GOURA, NUN
" , plover-like .... LAPWING
" , quail-like ... TINAMOU, TURNIX
" : rail .... CRAKE, SORA, MOHO,
        WEKA
" , ratite ...... MOA, EMU, OSTRICH

26

" : raven .. ALALA, CORBEL, RALPH
" : reed .... BOBOLINK
" : ring dove .... CUSHAT
" : ruff .... SANDPIPER, REEVE
" , Samoan .... IAO
" : sandpiper ..... REEVE, DUNLIN, TEREK
" , sea .... GANNET, MURRE, PETREL, SULA
" , sea; auk family .... PUFFIN
" , shore .... AVOCET, SORA, STILT, WILLET
" , short-tailed .... BREVE
" , Sinbad's .... ROC
" , small .... TIT, WREN, TODY
" : snake .... ANHINGA
" : snipe .... CURLEW, DOWITCHER
" , S. Amer. ...... GUAN, TOUCAN, WARRIOR
" , song .... SHAMA, LARK, OMAO, WREN, AMSEL, ROBIN, SERIN, VEERY
" ; song, organ of .... SYRINX
" : sorrel, wood .... OCA
" : starling .... MINO, MYNA, STARNEL
" : stib .... DUNLIN
" : stitchbird .... IHI
" : stork ..... MARABOU, ARGALA, SIMBIL
" , swallow-like .... MARTLET, MARTIN, TERN, SWIFT, HIRUNDINE
" , swimming ...... GREBE, SWAN
" , talking .... MINA, MINO, MYNA(H)
" , three-toed .... STILT
" : thrush .... OUSEL, SHAMA, ORIOLE, VEERY, MAVIS
" : toucan .... TOCO
" : towhee bunting ..... CHEWINK
" , trop. ...... TROGON, MANAKIN, JACANA, KAKA, MAKO, RURU, AGAMI
" , turkey-like .... CURASSOW, LEIPOA
" , unmusical .... TANAGER
" : vulture .... URUBU, PAPA, CONDOR, GEIR
" , wading .. COOT, CURLEW, HERN, HERON, IBIS, JACANA, RAIL, SORA, TERN, UMBRETTE, STORK, JACIRU
" : warbler .... PIPIT, REDSTART
" : waxwing .... CEDAR
" : weaver .... MUNIA, TAHA
" woman .... AVIATRIX
" : yellowhammer .. FINCH, FLICKER
birds .... . AVIS, ORNIS, AVIFAUNA

birds' eggs, scientific study of .... OOLOGY
bird's head, side of .... LORE
birds of given region .... ORNIS
birds, of the .. AVIAN, AVINE, OSCINE
birth . GENESIS, ORIGIN, BEGINNING, NATIVITY
birth, before .... PRENATAL
birth rate .... NATALITY
birthmark .... NAEVUS, BLAIN, MOLE, NEVUS
birthright .... HERITAGE, INHERITANCE
birthstone ....
    "   for Jan'y .... GARNET
    "   for Feb. .... AMETHYST
    "   for Mar. .... BLOODSTONE
    "   for Apr. .... DIAMOND
    "   for May .... EMERALD
    "   for June .... AGATE
    "   for July ...... CORNELIAN
    "   for Aug. .... SARDONYX
    "   for Sep. ...... CHRYSOLITE
    "   for Oct. .... OPAL
    "   for Nov. .... TOPAZ
    "   for Dec. .... TURQUOISE
bis ... AGAIN, ENCORE, TWICE, REPEAT
Biscay island .... RE, YEU
Biscay, language of .... BASQUE
biscuit . WAFER, BUN, PANAL, RATAFEE, RUSK, RATAFIA, SCONE, SNAP, PANTILE, CRACKER
bisect .... HALVE, CLEAVE, SPLIT
bishop ...... PRIMATE, PRELATE, ABBA, ALFIN
    "   of Alexandria .... ARIUS
    "   of Rome .... POPE
bishop weed .... AMMI
bishopric .... SEE, DIOCESE
bishopric, raise to .... MITRE
bishop's cap .... HURA
    "   seat .... APSE, BEMA, LAWN, CATHEDRA
    "   staff .... CROSIER
    "   vestment .. COPE, GREMIAL
bison .. BOVINE, BUFFALO, AUROCHS, GAUR
bistort .... SNAKEWEED
bistro .... BAR, TAVERN
bit .... ACE, IOTA, JOT, MOTE, ATOM, WHIT, MORSEL, SNAFFLE, WEE, ORT, SPECK
bite STING, NIP, WHEAL, EAT, CHAM, CHEW, GNAW, MORSEL
bite impatiently .... CHAMP
biting .. ACRID, CRISP, COLD, CAUSTIC, MORDANT
bito .... AGIALID
bitter ..... ACID, ACERB, ACRID, IRATE, AMAR

27

bitter sentiment ... ACRIMONY, HATE, RUE, ACOR, MARAH
bitter substance .... ALUM, AMARINE, ALOIN
bitter vetch .... ERS
bitters; Fr. .... AMER, AIGRE
bitumen .... ASPHALT, TAR, PITCH
bituminous shale .... BAT
bivalve ... PANDORA, MOLLUSK, CLAM, MUSSEL, OYSTER
bivalves, fresh-water; genus ... UNIO
bivouac .... ENCAMP, ETAPE, CAMP
bizarre .. GROTESQUE, ODD, ANTIQUE, EXOTIC, QUAINT, QUEER, OUTRE, DAEDAL
Bizet, opera by .... CARMEN
black .... JET, EBONY, INKY, NEGRO, RAVEN, NIGRINE, SMOOCH, ATROUS
   "   alloy .... NIELLO
   "   and blue .... LIVID
   "   art .... EVIL, MAGIC
   "   ; Celtic .... DHU
   "   ; comb. form ...... ATER, ATRO
   "   crystalline mineral .. KNOPITE
   "   diamond .... COAL
   "   gum .... TUPELO
   "   mineral ..... URANINITE, IRIDE
   "   pigment .... MELANIN
   "   rhinoceros .... BORELE
Black Plague .... BUBONIC
   "   Sea, old name for ... EUXINE, PONTUS
   "   " , per. to .... PONTIC
   "   " port .... ODESSA
blackball .... PILL, OSTRACIZE
blackbird . MERLE, RAVEN, ANI, OUZEL
blackboard .... SLATE
blacken .. JAPAN, INK, SOOT, SHINE, DEFAME
black-fin snapper .... SESI
blackfish .... TAUTOG
blackguard . GAMIN, KNAVE, VILLAIN, VILIFY
Black Hand .... CAMORRA, MAFIA
blackhead .... DUCK, COMEDO
blackheart .... CHERRY
black hole .....DUNGEON, CALCUTTA
blackish .... SWART
blackjack .... CARAMEL, SPHALERITE
blackleg .... CHEAT
blackmailing; law ...... CHANTAGE
black martin .... SWIFT
blacksmith . FARRIER, STRIKER, SHOER
black snake .... RACER, COLUBER
blackthorn .... SLOE
blackthorn, fruit of .... HAW
black vulture .... URUBU
blackweed .... RAGWEED
black widow ..... SPIDER, POKOMOO
blackwort .... COMFREY

blade ..... BIT, TOLEDO, GRAIN, LEAF, SPIRE, OAR, EDGE, TANG, DANDY
blah .... NONSENSE, RUBBISH
blain ....BLISTER, BULLA, SORE
Blaine, Miss .... VIVIAN
blame .... CENSURE, REPROACH, CALL, OBLOQUY, ODIUM, SHEND, SNAPE, GUILT, FAULT, ONUS
blanch .. ETIOLATE, BLEACH, WHITEN, LEAD
bland .... FLAT, AFFABLE, MILD, SOFT, SUAVE, GENTLE, URBANE
blandish ... COAX, CAJOLE, WHEEDLE
blank .... FORM, VOID, VACANT
blanket AFGHAN, BROT, COTTA, QUILT, MANTA, STROUD, CORONA, PONCHO, SERAPE, SHEET
blanket, small .... THROW
blare of trumpet . TANTARA, FANFARE
blast .... BANG, FLAW, GALE, ATTACK
blast furnace, section of ..... BOSH
blasted ..... RUINED, BLIGHTED, SERE
blat ....BLEAT, BLURT
blatant COARSE, NOISY, GLIB, GROSS, VOCAL
blaubok ....ETAAC
blaze .... FLAME, FLARE, MARK, GLOW
blazer .... JACKET
bleach .... BLANCH, ETIOLATE, PATCH, CHLORE, WHITEN
bleaching vat .... KEIR
bleak ... RAW, SPRAT, ABLET, DREARY
"Bleak House" heroine .... ADA
blear; of the eye .... DIM, SORE
bleared ....RHEUMY
bleater .... SHEEP
bleb . BULLA, BLISTER, PUSTULE, BUBBLE
bleffert .... SQUALL
blemish ... BLOT, MACULE, MAR, SCAR, FLAW, INJURY, SLUR, TACHE, BRUISE, FAULT, DEFACE
blemish in cloth DEFECT, AMPER, SULLY
blench .. FLINCH, PALE, QUAIL, SHUN, AVOID, SHIRK, RECOIL
blend ...... MERGE FUSE, GRADATE, TINCTURE, TINGE, MIX, COALESCE
blend colors .. RUN, FONDU, SCUMBLE
bless .... CONSECRATE, HALLOW, MACARIZE, SAIN, EXTOL, PRAISE, BEATIFY
blessed ..... HOLY, SACRE(D), DIVINE
blessing ..... BENISON, BOON, SAIN, GRACE, BENEFICE
blight .. NIP, ROT, RUIN, RUST, SMUT, MILDEW
blind .. SEEL, DECOY, SHADE, SHUTTER
blind alley ..... IMPASSE, CULDESAC
blind flower girl .... NYDIA
blind impulse .... ATE
blind; Span. .... CIEGO

28

blind, printing for the ...... BRAILLE
blind staggers .... GID
blindfolded one .... HOODMAN
blindness .... ANOPSIA, CECITY
blink . PINK, WINK, NICTATE, TWINKLE
bliss .... FELICITY, RAPTURE, ECSTASY
blissful ...... ECSTATIC, SEELY, HOLY
blister .... QUAT, BLEB, BLAIN, BLURE,
                                   BULLA
blithe .... AIRY, GAY, MERRY
blizzard .... PURGA, BURAN
bloat ...... SWELL, DISTEND, INFLATE,
                                   TUMEFY
bloated .... TURGID, CONVEX
blob .. MARK, SPLOTCH, BLOT, BUBBLE,
            WEN, DROP, MASS, BLEMISH
bloc .... RING, CABAL, FACTION
block .... BESET, DAM, NOG, HINDER,
           TYMIE, BAR, BITT, FOIL, QUAD,
                      DENTEL, DENTIL
block; falconry .... PERCH
    ″ , flat .... MUTULE
    ″ , ice .... SERAC
    ″ , iron stamp .... VOL
    ″ , mechanical .... PULLEY
    ″ , nautical .... DEADEYE
    ″ , small .... TESSERA
blockhead DUNCE, NINNY, DOLT, ASS,
      FOOL, IDIOT, OAF, CUIF, NOWT,
                                MOKE
blockhead board .... DOLL
blond(e) .... TOWHEAD
blood .. GORE, FLUID, SERUM, CRUOR,
                     ICHOR, PLASMA
blood-bank deposit .... PINT
    ″ color .... SANGUINE
    ″ , coloring matter of ... CRUOR
    ″ disease ... ANEMIA, LEUKEMIA
    ″ emulsion .... CHYLE
    ″ feud .... VENDETTA
    ″ fluid; comb. form ...... SERO
    ″ , fluid part of .... PLASMA
    ″ -letting .... PHLEBOTOMY
    ″ of the gods .... ICHOR
    ″ poisoning .... PYAEMIA
    ″ , per. to ..... HEMAL, HAEMAL,
                   HEMIC, HAEMIC
    ″ ; prefix .... HEMA, HEMO
    ″ , red .... VENOUS
    ″ slackening .... STASIS
    ″ , stagnation of .. CLOT, CRUOR,
                      GRUME, GORE
    ″ vessel ...... VAS, ARTERY, VEIN
bloodless .... ANAEMIC, ANEMIC
blood-like .... HEMATOID
blood money .... GALANAS, CRO
bloodsucker .... LEECH, VAMPIRE
bloody .. GORY, SANGUINARY, CRUENT
bloom .. PRIME, FUZZ, HEYDAY, DEW,
           FLOWER, YOUTH, DOWN

bloomer .. LAPSE, TROUSER, MISTAKE,
                           SLIP, ERROR
bloomery .... HEARTH, FORGE
blossom .... PROSPER, BLOOM
blossom keels .... CARINAE
blot .... BLUR, SULLY, SMEAR, ERROR,
              TAINT, STIGMA, STAIN
blot out .. DELETE, EFFACE, EXPUNGE,
                    DESTROY, DELE
blotch MOTTLE, MACULA, BLEB, BULLA,
                     BLAIN, SPLAT
blotch of color ..... GOUT, LIPSTICK
blotter .... BLAD, PAD
blouse .... SMOCK, TUNIC, WAIST
blow ..... DINT, PANT, SLOG, CLOUT,
      THWACK, BUFFET, CLUMP, CONK,
      COUP, CRIG, DEVEL, GALE, HIT,
                       DISASTER
blow cement on sculpture ... KIBOSH
blow; col. ..... ONER, RANT, VAUNT
blowzed ...... RUDDY, FLUSHED, RED
blubber ...... LIPPER, FAT, WEEP, CRY,
                     WAIL, SPECK
blubber, cut .... FLENSE
bludgeon ...... CUDGEL, MACE, BAT,
                SHILLALAH, CLUB
blue ..... BICE, CADET, DELFT, AZURE
blue-back .... TROUT, HERRING
    ″ cap .. SALMON, SCOT, TOMTIT
    ″ dye ... CYANINE, ANIL, WOAD
    ″ eagle agency .... NRA
    ″ -fin .... HERRING, TUNA
    ″ -gill .... SUNFISH
    ″ grass .... POA
Blue Grass State .....:.. KENTUCKY
    ″ jeans .... LEVIS
    ″ penciler .... EDITOR
    ″ pigment .. SMALT, IOLITE, BICE
    ″ -print .. MAP, PLAN, DIAGRAM,
                                DRAFT
    ″ vitriol .... BLUESTONE
Bluebeard's wife .... FATIMA
bluebottle .... CORNFLOWER
blues .... DISMALS, DUMPS, MEGRIMS,
                             LOWS
bluff .... BANK, CLIFF, CRUSTY, RUDE,
            BRAG, CURT, HOAX, STEEP
bluish gray .... CESIOUS
bluish green-blue .... CALAMINE
blunder ..... BULL, ERR, SLIP, BONER,
      ERROR, FAILURE, MISDO, GAFF,
                         BUNGLE
blunt .... ASSUAGE, BLATE, OBTUND,
              DULL, RUDE, OBTUSE
blur ..... BLOB, MACKLE, MACULE
blurb ... AD, RAVE, ANNOUNCEMENT
blush ...... COLOR, MANTLE, FLUSH,
                   TINGE, REDDEN
blushingly .... ROSILY

bluster ...... ROAR, BOUNCE, RANT, THREATEN, RODOMONTADE, BULLY, BRAVADO, SWAGGER
Blyth, actress .... ANN
boa .... BOMA, ABOMA, PYTHON
boar ..... APER, BARROW, HOG, SUS, TUCKER, HOGGET
board . COUNCIL, DEAL, EATS, LODGE, PANEL
boards .... STAGE, FEEDS, KEEPS
boar's head .... HURE
boast ... BRAG, GAB, VAPOR, VAUNT, BOG, RAVE, PREEN, BOMBAST, CROW
boaster .... RODOMONT, BRAGGART, BRAVADO, JINGO
boastful air .... PARADO
boasting .... GASCONADE
boat ..... GIG, ARK, BUSS, CAT, TUB, TROW, LST
" , African slave .... DHOW
" , anc. Britons' .... CORACLE
" , Bolivian .... BALSA
" brace .... THWART
" captain in the East ..... RAIS
" , Chinese .... SAMPAN, JUNK
" , dispatch ..... OOLAK, AVISO
" , Dutch .... PRAAM, HOOKER
" , Eskimo ...... OOMIAK, UMIAK
" , E. Ind. .... DONY, DINGEY, DINGHY
" , flat-bottom .. DORY, BAC, PUNT, SCOW, BATEAU, BARIS
" , French .... CARAVEL
" , half-decked .... WHERRY
" , heavy-decked ...... CANALER, CANALLER
" , Indian .... MASOOLA
" , Indian river .... LAMADIA
" , Italian .... GONDOLA
" , kind of raft .... BARGE, CATAMARAN
" , large .... ARGOSY, MOSES
" , man-of-war's .... PINNACE
" , Malayan .... TOOP, PROA
" , name of Jason's .... ARGO
" , part of .... DECK, KEEL, PROW, RAIL, SKEG, STERN
" propelled by three rowers..... RANDAN
" , ship's .... YAWL
" , small .. SHALLOP, SCULL, SKIFF, COG, DORY, PUNT
" , steam .. TUG, TENDER, LAUNCH, LIGHTER
" ; tender .... HOY
" , Venetian state .... BUCENTAUR
" , W. Ind. merchant ... DROGHER
boatman .... PHAON, CHARON
boat-shaped vessel ...... NAVICELLA

boat-shaped ornament .... NEF
boats, collection of .... TOW
boatswain of a lascar crew . SERANG
boatswain's whistle .... PIPE
boat timber .... KEEL
Boaz, son of .... OBED
Boaz, wife of .... RUTH
bob ... PENDANT, BAB, FLOAT, DUCK, JERK, SHILLING
bobbin .. SPOOL, PIRN, REEL, SPINDLE
bobcat .... LYNX
bobolink .... SUCKER, ORTOLAN, REEDBIRD, RICEBIRD
Boccaccio classic ...... DECAMERON
bode ... AUGUR, PORTEND, FORETELL, PRESAGE
bodice .... BASQUE, WAIST
body ...... PHYSIQUE, UNIT, CORPSE, TORSO, CORSE, BOLE, BULK, FORM, MASS, SOMA, STEM, CADAVER, CARCASS, STIFF, LICH(AM)
body motion.....................
" , of a .... GESTIC
" of a vehicle ...... BED, BOX
" of men ... ARMY, MASS, NAVY, CORPS, FORCE, POSSE
" , per. to ..... SOMAL, SOMATIC
" , small .... NANOID
Boer dialect .... TAAL, AFRIKAANS
Boer general .... BOTHA
Boeotian capital .... THEBES
" region .... IONIA
boeuf .... BEEF
bog .... FEN, MARSH, MOOR, OOZE, SWAMP, MORASS, QUAG, SYRT, MIRE, SLOUGH
bog manganese .... WAD
bog plant .... ABAMA
bogey . BUGABOO, BUGBEAR, GOBLIN, SPOOK, SPECTER, DEMON
boggle ..... ALARM, SCARE, JIB, BALK
boggy ..... MIRY, SOFT, WET, FENNY
bogus ... FAKE, FALSE, SHAM, PHONY
bohea .... TEA
Bohemia, district in .... EGER
Bohemian .. PICARD, HUS(S), GYPSY, ARTY
" character .... MIMI
" city .... PRAHA
" dance ... REDOWA, POLKA
" mountain range ..... ERZ
" vesuvianite ...... EGERAN
boil .... SEETHE, STEW, KYLE, ANGER, BUBBLE, STY, RAGE, SORE, TEEM, (DE)COCT
boiler .. CALDRON, COPPER, ALEMBIC, RETORT, TANK
boiler reinforcer .... SPUT
boiler-tube scaler .... SOOTER
bold . BRAZEN, RASH, PERT, FORWARD

bold style of type ...... TEST, DARK
bole ..... CRYPT, DOSE, STEM, TRUNK
bolero .... JACKET, DANCE, WAIST
bolide .... MISSILE, METEOR
Bolivia, dept. in .... ORURO
Bolivian coin ... TOMINE, CENTAVO
boll BULB, POD, ONION, SWELL, KNOB
bolt ..... SIFT, PAWL, RIVET, CLOSE,
    FASTEN, RUN, GULP, TOGGLE,
    NAB, PIN, PINTLE, BAR, LOCK,
    SLOT, ELOPE, FLASH, SCREEN,
    WINNOW
bolo .... MACHETE, KNIFE
bolter .... SIEVE, DESERTER
bolus .... CLOD, LUMP, MASS, CUD
bomb .... GRENADE, MARMITE
bombardment . CANNONADE, STRAFE,
    RAFALE
bombardon .. BASSOON, OBOE, TUBA
bombast ...... FUSTIAN, GAS, RAGE,
    BOASTING, RANT, ELA, TUMOR
bombastic .... INFLATED, OROTUND,
    TURGID, GRANDIOSE, TUMID,
    FLOWERY, POMPOUS
Bombay town .... MIRAJ, SURAT
bombproof chamber . ABRI, CASEMATE
bombyx .... MOTH, ERI, ERIA
bonasus .... AUROCHS, BISON
bond ...... DUTY, LINK, NEXUS, TIE,
    COMPACT, RELATION, VOW,
    PLEDGE, VALENCE, GLUE, YOKE
bond; Fr. .... RENTE
bondage SERVITUDE, YOKE, THRALDOM
bond land .... COPYHOLD
bondsman . CHURL, ESNE, PEON, SERF,
    SLAVE, HELOT, THRALL, VASSAL,
    VILLEIN, STOOGE, SURETY
bondstone .... PERPEND
bone(s) .... OS, OSSA, DIES,
    OCCIPITA, TIBIA
bone, anvil .... INCUS
bone, breast ...... RATITE, STERNUM
 " cavities .... ANTRA
 " , cheek .... MALAR
 " ; comb. form .... OSTEO
 " curvature .... LORDOSIS
 " decay .... CARIES
 " disease .... RACHITIS, RICKETS
 " , face .... MAXILLA
 " , flank .... ILIA
 " in finger .... PHALANGE
 " , inflamed .... OSTEITIS
 " in forearm .... ULNA
 " of a fish .... OPERCLE
 " of wrist .... CARPAL
 " , per. to ..... ULNAR, OSTEAL
 " , process of temporal . MASTOID
 " , plowshare .... VOMER
 " , small ...... OSSELET, OSSICLE
 " , thigh .... FEMUR

bone black .... ABAISER
boner .... ERROR, BLUNDER, SLIP
bones .... DICE, OSSA
boneset FEVERWORT, SAGE
bongo .... DRUM
boniata .... YAM
bonito .... AKU
bonnet . CAPOTE, MOBCAP, CHAPEAU,
    TOQUE
bonnet, resembling a ...... MITRATE
bonnet string .... BRIDE
Bonneville dam site ...... OREGON
bonus .... TIP, MEED, AWARD,
    CUMSHAW, PREMIUM
bony .... LANK, OSSEOUS, SCRAGGY,
    HARD, LEAN, STIFF, SKELETAL
boo .... LOW, MOO
boob .... DUNCE, FOOL, NITWIT, ASS
booby .... LOSER, PRIZE, STUPID
booed .... HOOTED
boojum .... SNARK
book(s) ...... ALDUS, BIBLE, TOME,
    MS, MSS, VOLUME, PRIMER, LIBER,
    MANUAL, OPUS, FOLIO, LOG
book awarded to undergraduate.....
    DETUR
 " , back of a .... SPINE
 " , handsomely printed ... ALDINE
 " , introduction to ..... ISAGOGE
 " of devotions .... MISSAL
 " of hours .... HORA, HORAE
 " of nobility .... PEERAGE
 " of psalms .... PSALTER
 " of rubrics .... ORDO
 " palm .... TARA, TALIERA
 " , shape and size of ... FORMAT
 " sheath .... FOREL
 " selection .... PERICOPE
bookkeeping entry .... DEBIT, CREDIT
boom . RESOUND, ROAR, SPAR, SPRIT,
    DRUM
boomerang .... RESILE, RECOIL,
    RICOCHET, BACKFIRE
boon ... GAY, JOVIAL, BENE, FAVOR,
    GRANT
boor .... LOUT, CARLOT, CHURL, CAD,
    OAF, CARL, CLOWN, TIKE, CLOD
boorish ... GAWKY, RUDE, UNCOUTH,
    VULGAR
boost . ABET, KITE, LIFT, EXULT, HOIST
boot ... KAMIK, KICK, RECRUIT, SOCK,
    SHOE, STOGA, CRUISER, OXFORD,
    BALMORAL, STOGY, PAC, OCREA
booth .... LOGE, SOOK, SOUK, SUQ,
    CRAME, STALL
bootlick .... FAWN, TOADY, FLATTER
bootlicker .... YESMAN
booty .... PREY, GAIN, LOOT, SWAG,
    GRAFT, SPOIL, PELF, FANG
borax .... TINCAL

31

border .. TIP, ABUT, EDGE, RAND, RIM,
FRAME, SKIRT, FRONTIER, FOREL,
FLANK, BRINK, VERGE, MARGIN
border, make a raised .... MILL
border on stamps .... TRESSURE
bordered .... LIMBATE, VERGED
bore .... PROSER, IRK, STOOD,
DIAMETER, TEWEL, PEST, EAGRE,
TIDE, ENNUI
bore; mil. .... CALIBRE, CALIBER
bore, to pierce .... HOLE, TEREBRATE
Boreas .... NORTHER
boredom .... TEDIUM, ENNUI
Borge .... VICTOR, DANE
boring tool .... AUGER, BIT, WIMBLE
Boris Godunoff char. .... DIMITRI
born .... NATE, NASCENT, NEE
born, well- .... FREE, EUGENIC
borne, was .... RODE
Borneo, aborigine of .... IBAN, DYAK
    "   ape .... ORANG
    "   , capital of .... BRUNAI
    "   , port of .... MIRI
    "   , river in .... BARAM
Borodin opera hero .... IGOR
borough .... BURG, BORG
borrow ... COPY, KICK, ADOPT, STEAL
borrower .... DEBTOR, OWER
borrowed stock .... DAER
borsht base .... BEETS
bos .... BREED, COW, NEAT, CALF
bosh .... SKETCH, TRIVIA, ROT, SPOIL,
END, JOKE, POOH
Bosnia, native of .... CROAT
boss DIRECTOR, FOREMAN, OVERMAN,
DEAN, STRAW, MASTER, BAAS,
KNOB, KNOP, STUD, UMBO
bot .... NIT, LARVA
botanical angle .... AXIL
    "   cell .... SPORE
    "   change .... PELORIA
    "   depression .... VARIOLE
botanist .... BROWN, RAY, BURBANK
botany .... PHYTOLOGY
botch .... BUNGLE, FAIL, MUX, MESS,
FLUB
bother . AIL, MOLEST, HARASS, PESTER,
FUSS, TODO, HARRY, MEDDLE,
TEASE
bottle .... VIAL, COSTREL, KIT, PHIAL,
CARBOY, PIG, JUG, CRUET, CRUSE,
FLASK, CARAFE, FLAGON, CANTEEN
bottom .... BED, LEED, NADIR, PLAYA,
BASE, SOLE, DREGS, FLOOR,
GROUND
bottom facet of a brilliant .... CULET
bough .... ARM, LIMB, TWIG, SHOOT,
SPRIG, SHROUD
bounce .... SACK, LEAP, EJECT, FIRE,
DISMISS, VERVE, RECOIL, SPRING

bound . CONFINE, DELIMIT, DART, HOP,
LOPE, SECURED, SCUD, SKIM, STEND
boundary . LINE, AMBIT, MERE, VERGE,
BOURNE, LIMIT, METE
bounded .... LEAPT, SPRANG
bounder RAKE, CAD, SNOB, CUB, ROUE
bounty ... BONUS, REWARD, LARGESS,
GIFT, MEED, GRANT, PRIZE
"Bounty" captain .... BLIGH
bouquet ..... AROMA, ODOR, POSEY,
NOSEGAY
Bourbon; modern name ... REUNION
bourgeois .... CITIZEN
bout . ESSAY, ROUND, SETTO, MATCH,
TURN
bovine .... BULL, OX, TAURINE, COW,
CALF, YAK, BISON, CATALO, TORO,
ZEBU, ARNI
bow ..... ARC, CONGE, NOD, BEND,
CURVE, PROW, STEM, DEFER,
CURTSY
bow, low ... SALAAM, BINGE, STOOP
bowdlerize .... EXPURGATE
bowed .... ARCATE, ARCUATE(D)
bowel .... PITY, COLON, RUTH
bower ..... ANCHOR, ARBOR, NOOK,
GROTTO, KNAVE
bowfin .... AMIA, LAWYER
bowl .. CRATER, KITTY, BASIN, MAZER,
PATINA, ARENA, PAN, DEPAS
bowler .... HAT, DERBY, KEGLER
bowling .... TENPINS
bowling pin .... JACK, NINEPIN
bowsprit, part of .. SHROUD, CHOCK,
HEEL, APRON, STEM, BEE
box .... COFFER, CAR, CASE, DORINE,
CARTON, MOUNT, LOGE, BIN,
CIST, CUFF, ETUI, SEAT, SLAP,
SLUG, SPAR, SWAT, CAPSA, CHEST,
CRATE, FIGHT, PUNCH
box, alms .... ARCA
box elder .... ACER
box for tea .... CANISTER
box of tools .... CHEST, KIT
boxer .... SPARRER
Boxer .... CHINESE
boxers (prize) .... BAER, BRADDOCK,
CARNERA, CORBETT, DEMPSEY,
JEFFRIES, JOHNSON, LOUIS,
SHARKEY, SCHMELING, SULLIVAN,
TUNNEY, WILLARD, CLAY, ALI,
LISTON, MARCIANO
boxing match .... SETTO
boxing term .... TKO, KAYO, KO
box-shaped tomb .... CIST
boxwood tree .... SERON
boy .. SHAVER, LAD, TOT, TAD, NINO,
GROOM, YOUTH
"Boy Scouts" founder ....
BADEN-POWELL

boycott .... SHUN, OSTRACIZE, BLACKBALL
brace .. LEG, PAIR, TWO, BIRD, GIRD, PROP, STAY, SHORE, TRUSS, CRUTCH, STIFFEN
brace and a half ..... LEASH, THREE, TIERCE
bracelet .... BANGLE, ARMIL, SANKHA
bracing ...... QUICK, TONIC, TIMBER
bracket ... CONSOLE, CORBEL, STRUT, CLASS, SHELF
bract ...... SPATHE, GLUME, PALEA, PALET, SPADIX
brad .... NAIL, PIN, SPRIG
Bradley .... OMAR
brag ... CROW, GASCONADE, VAPOR, BOAST, VAUNT, YELP, SWAGGER, STRUT, PREEN
Brahma .... CREATOR
Brahman ..... ZEBU, ARYAN, PUNDIT
Brahman deity .... AGNI, DYAUS
Brahman precept ... SUTRA, NETINETI
Brahman title .... AYA
braid .. CUE, LACET, PLAIT, TRESS, TRIM, INKLE
bramble .... THORN, THIEF, BRIER
brain box .... PAN
   " canal .... ITER
   ", external membrane of .. DURA
   " grooves .... SULCI
   " matter .... ALBA
   " membrane .... TELA
   " orifice .... LURA
   ", per. to .. CEREBRAL, ENCEPHALIC
   " tumor .... GLIOMA
   " wave .... ALPHA, BETA
brake ..... CURB, FERN, BURR, DRAG, BLOCK, DELAY
brake, part of .... DRUM, SHOE
brambly .... PRICKLY, SPINY
branch .. FORM, RAME, RICE, STOLON, RAMIFY, VIMEN, ARM, SPRIG, LIMB
   ", angle formed by ..... AXIL
   " of a nerve .... RAMUS
   ", per. to ...... COMAL, RAMAL
branched . RAMAL, CLADOSE, RAMOSE
branches .... RAMAGE
branchiae .... GILLS
brand .... MARK, STAMP, LABEL, STAIN, STIGMA, FLAW, CHOP, TAINT, SEAR
branding iron ... SEARER, CAUTER(Y)
brandish .... SHAKE, SWING
brandy .... COGNAC
   ", a content of .... ETHER
   ", cordial .... ROSOLIO
   ", French .... MARC
   ", mastic .... RAKI
brant .... CHEN, GOOSE, QUINK

brash ... BOLD, HASTY, SAUCY, SASSY
brass .... ALLOY, NERVE, OFFICER(S)
brass to imitate gold ...... ORMOLU
brassica ...... CABBAGE, COLE, KALE
brasslike alloy ...... PLATEN, LATTEN
brassy .... BRAZEN, BOLD
brat .... BAIRN, ELF, IMP, MINOR, GAITT, GETT
brave .... HEROIC, MANLY, FACE, DARE, GAME, DARING, INDIAN, STIFF, DEFY
bravo ..... BIS, OLE, BANDIT, GOOD, HEAR, RAH, THUG
brawl .... FRACAS, FRAY, RIOT, ROW, SHINDY, MELEE
bray ... MIX, HEEHAW, CRUSH, GRIND
brazen .... SASSY, NERVY, PERT
Brazil was first sighted by ————— CABRAL
   ", capital of ...... RIO, BRASILIA
   ", president of .... VARGAS
   ", rubber region of .... ICA
   ", rubber tree of .... HEVEA
   ", seaport of .... BAHIA, CEARA
   ", state in ...... CEARA, PARANA
   ", town in ..... BELEM, MANAOS, RECIFE, SANOS
Brazilian aborigine .... CARIB
   " cape .... FRIO
   " club moss .... PILLIGAN
   " dance ..... MAXIXE, SAMBA
   " drink .... ASSAI
   " fiber .... IMBE
   " forest .... MATA
   " lagoon .... PATOS
   " long-legged bird .. SERIEMA
   " money .... MILREIS, REI
   " plant .... CAROA
   " tree .... SATINE, ANDA, APA, MURURE
   " wood .... EMBUIA
breach ...... CLEFT, GAP, RENT, SLAP, CRACK, RUPTURE
bread ...... LOAF, PONE, RUSK, BUN, CUSH, DIKA, ROLL, BATCH, MONEY
bread crumbs .... PANADA
bread crust .... CAROB, RIND
bread, leavened; Afr. .... KISRA
bread of Passover .... MATZOS, AZYM
bread soaked in broth ...... BREWIS
bread spread .... BUTTER, OLEO
bread, toasted, small piece ... SIPPET
breadth .... SPAN, SCOPE, EXTENT, WIDTH
break .... HIATUS, RUIN, RUPTURE, BOON, CRACK, HINT, SNAP
break molten glass in water .... DRAGADE
break out ...... ERUPT, RASH, ESCAPE
breakable .... SHELLY, BRITTLE

break-bone fever .... DENGUE
breaker ... BILLOW, ROLLER, COMBER
breakwater ...... JETTY, DIKE, MOLE,
COB, DAM, PIER, QUAI
bream .... CLEAN, BROOM
breast .... CHEST, THORAX, STEM
breastbone .... STERNUM
breastbone, having flat ...... RATITE
breastpin ...... BROOCH, PECTORAL,
OUCH, CLASP
breastplate .... LORICA, POITREL
breastplate, objects in .... URIM,
THUMMIM
breastwork ...... PARAPET, RAMPART,
SCHERM, FORT, DICKEY
breath .... ANDE, PECH, PNEUMA,
PRANA, HALITUS, HUFF
breath, to catch the .... GULP
breathe ...... PANT, PUFF, ASPIRATE,
RESPIRE, LIVE, WHEEZE
breathe out .... SNORT, SUSPIRE
breathed .... SPIRATE
breather .... REST, BREAK, PAUSE
breathing .. GASP, PNEUMA, WHEEZE,
RALE, STRIDOR
breathing orifice .... SPIRACLE
breathing, painful ..... DYSPN(O)EA
breathing, smooth .... LENE
breech ..... BUTT, REAR, BORE, BLOCK
breech site .... HAUSSE
breeches .... TREWS, JODHPURS
breed .... ILK, KIND, RACE, REAR,
SIRE, BEGET, HATCH, PROGENY
breeding place .... NIDUS
breeze .... AIR, WIND, STIR, AURA,
FLAW, GUST, PIRR, ZEPHYR
breve .... WRIT, MINIM, ORDER,
MARK, NOTE, BRIEF
breviary .... COMPEND, EPITOME,
DIGEST, ORDO
brew ...... ALE, CONCOCT, FOMENT,
MIX, PLOT, CURE, STEW
brewer's grain .. MALT, BARLEY, CORN
brewer's yeast .... LEAVEN, BARM
brewery refuse .... DRAFF, DREGS
brewing .... GAAL, GYLE, GAIL,
MALTING
bribe .... SUBORN, BOODLE, SOP,
BAIT, GRAFT, TEMPT, PAYOLA
bric-a-brac ... CURIO, VIRTU, BIBELOT
brick ..... DOBE, MARL, DOBY, DOBIE
" carrier .... HOD
" of wood .... DOOK
" oven .... KILN
" , unburnt and dried .... ADOBE
bricklayer .... MASON
bridal wreath .... SPIREA
bride .... KALLAH
"bride of the sea" .... VENUS

bridegroom's gift to bride ....
HANDSEL
bridesmaid bonnet ...... CORONET
bridewell .... GAOL, JAIL, PRISON
bridge .... PONT(OON), PONS, SPAN,
LINK, ARCH, MAGAS
" , part of .... TRESSEL, TRESTLE
bridge expert ... GOREN, CULBERTSON
bridge term ...... TENACE, BID, BYE,
NIL, BOOK, SLAM, SET, PASS,
SUIT, VOID, RAISE, TRICK, TRUMP
bridle ...... STRUT, BID, CAPER, CURB,
BRANK(S), PILLORY, SNAFFLE
brief .... SHORT, TERSE, EPITOME,
COMPACT, CURT, PITHY,
LACONIC, CONCISE, SUMMARY
brigand .... BANDIT, CATERAN,
LATRON, PIRATE
bright ..... APT, NITID, NAIF, SUNNY,
SLEEK, ANIME, LUCID
bright-colored fish .... SERRANO
bright star .... SUPERNOVA
brighten .... BURN, FURBISH, ENGLID,
SMARTEN, CHEER
brightness .. ACUMEN, NITOR, SHEEN
brilliancy .... GLITTER, ECLAT
brilliant . EMINENT, SIGNAL, RADIANT
brilliant coterie .... GALAXY
brim .... POKE, BRINK, EDGE, MARGE,
SKIRT, VERGE
brine .... PICKLE, TEARS, BRACK,
MAIN, SALT, SEA, OCEAN
brine shrimp .... ARTEMIA
bring ..... APPORT, FETCH, INCUR,
COMMAND
bring forth ...... CAUSE, RISE, EAN,
YEAN, BEGET, HATCH
bring near, to .... APPOSE
briny .... SALTY, SALINE
brink .... EDGE, BORDER, MARGE,
DITCH, RIM, VERGE, EAVE
brioche .... CUSHION, SAVARIN
brisk .... SPRY, PERK, ALIVE, YARE,
ACTIVE, KEDGE, FAST, FLEET, ALERT,
CHEERY, NIMBLE, ALLEGRO
bristle .... CHAETA, HAIR, PALPUS,
BRUSH, SETA, PREE, PRIDE,
SPINE, STRUT
bristle-like tip .... ARISTA
bristly ...... SCOPAIE, HISPID, SETOSE
Britain, anc. people of ...... SILURES
" , old name for .... ALBION
British author ..... WELLS, PRIESTLEY,
SHUTE, GREENE
" cavalry .... YEOMANRY
" channel .... SOLENT
" chief; anc. ...... PENDRAGON
" general .... BRADDOCK,
HAIG, GORDON
" gum .... DEXTRIN

34

" gun ...... ENFIELD, STEN, BREN	Brontë .... EMILY, CHARLOTTE,
" isle .... MAN, BUTE, SARK,	ACTON, BELL
JERSEY, WIGHT	bronze .... BROWN, ALLOY, TAN
" king, legendary .... ARTEGAL,	bronze, colored like ...... AENEOUS
ARTHUR, LUD	bronze, gilded .... ORMOLU
" naturalist .... SLOANE	", Roman .... AES
" novelist .... (ARTHUR)MACHEN,	", variety of .. PATINA, LATTEN
FLEMING	brooch ... PIN, CLASP, OUCH, FIBULA,
" orator .... WILLIAM PITT	TIARA, PECTORAL, CAMEO
" order .... GARTER	brood .... FRY, HATCH, SIT, MOPE,
" parish official .... BEADLE	ISSUE, LITTER, PONDER
" Parl. record .... HANSARD	" buds .... SOREDIA
" poet ...... (WYSTAN) (HUGH)	" of pheasants .... NID, NYE
AUDEN	brook .... RUN, BECK, RILLET, RUNNEL,
" prime minister .... ATTLEE,	CREEK, BEAR, ABIDE, SUFFER,
HEATH, PITT, DISRAELI,	SIKE, STAND
WILSON, HOME	broom .... WHISK, BESOM, MOP,
" prince ..... ANDREW, CHARLES	SWAB, HIRSE
" princess .... ANNE	broom plant .... SPART
" pudding .... SUET	broth .... POTTAGE, BREE, BROO,
" race; anc. .... PICT, ICENI	POTAGE, SOUP
" Royal Guard officer ..... EXON	brothel .... KIP, BAGNIO
" saint .... ALBAN	brother .. FRIAR, FRA, OBLATE, MONK,
" seaport .... COWES	PAL, BILLY, FRATER, FELLOW, PEER,
" soldier .... TOMMY(ATKINS)	CADET, SIBLING
" statesman ..... EDEN, HOARE,	brought up by hand .... BRED, CADE
SAMUEL	brow .... TOP, BREE, EDGE,
" theorist .... LASKI	SNAB, CREST, RIDGE
Britons; anc. .... ICENI, JUTES, PICTS,	Brown; actress .... VANESSA
SCOTS	brown .... COOK, SEAR, TOAST
Brittany, per. to .... ARMORIC	" coal .... LIGNITE
brittle .... WEAK, CRISP, FRAIL,	" color . PUCE, CUBA, BAY, SEPIA,
FROW(Y), FICKLE	KHAKI, TENNE, TAN, BEIGE
broach ... AWL, REAMER, PIERCE, TAP,	" hematite .... LIMONITE
LAUNCH, BEGIN, PUBLISH, VENT,	" paper .... KRAFT
AIR, VOICE	" pigment .... PISTER, UMBER
broad .... VAST, AMPLE, GENERAL,	browned .... TANNED, RISSOLE
LIBERAL, LARGE	brownie .... ELF, KOBOLD, NIS,
broadbill .... RAYA, GAPER	GOBLIN, PIXIE
broadcast .... RADIO, TV, TEEVEE	Brownie .... CAMERA
broaden .... WIDEN, EXPAND, DILATE,	Brownian movement .... PEDESIS
ENNOBLE	Browning's home .... ASOLO
broad-minded .. TOLERANT, CATHOLIC	browse .... BRUT, CROP, NIBBLE,
broadsword .... BILL, CLAYMORE,	FEED, GRAZE, PASTURE
CUTLASS, FERRARA	Broz .... TITO
Brobdingnagian .... GIANT	Bruce; actor .... NIGEL
brocket .... PITA, DEER, SPITTER	Brubeck, Mr. .... DAVE
brogan .... BROGUE, SHOE, BOOT,	bruise ...... MAUL, CONTUSE, FRAY,
STOGY	BRAY, DENT, HURT, ICTUS
Brogi's wife .... IDUN	bruised .... HUMBLE, LIVID, HURT
broil .... GRILLADE, BRAISE, GRILL,	bruit .... RUMOR, NOISE, TELL,
FRACAS, SCORCH, MELEE,	REPORT, HEARSAY
SCRAP, ROW	brunt ..... JAR, JOLT, SHOCK, IMPACT
broken in back .... CHINED	brush ..... GRAZING, THICKET, FITCH,
broken pottery .... SHERD	COPSE, BROSSE, CLEAN,
broken wind .... HEAVES	FRAY, TIP
broker ... AGENT, FACTOR, CHANGER,	brushwood .... COPPICE, SCROG,
JOBBER	BOSCAGE, SCRUB
brokerage business ...... AGIOTAGE	brushy ..... HIRSUTE, HAIRY, SHAGGY

brusque .... GRUFF, BLUNT, CURT,
        RUDE, BLUFF, ABRUPT, TERSE
brutal .... MAD, CARNAL, INSENSATE,
        CRUEL, FERAL, BESTIAL,
        COARSE, SAVAGE
bryophyta .... MOSSES
bryophyte, place for cultivating .....
        MOSSERIE
Brythonic .... CORNISH
bryozoa .... RETERPORE, POLYZOA
bubble .... BEAD, BLEB, BOIL, CHEAT,
        BLAIN, AIR, SEETHE
bubble breaking sound of ..... BLOB
buccaneer .... CORSAIR, VIKING,
     PIRATE, MAROONER, PICAROON
Bucephalus .... STEED, CHARGER
buck .... STAG, PRICKET, ETAAC,
     SASIN, FOB, NOB, DUDE,
     DANDY, SWELL, RESIST
Buck; novelist .... PEARL
bucket .... PAIL, BOWK, SKEEL, STOP,
     SCOOP, TUB
buckle .... TACHE, TIE, BEND,
     WARP, CLASP
buckler .... RONDELLE
buck's antler .... ADVANCER
bucks in fourth year .... SORES
buckthorn .... CASCARA
bucolic .... ECLOGUE, RURAL, IDYL,
     RUSTIC, PASTORAL
bud ...... GEMMA, BULB, CION, GEM,
     BURGEON, SPROUT, KNOP,
     GRAFT, IMP, BEGIN
   " , blighted .... BLAST
Buddha .... JATAKA, GAUTAMA,
     SAKYAMUNI
   " , mother of the ...... MAYA
   " , wife of the .... AHALYA
Buddhism: cause of finite existence .
     NIDANA
Buddhism, center of Tibetan . LHASA,
     LASSA
Buddhism: will to live ...... TANHA
Buddhist angel .... DEVA
   " column .... LAT
   " delusion .... MOHA
   " evil spirit .... MARA
   " fate .... KARMA
   " festival .... BON
   " final liberation ... NIRVANA
   " form .... RUPA
   " gateway .... TORAN
   " hell .... NARAKA
   " monastery .... TERA
   " monk .... BO, TALAPOIN
   " novice .... GOYIN
   " pagoda .... TAA, TEE
   " priest .... LAMA, BONZE
   " relic mound .... STUPA
   " sacred language ...... PALI

   " shrine ..... DAGOBA, TOPE
   " stupa .... AMARAVATI
   " temple .... VIHARA
buddy .... PAL, CHUM, CRONY
budget, family ...... BUNCH, PACKET
buds, send forth .... BURGEON
buff .... FAN, SHINE, POLISH
buffalo .... TIMARAU, ZAMOUSE,
     BISON, CATALO, NIARE
   " meat .... BILTONG
   " , water .... CARABAO
   " , wild .... ARNA, ARNI, ARNEE
   " : wild ox; Celebes .... ANOA
buffet ... SLAP, TOSS, COUNTER, PLAT,
     SMITE
buffoon .. ANDREW, CLOWN, MIMER,
     ACTOR, HUMORIST, ZANY,
     FOOL, JAPE, DROLL
buffoonery .... JAPERY, DROLLERY
bug .... BOATMAN, CIMEX
bugaboo .... JUMBO, MUMBO, GOGA,
     GOGO
bugbear ... BOGEY, OGRE, BUGABOO
bugle call .... RETREAT, TANTARA,
     TAPS, REVEILLE, TATTOO
bugle, strain on .... TIRALEE, MOT
bugle weed .... INDIGO
bugle, yellow .... IVA
bugs; genus .... EMESA
build ...... REAR, CONSTRUCT, FORM,
     RAISE, STATURE, COOT, ERECT
build a nest .... NIDIFY
builder .... CARPENTER, ERECTOR
builder of Cretan labyrinth ....
     DAEDALUS
building ..... EDIFICE, ADOBE, TAPIA
bulb .... BUD, LAMP, TUBER,
     ONION, CORM, KNOB, GLOBE
Bulgarian capital .... SOFIA
   " coast town .... VARNA
   " coin .... LEV, LEW
   " early ruler .... ASEN
   " mountain .... RHODOPE
   " tsar .... BORIS
bulge .... BLOAT, SWELL, BUG, KNOB,
     JUT, HUMP, BAG
bulging ... TUMID, CONVEX, GIBBOUS,
     FULL
bulk .... MAJORITY, MASS, SIZE,
     VOLUME, WHOLE, BODY,
     GROSS, SHAPE, BOUK
bull ...... MINOTAUR, TAURUS, ZEBU,
     TORO, STOT, APIS, HAPI,
     COP, SLIP, BOBBY, ERROR,
     PEELER, BLUNDER, SOLECISM
bull, like a .... TAURINE
Bull; violinist .... OLE
bulldoze ..... DIG, BULLY, RAM, COW,
     FORCE, SCOOP, BROWBEAT
bullfight .... CORRIDA

bullfighter ...... TORERO, MATADOR, PICADOR
bullet .... TRACER, SHOT, SLUG, BALL, DUMDUM, PELLET
bulletproof shelter .. ABRI, MANTELET
bullfinch .... ALP, ALF, OLP, NOPE
bullion ... BAR, INGOT, BILLOT, MASS
bully .... HECTOR, SHANNY, COW, SCARE
bully tree .... BALATA
bulrush .... SCIRPUS, TULE
bulwark .... BAIL, RAMPART, SCONCE, FORT, BASTION, CITADEL, PARAPET
bum .... HOBO, IDLER, TRAMP
bumble .... BITTERN, BULRUSH, BEADLE, BLUNDER
bumper .... FINE, GOBLET, FACER, TOAST, GLASS, BUFFER
bumpkin .... SWAB, BOOR, LOUT, YOKEL, CLOD, RUBE, GAWK, CARL, RUSTIC
bun .... ROLL, WIG, JAG, TAIL, STEM, STALK
bunch .... FAGOT, LOT, SET, BALE, TUFT, WISP, CROWD
bund ..... DAM, DIKE, QUAY, LEAGUE
bundle .... BOLT, HANK, SHEAF, SHOOK, BALE, FAGOT, FADGE
bung ..... CORK, PLU, STOPPER, SHIVE
bungle .... ERR, GOOF, BOTCH, SPOIL
    ″   in hunting .... TAILOR
bunk .... HOKUM, SLEEP, DWELL, COT, BERTH
bunker .... BIN, SANDHOLE, CRIB, HAZARD
_____ Bunker .... ARCHIE
bunko .... CHEAT, SWINDLE
bunting .... ORTOLAN, PAPE
buoy .... DAN, DEADHEAD, LIGAN, FLOAT, HOPE, NUN, RAISER, CAN, LEVITATE
buoyant .... CHEERFUL
burbot .. EELPOUT, CUSK, LING, LOTA
burden .... BIRN, CUMBER, ONUS, TAX, CARE, CARK, LADE, FARDEL
burdock .... LAPPA, CLITE
bureau ...... DESK, DRESSER, OFFICE, CHEST, AGENCY
burfish .... ATINGA
burgeon .... BUD, SHOOT, SPROUT
burglar .... CRACK(SMAN), YEGG
burial .... INTERMENT, SEPULTURE
burial case .... CASKET, COFFIN, BIER
    ″ , one who wraps for ... CERER
    ″ pile .... PYRE
    ″ place .... LOW, TUMULUS, AHU, GRAVE, BARROW
buried ... HIDDEN, SUNKEN, IMBEDDED

burin .... GRAVER, ROD
burke .... LYNCH, MURDER, SLAY, KILL
burl .... PIMPLE, LUMP, KNOT
Burl .... IVES
burlesque .... FARCE, COMEDY, OVERDO, PARODY
burley .... TOBACCO
burly .... FAT, OBESE, STOUT, BULKY, HUSKY
Burma capital .... RANGOON
    ″   chief ... BO(H), WUN, WOON
    ″   district .... TOUNGOO
    ″ , division of .... YEU, ARAKAN, PEGU
Burmese Buddhist .... MON
    ″   dagger .... DOW, DAH
    ″   gate .... TORAN
    ″   gibbon .... LAR
    ″   girl .... MIMA
    ″   governor ..... WOON, WUN
    ″   language ..... KACHIN, KUKI, LAI, PEGU
    ″   native .... CHIN, KACHIN, LAI, SHAN, PEGUAN
    ″   river .. IRAWADI, IRRAWADDY
    ″   spirit or demon .... NAT
    ″   robber .... DACOIT
    ″   shelter .... ZAYAT
    ″   tree .... ACLE
    ″   weight .... RUAY, TICAL, KYAT, VIS
burn ..... CENSE, CHAR, SCALD, SERE, SEAR, ASH, RILL, SINGE, BROOK, CONSUME, CREMATE, BRAND
burn the midnight oil ... LUCUBRATE
burned .... USTULATE, ADUST
burning .... ARSON, FIRE, EAGER, AFIRE, CAUTERY, CALID, ARDENT, IRATE
burning bush .... WAHOO
burnisher .. AGATE, POLISHER, BUFFER
burnsides .... WHISKERS, BEARD
burnt sugar .... CARAMEL
burr .... CIRCLE, HALO, WHETSTONE, POD, NUT, RING, BRIAR, CORONA
burrow ... HOLE, MOIL, MINE, ROOT, DIG, TUNNEL, TUBE
burrowing animal .. WOMBAT, MOLE, ARMADILLO, SURICATE
bursar .... SAC, TREASURER
burst forth ..... REAVE, REND, ERUPT
Burundi, capital of .... USUMBURA
    ″ , king of .... BAGAYA
    ″   natives of .... BATWA, BAHUTU, WATUSI
bury .... INTER, INHUME, INURN, EARTH, CACHE, CLOAK, VEIL
bush .... BOSCAGE, TOD, SHRUB, CLUMP

37

" of hair .... SHAG
bushels, forty .... WEY
bushing .... SLEEVE, LINING
bushy .... DUMOUS, DUMOSE
bushwhacker .... PAPAW
business ...... CRAFT, GEAR, OFFICE,
INC., FEAT, GEAR, AFFAIR,
CHORE, ERRAND, STINT
business memo .... AGENDA
business, per. to .... PRAGMATIC
business trust .... CARTEL, TRADE
buskin .... TRAGEDY, SHOE
buss ...... DECK, DRESS, SMACK, KISS
bust .... RENT, ERUPT, REAVE,
SPLIT, EXPLODE
bustard(s) ...... OTIS, PAAUW, KORI,
OTIDAE
bustle ... POTHER, TUMULT, STIR, ADO,
FISK, FUSS, HYPER, FLURRY
busybody ...... MEDDLER, QUIDNUNC
but .... SED, HENCE, SAVE, WITHOUT,
MERE, ONLY, BAR, YET, STILL
butcherbird .... SHRIKE
butcher's hook .... GAMBREL
butler .. CELLARER, SPENCER, STEWART
butt .... RAM, TUP, CASK, PUSH,
BUNT, GOAD, STUB, TARGET
" , one third of ...... TERCE, TIERCE
butte .... HILL, DUNE, MOUND, KNOLL
butter ... GHI, GHEE, MAHUA, BEURRE
butter-and-eggs .. RAMSTED, TOADFLAX
buttercup, fruit of .... ACENE
butter-like substance .... CACAO,
MARGARINE
butter substitute ...... OLEO, SUINE
butterflies .... LEPIDOPTERA
butterfly .... IO, VANESSA, VICEROY,
ADMIRAL, URSULA
butterwort .... STEEPWEED
buttery ..... PANTRY, SPENCE, LARDER
button .. KNOP, STUD, BUCKLE, HOOK,
OLIVE, BADGE, BOSS,
FASTEN, KNOB
buttons .... PAGE (COL.)
Buttons, Mr. .... RED
button part .... SHANK
buttonhole stitch .... FESTON
buttress .... STAY, SUPPORT, PROP
buyer ...... EMPTOR, VENDEE, AGENT
buzzard ...... PREYER, HAWK, GLEDE,
OSPREY, BEEHAWK, PERN
buzzer ..... BEE, BELL, ALARM, SIGNAL
by ..... ASIDE, WITH, AGO, AT, PAST,
PER, NEAR, CLOSE
by heart .... MEMORITER
bygone . PAST, FORMER, OLDEN, YORE
Byronian hero .... LARA
byway .... LANE, ALLEY, PATH
byword ... PROVERB, PHRASE, SAYING
Byzantine coin .... BEZANT

" empress .... IRENE
" mosaic .... ICON, IKON

C

C mark .... CEDILLA
caama .... ASSE
cab .... TAXI, ARABA
cabal ..... PLOT, JUNTO, INTRIGUE,
CLIQUE, BLOC
cabbage ... CHOU, COLZA, KOHLRABI,
SAVOY
" broth ...... BORECOLE, KALE
" , any white ...... COLEWORT
" ; genus .... COS
" salad .... KRAUT, SLAW
" worm .... LOOPER
cabin .... COACH, HUT, SHED, SHACK,
BERTH, CABAN(A)
cabinet ...... ALMIRAH, BAHUT, BUHL,
BUREAU, CLOSET, ETAGERE,
MINISTRY
cable, per. to a type of .. COAX(I)AL
cabling ...... RUDENTURE, MOLDINGS
caboose .... HACK, CAR, CAB, GALLEY
cacao .... COCKER, BROMA
cache .. CONCEAL, STORE, HIDE, BURY
cachet .... WAFER, SEAL, STAMP
cacholong .... OPAL
cackle ...... LAUGH, CHATTER, CANK,
CHAT, GOSSIP, TALK
cactus (see "plant")
cad .... BOUNDER, HEEL
cadaver .... CORPSE, SKELETON,
CARCASS, STIFF
caddish .... ILLBRED
cadence .. MODULATION, TONE, LILT,
PACE, METER, RHYTHM
cade .... JUNIPER
cadet .... SON, YOUTH, JUNIOR, PLEB
cadge .... BEG, MOOCH, SPONGE
Cadmus' daughter ...... INO, SEMELE
" father .... AGENOR
" sister .... EUROPA
" wife .... HARMONIA
caduceus ..... WAND, SCEPTER, STAFF
Caesar's colleague .... BIBULUS
" death place .... NOLA
" foe .... BRUTUS, CASCA
" wife .... CORNELIA
Caesar-weed fiber .... ARAMINA
caesura .... BREAK, PAUSE, REST
cafe .... BARROOM, CABARET
caffeine .... THEIN(E), THEINA
cafila .... CARAVAN
cage .... GIG, HUTCH, MEW
cahoots, in .... LEAGUE, PARTNERS

38

Cain's son .... ENOCH
caisson .. BOX, CHEST, WAGON, CASE
    "   disease .... BENDS
caitiff .... BASE, DESPICABLE, VILE
                    MEAN, WICKED
cajole .... PALP, CHEAT, COAX,
    WHEEDLE, DECOY, TEASE, ENTICE,
    BEGUILE, BLANDISH, FLATTER
cake .... BATTY, CONCRETE, HARDEN,
          SUN, FLOE, SCONE, BAP
    " , corn .... PONE
    " , flat .... PLACENT
    " , rounded ..... CHARLOTTE, TART,
                    TORTE
    " , seed .... WIG(G)
    " , thin .. FARL(E), WAFER, JUMBLE
calamitous . EVIL, DIRE, HAPLESS, SAD
calamity .... BLOW, BALE, HYDRA,
          DISASTER, REVERSE,
          WRACK, MISERY, WOE
calash .... CALESA
calcar .... OVEN, SPUR
calcareous .... TRAVERTINE
calcareous deposit .... CORAL,
                STALAGMITE
calcium phosphate .... APATITE
calcium sulphate ... GYPSUM, HEPAR
calculate .... COUNT, AIM, RATE,
       FRAME, RECKON, COMPUTE
calculator .... TABLE, ABACUS
Calcutta weight .... PANK
calderite, variety of .... GARNET
caldron .... BOILER, KETTLE, VAT,
              POT, RED
Caleb's daughter .... ACHSAH
    " son .... IRU, HUR
Caliban, deity of .... SETEBOS
Caliban's witch mother .... SYCORAX
calendar ...... ORDO, MASS, DIARY,
    ALMANAC, JOURNAL, DOCKET
calf, motherless ... MAVERICK, DOGIE
calf of leg, per. to .... SURAL
calf, skin of .... KIP
caliber .... BORE, DEGREE, DIAMETER,
               GAUGE
calico .... SALLOO
    " printing of colors .... TEER
    " steam dye process ... TOPICAL
California .... ELDORADO
    " bay .... MONTEREY
    " city .... PALOMAR, NAPA,
    CHINO, PASADENA, SONORA,
        MADERA, UPLAND
    " college .. MILLS, UCLA, USC
    " county ...... INYO, KERN,
          LAKE, MONO,
        NAPA, YOLO, YUBA
    " evergreen shrub ..... SALAL
    " fruit .... KUMQUAT
    " lake .... CLEAR, EAGLE,

        GOOSE, HONEY, MONO,
        OWENS, TAHOE
    " motto .... EUREKA
    " mountain ...... PALOMAR,
               DONNER
    " pass .... SONORA
    " sea .... SALTON
    " spot (with Big) ...... SUR
    " wine area .... NAPA
caliph ... ALI, IMAM, OMAR, OTHMAN
calisthenics system .... DELSARTE
calk .... CHINSE, CLOSE, COPY,
            NAP, STOP
calker .... STAVER
call BAN, CLEPE, DUB, TERM, BID, CRY,
    CITE, NAME, SOOK, YELL, PHONE,
      ROUSE, VISIT, ELICIT
call out .... INVOKE, EVOKE
call together ..... CONVOKE, MUSTER
called .... YCLEPT, NAMED, DUBBED
calligrapher .... COPYIST, PENMAN
calling .... AVOCATION, METIER,
    PURSUIT, TRADE, NAME, JOB
callous .... HARD, HORNY,
          TORPID, TOUGH
    " , render ..... /. HARDEN, SEAR
Calloway, Mr. .... CAB
callus .... POROMA, TYLOMA
calm ..... BALMY, MILD, ABATE, LULL,
    QUIET, PLACATE, ALLAY, STOIC,
      STILL, SMOOTH, SEDATE
calming, act of .... SEDATION
calorie .... THERM(E)
calumet .... PIPE
calumniate ... BELIE, LIBEL, SLANDER,
    DEFAME, REVILE, VILIFY
calumniator, a; Gr. .... THERSITES
calumny .... SLUR, LIBEL,
      SLANDER, LAMPOON
Calvinist .... BEREAN
calyx .... COVERING, HUSK, CUP,
      SEPAL, PERIANTH
cam ..... LOBE, COG, WIPER, CATCH,
           TRIPPET
camarilla .... CABAL, CLIQUE, JUNTO
camass .... LOBELIA
Cambodia, anc. capital of .. ANGKOR
    " , great river of .. MEKONG
    " , native of .... KHMER
Cambria .... WALES
Cambrian zone .... OLENUS
Cambridge boat race .... LENT
    " honors exam ..... TRIPOS
    " student .... SIZAR, OPTIME
came down .... DESCENDED, ALIT
camel .... DROMEDARY, DELOUL,
      HAGEIN, MEHARI, BACTRIAN
camel's hair cloth ...... CAMLET, ABA
    " keeper ...... SARWAN, OBIL
    " thorn .... ALHAGI

39

cameo .... ANAGLPH, ONYX, RELIEVO
camera .... ————— OBSCURA,
————— LUCIDA, KODAK,
POLAROID, PANORAM
   "   part .... LENS, FINDER
   "   shot .... SNAP, STILL
Cameroons people, one of ..... ABO,
SARA
Camorra .... MAFFIA
camp .... BIVOUAC, ETAPE, TABOR,
POST
   " , per. to .... CASTRAL
campaign .... CRUSADE
campanula .... HAREBELL
camphor ALANT, BORNEOL, MENTHOL,
APIOL
campion .... SILENE
campus .... QUAD, FIELD, GATED
cam-wheel projection .... LOBE
can . CONSERVE, MAY, MUN, TIN, JUG,
JAIL, COULD
Canadian airport .... GANDER
   "   bay . GRIPER, HECLA, FUNDY
   "   canal .... WELLAND
   "   cape .... CANSO
   "   free-grant district MUSKOKA
   "   goose .... BRANT(A)
   "   highest peak ...... LOGAN
   "   Indian . DENE, TINNE, CREE
   "   island .... HARE
   "   lake ... GRAS, SEUL, TESLIN
   "   land measure ..... ARPENT
   "   lynx .... PICHU
   "   national park ..... JASPER
   "   penalty; law .... DEDIT
   "   peninsula .... GASPE
   "   physician .... OSLER
   "   policeman ...... MOUNTIE
   "   province; abbr. ALTA, QUE,
ONT
   "   river ... NELSON, OTTAWA
   "   scientist .... BANTING
   "   squaw .... MAHALA
   "   statesman ...... PEARSON,
TRUDEAU, MASSEY
canaille ..... RABBLE, MOB, RIFFRAFF
canal .... DUCT, SUEZ, PANAMA,
RACEWAY, MEATUS, KIEL
   " , bank of a .... BERM
   "   slack water .... LODE
   " , spiral, of cochlea ..... SCALA
Canal Zone city .... ANCON, COLON
canary seed .... ALPIST
Canary island ..... PALMA, GOMERA,
HIERRO
cancel . ANNUL, ERASE, DELE, QUASH,
RESCIND, REVOKE, BLOT, VOID,
EFFACE
cancer ... TUMOR, CARCINOMA, CRAB
Candia .... CRETE

candid . FRANK, OPEN, HONEST, PURE,
BLUNT, NAIVE, ARTLESS
Candiot .... CRETAN
candle ...... TEST, CIERGE, DIP, WAX
candleholder .... SCONCE
candle; melt and run down .. SWEAL
candle, wax .... TAPER, BOUGIE
candlenut tree .... AMA, KEKUNA
candlestick .... CRUSIE, LAMPAD,
GIRANDOLE, JESSE, PRICKET,
LUSTRE, TRICERIUM
candy ...... PRALINE, LOLLY, COMFIT,
FONDANT, SWEET, TAFFY
cane STEM, RATTAN, SCOURGE, STICK,
PUNISH, MALACCA
cane sugar .... SUCROSE
canine .. CUR, FICE, PUP, PUG, CANIS
canine tooth .... LANIARY
cannibalism, type of .... EXOPHAGY
cannikin .... CUP
cannon . MORTAR, HOWITZER, BERTHA,
DRAKE, MINNIE
   "   ball .... MISSILE, PELLET
   " , knob at breech end of.....
CASCABEL
   " , old-time ...... ASPIC, SAKER
   " , part of a .... CHASE, BORE,
RIMBASE, BREECH
   "   platform .... TERREPLEIN
   " , projecting boss of TRUNNION
   " , small; obs. MINION, ROBINET
canoe ... ROB ROY, ALMADIA, KAYAK,
PITPAN, PIRAGUA, PIROGUE,
OOMIAK, UMIAK, PROA, BUNGO,
TONEE, BIDAR
canon ...... CRITERION, LAW, RULE,
HYMN, LAUD, SONG, AXIOM,
NODUS, STATUTE
canonical hours NONE, SEXT, LAUDS,
VESPERS, PRIME, TIERCE, COMPLI(E)
canonize .... SAINT
canopy . VAULT, COPE, AWNING, SKY,
DAIS, TESTER
   "   over an altar .... BALDACHIN
canted position, in a ... ALIST, ATILT
canter .... RUN, PACE, RACK, GALLOP,
WHINER
Canterbury archbishop .... LANG
Canterbury gallop .... AUBIN
canthook .... PEAV(E)Y
canticle ... SONG, ODE, HYMN, LAUD
canto ... FIT, PACE, PASSUS, STANZA
Canton flannel .... NAP
canvas DUCK, SAIL, TARP, TENT, TUKE,
TILT, SCRIM, TEWKE, BURLAP,
PICTURE, CREEPER
canvas-like fabric .... WIGAN
Canyon of the comics .... STEVE
canyon mouth .... ABRA
   "   wall .... DALLE

caoutchouc, source of ... CEARA, ULE
cant JARGON, ARGOT, LINGO, SLANG,
        CAST, LEAN, TILT, TOSS, CAREEN,
        PATOIS, DIALECT, BEVEL, HIELD, TIP
cap . BOINE, CLOCHE, TAM, LID, TOP,
        CORK, BEANIE, CORNET, EXCEL
  " ; child's hood .... BIGGIN
  " , close .... COIF, TOQUE
  " , flat eccl. .... BARRET, BERET
  " ; Jewish headdress .... MITRE
  " , military ... SHAKO, BUSBY, KEPI,
        HAVELOCK
  " , night .... MUTCH
  " , oriental ... CALPAC(K), TURBAN,
        FEZ
  " , Roman .... PILEUS
  " , Scotch .... BALMORAL, TAM
  " -shaped .... PILEATE
  " , skull .... PILEUS, HOUVE
  " , square eccl. .... BIRETTA
capable .... ABLE, EFFICIENT, APT
capacious .... ROOMY, AMPLE, MUCH,
        WIDE
cape ... RAS, FICHU, TALMA, MANTLE,
        SAGUM, GAPE
  " , Jap. .... MINO
  " , large .... PELERINE, TALMA
  " ; of land NESS, NASE, RAS, COD,
        MAY, SQUAW, SKAW, HEADLAND
Cape Colony plateau .... KAROO
Cape of Good Hope discoverer .....
        DIAZ
Cape Verde island ...... FOGO, SAL
Cape Verde island native .... SERER,
        BRAVA
Čapek play .... RUR
  "   " , figure in .... ROBOT
caper ... SKIP, ANTIC, DIDO, PRANCE,
        HOP, ROMP, FRISK, TITTUP
capital ... BASIC, CITY, MAIN, STOCK,
        LETTER, PRIMAL, FATAL
capote .... BONNET, HOOD
_____ Capote .... TRUMAN
caprate .... RUTATE, SALT
caprice . WHIM, VAGARY, FAD, QUIRK,
        NOTION, WHIM(SEY)
Capricorn .... GOAT
capriole .... CAPER, HEADDRESS, LEAP
caprylate .... OCTOATE
capstan .... HOIST, LEVER, DRUM
capsule .... PILL, DETONATOR, THECA,
        SHEATH, CACHET, PERICARP
captain .... AHAB, RAIS, REIS, BLIGH,
        SOTNIK
captain, allowance paid to . PRIMAGE
  " to the host .... JOAB
  " 's boat .... GIG
caption ..... LEGEND, TITLE, HEADING
captious ... CRITICAL, CARPING, TESTY

captivate . CHARM, ENAMOUR, ALLURE,
        ENCHANT, ENSLAVE
capture .. NAB, BAG, PREY, COP, NET,
        SNARE, ARREST
captured, a thing .... PRIS, PRIZE
caput .... HEAD, CITIZEN, TOP
carabao .... BUFFALO
caracal .... LYNX
caracara .... HAWK
caradoc .... BALA
carapato .... TICK
caravan .. SAFARI, CAFILA, TRIP, TREK
caravansary .. HOTEL, IMARET, INN,
        SERAI, HOSTEL, CHAN, KHAN
caraway cookie .... SEEDCAKE
carbine .... MUSKET, RIFLE, ESCOPET
carbohydrate .... CELLULOSE, SUGAR,
        STARCH
carbolic acid .... PHENOL
carbon . LEAD, SOOT, COKE, CRAYON,
        COAL, COPY, REPLICA
carbonate of potash ..... PEARLASH
carboy .... BOTTLE, FLAGON
card .... ACE, DEUCE, JOKER, KNAVE,
        KING, QUEEN, JACK, TEN, POSTAL
  " ; as wool or flax . COMB, TEASE,
        TUM
card game ..... BACCARAT, BASSET,
        BEZIQUE, BUNKO, CRIBBAGE,
        ECARTE, FARO, GLEEK, HOC, LOO,
        MONTE, NAP, OMBRE, PAM, SKAT,
        PIQUET, ROUNCE, WHIST,
        SOLITAIRE, STUSS, TAROTS,
        MACAO, KENO, CAYENNE
card-playing term BID, CAT, PIC, POT,
        BOOK, DEAL, HAND, MELD, PASS,
        SUIT, VOID, RAISE, TRUMP,
        WIDOW, SLAM, RENEGE, VOLE
cardinal, office of .... DATARIA
  " , rank of .... HAT
cards .... DECK, PACK
care .... ATTEND, RECK, CARK, HEED,
        VIGIL, ROWAN, WORRY, CONCERN,
        CUSTODY
care of the aged .... MEDICARE
careen ... HEEL, LIST, TIP, CANT, TILT,
        SLOPE, UPSET, INCLINE
career LIFE, TRADE, PURSUIT, CALLING
careful .... WARY, CHARY, LEERY,
        DISCREET
careless . LASH, RASH, CASUAL, REMISS
caress .. FONDLE, DANDLE, HUG, PET,
        COSSET, CODDLE, EMBRACE
Carew's ladylove .... CELIA
cargo .... FREIGHT, LOAD, LADING,
        GOODS, MAIL, LAST, PORTAGE
cargo from wrecked ship .. FLOTSAM
Caribbean sea bight .... DARIEN
caribe .... PIRANHA, PIRAYA

41

caricature .. CARTOON, PARODY, SKIT,
    COPY, FARCE, MIMIC, SATIRE
carina, without a .... RATITE
Carmichael, Mr. .... HOAGY
carnage, place of .... SHAMBLES
carnation .... FLAKE, PINK
carnelian .... SARD
Carnivora .... FELIDAE
carnivore .. BEAR, CAT, DOG, GENET,
    HYENA, OTTER, PUMA, RATEL, SEAL,
    SERVAL, TIGER, MEERKAT
carob .... LOCUST, ALGAROBA
carol ...... LAY, TRILL, NOEL, SONG
Caroline island ... PALAU, TRUK, YAP,
    PELELIU
carom ... SHOT, REBOUND, RICOCHET
carousal . BINGE, FEAST, ORGY, SPREE,
    REVEL, WASSAIL, JAMBOREE, BIRL
carouse .... BIRLE, BOUSE, LIFT, TOPE
carp .. CAVIL, CENSURE, NIBBLE, NAG,
    DRUM, LAKER
carpel .... PISTIL, LEAF, SOREMA
carpenter .... WRIGHT, JOINER,
    FRAMER _____ ANT
carpenter bee .... XYLOCOPA
carpet .... KALI, MAT, TAPETE, HERAT,
    TAPIS, TAPET, FABRIC, AFGHAN,
    BAKU, USHAK, KIRMAN, RUNNER,
    WILTON, BOKHARA
cascara .... BUCKTHORN
carplike fish .... IDE
carpus .... WRIST
carriage .... CALASH, SURREY, MIEN,
    CHAISE, MANNER, GIG, JINGLE,
    SADO, POSTURE, SUPPORT
    " , baby ...... GOCART, PRAM,
    CLARENCE
    " , four-wheeled .. DEARBORN,
    LANDAU
    " , one-horse ...... TRAP, FLY,
    CARIOLE
    " , part of .... HORNBAR
    " , Russian . KIBITKA, TARANTAS,
    TROIKA
    " , two-wheeled ...... CISIUM,
    STANHOPE
carried .... BORNE, TOTED
carrier ...... HAMAL, PORTER, REDCAP
Carroll, Lewis; character ..... ALICE,
    DUCHESS, HATTER, RABBIT
carrot ...... DAUCUS, DRIAS, CARUM
carrow .... GAMESTER
carry . LUG, BEAR, TOTE, HOLD, URGE,
    FETCH, CONVEY
carry away; as property ..... ELOIN
carry on .... CAPER, WAGE, RANT
cart ... WAIN, DRAY, LORRIE, TONGA
    " , rough .... TUMBRIL
    " , end of a .... TIB
    " ladder .... RACK

    " , milkman's .... PRAM
    " , oriental .... ARABA
carte . MAP, CARD, LIST, MENU, CHART,
    DIAGRAM
cartel .. POOL, TRUST, PACT, CORNER,
    TREATY
Carthage; Sp. .... CARTAGO
    " , per. to ... . PUNIC
    " , citadel ...... BURSA, BYRSA
    " , foe of .... CATO
    " fort .... GOLETTA
    " , founder of .... DIDO
    " , head of government of.....
    SUFFETE
    " ruler .... BARCA, HANNIBAL
    " , subjects of ...... NOMADS,
    LIBYANS
    " , suburb of .... MEGARA
Carthaginian cap.; anc. .... CARALIS
    " god .... MOLOCH, VAAL
    " moon goddess ... TANIT
Carthusian .... EREMITE, MONK
    " monastery .... CERTOSA
    " , noted .... STBRUNO
cartoonist .. ARNO, LOW, HERBLOCK,
    CAPP, BUELL, KELLY, KIRBY, SCHULZ,
    SOGLOW, STEIG, NAST
cartridge holder .... CLIP
carve .. SCULPTURE, ENGRAVE, CHISEL,
    INCISE, FORM, SLIT
carving ..... SCULPTURE, ANAGLYPHY
carving in stone .... CAMEO, SCRIVE
casaba .... MUSKMELON
case ...... EVENT, INRO, PACK, SUIT,
    COVER, ACTION, DATIVE, PETARD,
    SHEATH, SATCHEL
    " for holding a book .... FOREL
    " for liquor bottles .... CELLARET
    " , small .... TYE, ETUI, ETWEE,
    TRUSSE
casein .... LEGUMIN
caseous .... CHEESY
cash . CLEAR, MONEY, HONOR, DARBY,
    DUST
cashew .... ACAJOU, NUT
    " -nut oil .... CARDOL
cashier .... TELLER, BURSAR, PURSER,
    EXPEL, DROP, OUST
casing .... COVER, SHEATH, LINER
casino .... TEN, PINK
cask . KEG, BARECA, BUTT, CADE, TUN,
    TUB, VAT
    " , bulge of .... BILGE
    " rim .... CHIMB, CHIME
    " stave .... LAG
    " support .... STILLAGE
    " , wine .... TIERCE
casket .. CIST, PYX, TYE, COFFIN, BOX,
    CHASSE, SHRINE

Caspian Sea, river to ... ARAS, EMBA, KUMA, KURA, TEREK, URAL, VOLGA
Cassandra .... SEERESS
Cassandra's father .... PRIAM
cassava product .... MANIOC
casserole .... STEW, RAGOUT
cassia . CINNAMON, LAXATIVE, SENNA
Cassiopeia's daughter .. ANDROMEDA
cassock .... GOWN, SOUTANE
cassowary .... RATITE, MOORUP
cast .. SUM, JILT, MOLT, MOLD, SHED, TOSS, SLING, SLOUGH, SPEW
castanea .... CHESTNUT
castaway ... DERELICT, PARIAH, WAIF, OUTCAST, MAROON, BUM, TRAMP, EXILE
cast away .... EXILED
caste DOM, MEO, MAK, AHIR, GOLA, JATI, KOLI, KULI, RANK, TELI, CLASS, GRADE, ORDER, SUDRA, VARNA, DEGREE, STATUS, PARIAH
caster ... CLOAK, CRUET, VIAL, CRUSE
castigate .. CENSURE, BEAT, CLOG, FINE, SCORE, PUNISH, CHASTISE
Castile province ...... AVILA, BORIA, BURGOS
    "   river .. DOURO, EBRO, JUCAR
castle .... CHATEAU, ROOK, CITADEL, ELSINORE, FORTRESS
    " , part of . DONJON, KEEP, MOAT
castor ... BEAVER, CRUET, HAT, BEAN
castor .... STAR
Castor and Pollux GEMINI, DIOSCURI, TWINS
castor-bean poison .... RICIN
Castor, mother of .... LEDA
Castor's slayer .... IDAS
casual ... CHANCE, RANDOM, STRAY
Castro, Mr. .... FIDEL
cat .... FELID, FELINE, GIB, MANX, MALTESE, FELIS, MEWER
    " , Amer. .... MARGAY, EYRA
    " cry . MEW, MEOW, MIAOU, WAUL
    " , house-working .... MOUSER
    " , old female .... GRIMALKIN
    " , Persian .... ANGORA
    " , wild TIGER, BALU, PUMA, JAGUAR, OCELOT, MANUL, CIVET, SERVAL, PANTHER
catacomb .. LOCULUS, VAULT, CRYPT, GROTTO, LOCULE
catafalque .... SCAFFOLD, BIER
catalog ... FILE, ROTA, ROSTER, INDEX
catapult .... ONAGER, BALLISTA, ROBINET, SLINGSHOT, SCORPION
cataract CASCADE, FALL, LINN, FLOOD
catarrah .... RHEUM, COLD
catch ... COP, CAP, NAB, NET, GRAB, HAUL, HOOK, SNAG, INCUR
catch-all .. BAG, BASKET, ETC, CLOSET

catchfly .... SILENE
catchword .... CUE, SLOGAN
catechu .... GAMBIER
category ...... CLASS, RANK, GENRE, SPECIES, GENUS, FAMILY
cater .... PROVIDE, PANDER, PURVEY, FEED, FURNISH
caterpillar . ERUCA, WOUBIT, CANKER, AWETO, WERI
caterpillar hair .... SETA
caterwaul .... MIAUL
catfish TANDAN, HASSAR, POUT, RAAD
catgut VIOLIN, STRING, CORD, THARM
cathedral ... DOME, MINSTER, SOBOR
Catholic, Greek ..... UNIAT, UNIATA
catkin .... AMENT, RAG, SPIKE
catmint .... NIP, NEP, CATARIA
catnip and ground ivy ..... NEPETA
cat-o'-nine-tails .... WHIP
cat's paw .. TOOL, CULLY, DUPE, GULL, STOOGE
cat's tail .... TIMOTHY, CLOUD
cat's whisker .... SMELLER
cattail .... TOTORA, DODD, MATREED, REREE
cattle . BOVINES, KINE, BEEVES, OXEN, STOCK, NOWT
    " , black .... KERRY, ANGUS
    " , dwarf .... DEVON, NIATA
    " genus .... BOS
    " , long-haired .... DISHLEY
    " pen .... BAWN, KRAAL, REEVE
    " stealer ...... ABACTOR, RUSTLER, ABIGEUS
Caucasian .. IRANIAN, OSSET, SEMITE, SLAV, SVAN, TARTAR, TURK
    "   dialect .... KARTHLI
    "   family .... ARYAN
    "   language UDI, ANDI, AVAR
    "   milk liquor .... KEFIR
    "   mountaineer .... LAK
Caucasus peak ...... ELBRUZ, KAZBEK
caucho tree .... ULE
caucuses ...... PRIMARIES, MEETINGS
caudal appendage .... TAIL
cauldron .. COPPER, POT, KETTLE, VAT
cause .... AIM, KEY, AGENT, BASIS, MOTIVE, ORIGIN, PURPOSE, SUIT
    " , med. .... AETIOLOGY
    " to arch .... ROACH
causerie .... PARLEY, CHAT
causeuse .... TETEATETE, SOFA
caustic .... SNAPPISH, MORDANT, PYROTIC, TART, BURNING, KEEN, LIME, ACRID, GRUFF, SHARP, BITING, BITTER, SEVERE
    "   agent .... ERODENT, LYE
cauterize .. CHAR, SINGE, BURN, SEAR
cautious ... CHARY, CANNY, FABIAN, WARY, DISCREET, ALERT

43

cavalcade .... PAGEANT, PARADE
cavalier .. PROUD, KNIGHT, HAUGHTY
"Cavalleria Rusticana" char. .. ALFIO,
LOLA
cavalryman .... DRAGOON, HUSSAR,
SOWAR, SPAHI, ULAN, UHLAN
cave .. ANTRE, CRYPT, DEN, GROT(TO)
CAVERN, LAIR, CROFT
cave dweller .... TROGLODYTE
cave enthusiast .... SPELUNKER
caves, inhabiting .... SPEL(A)EAN
caves, scien. study of .. SPELEOLOGY
caviar .... IKRA, OVA, ROE
caviar, fish yielding .... STURGEON,
STERLET
cavil . CARP, HAFT, BICKER, CENSURE,
QUIBBLE
cavities ...... ANTRA, AULAE, CARIES
cavity .... LUMEN, PIT, SINUS, VUG,
DENT, AULA, HOLE, ANTRUM
" , body ..... COELUM, COELOM
" , crystal-lined, per. to. GEODIC
" of skull .... FOSSA
" per. to heart .... ATRIUM
cavort . CAPER, DIDO, PRANK, PRANCE,
CURVET
cavy .. PACA, GUINEA(PIG), RODENT
caw .... KAAK, QUARK
cayenne .... WHIST, PEPPER, CANARY,
CAPSICUM
cease .. PETER, STINT, REFRAIN, STOP,
HALT, QUIT, STAY, AVAST, CLOSE,
DESIST
ceased .... DEAD, KILLED
Cecrops' daughter .... HERSE
cedar .... DEODAR, TOON, TOONA
cede GRANT, YIELD, SURRENDER, WAIVE,
RESIGN, ABANDON
ceiling, division in .... TRAVE
celebrity .... VIP, FAME, LION, NAME,
STAR, ECLAT, HONOR, RENOWN,
REPUTE
celerity ..... DISPATCH, HASTE, SPEED
celery .... SMALLAGE, ACHE
celestial .... HOLY, DIVINE, ANGELIC,
URANIC, HEAVENLY
celestial being ...... ANGEL, CHERUB,
SERAPH
celestial elev. of mind .... ANAGOGE
Celeus' daughter .... ANDROMEDA
cell ...... EGG, KIL, GERM, CYTODE,
NEURONE, SPORE, SERDAB, GAMETE,
NAOS, CELLA
" division .... SPIREME, AMITOSIS,
LININ
" structure, study of .... CYTOLOGY
cellaret .... TANTALUS
cells, honeycomb .... ALVEOLI
cellular ...... ALVEOLATE, FAVIFORM
celluloid .... XYLONITE

Celt .... GAEL
celt .... EOLITH, CHISEL
Celtic .... WELSH, MANX, ERSE
" abbot .... DOARB
" landholder .... TANIST
" language .. BRYTHONIC, CYMRIC
" priest .... DRUID
" word for mountain ...... BEN
cement .... PUTTY, GLUE, JOIN, LUTE,
PASTE, MORTAR, SOLDER, COHERE
cement, hydraulic .... PAAR, ROMAN
cemetery .... MORTUARY, LITTEN,
BONEYARD, NECROPOLIS
cenobite .... ESSENE, MONK, RECLUSE,
NUN
cenoby ..... ABBEY, PRIORY, CLOISTER,
CONVENT
censer .... INCENSORY, THURIBLE
censure FLAY, CHIDE, SLATING, BLAME,
TARGE, IMPEACH, REBUKE
census .... LIST, POLL, COUNT
cent .... SOU, COIN, PENNY
center CORE, FOCUS, NUCLEUS, HEART,
MIDST, PIVOT, NAVE, HUB
" , away from .... DISTAL
" line, along .... AXIATE
centerpiece .... EPERGNE
central . AXIAL, FOCAL, MID, NUCLEAR,
PIVOTAL
centuries, ten .... CHILIAD
century plant . AGAVE, ALOE, MAGUEY
ceorl .... CHURL, THANE, VILLEIN
cepa .... ONION
cephalopod .... OCTOPUS, CUTTLE
ceral .... WAXY
ceramic sieve .... LAUN
cerate .... LARD, WAX, SALVE
ceratose .... HORNY
cerberus .... HELLDOG
cereal .... RICE, HOMINY, OAT, RAGI,
RYE, BRAN, GRITS, FARINA, MAIZE
ceremonious STIFF, FORMAL, SOLEMN,
STATELY
" leave-taking .. CONGE
ceremony . FORM, RITE, RITUAL, POMP
cero fish .... DHURRA, CAVALLA
certainly ..... AMEN, YEA, TRUE, SURE
certify ...... VOUCH, ASSURE, ATTEST,
AFFIRM, DEPOSE, EVINCE
cerulean .... AZURE, BLUE
cervine .... STAG, ROE, DEER
cessation ..... DESITION, END, LETUP,
HALT, LULL, REST, STAY, PAUSE
cesspool .... SUMP, SINK(ER)
cetacean .. SUSU, APOD, INIA, WHALE
Ceylon aborigines ...... VEDDAA(H)S
" ape ...... LANGUR, MAHA
" governor .... DISAWA
" hill dweller .... TODA
" language .... PALI TAMIL

44

" lotus .... NELUMBO
" moss ..... AGAR, GULAMAN,
JAFFNA
" palm .... TALIPOT
" town ... KANDY, UVA, GALLE
Ceylonese .... TAMIL, TODA
" garment .... SARONG
" measure .... PARAH
" native .... SINGALESE,
SINHALESE
" sea sands .... PAAR
Ceylonite ...... PLEONASTE, SPINEL
chafe .... FRET, RUB, VEX, FROT, GALL,
ABRADE
chaff .... BANTER, TRASH, BRAN, HUSK,
HULLS, REFUSE
chaffer ..... DICKER, HIGGLE, HAGGLE
chaffy ... PALEATE, ACEROSE, TRIVIAL,
SCALY, WORTHLESS
chafing .... GALLING
chain . TORC, TORQUE, GYVE, RANGE,
CATENA, FILE, LINK, HOBBLE,
SHACKLE, FETTER
chair ... KAGO, SEAT, STOOL, SEDAN,
ROCKER, OFFICE, THRONE
chair part .... RUNG, SPLAT
chalcedon .... JASPER
chalcedony ..... AGATE, ONYX, SARD
Chaldean city .... UR
" time cycle .... SAROS
chalice .. AMA, CUP, GRAIL, BLOSSOM,
CALYX, AMULA, GOBLET, BOWL
chalice flower .... DAFFODIL
chalice, pall of .... ANIMETTA
chalk .... CAUK
challenge ... DEFY, CALL, DARE, GAGE
" to duel .... CARTEL
chamber ..... KIVA, ROOM, LOCULUS
" , judge's .... CAMERA
chambers, lawyers' .... INNS
chambers, two legislative . BICAMERAL
chamois .... AOUDAD
champion .... ESPOUSE, DEFEND, ACE,
HERO, PALADIN, SQUIRE, BACK
chance .... LOT, HAP(LY), ODDS, TIDE,
LUCK, FATE, BREAK, BETIDE, OCCUR,
CASUAL, HAZARD
" ; comb. form .... TYCHO
chancel .. BEMA, JUBE, SEDILE, SEDILIA
Chaney, Mr. .... LON
change ...... AMEND, SHIFT, MODIFY,
MUTATE, COINS, ALTER, VARY,
MOVE, FLUX
" ; mus. .... MUTA
changeable .. PROTEAN, GIDDY, FICKLE,
FITFUL, VARIANT
changeling . DOLT, OAF, FOOL, DUNCE
channel ... DIKE, SINUS, STRIA, DUCT,
ITER, LEAT, TUBE, CANAL, DITCH,
DRAIN, SLUICE, STRAIT, FURROW

" bone .... COLLAR
" island ...... JERSEY, SARK
" of a river .... FLUME, ALVEUS
" , sea .... TROUGH
" to inland .... GAT
" , water .... GURT
chanson .... LYRIC, SONG, BALLAD
chant .... INTONE, INTROIT
chanticleer .... COCK, ROOSTER
chantry ..... ALTAR, CHAPEL, SHRINE
chaos ... ABYSS, CHASM, GULF, BABEL,
APSU, MESS, IMBROGLIO, PIE, VOID
Chaos' son .... EREBUS
" wife .... NOX, NYX
chaotic . MUDDLED, SNAFU, CONFUSED
chap .. BOY, LAD, CHINK, KISS, SPRAY,
COVE, KIBE
chape .... CRAMPET
chapel .... ALTAR, BETHEL, ORATORY,
CHANTRY, SISTINE, CHOIR
chaplet .... ROSARY, ANADEM, FILLET,
CORONAL
Chaplin, Mrs. .... OONA
chaps .... CHOPS, JAWS, FLEWS
chapped ... KIBY, KIBED, SPLIT, ROUGH
chapter, per. to .... CAPITULAR
character ... QUALITY, TRAIT, REPUTE,
STRIPE, ROLE
" in Irish alphabet .. OGHAM
" of a community .... ETHOS
" of Teutonic alphabet . RUNE
" to indicate pitch ... NEUME
characterize .... DEPICT, ENTITLE
charcoal .... FUSAIN, LIGNITE
charcoal ingredient .... PEAT
charge INDICT, ONUS, TAX, FEE, COST,
ADJURE, INDICT, DEBIT
charger .... PLATE, STEED, HORSE
chariot ... CURRE, ESSED, RATH, WAIN,
CALASH, BIGA, ESSEDA
charioteer ...... AURIGA, HUR, PILOT,
DRIVER
Charisse; actress .... CYD
charity .. LOVE, ALMS, DOLE, BOUNTY,
PITY, LARGESS, GIFT, RUTH, MERCY,
LENITY
charlatan EMPIRIC, QUACK, IMPOSTOR,
FAKER
Charlemagne, knight of ......GANO
Charlemagne's kin CARLOMAN, PEPIN,
ORLANDO
Charles's Wain .... DIPPER, BEAR
charlock .... KRAUT, MUSTARD
charm ...... SPELL, GRACE, AMULET,
PERIAPT, FETISH, FETICH, TALISMAN
" ; Afr. . JUJU, OBE, OBI, GRIGRI
" ; jewel BRIMBORION, BRELOQUE
" , to .... ALLAY, ENAMOR, TAKE,
PLEASE

45

charmer .. SORCERER, EXORCIST, MAGI,
SIREN, MAGICIAN
charnel house .... OSSUARY
Charpentier, opera by .... LOUISE
chars .... BURNS, COALS
chart .... GRAPH, MAP, PLAT,
SCHEME, DIAGRAM
charter .... LET, DEED, HIRE,
RENT, GRANT, LEASE
Charybdis, rock opp. to ...... SCYLLA
chase .... PURSUE, CHEVY, TRACK
Chase; authoress .... ILKA
chaste .... PURE, CLEAN, MODEST,
VESTAL
chat ... PRATE, CONFAB, COZE, TOVE,
GAB, CHIN, BABBLE, GOSSIP,
CAUSERIE
chatelaine ... ETUI, BROOCH, TORQUE,
PIN, CLASP
chattel .... GOODS, SLAVE
" , to recover .... DETINUE
chatter .... BABBLE, PRATE, GIBBER,
CLACK, JABBER, TATTLE, GAS
chastise ..... SPANK, TRIM, SWINGE,
BLAME, SLAP, TAUNT, WHIP,
SCOLD, CENSURE
Chatham .... PITT
Chaucer's inn .... TABARD
" title .... DAN
cheap .... VILE, PALTRY, LIGHT
chatterer .... MAG, JAY, PIET
cheat ... COZEN, FLEECE, BAM, DISH,
GYP, CON, SHARP, CHISEL,
RENIG, MUMP
" by trick .... THIMBLERIG
cheater .... BILKER, GULL
check .. NIP, REIN, DETENT, BIT, TAB,
STEM, BLOCK, CURB, IMPEDE,
VERIFY, BRIDLE
checkered .... VAIR, PLAID, PIED
checkerwork .... TESSEL, MOSAIC
checkmate .... BAFFLE, DEFEAT, LICK,
STOP, STYMIE, THWART, UNDO
checks by rein .... SACCADES
cheder .... SCHOOL (JEWISH)
cheek ...... TEMERITY, GENA, NERVE,
SAUCE, JAWL, GALL, BUCCA, BRASS
" , per. to .... GENAL, MALAR,
BUCCAL
cheek of spearhead .... JAMB
cheeks distended .... BUCCATE
cheep .... CHIRP, SQUEAK, PEEP, PULE
cheer ... CRY, OLE, RAH, CLAP, GLEE,
LAUD, ROOT, VIVA, BRAVO, ELATE,
HUZZA, HURRA, ACCLAIM, APPLAUD
cheerful ...... ROSY, GLEG, JOCUND,
SUNNY, PEART, BLITHE, HICARY
cheese .... CEMENT, GLUE,
CAMEMBERT, COTTAGE, MYSOST
" , Belgian .... LIMBURGER

" dish ...... FONDUE, RAREBIT,
SOUFFLE
" , Dutch .... EDAM, GOUDA
" , French .... BRIE, ROQUEFORT
" , green .... SAPSAGO
" , Italian .... PARMESAN,
GORGONZOLA
" spreader .... SPATULA
" magot .... SKIPPER
" , main constituent of . CASEIN
" , soft .... BRIE
" , Swiss .... GRUYERE, SAPSAGO
" , Scotch .... DUNLOP
" , whole-milk .... DUNLOP
cheesy .... CASEOUS
chemical compound .... AMID(E),
AMIN(E), AZIN(E), AZOLE,
BORID(E), CERIA, INOSITE, IODIDE,
ISOMER, LEUCINE, METOMER,
STEARATE, TOULENE, ELATERIN,
ESTER
" element . ARGON, HALOGEN
" radical ..... BUTYL, ETHYL,
TOLYL, BENZYL
" salt ..... SAL, ESTER, NITER,
BORATE
" substance ... IRIDOL, LININ
" suffix .... YL, ANE, OLIC
" test .... TITER, TITRE
chemise .... SHIFT, LINGERIE
chemist .... ANALYST, DRUGGIST
cherish .. ADORE, PET, FOSTER, NURSE,
LOVE, PRIZE, DOTE (WITH "ON"),
ESTEEM, REVERE
cherry ... CAPULIN, RUDDY, MORELLO,
AMARELLE, LAMBERT, OXHEART,
DUKE, GEAN, MARASCA,
MAZZARD, MOREL
" gum, part of .... CERASIN
" red .... CERISE
Cheshire district ...... HALE, HOOLE,
MARPLE
chess, opening in ..... MOVE, DEBUT,
CHASSE, GAMBIT
" term .... FIDATE, DUALS
chessman .... BISHOP, CASTLE,
KNIGHT, PAWN, ROOK, QUEEN
chest ...... ARCA, ARK, CIST, LOCKER,
CASE, COFFER, BAHUT
" of an animal .... BRISKET
" for supplies .... WANIGAN
" , human .... THORAX
" sound .... RALE
Chester, per. to .... CHESTRIAN
Chesterfield .... COAT, SOFA
chestnut, Poly. .... RATA
chestnut-colored .... MARRON,
CASTANEOUS
" , water .... LING

46

chevron .... STRIPE, VEE, MARK,
        RANK, MOLDING
chevrotain .... DEERLET, NAPU
chew . CHAM(P), MUNCH, BITE, CHAW,
        QUID, CRAVEL, MASTICATE
chewing-gum ingredient .... CHICLE
chewy confection .... GUM
Chian turpentine .... ALK, TEREBINTH
Chiang Kai-shek's wife .... MEI, LING
        SOONG
chic .... POSH, NATTY, MODISH,
        STYLISH, SPRUCE, NIFTY
Chicago play district .... LOOP
chicanery ...... TRICKERY, SOPHISTRY,
        RUSE, WILE, FEINT
chickadee ...... TITMOUSE, BLACKCAP
chicken .... FRYER, POULT, HEN,
        LAYER, PULLET, BROILER
chick-pea .... GRAM, CICER
chickweeds .... ALSINE
chicle .... GUM, LATEX
chicory .... ENDIVE
chide ..... BLAME (BE)RATE, REPROVE
chief . STAPLE, ARCH, CAPTAIN, HEAD,
    MAIN, TYEE, YARL, ELDER, PRIME,
    RULER, THANE, CAPITAL, SUPREME,
    VITAL, DATTO, HETMAN, ATAMAN
    " , oriental ..... IMAM, REIS, RAIS,
    KAHN, SIRDAR, AGHA,
    EMIR, AMEER
chigoe .... FLEA
chilblain .... PERNIO, KIBE
child ... BAIRN, BATA, CHIT, TAD, TOT,
    TIKE, BABE, BRAT, PEEWEE, KID,
    ARAB, GAMIN, INFANT, PROGENY
childish ... IMMATURE, PUERILE, NAIVE
childlike ...... MEEK, NAIVE, DOCILE,
        INNOCENT
childlike adult .... MORON
children of heaven and earth TITANS
children's patron saint ...... SANTA
Chile aborigines .... INCAS
    " , capital of .... SANTIAGO
    " , province in .... ATACAMA,
    ARAUCO, MAULE, ATALCA
    " , rivers in .. BIOBIO, ITATA, LOA
Chilean city .... ANGOL, LOTA, TALCA
    " desert .... ATACAMA
    " island .... HOSTE
    " mountain peak ...... JUNCAL
    " pass .... MAIPU
    " seaport .... LOTA
    " tree .... ALERCE, LITHI
    " winds .... SURES
chili con .... CARNE
chill ...... COLD, ICE, RIGOR, SHIVER,
    AGUE, ALGOR, FROST, SHAKE,
    FRAPPE, FRIGID, NIP
chilly .... BLEAK, RAW, ALGID, LASH,
    ICY, GELID, ARCTIC

chime ..... CYMBAL, EDGE, RIM, BELL,
    AGREE, ACCORD, JINGLE,
    HARMONY
    " of nine bells, changes on .....
        CATERS
chimerical .... UTOPIAN, VAIN
chimney .... LUM, TEWEL, FLUE, PIPE,
    STACK, FUNNEL, VENT
chimney piece ...... PAREL, MANTEL,
        INGLE
chimpanzee .... NCHEGA, JOCKO
chin .... MENTUM, MENTA (PL.)
    " ; comb. form .... GENIO
China, anc. ... SERICA, CATHAY, KITAI
china ...... DELFT, DISHES, DRESDEN,
    CROCKERY, PORCELAIN,
    SEVRES, MEISSEN
    " blue .... NIKKO
chine ... FISSURE, RAVINE, SILK, CREST
Chinese ...... SERIC, SINIC, CATAIAN,
    CATHAY, JOHNNY, MONGOL,
    SERES, SERIAN, SINAEAN
Chinese aborigine .... MANS, MANTZU
    " arch .... PAILOO, PAILOU
    " aromatic root ..... GINSENG
    " black tea .... OOLONG
    " boat .... JUNK, SAMPAN
    " Caucasian ..... LOLO, NOSU
    " city HANKOW, TSINAN, SIAN,
    ICHANG, PEIPING, PEKING
    " cautery .... MOXA
    " civet .... RASSE
    " ; comb. form .... SINICO
    " dependency .... TIBET
    " desert .... GOBI, SHAMO
    " dialect .... CANTON, WU
    " district .... HSIEN
    " divinity .... JOSS
    " dog .... CHOW, PEKE
    " duck eggs, preserved . PIDAN
    " early race .... KHITANS
    " , enemies of the ..... TATARS
    " exchange .... SYCEE
    " extra tax .... SQUEEZE
    " factory .... HONG
    " feudal state .... WEI
    " flute .... TCHE, CHE
    " gateway .... PAILOU
    " glue .... AGAR
    " god .... SHEN, JOSS
    " gong .... TAMTAM
    " grass .... RAMEE
    " guild .... TONG
    " harbor .... CHEFOO
    " immigrant .... HAKKA
    " island ..... AMOY, QUEMOY
    " knock-head ...... KOWTOW
    " laborer .... COOLIE
    " language .... SHAN

" leader MAO TSETUNG, CHOU ENLAI, SUN YATSEN
" mandarin's residence . YAMEN
" measure ...... CHANG, CHIH, FUN, TSUN
" money ..... PU, MACE, TAEL, TIAO YUAN
" Mongol dynasty ...... YUAN
" mus. instrument ... URHEEN, KIN, CHENG
" negative principle ...... YIN
" nest of boxes .... INRO
" noodles .... MEIN
" nurse .... AMAH
" official .... AMBAN, TAOYAN
" oil tree .... TUNG
" orange .... MANDARIN
" ounce .... TAEL
" pagoda .... TAA
" , per. to .... SINESIAN
" philosopher .... LAOTSE, LAOTZU, MOTI, MOTZU, YUTANG, LIN
" plant ..... RAMEE, GINSENG
" poet .... LIPO
" positive principle .... YANG
" pound .... CATTY
" province ... CHIHLI, SHANSI, KIANGSI
" race .... DARD, SINIC
" red .... CHROME, SCARLET
" religion .... TAOISM
" rich earth .... LOESS
" river .. HAN, ILI, TARIM, WEI
" roller .... SIRGANG
" root .... GALANGA
" sauce .... SOY
" sedge .... KALI
" servant .... AMAH
" silk .... PONGEE, SHANTUNG, TASAR, TUSSAH
" silkworm .... ERIA
" silver, uncoined ...... SYCEE
" skiff .... SAMPAN
" sky .... TIEN
" sleeping platform .... KANG
" society ... HUI, HOEY, TONG
" sovereigns, anc. .. KEE, YAOU
" tax .... LIKIN
" tea .... CHA, OOLONG
" temple . SHA, TAA, PAGODA
" toy .... TANGRAM
" treaty port .. AMOY, ICHANG
" vegetable .... UDO
" wax-secreting insect ... PELA
" weight ... CHEE, LIANG, YIN, CATTY, PICUL, HAO, SHIH, MACE
" wormwood .... MOXA

chink ...... CRACK, INTERSTICE, BORE, CASH, COIN, RIFT, RIMA, RIME
chinks full of .... RIFTY, RIMOSE
Chinook chief .... TYEE
chinquapin .... RATTLENUT
chinse .... CLOSE, CALK
Chios inhabitant .... SCIOT
chip .... GALLET, FLAKE, BIT, NICK, SPALL
chipmunk .... HACKEE
chipper .... GAY, SPRY, LIVELY, COCKY
chip stone, to .... NIG
Chips, Mr. .... DONAT
chiropter .... ALIPED, BAT
chirp .... CHEEP, PULE, PEEP
chirrup .... PEEP, TWEET
chisel .... CUT, GOUGE, FORM, PARE, CHEAT
" , broad .... DROVE
" , mason's .... POMMEL
" , paring .... SLICK
" , stone .... CELT
chiseled appearance .... CISELE
chit ..... IOU, NOTE, CHILD, VOUCHER
chiv.............. GARLIC, ALLIUM
chivy .... GAME, CHASE, NAG, HUNT, RUN, CRY, TEASE, PURSUE
chlorine family .... BROMINE, FLUORINE, IODINE
chlorophyl .... LEAFGREEN
chock .... CLEAT, WEDGE, BLOCK
chocolate, powder for ...... PINOLE
chocolate trees .... COLA
choice ...... OPTION, SELECT, CHARY, RARE, AONE, PICKED, PRIME, ELITE, CREAM
" ; in a lottery .... GIG
" ; make a .... OPT
choir vestments .... COTTA
choke .... BURKE, CLOSE, STIFLE, WORRY, DAM, GAG, PLUG
choler ...... IRE, ANGER, RAGE, BILE, FURY, SPLEEN
choler ...... IRE, ANGER, RAGE, BILE, FURY, SPLEEN
choleric ...... IRATE, IRACUND, TESTY
choose ...... (S)ELECT, OPTATE, CULL, LIST, PREFER, ESPOUSE, OPT
" jointly .... COOPT
chop ...... HEW, JOWL, MINCE, DICE, AXE, CARVE, SPLIT
Chopin's country ... POLAND, FRANCE
chord .... MAJOR, MINOR, TRINE, TRIAD, STRING, HARMONY
chore .... JOB, DUTY, CHARE, STINT
chortle .... CHUCKLE, SNORT
chorus .... ACCORD, UNISON, REFRAIN
Chosen .... COREA, KOREA
chosen .... OPTED

48

chowchow .... DOG, OLIO
Christ stopped at .... EBOLI
Christ, picture of .... VERONICA
christen .... CLEPE, NAME
Christian, oriental .... UNIAT
Christian unity .... IRENICS
Christmas .... XMAS, YULE(TIDE),
NOEL, NOWEL
chromosome .... IDANT
chronicle .. ACCOUNT, ANNAL, DIARY,
RECORD, ANNALS, RECITAL
chrysalis .... AURELIA, KELL, PUPA
chrysolite .... OLIVIN, PERIDOT
chub .... SKELLY, CHEVIN
chuck ..... GRUB, FOOD, LUMP, LOG,
HURL, TOSS, PITCH
chuckle .... CHORTLE, CLUCK, LAUGH,
TITTER, GIGGLE
chum .... BUDDY, CRONY, PAL
chunky .... STOUT, THICK, SQUAT,
STOCKY
church ...... FANE, TEMPLE, MINSTER,
KIRK, KURK, TERA, KIL, MALID,
SAMAJ, BETHEL, CHAPEL, MOSQUE,
PAGODA, BASILICA, CATHEDRAL,
SYNAGOGUE, TABERNACLE
    "   and state .... ERASTIAN
    "   calendar .... ORDO
    "   chapel .... ORATORY
    "   council .... SYNOD
    "   dignitary ... PRIMATE, BISHOP,
DEAN, POPE, PRELATE,
CARDINAL, ABBOT
    "   dissenter .... SECTARY
    "   district .... SEE, PARISH,
DEANERY, DIOCESE
    "   , division in a .... SCHISM
    "   doorkeeper .... OSTIARY
    "   judicatory .... CLASSIS
    "   , land belonging to a .. GLEBE
    "   leader .... HIERARCH
    "   officer .... ELDER, BEADLE,
SEXTON, SACRIST,
PRESBYTER, VERGER
    "   , one of a millennial . SHAKER
    "   , part of a .. NEF, PEW, BEMA,
APSE, NAVE, ALTAR,
PULPIT, TRANSEPT
    "   peace device ...... IRENICON
    "   reading desk .... AMBO,
LECTERN
    "   revenue .... BENEFICE
    "   rite .... LAVABO
    "   stipend .... PREBEND
    "   traffic in anything sacred....
SIMONY
    "   warden's assistant . SIDESMAN
Churchill's daughter .... SARAH
    "   trademark .... CIGAR

churl ..... BOOR, KNAVE, OAF, CARL,
CEORL, VILLEIN, NIGGARD,
VASSAL, LOUT
churlish ..... RUSTIC, SORDID, GRUFF,
SURLY
ciborium ...... PYX, CANOPY, COFFER
cicatrice .... SCAR
cicely .... MYRRH
Cicero, target of .... CATILINE
cicerone ..... PILOT, GUIDE, COURIER,
DRAGOMAN, CONDUCTOR
Cid .... POEM, CHIEF, LEADER
Cid's sword .... COLADA
cigar ...... CULEBRA, CHEROOT, TOBY,
PANATELA, STOGY, CLARO,
ROPO, CORONA, SCAD, SMOKE
cigarette .... CUBEB, FAG, GASPER
cinch .... GRIP, FASTEN
cinchona, yield from ...... QUININE
cinder SLAG, ASH(ES), CLINKER, SCAR,
DROSS, EMBER, SCORIA, LAPILLI
cinnamon .... CANEL, CASSIA
    "   stone .. GARNET, ESSONITE
cinquefoil .... FRASIER, CLOVER
cipher .... AUGHT, CODE, ZERO,
NIL, NOBODY
Circe .... TEMPTRESS
Circe's brother .... AEETES
    "   father .... HELIOS
    "   island .... AEAEA
circle .... ORB, RHOMB, RIGOL, LOOP,
CLASS, RING, SET, DISK, HOOP,
NIMB, TURN, SWIRL, COLURE,
CORDON, COTERIE, RONDURE
    "   , part of . ARC, CHORD, RADIUS,
SECANT, SECTOR, SEGMENT
circuit .... AMBIT, ZONE, EYRE,
LAP, TOUR, ORBIT, ROUTE
circular .... BILL, ORBED, ROUND,
ANNULAR, DISCOID, PAMPHLET
    "   letter .... ENCYCLICAL
    "   ornament .... PATERA
    "   tread .... VOLT
circulate ..... SPREAD, DIFFUSE, PASS,
ROTATE
circumference .. AMBIT, VERGE, GIRTH
circumlocution .. AMBAGE, VERBIAGE
circumspect .... WARY, ALERT, CHARY,
PRUDENT, DISCREET
circumstance .... STATE, FIX, FACTOR,
PHASE, EPISODE
circus rider .... DESULTOR
cistern .... RAINTUB, BAC, URN,
WELL, VAT, CUVETTE
citadel ..... TOWER, ALAMO, CASTLE,
FORT, ARX
cite .... MUSTER, SUMMON, CALL,
QUOTE, ARRAIGN, ADDUCE
citizen ...... DENIZEN, DWELLER, CIT,
BURGHER, RESIDENT, NATIVE

49

citron .... LIME, LEMON, CEDRAT, ETHROG
citrus fruit ..... CITRON, GRAPEFRUIT, SHADDOCK, LEMON, ORANGE, LIME
city ...... URBS, BURGH, POLIS, STADT
" , cathedral .... LINCOLN, YORK
" court .... MUNICIPAL
" of masts .... LONDON
" of palm trees .... JERICHO
" of the dead .... NECROPOLIS
" of the gods .... ASGARD
" , per. to .... CIVIC, URBAN
" ward .... WATCHMAN
civet ..... —————— CAT, NANDINE, PERFUME, RASSE
" palm .... MUSANG
civet-like animal .... GENET
civic .... LAY, OPPIDAN, URBAN, SUAVE, SECULAR, CIVIL
civil ...... DECENT, POLITICAL, HENDE, COURTLY, URBANE
" wrong .... TORT
Civil War battle .... GETTYSBURG, ATLANTA, BULLRUN, ANTIETAM
Civil War commander .... LEE, POPE, BARRON, BRAGG, BUELL, FLOYD, EWELL, HOOKER, MAURY, MEADE, MOSBY, PICKETT, SLOCUM
civilian dress .... MUFTI
clad .... ATTIRED, ROBED
claim .... LIEN, TITLE, ASSERT, RIGHT, EXACT, ALLEGE, DEMAND, ARROGATE
Clair; director .... RENE
Claire, Miss .... INA
clairvoyant .... SEER, PROPHET
clam ..... WINKLE, QUAHOG, SOLEN, MYA
" shell opening .... GAPE
" like animal .... CHAMA, COCKLE
clamor .... BUNK, DIN, BERE, CRY, WAIL, ROAR, NOISE, RACKET
clamp ..... CLOTHESPIN, GLAND, VISE, VICE, NIP, CLASP, NAIL, TIE, GRIP
clan ...... TRIBE, RACE, CLIQUE, GENS, SEPT, FAMILY, PARTY, GENUS, GROUP
clan, head of .... ALDER
clang .. TONK, DING, JANGLE, STROKE
clandestine . SECRET, SLY, PRIVY, FOXY, COVERT, FURTIVE
clangor .... HUBBUB, UPROAR, DIN
clannish .... SECRET, TRIBAL
clarify . PURIFY, FREE, CLEAR, DEPURATE
clarinet .... REED, AULOS, PUNGI
" mouthpiece socket .... BIRN
clasp ...... HASP, MORSE, GELT, STICK, TACHE, BUCKLE, CLUTCH, ENFOLD
class CASTE, GENUS, ILK, ORDER, RANK,

KIND, RACE, TYPE, FAMILY, HEIMIN, SPECIES, GROUP, BREED, SORT
classical .... CHASTE, PURE, ATTIC
classification .. SYSTEM, SORT, GENUS, ANALYSIS, TAXIS, CATEGORY
classify ... TICKET, LIST, DIGEST, TYPE, REGISTER, CATALOG, LABEL
clause .... PLANK, PASSAGE, PROVISO
claw ... NAIL, TALON, UNGUIS, UNCI, GRIFF, SCRAPE, UNGULA, HOOK
clay ADOBE, BRICK, TILE, TASCO, BOLE, LOAM, LOESS, KAOLIN, ARGIL, PUG
" beds .... GAULT
" box .... SAGGER
" and calcium carbonate .... MARL
" composition .... LUTE
" , constituent of .... ALUMINA
" , fine yellow EAGLESTONE, OCHRE
" manure .... MALM, MARL
" pigeon .... TARGET
" , polishing .... RABAT
" , potter's .... ARGIL, PETUNTSE
" , prepare, for pottery . PUG, BOTT
clayey ...... LUTOSE, MALMY, BOLAR
clean . FAY, DUST, KOSHER, CHASTE, DECENT, BREAM
cleaner .... SOAP, SWEEPER, VACUUM, SCALER, PURER, RAMROD
cleanse .. ABSTERGE, DEPURATE, PURGE, DETERGE, RINSE
clear LUCENT, LUCID, NET, RID, SIMPLE, ACQUIT, AUDIBLE, AWEIGH, FAY
clearing of land . SART, ASSART, MILPA
cleat . BATTEN, STRIP, KEVEL, BOLLARD, CHOCK
" , make fast around ...... BELAY
cleave ... SPLIT, REND, CLING, COHERE, RIVE, DISPART, SUNDER, BISECT
cleaver ...... FROE, FROW, BILLHOOK
cleft .... CHAPPY, GAP, REFT, RIMA, CLOVEN, FORKED
Clemens .... (MARK)TWAIN
clement ..... MILD, LENIENT, BENIGN, HUMANE
Cleopatra's attendant .... IRAS
" downfall .... ASP
" river, of .... NILOTIC
" lover .... ANTONY
clergy .... CLOTH, PULPIT
clergyman ..... ABBE, DEAN, CANON, PADRE, PRIOR, RABBI, VICAR, CURATE, PARSON, RECTOR, PASTOR
" , residence of .... MANSE, PARSONAGE
cleric (see "clergyman")
cleric, non .... LAIC, LAICAL, SECULAR
clerical .... SCRIBAL, MINISTERIAL
" vestment .... AMICE, ALB, FANON, ORALE

50

clerk .... AGENT, SCRIBE, TELLER
clever ADROIT, DEFT, SMART, SLICK, SLY,
      ARTFUL, HABILE
clew .... GLOBE, KEY, TINT, SKEIN
cliché .... BANAL, TRITE
click .. TICK, PAWL, RATCHET, DETENT,
      AGREE
cliff .. CLEVE, SHORE, KLIP, SCAR(P),
      BLUFF
climax .... ACME, APOGEE, EPI, PEAK,
     ZENITH, TOP
climb . GRIMP, SHIN, SPEEL, CLAMBER,
     CREEP, ASCEND
climbing .... SCALING, SCANDENT
  " , adapted for .. SCANSORIAL
  " fern .... NITO
  " vine .. BINE, CUPSEED, HOP,
     BRYONY, LIANA
clime .... REALM, REGION, ZONE
clinch ... CLUTCH, GRIP, NAIL, CLAMP,
    RIVET, SECURE, SEAL, HUG
cling .... ADHERE, CLEAVE, COHERE
clingfish .... SUCKER, TESTAR
clink .... PRISON, TING
clip .. BARB, SHEAR, SNIP, TRIM, MOW,
    PRUNE, WHACK
clique .... RING, COTERIE, SET, CABAL,
  JUNTO, PARTY, CIRCLE, GANG, CLUB
Cloaca Maxima of Rome .... SEWER
cloak HIDE, MASK, VEIL, WRAP, BLIND,
     SHIELD
  " , anc. Irish .... IZAR
  " , hooded ...... CAPOTE, CAMAIL
  " , loose ...... ABOLLA, PALETOT,
    PONCHO, PELISSE
  " ; Span. .... MANTA
clock . METER, KNOCK, NEF, TIME, BELL,
    DIAL, GONG, WATCH
  " , ancient water ..... CLEPSYDRA
  " , astronomical .... SIDEREAL
  " weight .... PLUMB, PEISE
clod ... DOLT, EARTH, LOAM, GROUND
clog ...... CHOPINE, HAMPER, SABOT,
   PATTEN, GETA, DAGGLE, JAM,
    CHOKE
cloister ..... NUNNERY, ABBEY, FRIARY,
  STOA, ARCADE, PRIORY, CONVENT
"Cloister and Hearth" author . READE
cloistress .... NUN, RELIGIEUSE
close . FINALE, STIVY, END, OCCLUDE,
  SEAL, AREA, DENSE, SHUT, YARD,
  DAM, HUG, MUGGY, ESTOP, CHINSE
  " ; poet. .... ANEAR
  " the eyes .... SEEL
closely .... ALMOST, BARELY, JUST
closet AMBRY, EWRY, LOCKER, SECRET,
    PRIVATE
closing measure in music ..... CODA
clot ... COAGULATE, LUMP, MASS, GEL,
  JELL, SOLIDIFY, THICKEN

cloth .... CREPE, TAPET, CHEYNEY,
    NANKEEN
 " , a blister in .. AMPER, RIP, TEAR
 " , camel's hair .... CAMLET
 " , checkered .... PLAID
 " , coarse hemp .... GUNNY
 " , coarse linen .... DOWLAS
 " , dealer in ..... HOSIER, DRAPER
 " finisher .... BEETLER
 " , flaw in .... BRACK
 " , homespun .... KELT
 " measure .... ELL, NAIL
 " , metallic .... LAME
 " , mulberry-bark .... TAPA
 " , muslin .... ADATI
 " of camel's hair .... ABA
 " selvage .... LISTING
 " , synthetic ... DACRON, ORLON,
    NYLON, RAYON
 " , Tibet .... CAMLET
 " , twilled .... JANE, JEAN, SERGE
 " , twilled cotton .... DENIM
 " , used as a dressing .... STUPE
 " , used for straining .... TAMIS
 " , woollen ..... KELT, TARTAN
 " , wrapping ..... BURLAP, TILLOT
clothe DRAPE, GARB, GIRD, ROBE, TOG,
  DECK, ARRAY, SWATHE, VESTURE
clothes ... ATTIRE, REGALIA, TOGGERY,
    RIG, TOGS
 " moth .... TINEA
clothing .... RAIMENT, BUREL, FRIPPERY
 " spy .... KEEK
cloud(s) ... NUBIA, CIRRUS, CUMULUS,
  CUMULI, HAZE, MIST, FOG, SCUD,
  SMUR, STRATUS, VAPOR, NIMBUS
 " ; group of stars ..... NEBULA
 " ; to bewilder .... OBFUSCATE
 " masses ..... STRATA, RACKS
cloudberry .... AVERIN, MOLKA
cloudy .... FILMY, DIM, MURKY, HAZY,
    OVERCAST
clout SWAT, SLAP, BUMP, CUFF, THRASH,
    WASHER
cloven .... CLEFT, SPLIT
cloven-hoofed .... FISSIPED
clover ..... LUXURY, MELILOT, ALSIKE,
    TREFOIL
clown ..... HOB, MIME, ZANY, COMIC,
  JESTER, BUFFOON, RUSTIC, ANTIC,
    HODGE
 " in "Twelfth Night" ..... FESTE
clownish .. CHURLY, GAWKY, LOUTISH
cloy . FILL, GLUT, PALL, SATE, SATIATE,
    SURFEIT
cloyed .... AMPLE, FULL, GORGED
club ..... MACE, POLT, THUMP, BILLY,
    TEAM, LODGE
 " , Maori .... MERE

51

" , service .. KIWANIS, USO, LIONS, ROTARY
" -shaped .... CLAVATE
" , social .... FRIARS
" , woman's ... SOROSIS, SORORITY
clubfoot .... TALIPES
clue ..... HINT, INTIMATION, KEY, TIP
clump .... TUFT, MOTTE, HEAP, MASS
clumsy INEPT, UNCOUTH, MALADROIT, GAUCHE, UGLY, OAFISH
clumsy thing .... JUMBO
Cluny, product of .... LACE
cluster ... CYME, CLUMP, TUFT, UMBEL, NEP, PANICLE, RACEME, KNOT, BUNCH
" of seven stars ...... PLEIADES
clustered ... ACINIFORM, GLOMERATE
clustered grains, formed of GRUMOSE
clutch lifting device .... CRAMPON
Clytemnestra's mother .... LEDA
coach ..... DILIGENCE, TEACH, TUTOR, PRIME, STAGE, TRAIN
" , hackney .... JARVEY
" dog .... DALMATIAN
" -man .. WHIP, JEHU, FISH, PILOT
coagulant .... RENNET, STYPTIC
coagulate .. CAKE, CLOT, GEL, POSSET, CURD, CONGEAL, CLABBER
coal ..... EMBER, CARBON, BASS, DUFF
" , bad soft .... SWAD, SMUT
" bin .... BUNKER
" carrying box .... DAN, HOD, SCUTTLE
" deposit .... BORD
" derivative .... CRESOL
" , immature form of ... LIGNITE
" refuse ... GOB, COOM(B), CULM, GOAF, SLAG, SOOT, CINDER
" size .. EGG, NUT, PEA, CHESTNUT
" tar, derivative of .... PITCH
" tar distillate .... TOLUENE
" tar, product of .... LYSOL
" , volcanic .... SCORIA
" wagon ...... CORB, CORF, TRAM
coalesce .. MERGE, UNITE, FUSE, BLEND
coalescence FUSION, LEAGUE, UNION
coalfish .... SEY, PARR, GLASHAN
coal-like substance .... JET
coal miner .... COLLIER
coarse .. RIBALD, RUDE, BAWDY, CRASS, CRUDE, GROSS, RANDY, VULGAR
coarse grass .... QUITCH, REED
coast ... SEASIDE, BEACH, RIPA, GLIDE, SLIDE, LITTORAL
coast dweller .... ORARIAN
" guard .... SPAR
" , per. to ... COASTAL, ORARIAN, LITTORAL, RIPARIAN
coat .... FUR, HAIR, HIDE, FELT, RIND, SKIN, WOOL, CRUST, GLAZE, LAYER, TERNE
" , anc. Roman .... TOGA
" , coarse .... CAPOTE
" , double-breasted ... REDINGOTE, REEFER
" , long-sleeved .... CAFTAN
" , men's close-fitting .. SURTOUT
" , monk's .... MELOTE
" of a mammal .... PELAGE
" of mail ...... ARMOR, HAUBERK, HABERGEON
coati .... NARCIA, NUTRIA
coating for wounds ..... COLLODION
coating on copper and bronze PATINA
" on inside of boiler ...... FUR
coax .... CANT, CAJOLE, COG, TEMPT, LURE, URGE, ENTICE, WHEEDLE
cobalt bloom .... ERYTHRITE
" symbol .... CO
cobaltiferous arsenopyrite .. DANAITE
cobble ... DARN, MEND, PATCH, PAVE, BOTCH, BUNGLE
cobbler ..... SOUTER, SUTER, CRISPIN
cobra .... SNAKE, VIPER, NAJA
cobweb ... NET, FICTION, TRAP, SNARE
cobwebby .. ARACHNOID, ARANEOUS
cochleate .... SPIRAL
cock . TAP, RICK, YAWL, FAUCET, HEAP, VALVE, ROOSTER
cockade ..... KNOT, ROSETTE, BADGE
cock-and-bull story .... CANARD
cockatoo .... ARARA, GALAH
cockatrice .... BASILISK
cocker .. _____ SPANIEL, PAMPER, CODDLE, PET, FONDLE, BOOT, SHOE, LEGGING
cockle ...... GITH, KILN, OAST, SHELL
cockpit .... NOSE, ARENA, CABIN
" of Europe .... BELGIUM
cocktail ... MARTINI, SIDECAR, BRONX
cocky .... SMART, PERT, SAUCY
cocoa, oilless .... BROMA
" plum .... ICACO
coconut husk fiber COIR, KYAR, KOIR
" , meat of dried .... COPRA
cocoon .... KELL, CLEW, POD
" thread .... BAVE
cocuswood .... EBONY
cod .... COR, CULTUS, SCROD
" , per. to .... GADOID
coddle .... HUMOR, PAMPER
code .. CANON, LAW, CODEX, PILLOW, SALIC, FLAG, RULE, CIPHER, PRECEPT
coded message .... CRYPTOGRAM
codfish .... CUSK, TORSK, GADUS
codger .... MISER, NIGGARD, CRANK, CHURL
codicil ..... DIPLOMA, RIDER, SEQUEL

52

codify ....CODE, DIGEST
cod-like fish ....BURBOT, HAKE
coerce ....COMPEL, CURB, DRAGOON
coercion ....CONSTRAINT
coffee ...JAVA, MOCHA, RIO, BRAZIL,
             SUMATRA, SANTOS
   "   berry, exterior of   PULP
   "   cup holder ....ZARF
   " , extract from ....CAFFEINE
   "   house ....CAFE, INN
   "   pot ....BIGGIN
   " , root used with .....CHICORY
coffer ..CHEST, ARK, CAISSON, TRUNK,
             CASKET, DAM
coffin ....CIST, CHEST
   "   cloth ....CLOAK, PALL
cog .....GEAR, CAM, CATCH, TOOTH,
          CHEAT, CHUCK, WHEEDLE
cogitate ....MULL, MUSE, PONDER
cognate .....RELATIVE, ALLIED, AKIN
cognizance ......KEN, HEED, NOTICE
cognize ....KNOW, PERCEIVE
cognomen ..SURNAME, EPITHET, TITLE,
             YCLEPT
coheir ....PARCENER, JOINT
cohere ..ADHERE, STICK, GLUE, CLING,
             UNITE
coiffure ....HAIRDO, UPSWEEP
coil .CURL, ANSA, MESH, QUERL, TOIL,
          TWINE, TESLA, LOOP
   " into ball ......CONVOLVE, CLUE
coiled ....TWIRLED, TORTILE
coin ..JOE, TRA, CASH, MINT, MONEY,
        SCEAT, QUOIN, INVENT, SPECIE
coin (see also "gold coin")
   " , Angola ....MACUTA, ESCUDO
   " , Anglo-Saxon ......ORA, SCEAT
   " , Arabia ..CARAT, KABIK, TALLARI
   " , Argentina .....CENTAVO, PESO
   " , Australia ....DUMP
   " , Austria .DUCAT, HELLER, KRONE
   " , Brazil CONTO, MILREIS, REE, REI
   " , Bulgaria ......LEV, LEW, DINAR
   " , Chile .ESCUDO, CENTAVO, PESO
   " , China .TAEL, TIAO, YUAN, LI, PU
   " , Colombia .PESO, REAL, CONDOR
   " , copper ....BATZ, CENT
   " , debased ....RAP
   " , Denmark ....ORE, KRONE
   " , Dutch ....DOIT, CORD, FLORIN,
             GULDEN
   " , E. African ....RUPIE, PESA
   " , Ecuador ......SUCRE, CONDOR
   " , Egypt ....RIYAL, GIRSH, PIASTER
   " , English ......GROAT, GUINEA,
           CAROLUS, PENNY
   " , Ethiopia TALARI, ASHRAFI, BESA
   " , French ECU, OBOLE, SOU, LOUIS,
             AGNEL

   " , front of ....OBVERSE
   " , German MARK, THALER, PFENNIG
   " , Greek LEPTON, OBOL, DRACHMA
   " , Hungary .PENGO, GARA, FILLER
   " , India ..RUPEE, ANNA, PICE, PIE,
             LAKH
   " , Ireland ....POUND, RAP
   " , Italy LIRA, LIRE, SCUDO, TESTONE
   " , Japan BU, RIN, SEN, YEN, OBAN
   " , Jewish ....GERAH, SHEKEL
   " , metallic ....SPECIE
   " , Mexican .....CENTAVO, PESO,
             AZTECA
   " , Morocco ....OKIA, RIAL
   " , Nepal ....MOHAR
   " , Norway ....KRONE, ORE
   " , Persia .DARIC, DINAR, KRAN, PUL,
             TOMAN
   " , Peru ....DINERO, SOL
   " , Poland .....ZLOTY, GROSZ
   " , Portugal ....DOBRA, MILREIS
   " , roll of ....ROULEAU
   " , Rome .....AS, AES, SESTERCE,
             SEMIS
   " , Rumania ....BAN, LEU, LEY
   " , Russia ..COPECK, ALTIN, RUBLE
   " , Serbia ....DINAR, PARA
   " , shekel, 1/20 of ....GERAH
   " , Siam .AT(T), BAT, FUANG, LOT,
             TICAL
   " , silver amalgam ...TESTER, PINA
   " , Spain .....PESETA, PESO, REAL
   " , Sweden ....KRONA, ORE
   " , Switzerland BATZ, FRANC, RAPPE
   " , trifling ....DOIT
   " , Tripoli ....PIASTRE
   " , Turkey ...ALTILIK, ASPER, PARA
   " , United States ......DIME, CENT,
         NICKEL, EAGLE, BIT, DOLLAR
   " , Venice ....OSELA, BETSO
coincide .....FIT, JIBE, AGREE, TALLY
coiner ....NEOLOGIST, NEOTERIST
coins, per. to ....NUMISMATIC
col ....NECK, NEK
cold ..BLEAK, FRIGID, ICY, NIP, GELID,
             ALGID
   " , a ....CATARRH, RHEUM
   "   chap ....KIPE
   "   mist ....DROW
   " , per. to ....FRIGORIC, ICY
   " ; Sp. ....FRIO
   "   wind ....BISE
Cole, Mr. ....PORTER, NAT
Coleridge's "sacred river" ......ALPH
colewort ....KALE
colic ..GRIPES, ENTERALGIA, TORMINA
collapse ......CAVE, FALL, FAIL, RUIN
collapsible boat ....FALTBOAT

collar ETON, RABAT, RUFF, CARCANET,
RUCHE, RABATO, TORQUE, FICHU,
CATCH, RING, CANG, NAB
" bone .... CLAVICLE
" , papal .... FANON, ORALE
collect PRAYER, COMPILE, LEVY, AMASS,
TAX, BAG, SHEAVE, GARNER
collection(s) SET, LEVIES, ANA, STACK,
SORITES, CORPUS, DOSSIER,
ANALECTA, TROUSSEAU
collector of bird eggs .... OOLOGIST
colleen .... GIRL, MAID
college .. ACADEMY, LYCEE, SEMINARY,
ETON, SORBONNE, HARROW,
HARVARD, OXFORD, YALE, ADELPHI,
HUNTER, PURDUE, VASSAR,
HOFSTRA, CORNELL, FORDHAM, COE,
SETON(HALL), BEREA, EMORY
" girl .... COED
" graduate . ALUMNUS, ALUMNA
" grounds ...... QUAD, LAWN,
CAMPUS
" half year .... SEMESTER
" license for absence .... EXEAT
" mode of training .. DRESSURE
" officer . PROCTOR, DON, DEAN,
BEADLE, BURSAR, DOCENT
" servant .... GYP
collide CLASH, CRASH, HURTLE, BUMP,
WRECK
collier .... MINER
colloquy .... CHAT, PARLEY, TALK
Cologne, one of three kings of .....
GASPAR
Colman, Mr. .... RONALD
Colombian town .... CALI, PASTO
colonizer ...... ANT, OECIST, SETTLER
colophonite .... GARNET
colophony .... ROSIN
color .. TINT, CAST, FLAG, TONE, HUE,
PAINT, SHADE, TINGE, DYE
" , auburn .... TITIAN
" , bark .... MOCHA
" , bay .... MALABAR
" , beige .... ECRU
" , bittersweet .... LOBSTER
" , black .... EBON, JET, SABLE
" , blue .... PERSE, AZURE, CHING,
SMALT, ORIENT, SEVRES
" , blue-greenish ... BERYL, CYAN,
MESANGE, GOBELIN
" , blue, marine .... NAVY
" , pearl .... METAL
" , brown .. ESKIMO, SEDGE, TAN,
VERONA, BAY, FOX, LIVER, MOCHA,
PABLO, FAWN, CUBA, TEAK
" , gray ... RESEDA, PONGEE, ASH,
GULL, IRON, PLOMB, MOUSE
" , green .. EMAIL, RESEDA, PARIS,
IVY, PARROT, MIGNONETTE, JADE,
PERIDOT, HUNTER, MOUSSE

" markings .... RIVULATIONS
" , natural BEIGE, GREIGE, GREGE
" , nude .... SEASAN
" , oakwood .... MESA
" , purple-brown .... PUCE
" , red .. RUFOUS, TAWNY, GOYA,
FLEA, SCARLET, LAKE, ANEMONE,
MAGENTA, LAMA, CERISE,
BAPHE
" , spectrum .... VIBGYOR
" , streak of .... FLECK
" , striped .... PLAGA(TE)
" , to paint .... IMPASTE
" vehicle .... MEGILP
" , white .... ERMINE, SNOW,
BAWN, CHALKY, LABAN
" , yellow .. DEER, BOLE, MIMOSA,
ACORN, ALOMA, TOTEM, RED,
BUFF, CLAY, DORE, FLAX,
LEMON, OCHER, ACACIA,
TAUPE
Colorado city .... LAMAR, DENVER
" , county in .. LARIMER, OTERO
" Indian .... ARAPAHOE
" mountain .... RATON, ESTES,
PTARMIGAN
" river .... GILA
colored highly .... PRISMAL
coloring matter in fustic ..... MORIN
colorless .. ASHEN, WAN, DRAB, DULL,
PALE, CLEAR, PALLID,
ACHROMIC, WHITE
" liquid ...... PYRROL, ACETAL
colors .... ENSIGN, FLAG
" , blending of in calico print ..
FONDU
" , spectrum .... BLUE, GREEN,
INDIGO, ORANGE, RED,
VIOLET, YELLOW
" , to blend ... SOFTEN, SCUMBLE
colossal beast .... BEHEMOTH
colt .... FILLY, HOGGET
Columbia University symbol ... LION
columbium .... NIOBIUM
Columbus' birthplace .... GENOA
" port of embarkation ....
PALOS
column .... PILLAR, ANTA, DORIC,
IONIC, SHAFT, STELE, TORSO,
PILASTER, CARYATID
" base .... PLINTH
" , Buddhist .... LAT
" , outward form of .... ENTASIS,
GALBE
" , ring of an annulated .. BAGUE
" , shaft of .... FUST, SCAPE
" support .... SOCLE
columnar .... TERETE
columns, subbase of ..... STYLOBATE
comate .... HAIRY

54

comb ..... CARD, CARUNCLE, CREST,
TEASE, KAME, CURRY, RIDGE
" , shaped like a ..... PECTINATE
combat .... ACTION, COPE, JOUST,
BRUSH, CONTEST, SKIRMISH
combine ...... BLEND, AMALGAMATE,
CARTEL, MIX, WED, JOIN, POOL,
RING, MARRY, SPLICE, FACTION
combining form for equal ...... ISO
"   form for far .... TELE
"   form for hundred . HECTO
"   form for private .... IDIO
"   form for tooth .. ODONTO
"   form for weight .... BARO
come ... ARRIVE, NEAR, ENSUE, ISSUE,
REACH, ACCRUE, ADVENE
"   before .... PREVENE
"   down .... ALIGHT, LAND
"   out .... EMERGE, SPRING
"   under .... SUBVENE
comedian . COMIC, WIT, BUFF(OON),
WAG, ANTIC, CLOWN,
JESTER, STOOGE
comedy . SLAPSTICK, FARCE, TRAVESTY
"Comedy of Errors" character ......
ADRIANA, ANGELO, LUCE,
LUCIANA, PINCH, SOLINUS
comet .. BIELA'S, HALLEY'S, HOLMES'S,
OLBERS', SWIFT'S
" , envelope of .... COMA
" , tail of .... STREAMER
comfit .... CONFECT, PRALINE, CANDY,
CONSERVE, SWEETMEAT
comfort ...... EASE, SOLACE, REPOSE,
CHEER, QUILT, RELIEF
comfortable ..... COSH, SNUG, LITHE
comforter .... SCARF
comic .... DROLL, FUNNY, RISIBLE
" strip .. PENNY, ABNER, CANYON
comity .... URBANITY
command .... BECK, BEHEST, BID,
MANDATE, FIAT, HEST, ENJOIN,
GOVERN, ORDER, COMPEL,
DICTATE
"   (market) .... CORNER
"   to a horse .... GEE, HAW,
HUP, WHOA
commander . CID, CHIEF, AGA, AGHA,
CAID, QAID, LEADER, MASTER,
SIRDAR, ALCAIDE, CAPTAIN,
OFFICER
" , USA .. HODGES, PATTON,
PATCH, SIMPSON, BRADLEY,
SPAATZ
commandment(s) .... LAW, RULE,
ORDER, PRECEPT, DECALOG(UE)
commence ..... ARISE, OPEN, SPRING,
FOUND
commend ... COMMIT, PRAISE, EXTOL,
KEN, LAUD, APPROVE,
BESPEAK, INTRUST

commensurate .... EQUAL, EVEN
comment .... POSTIL, ANNOTATE,
DESCANT, ASIDE, GLOSS, REMARK
commentator .... GLOSSATOR
commerce ... TRADE, BARTER, TRAFFIC
commingle .... INMIX, BLEND
comminute ...... MILL, CRUSH, GRIND
comminuted .... FINE, PULVERIZED
commiseration .. RUTH, PITY, EMPATHY
commission .. BREVET, TASK, CHARGE,
DEPUTE, ORDAIN,
WARRANT, DELEGATE
commit .... ALLOT, ASSIGN, CONSIGN
commodity .... GOODS, ARTICLE,
PRODUCT, WARE, STAPLE
common GENERAL, ORNERY, PLEBEIAN,
AVERAGE, BASE, BANAL, JOINT,
TRITE, USUAL, COARSE, VULGAR
"   people; Sp. .... GENTE
"   to both sexes ...... EPICENE
commonly accepted .... VULGATE
commonplace ..... HUMDRUM, STALE,
DAILY, PROSY, TRUISM,
PROSAIC, TEDIOUS, DULL
commonwealth ..... REPUBLIC, STATE
commotion ADO, FLARE, RIOT, FUSS,
STIR, BUSTLE, POTHER, WELTER
commune .. CONVERSE, SHARE, AREA,
REALM, SOIL, IMPART, TOWNSHIP,
DISTRICT
communication satellite ... SYNCOM,
TELSTAR
communion .... EUCHARIST, HOST,
VIATICUM, MASS, ANTIPHON
"   plate .... WAFER, PATEN
Communist council .... SOVIET
"   curtain ..... WALL, IRON,
BAMBOO
community .... DEME, DEMOS, MIR
Comoro island .... MOHELI
compact ... ETUI, PRESS, FAST, DENSE,
TERSE, SOLID, TRIG, TREATY,
CARTEL, COVENANT
companion ... MATE(Y), ALLY, CRONY,
ESCORT, SPOUSE, COMATE, FERE
" , an equal ...... COMPEER
" , constant ...... SHADOW
" , faithful .... ACHATES
" ; Sp. .... AMIGO
company ...... BAND, TEAM, TROOP,
BODY, CREW, TROUPE, BATTERY,
PHALANX, VISITOR
compare .... COLLATE, EVEN, SEMBLE,
LIKE, RELATE
comparison .... PARABLE, SIMILE,
ANALOGY, METAPHOR
compartment .... BIN, CELL(ULE)
compass .... REACH, SWEEP, GYRO
"   beam .... TRAMMEL
"   part ...... AIRT, ROSE, VANE,
RHUMB, GIMBAL, AZIMUTH

"   point . ENE, ESE, NNE, NNW,
SSE, SSW, WNW, WSW
compassion .... PITY, RUTH
compel ... COERCE, DRIVE, DRAGOON,
PRESS, ENJOIN, OBLIGE
compendium ...... DIGEST, EPITOME,
SUMMARY
compensate .... REPAY, RECOUP,
SATISFY
compensation . SOLATIA, REPARATION,
HIRE, PAY, UTU, BALM, OFFSET
compete .... EMULATE, COPE, MATCH,
CONTEND, STRIVE, VIE, PIT
competent ..... SMART, CAPAX, ABLE,
SANE, APT, FIT
competition .... FEIS, RIVALRY, STRIFE,
MATCH, CONTEST
competitor .... RIVAL, OPPONENT
Compiegne's river ...... AISNE, OISE
compilation .... DIGEST
complain ... CROAK, REPINE, YAMMER,
MOAN, FRET, FUSS, GRIPE,
LAMENT, WAIL, GRUMBLE
complaisant .... KIND, LENIENT
complete . FULL, PLENARY, SOLE, END,
MATURE, UTTER, CLOSE,
QUITE, FULFIL(L)
complexion .. BLEE, TINGE, HUE, TINT,
VEIN, ASPECT, TENOR
complicate .... INTORT, TANGLE
complication .. NODE, SNARL, NODUS
comply .... ASSENT, YIELD, OBEY
component ...... ELEMENT, INTEGRAL
comport ..... ACCORD, ACT, DEMEAN,
CONDUCT, BEHAVE
composed ..... WOVE, WROTE, CALM,
COOL, PLACID, SEDATE
composer ...... VERDI, BIZET, WEBER,
BARTOK, LEHAR, ARNE, BACH,
KERN, WOLF, ELGAR, GLUCK,
GRIEG, GUIDO, HAYDN, LISZT,
MOZART, BEETHOVEN, RAVEL,
LALO, REGER, WEILL, BRAHMS,
CHOPIN, DELIUS, DVORAK,
HANDEL, KALMAN, MAHLER,
ROGERS, PORTER, WAGNER,
BERLIOZ, COPLAND, DEBUSSY,
MENOTTI, STRAUSS, GERSHWIN
composition .... OPUS, PIECE, THEME,
SCENA, ESSAY, NOME
"   for nine instruments ...
NONET
"   of ivory dust .. EBURINE
"   , premise of .... LEMMA
"   , of selected works .....
CENTO
compositor .... TYPO, PRINTER
compound ..... MIX, FARRAGO, OLIO,
BLEND, JUMBLE
"   , chem. .... PYRAN

"   in asarabacca root ....
ASARONE
"   in fleshy fruits .... PECTIN
"   in incandescent mantles ..
CERIA
"   of iron and sulphur ......
PYRITE
"   used for arthritis .. ACTH,
CORTISONE
"   , yellow .... ANISIL
comprehend . GRASP, SENSE, FATHOM,
SEE, REALIZE, IMAGINE, SAVVY,
LATCH, DISCERN
compress .... CROWD, STUPE, DIGEST,
REDUCE, SHRINK, CURTAIL,
CONDENSE, SQUEEZE, PLEDGET
compulsion ..... COACTION, DURESS,
FORCE
compulsory service .... ANGARIA,
SLAVERY
compunction .... PENITENCE, QUALM,
REMORSE, REGRET, RUE
compute ...... TALLY, ASSESS, FIGURE
computing device .... ANALOG
comrade .... FRATER, BUDDY, PAL,
CRONY, BILLY, PEER, ALLY, MATE
con ...... ANTI, SCAN, CHEAT, LEARN,
AGAINST, VERSUS, STUDY
concatenate ... CHAIN, STRING, UNITE
concave .... DISHED
"   mirrors .... SPECULA
conceal .... CLOAK, PALM, WRY,
ELOI(G)N
concealed .. LATENT, VEILED, DOGGO,
PERDUE, INNER, MASKED, LARVATE
concede ...... ADMIT, AGREE, GRANT,
YIELD, OWN
conceit .... FLAM, PRIDE, VANITY,
EGO(TISM)
conceited .... VAIN
conceive ...... THINK, BRAIN, IDEATE
concentrate .... AIM, FOCUS, CENTER,
GATHER
conception ... IDEA, NOTION, FANCY,
IMAGE, THOUGHT
concern .. AFFAIR, CARE, SAKE, EVENT,
GRIEF, WORRY, MATTER,
REGARD, FIRM, INTEREST
concerning ..... ABOUT, ANENT, FOR,
INRE
concert .... ACCORD, HARMONY,
RECITAL
"   hall .... ODEON, ODEUM,
CARNEGIE
conch .... PUNK, STROMBUS
conciliate .... (APP)EASE, PACIFY,
PLACATE
conciliatory .... GENTLE, IRENIC,
LENIENT
concise ...... CURT, PITHY, SUCCINCT,
PRECIS, LACONIC

conclude ... CLOSE, END, INFER, REST, DEDUCE, REASON, SETTLE, GUESS
conclusion ...... END, CODA, RESULT
conclusive .. COGENT, FINAL, TELLING
concoct .... COOK, BREW, MIX, PLAN, INVENT, COMPOSE
concord ...... AMITY, PACT, RAPPORT, GRAPE
concordat .... TREATY
concrete ..... ACTUAL, SOLID, BETON, REAL
concur .... ACCORD, CHIME, JIBE
concurrent ..... SYNERGETIC, COEVAL
concuss .... JAR, JOLT, SHAKE, CHOCK
condemn .. BAN, DECRY, DOOM, FILE, BLAME, CONVICT
condense . SHRINK, DECOCT, ABRIDGE, DEFLATE, THICKEN, DISTIL(L)
condescend ... DEIGN, STOOP, FAVOR
condiment ..... SAUCE, CURRY, MACE, SAGE, HERB, RELISH
condition ... IF, COVIN, TERM, MODE, ANGLE, FACET, PHASE, PROVISO
condone ... ABSOLVE, REMIT, PARDON
conduce ...... ADVANCE, LEND, TEND
conduct .. ACTION, CONVEY, DEMEAN, RUN, GUIDE, ESCORT, CONVOY, MANAGE
conductor . CICERONE, GUIDE, GUARD, LEADER, CATHODE, MAESTRO, TOSCANINI, WALTER, BERNSTEIN, FIEDLER
conduit ..... MAIN, PIPE, DUCT, RACE, CANAL, CHANNEL, SEWER
cone ... COP, FUNNEL, STROBILE, PINA
Conestoga wagon .... FREIGHTER
coney .... DAMAN, RABBIT
confection .... CIMBAL, NOUGAT, PRALINE, DULCE, FONDANT, SWEETMEAT, CARAMEL
confederate .... ALLY, ABETTOR, PARTNER, AIDE, UNITE
Confederate .... REBEL
confer .... DUB, AWARD, ENDOW, BESTOW, DONATE, PARLEY
conference .... SYNOD, CONFAB, PALAVER
confess .... ADMIT, REVEAL, OWN, ATTEST, SHRIVE, CONCEDE, DIVULGE
confession .... CREED, CREDO, SHRIFT
confetti .. BONBONS, CANDY, RIBBON, TAPE
" , eggshell filled with .... CASCARON
confidential . ESOTERIC, SECRET, PRIVY
confine .. CAGE, DAM, LIMIT, IMMURE, STRAITEN, PEN, CURB, JAIL, CHECK, CRAMP, BORDER, FETTER
confined .... ABED, BOUND, PENT

confirm ..... ASSURE, PROVE, RATIFY, ENDORSE
confiscate .... USURP, SEIZE
conflict .. BOUT, FRAY, WAR, DISCORD
confront .... DEFY, FACE, OPPOSE, MEET, BRAVE
confuse ... ABASH, FUDDLE, DERANGE, NONPLUS
confused .... ASEA, ADDLED, RATTLED, MUSSY
confusion .... ADO, CHAOS, DIN, SNAFU, PIE, BABEL, WELTER
congeal .... PECTIZE, SET, DENSEN
congealed, capable of being .... GELABLE
congenital . INBORN, INNATE, NATIVE
congenitally attached ...... ADNATE
conger trap .... EELPOT
" young .... ELVER
congo _____ .... EEL
" snake .... AMPHIUMA, SIREN
Congo capital .... KINSHASA
" river .... ZAIRE, LULUA
Congolese councilor .... MACOTA
" plant .... MANIOC
congratulate ..... MACARIZE, SALUTE, LAUD
congregate .. ASSEMBLE, HERD, TROOP, MEET, CONVENE
congregation ... FOLD, FLOCK, PARISH
congress .... DAIL, DIET, SYNOD
congruous ... FIT, MEET, CONSONANT
conies .... HYRACES
conifer ... TORREY, CEDAR, PINE, YEW, PINAL, FIR, LARCH, SPRUCE
conjecture ...... ETTLE, GUESS, POSIT, SUPPOSAL, SURMISE, THEORY
conjoined parts .... ADNEXA
connect .. GLUE, LINK, CEMENT, JOIN
connection .. NEXUS, BOND, AFFINITY
connective .... SYNDETIC
connive . WINK, BLINK, ABET, FOMENT
conquer .... LICK, BEST, SUBDUE, PREVAIL
conquistador .... CORTEZ
consanguineous .. KINDRED, RELATED, AKIN
conscience .... INWIT
conscientious conduct ...... CRICKET
conscious .... AWARE, AWAKE, KEEN, SENTIENT
conscript ..... DRAFT, ENROL, ENLIST, MUSTER, RECRUIT
consecrate .... ANOINT, BLESS, HALLOW, SAIN, DEVOTE
consecrated .... SACRED
" oil ..... OBLATE, CHRISM
consent ..... ACCEDE, AGREE, GRANT, CONCUR
consequence .... END, ISSUE, SEQUEL, RESULT, OUTCOME

conservative . TORY, DIEHARD, STABLE
conserve .... CAN, SAVE, GUARD,
                          SHIELD
   " , grape .... UVATE
consider ... HEED, RATE, DEEM, MUSE,
                   REFLECT, PONDER
consort .... MATE, MINGLE, WIFE
   "   of Siva .... DEVI
consign ... ALLOT, COMMIT, CONFIDE,
    DELIVER, ENTRUST, REMAND, REMIT
consignee .... FACTOR, BROKER,
                        RECEIVER
consolation .... SOP, SOLACE
console ... COMFORT, CHEER, SOLACE
consolidate .. KNIT, COMBINE, MERGE,
      HARDEN, POOL, COALESCE
consonant ... DENTAL, LENIS, SPIRANT
   " , aspirated .... SURD
   " , per. to .... FRICATIVE,
                        PALATAL
   "   producing hissing sound ..
                        SIBILANT
   " , voiceless .. ATONIC, LENE
conspicuous .... SALIENT, SIGNAL,
    BLATANT, OVERT, PATENT, MARKED
conspiracy .. INTRIGUE, CABAL, COUP
conspire .... PLOT, COLLUDE, SCHEME
constable . TIPSTAFF, BAILIFF, BEADLE,
    BULL, COP, SLOP, KEEPER, WARDEN
constant .... STILL, FAST, LOYAL,
                        STAUNCH
Constantine's birthplace .... NIS(H)
Constantinople caravansary .. IMARET
   "   ; Turkish name .. ISTANBUL
constellation ....
   " , altar .... ARA
   " , balance .... LIBRA
   " , bull .... TAURUS
   " , crab .... CANCER
   " , crane .... GRUS
   " , cross .... CRUX
   " , dipper .... URSA
   " , dog .... CANIS
   " , dragon .... DRACO
   " , eagle .... AQUILA
   " , fish .... PISCES
   " , Halley's ... APUS, GRUS,
              MUSCA, PHOENIX
   " , herdsman ..... BOOTES
   " , Hevelius' .... CERBERUS,
               LACERTA, LYNX
   " , hunter .... ORION
   " , lion .... LEO
   " , long, winding ....
                     ERIDANUS
   " , northern ...... AURIGA,
    BOOTES, CYGNUS, DRACO,
    LYRA, PERSEUS, SAGITTA,
    ANDROMEDA, PISCES
   " , peacock .... PAVO

   " , ram .... ARIES
   " , sails .... VELA
   " , southern ... PAVO, ARA,
    ARGO, CANIS, CETUS,
    HYDRA, LEPUS, LUPUS,
    ORION, ALTAR
   " , water-bearer AQUARIUS
   " , whale .... CETUS
constellation's brightest star .... COR
constituent .... DETAIL, ELEMENT,
    FACTOR, PIECE, VOTER
constitute ...... APPOINT, COMPOSE,
                        DEPUTE
constitution ..... LAW, CODE, STATE,
    HEALTH, NATURE, TEMPER
Constitution .... IRONSIDES
constraint .... FORCE, BOND, DURESS
constrict ....ASTRINGE, NARROW,
                  SHRINK, CRAMP
construe ...... INFER, PARSE, DISSECT
consuetude ... CUSTOM, USAGE, HABIT
consume ..... BURN, EAT, SPEND, USE,
                  WASTE, WEAR
consummate ...... WHOLE, ACHIEVE,
              IDEA, END, ARRANT
consumption .. USE, PHTHISIS, WASTE
contact .... IMPACT, ABUT, TOUCH
contain .... CHECK, EMBODY, SUBSUME
container .... PAIL, TEACUP, CAN,
    CARTON, BAG, COMPACT, POUCH,
    VAT, TIN, JAR, BASKET, BOX
   " , large glass ...... CARBOY
contaminate ... DEFILE, SULLY, TAINT,
    DEBASE, CORRUPT,
    POLLUTE, TARNISH
contemplate .... MEDITATE, MUSE,
                     PONDER
contemporaneous .. COEVAL, CURRENT
contempt .... DISDAIN, GECK, SCORN,
                        BAH
   "   ; Ital. .... FICO, FIGO
contemptible ..... BASE, LOW, MEAN,
                  VILE, ABJECT
contend ..... COPE, WAR, BATE, VIE,
    ARGUE, STRIVE, OPPOSE
contender .... BATTLER, STICKLER
content .... GIST, SATED, PLEASED,
                        REPLETE
contest ...... TOURNEY, AGON, BOUT,
                     COPE, SUE
   "   in law ..... DEFEND, LITIGATE
continent, hypothetical ... ATLANTIS,
    LEMURIA, CASCADIA
contingency ... CASE, CHANCE, EVENT
contingent .... PROVISORY
continue . LAST, PERDURE, ABIDE, STAY
continued ...... PROTRACTED, SERIAL,
    CHRONIC, LASTING
continuously .. ETERNAL, EVER, STEADY
contort .... TWIST, GNARL, COIL,
                        WRITHE

contract .. INCUR, SHRIVEL, STRAITEN, INDENTURE, CATCH
contradict .... BELIE, IMPUGN, REBUT, GAINSAY
contradiction ...... PARADOX, DENIAL
contraption .... GISMO
contravene .... OPPOSE, HINDER, THWART
contribution ...... BOON, GIFT, ALMS
contrite ..... SORRY, HUMBLE, RUEFUL, PENITENT
contrivance .. GADGET, DEVICE, GEAR
control .... MANAGE, REGIMEN, REIN, POWER, RULE, SWAY, CURB, REGULATE, HANK
controversial ...... POLEMIC, ERISTIC
controversy SPAT, WRANGLE, DEBATE
controvert .... MOOT, ARGUE
contuse .... BRUISE
conundrum .. ENIGMA, RIDDLE, PUZZLE
convened ... SAT, CAME, MET, UNITED
convent .. ABBEY, NUNNERY, CLOISTER
conventional .... NOMIC, FORMAL
conversation .... CAUSERIE, CHAT, DIALOG, PALAVER, TRIALOG
converse .... COMMUNE
convert .... THEIST, PROSELYTE, ALTER, GER, REFORM, REVERSE
convex .... ARCHED, GIBBOUS
convex molding .... OVOLO, TORUS
convexity of column shaft ....
ENTASIS
convey .. DEED, CEDE, PASS, TRANSFER, TOTE
conveyance .... TAXI, CAR, NORIMON, TRAILER, VAN, LOAD, DEMISE, CESSION
convict ...... TERMER, TRUSTEE, LIFER, FELON, CONDEMN, DOOM, SENTENCE
conviction .... CREED, DOGMA, TENET
convincing . COGENT, TELLING, VALID
convivial .... BOON, FESTAL, GAY
convocation .. DIET, SYNOD, COUNCIL
convolution of the brain ..... GYRUS
convoy ..... PILOT, ESCORT, CONDUCT
cony .... DAS, FUR, PICA, RABBIT
    " ; Lat. .... LAPUS
    " ; Script. ..... ASHKOKO, DAMAN, GANAM, HYRAX
cook ..... STEAM, SEETHE, FRY, GRILL, STEW, SHIRR, CHEF, HEAD
    " lightly .... BRAISE, SAUTE
cook room .... CUDDY, GALLEY
cookie .... SNAP, BISCUIT
cooking, art of ... MAGIRICS, CUISINE
cooking vessel ... SPIDER, AUTOCLAVE
cool .. NERVY, FAN, CHILL, ICE, CALM, PLACID
Coolidge's vice-president ..... DAWES

coop .. COTE, HUTCH, MEW, PEN, STY, ENCASE
cooper .... TUBMAN
Cooper, Mr. .... GARY
cooper's plane .... HOWEL
co-ordinate .... ADAPT, ADJUST, SYNTONY
coot .... SCOTER, GOTHEN, RAIL
cop .... BULL, BOBBY, PEELER, OFFICER
copal .... ANIME, RESIN
copius .... LUSH, AMPLE, PLENTY
Copland, composer .... AARON
copper ... BOBBY, BULL, CENT, PENNY, CAULDRON, CUPRUM, AES
    " alloy ...... BRASS, RHEOTAN, OROIDE
    " cup .... CHALCO
    " , engraving on a variety of ...
MEZZOTINT
    " , green, phosphate ..... EHLITE
    " sulphate .... VITRIOL
Copperfield .... DAVID, DORA
copse .... HOLT, BOSK, BOSCAGE
copy ...... ECTYPE, REPLICA, EXTRACT, ESTREAT, APE, ECHO, MODEL, CARBON, EFFIGY, DUPLICATE
coral .. MADREPORE, OCULINA, POLYP, PEARL
    " branch .... RAMICLE
    " island .... KEY, ATOLL, REEF
    " septa .... PALI
    " snakes .... ELAPS
    " with porous walls ..... PORITE
corbel .... STRUT, ANCON
corbie .... CROW, RAVEN
cord .... LINK, RAIP, ROPE, WELT, TENDON
    " of goat's hair .... AGAL
cordage fiber ..... SISAL, HEMP, PITA, ERUC
corded .... REPPED, TIED
cordial ...... GENIAL, LIQUEUR, REAL
cordon .... BADGE, ENSIGN, COPING
core .. AME, HEART, NAVE, GIST, PITH
    " of a mold ..... MATRIX, NOWEL
    " of ear of maize .... COB
corf .... BASKET, CORB, SKIP
corin .... GAZELLE
Corinth king .... POLYBUS
cork .... PLUG, SHIVE, STOPPER, STOPPLE, SPILE, BOBBER
    " , noise of drawing ...... CLOOP
    " tissue .... SUBER
    " , wax in .... CERIN
corkwood .... HAREFOOT, BALSA
cormorant ..... NORIE, SCARG, SHAG
cormorant-like bird ...... SNAKEBIRD
corn ..... CLAVUS, MAIZE, SALT, ZEA, SAMP
    " flag .... GLADIOLUS

" , hulled .... HOMINY
" juice .... WHISKEY
" meal .... MASA
" meal bread .... PONE
" meal, fried .... HOECAKE
" meal mush .... ATOLE
corned .... SALE, SALTED
corner ...... COIGN, INGLE, QUOIN,
NOOK, CANTLE
" , to .... TRAP, TREE, POSE
corners .... HERNES, NICHES
cornerstone ...... COIN, CURBSTONE,
COIGN(E)
cornice ..... ASTRAGAL, DRIP, CROWN
Cornish diamond .... QUARTZ
" prefix of town . TRE, POL, PEN
Cornwall mine .... BAL
corolla ... PETAL(S), PERIANTH, GALEA
corollary .... PORISM, ADJUNCT,
THEOREM, TRUISM
corona ... AUREOLE, SCYPHUS, CIGAR,
CIRCLET, FILLET
coronal .... ROSARY, GARLAND
coronet .. DIADEM, ANADEM, CROWN,
TIARA
Corporal .. NCO, REAL HYLIC, ACTUAL,
BODILY, SOMATIC
coporate; law .... UNITED
corpse ..... CADAVER, CARCASS, STIFF
corpulent .. FAT, OBESE, BULKY, BURLY
corpuscles, lack of red ...... ANEMIA
corral . POUND, STOCKADE, STY, PEN,
ATAJO
correct ...... CHASTEN, EDIT, EMEND,
PUNISH, ADJUST, EXACT, REPAIR,
REVAMP, REVISE, PRECISE, RECTIFY,
TRUE, OKAY
correct; abbr. .... OK, RT
correlative .... MUTUAL, NOR, OR
correspond .... FIT, EQUAL, TALLY
correspondence .... HOMOLOGY
corresponding part .... ISOMERE
corridor ...... HALL, AISLE, ARCADE,
GALLERY, PASSAGE
corrode .... RUST, EAT, BURN, GNAW,
DECAY, ABRADE, CONSUME
corrosive .. MORDANT, ACID, CAUSTIC
corrugated CRIMPED, RUGATE, FOLDED
corrugation CREASE, WRINKLE, PUCKER
corrupt POISON, ROT, AUGEAN, BRIBE,
DEBASE, SPOIL, VENAL, POLLUTE,
VITIATE
corsair ..... FREEBOOTER, PICAROON,
PIRATE
corselet .... BODICE
" , body .... ARMOR, COVER
corset strip .... STAY(S), BUSK
Corsican seaport .... BASTIA
cortege .... RETINUE
cortex .... BARK, RIND, PEEL, PERIDIUM

corundum ...... SAND, EMERY, RUBY,
SAPPHIRE
coryza sign .... COLD, SNEEZE
cosmetic ...... HENNA, PAINT, KOHL,
ROUGE, MASCARA, POWDER,
LIPSTICK
cosmetic, medicated .... LOTION
" , white-lead .... CERUSE
cosmic order .... RITA
cosmos ... EARTH, GLOBE, HARMONY,
ORDER, WORLD
Cossack ...... RUSS, CAVALRYMAN
" captain .... SOTNIK
" chief ..... ATAMAN, HETMAN
" organization unit .. STANITSA
" regiment .... POLK, PULK,
SOTNA, SOTNIA
" whip .... KNOUT
cost .... CHARGE, LOSS, PRICE
costa .... RIB, VEIN
costard .... HEAD, APPLE
costume .. SHAPE, TOILETTE, RIG, TOG
cot .... CHARPOY
Côte d'Azur .... RIVIERA
coterie .... CIRCLE, CLIQUE, SET,
CAMARILLA, JUNTO
cottage .... HUT, BARI, CHALET, LODGE
cotton, a dye for .... SULPHIDE
" clearer .... GIN
" cloth .... DORIA, KHAKI, SURAT
" drilling .... DENIM
" fabric ..... GALATEA, PERCALE,
SCRIM, TERRY, WIGAN, SILESIA,
DIMITY, NANKIN
" fiber .... LINT(ER)
" gauze .... LENO
" gin attachment .... MOTER
" lawn .... BATISTE
" machine .... MULE
" material .. MALABAR, JACONET
" seed vessel .... BOLL
" thread .... LISLE
" tree .... SIMAL
" , twilled .... JEAN
cottontail .... HARE, LEVERET
cotton-warp cloth .... SATINET
couch ... DIVAN, SOFA, LAIR, CANAPE,
SETTEE, DAVENPORT, SKULK, SNEAK
" , per. to .... SOFANE
Coué, Mr. .... EMILE
cougar .... PUMA, PAINTER
cough ..... HACK, TUSSIS, PERTUSSIS
council ...... JUNTA, SENATE, FONO,
CABINET, SYNOD, DIET
" , rel. to .... CAMERAL
" table cover .... TAPIS
counsel .... CHIDE, WARN, REDE
counselor EGERIA, PROCTOR, MENTOR
count ..... TALLY, CENSUS, TOT, EARL,
FOOT, GRAF, SCORE, RELY, CENSUS,
RECKON, COMPUTE

Count of Mayence ...... GAN(ELOW)
" of Monte Cristo ...... DANTES
" of Rousillon .... BERTRAM
countenance .... ABET, FACE, VISAGE,
    MUG, MIEN, FAVOR, ASPECT
counter ... SHELF, CHIP, GEIGER, BAR
counterfeit .... FALSE, FORGE, SHAM,
    BOGUS, FRAUD, PHONY, SIMULAR
counterirritant .. MOXA, SETON, STUPE
countermand ..... ABOLISH, CANCEL,
    ABROGATE
counterpart ... COPY, IMAGE, DOUBLE,
    TWIN, REPLICA
counting frame .... ABACUS
country ... VALE, PAIS, LAND, WEALD,
    TRACT, REGION
" , ancient .... ELIS, GAUL
" bumpkin CLOD, CARL, YOKEL,
    YAHOO, CHURL
" gallant .... SWAIN
" , per. to .... AGRESTIC, RURAL,
    RUSTIC
" , Rom. .... CAMPAGNA
countryman .... PATRIOT
county . DOMAIN, SHIRE, SEAT, AMT,
    LAN, FYLKE, PARISH
coup . SCOOP, STROKE, BLOW, PUTSCH
couple ... BRACE, DYAD, SPAN, TWAIN,
    TWO, PAIR, TEAM, TWINS, GEMINI
coupled ... YOKED, WEDDED, GEMELED
couplet .... PAIR, DISTICH, BRACE
courage .. GRIT, HEART, METAL, NERVE,
    VALOR, GUTS, SPUNK
courageous . HARDY, SPARTAN, GAME,
    BOLD, FIERY, FEARLESS
courier ..... ESTAFET, SCOUT, GUIDE
course PATH, ROTE, SERIES, HEAT, RUN,
    ROUTE, CYCLE, LAP, LEG, ENTREE
court .... PARVIS, CURRY, BAR, SPARK,
    WOO, ASSIZE, SOC, LEET,
    GEMOT(E), EYRE, CURIA, DAIRI,
    ATRIUM, PATIO, GATE
" assistant ..... ELISOR, TALESMAN
" crier .... BEADLE
" exemption .... ESSOIN
" hearing .... OYER
" minutes .... ACTA
" , royal, per. to .... AULIC
courteous . DEBONAIR, URBANE, SUAVE,
    CIVIL
courtly .. AULIC, HEND(E), ELEGANT
courts, belonging to ...... FORENSIC
courtship .... ROMANCE, SUIT
court writ ..... SUBPOENA, SUMMONS
courtyard CORTILE, CURTILAGE, PATIO
cove ... FELLOW, NOOK, BIGHT, SUMP
covenant . AGREEMENT, PACT, CARTEL,
    TREATY, ACCORD
cover .. CEIL, TOP, CAP, LID, THATCH,
    HIDE, LAP, COSY, CONCEAL
" scatteringly .... STREW

" with horny plates .... SCUTATE
" with silky down .... SERICATE
covered meat with bacon ... LARDED
" with small figures .... SEME
covering ... PELAGE, TEGUMENT, TILT,
    CAPARISON, HIDE, HUSK, PEEL,
    PELT, RIND, SKIN
" continents .... EPEIRIC
covers a bet .... FADES
covert .... SECRET, SHELTER
covet ... ASPIRE, ENVY, YISSE, CRAVE,
    YEARN, HANKER
covetous .. GREEDY, MISERLY, FRUGAL,
    AVID, EAGER
covey .... BEVY, BROOD, FLOCK
cow, to .... AWE, THREATEN,
    INTIMIDATE, DAUNT, BULLY
cow HEIFER, BOVINE, BROCK, VACHE,
    SUSSEX, BOS, KERRY, MILCH, ANGUS,
    AYRSHIRE, KEE, KINE, STIRK
" barn .... BYRE
" , hornless .... MOIL
" , lowing of .... MOO
" , mother .... CALVER
" , order of sea .... SIRENIA
" , sea .... MANATEE
" , unbranded .... MAVERICK
coward(ly) CRAVEN, SHY, POLTROON
cowboy . LLANERO, VAQUERO, ROPER,
    HERDER, GAUCHO
cower ...... CRINGE, FAWN, WINCE
coxcomb .. DANDY, DUDE, FOP, NOB,
    BUCK, TOFF, SWELL
coy . DEMURE, BASHFUL, MODEST, SHY,
    PAT, WARY
coze .... CHAT, TALK
cozen .... BEGUILE, CHEAT, TRICK
cozy .... SNUG, QUILT, EASY, HOMEY
cozy retreat NUCK, DEN, NEST, INGLE
crab ...... CANCER, UCA, OCYPODE,
    FIDDLER, MAIA, HORSEMAN, BUSTER
" , claw of .... CHELA
" , king .... LIMULUS
" , middle portion of .... METOPE
crab apple .... SCROG
crack . CHAP, KIBE, RIFT, RIME, CHINK,
    CLEFT, SPLIT, CRANNY
cracker .... BISCUIT, WAFER
crackle ..... CREPITATE, CRINK, SNAP
cracksman .... BURGLAR, YEGG
cradle .... CADER, CRECHE, SLEE,
    CUNABULA, SOLEN
craft .... ART, TRADE, METIER, TALENT
crafty .... SLY, WILY, WISE, FOXY
crag . TOR, ARETE, BRACK, CLIFF, SCAR
crake .... RAIL, CROW, RAVEN, SORA
crakow .... BOOT, SHOE
cram ..... JAM, STUDY, PACK, BONE,
    GOUGE, STUFF, FILL
crane .. SARUS, GRUS, TITAN, JENNY,
    GIB, JIB, DAVIT

```
"    fly ................. TIPULA
craniometrical point ........ INIOM,
              STENION, PTERION
cranium .... SKULL, BRAINPAN, HEAD
crank ...... WINCH, BRACE, HANDLE,
                     CRACKPOT
cranky ..... CROSS, TESTY, GROUCHY
crape ..... CLERGY, CRIMP, FRIZ, CURL
crash . BURST, CLOTH, FAILURE, LINEN
crass ........ CRUDE, THICK, COARSE
crate ..... CRADLE, ENCASE, HAMPER
crater ... PIT, CONE, CALDERA, LINNE
cravat ...... TIE, ASCOT, STOCK, TECK
crave .. BEG, HANKER, YEARN, LONG,
                     PINE, DESIRE
craven .. POLTROON, COWARD, TIMID
craw ............. CROP, MAW
crawfish ................... YABBY
crawl ...... CRINGE, FAWN, GROVEL,
              CREEP, INCH, SWIM
crawler .................... REPTILE
crayon ..... PENCIL, PASTEL, CHALK
craze ... FUROR, FAD, MANIA, MAZE,
              VOGUE, RAGE, MADDEN
crazy AMOK, LOCO, REE, MAD, POTTY,
       WACKY, DAFFY, BALMY, MANIC,
                          LUNATIC
creak . GRATE, GRIND, RASE, SQUEAK
cream ........... ELITE, BEST, GIST
"   mixed with wine .... SILLABUB
crease . WRINKLE, FOLD, RUCK, SEAM,
                     CRIMP, PLEAT
create CAUSE, DESIGN, INVENT, REAR,
                          SHAPE
creation . MAKING, COSMOS, WORLD
creator of the world ..... DEMIURGE
creature ... BEING, MINION, WRETCH
credit .. IMPUTE, TICK, TRUST, HONOR,
                     ASSET, ASCRIBE
"    transfer ............... GIRO
creditor ..... SHYLOCK, DUN, LENDER
creed ... ISM, CREDO, DOGMA, TENET
creek .... ESTERO, RIO, SPRUIT, WICK,
                     VLEI, RUN, KILL
creel ............. TRAP, BASKET, RIP
creep ........ SKULK, WORM, TINGLE,
              FAWN, INCH, CRINGE
creeper ..... IVY, SHOE, VINE, WORM
creeping ........... REPTANT, REPENT
creese ................ SWORD, KRIS
cremation ................. SUTTEE
Cremona ............ AMATI, VIOLIN
crescent .. HORN (SEMI)LUNAR, CUSP,
       LUNE, MOON, LUNULA, LUNULE
"    , per. to ... LUNATE, LUNULAR
crest ....... COMB, COP(PLE), RIDGE,
       TUFT, PEAK, CROWN, ARETE
_____ Crest College ...... CEDAR
crested ....... CORONATED, PILEATE,
                     CRISTATE
```

```
Cretan earth spirits ........ CURETES
"    monster .......... MINOTAUR
Crete ...................... CANDIA
"  , capital of ............. CANEA
"  , king of .............. MINOS
"  , mountain in ............. IDA
"  , watcher of ............ TALOS
cretin .......... IDIOT, MONGOLOID
crevice ........ RIME, CLEFT, CRANNY
crew ...... MEN, MOB, GANG, TEAM,
                          OARS
crib ........ PONY, RACK, STEAL, BIN,
       CRATCH, MANGER, CRECHE,
                     PILFER, PURLOIN
cribbage points ....... NOB(S), PEG
cricket ...................... GRIG
"  , sound of ...... STRIDULATE
"  , term in . MIDOFF, SNICK, BYE,
              OVER, TICE, EDGER, YORK
crime ...... FELONY, SIN, EVIL, VICE,
                     ARSON, OFFENSE
Crimean city ... SEVASTOPOL, YALTA,
                          KERCH
"    river ................ ALMA
"    sea ........... AZOF, AZOV
criminal .. CONVICT, FELON, NOCENT,
                          CULPRIT
criminal intent ............. DOLE
"       "  , characterized by....
                          DOLOSE
crimp ........ CURL, FRIZZ, CRINKLE,
              WRINKLE, GOFFER, PLAIT
crinkle .......... CURL, KINK, CRIMP
crimson ... LAC, RED, CARMINE, PINK
cringe ...... QUAIL, FAWN, TRUCKLE,
              CRAWL, STOOP, COWER
cripple(d) ..... HOCK, LAME, IMPAIR,
                     HOBBLE, HALT
crisis ............ CRUX, PINCH, TURN
crisp ....... FRIABLE, BRITTLE, SPALT,
                          CUTTING
Crispin ................ SHOEMAKER
criteria .................... METRICS
criterion .... CANON, MODEL, NORM,
              STANDARD, TYPE, TEST
critical ..... EDGY, ZOILEAN, CRUCIAL
"    mark ...... OBELISK, OBELUS
critic ....... ZOILUS, CARPER, BOOER,
              LITERATOR, CENSOR,
              CRITICASTER, SLATER
criticism ................. ZOILISM
criticize .... CENSURE, ROAST, SLATE,
              CAVIL, FLAY, PAN
Croatian capital ............ ZAGREB
"    city ........ AGRAM, EIUME
"    mountain .......... KAPELA
"    territory ............ BANAT
"    tribe ...... WENDISH, SLAV
crock ............. SMUT, SOOT, JAR
Crockett; Texan ............. DAVID
"  , chapel of .......... ALAMO
```

crocodile .... SAURIAN, MUGGER,
　　　　　　VULGARIS, GOA, YACARE
　　" 　bird ...... PLOVER, SICSAC,
　　　　　　　　　　　TROCHILUS
　　" 　like .... GAVIAL, NAKO
croft .... COTTAGE, FARM, BOTTLE
cromlech .... DOLMEN
Cromwell, Oliver .... NOLL
　　" 　; site of victory ... NASEBY
crone ... BELDAM, HAG, EWE, WITCH
crony .... EME, PAL, CHUM, BUDDY
crook .... STAFF, CROSIER, CURVE
crooked ..... BENT, ASKEW, AKIMBO,
　　　　　　　WRY, ZAG, CORRUPT
crop ... REAP, CROW, MAW, HARVEST
　　" 　of a fowl .... GEBBIE
　　" 　, out .... BASSET
　　" 　; to cut .... CLIP, LOP
crops for cattle .... BOILAGE
Crosby .... BING, BINGLE
cross ... CELTIC, ROOD, TRACE, IRATE,
　　　FYLFOT, SWASTIKA, CRUCIFIX
　　" 　, tau .... ANKH, CRUX
crossbeam .... TRAVE
crossed beet and carrot .... WOBBLE
crosspiece .... BAR, RUNG
cross-question ...... EXAMINE, TARGE
crossroads of the world .... LISBON
crossrow .... ALPHABET
cross-shaped .... CRUCIAL
cross stroke .... SERIF
cross timber .... SPALE
cross threads .... WEFT, WOOF
crotchet .... FAD, VAGARY, WHIM,
　　　　　　　　　　　CAPRICE
Croton bug .... COCKROACH
crouch ...... FAWN, SQUAT, TRUCKLE
croup .... CATARRH
crouton .... BIT, SIPPET
crow .... CORBIE, ROOK, CAW, DAW,
　　HOODY, CORVINE, AYLET, CORBLE
　　" 　, to .... VAPOR, BOAST,
　　　　　　　　　VAUNT, BRAG
crowd .. SWARM, DROVE, HORDE, MOB,
　　RUCK, JAM, FLOCK, SERRY, RABBLE
crowded ... ELBOWED, FILLED, PACKED
crown ..... DIADEM, CORONA, MITER,
　　　TIARA, PATE, LAUREL, TROPHY
　　" 　, to .... CORONATE, CAP
crown prince .... ATHELING, HEIR,
　　　　　　　　　　　CHARLES
crown wheel .... CONTRATE
crowned .... CRESTED, CRISTATED
crucial ..... SEVERE, FINAL, CRITICAL
crude .... CRASS, ROUGH, RAW,
　　　　　　　　　　　CALLOW
crucible ...... ETNA, RETORT, CRUSET
cruel .... SAVAGE, BRUTAL, FELL,
　　TYRANNIC, FERAL, BESTIAL, SAVAGE
cruet .. AMA, AMPULLA, CASTER, VIAL

crumbly .... BRASHY, FRIABLE
crumple .... WRINKLE, RUFFLE,
　　　　　　　　　CREASE, RUCK
crunch ...... CHAMP, MUNCH, CRUMP
cruor .... BLOOD, GORE
crural joint .... KNEE
"Crusade in Europe"; by ....
　　　　　　　　　EISENHOWER
crusader .... TEMPLAR, PILGRIM
　　" 　, foe of .. SALADIN, SARACEN
　　" 　, port of .... ACRE
crush .... CROWD, PRESS, SINK,
　　　　　MESH, HORST, SUBDUE
crushed sugar .... BAGASSE
crust ... CAKE, COATING, HULL, SHELL
crustacean .. LOBSTER, CRAB, PRAWN,
　　　ISOPOD, DECAPOD, ERYON,
　　HIPPA, LIMULUS, COPEPOD, SHRIMP,
　　　　　　　MAIAN, YABBY
　　" 　feeler .... ANTENNA
　　" 　, footless .... APUS
　　" 　, fossil .... TRILOBITE
　　" 　larva form .... ALIMA
　　" 　, limb of .... PODITE
crustaceous .... SHELLY
crux .. PUZZLE, RIDDLE, ANKH, CROSS
cry .... FAD, COOEY, RAGE, PISH,
　　　AVAST, HEP, WEEP, YELP,
　　　SOB, PULE, MEWL, LAMENT,
　　　WHOA, OYEZ, COOEE, HOY
　　" 　, a party ... SHIBBOLETH, SLOGAN
　　" 　, mystic .... OM
cry to urge on ... TANTIVY, IMPLORE,
　　　　　　　　　　　YOICK
crying .... PULING, CLAMANT
cryptic ..... HIDDEN, OCCULT, VAGUE
cryptogam .... ACROGEN, FERN
cryptogamic .... AGAMOUS
crystal ..... ICE, HARD, CLEAR, LUCID
　　" 　, twin .... MACLE
crystal gazing, do .... SCRY
crystalline .... PELLUCID
　　" 　alkaloid poison ....
　　　ATROPINE, AMARINE,
　　　DATURINE, JERVINE
　　" 　base .... ALANINE
　　" 　compound .... SERINE,
　　　OSCIN, PABA, TYRAMINE
　　" 　globulin .... VITELLIN
　　" 　hollow nodule .... GEODE
　　" 　pine tar .... RETENE
　　" 　rock .... DIORITE, GREISEN
　　" 　salt .... BORAX
　　" 　structure .... SPARRY
　　" 　substance ... ALBINE, UREA
　　" 　substance, colorless ......
　　　　　　　　　　ORCINE
　　" 　substance, sugarlike .....
　　　　　　　　　　DULCIN
crystals, dewy with .... DRUSY

63

cub .... CODLING, FRY, PUP, LIONET, WHELP
Cuban bird .... TOCORORO, TROGON
" castle .... MORROW
" coin .... PESO
" dance .... RUMBA, CONGA
" ex-president .... BATISTA, MACHADO
" fish .... DIABLO
" municipality .... PALMIRA
" mus. instrument ..... MARACA
" premier .... CASTRO
" rodent .... HUTIA, PILORI
" tempest .... BAYAMO
" tobacco .... CAPA, VUELTA
" town ..... GUINES, HAVANA, MANTUA
" tree .... CUYA
" ward .... BARRIO
cube .... TESSERA, DIE
cubic decimeter .... LITRE
" measure .... CORD
" meter .... STERE
cubicle .... NICHE, ALCOVE, CELL, BOOTH, BAY
Cuchullin's wife .... EIMER, EMER
cuckoo .... ANI, GAWK, HUNTER, RAINBIRD, CHATAKA, KOEL
cuckoopint .... OXBERRY, ARUM
cucumber .. PEPO, CONGER, GHERKIN
" ; Sp. .... PEPINO
cucumbers, sea .... PEDATA
cucurbit .... GOURD
cud .... QUID, RUMEN, BOLUS, CHEW
cuddle .. SNUGGLE, HUG, NESTLE, PET
cudge ..... STAFF, SHILLALAH, STAVE, BASTE, DRUB
cue .... HINT, TAIL, ROD, TIP, PIG, NOD, PRESA, SIGNAL
cuff ...... BOX, CLOUT, BUFFET, SLUG, SWAT
Cugat, Mr. .... XAVIER
cuirass ..... ARMOR, MAIL, LORIC(A)
cull .. DUPE, SELECT, PLUCK, WINNOW
culmination ... ACME, AUGE, NOON, APOGEE, CLIMAX, VERTEX, ZENITH
cultivate .... FARM, TILL, PLOW, HARROW, NURSE, RAISE, FOSTER, EAR
cultivation .... JUM, JOOM, TILTH
cultivated ..... HOED, TILLED, URBAN
culture .. AGAR, ART, POLISH, TILLAGE
cummerbund .... SASH
cunning ...... ARTFUL, CRAFT(Y), SLY, WILY, DAEDAL, DEDAL, ASTUTE, DECEIT, GUILE
cup .. TOSS, GODET, TIG, TASS, MUG, BEAKER, CUPEL, GRAIL, JORUM, CHARK, CRUSE, NOGGIN, CANNIKIN, AMA, SHOT, CYLIX, FACER, HOLMOS

" of a flower .... CALYX
" to hold precious stones .... DOP
cupbearer .... HEBE, SAKI
cupboard ..... ARMOIRE, AMBRY, KAS
cupel .... REFINE, TEST
Cupid ...... DAN, AMOR, EROS, LOVE
Cupid's sweetheart .... PSYCHE
cupidity ...... AVARICE, LUST, GREED, AVIDITY
" demon .... MAMMON
cup-like .... CALICULAR
cup-like stone .... GEODE
cup-like vessel .... ZARF
cupola .... LANTERN, DOME
cur .... MUTT, MONGREL
curare .... OORALI, URALI
curassow .... CRAX, MITU, BIRD
curate .... DOMINIE, PRIEST, ABBE
curative .... REMEDIAL
curb .... BIT, CHECK, REIN, BALK, FOIL, BRIDLE, REPRESS
curd .... CONGEAL, CRUD, CASEIN
curdle .... POSSET, SAM, RENNET, CLABBER
cure .... CORN, HEAL, SALT, SAVE, REEST, SMOKE
cure-all .... ELIXIR, PANACEA
"Curfew Shall Not Ring Tonight"
author .... THORPE
Curie .... PIERRE, EVE, MARIE
curio ...... VIRTU, BIBELOT, KEEPSAKE
curious .. UNUSUAL, ODD, RARE, NOSY
curl ...... KINK, TOUPEE, TRESS, COIL, FEAK, FRIZ, SPIRAL, BERGER
curled ...... SPIRY, CRIMPED, TWISTY
curlew .... FUTE, SNIPE, WHAUP, MARLIN, BUSTARD, KIOEA
curling mark .... TEE
curly .... KINKY, WAVY, OUNDY
curlycue .... FLOURISH, PARAPH
currant .... RISSEL, RIBES
current .... GOING, RAPID, FLOW, EDDY, RIFE, TIDE, USUAL, COEVAL, GENERAL, TREND
curse .... OATH, HEX, BAN(E), ANATHEMA, MALEDICT, MALISON
cursed .... ODIOUS, EXECRABLE
curt .... BLUNT, BRIEF, GRUFF, SHORT
curtail .... LOP, PARE, REDUCE
curtain .... BLIND, SHADE, VEIL
curvature ...... LORDOSIS, CYRTOSIS
curve ..... ARC, BEND, CROOK, TURN, ESS, OGEE, EXTRADOS, TOROID, ELLIPSE, SINUS
" , cusp of a .... SPINODE
" , double point of ...... ACNODE
curved .. NOWY, CONVEX, CONCAVE, ARCUATE, ADUNC
" processes .... HAMI
" wedge .... CAM

64

cuscuta .... DODDER
Cush's father .... HAM
    "   son .... NIMROD, SEBA
cushion .... DASHPOT, PAD, BOLSTER,
                            HASSOCK
cusk .... CATFISH, FISH
cusp .... APEX, CORNER, END, POINT,
            HORN, ANGLE, PEAK, TOOTH
custard .... FLAN, FOOL
    "   apple .... ANONA
custody .... CHARGE, TRUST, DURANCE
custom(s) .... URE, WONT, USE,
            USAGE, MOS, RITUS, MORES
cut ...... LOP, MOW, CARVE, SNEE(D),
            CLEAVE, DOCK, SNIP, ESCARP(E),
            SLICE, SEVER, SLASH, SERRATE
    "   down .... RASEE, RAZEE
    "   in half .... HALVE, BISECT,
                            DIMIDIATE
    "   in cubes .... DICE
    "   of an ax .... HACK, GASH, KERF
    "   off .. BOB, SNICK, SCIND, SHORN
    "   off, as a mane .... ROACH
    "   off wool .... DOD
    "   or pare off .... RESECT
    "   out .... EXCIDE, EXCISE
    "   short .... POLLED
    "   up .... GRIEVE, DICE, HARRY
    "   with geometric surfaces ....
                            FACETED
    "   with shears .... SHIRL
cutaneous .... DERMAL
cutter ...... FACER, INCISOR, SLEIGH,
                        SLICER, SLOOP
cutting .... MORDANT, TART, SCION,
            SNEEING, TRENCHANT, KEEN,
                    SHARP, APOCOPE
    "   into two parts ...... SECANT
cuttlefish .... SEPIA, SQUID, CATFISH
cuttlefish fluid .... INK
cyanite .... BLUE, DISTHENE
Cyclades .... IOS, NAXOS, TENOS,
            ANDROS, PAROS, MELOS
cycle ..... SAROS, AGE, EON, WHEEL
cyclone .... TORNADO, TWISTER
Cyclops .... GIANT
cyclostome .... LAMPREY
cygnet .... SWAN
cylinder ... GABION, ROLLER, PLATEN,
                INKER, PRISM, PISTON
cylindrical saw .... CROWN
    "   transverse section . TERETE
cyma .... GOLA, GULA, OGEE,
                        MOLDING
cymbal .... TAL, ZEL
cymbalo .... DULCIMER
Cymbeline's daughter ...... IMOGEN
Cymric .... WELSH
    "   bard ..... ANEURIN, ANEIRIN
    "   god ...... DYLAN, GWYDION,
                    PWYLL, LLEU

cynic ... DOGLIKE, SNARLER, TIMON,
                    ASCETIC, MOROSE
cynosure ...... LODESTAR, LOADSTAR,
                        POLESTAR
cypress, mock .... BELVEDERE
cyprinoid fish ..... IDE, SMELT, DACE
Cyrenaic .... HEDONIC
    "   measure .... DRA
Cyrus .... SUN
    "   , daughter of .... ATOSSA
    "   , son of ... CAMBYSES, SMERDIS
cyst .... BAG, POUCH, SAC, WEN
Cythera .... VENUS
czar .... IVAN, PETER, TSAR
Czech .... SLOVAK
    "   capital .... PRAHA, PRAGUE
    "   city .... BRNO, PILSEN
    "   composer ..... FRIML, DVORAK
    "   county .... UNG
    "   leader .... BENES, MASARYK
    "   mountain .... TATRA
    "   munition plant .... SKODA
    "   river .... ISER, MOLDAU

D

dab .... PAT, PINCH, SPOT
dabbler .... DILETTANTE, TRIFLER,
                        SCIOLIST
dabchick .... GALLINULE, GREBE
Dacian, early .... AVAR
dacoit .... BANDIT
daddle ...... TODDLE, WADDLE, WALK
daddy longlegs .... SPINNER, TIPULID
Dadaist .... ARP, ERNST, PICABIA
dado ..... SOLIDUM, DIE, WAINSCOT,
                            BASE
Daedalus slew _____ .... TALOS
    "   , son of .... ICARUS
Dagda's son .... AENGUS
dagger ... BAYONET, PANADE, SKEAN,
            BODKIN, PONIARD, ANLACE,
            DIESIS, CREESE, CRIS, KRIS,
                DIRK, STILETTO, KATAR
    "   handle .... HILT
    "   stroke ...... STAB, STOCCADO
Dahomey tribe .... EWE, FONG
daily .. ADAY, DIURNAL, QUOTIDIAN
dainty .... CATE, BONNY, FUSSY,
                CHOICE, PETITE, TIDBIT
dairy .... LACTARIUM
dairymaid .... DEY
dais ..... ESTRADE, PLATFORM, TABLE,
                CANOPY, ROSTRUM
daisy ... GERBERA, GOWAN, MORGAN
    "   , oxeye .... SHASTA
dale ..... DELL, DINGLE, DENE, GLEN,
                    VALE, VALLEY

dally .... DAWDLE, PINGLE, TOY, BIDE, LOITER, TRIFLE
Dalmatian .... SERB
" island .... SOLTA
dam ...... GIRTH, SAAD, SPUR, STEM, OBSTRUCT, RESTRAIN, WEIR
", Arizona-Nevada .... DAVIS, HOOVER
", Australian .... HUME
", California .... SHASTA
", Canal Zone .... GATUN
", Egyptian .... ASWAN
", Missouri .... OSAGE
", South Carolina .... SALUDA
", South Dakota .... OAHE
", Tennessee .... NORRIS
", Virginia .... KERR
damage ...... LOSS, NOXAL, SCATHE, HURT, IMPAIR, MAR, STRAFE, WRECK
daman .... HYRAX
Damascus, river of .... BARADA
damask .... ROSE, CLOTH, PINK
damp .... HUMID, MOIST, DANK, WET
", become .... EVE
dance .. BALL(ET), TOE, FARANDOLA, HOP, GALOP, GAVOT, PARTY, PROM, HORA, HULA
", ancient .... CORANTE
", Bohemian ... REDOWA, POLKA
" clumsily .... BALTER
", Cuban ...... RUMBA, CONGA
", English ...... ALTHEA, MORRIS
", folk, Eur. . KOLO, TARANTELLA
", formal ... PAVAN, FARANDO
", French ...... BOREE, GAVOTTE
", Italian .... COURANT(E)
", gay ... RIGADOON, GALLIARD GALOP, CONGA, CAPER
", modern ...... SHÁG, TANGO, TWIST, MAMBO
", motion per. to ...... GESTIC
", New Zealand ...... HAKA
", old-fashioned ... ALLEMANDE, VOLTA, HORNPIPE, LOURE
", Spanish .... CABALLERO, FANDANGO, POLO
", weird .... ———— MACABRE
dancer ..... ALMEH, ALMA, CHORINE, KELLY, BOLGER, DUNCAN, GEISHA, NAUTCH, ASTAIRE, PAVLOVA, DANSEUSE
dancing, art of .... ORCHESIS, CHOREOGRAPHY
" girls .... DEVADASIS
", muse of ...... TERPSICHORE
" partner .... GIGOLO
", rel. to .... GESTIC, SALTANT
" step . PAS, CHASSE, GLISSADE
" term .... PLIE

dandelion .... DINDLE, BLOWER
dandify .... ADONIZE, SPRUCE
dandle ..... NURSE, PET, PAT, CARESS
dandruff .... SCURF
dandy .... FOP, TOFF, DUDE, BEAU, BUCK, JAKE, BLAD, SWELL
danger .... PASS, RISK, PERIL, HAZARD
dangerous .... DIRE, CRITICAL, FERAL, OMINOUS, PARLOUS, RISKY
dangle .... DROOP, HANG, SWAY, SWING
Danish anatomist .... STENO
" artist .... BLOCH
" astronomer .... BRAHE
" chief .... JARL, YARL
" county .... SORO
" early ruler .... SWEYN
" fjord .... ISE
" island .... AERO, FALSTER, FAROE, FYN
" king .... CANUTE
" measure ..... ALEN, FOD, LAST
" monetary unit ...... SKILLING, KRONE, ORE
" parliament .... RIGSDAG
" peninsula .... JUTLAND
" physician .... FINSEN
" physicist .... BOHR
" pianist .... BORGE
" prince ...... HAMLET, OGIER, HAVELOK
" sand ridge .... SCAW
" seaport .... VEJLE
" speech .... STOD
" ter. division .... AMT
" trading post .... THULE
" trumpet .... LUR(E)
" weight .... CENTNER, LOD
danseuse ..... BALLERINA, CORYPHEE
Dante's friend ...... BEATRICE SCALA
" verse form .... SESTINA
Dantes, Ed. .... COMTE
Danube fish ..... HUCH(O), HUCHEN
Daphne's father .... LADON
Daphnis, lover of .... CHLOE
dappled .... SPOTTED, PIEBALD, SORREL, PIED, FLECK
dare .... OSSE, RISK, BRAVE, DAUR
dark ... MELANIC, OCCULT, STYGIAN, BLACK, DIM, JOYLESS, WAN, SWART, SOMBRE, UNLIT, INKY, EBON
darken .... OBFUSCATE, BECLOUD, SADDEN
darkness .... TENEBRES, MURK, SHADE, EREBUS, MIRK, UMBRA, GLOOM
darling .... CHERI, LIEVE, PET, ACUSHLA, ARUIN, ASHTORE
darnel .... COCKLE, TARE

dart .... ELANCE, FLIT, MISSILE, SCOOT, LICK, CAST, FLIT, BOUND
Darwin's boat .... BEAGLE
das .... BADGER
dash .... PLASH, ARDOR, ELAN, LACE
dashes .... OBELI
dashing ... CHIC, NATTY, NIFTY, POSH
dastard ... CRAVEN, CAD, POLTROON, MILKSOP
datary .... CARDINAL
date .... IDES, TRYST, NONES
date plum .... SAPOTE
daub ..... GAUM, SMEAR, BLOB, SOIL, SULLY, TEER, PLASTER
daunt ..... FAZE, AMATE, AWE, COW
dauphin, rel. to .... DELPHINE
David; actor .... NIVEN
David Copperfield's "child wife" .... DORA
David's general ... IGAL, ABNER, REI, SHAMMAH
Davis .... BETTE, JEFFERSON
davit .... CRANE, SPAR
dawdle .... IDLE, LAG, POTTER, POKE, LOITER, QUIDDLE
dawn .... DEW, SUNRISE, AURORA, UPRISE, EOS, ORIGIN
    ″ , per. to .... EOAN
day .... AGE, EPOCH, ERA, YOM, DIES
daydream .... REVERIE, FANCY
daylight vision .... PHOTOPIA
day nursery .... CRECHE
day scholar .... EXTERN
day's work .... DARG
daze ..... ASEA, BEMUSE, FOG, MAZE, STUN, STUPEFY
dazzling .... SHOWY, GARISH
dead . FEY, NAPOO, OBIT, FLAT, GONE, LATE, AMORT, DEFUNCT, EXPIRED
deaden .... DAMP, OPIATE, MUTE, BLUNT, MUFFLE
deadhead .... SINKER
deadhouse .... OSSUARIUM
Dead Sea, country near ...... MOAB
    ″   ″ , river to .. JORDAN, ARNON
dead tree ... RAMPICK, RAMPIKE, DRIKI
deadly . FATAL, KILLING ———— SIN, LETHAL, MORT, TOXIC
deadly sins ..... LUST, ENVY, ANGER, PRIDE, SLOTH, GLUTTONY, COVETOUSNESS
deafness .... AMUSIA, SURDITY
deal .... TRADE, SALE, ALLOT
dealer ..... AGENT, MERCER, MONGER
dean .... DOYEN, ELDER, DECAN
    ″ , per. to .... DECANAL
dearth ...... FAMINE, WANT, PAUCITY
death .... OBIT, MORT, FINIS, DEMISE, QUIETUS

    ″ , bringing .... FUNEST
    ″ , mercy .... EUTHANASIA
deathlessness .... ATHANASIA
debase ..... ABASE, CORRUPT, ALLOY, LOWER, SPOIL, DEGRADE
debased .... VITIATED, VILE
debate ..... ARGUE, CANVASS, MOOT, REASON, TALK, PLEAD
    ″ , cutting off of .... CLOSURE
    ″ , per. to .... QUODLIBET, FORENSIC
debauch .... BOUT, ORGY, SPLORE
debauchee ...... RAKE, ROUE, SATYR, LIBERTINE
debilitate ..... WEAKEN, UNMAN, SAP
debility .... INFIRMITY, ATONY
debonair .. SUAVE, URBANE, BUOYANT, LITHE
debris ...... SCREE, DRIBLETS, TRASH, RUBBISH
debt(s) ..... LIABILITY, DUE, ARREARS, IOU, DUTY
debutante .... BUD, DEB
decade .... TEN, DECENNIUM
decamp . FLEE, ABSCOND, LAM, BOLT, ELOPE, SCRAM, VAMO(O)SE
decanter ...... CARAFE, CROFT, EWER
decapod ...... CRAB, PRAWN, SQUID, HOMARUS
decay .... CONK, BLET, CARIES, PUTRIFY
decease .... DEMISE, FAIL, OBIT
deceased .... LATE, DEAD, GONE
deceit .. GUILE, CONVIN, COZENAGE, SHAM, WILE, FRAUD, FEINT
deceitful .... ARTFUL, WILY
deceive .... SILE, HOCUS, FLAM, GULL, ILLUDE, DUPE, BILK
deceiver .... TRAPAN, TRICKSTER, SHARPER, LIAR, SHAM, IMPOSTOR
deception .... ILLUSION, JAPE, LIE
deceptive . SIRENIC, HOLLOW, VAGUE
decibles, ten .... BEL
decide .... ELECT, VOTE, RESOLVE, FIX
decimal .... TEN, TENTH
decision ..... METTLE, REDE, VERDICT, ARRET, RULING
decisive .... FINAL, CRITICAL, CRUCIAL
deck .... ORLOP, COAMING, POOP
    ″ out .... ARRAY, ADORN, DIZEN, ENRICH, GILD, ATTIRE
declaim ...... ORATE, SPOUT, BLEEZE, HERALD, MOUTH, PERORATE, RAVE, RECITE
declaimer .... RANTER
declare .... ALLEGE, AVER, AVOW, PUBLISH, SPREAD, MELD, SAY, STATE, BID
decline ...... ABATE, TABES, DIP, EBB, REFUSE, REJECT, WANE, SLUMP

declivity .. DESCENT, SCARP, CALADE, SLOPE
decompose and melt .... FRIT
decorate .... TRIM, SCRIMSHAW, BEDIZEN, GARNISH
   "   with letters .... MINIATE
   "   with raised pattern .... BROCADE
decorated .... NIELLED, ADORNED, SIGILLATE
   "   initial letter .... FAC
decoration .... RIBBON, TINSEL, PURFLE, MEDAL, TROPHY, CUP, DSC, DAM, DSO
   "   , per. to .... MEDALLIC
decorative metalware .... TOLE
decoy .... LURE, STOOLPIGEON, BAIT, CAPPER, RINGER, DECEIVE
decrease ...... ABATE, EBB, DWINDLE
decree ..... NISI, ACT, EDIT, CANON, ARET, ARRET, ORDAIN, DICTUM, MANDATE, ACT, LAW
   " , imperial .... FIAT, IRADE
   " , papal .... BULL
   " , Russian .... UKASE
decrepit .... WORN, RAMSHACKLE, FRAIL, FEEBLE, INFIRM
decry .... BELITTLE, DISCREDIT
deduce .... DEEM, INFER, DERIVE
deduct .... BATE, FAIK, TAKE, RETRENCH, DELATE, REBATE
deed(s) ACT(A), FEAT, GEST, RECORD
deed, one who grants by ... REMISER
deem ..... CONSIDER, JUDGE, REPINE
deep dish, fruit pie .... COBBLER
deer .... CERVIDAE, ELK, CARIBOU, WAPITI, MOOSE, AXIS, KAKAR, RUSA, MARAL, PLANDOK, MUNTJAC, RATWA, ROE, PITA, GUEMAL
   " , female of ..... DOE, HIND, ROE
   " , like the fallow .... DAMINE
   " , male .. STAG, HART, OLEN, BUCK
   " , tail of .... SCUT
   " , track of .... SLOT
   " , young .... BROCK(ET), FAWN, SPITTER
deerlet .... CHEVROTAIN, NAPU
deer-like giraffe .... OKAPI
deer's cry .... BELL
deface .... MAR, MUTILATE, INJURE
defame .... SPATTER, LIBEL, VILIFY, ASPERSE, MALIGN, DECRY
default .... DEFICIT, LACK, WANT, MORA, LOSS
defeat .. REVERSE, BEST, WORST, FOIL, LICK, MATE, ROUT, FAILURE
defect .. BUG, SNAG, FLAW, FOIBLE
   " in timber .... LAG
defend .... GUARD, SHEND, WARD, BACK, JUSTIFY, UPHOLD

defendant .... REUS, CHAMPION
defender of the people ..... TRIBUNE
defense ...... SEPIMENT, ALIBI, PLEA, BULWARK, EXCUSE, GUARD
defense making an angle .. RAVELIN
   " , means of .... ABATIS
defer ...... ACCEDE, DELAY, REMAND
deference .... FEALTY, HOMAGE
deficiency ...... SHORTAGE, ULLAGE
   " of oxygen ...... ANOXIA
defile .... TAINT, POLLUTE, MOIL, PASS, SULLY
deflect .. VEER, CURVE, SWERVE, TWIST
Defoe character ..... FRIDAY, CRUSOE
Defoe; essayist .... DANIEL
deform .... CRIPPLE, DISFIGURE, MAR, WARP, MANGLE
deformity of foot .... TALIPES, VARUS
defraud ..... GULL, SWINDLE, CHEAT, BILK, COZEN, GYP, CHOUSE
deft .... ADROIT, CLEVER, EXPERT, APT, FIT, MEET, PAT, NIMBLE
defy .... BEARD, CARTEL, DARE, BRAVE, FLOUT, SPURN, SLIGHT
degrade ... DEBASE, SHAME, DEMOTE, LOWER, DEPOSE
degree ..... STEP, RANK, RATE, CLASS, HONOR, TERM, STAGE
dehydrate ... DRY, PARCH, DESICCATE
deification .... APOTHEOSIS
deiform .... DIVINE, GODLIKE
deify .... EXALT, BEGOD
deity (see also god) .. NUMEN, GOD, BAAL
   " Assyrian .... ASHUR, ASUR, EA, NEBO, NERGAL, SHAMASH, SIRSI
   " at Ephesus .... DIANA
   " , avenging .. ALASTOR, ANTEROS
   " , Babylonian .... ANU, BEL, DAGAN, EA, HEA, ALALU, MARDUK, MERODACH
   " , Celtic .... ARAWN, BELI, TARANIS, ESUS
   " , classic woodland .. FAUN, PAN
   " , Egyptian .. AMEN, AMON, BES, MENT, MIN, HERSHEF, NU, OSIRIS, PASHT, PAKHT, SET, SEB, SERAPIS
   " , Germanic .... DONAR
   " , Greek .... ATHENA, CHAOS, CYBELE, INO, MORS, SATYR, ZEUS
   " , Hindu . KRISHNA, MANU, RAMA, DEVA, SIVA, VARUNA, VISHNU
   " , holidays .... FERIA
   " , Italian ...... CONSUS, FAUNUS, FLORA
   " , Japanese .... EBISU, SHA
   " ; Lat. .... DEUS, DEA

" , lesser .... BUNENE
" , Norse .. FREY, THOR, LOKI, VALI
" of human sacrifice ... MOLOCH
" of music .... APOLLO
" of underworld ..... DIS, GWYN,
                                    OSIRIS
" , Phrygian .... ATTIS, ATYS
" , Roman .... FAUN, JUNO, MORS,
              PALES, JANUS, VACUNA,
                       PICUS, MINERVA
" ; Skr. .. ADITI, MANU, DEVI, UMA
" , Welsh .... DYLAN
dejected .... DROOPY, AMORT
delate .... ACCUSE, DENOUNCE
Delaware county ...... KENT, SUSSEX
delay .... RETARD, LATEN, DALLY, LAG,
             MORA, SLOW, DEFER, STALL,
             ARREST, LINGER, DETAIN
delayed reaction .... DOUBLETAKE
dele .... DELETE, EFFACE, REMOVE
delegate .... DEPUTE, LEGATE, DEPUTY,
                       AGENT, ENVOY
delete ... CANCEL, OMIT, DELE, ERASE
deliberate ... PREPENSE, COOL, THINK
Delibes, opera by .... LAKME
delicacy .... GATE, TITBIT, KNACK,
              TACT, NICETY, FINESSE
delicate ...... DAINTY, MINIKIN, SLY,
              LACY, FRAGILE, SOFT
delicious ...... TASTY, SAPID, SAVORY
delight ...... BLISS, GLEE, JOY, MIRTH
delineate ...... DEPICT, LIMN, PAINT,
             MAP, OUTLINE, PLOT, PORTRAY
delirium tremens .... HORRORS,
                            OENOMANIA
deliver ...... HIT, COUGH, RID, UTTER,
              REDEEM, YIELD, VENT
" of an evil spirit ... EXORCISE
dell ...... DENE, SLADE, VALE, BLADE,
            DINGLE, RAVINE, VALLEY
Delphi, modern name of .... KASTRI
" , priestess of .... PYTHIA
delude .... DUPE, FLAM, DECEIVE
delusion .... MIRAGE, PHANTASM,
                   MOHA, DREAM
" of grandeur . MEGALOMANIA
delve .... DIG, MINE, TILL,
              SPADE, PROBE
demand ... DUN, ASK, SOLICIT, EXACT
demeanor ..... CARRIAGE, MIEN, AIR
demented .... LOONY, LUNY, MAD,
              DAFT, MANIC, CRAZED
demigod .... HERO, SATYR, IDOL,
                          GODLING
demolish ... RAZE, RUIN, UNDO, LEVEL
demon .... DEUCE, FIEND, OGRE, IMP,
          DAEDAL, ASURA, ATUA, EBLIG,
          ASMODEUS, IMP, JINN, RAHU,
          GOBLIN, TROLL, GENIE

" , female .... LAMIA, MARA
" , wood .... NAT
demons, assembly of .... SABBAT
" in Arabian legends ....
                    AFREETS, AFRITS
" , worship of . DEMONOLATRY
demonstrate .... EVINCE, PROVE
demonstrative ...... GUSHING, THAT
demur .... DELAY, PAUSE, WAVER,
                            OBJECT
demure .... STAID, COY, GRAVE, MIM,
             PRIM, SOBER, MODEST
den .... CAVEA, STUDY, TAVERN, DIVE,
                       LAIR, HAUNT
denary .... TEN
denizen .... CIT(IZEN), HELLION
Denmark (see "Danish")
" , ancient name of ... THULE
" , capital of ... COPENHAGEN
" , dry wind of .... SKAI
" , port of .... KORSOR
" , ter. division of .. ALT, AMT
denominate .... STYLE, CALL, DUB,
                            TERM
denomination .. PARTY, SCHOOL, SECT
denote .... MEAN, IMPLY, SIGNIFY
denounce ... ASSAIL, SCATHE, INDICT,
                            DECRY
dense ..... POPULOUS, CRASS, GROSS,
             OBTUSE, COMPACT, HEAVY, DULL
dent ... NICK, DINGE, HOLLOW, DINT
dental .... ORAL, ODONTIC
dentate .... SERRATE, TOOTHED
dentine .... IVORY
denture .... BRIDGE, PLATE, TEETH
denude . STRIP, UNROBE, BARE, DIVEST
deny .... NEGATE, ABJURE, GAINSAY,
             REFUSE, DISOWN, NEGO
depart .... MOSEY, VAMO(O)SE, DIE,
             EXIT, VADE, SCRAM, BEGONE
departed ..... NAPOO, OFFED, DEAD,
                            LATE
depend ... HINGE, RELY, HANG, LEAN,
                            REST
dependency .... APPANAGE, COLONY,
                            TALUK
dependent .... CLIENT, MINION,
              SPONGER, SERVILE
depict .... DELINEATE, HUE, LIMN,
              PAINT, PORTRAY
depilate .... HUSK, SHAVE, PLUCK
depilatory .... RUSMA
deplore .... BEWAIL, REGRET, RUE
deport .... EXILE, CARRY, BANISH
depose ...... AVER, TESTIFY, UNSEAT,
                            OUST
deposit .... BED, MARL, OOZE, PLACE,
             LEES, LODE, SILT, CACHE,
             GEEST, ALLUVIA, SEDIMENT
" box for coins ... PYX, METER

69

      "   containing gold ...... PLACER
      "   of black tissues .. MELANOSIS
depository ..... SAFE, CACHE, DEPOT,
                           VAULT
depot .... STATION, GARE
depravity .... LICENSE, VICE
deprecate .. BEWAIL, PROTEST, REGRET
depreciated .... SHRUNK, FALLEN
depredate .... MARAUD, PILLAGE,
                           WASTE
depress .... ABATE, DAMPEN, DENT
depressed .... DIRE, DISMAL, LOW,
                        BLUE, SAD
depression ..... TROUGH, COL, DENT,
              FOSSA, PIT, VAPORS,
                DUMPS, ENNUI
deprive .... MULCT, TAKE, DIVEST
deprived ..... REFT, SHORN, AMERCED
depth ...... ABYSS, EXTENT, ACUMEN,
                     GULF, HOLL
deputies, sheriff's .... POSSE
deputy ...... AGENT, VICAR, ENVOY,
           PROXY, FACTOR, LEGATE
derby .... HAT, RACE, BOWLER
derelict .... ABANDONED, WRECK,
             CASTAWAY, TRAMP
deride ...... FLEER, JEER, JIBE, MOCK,
            SCOFF, TAUNT, TWIT
derive ... DRAW, EVOLVE, CONCLUDE,
         EDUCE, INFER, STEM, ISSUE
derived, to be .... DESCAND
derogate ..... DECRY, REPEAL, ANNUL
derrick .... CRANE, RICK, STEEVE
      "   for execution .... HANGMAN
      " , part of .... BOOM, GIN, LEG
dervish .... FAKIR, HERMIT, MONK
descant .... EXPATIATE, SOPRANO
descendants ... POSTERITY, PROGENY,
      BREED, LITTER, SCION, SONS,
               GENES, ISSUE
descended .... ALIT, STOOPED, SANK,
                         FELL
descent ...... BIRTH, ORIGIN, SCARP,
         SLOPE, DROP, LINEAGE
describe .... DEPICT, POINT, LIMN,
      STATE, PORTRAY, OUTLINE
description ..... VERSION, ACCOUNT
descry .... KEN, SIGHT, SEE, ESPY,
           DETECT, REMARK
Desdemona, husband of ... OTHELLO
desert .... RENEGE, MEED, EMPTY,
      MERIT, QUIT, WILD, WASTE,
      BARREN, REWARD, FORSAKE
      " in Africa .. SAHARA, REG, ERG
      " in Asia .... GOBI
      " in Russia .... TUNDRA
      " , per. to .... EREMIC, SERE
      " plant(s) .... ALHAGI, CACTUS,
                         CACTI

deserter .... APOSTATE, RAT,
    RENEGADE, RECREANT, TURNCOAT
desiccated .... ARID, DRY, SERE
design ... FORM, PLAN, ETTLE, DRAFT,
      MOTIVE, SCHEME, DIAGRAM
designate .... MARK, CALL, STYLE,
    DENOTE, PICK, ASSIGN, SPECIFY
desire ...... COVET, EYE, CARE, YEN,
      CRAVE, ITCH, LUST, PINE,
              URGE, HANKER
desirous .... FAIN, EAGER
desolate .... BLEAK, LORN, ALONE
Desmanthus .... ACUAN, MIMOSA
despair .... GLOOM, GRIEF, SADNESS
desperate .... FRANTIC, HOPELESS
despise ... ABHOR, SPURN, CONTEMN
despoil .... FLEECE, REAVE, DIVEST,
           INJURE, RAVAGE
despot ..... AUTOCRAT, TSAR, TYRANT
dessert .... COURSE, MOUSSE, SNACK
destiny .... DOOM, EURE, FATE, LOT,
                     BAHI
    " , oriental ..... KARMA, KISMET
destitute ...... NEEDY, VOID, BARREN,
                   BEREFT
destroy .... RAZE, RUIN, SACK, UNDO
destroyer .... HUN, ICONOCLAST
"destroying angel" fungus . AMANITA
"destroying angel", Mormon . DANITE
destruction ..... HAVOC, PERDITION,
      HOLOCAUST, TALA, STRY
    " of species .... GENOCIDE
destructive insect .. TERMITE, LOCUST
desultory .... CASUAL, CURSORY,
                   FITFUL
detach ..... ISOLATE, SEVER, SUNDER,
               UNFIX, WEAN
detachment .... DISUNION, PARTY
detail .... NARRATE, ITEM
detain .... NAB, CURB, DELAY, INTERN
detains; law .... DETINET
detecting device ..... RADAR, SONAR
detection .... SCENT, ESPIAL, SPOT
detective .. BEAGLE, SLEUTH, SPY, TEC,
      SPOTTER, TAILER, SHADOW
detective-story character ... NERO,
      MOTO, LUPIN, HOLMES
detent ...... CLICK, PAWL, PIN, STUD
detergent . SAPONIN, SOAP, CLEANER
deteriorate .... CORRUPT, WORSEN
determine .. FIX, FIND, IMPEL, JUDGE,
    LIMIT, DECIDE, SETTLE, RESOLVE
detest ..... EXECRATE, HATE, ABHOR,
                 LOATHE
detonator .... CAP, EXPLODER
detour .... WINDING, DIVERT, BYPASS
detract ... DECRY, DEROGATE, ASPERSE
detriment ...... HURT, INJURY, LOSS
devastate .... RAZE, SACK, STRIP,
      RAVAGE, DESPOIL, RUIN

devastation .... HAVOC, RAPINE
develop .... EVOLVE, RIPEN, MATURE,
DILATE, UNFOLD
developing early .... PRECOX
development, per. to .... GENETIC
Devi .... GAURI, UMA, DURGA,
CHANDI, KALI
" , consort of .... SIVA
" , parent of .... HIMAVAT
deviate ...... YAW, ERR, RUN, STRAY,
DIGRESS, HADE, MUTATE, SHIFT,
SWERVE, DEFLECT, DIVERGE
device for amplifying sound . MASER
" to determine height of clouds .
CEILOMETER
devil .... SATAN, AZAZEL, BELIAL,
BEELZEBUB, DULE, DEUCE, DICKENS,
IMP, LUCIFER, OGRE, DEMON,
DEMONESS, ABLIS, FIEND, HUGON,
APOLLYON, SHAITAN
devil dog .... MARINE
devilfish ...... MANTA, OCTOPUS, RAY
devil's bones .... DICE
" godmother .... BABA
devious ...... MAZY, ERRATIC, FOXY,
SLY, CROOKED
devise .. FRAME, ARRAY, AIM, INVENT,
SCHEME, CONCOCT
devised, not .... INTESTATE
devoid ...... BARE, BARREN, VACANT
devote .. ADDICT, CONSIGN, HALLOW
devoted ... DOCILE, PLIANT, YIELDING
devotee ..... BUFF, FAN, IST, VOTARY,
ZEALOT, FANATIC
devotion ...... ADORATION, PIETISM,
ZEAL, WORSHIP, LOVE, ARDOR,
FERVOR, NOVENA, FEALTY
devotional exercise .... AVES
devour .... WOLF, GULP, GORGE,
SWALLOW
devouring; her. .... VORANT
devout ...... GODLY, FERVENT, HOLY,
PIOUS, SOLEMN
De Witt .... CLINTON
dewlap .... FOLD, PALEA, WATTLE
dewy .... RORAL, RORIC, ROY, MOIST
dexterity .... SLEIGHT, FINESSE, ART,
KNACK, TACT, SKILL
dexterous . APT, ADROIT, DEFT, ADEPT,
AGILE, FACILE, NIMBLE, HANDY
dextrose .... SUGAR
diabetic remedy .. INSULIN, ORINASE
diacritic .... DIAERESIS, MARK
diadem .... TIARA, CROWN
diagram .... EPURE, CHART, DRAFT,
GRAPH, SKETCH
dialect . IDIOM, LINGO, CANT, ARGOT,
DRAWL, JARGON, PATOIS, PATTER
diameter ...... CALIBER, MODULE, PI,
BREADTH, BORE, WIDTH

diamond .. GEM, ADAMANT, CARBON,
LOZENGE, RHOMB
" crystal .... GLASSIE
" , cup for cutting .... DOP
" , cut a .... FACET
" , famous ... MOGUL, MATAN,
HOPE, ORLOFF, PITT, KOHINOOR
" , true luster of .... NAIF
" , inferior .... BORT
" , small splinter-like ... ROSE
" wheels .... SKIVES
diamonds .... ICE
Diana .... DELIA
" , parents of .. JUPITER, LATONA
diaphanous ...... SHEER, THIN, LUCID
diary .... LOG, RECORD, CHRONICLE,
JOURNAL
diaspora .... GOLAH, GALUTH
diatribe ... TIRADE, PHILIPPIC, SCREED,
HARANGUE
dib .... BOB, DIP, DAP
dice .... BONES, CRAPS, CUBES
" game naturals .... SEVENS
" , cheat in throwing .... COG
Dickens character ...... TIM, FAGIN,
GAMP, MICAWBER, OLIVER,
TWIST, URIAH, HEEP
" pseudonym .... BOZ
dicker .... BARTER, HAGGLE, TRADE
dickey .... COLLAR, SEAT, APRON
dictionary .... LEXICON, CALEPIN,
GRADUS, THESAURUS, GLOSSARY
dictum .. MAXIM, SAYING, APOTHEGM
didactic ...... TEACHING, MENTORIAL
diddle .... CHEAT, SWINDLE
dido .... ANTIC, CAPER, TRICK, PRANK
Dido's sister .... ANNA
" wooer .... AENEAS
die ..... DADO, STAMP, DOD, SICCA,
EXPIRE, PERISH, TESSERA, CUBE,
MOLD
" , highest number on a .... SISE
" , number six on a ..... SISE, SICE,
BOXCAR
"die-hard" .... TORY
"Dies _____"; Latin hymn .. IRAE
diet ..... BANT, FARE, FAST, AILMENT,
REGIMEN, CONGRESS, RATION
differ ...... VARY, DEVIATE, DISSENT,
DIVERGE
difference .... NUANCE, ODDS, EPACT
different .... OTHER, SUNDRY,
DIVERS(E), UNLIKE
difficulty .... KNOT, RUB, SCRAPE,
FIX, JAM, CRUX, NODUS, PICKLE,
DILEMMA
difficulty, per. to .... CRUCIAL, SPINY
diffident .... COY, SHY, MODEST,
BASHFUL

diffuse .... PERVADE, LAVISH, PROLIX, SCATTER, VERBOSE, WORDY
diffusion through membranes .... OSMOSIS
diffusive .... AMPLE, OSMOTIC
dig ... DELVE, JAB, EXCAVATE, HOWK, PION, MINE, EXHUME
digest .... ABSTRACT, PANDECT, BRIEF, ABSORB, APERCU, PRECIS, EPITOME
digestion .... EUPEPSIA, PEPSIS
" , having good .... EUPEPTIC
digestive tract .... ENTERON, COLON
digger .... SAPPER
digging, adapted for ..... FOSSORIAL
" , fitted for .... FODIENT
" tool .... LOY, SPADE
digit ..... FINGER, TOE, UNIT, CIPHER, THUMB, PINKY
" on dog's foot .... DEWCLAW
digitus .... DACTYLUS, TARSUS
dignified .... ELEVATED, AUGUST, DECOROUS, STATELY
dignities .... DECORA
dignity .... DECORUM, GRACE, REPUTE, STATUS, VIRTUE
digression . DETOUR, ECBOLE, EPISODE
dike ...... DITCH, LEVEE, GAP, JETTY, MOUND, ESTACADE
" rock .... ODINITE
diked land .... POLDER
dilapidate ..... HAVOC, RUIN, WRECK
dilate .... SWELL, WIDEN, DISTEND
dilation of a hollow organ .... ECTASIA, ECTASIS
dilatory ... LAX, SLOW, TARDY, REMISS
dilemma .... NODE, FIX, JAM, SNARE, PICKLE, SCRAPE, BRIKE
dilettante .. AMATEUR, DABBLER, TYRO
diligence .... STAGECOACH, SEDULITY
diligent .... OPEROSE, ACTIVE, STUDIOUS, SEDULOUS
dill seed .... ANISE, ANET
dilute .. LENGTHEN, RAREFY, WEAKEN, THIN
dim ... BLEAR, FAINT, OBSCURE, DULL, ECLIPSE, FADE, DUSKY, DARKLE
diminish .... PLOY, BATE, PETER, CURTAIL, TAPER, WANE, EBB, SINK
diminution .... DECREMENT
diminutive ...... RUNTY, PETITE, WEE, PUNY
" breed of fowl ... BANTAM, BANTY
" ; suffix ...... ET(TE), ULE, KIN, LET
din .... HUBBUB, NOISE, UPROAR, CLAMOR
diners, group of .... MESS
dingle ...... DALE, GLEN, VALE, DELL
dingy ... DUSKY, GRIMY, OURIE, BOAT

dining room ..... SPENCE, CENACLE, OECUS
dinner, per. to .... PRANDIAL
dinosaurs, per. to .... SAUROPODOUS
" , era of .... MESOZOIC
Dinsmore, Miss .... ELSIE
dint .... NICK, NOTCH, POWER
diocese .... BISHOPRIC, SEE
Dione .... VENUS
" , consort of .... ZEUS
Dionysus .... BACCHUS
" , mother of .... SEMELE
" , surname of ..... ZAGREUS
diopter .... ALIDADE, LEVEL
Dioscuri .. CASTORES, TWINS, ANACES
" , one of .... ANAX, CASTOR, POLLUX
dip ... BAIL, DAP, DOUSE, LADE, DUNK
" in liquid .... MERSE
diploma .... DEGREE, SHEEPSKIN
diplomacy .... TACT, FINESSE
diplomat ... ENVOY, CONSUL, LEGATE, NUNCIO, ATTACHE, MINISTER
diplomatic .... CRAFTY, POLITIC, TACTFUL, ARTFUL
" corps leader ..... DOYEN
dipody .... SYZYGY
dipper ... GRAB, PIET, SCOOP, PIGGIN
dipsomaniac .... SOT, DRUNKARD, TOSSPOT, TOPER
Diptera, one of the ...... FLY, GNAT, MOSQUITO, ANOPHELES
" , lobe of wing of ...... ALULA
dire ...... FUNEST, BANEFUL, FEARFUL
direct ... BOSS, MARSHAL, AIM, LEAD, STEER, MANAGE, CON, OPEN, BLUNT, PILOT
" a squadron of planes AVIGATE
" lines of descent .... PHYLA
direction ...... AIM, TENOR, BEARING
" , without fixed ..... ASTATIC
directly ... ANON, FLAT, SPAN, SOON
dirge .... CORONACH, HEARSE, THRENODY, LAMENT, GRIEF, SONG, LINOS, LINUS
dirigible ... SHENANDOAH, BALLOON, ZEP(PELIN)
" framework .... NACELLE
dirk .... DAGGER, SNEE, OBELISK
dirty .... FOUL, SORDID, VILE
disable .... MAIM, GRUEL, SAP
disappear ... VANISH, DISSOLVE, PASS
disapproval .... BOO, HISS
disbeliever .... ATHEIST
disc ...... MEDALLION, DIAL, MEDAL, PATEN
discard ... SCRAP, SHED, SLUFF, JUNK, MOLT, REJECT, CASTOFF
discern ..... READ, DESCRY, KEN, SEE

discerning .... ASTUTE, NICE
discernment .... SAGACITY, TACT,
    ACUMEN, INSIGHT
discharge .. EMIT, FIRE, BLAST, SALVO,
    VOLLEY, SPEED, EJECT, EXPEL, OUST
    "   from office .... QUIETUS
disciple . ADHERENT, SCHOLAR, CHELA,
    MUKID, PUPIL, VOTARY, APOSTLE
disciplinarian .... TYRANT, MARTINET
discipline .... TRAIN, CHASTEN,
    CHASTISE, CONTROL, CURB,
    CORRECT, DRILL
discolored ...... USTULATE, STAINED,
    DOTY, LIVID
discomfort .. MISEASE, AGONY, PAIN,
    MALAISE
disconcert ...... FAZE, ABASH, RATTLE
discord ..... CACOPHONY, VARIANCE
discordant music .... SCORDATO,
    CHARIVARI
Discordia .... ERIS
discourage .... DETER, OPPOSE, DASH,
    DAUNT, DEJECT, DISSUADE
discourse .... DESCANT, PRELECT,
    SCREED, SERMON, DISSERT, HOMILY
discover ...... ESPY, LEARN, UNEARTH
discoverer .... COLUMBUS, ERIC,
    PEARY, AMUNDSEN, GAMA,
    TASMAN, NANSEN
discovery .... ESPIAL, DETECTION
discredit .... ASPERSE, REVILE, ODIUM
discreet .... HEEDFUL, POLITIC, WARY
discretion .... PRUDENCE, TASTE, TACT
discriminate ..... RECOGNIZE, SECERN
discrimination . ACUMEN, TASTE, BIAS
discus .... QUOIT, DISK, PLATE
discus thrower .... DISCOBOLUS
discuss .... DISSERT, MOOT, SIFT,
    ARGUE, DEBATE, DILATE
disdain .... CONTEMPT, SCORN,
    HAUTEUR
disease .... MAL(ADY), AILMENT,
    DISTEMPER
    " ; abbr. .... TB
    " , animal .... HOOSE, NAGANA
    " , cause of ...... GERM, VIRUS,
    BACTERIA
    " , fatal ... PEST, LYSSA, PLAGUE
    " germ killer ...... ANTIBIOTIC
    " , investigator of ... ETIOLOGIST
    " , jumping .... LATA, TIC
    " , malignant .... CANCER,
    SARCOMA
    " , nervous ..... PELLAGRA, TIC,
    NENTA
    " of apple .... STIPPEN
    " of chickens ...... ROUP, PIP
    " of hock of horses ... SPAVIN
    " , origin of .... ETIOLOGY

    " , per. to ...... CLINIC, LOIMIC
    " , plant ... ESCA, SMUT, ERGOT,
    SCALD, ERINOSE
    " , rel. to .... ENDEMIC
    " spreader ... VECTOR, CARRIER
    " , kind of ...... POX, STY(E),
    COLIC, CROUP, LEPRA, ULCER,
    ASTHMA, SCURVY, TETANY
diseased .... MORBID, SICKLY
disembark .. DETRAIN, LAND, DEPLANE
disembowel :. EVISCERATE, GUT, HULK
disencumber .. RELEASE, BID, DETACH,
    LIGHTEN, FREE
disentangle . UNRAVEL, SLEAVE, TEASE
disfigure .... SCAR, MAR, MANGLE,
    DEFACE
disgrace ... ATTAINT, ODIUM, SHEND,
    ABASE, SULLY, STIGMA, INFAMY
disguise .... CAMOUFLAGE, MUMM,
    SHAM, HIDE
disguised .... COVERT, CLOAKED
dish .... BOAT, CHARGER, CRUSE,
    PATINA, BOWL, FOOD, PATERA,
    SAUCER, TROUGH
dishearten .... AMATE, DOWN, DETER,
    DEJECT
dishonest lawyer ..... PETTIFOGGER,
    SHYSTER
disinfectant . IODIN(E), LYSOL, PHENOL
disinherit . DEPRIVE, UNGET, DISOWN
disintegrate .... ERODE, CORRODE,
    DECAY, PUTREFY, ROT
disinter .. EXHUME, UNBURY, UNEARTH
disk .. ATEN, SEQUIN, DIAL, HARROW,
    MEDAL, RECORD, PUCK, SPUT,
    WAFER
dislike .... ANTIPATHY, ODIUM,
    AVERSION
dislocate .... SPLAY, LUXATE
dislodge EJECT, OUST, TOPPLE, EXPEL
dismal DREAR, JOYLESS, BLUE, SOMBRE
dismantle .... RAZE, STRIP, UNRIG
dismay ... APPAL(L), DAUNT, TERRIFY
dismiss .... AMAND, RELEGATE, REMUE,
    CASHIER, GATE, SHELVE, FIRE, OUST
dismissal .... CONGE
dismounted .... ALIT, DESCENDED
disorder .... DERAY, SNARL, MESS,
    SNAFU, UPSET, JUMBLE, LITTER
disorderly .... CHAOTIC, MESSY,
    TUMBLY, RIOTOUS
disparage ...... DECRY, BLUR, MALIGN
disparaging .... DEFAMATORY, SNIDE,
    PEJORATIVE
dispatch ..... POST, KILL, SEND, SLAY
dispense ...... DOLE, PARCEL, RATION
    " with EXEMPT, EXCUSE, FORGO
dispenser of alms .... ALMONER
displaced person .... DP, EVACUEE

display .... AIR, SHOW, SPLURGE,
　　　　FLAUNT, UNCASE, EXPOSE,
　　　　PARADE, VAUNT
displease ...... OFFEND, PIQUE, MIFF
disposed .... PRONE, READY, SOLD
disposition ...... BENT, BIAS, MOOD,
　　　　ANIMUS, MORALE, NATURE
　　" 　toward work .... ERGASIA
dispossess ..... DIVEST, EVICT, OUST
disprove .... NEGATE, CONFUTE,
　　　　REFUTE, REBUT
disputant .... ARGUER, DEBATER
disputation .... POLEMIC
disputatious .... ERISTIC, SASSY
dispute .... DISSENT, BICKER, HAGGLE,
　　　　SPAR, ARGUE, TIFF, BRAWL
disputer .... MOOTER
disqualify ... DEPRIVE, DISBAR, DIVEST
Disraeli nickname .... DIZZY
disregard .... DEFY, OMIT, SLIGHT
disrepute .. ODIUM, SHAME, SCANDAL
disseminate ... EFFUSE, SPREAD, SOW
dissenter .... HERETIC, RECUSANT,
　　　　SECTARY
dissertation ..... THESIS, DISCOURSE,
　　　　TRACT, STUDY, SERMON, TREATISE
dissipate .... DISPEL, SCATTER, LAVISH
dissociate .... SEVER
dissolute ..... LOOSE, LEWD, RAKISH,
　　　　WANTON, CORRUPT
dissolve .. FADE, MELT, ANNUL, THAW
dissonant .... ATONAL
distal angle .... AXIL
distance ..... SHAVE, MILEAGE, STEP,
　　　　OFFING, RESERVE
　　" 　, at a .... YOND
　　" 　, inst. for determining ....
　　　　TELEMETER
distant FOREIGN, AFAR, ALOOF, COLD,
　　　　REMOTE, AWAY, HAUGHTY, YON
distended .... PATULOUS, BLOATED
distich .... COUPLET
distil .... DROP, TRICKLE, EXTRACT
distilling device ..... STILL, MATRASS,
　　　　ALEMBIC
distort .... DEFORM, TWIST, WARP
distortion .... WRYNESS, LOXIA
distract ..... ADDLE, AMUSE, PERPLEX,
　　　　DIVERT, PUZZLE
distracted ..... FRANTIC, CRAZY, MAD
distraint .... NAAM, POIND
distress .... AIL, DISASTER, DOLOR,
　　　　HARASS, MISERY, PANG, RACK,
　　　　TORMENT, TRY
distribute ...... DOLE, ASSIGN, METE,
　　　　ALLOT, RATION, PRORATE
district .... CANTON, DEMESNE, PALE,
　　　　REALM, REGION, WICK, GAU,
　　　　SOKE, WARD, ZONE, QUARTER,
　　　　SECTOR, AREA, SLUM

District of Columbia flower .... ROSE
disturb .... MOLEST, FAZE, ROIL
disturbance ... ROW, FRACAS, TUMULT
disyllabic foot .... TROCHEE
ditch .... DIKE, FOSS, MOAT, SAP,
　　　　TRENCH, RIME, FLUE, SWILE,
　　　　ZANJE, RELAIS
　　" 　, part of a .... GRAFFAGE
　　" 　, slope of a .... SCARP
dithyramb ...... HYMN, POETRY, ODE
diurnal .... DAILY, JOURNAL
divan .... SETTEE, SOFA, CANAPE
dive .... DEN, HEADER, SPIN
diverge .... FORK, ALTER, DEVIATE
diver's gear .... FLIPPERS, AQUALUNG
diversify .... MODIFY, VARY, VARIATE
diversion . PLAY, (DI)SPORT, PASTIME
divert .... AMUSE, AVERT, PARRY,
　　　　DISTRACT
divest ...... DOFF, STRIP, TIRL, BARE
divide ...... SEPARATE, CLEAVE, FORK,
　　　　SEVER, SHARE, RENT, RIVE, ALLOT,
　　　　HALVE, BISECT
　　" 　into feet .... SCAN
　　" 　into number of parts ....
　　　　MULTISECT
divided .... SPLIT, ZONED, REFT,
　　　　BIFID, PARTIAL, PARTITE, APART
dividend ..... BONUS, SHARE, MELON
dividing walls .... SEPTA
divination .... AUGURY, SORS, OMEN,
　　　　PRESAGE, SORTS
　　" 　by dreams ONEIROMANCY
　　" 　by figures .... GEOMANCY
　　" 　by forehead ....
　　　　METOPOMANCY
　　" 　by burning straws ....
　　　　SIDEROMANCY
divine ... ANGELIC, FORESEE, PASTOR,
　　　　PREDICT, GUESS
　　" 　word, ... GRACE, LOGOS
　　" 　work, a ...... THEURGY
"Divine Comedy" author ..... DANTE
divinely inspired .... ENTREAL,
　　　　ENTHEATE
diving bell .... NAUTILUS
　　" 　sphere ...... BATHYSCAPH(E)
divining rod .... DOWSER
divinity .... DEITY, IDOL, ADONAI,
　　　　ELOHIM, JAH, JEHOVAH, NORN
division .... PART, SCHISM, HIEN,
　　　　COHORT, SEGMENT
　　" 　in ceiling .... TRAVE
　　" 　of a leaf .... LOBE
　　" 　of land .... CANTON
　　" 　of shield ...... PALY, ARGOL
　　" 　of the Koran .... SURA
　　" 　, restricted ...... MERE, MEER
divorce law .... TALAK, GET(T)
divot .... SOD, TURF, CLOD

74

divulge .... CONFIDE, TELL, BLAB,
GOSSIP, TATTLE
dizziness .... VERTIGO, WHIRLING
    " , per. to .... DINIC(AL)
Dnieper tributary ...... BUG, DESNA,
PSEL, SULA
do DAE, DIV, COMMIT, PERFORM, SERVE
do again; Lat. .... ITERA
do not know .... KENNA
dock .... JETTY, PIER, WHARF, BANG,
BASIN, SLIP, CLIP, CURTAIL
    " post .... BOLLARD
doctor .... LEECH
    " , young .... INTERN(E)
doctrine . LOGIC, DOGMA, ISM, LORE,
TENET, CABALA, MAXIM, CREED
    " , secret .... ESOTERIC
    " , single-princ. ..... HENISM
document .... DRAFT, DEED, MEMO,
RECORD, WILL, SCRIPT
    " , provisional .... SCRIP
    " , true copy of .... ESTREAT
documents, place for ..... ARCHIVES,
CARTULARY
Dodecanese island .. COO, COS, KOS,
PATMOS, RHODES
dodge ... PALTER, PARRY, DUCK, ELUDE,
JOUK, TRIFLE
Dodgson, Chas. .... CARROLL
doff .... DIVEST, STRIP, VAIL
dog .... SHADOW, CUR, WHELP, ALCO,
FEIST, FOOT, TRACK, TAIL, CUR,
DANE, CHOW
    " , Buster Brown's .... TIGE
    " , coach .... DALMATIAN
    " , duck-hunting .... TOLLER
    " , extinct breed of .... TALBOT
    " family, genus of .... CANIS
    " , famous ..... FALA, ASTA, LAIKA,
BELKA, LASSIE, RINTINTIN
    " guarding underworld .. CERBERUS
    " house .... KENNEL, LAIR
    " , howling of a ... ULULATION, ARR
    " , hunting ...... BASSET, RETRIEVER,
TALBOT, GRIFFON
    " , in Punch and Judy show . TOBY
    " , nondescript .... POOCH
    " of India .... DHOLE
    " rose .... CANKER
    " rose, fruit of .... HEP, HIP
    " salmon .... KETA, HOLIA
    " , Scottish .... SEALYHAM
    " , short-eared .... ALAN
    " , short-legged .... BEAGLE
    " , small ..... FEIST, TIKE, ALCO,
SCHIPPERKE
    " star ...... SIRIUS, SOTHIS, SOPT
    " , wild .... DINGO, AGOUARA
dog days .... CANICULE
dog fennel .... HOGWEED

doggerel .... MEAN, TRIVIAL, RIME
dogie .... CALF, MAVERICK
dogma ..... ISM, CANT, CREED, TENET,
BELIEF, DOCTRINE
dogmatic saying .... DICTUM, LEVITIC
"Dogpatch" depicter .... CAPP
dogwood .... OSIER, CORNEL
doing .... ADO, BUSY, HUSTLE
doldrum ...... CALM, TEDIUM, DUMPS,
ENNUI
dole ... ALMS, PITTANCE, METE, GRIEF,
MISERY, SORROW
doleful .. DISMAL, DREE, SAD, DREARY
doleman; Alger. .... SENAM
doll .. PUPPET, PRIMP, TOY, PREEN, GIRL
dollar .... BILL, TALER
dollar; slang ..... BEAN, BERRY, BUCK,
PLUNK
dolphin .... SUSU, UNIE
dolt .. DUNCE, ASS, CLODPATE, NINNY,
OAF, LOUT
domain ..... EMPIRE, REALM, BARONY,
BOURN(E)
"Dombey and Son" char. ... CUTTLE
dome . HEAD, ROOF, CUPOLA, THOLUS
domestic .... TAME, DOMAL, SERVANT,
MAID, NATIVE, LOCAL
    " establishment ..... MENAGE
dominate .... RULE, SWAY
domineer ..... BOSS, BLUSTER, LORD
domino CLOAK, AMICE, MASK, IVORY,
HOOD
    " , spot on .... PIP
"Don Juan" girl .... HAIDEE
"Don Quixote," doctor in ... PEDRO
    "   " , steed of ..... ROSINANTE
Donets area; capital .... STALINO
donkey ..... ANE, ASS, BURRO, MOKE,
NEDDY
doohickey .... DINGUS
Dooley, Mr., creator of ...... DUNNE
doomed .... FATED, FEY, GONER
doomsday; Norse .... RAGNARAK
Doone .... LORNA
door ..... ENTRY, JANUA, GATE, DAR,
PORTAL, INLET
    " , part of ...... JAMB, RAIL, STILE,
LINTEL, SASH
doorkeeper .... OSTIARY, HASP, TILER,
TYLER, JANITOR
Doric capital, part of .... ABACUS
    " fillet at bottom of frieze TAENIA
    " frieze space .... METOPE
dormancy .... LATENCE, TORPOR
dormant ...... ASLEEP, TORPID, INERT,
LATENT, IDLE
Dorsetshire borough .... POOLE
dose .... BOLUS, POTION
dosseret .... ABACUS, PULVINO

dot ... PERIOD, POINT, DOWRY, SPECK, IOTA, WHIT, STIPPLE
dotted ... PIEBALD, PINTO, SEME, PIED
dotterel .... DUPE, GULL, MORINEL
double . DUAL, BINATE, DUPLEX, TWIN, PAIRED
" course for races .... DIAULOS
" dagger .... DIESIS
" faced .... ANCIPITAL
" ring .... GEMEL
double-ripper .... SLED, BOBSLED
doubletree .... EVENER
doubloon .... ONZA
doubt ..... WAVER, DISTRUST, DUBIETY
dough ...... NOODLE, DUFF, LEAVEN, PASTE, SPUD, MONEY, PASTA
doughnut .. SINKER, CYMBAL, CRULLER
Douglas is its capital (Isle of
————) .... MAN
dour .... GLUM, STERN, SURLY
dove ... INCA, NUN, CULVER, TUMBLER, COLUMBA
dovekie .... ALLE, AUK, ROTCHE, GUILLEMOT, ROTGE
dovetail .... FIT, JOIN, TENON
dowel .... COAK, PIN, PINTLE
dower . DOS, ENDUE, BEQUEST, GRANT
down .... NAP, DOWL, FUZZ, BELOW, DUNE, BAS, PLUMULE
" ; comb. form . CAT, CATA, CATH
" quilt .... DUVET
downfall .... RUIN, DESCENT, REVERSE
downright ..... BLUNT, FLAT, STARK, ARRANT, SHEER
downy FLOCCULENT, PUBESCENT, SOFT, FLUFFY, LANATE
dowry ...... GIFT, MONEY, DOS, DOT
doyen .... DEAN
doze .... (CAT)NAP, DROWSE, DORM
drachma, 1/20 of .... OBOL
draft PLOT, CHECK, COPY, PROTOCOL, DRAM, SKETCH, LEVY, MUSTER
drag .. HAUL, HALE, LUG, TOW, TUG, SNIG
" (deer) .... TOLL, TUMP
dragoman .... INTERPRETER
dragon .... DRAKE, OGRE, RAHAB, ATI, FAFNIR, BASILISK
" flies .... ODONATA
" tail .... KETU
drain . DITCH, EMPTY, GAW, SAP, SUMP, SEWER, CULVERT
dram .... NIP, SLUG, DRAFT
drama ... PLAY, OPERA, KABUKI, AUTO
" , introduction of a .. PROTASIS
" , main action of a .. EPITASIS
dramatic ...... SCENIC, STAGY, VIVID
dramatize .... ENACT
drapery .... VALANCE, PAND

drastic ...... RADICAL, SEVERE, STERN
draughts .... CHECKERS
Dravidian tongue .... TAMIL
draw .. DRAFT, TIE, ETCH, TOLE, LIMN, TOW, TUG, DEPICT, ELICIT, SIPHON
" away .... ABDUCE, DIVERT
" back .... WINCE, RESILE
" close .... NEAR, APPROACH
" forth .... EDUCE, DERIVE
" out ...... PROTRACT, CONTINUE
" tight ...... THRAP, COUL, PULL
drawback .... DEFECT, FAULT
drawer .... TILL, ARTIST
drawing back .... RETRAHENT
dread ..... AWE, FEAR, GRISE, ALARM, PANIC
dreadful .... DIRE, HORRID
dream REVE, FANCY, SCHEME, VAGARY, VISION, DELUSION, FANTASY, MUSE
" , per. to . ONEIRIC, ONEIROTIC
dreamy tranquillity ..... REVERIE, KEF
dreary DISMAL, DULL, ALANGE, OURIE, BANAL, SOMBER
dredge .... TRAIN, SIFT, RAISE
dredger .... DUSTER
dregs .... SORDOR, SILT, DRAFF, LEES, DIRT, REFUSE, SLUDGE, SCUM, MAGMA, FAEX, SEDIMENT
drench .. DOUSE, IMBUE, HOSE, SOUSE, SOAK
drenched .... WET, ASOP, DEWED
dorsal . NEURAL, NOTAL, TERGAL, BACK
" , opposed to ...... VENTRAL
dress ATTIRE, DECK, DIGHT, RIG, DAB, DUB, TOGS, PREEN, CLOTHE
" a wound .... PANSE
" , as stone .... NIG, NIDGE
" flax .... TED
" gaudily .... BEDIZEN, PRANK
" leather .... CURRY, TAW, TEW
" , looped part of .... POUF
" , riding .... HABIT
" up .... ARRAY, PRIG
" worn by pilgrims .... IHRAM
dressed .... TITIVATED, CLAD, DECKED
dresser ... LEVANTER, BUREAU, CHEST, VANITY, TABLE
dressmaker .... MODISTE, SEAMSTRESS
dressmaker's term .... GODET, GORE, GUSSET
Drew's costar .... REHAN
Dreyfus, champion of ... EMILE, ZOLA
dribble .... TRICKLE, GUSH, SPOUT
dried .... ARID, SERE, DESICCATED
drift .. TENOR, INTENT, TREND, FLOAT, COURSE
drill ... BORE, PIERCE, TRAIN, AUGER, EXERCISE
drilling .. TRAINING, NURTURE, DENIM

drink ...... ALE, ADE, NIPA, SILLABUB,
    IMBIBE, GUZZLE, GULP, SIP, PEG, SOT,
    BEER, BOOZE, CAUDLE, STINGER,
    BRACER, TIPPLE, DRAM, TOT, NIP,
    SLUG, QUAFF, NEGUS, TODDY, DRAM,
                                RATAFIA
" , ancient .... MORAT
" , Arabian .... BOZA
" , brandy (spiced) .. SANGAREE
" , fermented ..... MEAD, PTISAN
" , gruel-like .... CAUDLE
"   made of gin or rum .. GROG,
                                BUMBO
"   of the gods .... NECTAR
"   of the Tatars .... KUMISS
" , oriental .... SAKI
" , plant-juice .... SOMA
" , Russian .... VODKA
" , S. Sea Island .... AVA
" , sweetened .... JULIP, ORGEAT,
                                POSSET
drinker .. SOAKER, POTER, TOPER, SOT
drinking bout .... POTATION
"   bowl .... MAZER
"   cup .... CYLIX, FACER
"   horn .... RHYTON
" , pledge in .... PROPINE
drip .... LEAK, SILE, SEEP, OOZE
drive .... FORCE, IMPEL, LANE, MOVE,
                    RIDE, URGE, MOTOR
"   away .... SHOO, DISPEL
"   back .... ROUT, REPEL, REPULSE
"   in .... TAMP
"   in waitress .... CARHOP
drivel ..... DOTE, DROOL, SLOBBER
driver ...... JEHU, MOTORIST, WHIP,
                    HAMMER, SARWAN
drizzle .... MISLE, MIST, MIZZLE, SMUR
droll .... ZANY, WAGGISH, ODD
dromedary . CAMEL, BACTRIAN, DELUL,
                                MEHARI
drone .... BEE, HUM, IDLER
drool .... DRIVEL, SLABBER
droop LOP, FADE, SAG, WILT, SLOUCH,
                        LAG, NUTATE
drop BEAD, GUTTA, BLOB, FALL, OMIT,
        SINK, SIE, SYE, MINIM, PLOP,
        GLOBULE, BLUB, DREPE, DAP, DRIB
"   by drop .... GUTTAT
" , sudden .... HANCE
dropsical .... EDEMIC
dropsy .... EDEMA, TUMOR
dross .. SCORIA, SCUM, SCOBS, SPRUE,
        SLAG, SINTER, SULLAGE, REFUSE
drove .. CROWD, FLOCK, HERD, RODE,
                    BEVY, PACK, ATAJO
drowning ...... NOYADE, DEMERSION
drowse .... SLEEP, DOZE, DOVER, NOD
drowsiness ... LETHARGY, OSCITANCE

drudge .... HACK, PLOD, SLAVE, FAG,
                        LABOR, MOIL
drug . DOPE, DOSE, OPIATE, ATROPIA,
        COCAINE, NARCOTIC, SINA, SULFA,
                    REMEDY, DILANTIN
" , active principle of ...... ALOIN
" , addict .... JUNKIE
" , ataractic .... RESERPINE
" , nux-vomica .... TETANIC
drum ...... BEAT, RIDGE, DUB, DRUB,
                                REPEAT
"   call RAPPEL, RATAPLAN, TATTOO,
                                DIAN
" , hand .... TABOR, TIMBREL
" , Indian .... NAGARA
" , low beat of .... DUB, RUFF
" , Moorish .... ATABAL
" , oriental .. ANACARA, TOMTOM
" , string .... SNARE
" , tighten a .... FRAP
drum-like ... TABARET, BARREL, NAKER
drummer .... KRUPA, RICH, TIMPANIST
drunkard .... DIPSOMANIAC, SOT,
                TOSSPOT, SOUSE, TIPPLER
drunkenness detector ... ALCOMETER,
                        DRUNKOMETER
dry .... ARID, SICCATE, BLOT, AERIFY,
                WIPE, JEJUNE, SEC, SERE
" ; comb. form .... XERO
dryad .... NYMPH, DEITY
drying frame .... SESS, AIRER
"   machine .... TEDDER
" , spread for .... TED
dryness of skin ... XEROSIS, ARIDITY
" , period of DROUTH, DROUGHT
dry-stone diker .... COWAN
Du Maurier, Miss .... DAPHNE
dual ...... DUAD, DYAD, TWO, TWIN,
                                BINARY
dub . CALL, NAME, POKE, STYLE, TITLE,
                                KNIGHT
dubious ...... SHADY, SEAMY, VAGUE
duck .... REDHEAD, SHELDRAKE, NENE,
        NENI, MUSCOVY, HARLE, SCOTER,
        SMEE, PINTAIL, TEAL, EIDER, SCAUP,
                                MALLARD
"   genus .... ANAS, ANSER
"   hawk .... FALCON
"   litter .... TEAM
" , per. to .... ANATINE
"   with swollen bill ...... SCOTER
duck, to . DIP, STOOP, DODGE, EVADE,
                                MERSE
duckbill .... PLATYPUS
duck-like bird .... COOT
"   object .... DECOY
duckweed .... LEMNA
ducks, flock of .... SORD
duct .. CANAL, TYPE, TUBE, RACE, VAS,
                FLUE, AORTA, CONDUIT

ductile .... TENSILE, ELASTIC
ductless gland ...... THYMUS, PINEAL
dude ...... JOHNNIE, COXCOMB, FOP,
DANDY, MACARONI
due ...... DEBT, HAK(H), FIT, OWED,
LAWFUL, PROPER
duel .... CONTEST, TILT
dugong .... HALICORE
dugout .... FOXHOLE, ABRI
" canoe .... PIROGUE
dulcet ...... ARIOSE, SWEET, TUNEFUL
dulcimer .... PSALTERY, CITOLE, SITAR,
SITOL, CANUN, SANTIR
dull ...... INERT, DIM, DRAB, BLUNT,
JEJUNE, OBTUND, VAPID, LEADY,
STOGY, DRY, LOGY, BORING, OBTUSE
" finish .... MATTE, MAT
" ; of cloth .... STARY
" statement .... PLATITUDE
dullard .... DUNCE, MOPE, OAF
dullness .... COLDNESS, PHLEGM
Dumas char. .... ATHOS, ARAMIS,
PORTHOS, DANTES
dumb .... MUTE, APHONIC, SILENT
dummy ... SHAM, SUBSTITUTE, MORT
dump ...... PLUMP, THUD, DROP, SELL
dun ... PRESS, ASK, FAVEL, TAN, URGE
dunce ..... COOT, DOLT, OAF, GONY,
FOOL, HOBBIL, ASS, IGNORAMUS,
NUMBSKULL, HALFWIT
dune .... BANK, DENE, RIDGE
dunk .... DIP, SOP, SOUSE, SOAK
dunlin ...... SANDPIPER, STIB, PURRE
Dunne, Miss .... IRENE
dupe .... CHEAT, DELUDE, TRICK, BILK,
FRAUD, HOAX, COZEN, SUCKER
" , a .... TOOL, FOX, CATSPAW
duplicate .... BIS, DUPLEX, COPY,
REPLICATE, TWIN, CARBON
duplicity .... FRAUD, GUILE
durable .... FIRM, TOUGH, STOUT
duration . SPACE, DATE, PERIOD, SPAN,
TIME, TRICE, TERM
Durocher, Mr. .... LIP, LEO
durra .... MILLET, SORGHUM
dusky .. DARK, DIM, SWARTHY, MURKY,
TAWNY
dust ... COOM(B), BRISS, PILM, STIVE,
TRASH, STOUR, ASH, LINT, SOOT
" , reduce to .... MULL, GRIND
Dutch botanist .... VRIES
" coin .... DOIT, DAALDER
" colonist .... BOER
" commune .... EDE, EPE
" family of printers .... ELZEVIR
" judge .... SCHOUT
" liquid measure ... AAM, DUIM,
KAN, EL
" merchant vessel ..... GALLIOT
" news agency .... ANETA

" painter .... HALS, STEN
" poet .... DACOSTA
" political party .. HOEK, HOOK,
COD
" promoter .... PATROON
" scholar .... ERASMUS
" statesman .... KUYPER
" town ..... TIEL, HAARLEM, EDE
" uncle .... EME, OOM
" weight .... LOOD, POND
" writer .... BEKKER, VONDEL
dutchman .... HEER, HOGEN, MOGEN
duty .. LASTAGE, EXCISE, FEU, OFFICE,
TAX, TOLL, IMPOST, DEVOIR, ONUS,
TASK, DHARMA, TARIFF, CHORE
Dvořák; comp. .... ANTON
dwarf .. ELF, GNOME, MANIKIN, RUNT,
PIGMY, TROLL, CRILE, CRUT,
DURGAN, GRIG, DROICH, URF
" ; archaic .... DANDIPRAT
" cattle .... NIATA
" , fish-shaped .... ANDVARI
" ; Sigurd's foster father .. REGIN
" , to .... STUNT
dwarf; Scot. .... BLASTIE
dwarfishness .... NANISM
Dwarfs, The Seven .. BASHFUL, DOC,
DOPEY, GRUMPY, HAPPY,
SNEEZY, SLEEPY
dwell .... (A)BIDE, LIVE, LODGE
dwelling .... DAR, QUARTER, FLAT,
HUTCH, IGLOO, TEEPEE,
MANSION
dwelling house complete .. MESSUAGE
dwindle .... SHRINK, LESSEN, PINE,
ABATE, PETER, EBB
dwindling .... AWASTE
Dyak .... IBAN
" blowgun .... SUMPITAN
dye ..... KINO, COLOR, IMBUE, STAIN,
TINT, WOAD, WOLD, TINGE
" , coal-tar .... EOSIN, AZARINE
" component .... AZO, DIAZO
" cosmetic, oriental .. RED, HENNA
" , crimson .... REDBUN
" , for silk .... LUTEOLIN
" , indigo .... ANIL
" , morindin .... AL
" plant ... CHAY, SUMAC, ALKANET
" preparation of soot .... KOHL
" , red ... CERISE, AAL, ALT, EOSINE
" , red poison .... AURINE
" , reddish-brown .... ERIKA
" , root-pigment .... MADDER
" , rose-red .... RHODAMIN
" , source of purple .... MUREX
dyestuff .. ORPIMENT, ISATIN, MADDER
" , substance in ..... MORDANT
" , violet ..... ORSELLE, ARCHIL

   " , yellowish pulp .... ANATO, ANATTO
dyeing apparatus .... AGER
   "   chamber .... OVEN
   "   producing marble effects .... BATIK
dyer's furze .... DYEWEED
   "   grape .... POKEWEED
dynamite .... SAWDUST, TNT
   "   inventor .... NOBEL
   "   projectile .... DUALIN
dynamo .... GENERATOR
   " , inventor of .... FARADAY
   " , part of ...... LIMB, STATOR, YOKE
dynasty, Chin ...... FO, HAN, MING, SUNG, TANG, YIN
Dzhugashvili .... STALIN

E

ea .... RIVER
Ea .... DEITY
ea .... EACH
each .... PER, ALL, EVERY, APIECE, EITHER
eager ..... AGASP, AGOG, APT, AVID, ARDENT
eagle ...... NRA, ERNE, BERGUT, ERN, GIER, AQUILA, ETANA
   "   ray .... OBISPO
eagles, brood of .... AERIE
   " , nest of .. AERIE, EYRIE, EYRY
eaglewood .... AGALLOCH, ALOES
eagre .... BORE, HYGRE
ear, anvil of .... INCUS
   " , auricle of .... PINNA
   "   bone .... STAPES, STIRRUP
   "   cavity .... COCHLEA
   " , elongated depression in .... SCAPHA
   " , external .... AURICLE
   "   hammer .... MALLEUS
   " , inflammation of .... OTITIS
   " , lobe of .... EARLAP, LUG
   " , membrane of .... TECTORIUM
   "   of corn; S. Afr. .... MEALIE
   "   of grain .... SPIKE, SPICA
   " , outer .... CONCHA
   " , parts of .... LOBE, TRAGI
   " , per. to ...... LOBAR, (PAR)OTIC, AURAL
   " , per. to interior of ..... ENTOTIC
   " , science of the .... OTOLOGY
   "   specialist .... OTOLOGIST, AURIST
   " , thin bony plate in ..... TEGMEN

earache .... OTALGIA, OTALGY
earring .... PENDLE, GIRANDOLE
ears, ringing in .... SYRIGMUS
ear-shaped gastropod ..... ABALONE, ORMER
ear-stone .... OTOLITE
ear trumpet, double .... TOPOPHONE
earwax .... CERUMEN
earl .... NOBLEMAN
earliest .... FIRST, ALERT, CHIEF
early .... MATUTINAL, BETIME, SOON, AHEAD, OLD
   "   origin, of .... ANCIENT
   " ; poet. .... RATH, RATHE
earn .... GAIN, WIN, MERIT, PROCURE
earnest ..... SOBER, ARDENT, INTENT, SINCERE
earnest money ..... ARLES, HANDSEL, ARRHA
earnings ... INCOME, STIPEND, WAGES
earth ..... CLAY, DIRT, GLOBE, TERRA, WORLD, LOAM, SOIL, GEO
   "   born .... TERRIGENOUS, MORTAL
   " , center of ..... CENTROSPHERE
   "   deposit .... MARL, MOLD
   "   goddess .... TARI, DEMETER, SEMELE, GE
   "   layers .... SLOAM
   "   metal .... ERBIUM, PROTORE
   " , occurring at surface of .... EPIGENE
   " , of the .... GEAL, TERRENE
   " , the; poet. .... VALE
   " , volcanic .... TRASS
earthborn .... LOW, VULGAR
   " ; deified .... SEB
earth drake .... DRAGON
earthen jar .... OLLA
earthenware .... DELFT, JASPER, PORCELAIN, CHINA, CROCKERY, ECHEA
earthflax .... AMIANTHUS
earthiness .... TERROSITY
earthkin .... TERELLA
earthnut ..... CHUFA, PIGNUT, ARNUT
earthquake .... SEISM, TEMBLOR, TREMOR
earth satellite, U.S. .... EXPLORER, VANGUARD, ATLAS, DISCOVERER, PIONEER, MIDAS, ECHO, COURIER, TYROS, SAMOS, RANGER, MERCURY, ARIEL, MARINER, TELSTAR
   "   " , U.S.S.R. ...... SPUTNIK LUNIK, VOSTOK, COSMOS, MARS
earth's axis .... HINGE
   "   crust tract .... HORST
   "   surface above earthquake .... EPICENTER
earthstar .... GEASTER

earthwork .... AGGER, DIKE, FORT, MOUND
earthworm .... DEWWORM, MAD, MADDOCK
earthy .. CARNAL, MORTAL, MUNDANE, TEMPORAL
ease ...... MOLLIFY, RELIEVE, SOOTHE
easiest; Shak. .... EFTEST
East .. ORIENT, LEVANT, SUNRISE, ASIA
" , per. to .... ORIENTAL, ASIAN, EOAN
E. African native house ...... TEMBE
"   "   negro tribe .... BARI
"   "   slave vessel .... DHOW
"   "   tree .... MOLI
E. India discoverer .... GAMA
"   " , founder of British ..... CLIVE
" Indian aborigines .... ARYANS, BENGALI
"   "   army servant .... LASCAR
"   "   berry-like fruit .... LANSEH, LANSA
"   "   broadbill bird .... RAYA
"   "   chief .. DATO, RANA, SIRDAR
"   "   city .. AGRA, BENGAL, SURAT
"   "   coin ..... ANNA, PICE, RUPEE
"   "   disease .... LANAS
"   "   dodder .... AMIL
"   "   drink .... NIPA
"   "   early tribe ... DASA, DASYUS
"   "   embanked road ...... PRAYA
"   "   fabaceous tree .... DHAK
"   "   fabric; var. .... ROMAL
"   "   fan .... PUNKAH
"   "   farmer .... RYOT
"   "   fiber plant .. OADAL, NILGIRI
"   "   fruit .... BEL
"   "   fruit pigeon .... TRERON
"   "   fruit tree .... PAPAW
"   "   garment .... SARI
"   "   groom .... SYCE
"   "   gum tree, deriv. of ... KINO
"   "   herb ..... ROSELLE, SESAME
E. Indian island(s) .. JAVA, SUMATRA, BALI, CELEBES, ADI, LETI
"   "   kingdom ..... NEPAL, SIKKIM
"   "   mail .... DAK
"   "   mammal .... TARSIER
"   "   money .... ANNA, RUPEE
"   "   mountain .... GHAT
"   "   mus. instrument ..... SITAR, BINA, SAROD, VINA
"   "   muslim .... JAMDANEE
"   "   nation, anc. .... TAMIL
"   "   nurse .... AMAH
"   "   plant ..... CHAV, SILA, SUNN
"   "   plant, fiber of .... JUTE
"   "   poison .... BISH, BIKH
"   "   race or caste .... VARNA
"   "   rat .... BANDICOOT

"   "   region .... MALABAR
"   "   root .... ATEES, ATIS
"   "   ruminant .... ZEBU
"   "   sacred city .... BENARES
"   "   screen .... TATTIE
"   "   seaman .... LASCAR
"   "   sect .... JAIN, JAINA
"   "   servant .... MATY
"   "   shrub .... MUDAR, ODAL
"   "   snuff .... RAPEE
"   "   soldier .... SEPOY
"   "   title ...... RAJA, SAHIB, SRI, RANI, RANEE
"   "   tree .. BANYAN, SISSOO, SAL, TOON, MARGOSA
"   "   tree bark .... NIEPA
"   "   tribe .... MARIS, PULIARS
"   "   vessel .... PATAMAR
"   "   vine .... ODAL
"   "   viol .... RUANA
"   "   warrior .... SINGH
"   "   water vessel .... LOTA
"   "   weight ... CATTY, RATTI, SER, TOLA
"   "   xylophone .... SARON
east wind .... EURUS
Easter ... EED, PAAS, PACE, PASCH(A)
" , per. to .... PASCHAL
eastern ... ORIENTAL, ASIATIC, ORTIVE
"   palace .... SERAI
"   people .... SERES, AVARS
"   ruler ..... EMIR, AMIR, AMEER, AGHA, (MAHA)RAJA, NIZAM, JAM, MIRZA, DEWAN, SIRDAR, NAWAB
easy .... EATH, FACILE, GLIB
" job ..... SNAP, CINCH, SINECURE
eat ... SUP, CORRODE, ERODE, INGEST, GNAW, FRET, RUST, DEVOUR
" between meals .... BEVER
" greedily .... GORGE, RAVEN
" heartily .... THORN
" immoderately .... GLUT
" in gulps .... LAB
eaten away .... EROSE
eating .... BIT, CANKERING
"   away ...... CAUSTIC, ERODENT
" , excessive .... EDACITY
" hall .... MESS
" place .... CAFE(TERIA), BISTRO, AUTOMAT, DINER
Eban, diplomat .... ABBA
ebb .... NEAP, RECEDE, REFLUX, WANE, ABATE, LESSEN
" and flow .... TIDE, AESTUS
Eber's son .... PELEG
eccentric .... ERRATIC, ODD, GINK, CRANK, QUEER, BIZARRE
" piece .... CAM

ecclesiastic ..... ABBE, ABBOT, CLERIC, DIVINE, PADRE, PASTOR, PRIEST, PRIOR, VICAR
     "   attendant ...... ACOLYTE
     "   banner .... LABARUM
     "   benefice .... GLEBE
     "   cape .... CAPPA
     "   council .... SYNOD
     "   court ..... CLASSIS, ROTA
     "   hood .... AMICE
     "   order of widows .... VIDUATE
     "   seat .... DEANERY, SEDILE
     "   skullcap .... BIRETTA
     "   surplice .... COTTA
     "   vestment .. AMICE, STOLE, VAGAS
echidna .... ANTEATER
echinate .... BRISTLY, SPINY
echoing .... ITERANT
     "   back .... RESONANT
éclat .... GLORY, RENOWN, PRAISE
eclipse ...... OBSCURE, SURPASS, DIM, DARKEN
     " , part .... PENUMBRA
ecology .... BIONOMICS
economize .. SCRIMP, STINT, HUSBAND, SAVE, RETRENCH, PARE
ecru .... BEIGE, TAN, YELLOW
ecstasy ..... TRANCE, RAPTURE, BLISS, FRENZY
ectad, opposed to .... ENTAD
écu .... COIN, SHIELD
Ecuador, capital of .... QUITO
     "   city or town .... AMATO, CUENCA, IBARRA, LOJA, NAPO
     "   seaport .... MANTA
ecumenical council .... TRENT
eczema .... HERPES, TETTER
eddish .. ARRISH, AFTERMATH, EDGREW
eddy ... SWIRL, WHIRL(POOL), TWIRL, VORTEX, BORE, GYRATE
edema .... DROPSY, TUMOR
Eden ..... GLORY, HEAVEN, PARADISE, ANTHONY
Ederle, Miss .... GERTRUDE
edge ..... LABRUM, BRIM, HEM, RAND, RIM, MARGIN, SELVEDGE, ARRIS, LIP, SIDLE, ZEST
edged irregularly .... EROSE
edging .... RUCHE, TATTING
     " , make .... PICOT, TAT
edible .... COMESTIBLE, ESCULENT
     "   fungus .... MOREL
     "   nut .... CASHEW
     "   seed ...... BEAN, PEA, PEANUT
     "   tuber ... TARO, UVA, YAM, OCA
edict .... ARRET, ACT, DECREE, UKASE, MANDATE, LAW, BULL, FIAT, WRIT

Edinburgh magazine .... MAGA
     " , part of .... LEITH
     " ; poet. name .... EDINA
edit ...... REVISE, REWORD, ARRANGE
editor .... REVISER, REDACTOR
editorial .... ARTICLE, LEADER
Edom, land of ...... IDUMEA, TEMAN
Edomite chieftain .... IRAM
educated .... ERUDITE, LITERATE, LETTERED
educe .... DRAW, EVOLVE, ELICIT, EVOKE, INFER
eel .... MORAY, ELVER, GRIG, LAUNCE
eelfish .... TANDAN
eelpout .... BURBOT, LING
eels, fish for .... SNIGGLE
     " , migration of .... EELFARE
eelware .... CROWFOOT
eelworm .... NEMA, NEMATODE
eerie ..... UNCANNY, WEIRD, BIZARRE
efface .... EXPUNGE, ERASE, DELE(TE), SPONGE
effect .... SEQUEL, ACHIEVE, PURPORT, UPSHOT
effeminate .... COCKNEY, EPICENE, UNMANLY, WEAK
effervesce .... BUBBLE, HISS, BOIL, FOAM, FIZZ, AERATE, FERMENT
effete .... BARREN, IDLE, SERE
efficacy .... POTENCY, POWER
effigy .... ICON, GUY, FACSIMILE
effluvium .... AURA, REEK, FLATUS
effort ... BURST, CONATUS, JUMP, TUG, STRAIN, NISUS, DINT, ASSAY, TRIAL
effrontery ...... BRASS, CHEEK, GALL, GUTS, NERVE
effusive, be .... GUSH, RANT
eft .... LIZARD, NEWT, TRITON
egest .... DISCHARGE, VOID
egg ... NIT, OVUM, ROE, OVULE, OEUF
     " ; comb. form .... OVI, OO
     " , fertilized .... OOSPERM
     " , part of .... LATEBRA, YELK, YOLK, GLAIR, SHELL, ALBUMEN
eggs .... BOMBS, URGES, GOADS
     " , fish .... BERRIES, ROE
     " , preserved; Chin. .... PIDAN
     " , tester of .... CANDLER
egg-shaped .... OOID, OVAL, OVATE, OVOID
eggshell color .... ECRU
Egil, brother of .... VOLUND
ego .... JIVATMA, ATMAN, SELF
egress .... OUTLET, ISSUANCE
egret .... HERON
Egypt, anc. Christians of ..... COPTS
     " , capital of Upper .... ASYUT
     " , city of; anc. .... ABYDOS
     " , in Hebrew .... MIZRAIM
     " , lower division of ..... MAZOR

Egyptian .... NILOT, GYPSY
    " ape; myth. .... AANI
    " astral body .... KA
    " bull; myth. .... APIS
    " cape .... SUDR
    " captain .... RAIS, REIS
    " catfish .... BAGRE, DOCMAC
    " chaos .... NU
    " cobra .... HAJE
    " commander in chief SIRDAR
    " cosmetic powder .... KOHL
    " cotton .... PIMA
    " cross of life .... ANKH
    " currency ... FODDA, GERSH,
                GIRSH, PIASTRE
    " dancing girl .... ALMA
    " deity (see "deity")
    " Diana ...... PAKHT, SEKHET
    " divinity .... HOR, PTAH
    " dog .... SALUKI
    " dye plant .. HENNA, HINNA
    " fabled monster .... SPHINX
    " falcon-headed deity . HORUS
    " fertile land .... GOSHEN
    " for "father" .... ATEF
    " fruit of the cactus ..... FIG
    " gate .... PYLON
    " god (see god) .... ANUBIS
    " goddess (see goddess) .....
                APET, ISIS
    " governor .... BEY
    " guard .... GHAFIR
    " hare-like animal .... HYRAX
    " headdress of ruler . URAEUS
    " heaven .... AARU
    " island .... ELEPHANTINE
    " jar .... CANOPIC
    " jinee .... AMSET, HAPI
    " judge of dead ...... OSIRIS
    " khedive's estate ..... DAIRA
    " king .... PTOLEMY
    " lake .... MOERIS
    " land .... FEDDAN
    " leaping mouse .... JERBOA
    " lighthouse .... PHAROS
    " lizard .... ADDA
    " lute .... NABLA
    " measure .... ARDEB, CUBIT,
              KELEH, KHET, PIK
    " monarch ... RAMESES, FUAD,
        NIKI, PEPI, SETI, KUFU,
          MENES, CHEOPS
    " month ..... APAP, HATHOR,
      MECHIR, MESORE, PAYNI,
            TYBI, THOTH
    " mus. performer .... ALMEH
    " oasis .... KHARGA, SIWA
    " peasant .... FELLAH
    " pebble .... JASPER
    " peninsula .... PHAROS

    " Pharaoh's hen .... VULTURE
    " physician .... IMHOTEP
    " plant .... KUMIN
    " plateau .... TIH
    " policeman .... GHAFIR
    " port .... SAID
    " pound .... ROTL
    " queen .... CLEO(PATRA)
    "   " of the gods .... SATI
    " rattle .... SISTRUM
    " reed .... BYBLUS, BIBLUS,
                PAPYRUS
    " royal symbol .... ASP
    " ruler ..... KHEDIVE, CALIPH
    " scribe .... ANI
    " serpent; myth. .... APEPI
    " solar disk .... ATEN
    " soul .... BA, BAHU
    " sultan .... SALADIN
    " symbol .... ANKH, SCARAB,
             SERAPIS, URAEUS
    " temple site .... KARNAK
    " thief; Shak. .... DOXY
    " thorn .... BABUL
    " title .. CALIPH, PASHA, VIZIR
    " tomb, cell in ...... SERDAB
    " town .. SYENE, ASWAN, SAIS
    " unit of capacity .... ARDEB
    " viceroy .... KHEDIVE
    " village .. ABYDOS, ABOUKIR,
               EDFU, IDFU
    " water bottle ...... DORUCK
    " water-raising device ....
        SAKIEH, SHADOOF, TABUT
    " weight .. KET, KAT, KANTAR,
       OCHA, OKIEH, OKE, UCKIA
    " wind ... KAMSIN, KHAMSIN
eider .... DOWN, WAMP, DIVER, COLK
eidolon .... IMAGE, APPARITION,
                PHANTOM
eight; comb. form .... OCTO
eightfold .... OCTUPLE
    " performers .... OCTET
    " , series of .. OGDOAD, OCTAD
    " ; Sp. .... OCHO
    " tones .... DIATONIC, UNCAE
eighteen-inch meas. .... CUBIT
Eire (see "Ireland, Irish")
Eisenhower .... DWIGHT, IKE, MAMIE,
                DAVID
eject ...... EMIT, EXPEL, EVICT, OUST,
     DISLODGE, VOID, CAST, SPEW,
      BANISH, EXILE, BOUNCE,
            CASHIER
eke .... ADD, ETCH, IMP, TAB
elaborate .... ORNATE
Elam capital .... SUSA
elan .... ARDOR, DASH, SPIRIT
elapse .... DIE, GO, PASS, GLIDE

elastic .... LIMBER, LITHE, PLIANT, SPRINGY
elasticity .... GIVE, SPRING
elasticize .... STENT, STRETCH
elate .... ENLIVEN, EXALT, FLUSH
elated .... GLEEFUL, PERKED, RAD, JOYOUS
Elbe, tributary of .... EGER, ISER, HAVEL, ELDE, SAALE
elbow .. ANCON, BEND, PUSH, ANGLE, CROWD, JOSTLE, NUDGE, JOINT
" ; per. to .... ULNAR
elder .... MORMON, IVA, PRIOR, SENIOR, FIRST
elder statesman ..... GENRO, BARUCH
elderly .... GRAY, OLD, VETERAN
eldest .... EIGNE, SENIOR
eldritch .... EERIE, WILD
elect .... CHOOSE, NAME, ELITE, OPT, CULL, PICK
electioneer .... STUMP, CAMPAIGN
elector .... ELISOR, VOTER
Electra's brother .... ORESTES
electrical appliance .... SPARKER, STEPUP, DRYER, HEATER, IRON, TOASTER, FAN
"   atmosphere .... AURA
"   atom .... ELECTRON
"   circuit regulator .. BOOSTER
"   constituent .... ANION
"   measure .... MEGADYNE
"   odic force .... ELOD
"   particle ...... ION, CATION
"   pressure detector TASIMETER
"   terminal .... ELECTRODE
"   unit .. HENRY, VOLT, WATT, JOULE, FARAD, COULOMB, OERSTED, REL, AMPERE, OHM, MHO
electromagnet .... GROWLER
"   , discoverer of principle of .... OERSTED
electronic detector .... RADAR
"   tube .... STROBOTRON
electrum .... AMBER
eleemosynary .... DONEE
elegance .... GRACE, LUX, BEAUTY, POLISH
elegant .... FINE, POSH, RICH
elegy ...... LAMENT, DIRGE, REQUIEM, NENIA
element .... COMPONENT, METAL, FACTOR, SILICON, ITEM, PART, RECT, DETAIL
"   , even-valence .... ARTIAD
"   ; inert gas .... NEON, XENON
"   , non-volatile .... BARIUM
"   of air .... ARGON
"   of a plane .... RAY
"   of the earth group .. ERBIUM

"   , poisonous .... ARSENIC
"   , rare metallic ..... YTTRIUM, IRIDIUM
"   , rare white .... INDIUM
"   similar to another .. ISOTOPE
"   , very rare .... HAFNIUM
elemental spirit .... GENIE
elementary ..... INCHOATE, PRIMARY, BASIC, PRIMAL, SIMPLE
elemi .... RESIN
elephant ..... HATTY, MAKNA, TUSKER
"   boy .... SABU
"   cry .... BARR
"   , extinct .... MASTODON
"   , keeper of .... MAHOUT
"   pen .... KRAAL
"   per. to ... PACHYDERMATOUS
"   seat .... HOWDAH
"   staff for goading ... ANKUS
"   tusk ..... IVORY, SCRIVELLO
"   young .... CALF
elevate ..... RAISE, EXALT, PROMOTE, ADVANCE, BOOST, HEAVE, HOIST, SOAR
elevating muscle .... LEVATOR
elevation ... HILL, MESA, RISE, HEIGHT, RIDEAU, MOUNT, STATURE
elevator car .... CAGE
elf . NIX, GNOME, IMP, OAF, OUPH(E), SPRITE, PERI, GOBLIN, ERLKING
elfkin .... FAIRY, FAY
elicit .... EDUCE, EXTRACT, DRAW
eligible ... APT, MEET, COMPETENT, FIT
eliminate ERASE, RID, DETACH, DELETE, OMIT, REMOVE
Eliot character .... MARNER, ROMOLA
Eli's son .... HOPHNI
elision ... SYNCOPE, ABRIDGMENT
elite .. BEST, CREAM, CHOICE, FLOWER
Elizabeth I .... ORIANA
"   , mother of .... BOLEYN
elixir ... AMRITA, ARCANUM, CUREALL, PANACEA
elk ..... MOOSE, ALCE, ELAND, LOSH, WAPITI, SAMBAR
"   bark .... BAY, MAGNOLIA
ell .... ANNEX, WING
ellipse .... CURVE, OVAL, OVATE
elm .... ULMUS
" , fruit of the .... SAMARA
Elmo's fire .... CORPOSANT
elongated .... LANK, LINEAR, PROLATE
elope .... DECAMP, LEVANT
eloquent .. CICERONIAN, ORATORICAL, FLUENT, GLIB, VOLUBLE
else .... ENSE, OTHERWISE
elude . SHUN, AVOID, EVADE, DODGE, FOIL, OUTWIT
elusive ... EQUIVOCAL, EVASIVE, EELY, SLICK, SLIPPERY

Eluthera bark .... CASCARILLA
elver .... CONGER, EEL
elytrin .... CHITIN
elytrum .... SHARD
emaciation ... TABES, WASTE, MACIES,
ATROPHY
emanate .... ISSUE, SPRING, RISE
emanation .... NITON, AURA, VAPOR
emancipate .. FREE, MANUMIT, RELEASE
emancipator .... FREER, LINCOLN
embankment DIKE, LEVEE, DAM, BUND,
DIGUE
" in rice fields ... PILAPIL
embark .... BEGIN, BOARD, SAIL
embarrass .... FAZE, HARASS, SHAME,
FLUSTER
embattled .... CRENELED
embellish ...... DRESS, ADORN, GILD,
GARNISH, ROUGE, BEDECK, ENRICH
ember ..... COAL, ASH, CINDER, IZLE,
CLINKER
embitter . ACERBATE, ENVENOM, SOUR
emblem .. FLAG, MARK, DESIGN, SIGN,
STAR, FASCES, SYMBOL, INSIGNE,
BAR, BADGE, EAGLE, MOTIF
" of a clan .... TOTEM
" of authority .... MACE
emblic .... AMLA
embodiment .... AVATAR, MATTER,
EPITOME
embrace CARESS, HUG, CLASP, ACCOLL,
CLASP, ENARM, CLUTCH
embroider ...... TAT, DECORATE, PURL
embroidery frame .... TABORET
emend . CORRECT, RECTIFY, EDIT, RIGHT
emerald ..... BERYL, GREEN, SMARAGD
Emerald Isle ..... EIRE, ERIN, IRELAND
emerge .... EMANATE, ISSUE, RISE
emery .... CORUNDUM, ABRADANT
emesis .... VOMITING
emetic .... IPECAC, MUSTARD
emigree .... REFUGEE
Émile Herzog ...... (ANDRE)MAUROIS
Émile Zola, book by .... NANA
eminence ..... DIGNITY, HILL, RIDEAU,
CARDINAL, FAME, RENOWN, REPUTE,
TOR
eminent .... HIGH, LOFTY, FAMED
emissary AGENT, SCOUT, SPY, ENVOY,
LEGATE
emit ... EMANATE, PLUFF, SHED, UTTER,
ERUCT, EXHALE, REEK, SQUIRT, SPURT
emmer .... SPELT
emmet .... ANT, PISMIRE
emolument .... FEE, GAIN
Emory Univ. site .... ATLANTA
emotion IRE, PATHOS, ONDE, PASSION,
ELAN
emotionless ... APATHETIC, UNFEELING

emperor ..... CZAR, TSAR, IMPERATOR,
INCA, AKBAR, TENO, MIKADO
emphasis .... ACCENT, STRESS
empiric ... CHARLATAN, QUACK, FAKER
employ ... USE, HIRE, PLACE, ENGAGE,
OCCUPY, ENGROSS, UTILIZE
emporium .... MART, STORE
emptiness .... VACUUM, VOID
empty .... IDLE, INANE, VOID, TOOM,
VACUOUS, VACANT, UNLOAD,
DRAIN, DEPLETE
emu wren .... STIPITURE
emulate .. COMPETE, RIVAL, VIE, APE,
COPY, STRIVE
enact ...... DECREE, ORDAIN, ENJOIN
enactment .. CANON, EDICT, STATUTE,
LAW, ORDINANCE
encamp .... BIVOUAC, TENT
enchain .... FETTER, FASTEN
enchant . BEWITCH, ENSORCEL, ALLURE,
ENAMOR, CHARM
enchantment .. CHARM, SPELL, MAGIC,
SORCERY, WITCHERY
enchantress .... CIRCE, SIREN, WITCH,
MEDEA, CHARMER
encircle ENVIRON, GIRD, ORB, INORB,
EMBAY, RING
enclose CORRAL, ENCLAVE, HEM, CAGE,
CASE, WRAP
enclosure ... STOCKADE, YARD, BAWN,
PEN, MEW, CORRAL, CANCHA,
ATAJO
encomium TRIBUTE, ELOGE, PANEGYRIC
encore ..... AGAIN, BIX, ECHO, OVER,
TWICE, REPEAT
encourage . ABET, BOOST, EGG, URGE,
CHEER, INCITE, FOSTER
Encratites, founder of .... TATIAN
encroach ... INVADE, USURP, INFRINGE
encumber .... LOAD, SADDLE, CLOG
encyclic .. PANDECT, TREATISE, LETTER
end AIM, CEASE, CLOSE, OMEGA, TOE,
LIMIT, TAIL, DIE, CODA, STUB,
EXPIRE, FINALE
" (boundary) .... BOURN, ABUTTAL
" , tending to an .... TELIC
endeavor ... SEEK, AIM, STRIVE, ESSAY,
VIE, EFFORT, ETTLE, NISUS
ending .... CONCLUSION, DESINENT
endless ... ETERN, LASTING, UNDYING
endorse ..... SIGN, RATIFY, SANCTION
endow ..... (IN)VEST, BESTOW, DOTE
endowment ..... APPANAGE, DOWER,
GRANT, GIFT, TALENT, LARGESSE,
BOON
endue .... DIGEST, DOWER, ENRICH
endure ..... BEAR, LAST, LIVE, BROOK,
DREE, ABIDE, UNDERGO
enemy ... HATER, FRENNE, FOE, RIVAL,
ADVERSARY

84

energize ...... BRACE, FORTIFY, NERVE
energy ... PEP, STHENIA, BENT, ERGAL,
    MIGHT, VIGOR, METTLE, POTENCY
    "   of the mind ...... PSYCHURGY
    "   unit .. (MEG)ERG, JOULE, RAD
    "   , want of ... ATONY, ANEURIA,
        INERTIA
enervate .... DRAIN, EXHAUST, SAP
engage .... PLIGHT, PROMISE, HIRE,
    BETROTH, CHARTER, ENLIST
engender .... BEGET, BREED, SIRE
engine . MOTOR, MOGUL, GIN, DIESEL,
    YARDER, TURBINE
    "   of warfare ONAGER, CATAPULT,
        RAM
engineer ...... EADS, SAPPER, SEABEE
England; anc. name .... ALBION
    "   ; district of York ...... ILKLEY
    "   , early conqueror of ....
        HENGEST, HORSA
    "   , forest in .... ARDEN
    "   , headland of .... NAZE
    "   , southernmost port of LIZARD
    "   , northwest; anc. .... ARGYLL
    "   , symbol of ...... LION, BULL
English .. SILURES, ANGLO, ANGLICAN
    "   actor ..... OLIVIER, COWARD,
        BURTON
    "   actress . ANDREWS, REDGRAVE,
        BLOOM
    "   address to queen ..... MAAM
    "   Antarctic explorer ... SCOTT
    "   archbishop .... LAUD, BECKET
    "   architect ADAM, SCOTT, WREN
    "   author . ROLLE, LANDOR, OPIE,
    COWARD, FLEMING, WELLS,
    BRONTE, KIPLING, FOX, HENTY
    "   aviators .... RAF
    "   bailiff .... REEVE
    "   canal laborer .... NAVVY
    "   castle site .... ARUNDEL
    "   cathedral city .... ELY
    "   Channel, river to . EXE, ORNE,
    RANCE, SEINE, SOMME
    "   circuit court .... EYRE
    "   city . LEEDS, BOLTON, BRISTOL,
    OXFORD
    "   clergyman .... INGE, NEALE,
    WESLEY
    "   coin . GEORGE, GUINEA, ORA,
    CAROLUS, RIAL, GROAT
    "   college ...... BALLIOL, ETON,
    HARROW
    "   comedienne .... GINGOLD
    "   commander .... HAIG
    "   composer ...... ELGAR, ARNE,
    DELIUS
    "   conservative party ..... TORY
    "   conspirator .... FAWKES
    "   country festival .... ALE

"   county .... ESSEX, YORK, KENT,
    SHIRE
"   county hundreds .... LATHES,
    RAPES
"   court EYRE, SOC, GEMOT, LEET
"   dandy .... TOFF
"   diarist .... PEPYS
"   diplomat . HOARE, EDEN, PITT,
    DISRAELI
"   district court, per. to ... SOC,
    SAKE
"   divine .... PALEY
"   domain .... MANOR
"   dramatist ..... PINERO, READE
"   emblem .... ROSE
"   essayist .. LANG, ELIA, STEELE,
    ADDISON, LAMB, RALEIGH
"   etcher .... HADEN
"   executioner .... KETCH
"   explorer .. RALEIGH, HUDSON,
    CABOT
"   forest .... SHERWOOD, ARDEN
"   founder of Northumberland .
    DEIRA
"   franchise .... SOC
"   free tenant .... DRENG
"   freeman ...... CEORL, THANE
"   freemen ...... CHURLS, LOETS
"   hamlet .... DORP
"   headland .... NAZE
"   heathen ruler .... PENDA
"   hills .... CLEE, WOLDS
"   historian .. TOYNBEE, GIBBON,
    GROTE, BEDE
"   hog .... ESSEX
"   honor exam .... TRIPOS
"   humorist .... LEAR
"   hymnodist .... NEALE
"   impresario .... CARTE
"   king ...... INE, HAL, HAROLD,
    EDRED, EGBERT, EADGAR
"   kingdom, early .... DEIRA
"   landed proprietor .... SQUIRE
"   lawn billiards .... TROCO
"   legendary king ...... ARTHUR
"   legislature ...... PARLIAMENT
"   letter .... EDH, AR
"   liberal party .... WHIG
"   measure of coal .... CORF
"   mendicant orders ..... FRIARS
"   mine wagon .... ROLLEY
"   minister of state ...... PITT,
    WALPOLE, BEDE
"   monk .... BEDE
"   mountain peak ..... CHEVIOT
"   musician ..... ARNE, PURCELL
"   navigator ...... DRAKE, ROSS
"   nobility THEGNS, EARLS, LORDS
"   noble . DUKE, EARL, PRINCE, SIR
"   northern tribe .... PICTS

" novelist ...... CAIN, CRONIN, HUXLEY, PRIESTLEY, WELLS
" order .... GARTER
" painter .... OPIE, CONSTABLE, HOGARTH, ROMNEY
" pamphleteer ... DEFOE, SWIFT
" party . LABO(U)R, TORY, WHIG
" patron saint .... GEORGE
" philosopher ... BACON, HUME, RUSSELL, SPENCER, LOCKE
" pianist .... HENDERSON
" poet ..... GRAY, KEATS, LANG, AUDEN, MASEFIELD, CAREW, SHELLEY, POPE, TENNYSON, CIBBER
" poetess .. BROWNING, SITWELL
" political philosopher ... BURKE
" pot herb .... CLARY
" pottery .... SPODE
" prelate .... INGE
" printer .... CAXTON
" prose writer ... BEDA, BAEDA, BEDE
" race course ... EPSOM, ASCOT
" ready money .... PREST
" reformer .... SPENCE
" region .... WEALD
" river . AVON, ESK, EXE, NEN, EDEN, OUSE, CAM, URE, TEES, TRENT, TYNE, YARE
" rock strata .... PERMIAN
" royal house BLOIS, HANOVER, YORK, STUART, WINDSOR
" ruler, early .... OFFA
" scholar .... ALCUIN
" school .... ETON
" schoolboy .... ETONIAN
" scientist ... DARWIN, FLEMING
" serf .... THRALL
" settlers, early .... JUTES
" sheep .... LONK
" ship money .... PREST
" slave .... ESNE
" socialist .... FABIAN
" statesman . BURKE, CRANMER, PITT, EDEN
" stone monument .. CROMLECH
" surgeon ...... HADEN, PAGET
" thicket .... PSINNEY
" traveler and author ... LIGON
" treaty .... TROYES
" village .... BOURG
" warrior and king CNUT, KNUD
" weight .. MAST, STONE, TOD
" woman soldier .... WAAC
engrave .. CHISEL, CUT, INFIX, STIPPLE, ETCH, RIST, CARVE, INCISE
engraver .... CHASER, GRAVER, ETCHER
" , tool of .... BURIN
engraving . CHASING, PRINT, CELATURE

" on wood ..... XYLOGRAPH
" on stone .... INTAGLIO
engrossed ... RAPT, INTENT, ABSORBED
enhance .... INCREASE, WAX, ELEVATE
enisled .... ALONE, APART, ISOLATED
enigma ..... REBUS, CHARADE, GRAPH, RIDDLE, MYSTERY, WHY, SECRET, CONUNDRUM
enigmatic ..... MYSTIC, CRYPTIC, DARK
enjoin .. BAN, FORBID, DIRECT, ORDER, RESTRAIN, WARN
enjoyment ...... GUSTO, RELISH, ZEST
enlarge .... REAM, DILATE, EXPAND
enlarged mass in nose ..... ADENOID
enlighten .... EDIFY, ILLUME
enliven .... ANIMATE, REFRESH
enmesh ..... ENSNARE, KNOT, SNARL
enmity HATRED, RANCOR, FEUD, COLD, DISCORD, MALICE, ANIMUS
ennead .... NINE
ennui ...... FATIGUE, LANGUOR, BORE
enormous ...... HUGE, VAST, TITANIC
" number .... GOOGOL
Enos' father .... SETH
" grandmother .... EVE
" uncle .... ABEL, CAIN
enough .... FULLY, QUITE, BUS, BASTA, AMPLE
enrage ... ANGER, IRE, ROIL, MADDEN
enraged .... IRATE, INCENSED
enraptured .... ECSTATIC, BEATIFIC
enrich ...... ENDOW, INCREASE, LARD
enrol . ENTER, IMPANEL, MATRICULATE, ENLIST, REGISTER
ens .... ENTITY, BEING
ensign .... BADGE, COLORS, JACK, PENNANT, GONFALON, PENNON, REGALIA
" of Othello .... IAGO
ensilage .... FODDER
ensiled .... SILOED
ensnare .... SNIGGLE, BENET, NOOSE, WEB, TRAP, TRICK, SEDUCE, DECOY
entad, opposed to .... ECTAD
entangle WEB, MAT, RAFFLE, TRAMMEL, RAVEL, MESH, CONFUSE
entanglement ... LIMING, IMBROGLIO, SNARE
enter .... RECORD, BORE, LIST, ADMIT, ENROL, START, EMBARK, INSERT
enterprise .... EXPLOIT, FEAT, SCHEME
entertain .... DIVERT, REGALE, AMUSE, TREAT
entertainment FEAST, FETE, BANQUET, FIESTA, FESTIVAL, PLAY, GAME, SHOW, PASTIME, SPORT
enthusiasm .... ARDOR, ENVY, VERVE, MANIA, ZEAL, FERVOR
enthusiast .. ZEALOT, FAN, BUG, BUFF, FANATIC, DEVOTEE

entice .. INVEIGH, TEMPT, LURE, TOLE, COAX
enticer .... SEDUCER, DECOYER
entitle ..... NAME, DUB, CALL, STYLE
entity ...... SOUL, ENS, UNIT, BEING
entomb .... BURY, HEARSE, INURN
entourage .... ATTENDANTS, RETINUE, TRAIN
entrance .... PORTAL, ADIT, INLET, POSTERN, GATE, INGRESS, STILE
entreat ..... ADJURE, BESEECH, HALSE, SOLICIT, IMPLORE, COAX, PRAY
entree ..... ADMISSION, ACCESS, DISH
entwine .... ENLACE, WEAVE, TWIST
enumeration ..... TALE, CENSUS, LIST
envelop ..... WRAP, ENFOLD, INFOLD, SHROUD
envelope .... BURR, CASE, SHROUD, CAPSULE, VESTURE, WRAPPER
envenom .... TAINT, POISON
environ ..... HEM, OUTSKIRT, PURLIEU
environment .. TERRAIN, AREA, MILIEU
envoy .... LEGATE, NUNCIO
envy .... RANKLE, COVET, GRUDGE
enzyme ...... ASE, DIASTASE, PEPSIN, PTYALIN, OLEASE, MALTASE, RENNIN
    " , leather making ... TANNASE
    " , opposed to .... AZYM
eolith .... CELT, AXE
eon .... ERA, AGE, OLAM
eonic .... ERAL
ephah, tenth of .... OMER
epic ..... POEM, EPOS, SAGA, EPOPEE, ENEID, ILIAD, CID, HOMERIC, HEROIC
Epictetus was one .... STOIC
epicure . FRIAND, GOURMET, GLUTTON, SYBARITE
epicurean ...... APICIAN, LUXURIOUS
epicurism . GASTRONOMY, HEDONISM
epidemic .... FLU, PEST, PLAGUE
epidermal tissue .... KERATIN
epidermis .... BARK, CUTICLE, SKIN
epigram ... ADAGE, POSY, QUIP, MOT
epigram couplet .... DISTICH
Epimetheus' wife .... PANDORA
epinephrine .... ADRENALIN
Epirus, native of .... EPIROTE
    " , town in .... DODONA
epistle . LETTER, MISSIVE, NOTE, BILLET, POST
epithet . AGNOMEN, (BY)NAME, CURSE
epitome .... BRIEF, DIGEST, ABSTRACT, BREVIARY, SYNOPSIS
epoch ..... EON, AGE, DAY, ERA, TIME
Epsom event .... DERBY
equal ... BOTH, EVEN, FERE, TIE, SAME, QUITE, LIKE
    " , an .... MATCH, MEET, PAR
    " -angled figure .... ISAGON
    " ; comb. form .... ISO, PARI

equality .... PAR, PARITY, EGALITE
    " of civil right ..... ISONOMY
equatorial .... TORRID
equestrian .... HORSEMAN, RIDER
equilateral parallelogram .... RHOMB
equilibrist .... BALANCER
equilibrium, want of .... ASTASIA
equine cry .... NEIGH, FARCY
    " disease .... FARCY
equip . RIG, FEAT, GIRD, IMP, ENDOW, OUTFIT, PROVIDE, ACCOUTRE
equipment ...... ARMS, GEAR, TACKLE
equitable .... HONEST, FAIR, JUST
equivocate .. FENCE, PALTER, FIB, LIE, HEDGE, EVADE, QUIBBLE
era .... AGE, CYCLE, DATE, EON, TIME, EPOCH
eradicate ..... EPILATE, ANNUL, LEVEL, ROOT, BLOT
erase DELE(TE), EFFACE, BLOT, CANCEL
ere ..... BEFORE, PRIOR, RATHER
Erebus .... HADES
    " , brother of .... NOX
    " , father of .... CHAOS
    " , children of ... DAY, AETHER
erect .... REAR, STAY, RAISE
Eretrian .... ELIAN
ergo .... HENCE
Eric the _____ .... RED
erica .... HEATH(S)
Eridanus, star in .... KEID
Erin .... HIBERNIA, IRELAND
ermine .. STOAT, WEASEL, VARE, VAIR, MINIVER, FUR
eroded .... EATEN, EROSE, ATE
Eros .... CUPID, AMOR
erotic .. AMATIVE, AMOROUS, LOVING, ARDENT, AMATORY
err ...... SIN, SLIP, TRIP, FALL, LAPSE, WANDER, MISTAKE
erratic .. VAGRANT, NOMADIC, FICKLE, QUEER
erring .... ASTRAY, PECCABLE
error(s) .... ERRATA, LAPSE, SIN, SLIP, BONER, MISCUE, BULL, TYPO, GAFFE
ersatz .... SUBSTITUTE
Erse .... CELT, GAEL(IC)
erudition .... WISDOM, LETTERS, LORE
eruption .... RASH
erythrina, tree of .... DADAP
Esau, descendant of ...... EDOMITE
    " , later name of .... EDOM
escapade .... FROLIC, PRANK, VAGARY
escape ... ELOPE, EVADE, FLEE, AVOID, LAM, BOLT, DECAMP, ABSCOND
escargot .... SNAIL
escarpment .... SLOPE, STEEP
Escaut .... SCHELDT, SCHELDE
eschew ...... ABSTAIN, AVOID, SHUN
escolar .... ROVET

87

escort ...... GUARD, ATTEND, BEAU(X), USHER, CONVOY, GALLANT, CAVALIER, SQUIRE
escrow .... BOND, DEED
escutcheon .... ARMS, CREST, ORLE
Esdras .... APOCRYPHA
Eskimo ALASKAN, ALEUT, INNUIT, YUIT, ITA
   " descent .... TURANIAN
   " dog .... HUSKY, MALEMUTE
   " fur coat .... TEMIAK
   " garment .... PARKA
   " house .. TOPEK, TUPEK, IGLOO, IGLU
   " knife .... ULU
   " male attire, per. to ... LABRET
   " memorial post .... XAT
   " open skin boat ...... UMIAK, OOMIAK
   " settlement .... ETAH
   " skin-covered canoe .. BAIDAR, BIDAR, KAYAK
esophagus .... GULA
esoteric ... ABSTRUSE, INNER, ARCANE, MYSTIC, SECRET, OCCULT
esoteric knowledge GNOSIS, CABALA
espalier .... TRELLIS, PALISADE
esparto .... ATOCHA
espouse ... ADOPT, BETROTH, PLIGHT, WED
esprit de corps .. MORALE, WIT, SPIRIT
ess .. CURVE, SIGMOID, SIGMA, WORM
essay .. CHRIA, THESIS, TRACT, PAPER, THEME, TEST, TRY, TREATISE
essays of _____ .... ELIA
essence . ATTAR, GIST, ENS, MARROW, PITH, CORE, BEING, SCENT, ENTITY
essential . INHERENT, INTRINSIC, VITAL, BASAL, PRIMARY
establish ...... FOUND, RADICATE, FIX
establishment, domestic ... MENAGE
estate ...... ASSETS, MANOR, RANK, ALLOD(IUM), DAIRA, STATUS, ALOD
   " , per. to an .... PRESS, DEMESNE
esteem ... AIM, HONOR, PRIDE, VALUE, ADMIRE, REGARD, REPUTE, REVERE, CHERISH
ester .... TROPATE, SILICATE, STEARIN, ACETIN, IODIDE, OLEATE
Esther's husband .... XERXES
estimate .... AUDIT, METE, RATE, MEASURE, JUDGE, ASSAY, BUDGET
estivate .... SUMMER
Estonia, capital of .... REVAL, TALLIN
   " , island of .... SAREMA, OESEL
   " , measure of .... LIIN
   " , peasant of .... KULAK
estrange ..... ALIENATE, WEAN, PART
estray .... DOGIE, WAIF

estuary BAY, FIRTH, FRITH, RIA, FIORD, INLET
   " of Amazon .... PARA
etch ... BITE, CORRODE, CUT, ENGRAVE
eternal .... AGELESS, EONIAN
eternity (A)EON, OLAM, TIME, AEVUM
ether .... AIR, SKY
   " compound ... ANISOL, ESTER
ethereal ..... AERY, AIRY, RARE, THIN, FAIRY, LIGHT, AERIAL, DELICATE, HEAVENLY, CELESTIAL
Ethiopia, anc. capital of ..... MEROE
   " , queen of .... CANDACE
Ethiopian ape .... GELADA
   " battleground ...... ADOWA
   " breed of cattle ..... SANGA
   " cereal .... TEFF
   " coin ... TALARI, BESA, GIRSH
   " division ...... SHOA, TIGRE
   " drink .... BOUSE
   " emperor .... NEGUS, HAILE, SELASSIE
   " fly .... ZIMB
   " governor .... RAS
   " Hamite .... AFAR
   " lake .... TANA, TSANA
   " language .... AMHARIC, GALLA, GEEZ, SAHO
   " native ...... DOKO, NEGRO
   " primate .... ABUNA
   " river ... OMO, ABAI, GASH, MAREB
   " tree .... CUSSO, KOSO
   " wolf .... KABERU
ethyl derivative .... ALCOHOL, ETHER
   " hydride .... ETHANE
etiquette .... CUSTOM, DECORUM, MANNERS
Etruscan title .... LARS, LAR
etui .... CASE, TROUSSE
Etzel .... ATTILA, HUN
eucalypt .... MALLEE, YATE
eucharist box .... PIX, PYX
   " vessel .... PATEN, AMA, AMULA
eucharistic plate .... PATINA
   " wine .... KRAMA
euchite .... SATANIST
Euclid's origin .... MEGARA
eulachon .... CANDLEFISH
eulogize .... EXTOL, LAUD, BOOST
eulogy ... ELOGE, PRAISE, ENCOMIUM, PANEGYRIC
euphonium .... TUBA
euphony .... MELODY, METER
Euphrates tributary .... TIGRIS
Eurasia, region in .... TATARY
Eurasian range .... URAL(S)
eureka .... AHA, TRIUMPH

Euripides play ...... HELENA, MEDEA,
ALCESTIS, HECUBA
European .... LAPP, DANE, SLAV, BALT,
FINN, POLE, ESTH, SCOT, SERB,
WEND, CZECH, NORSE, WELSH
"   battlefield .... MARNE,
VERDUN, ARDENNES,
WATERLOO, BULGE,
MARENGO, YPRES, SEDAN
"   coal basin ..... RUHR, SAAR
"   health resort .. BADEN, AIX,
VICHY
"   river ... RHINE, ELBE, SEINE,
ODER, DANUBE, VISTULA, ISAR,
EBRO, ARNO, PO, MOLDAU
Eurytus' daughter .... IOLE
evade .... BILK, SHIRK, ELUDE, SHUNT,
AVOID, DODGE, PARRY, PALTER
evaded .... GEED, EXEMPT
evade work .... GOLDBRICK
evaluate ... APPRAISE, ESTIMATE, RATE,
ASSESS, JUDGE
evanesce .... FADE, VANISH
evangelist .... GRAHAM, JOHN, LUKE,
MARK, APOSTLE, MATTHEW,
DISCIPLE, ROBERTS, SUNDAY,
MCPHERSON
Evans, Mary Ann .... ELIOT
evaporate DRY, EXHALE, DISTIL, VANISH
eve .. DAMPEN, WET, IVA, FEMALE, RIB
even ... EQUABLE, PLANE, TIED, LEVEL,
CALM, STEADY, TRUE, FLUSH,
SQUARE
evened .... SMOOTHED
even if .... THOUGH, THO, SPITE
evening .. SOIREE, DEN, ABEND, ERES,
DUSK, SUNSET, TWILIGHT, SOIR,
VESPER
"   star .... HESPER, VENUS
event ... CASUS, FEAT, EFFECT, RESULT,
UPSHOT, HAPPENING
eventuate .... CLOSE, HAPPEN, OCCUR
ever .... EER, ONCE, ANON
Everest peak .... LHOTSE
evergreen .... BARETTA, SPRUCE,
ABELMOSK, TARATA, PINE
"   , cedar-like ...... DEODAR
"   shrub ... OLEANDER, SAVIN
evergreens ... OLAX, TARAIRI, CAROB,
TOYON
everlasting ...... AGELONG, ETERNAL,
ETERNE, OLAMIC
everted .... ECTOPIC, TURNED
every .... EACH, ILK, ANY
everything .... ALL, TOTAL, SUM
evict ... EJECT, EXPEL, OUST, REMOVE,
SACK, CASHIER
evidence .. PROBATE, DEPONE, ATTEST,
DATA, PROOF, EVINCE
evident .... CLEAR, PALPABLE, PATENT

evil .... BASE, HARM, VICE, VILE,
MALUM, WRONG, MALIGN,
CORRUPT
"   doer .... CHEAT, MISCREANT,
CULPRIT, SINNER, FELON,
VILLAIN
"   intent .... DOLUS
"   omen .... KNELL
"   spirit ..... BUGAN, CACODEMON,
DEVIL, AMAIMON,
ASMODEUS, OTKON,
OKI, MOMUS, GHOUL
evils .... ILLS, MALA, ERRS
evoke .... EDUCE, CALL, VOICE
evolution, doctrine of ..... BIOGENY,
COSMISM
evolve ...... DEDUCE, UNFOLD, DERIVE
ewe .... KEB, THEAVE, CRONE
ewer .... CROCK, URN
exacerbate ... IRK, ENRAGE, WORSEN,
PROVOKE
exact LITERAL, ESTREAT, JUST, MINUTE,
STRICT, SEVERE, LEVY, BLEED,
WREST, WRING
exaggerated ...... OUTRE, MAGNIFIED
exalt ... CROW, ELATE, BOAST, GLOAT
exalted ..... ELATED, SHEEN, SUBLIME
examination ...... ORAL, QUIZ, TEST,
AUDIT, PROBE, TRIAL,
SEARCH, TRIPOS
examine .... TRY, APPOSE, LAIT, PORE,
TEST, EXPLORE, PRY
examiner .... CONNER, CENSOR
example .... PINK, BYSEN, PARADIGM,
SPECIMEN, STANDARD, MODEL
exasperate .. GALL, INCENSE, ENRAGE,
NETTLE, PEEVE, VEX
excavate ... DIG, SCOOP, GRUB, PION,
DELVE, DREDGE
excavation .. MINE, MUCK, PIT, STOPE,
HOLE, CAVITY, SHAFT
"   , surface ...... OPENCAST
exceed ..... CAP, TOP, OUTDO, DING,
BEST, ECLIPSE, SURPASS
excellence .... MERIT, VIRTUE
excellent .... BRAVO, AONE, TOPS,
PRIME
except ...... BESIDES, BUT, BAR, SAVE
exception, take ...... DEMUR, DOUBT,
QUALIFY, RESENT
excess ...... SURPLUS, NIMIETY, TOO,
OVER, PLUS, LUXUS
excessive .. EXTREME, UNDUE, EXTRA
excessive admiration of mothers ....
MOMISM
exchange ..... BANDY, BOURSE, SWAP,
PIT, BARTER, AUCTION
exchequer .. FISC, FISK, BANK, PURSE
excise ...... TOLL, TAX, IMPOST, CESS,
TITHE, LEVY

excite . BESTIR, AGITATE, ELATE, ROIL, INFLAME, WHET
excited ..... AROUSED, AGOG, ASTIR, MANIC, AVID
exclamation .. AH, AHA, AHEM, ALAS, BAH, EGAD, FIE, HIP, OHO, OW, PAH, PHEW, PHO, TUT, HAH, HEY, EVOE, YAH, DRAT
" pledging a toast .. SKOAL
exclude .... EJECT, OMIT, BAR
exclusive .... LIMITED, ALONE, ONLY, POSH, SOLE
excommunicate .... UNCHURCH
excoriate .... ABRADE, FLAY
excrescence ...... BOSS, STUD, LUMP, KNOB
excursion .... JAUNT, TOUR, OUTLOPE, SALLY, CIRCUIT, TREK, CRUISE
excuse .... ALIBI, CONDONE, PRETEXT, PLEA, ASSOIN, REMIT
" of sickness .... AEGER
execrate .. DETEST, ABOMINATE, HATE
execute .... HANG, ACT, ACHIEVE, EFFECT, (EN)FORCE
exegete .... INTERPRETER
exemplar .... MODEL, PATTERN
exempt .... IMMUNE, FREE, APART, REMOVED, RELIEVE, EXON
exemption .... ESSOIN
exercise ..... PRAXIS, URE, USE, DRILL, NISUS, TASK
Exeter, per. to .... EXON
exhalation .... AURA
exhale ..... BREATHE, EMANATE, EMIT, EXPIRE
exhaust .... JADE, EMIT, FAG, SAP, DRAIN, DEPLETE, EMPTY, SPEND, WASTE
exhausted .... TIRED, PETERED, DONE, SPENT, BEAT, EFFETE, WEARY
exhibit .. STAGE, SHOW, AIR, EVINCE, STATE, EXPOSE, FLAUNT
exhibiting .... OSTENSIVE
exhilarate .... BUOY, ELATE, TITILLATE
exhilaration ...... GAIETY, GLEE, JOY
exhort .... PREACH, URGE
exhume .... UNEARTH, DISINTER
exigency ..... NEED, URGE, PRESSURE, CRISIS, WANT
exile .... BANISH, DEPORT, EXPATRIATE
exist .... ARE, LIVE, BE
existence .... ESSE, ENTITY, BEING, STATE, STATUS, DURATION
existent ...... EXTANT, BEING, LIVING
exit ...... EGRESS, END, VENT, DEATH
ex libris .... BOOKPLATE
exodus ...... GOING, FLIGHT, HEGIRA
exonerate .. ACQUIT, CLEAR, RELEASE, REMIT, ABSOLVE, PARDON
exorcism .... EXPULSION, SPELL

exotic ... ALIEN, FOREIGN, PEREGRINE
expand .. SPLAY, DILATE, FLAN, SWELL, DISTEND, INFLATE
expanding bullet .... DUMDUM
expanse .... SEA, OCEAN, SPREAD, REACH, STRETCH, ORBIT, RANGE, SCOPE, SWEEP, TRACT, SPHERE
expatiate .... ENLARGE, DESCANT
expect .... (A)WAIT, HOPE
expecting .... ATIP, PREGNANT
expedient .... RESSORT, STOPGAP
expedition .. CRUSADE, DRIVE, SAFARI, TOUR, TRIP, JAUNT, QUEST, CARAVAN, CAMPAIGN
expel ... EXILE, EJECT, EXTRUDE, SPURT, BANISH, DISBAR
experiment .. PROOF, TEST, TRIAL, TRY
expert .. ACE, ADROIT, ADEPT, MASTER, WHIZ, CRACK
expiate .... ATONE, PURGE, SHRIVE
expiation, rel. to .... PIACULAR
expire ..... DIE, ELAPSE, PERISH, END, EXHALE
explain .... CLEAR, DEFINE, WISE
explanation .... ALIBI, ANSWER, EXCUSE, EXEGESIS, SCHOLIA, SOLUTION, KEY
explanatory inscription ..... TITULUS
expletive .... VOILA, CURSE, OATH
explode ...... POP, DETONATE, BURST, FIRE
exploding meteor .... BOLIDE
" sun .... NOVA
exploit ...... ACT, BLEED, MILK, FEAT, GEST(E), DARE, DEED, HEROISM, CLIP
explore ... EXAMINE, PROBE, FATHOM, PLUMB, SEARCH, SCOUT, TEST
explorer ... BALBOA, DESOTO, HEDIN, DRAKE, ERIC, RAE, BYRD, GAMA, ROSS, LEWIS, PERRY, DELEON, DELONG, SCOTT, CORTES, PIZARRO
explosion ...... OUTBURST, POP, BLAST
explosive .... AMATOL, DYNAMITE, MINE, TNT, CORDITE, POWDER, TONITE, CAP, AMMO, GAINE, PENTHRITE
" isometric mineral .. THORITE
" picric acid .... LYDDITE
" produced by lightning ...... FULGURITE
" sound .... CHUG, PLUFF
expose .... BARE, UNMASK
express ...... AIR, ASSERT, SHIP, VENT
expression .... LOCUTION, ASPECT, TERM, IDIOM, PHRASE, ATTICISM
expunge .... DELE(TE), EFFACE, ERASE
expurgate .... CENSOR, PURGE, BATHE

exquisite .... DELICATE, RARE
extend .. EKE, JUT, PROTRACT, RENEW,
                 SPAN, LIE, REACH
extent .. RANGE, SCOPE, AREA, SWEEP
exterior .... ECTAL, EXTRINSIC,
                 CORTICAL, OUTER
    " , toward the .... ECTAD
external world .... NONEGO
extermination of groups .. GENOCIDE
extinguish .... CHOKE, DOUSE, QUELL,
           QUENCH, STIFLE, SMOTHER
extirpate .... DELE, ROOT, STUB
extol .... PRAISE, LAUD, GLORIFY,
          COMMEND, EULOGIZE, EXULT
extort .... WRING, COMPEL, EXTRACT,
     BLEED, WREST, WRENCH, SQUEEZE
extortioner .... BLACKMAILER, HARPIE
extra .... ODD, ORRA, OVER, SUPE
extract .... CITE, ELICIT, ESTREAT,
     EVULSE, PERICOPE, DRAW, PUMP
extraction .... LINEAGE, ORIGIN,
                  DESCENT
extraneous .... EXOTIC, OUTER, ALIEN
extraordinary ..... UNCO, ONER, BIG
extravagant .... BAROQUE, OUTRE,
                  LAVISH
extreme .. RADICAL, LAST, ULTRA, END,
             DRASTIC, UTMOST
extremities .... POLES, TIPS
extremity ...... LIMB, LIMIT, BOUND,
                  VERGE
exudation ...... GUM, LAC, SAP, TAR,
     SUDOR, AURA, RESIN, SWEAT
exude ..... EMIT, OOZE, REEK, FLOW
exultant .. OVANT, SANGUINE, AGOG
eye(s) .. OPTIC, ORB, OGLE, SEE, UTA,
     EEN, EES, GLIM, HILA, HILUM,
         SIGHT, STARE, PEEPER
    " , a black ...... MOUSE, SHINER
    " , cavity of the .... ORBIT
    " , colored portion of ...... IRIS
    " disease .... GLAUCOMA
    " dropper .... PIPETTE
    " flap ... VISOR, BLINKER, PATCH,
                  BLINDER
    " , German for .... AUGE
    " glass .... LENS, LORGNON,
                  MONOCLE
    " , inner coat of .... RETINA
    " , magic .... RADAR
    " , opening in the .... PUPIL
    " , part of .... IRIS, UVEA
    " , per. to the .... IRIAN
    " thread worm .... LOA
eyeball portion .... CORNEA
eyebrow .... SUPERCILIUM, BREE
eyelashes .... CILIA
    " , dye for .... MASCARA
eyelet .... GROMMET

eyelid darkener .... KOHL
    " , incision of .... TARSOTOMY
    " , droop of upper .... PTOSIS
eye-like .... OCELLATED, OCELLUS
eyes, close the .... SEEL
    " , films in the .... NEBULAE
    " , furnished with ..... OCULATE
    " of beans .... HILA
eyesore .... BLEMISH, DEFECT
eyewash .... EXCUSE, APPLESAUCE
eyewater ... COLLYRIUM, BORIC(ACID)
eyot .... AIT, ISLE, ISLET
eyrie .... NEST
Ezraite .... HEMAN

F

F.D.R.'s mother .... SARA
fable ..... LEGEND, LIE, APOLOG(UE),
              MYTH, PARABLE
    " , teller of .... PARABOLIST
    " writer .... AESOP
fabled bird .... RUKH, ROC
    " fish .... MAH
Fabray, Miss .... NANETTE
fabric .... CLOTH, TEXTURE, MATERIAL,
     FELT, WEB, ATLAS, RAS, FAILLE,
   LANSDOWNE, LAME, LENO, PILE,
     TULLE, TOILE, BOUCLE, CALICO,
     MADRAS, MUSLIN, TARTAN,
       CHIFFON, ORGANDY
    " , coarse ... CRASH, MAT, RADIS,
               CADIS, RATINE
    " , cotton and worsted ....
             PARAMATTA
    " , crinkled .... CREPE, CRAPE
    " design with wax .... BATIK
    " , figured .... MOREEN
    " , heavy ...... BROCADE, DENIM
    " , hempen .... BURLAP
    " , light worsted .... ETAMINE
    " , linen .... SCRIM
    " ; of waste fabrics ..... MUNGO
    " , printed ..... PERCALE, CHALLIS
    " , ribbed .... REP, TWILL
    " , shiny ...... SATEEN, SATIN(ET)
    " , silk ..... ALACHA, SURA, GROS
    " , silk-and-gold ... ACCA, SAMITE
    " , striped .... GALATEA
    " , textile .... DELAINE
    " , velvet-like ..... TERRY, PANNE
    " , watered silk .... MOIRE
    " , woollen .... PRUNELLA, BEIGE,
               TABINET
    " , woven silk TRICOT, SARSENET,
               PIQUET

fabricate .... COIN, MAKE, MINT, SCHEME, FALSIFY, CONCOCT
fabrication ... ROMANCE, LIE, TISSUE, WEB, COGGERY, DECEIT, GUILE
fabricator .... FORGER, INVENTOR
fabrics, method of ornamenting .... FAGOTING
   " , dealer in .... MERCER
fabulist ... AESOP, GRIMM, ANDERSEN
fabulous being .... ROSMARIN, UNICORN, CENTAUR, BASILISK, HYDRA, DRAGON, GORGON, GRIFFIN, SPHINX, CHIMERA
façade .... FACE, FRONT, REAR
face .... MEET, ANSWER, GRIMACE, MOUE, SNOOT, MAP, MUG, PHIZ, PUSS, VISAGE, ASPECT
   " downward .... PRONE, PRONATE, PROSTRATE
   " with masonry .... REVET
facer .... POSER, SOCKDOLAGER
facet .... BEZEL, CULET
facetious .... COMICAL, DROLL, WITTY
facile ...... EASY, PLIABLE, APT, DEFT
facilitate .... EASE, FURTHER
facility .... ART, MEANS, KNACK, POISE, SKILL, TACT
facsimile .... COPY, MATCH, REPLICA, TWIN
fact(s) .... DATUM, DATA, TRUTH, DEED, FEAT, FAIT
   " , pose as a .... POSIT
faction .... BLOC, CABAL, JUNTO, SIDE, CLAN, SECT, CLIQUE
———— facto .... IPSO
factor .... AGENT, BROKER, GENE, REEVE, ELEMENT
factory .... HONG, MILL, PLANT
factotum .... SERVANT, AGENT
faculty .... BENT, KNACK, SENSE, TALENT
fad .... ISM, CRY, MODE, RAGE, WHIM
fade ...... PETER, WILT, DAVER, DOW, PALE, DIM
faded .... DULL, FAINT, PASSE
Fadiman, Mr. .... CLIFTON
"Faery Queen" char. .. AMORET, ATE, UNA, ACRASIA, DUESSA, TALUS, GUYON
Fafnir's brother .... REGIN
   " slayer .... SIGURD
fag ...... HACK, SLAVE, TIRE, DRUDGE, JADE, MENIAL, TOIL
fail .. DEFECT, ERR, FLOP, LOSE, FLUNK
   " to follow suit ... RENEGE, RENIG
failing .... BLOT, FOIBLE, CADENT
failure ... DUD, LACK, BUST, COLLAPSE
faint .... DIM, SWELT, SWOON, SOFT, WEAK, SYNCOPE, FEEBLE

fair .... BAZAAR, BLONDE, FERIA, KIRMESS, EVEN, JUST, SOSO, CLEAR
   " , per. to a .... NUNDINAL
fairies, queen of the .... MAB
fairness .... BEAUTY, CANDOR
fairy ...... ELF(KIN), FAY, PERI, PIXY, SYLPH, SPRITE, NIX(IE)
   " fort .... LIS, SHEE
   " king .... OBERON
   " queen .... TITANIA, UNA
   " shoemaker ... LEPRECHAUN
   " spirit of death ...... BANSHEE
   " story .... ALLEGORY
   " , tricky .... PUCK
faith .. BELIEF, CREDO, TROTH, DOGMA, TENET, FIDELITY
faithful ... FAST, LEAL, LIEGE, LOYAL, STAUNCH
   " friend .... ACHATES
fake .... CHEAT, TRICK
fakes of a cable, ranges of .... TIER
fakir ..... MENDICANT, MONK, YOGI
falcon KESTREL, GYR, LANNER, HOBBY, PEREGRINE, SAKER, TERCEL, ANATUM
   " of India ... LAGGAR, LUGGER, LUGGAR, SHAHIN
   " , rapacious; genus . RAPTORES
   " , ribbon to secure .... JESS
   " , small .... BESRA, MERLIN
fall .. DROOP, PLOP, RUIN, SIN, SAG, SPILL, AUTUMN, TOPPLE, CASCADE
fall guy .... PATSY
fallacy .... IDOLUM, SOPHISM, ERROR
falling .... CADENT
   " sickness .... EPILEPSY
false ... LUKE, BOGUS, PSEUDO, FAKE, SHAM
   " friend .... TRAITOR, JUDAS
   " hair .... TETE, TOUPEE, WIG
   " items .... SPURIA
   " , show to be .... DEBUNK
   " swearing .... PERJURY
   " wing .... ALULA
falsehood .. CANARD, FLAM, LIE, TALE, FIB, FRAUD, PERJURY
falsify ...... FORGE, PERVERT, BELIE, GARBLE, DISTORT, FAKE
falter ...... WAVER, QUAIL, QUAVER
fame NOTE, RENOWN, GLORY, REPUTE, ECLAT, KUDOS, LUSTER, HONOR
famed .... EMINENT, NOTORIOUS
familiar .... CLOSE, COSY, VERSANT, HABITUAL, INTIMATE
family LINE, GENS, ILK, STIRPS, TRIBE, STOCK, BREED
   " , Italian . ESTE, MEDICI, BORGIA, DORIA
   " name .... SURNAME
   " , per. to .... LINEAL
famous ... NAMED, NOTED, EMINENT

fan .. COOL, FOMENT, WINNOW, OGI, BUFF, DEVOTEE
" form .... PLICATE
" light .... TRANSOM
", oriental .... OGI, PUNKA(H)
" palm ... INODES, TALIPOD, YARAY
" stick .... BRIN
fanatic ...... BIGOT, LUNATIC, MAD, ZEALOT, FRENETIC, RABID
fancy ...... DREAM, FAD, IDEA(TE), MEGRIM, FOIBLE, CHIMERA, NOTION, VISION, CONCEPT, CAPRICE
fandango .... DANCE
fanfare .... TANTARA
fang ..... CLAW, TALON, TUSK, TINE, TOOTH, NAIL
fanon .... MANIPLE, ORALE
fantastic . OUTRE, BAROQUE, ROCOCO
fanwort .... WATERLILY
far; comb. form .... TELE
farce . EXODE, SKIT, PARODY, MOCKERY, SHAM
farcical ..... ATELLAN, RIBALD, DROLL
fare . FOOD, DIET, RATE, PAY, THRIVE, TOKEN, MENU, BOARD, TRAVEL, PROSPER
farewell . ADIOS, AVE, CONGE, VALE, ADIEU, LEAVE
farinaceous .... MEALY, STARCHY
" food ...... SAGO, SALEP
farm ...... COTLAND, CROFT, MAINS, GRANGE, HACIENDA, RANCH, PLOW, TILL
" fee .... MANOR
" house ...... ONSTEAD, VILLA
" outbuildings .... STEADING
" tenant .... COTTER
farmer PLANTER, COCKY, RYOT, BOER, OKIE, KULAK, MEO, TILLER, CROPPER
farming ..... HUSBANDRY, FRUGALITY
farmstead .... BYRE, FARM
faro, form of ...... MONTE, STUSS
Faroe island ...... BORDO, OSTERO, BANDO, STROMO, VAAG
" Islands judge .... FOUD
farrow .... DRAPE, LITTER, PIG
Fascist theory, founder of .. PARETO
fashion . RAGE, CRAZE, MODE, VOGUE, MOLD, SHAPE, STYLE, DESIGN
fashionable . ALAMODE, CHIC, DAPPER, MODISH, NATTY, NIFTY, POSH, SMART, SPRUCE
fast .... APACE, DHARNA, LENT, RAMADAN, FLEET, HASTY, CARENE, EMBER
fasten TACK, NAIL, LACE, PIN, CHAIN, ROPE, RIVET, BOLT, GLUE, MOOR, SEAL, AFFIX
fastener .... PEG, CLAMP, HALTER

fastening; comb. form ...... DESMO
fastidious .. CRITICAL, DAINTY, FUSSY, PRISSY
fastness .... CELERITY, CITADEL, FORT
fat .. OILY, ESTER, LIPA, OBESE, SAIM, SUET, PINGUID, ADIPOSE, ADEPS, GREASE, PLUMP, PUDGY, STOUT
"; comb. form .... STEAT
", constituent of .... STEARIN
", deriv. of .... OLEO, SEBUM
" in butter .... CAPRIN, OLEO
", liquid part of ..... ELAIN, OLEIN
" of geese .... AXUNGE
" of swine .... LARD
" of wool .... SUINT, LANOLIN
", true .... LIPID
" -yielding tree .... SHEA
fata morgana .... MIRAGE
fatal .... MORT, FUNEST, LETHAL
fate .. DOOM, DESTINY, KISMET, LOT, KARMA, FORTUNE
fate; myth. .... LACHESIS, ATROPOS, CLOTHO, MOIRA, DECUMA, MORTA, NONA, PARCA
fated ..... DOOMED, FEY, FINAL, LAST
Fates, the .... MOIRAI, PARCAE
father .. ABBA, ABU, AMA, DAD, PERE, SIRE, PAPA, VATER, PATER, PADRE, BEGET
", a wise .... MENTOR
" of Agamemnon .... ATREUS
" of English learning ...... BEDE
"Father of Mankind" ...... IAPETUS
"Father of the Gods" . AMEN, AMON
father of the hydrogen bomb . TELLER
father, rel. to ... PATERNAL, AGNATE
fatherless .... ORBATE
fathom .... DELVE, PROBE, TEST, TRY, PLUMMET, PLUMB, SOUND
fatigue .... WEARY, BORE, FAG, JADE, TIRE, TUCKER
Fatima, descendant of ... SAYID, SEID
", stepbrother of .... ALI
fatty .... OILY, GREASY, ADIPOSE
" acid .... ADIPIC, VALERIC
" tumor .... LIPOMA
fatuous ... IDIOTIC, INANE, VACANT, ASININE, WITLESS
faucet ..... COCK, HORSE, PEG, TAP, ROBINET, SPIGOT
fault .... CULPA, FOIBLE, LAPSE, FLAW, SLIP, BLEMISH
", find .... CARP, CAVIL, CENSURE
" in mining ... HADE, LEAP, LODE
faultily .... AMISS, WRONGLY
faultless .... IMPECCABLE, PERFECT
faun .... SATYR, DEITY
Fauntleroy's mother .... DEAREST
Faunus' son .... ACIS

93

faux pas . ERROR, MISSTEP, SLIP, BULL,
        BONER, GAFFE, BLUNDER
favor . BIAS, BOON, OBLIGE, BENEFIT,
        INDULGE, SUPPORT
favorite ... MINION, PET, IDOL, HERO
favoritism .... NEPOTISM, BIAS
fawn ... CRINGE, BUCK, DOE, TOADY,
        GROVEL
fawning ...... SERVILE, OBSEQUIOUS
fay .... ELF, FAIRY, SPRITE
faze .... DAUNT, DISTURB
FBI director .... HOOVER
  " agent .... FED, GMAN
fealty ...... HOMAGE, DUTY, RESPECT
fear ... AWE, PHOBIA, DREAD, FUNK,
        PANIC
  " of crossing road . DROMOPHOBIA
  " of darkness ...... NYCTOPHOBIA
  " of drafts .... AEROPHOBIA
  " of fire .... PYROPHOBIA
  " of heights .... ACROPHOBIA
  " of pain .... ALGOPHOBIA
  " of poisons .... TOXIPHOBIA
fearful .. OVERAWED, CRAVEN, PAVID,
        TIMID, TREPID, ANXIOUS
fearless ...... BOLD, BRAVE, DARING,
        IMPAVID, VALIANT
feast ... JUNKET, PICNIC, REVEL, BON,
        REGALE, BANQUET
  " ; comb. form .... MAS
  " , funeral .... WAKE, ARVAL
  " of St. Martin ...... MARTINMAS
feat .. STUNT, DEED, EXPLOIT, GEST(E)
feather ..... PENNA, PINNA, TONGUE
  " ; as an arrow . FLETCH, FLEDGE
  " , barb of ...... PINNULA, HERL
  " , filament of .... DOWL
  " key .... SPLINE
  " , large strong .... QUILL
  " , quill .... REMEX
  " , shaft of a .... SCAPE
  " star .... ANTEDON
feathered PENNATED, FLEDGED, PLUMED,
        PLUMOSE
feathered keys .... FINS
feathering .... ENDYSIS
featherless .... CALLOW
feathers .... DOWN, SLEY
  " , adorn with .... IMPLUME
  " , adjust the .... PLUME
  " at bird's wing ...... ALULA
  " , yellow .... HULU
feature . MOTIF, TRAIT, ASPECT, FORM,
        ITEM, MIEN
feaze .... UNRAVEL, UNTWIST
feculent .... ROILY, TURBID
federation . ALLIANCE, BODY, FUSION,
        UNION, LEAGUE
fee ... FIEF, HONORARIUM, RETAINER,
    TIP, DUES, TOLL, GRATUITY, PAP

feeble .. DOTTY, INFIRM, PUNY, FAINT,
        ANEMIC, FEEBLE, DEBILE
feed .... AGIST, CATER, HAY, MASH,
        GRAZE, FODDER
feeding, forced .... GAVAGE
feel ... PALP, SENSE, GROPE, SUFFER
feeler(s) ...... ANTENNA, TENTACLE,
        PALPUS, PALPI, ANTENNAE
feeling ARDOR, EMOTION, LOVE, PITY
  " , capable of ...... SENTIENT
  " , show .... EMOTE
feet, combining two metric . DIPODIC
  " , having .... PEDATE
  " , number of .... FOOTAGE
  " , per. to .... PODAL, PEDAL
  " , without .... APOD
feign .... SHAM, ACT, SIMULATE
  " illness .... MALINGER
feint . PRETENSE, BLIND, APPEL, GEM,
        WILE
feldspar ... ALBITE, KAOLIN, ODINITE
felicitate .... BLESS, MACARIZE
felicity ...... BLISS, ECSTASY, JOY
feline .. JAGUAR, OUNCE, CAT, TOM,
        MOUSER, TIGER, SLY, CATTY
fell .... BRUTAL, CRUEL, FIERCE, PELT,
        GRIM, HEW, SAVAGE, SKIN
fellow .... WAT, CHAP(PY), GUY, LAD
  " , brutish .... YAHOO
  " , queer old .... GEEZER
  " , worthless .... SPALPEEN, CAD,
        LOSER
  " , young ..... YOUNKER, BLADE,
        GALLANT
fellowship .... SODALITY, UNION,
        COMPANY
felon .. WHITLOW, OUTCAST, CONVICT,
        CRIMINAL
felony .... BURGLARY, CRIME
felt-like .... PANNOSE
feltwort .... GENTIAN, MULLEIN
female figurine .... ORANT
  " fox .... VIXEN
  " of red deer .... HIND
  " warrior .... AMAZON
feminine suffix .... ETTE
femme fatale . VAMP, LORELEI, CIRCE
femur .... THIGH
fen .... MORASS, BOG, SUMP, SWAMP
fence PALISADE, RADDLE, AHA, HAHA,
    STILE, GLANCE, HURDLE, PALING,
        STOCKADE, RAIL
  " , picket of a .... PALE
  " , to ...... SCRIME, SWORDPLAY
fencer's cry .... HAI, HAY, SASA
fencing; breastplate ...... PLASTRON
  " , foot tap in .... APPEL
  " , hit in .... PUNTO
  " , parrying position in SECONDE
  " posture ... CARTE, PEL, SEPTIME

" ; redoubling of attack . REPRISE
" stroke .... BUTT, APPEL
" sword ..... EPEE, RAPIER, FOIL
" term ..... QUARTE, RIPOSTE,
    TIERCE, PALING
" thrust .. FOIBLE, FORTE, PUNTO,
    REMISE
fend .... AVERT, PARRY, WARD, SHIFT
fennel .... ANIS, MAYWEED
" flowers; genus ...... NIGELLA
Ferdinand II, sobriquet of ... BOMBA
ferment ... SEETHE, YEAST, LEAVEN,
    BARM, FRET, BREW, AGITATE,
    TURMOIL
" , active principle of a ......
    ENZYME
fermenting, stop from .. STUM, MUST
fern .... NARDOO, BRAKE, BRACKEN,
    TARA, OSMUND, TODEA, ANEMIA,
    POLYPODY
" leaf .... FROND
" owl .... NIGHTJAR
" patches .... SORI, SPORES
fern-like plant .. PETROID, ACROGEN
ferocious .. CRUEL, FELL, FERAL, GRIM
ferret .... GIL(L), HOB(B)
ferric-oxide powder .... ROUGE
ferrotype .... TINTYPE
ferry .... PONT, TRAJECT, BAC
fertilizer .. COMPOST, GUANO, MARL,
    MANURE
fervid .... FIERY, HOT, EXCITED
fervor .. ARDOR, ZEAL, ZEST, PASSION
fester .... ABSCESS, RANKLE, ROT,
    ULCERATE, PUTRIFY
festival .. FEIS, BEE, ALE, FEAST, FETE,
    GALA, BAL, FAIR, PICNIC, JUBILEE
" day, last .... APODOSIS
" in Holland .... KERMIS
" , Jewish PURIM, SEDER, SUCCOTH
" of Apollo .... DELIA
" procession .... CORSO
festivity .... JOY, REVEL(RY)
festoon GARLAND, SWAG, LEI, WREATH
fetch .... RETRIEVE, BRING
fetid .... NOISOME, OLID, FUSTY
fetish ..... IDOL, OBI, TOTEM, JUJU,
    MASCOT, AVATAR, MOJO, ANITO,
    CHARM, GRIGRI, AMULET
fetter .. CHAIN, HOBBLE, BOND, GYVE
" , to .... SHACKLE, THRALL
feud ...... QUARREL, FIEF, VENDETTA
feudal land ..... FEOD, FEOFF, SOC,
    SOKE
" , opposed to ...... ALLODIAL
" tax ...... TALLAGE, TAILAGE
" tenant ..... SOCAGER, VASSAL
" tribute .... HERIOT
fever .... AGUE, ARDOR, FRENZY,
    PYREXIA, CAUMA, TERTIAN,
    QUARTAN, OCTAN, TAP, DENGUE

" , affected with .... PYRETIC
" , kind of .. HAY, MARSH, MALTA,
    SPOTTED, UNDULANT, YELLOW
feverish .... FEBRILE, HECTIC
few; Sp. .... POCOS
fez .... CAP, TARBOOSH
fiat .. SANCTION, EDICT, ACT, ORDER
fiber .... NOIL, STRAND, THREAD
" , cordage ... HEMP, ERUC, ADAD,
    FERU
" , kind of .... FILASSE, SISAL
" knots in cotton .... NEP
" of century plant CLUSTERS, PITA
" of E. Indian plant ...... RAMIE
" of wool .... PILE, KEMP
" palm .... AGAVE, RAFFIA
" , Tampico .... ISTLE
" , wood .... BAST
fickle .... VOLATILE, ERRATIC
" girl .... JILT
fictitious .... FALSE, POETIC, BOGUS,
    UNREAL, SPURIOUS
fiddle .. VIOLIN, KIT, CROWD, SCRAPE
fiddler .... TWEEDLEDEE, NERO
fidelity ...... TROTH, FEALTY, LEALTY
fidget ... FANTOD, FRET, FUSS, TWITCH
fidgety ... RESTIVE, UNEASY, NERVOUS
field . ACRE, GLEBE, LEA, GRID, AGER,
    CROFT, WONG
" duck .... BUSTARD
" , extensive ...... SAVANNA(H)
" glass ...... BINOCLE, TELESCOPE
" mouse .... VOLE
" of work .... METIER
" , stubble .... ROWEN
"Field of Blood" .... ACELDAMA
fields, of the .... AGRAL
fiend; Shak. .... AMAIMON
fiendish .... AVERNAL, DEMONIAC,
    SINISTER
fiery ANGRY, HOT, ARDENT, IGNEOUS,
    FERVID
" cross .... CRANTARA
fiesta .... FESTIVAL, HOLIDAY
fife .... FLUTE, PIFERO
fig ...... PIPAL, FICO, CARICA, ELEMI,
    ELEME
" basket .... CABAS, SERON
fight .. BATTLE, MELEE, BARNEY, ROW,
    STRIFE, WARFARE, FRAY, BOUT,
    DUEL, SPAR, TILT, SCRAP, SCUFFLE
" , desire to .... ANIMUS
fig-like .... CARICOUS
" fruit .... SYCONIUM
figs, one cured by: Bib. .. HEZEKIAH
figure ... SYMBOL, BOSH, DIGIT, DOLL,
    FORM, TYPE, ENTAIL, COUNT,
    EFFIGY, SOLID, DECAGON,
    HEXAGON, OUTLINE, STATUE
" , arch. ... CARYATID, TELAMON

" , equal-angled ..... ISAGON, ISOGON
" of speech .... LITOTES, TROPE, METAPHOR, SIMILE
" of the earth .... GEOID
" , part of human . BUST, TORSO, TRUNK
" , to cut a .... DASH
figured .... FACONNE
figurine .... TANAGRA, STATUETTE
filament . STRAND, DOWL, HAIR, HARL, BRIN, FIBER, TENDRIL
filbert .... HAZEL
filch .... NIM, ROB, PILFER, STEAL
file ENTER, ROW, LIST, POLISH, RASP, RECORD, QUANNET, GRAIL
" , combmakers' .... CARLET
" finisher .... ENDER
" fish .... TRIGGERFISH
" of six soldiers .... ROT
filigree ... LACE, DESIGN, OPENWORK
filing .... LIMATION
Filipino .... TAGAL, MORO, ATA
" food staple .... TARO
" knife .... BOLO
" native language ... TAGALOG
fill ... PAD, STUFF, CALK, GLUT, SATE, GORGE, PLUG
filled .... REPLETE, SATED
fillet . SNOOD, BAND, TAENIA, REGULA
" , jeweled .... DIADEM, TIARA
" , narrow .. ANADEM, ORLE, STRIA
fillip .... EXCITE, STIMULUS
filly .... COLT, FOAL, GIRL, MARE
film .... PATINA, PELLICLE, COATING, XRAY, CINEMA, NEGATIVE, BRAT, SCUM
filter .. PERCOLATE, COLATURE, OOZE, CLEAN, SEEP, COLANDER
filth .... SQUALOR, MUCK, LUCRE
fin-footed animal .... PINNIPED
fin, spinous .... ACANTHA
" , under .... VENTRAL
final .... DERNIER, BEALL, END, TELIC, TERMINAL
finale ..... CODA, SWANSONG, FINIS
finch .... SPINK, FRINGILLA, REDPOLL, SISKIN, CHEWINK, JUNCO, TOWHEE, CHAFFINCH, DRAWBIRD, LINNET, BURION, MORO, SERIN, TARIN
finchlike bird .... TANAGRA, CANARY
find faults .... BEEF, CARP
" out ... DETECT, SOLVE, UNRIDDLE
finding, a .... SERENDIPITY
fine ... LEGER, AMERCE, SCOT, MULCT, ABWAB, AMENDE, CRO, EXACT, DELICATE, FORFEIT, PENALTY, TENUOUS, WERGILD, SCONCE
finery . GEEGAWS, FRIPPERY, GAUD(Y)

finesse .... ART, SKILL
Fingal's Cave island .... STAFFA
" kingdom .... MORVEN
fingan stand .... ZARF
finger .... DACTYL, DIGIT
" , fore .... INDEX
" , little .... PINKIE
" , middle .... MEDIUS
" , per. to .. ANNULAR, DIGITAL
" , ring .... ANNULARIS
" stall .... COT, THIMBLE
fingerling .... PARR
fingernail, mark at base of .. LUNULE
fingerprint .... ARCH, LOOP, WHORL
finial .... EPI, TEE, TOP, APEX
finical . PRUDISH, NICE, SPRUCE, FUSSY, FASTIDIOUS
finish ...... POLISH, SHINE, VENEER
finished ...... DONE, OVER, CLOSED, SMOOTH, RIPE
finisher .... EDGER, ENDER
fink SPY, STRIKEBREAKER, SCAB, FINCH
Finland, per. to .. SUOMIC, SUOMISH
Finnish bath .... SAUNA
" coinage ..... MARKKA, PENNI
" dialect .... KAREL
" harp .... KANTELE
" lake .... ENARE
" legislature ...... EDUSKUNTA
" musician .... SIBELIUS
" novelist .... WALTARI
" seaport .... TURKU, ABO
Finno-Ugric language, per. to........ URALIAN
Finns .... SUOMI, VOD
fire ... KINDLE, IGNIS, FLAME, IGNITE
" , artillery .... BARRAGE
" basket .... CRESSET, GRATE
" cracker .... PETARD
" extinguishing substance FOAMITE
" , having power over . IGNIPOTENT
" , miss .... SNAP
" opal .... GIRASOL(E)
" , swamp .... METHANE, GAS
firearm ..... GAT, GUN, COLT, RIFLE, CARBINE, PISTOL, MAUSER, LUGER, MAXIM
firecrackers, box for ..... MARROON
fireman .... VAMP, STOKER
fireplace INGLE, HOB, SHELF, POGON, GRATE, HEARTH
" part ...... MANTEL, REREDOS
firewood ...... LENA, BARIN, FAGOT
fireworks ..... GIRANDOLE, SERPENTS, RIPRAP, GERB(E), FIZGIGS
firm ..... COMPANY, STABLE, STEADY
firmament ..... HEAVEN, SKY, VAULT
firmness, want of .... LAXITY, LOOSE
firn .... ICE, SNOW, NEVE
firs, the .... ABIES

first ...... CAPITAL, INITIAL, PRIMUS,
      CHIEF, NEW, MAIDEN
" born .... HEIR
" day of Roman month .. CALENDS
" installment ... HANDSEL, EARNEST
" letter of alphabet ... ALPHA, ALIF,
      ALEPH
" mate .... EVE
" rate . OK(AY), AONE, TOPS, SUPER
" year's revenue .... ANNAT
" -year man at West Point .... PLEB
firth .... FRITH, KYLE, ARM, FIORD,
      ESTUARY
fish ...... FIN, ANGLE, DRAIL, TRAWL,
      TROLL
" , Amer. fresh-water ..... DARTER
" , Amer. genus; Hyodon ....
      MOONEYE
" , aquatic mammal ..... MANATEE
" , Arctic .... BIB
" , bait .... KILLY
" , barracuda .... SPET, SENNET
" , bin for salting .... KENCH
" , bivalve .... SCALLOP
" , bleak .... BLAY
" , bonito .... SKIPJACK
" , brook trout ...... CHAR, CHARR
" , burbot .... EELPOT, LOTA
" , butter .... GUNNEL
" , caribe .... PIRAYA
" , carp family .... CHUB, IDE, RUD,
      LOACH
" , cat, electric .... RAAD
" , catch of .... SHACK
" , cephaloptera .... MANTA
" , chopped .... CHUM
" , cigar .... SCAD
" , climbing ...... ANABAS, SKIPPER
" , coal .... PARR
" , cobia .... SERGEANT
fish, cod, the .... BACALAO, TORSK
" , cod-like ... CUSK, GADOID, LING
" , condiment .... PASTE
" , cow .... MANATEE
" , crab and fiddler .... UCA
" , Cuban .... ESCOLAR
" , cuttle; genus .... SEPIA
" , cyprinoid .. BARBEL, BREAM, CHI,
      DACE, ID, IDE, TENCH
" , devil .... MANTA, RAY
" , dog .... HOUND, SCYLLIUM
" , dolphin .... COWFISH, INIA
" , E. Ind. .... ARCHER, DARTER,
      DORAB, GOURAMI
" , edible ...... COD, ID, HADDOCK,
      LOACH, TAUTOG, TILE,
      WEEVER, WRASSE
" , eel, bright-colored ..... OPAH,
      MORAY
" , eel, conger .... ELVER

" , eel, marine .... CONGER,
      LAMPREY, LING
" , eel-like .... APOD, LANT
" , eggs .... ROE
" , elasmobranch .... SAWFISH
" , Eur. ..... BARREL, BOCES, DOREE,
      DORY, PICAREL, TENCH
" , Eur. food .... MAIGRE, MEAGRE
" , Eur. shad .... ALOSE
" , Eur. spine .... LYRIE
" , Eur. white .... LAVARET
" (fabled) upholding world ... MAH
" , female .... RAUN
" , fence .... WEIR
" , flat .... DAB, TURBOT, SKATE,
      SOLE, PLAICE
" , flying .... SAURY
" , food .... BAYA, CARP, CERO,
      GROOPER, HAKE, MEAGRE,
      MULLET, PLAICE, POMPANO,
      SARDINE, SCUP, SESELE,
      SHAD, TROUT, TUNA, SMELT
" , fresh-water ... ANABAS, CRAPPIE,
      BURBOT, LOACH, DARTER,
      REDEYE
" , fresh-water; genus .... ESOX
" , frog .... ANGLER
" , game .... MARLIN, SALMON,
      SWORD, TARPON
" , ganoid, large ..... GAR, DIPNOI,
      STURGEON
" ; genus ...... MOLA, PERCA, ELOPS
" ; genus, N. Am. .... AMIA
" , gig .... SPEAR
" , globe .... DIODON
" , gobylike .... DRAGONET
" , grampus .... ORC
" , grouper, red .... MERO
" , grunt .... CROAKER, RONCO
" , halfbeak .... IHI
" hawk .... OSPREY
" , herring .... ALEWIFE, ALOSA,
      SPRAT
" , herring, barrel for .... CADE
" , herring family .... PILCHARD
" , herring-like ... ANCHOVY, CISCO
" , herring, measure .... CRAN
" , herring, young .... BRIT
" hook .... GAFF, SPROAT
" , hound .... GARFISH
" , imperfect .... BARB, THOKE
" , Japanese .... TAI, FUGU
" , jelly .... MEDUSA, ACALEPH
" , jew .... MERO, TARPON
" , king, ocean .... BARB, OPAH
" , ladder .... DAM
" , lake .... LAKER
" , land-traveling .... ANABAS
" , largest fresh-water ... ARAPAIMA
" line, short .... SNELL

97

"	line with series of hooks .. TROT	"	, shad-like .... ALEWIFE
"	, little ...... MINNOW, SARDINE, SMELT	"	, shark .... MAKO, TOPE
"	, mackerel, horse TONNY, TUNNY	"	, shark family .... ANGEL
"	, mackerel-like ... BONITO, CERO, ESCOLAR	"	, shark's pilot .... REMORA
"	, marine .... SCUP, BLENNY, CUSK, LING, GRUNT, CHOPA, MENHADEN, TARPUM	"	, shell ABALONE, LIMPET, SCALLOP

" line with series of hooks .. TROT
" , little ...... MINNOW, SARDINE, SMELT
" , mackerel, horse TONNY, TUNNY
" , mackerel-like ... BONITO, CERO, ESCOLAR
" , marine .... SCUP, BLENNY, CUSK, LING, GRUNT, CHOPA, MENHADEN, TARPUM
" , marine, of W. Indies .. ROBALO
" , maskanonge .... LONGE
" , Medit. .... SARGO
" , milk .... ANGED, AWA, SABALO
" , mollusk, giant OCTOPUS, SQUID
" , mutton; Porto Rico ...... SAMA
" net, bagging of a .... BUNT
" net support .... METER
" , New Zealand .... IHI
" of the Nile .... BICHIR, SAIDE
" , olive-green ... BLENNY, SHANNY
" , ornamental .... PARADISE
" , oyster .... TAUTOG
" , parrot .... LORO, SCAR
" , per. to certain .... TELEOST
" , pen for .... CRAWL
" , perch-like .... DARTER
" , perch-like; genus ...... ANABAS
" , pike .... DORE, GED, LUCE
" , pike-like ...... ARAPAIMA, GAR, LUCE, ROBALO
" , place for .... WARREN
" , pond .... BREAM
" , porgy .... SCUP
" , porgy; Jap. .... TAI
" , pork .... SISI
" , porpoise .... DOLPHIN, INIA
" , poison; Jap. .... FUGU
" , ray .... DOM, MANTA, SEHEN, SKATE
" , red .... CLEE, FATHEAD
" , redmouth .... GRUNT
" , remora .... PEGA
" -rice dish .... KEDGEREE
" , river-ascending ..... ANADROM
" , rock; Cal. .... RENA, REINA
" , sail .... BOOHOO
" , sailor's choice .... PORGY
" , salmon, adult .... GILLING
" , salmon; Jap. .... MASU
" , salmon, second year .... SPROD
fish, salmon, young ... ALEVIN, PARR
" , salmonoid .... POWAN, TROUT
" , salt-water ...... HAKE, TOMCOD, TUNA
" , sandshark .... BONEDOG
" sauce ..... ALEC, ANCHOVY, SOY
" scale .... GANOID
" , scallop .... CRENA
" , sea .... TUNA
" , shad; Eur. .... ALOSE

" , shad-like .... ALEWIFE
" , shark .... MAKO, TOPE
" , shark family .... ANGEL
" , shark's pilot .... REMORA
" , shell ABALONE, LIMPET, SCALLOP
" , shiner .... ROACH
" , shiny, enamel-like .... GANOID
" , silvery; Samoan .... SESELE
" , slender .... SAURIES, GAR, SAURY
" , smelt family .... CAPELIN
" , snapper, black fin .... SESI
" , soap .... JABON
" , S. Amer. .... ACARA, CARIBE
" , spade .... PORGY
" , Spanish .... RONCO
" , sparoid ..... NAPA, PORGY, TAI, SARGO
" spear .... GIG
" , spotted trout .... MALMA
" , squirrel .... MARIAN
" , sturgeon .... STERLET
" , sucking .... REMORA
" , surf .... ALFIONA
" , surgeon .... TANG
" , tarpon family; genus .... ELOPS
" , teleost .... APODA, EEL
" , tench .... TINCA
" , threadfin .... BARBUDO
" , to .... ANGLE, TROLL
" , toad .... SAPO
" trap .... FYKE
" tropical ... BARRACUDA, CHROMID, ROBALO
" , tropical; genus .... GERRES
" , trout family ... OQUASSA, CHAR
" upholding universe .... MAH
" , voracious .... CARIBE, SHARK
" , W. Indian .... SESI
" , whale or sturgeon ..... BELUGA
" , whales, order of .... CETE
" with gaff through ice ..... CHUG
" , whiting ..... LAVARET, GWYNIAD
" with spear-like snout ...... GAR
" , young .... ALEVIN, FRY, PARR
fisher .... WEJACK, PEKAN
fisherman . EELER, SQUAM, ANGLER, SEINER, PISCATOR
" (author) IZAAK WALTON
fishhook ..... ANGLE, BARB, SPROAT, GANGE, HACKLE, FLY, SEDGE
" leader .... SNELL
fishing .... SNELLING, SPILLET
" basket .. SLARTH, CREEL, SLATH
" fly ..... SEDGE, HARL, CAHILL
" , living .... PISCATORY
" smack .... DOGGER
fishlike .... ICHTHYIC
fishline, part of .... BOB, SNOOD
fishman .... HERRINGER
fishpond .... PISCINA

fishwife .... FAG
fissure ...... RIFT, RENT, CLEFT, RIMA,
    CHINK, SLIT, CREVICE, CRACK,
    SPLIT, CHASM, SULCUS
fist MAULEY, MITT, NEIF, NIEVE, NEAF
fit .. COMPETENT, DUE, ELIGIBLE, PAT,
    APT, FAY, HUFF, SPASM,
    TANTRUM, ADAPT
" an arrow on a string ..... NOCK
fitchew .... POLECAT
fitly .... DULY, RIGHT
fitted .... GIFTED, CLEVER, ABLE
" for digging .... FODIENT
fitting .... APT, MEET, JUST, PAT
Fitzgerald, Miss .... ELLA
Fiume .... RIJEKA
five books of Moses .... PENTATEUCH
" finger .... OXLIP
" fold .... QUINTUPLE
" lines of nonsense ..... LIMERICK
" of trumps at cinch ...... PEDRO
" year period ... LUSTRUM, PENTAD
fix ... AMEND, DILEMMA, SET, DEFINE,
    LIMIT, PICKLE, PLIGHT, RIVET,
    SCRAPE, REPAIR
fixed .... FIRM, STABLE, SETTLED
fiordlike passage .... GAT
flaccid ..... LAX, LIMP, FLABBY, WEAK
flag .... GONFALON, BUNTING, SIGN,
    WEAK, FANE, LAG, SINK,
    PENNANT, BANDEROLE,
    ENSIGN, GUIDON, PENNON,
    STREAMER, STANDARD, JACK,
    FANION, BURGEE
" , flower .... IRIS
" , pirate .... ROGER
" , signal .... CORNET
" , sweet .... CALAMUS
flagellants .... ALBI
flageolet ...... LARIGOD, BABAREE
flagon .... JUG, EWER, DEMIJON,
    CANTEEN, CARAFE
flagmaker .... BETSY ROSS
flagstone .... SHALE, SLAB
flail .... SWINGLE, THRESH, BEAT
" , part of ...... SWIPLE, CAPLING
flair .... TALENT, TASTE, BENT, SCENT
flake ... CHIP, FLOCK, LAMINA, SLAKE
flaky .... SQUAMOUS, SCALY
flambeau .... CRESSET, TORCH
flame ..... ARC, BEAM, LEYE, FERVOR,
    GLAZE, ZEAL
flamenco dancer .... AMAYA, GRECO
flaneut .... LOITERER, STROLLER
flank .... LEER, LISK, SIDE
flannel .... DOMMETT
flap .... LAPPET, BANGLE, TAB, LOMA,
    FLUTTER, SLAT, LOBE
flapper .... SNICKET

flare .... BLAZE, FLICKER, GLARE,
    FUSEE, FLASH, SIGNAL, TORCH,
    SPLAY, WIDEN, GLOW
flash .. BLAZE, DAZZLE, SPEED, SPARK,
    GLINT, INSTANT, SHINE
flashy .... GAUDY, SHOWY, LOUD
flask .. CANTEEN, BETTY, CRUSE, OLPE,
    CARAFE, EWER, FLAGON, MATRASS,
    GIRBA
flat .... BANAL, PLANE, PRONE, STALE,
    LOW, SHOAL, JEJUNE, INSIPID,
    FLUSH
" , a .... SUITE
" boat .... PUNT
" canopy .... TESTER
" ; mus. .... BEMOL, MOLL
" part of wine .... VAP
" suface ...AREA, TABULA, PAGINA
flatiron .... SADIRON
flat-nosed .... SIMOUS
flattened ... OBLATE, PLANATE, PLANE
flatter ... PALP, ADULATE, BLAND, OIL,
    EVENER, PLEASE, FAWN, GLOZE
flatterer .... COURTIER, FLUNKY,
    PARASITE, JENKINS
flattery ... BLARNEY, PALAVER, TAFFY,
    OIL, SOAP
flatworm .... TREMATODE
flaunt .. TRAIPSE, BOSH, BOAST, BRAG,
    PARADE, WAVE
flavor SAUCE, AROMA, GUST, SAPOR,
    SEASON, LACE, RELISH, TANG, ZEST,
    SMACK
flavored .... RACY, TINCT
flaw .... FAULT, MAR, RASE, WEM,
    BLEMISH, CRACK, DEFECT
flax .... LINEN, LINT, LIN, LINUM
" bundle .... HEAD
" capsule .... BOLL
" , coarse tow of .... CODILLA
" , comb. .... CARD, HATCHEL
" , dust from .... POUCE
" , earth .... AMIANTHUS
" , fibrous part of .... TOW
" filaments .... HARL
" , like .... TOWY
" , place for process of .... RETTERY
" , prepare .... RET
" , refuse of ... HARDS, HURDS, POB
" seed .... LINSEED
flay ..... EXCORIATE, SCARIFY, CHAFE,
    PARE, PEEL, RACK, SKIN
flea .... PULEX, CHIGOE, CYCLOPS
flee ELOPE, RUN, LAM, BOLT, DECAMP
fleece .... NAP, PILE, SKIN, MULCT,
    ABB, CLIP, HAIR, CHEAT, SHEAR,
    WOOL
fleer .... GIBE, MOCK, SNEER
fleet RAPID, NAVY, ARMADA, ARGOSY,
    ARMADO, FAST

Fleet prison in London .... FLETA
Flemish painter .... RUBENS
flesh, per. to .... CARNOSE, SARCOUS
fleshly ... CARNAL, LUSTFUL, SENSUAL
fleshy ... ADIPOSE, FAT, OBESE, BURLY
" fruit ..... PERA, BACCA, DRUPE,
POME
Fletcher's drama hero ...... AMORET
fleur-de-lis .... LUCE, LUCY, IRIS
flex .... BEND, CURVE, DEFLECT
flexible ..... LIMBER, LISSOME, LITHE,
PLIANT, SUPPLE, WILLOWY
flexion of a limb .... ANACLASIS
flexure .. GENU, CROOK, FOLD, BEND,
CURVE, TURN
flight ..... EXODUS, HEGIRA, GAGGLE,
HOP, BEVY, COVEY
flightless .... RATITE
flighty ..... BARMY, FICKLE, VOLATILE
flimflam .... HOCUS, TRICK, HOAX,
HUMBUG
flimsy ... FRAGILE, SHALLOW, SLEAZY
flinch ...... QUAIL, BLENCH, WINCE,
WONDE, SWERVE
fling about .... AGITATE, BETOSS
flint .... CLINT, CHERT, SILEX
flippant .... GLIB, PERT, BOLD, SASSY
flirt .. FIKE, JILL, COQUET(TE), DALLY,
TOY, TRIFLE
flit .... FLICKER, HOVER, FLY, GAD,
DART, SCUD, SKIM
flittermouse .... BAT
float .... BUOY, QUILL, LURE, RAFT,
CORK, SELL, WAFT, SWIM
floating ... AWASH, NATANT, ADRIFT
" plant .... FROGBIT
flock .. COVEY, BEVY, DROVE, HIRSEL,
HERD, GAGGLE, RAFT, SEDGE,
SCHOOL, TROOP, GATHER, SWARM,
HORDE, HATCH, BROOD, MOB
" , of a .... GREGAL
flog LARRUP, WALE, CAT, TAN, YANK,
WELT, WHIP, BALEISE, LASH
flogging .... TOKO, TOCO
flood ... CATARACT, CATACLYSM, SEA,
BORE, SPATE, DELUGE, EAGRE,
TIDE, TORRENT
" gate ..... CLOW, SLUICE, GOOL
" lights .... KLIEG
floor ..... PAVE OVERTHROW, PLAYA,
BEAT, DECK, STORY, DEFEAT,
COAMING
" leader .... WHIP
flooring .... BATTEN, SLAB, TILE
" slab .... DALLE
flop .... FAIL, FAILURE, LEMON, SLUMP
Flopsy .... COTTONTAIL, RABBIT
flora and fauna .... BIOTA
floral leaves .... PERIANTH

Florence gallery .... PITTI, UFFIZI
" river .... ARNO
" family .... MEDICI
florid .... ORNATE
" style .... MELISMA, ROCOCO
Florida city .. MIAMI, TAMPA, NAPLES
" county .... BAY, CLAY, DADE,
GULF, LAKE, LEE, LEON, LEVY,
PASCO, POLK
" plant .... COONTIE
" river fish .... TETARD
floss .. RUSHES, SLEAVE, STREAM, SILK,
THREAD
Flotow opera .... MARTHA
flounder .... PLAICE, TURBOT, WELTER,
DAB, FAIL, ROLL, WALLOW
flour .... ATA, ATTA, FARINA
" and butter mix .... ROUX
" pudding .... DUFF
flourish .... PARAPH, WAVE, FUSTIAN,
TANTARA, ROULADE, VAUNT,
PROSPER
flout .... JIBE, JEER, SCOFF, FLEER,
SCORN, TRUSS, TAUNT
flow ...... OOZE, SPOUT, WELL, RUN,
FLUX, GUSH, TEEM
" of the tide .... EBB, NEAP
" out .... EXUDE, ISSUE
flower .... BLOOM, ELITE, POSY
flower, aromatic .... CAMOMILE
" , August .... POPPY
" , avens, yellow ...... BENNET
" , buckwheat, fragrant ..... TITI
" bud .... KNOT
" , burry .... TEASEL
" , butterfly lily ..... MARIPOSA
" , cardinal .... LOBELIA
" center .... EYE
" cluster .... UMBEL
" cluster, elongated .... RACEME
" cluster, flat top .... CYME
" cluster, leaf in a ...... BRACT
" clusters, arranged in
PANICULATE
" , cormus .... CROCUS
" , delicate pink ...... RHODORA
" , dogrose, fruit of .... HIP
" , dry .... AZALEA
" , Egypt, sacred .... LOTUS
" envelope .... PERIANTH
" , erica; genus .... HEATH
" extract .... ATTAR, OTTO
" , felwort .... GENTIAN
" , field .... GOWAN
" , fragrant .... JASMINE
" , full bloom .... ANTHESIS
" , garden .... FREESIA
" garden .... GREENERY
" ; genus .. ROSA, ADONIS, VIOLA
" growing in meadows .. PRATAL

100

" having leaves in sets of three .. TRILLIUM
" head .... PANICLE, TEASEL
" , heath .... AZALEA
" , hibiscus; E. Ind. .... ROSELLE
" , honeysuckle .... ELDER
" , hyacinth, wild .... CAMAS
" , in .... BELL
" , indigo .... ANIL
" , iris .... ORRIS
" , Japanese .... UDO
" , jasmine; Arab. .... BELA
" , large white .... BARTONIA
" leaf .... BRACT
" , lily .... ARUM, LOTUS, SEGO
" , lily, butterfly ...... MARIPOSA
" , lily, corn .... IXIA
" , lily, palm .... TI
" , marigold .... COWSLIP
" , meadow .... BLUET
" , New York State .... ROSE
" , nightshade .... TRILLIUM
" , Oklahoma .... MISTLETOE
" of forgetfulness .... LOTUS
" of kings .... ARTHUR
" of poets .... CHAUCER
" , orchid; N. Am. .... ARETHUSA
" , part of ...... ANTHER, BRACT,
        PISTIL, SEPAL, STAMEN
" , passion .... MAYPOP
" , pinks, the .... SILENE
" pistil .... CARPEL
" plat .... BED
" , ragwort, purple ..... JACOBY
" , reseda .... MIGNONETTE
" rootstock .... TARO
" , rose of Sharon .... LOTUS
flower, rose, Persian .... GUL
" , rose, wild .... SWEETBRIAR
" , seed, a .... OVULE
" , sheath of a .... SPATHE
" , showy, peren. .... AZALEA,
        ORCHID, CAMELLIA
" sifter .... BOLTER
" spicule, star-shaped ..... ASTER
" spike .... AMENT, SPADIX
" , spring .... HYACINTH
" stalk PEDUNCLE, KEMP, PETIOLE
" stand .... EPERGNE
" , starwort .... ASTER
" ; summit of stamen .... ANTHER
" , Swiss .... EDELWEISS
" , Syrian .... RETEM
" , genus; syringa .... LILAC
" , the .... ELITE
" , turban .... TULIP
" , unfading .... AMARANTH
" , water lily .... LOTUS
" , white weed .... DAISY
" , willow, bed .... OSIERY

" , wind .... ANEMONE
" , wood sorrel .... OXALIS
" , yellow, medicinal ...... RUE
flowering grasses; genus ..... STIPA
flowerless plant FERN, LICHEN, MOSS,
        ACROGEN
flower-like .... ANTHOID
"Flower of My Heart" .... ADELINE
flowers, bunch of .. POSY, NOSEGAY,
        BOUQUET
flower-shaped .... FLEURON
flowing .... AFFLUX, CURSIVE,
        EMANANT, FLUX
flowering again .... REMONTANT
fluctuate .... SWAY, WAVER, VIBRATE,
        UNDULATE, VACILLATE
fluctuating; mus. .... RUBATO
fluent .... FREE, FACILE, APT, GLIB,
        COPIOUS, VOLUBLE
fluff .. FLOSS, LINT, FLOCK, PRIMP, ERR,
        NAP, DOWN
fluid .... FLUX, STEAM, SAP, GAS,
        LIQUID, PLASMA, SALIVA
" ; myth. .... ICHOR
fluidity unit .... RHE
fluke ...... BLADE, HOOK, FLOUNDER
flume ...... CHUTE, SLUICE, CONDUIT
flunk ...... FAIL, FLINCH, SLIP, SHIRK
flunk(e)y .... TOADY, FOOTMAN,
        LACKEY
flurry ... FRET, ADO, FLUSTER, POTHER
flush ... EVEN, BLUSH, LEVEL, REDDEN
flushed ... AGLOW, FLORID, RED, RUBY
fluster POTHER, FAZE, RUFFLE, ADDLE,
        UPSET
flute .... CRIMP, GROOVE, SHUTTLE
" , nose .... PUNGI
" of bagpipe .... CHANTER
" player .... TOOTLER, AULETE
" stop .... VENTAGE
" , transverse .... FIFE
fluting .... STRIX, GADROON
flutter .... AGITATE, FLIT, WAVE, FLAP,
        HOVER, QUIVER
flutteringly .... PITAPAT
fly .... AVIATE, SOAR, WHIR, WHEW,
        WING, DART, FLAP, FLIT, HERL,
        SCUD, GLIDE
" ; Afr. ... TSETSE, ZIMB, SEBUB, MAU
" , artifical .... SEDGE, CLARET
" block .... PULLEY
" close to the ground .. HEDGEHOP
" , golden-eyed .... LACEWING
" , very small .... GNAT, MIDGE
flyaway .... GIDDY
flybane .... SILENE
flyblow .... LARVA
flycatcher .... PEEWEE, PHOEBE,
        KINGBIRD, TODY
flying .... VOLANT, AWING

101

```
"     condition ............. YARAK        foolhardy ....... (B)RASH, RECKLESS,
"Flying Finn" ............... NURMI                                     ICARIAN
flying signal ............... ROGER        foolish ... HARISH, INEPT, RACA, MAD,
flywheel ................... WHORL                     ASININE, PUERILE, ZANY
Flynn, Mr. ................. ERROL         "    fancy ............. CHIMERA
foam ... SCUM, BARM, FROTH, SPUME,         fool's bauble ............ MAROTTE
          SUDS, BOIL, RAGE, LATHER,        "     gold .................. PYRITE
                FERMENT, YEAST             "     stitch ............... TRICOT
fob ............ CHEAT, TRICK, SHAM        foot ... PAW, PES, PAD, PUD, TOTAL,
Foch, actress ............... NINA                                   HOOF, DOG
focus ... HUB, CORE, HEART, NUCLEUS        "   of three morae ....... TRISEME
fodder .......... (EN)SILAGE, FORGE        " , part of a ............. INCH
fodder, rel. to ...... FORAGE, VETCH       " , per. to .......... PEDI, PODAL
"    straw ............... STOVER          " , per. to the sole of a .. PLANTAR
fog .. AEROSOL, SMOG, BRUME, HAAR,         " , poetic ..... IAMB(US), ANAPEST,
          ROKE, VAPOR, RAG, MIST, MURK               DACTYL, TROCHEE, SPONDEE
foghorn ..................... SIREN        " , study of ............ PODIATRY
fogdog ..................... STUBB         foot-and-mouth disease .... MURRAIN
foggy .......... CLOUDY, NUBILOUS          football field ................. GRID
fogy .. FOGRAM, HUNKER, MOSSBACK,          "     team ............... ELEVEN
                                 DODO      "     term .... PASS, END, DOWN,
foil BALK, EPEE, STOOGE, LEAF, FAZE           GOAL, PUNT, TACKLE, LATERAL
fold ... PLEAT, CRIMP, LAP, PLY, RUGA,     footed, large- ............ MEGAPOD
      WRAP, CLASP, PLICA, DRAPE, PEN,      footing ............... BASIS, TERMS
                        CREASE, COTE       footless ...... APOD, FREE, NOMADIC
folded; fan ................ PLICATE       foot-like ................... PEDATE
foliage ... SPRAY, LEAFAGE, BOUQUET        footpad ..... THUG, WHYO, BRIGAND,
foliated .................... SPATHIC              HIGHWAYMAN, HOOD, ROBBER,
folio .......... PAGE, BOOK, ATLAS                                    BANDIT
folksinger ......... (BURL)IVES, BAEZ      footprint ....... SPOOR, TRACK, SLOT
folkways .......... CUSTOMS, MORES         foot-race, double-course ... DIAULOS
follow ..... HEED, DOG, ENSUE, TAG,        footstalk ............ PEDICEL, STRIG,
      TRACE, IMITATE, PURSUE, HOUND,                     PEDUNCLE, PETIOLE
                OBEY, TRAIL, TAIL          footstool ....... HASSOCK, OTTOMAN
follower .. COPIER, SEQUENT, VOTARY,       footway in airship ........ CATWALK
      FAN, IST, ITE, APER, BUFF, PUPIL,    fop ....... DUDE, NOB, ADON, BUCK,
                              ADDICT              PUPPY, DANDY, SWELL, TOFF
following RETINUE, NEXT, SECT, SINCE       for .................. BECAUSE, PRO
folly ....... FATUITY, LEVITY, LUNACY      "   example; Lat. ............. VIDE
foment ..... BREW, ABER, SPUR, STUPE       "   fear that ................. LEST
fondle .. COSSET, INGLE, PET, CODDLE       "   this reason ....... HENCE, ERGO
fondling ......... CARESSANT, NINNY        forage ........ FOOD, PLUNDER, RAID,
fondness ......... GRA, LOVE, DESIRE                       MARAUD, FODDER
font ..... ORIGIN, TYPE, BASIN, LAVER,     foray .... INCURSION, RAID, PILLAGE,
                    STOOP, SOURCE                          INROAD, SALLY
food ..... PEMMICAN, ALIMENT, DIET,        forbear ..... ANCESTOR, SPARE, STOP
      FARE, ORT, PAP, POI, VIANDS,         forbearance ..... MERCY, GRACE, PITY
      TUCKER, SCUFF, CHYME, SCRAN,         forbearing ..... TOLERANT, LENIENT
          CHOW, EATS, GRUB, SNACK,         forbid .. TABOO, BAN, INHIBIT, VETO,
                AMRITE, PABULUM                             ENJOIN, DEBAR
" ; cocoa preparation ..... BROMA          forbidden city ............... LHASA
" , lack of desire for ...... ASITIA       forbidding . GRIM, PLAIN, STERN, UGLY
" , miracle .............. MANNA           force .... COMPEL, DINT, VIS, POWER,
" of the gods .......... AMBROSIA                       VIGOR, ENERGY, ARMY
" room .................. SPENCE           "   alleged ....... OD(YLE), ELOD
" source .................. TARO           " , brief and sudden ..... BRUNT
fool ....... IDIOT, DUPE, NIZY, ZANY,      " , by ................. AMAIN
      DOTARD, OAF, JERK, RACA, MORON       "   down ............. DETRUDE
" hen .................. GROUSE            " , unit of ............... DYNE
" of the court ............ JESTER         forced feeding ........... GAVAGE
```

forcemeat .... FARCE
forcing substance .... CATALYST
Ford .... EDSEL, HENRY
Fordham's team .... RAMS
fore .... PRIOR, VAN
forearm, per. to .... ULNAR
foreboding .... OMEN, AUGURY,
PORTENT, MENACE
forecaster ...... SEER, NOSTRADAMUS,
TOUT, TIPSTER
forefather .... PROGENITOR
forefoot .... PAW
forefront .... VANGUARD, VAN
foregoing .... ABOVE, PAST
forehead .... BROW, SINCIPUT
forehead, of the .... METOPIC
foreign .... ECDEMIC, PEREGRINE,
EPIGENE, FORANE, EXOTIC, FREMD
foreign quarter ...... ENCLAVE, PARA
foreigner ...... HAOLE, EMIGRE, ALIEN,
GRINGO
foreordain .... DESTINE
foremost part .... BOW, VAN, ACRON
forerun .. ANTECEDE, HERALD, PIONEER,
SCOUT
foreshank .... SHIN
foreshadow ..... ADUMBRATE, PRESAGE
forest .. COPSE, GAPO, ARDEN, GROVE,
GUBAT, SHERWOOD, SYLVA, TAIGA
    " keeper .... RANGER
    " , open space in ...... CLEARING,
GLADE
    " , per. to ..... NEMORAL, SILVAN
    " road .... RIDE
foretell .... READ, AUGUR, BODE, SPAE,
PRESAGE, INSEE, VATICINATE
foretoken .... OMEN, AUGURY
forever .... AKE, ETERN(E), AYE
forfeit .... FIN, KEN, LAPSE, LOSE
forfeiture .... FINE, DEDIT, LOSS, TORT
forge .... MINT, STITHY, IMITATE,
BLOOMERY
forget .... LAPSE
forgetfulness .... LETHE, OBLIVION,
MANASSEH, AMNESIA
forgive ...... EXCUSE, ABSOLVE, REMIT,
PARDON
forgiving .... CLEMENT
forgo . NEGLECT, RESIGN, WAIVE, DENY
fork .... GRAIP, PRONG, TINE
forked .... FURCATE
form .. CAST, CONTOUR, MOLD, EIDOS,
RUPA, MODEL, TAILLE, RITUAL
    " , per. to .... MODAL
formal .... PRIM, STIFF
    " entrance .... DEBUT
formation ... HERSE, FILE, LINE, BIOME
former(ly) ... ERST, NEE, PRIOR, ONCE,
QUONDAM, WHILOM, ANTERIOR,
PASSE, THEN

former days .... ELD, OLD, YORE
formless .. ANIDIAN, CHAOTIC, ARUPA
formula .... CREED, LAW, RULE, LURRY,
RITUAL, MAXIM, MANTRA
forsaken .... LORN, DESERTED
Forsyte _____ .... SAGA
fort .... ABATIS, DUN, BULWARK, POST,
REDAN, CASTLE, COTTA, CITADEL,
REDOUBT, DIX, ORD, PAH,
GARRISON
    " , sloping bank of .... GLACIS
fortification ...... PARADOS, BASTION,
RAVELIN, TALUS
fortified landing place ... BEACHHEAD,
BRIDGEHEAD
fortify .... GIRD, ARM, MAN, STANK
fortress .... ALCAZAR, KAME, KEEP,
BASTILLE, DONJON, CAMP
    " , outwork of a .... TENAIL
fortunate ... DEXTER, FAUST, BLEST, SRI
fortune .... HAP, LOT, BAHI, STAR,
HAZARD, RICHES, ESTATE
    " teller .... SEER, SIBYL, ORACLE,
PALMIST, PROPHET(ESS), SPAEMAN
forty-five-degree angle ...... OCTANT
forty-two-gallon cask .... TERCE
forty winks .... NAP
forward .... PERT, FRONT, AHEAD,
ACTIVE, EAGER
    " , moving .... PROAL
fossil .... BALANITE
    " egg .... OVULITE
    " footprint .... ICHNITE
    " resin .... AMBER
    " shell .... DOLITE
    " , toothlike .... CONODONT
    " tubular structure .... SCIOLITE
    " worm track .... NEREITE
foster .... REAR, BREED, NURSE
    " child ... STEPSON, DALT, NURRY
foul-smelling ...... OLID, FETID, REEKY
foundation ..... BEDROCK, BASE, BASIS
founder .. AUTHOR, FAIL, SINK, WELTER
fountain .. WELL, FONT, HEAD, GENESIS,
SPRING, SPA, SYKE, FONS
    " nymph ...... NAIAD, EGERIA
    " of youth .... BIMINI
four-footed .... TETRAPOD
four-bagger .... HOMER
four-in-hand .... ASCOT, SCARF
fourpence .... GROAT, FLAG, JOEY
foursome .... TETRAD
fourteen pounds .... STONE
fourth calif .... ALI
fourth-century saint .... BLAISE
fourth estate .... PRESS
fourth gate, founding .... GIT
fowl .... CAPON, POULT, COCK, HEN,
DORKIN, LEGHORN, MINORCA

103

fox .. ASSE, FENNEC, ADIVE, CORSAC, KARAGAN, KALONG, STAG
", female .... VIXEN
" hunter's coat .... PINK
" " hazard .... OXER
" killer .... VULPECIDE
", paw of .... PAD
foxglove .... POPPY, THIMBLE
" leaves .... DIGITALIS
foxtail .... CAUDA, CHAPE
fraction .... PART, DECIMAL
fragile .... FRAIL, FROUGH, SLATTERY
fragment .. SNIP, ORT, SCRAP, SHARD, WISP, ANA
fragment(s) FLINDER, FARDEL, GROTS
fragrance .. AROMA, INCENSE, ATTAR
fragrant ...... BALMY, ODORIFEROUS, REDOLENT
fragrant ointment .. VALERIAN, NARD
" wood MIMOSA, ALOE, CEDAR
frail .... FLIMSY, SEELY, FEEBLE
frailty .. ADAM, FAULT, DEFECT, FLAW, FOIBLE
frambesia .... YAWS
frame . CHASSIS, RACK, SESS, TENTER, FORM, TRESSEL, TRESTLE, TRUSS
" , counting .... ABACUS
" for fishline .... CADRE
" for glassmaking .... DROSSER
" on ship's table .... FIDDLE
" , skin-drying .... HERSE
framework .. CRADLE, SHELL, STILLAGE
France (see also "French")
" , anc. name .. GALLIA, GAUL
" , dialect in .... PATOIS
" , early conqueror of .. CLOVIS
" , edict in; law .... ARRET
" , nickname of .... MARIANNE
" , patron saint of ...... DENIS
" , Southern .... MIDI
" , symbol of .... COCK
franchise RIGHT, LICENSE, VOTE, SOC, SOKE, BALLOT, CHARTER
Franciscan .... MINORITE
Franciscan mission .... ALAMO
francolin .... TITAR
frank .... FREE, MARK, OPEN, EXEMPT, CANDID
frankincense ...... OLIBANUM, THUS
Frankish dynasty .... MEROVINGIAN
" king .... CLOVIS
" vassal .... LEUD
Franklin sobriquet .... BEN
Franks, per. to .... SALIC
frantic, become .... MANG
fraud ... DECEIT, IMPOSTURE, COVIN, SHAM, BUNCO, GUILE
fraught .... FILLED, LADEN
fray .. RUCTION, TIFFLE, CHAFE, RAVEL, HASSLE, MELEE

freak .... CAPRICE, FLAM, WHIM
freckle ...... SPOT, TACHE, LENTIGO
Frederick .... BARBAROSSA, FRITZ
free .... ABSOLVE, LAX, FRANK, LIBRE, RID, MANUMIT, RELEASE, LIBERAL, GRATIS
" from restraint .... UNTIE
freebooter .... CATERAN, PIRATE
freedman .... THANE, LAET
freedom from doubt ..... CERTITUDE
" from infection .... ASEPSIS
freehold .... LAND, ODAL
freeholder .... YEOMAN
freeman .... CEORL, CHURL, THEGN, THANE
Freeman, Miss .... MONA
freemason .... TEMPLAR
freeze .. BEICE, ICE, STEEVE, CONGEAL
fremd .... FOREIGN, STRANGE, ALIEN
French ... GASCON, GAUL, NORMAN, PICARD
" abbott .... ABBE
" according .... SELON
" actor .. FERNANDEL, AUMONT, CHEVALIER, MONTAND
" again .... ENCORE
" alb .... AUBE
" all .... TOUT(E), TOUS
" alone .... SEUL
" almost .... PRES
" also .... AUSSI
" among .... ENTRE, PARMI
" angel .... ANGE
" annuity .... RENTE
" arm .... BRAS
" article ...... LE, LA, LES, UN, UNE(S)
" artillery officer .... DREYFUS
" artist MANET, MONET, DEGAS, COROT, RENOIR, MILLET, RAPIN, GAUGUIN, MARIN, DORE
" at the home of .... CHEZ
" aunt .... TANTE
" author RENAN, DUMAS, HUGO, LOTI, GIDE, CAMUS, SARTRE
" awkward .... GAUCHE
" ax .... HACHE
" baby . BEBE, ENFANT, POUPEE
" bath .... BAIN
" bay .... BISCAY
" beach .. PLAGE, RIVE, RIVAGE
" bean ... HARICOT, PHASEOLE, FEVE
" beast .... BETE
" be(ing) .... ETRE
" bed .... COUCHE, LIT
" beef .... BOEUF
" beer .... BIERE
" before .... AVANT
" better .... MIEUX

"	between	ENTRE	"	deed	FAIT

" between .... ENTRE
" beware .... GARDE
" bicycle .... VELO
" bitter .... AMER
" black .... NOIR(E)
" blest .... BENI, SACRE
" blue .... BLEU
" blunder .... GAFFE
" book .... LIVRE
" bread .... PAIN
" bridegroom .... MARIE
" bridge .... PONT
" brother .... FRERE
" brown .... BRUN(E)
" but .... MAIS
" cabbage .... CHOU
" cake ...... GATEAU, DARIOLE
" cardinal . MAZARIN, RICHELIEU
" chalk .... TALC
" chanteuse .... PIAF
" cheese ...... FROMAGE, BRIE
" chemist . HOLBACH, PASTEUR,
                        CURIE
" chicken .... POULE
" city ... ARLES, NIMES, TOURS,
       RIOM, CANNES, NICE, LYON,
                        DIJON
" cleric .... ABBE
" cloth .... DRAP, TOILE
" coin LIARD, ECU, OBOLE, SOU,
                        RIAL
" cloud .... NUAGE
" coach .... FIACRE
" cold .... FROID
" comfort .... AISE
" commune .... NERAC, ANCRE,
                TARARE, USSEL
" company .... CIE
" composer .... LALO, HALEVY,
                RAVEL, INDY
" cop .... FLIC
" corn .... BLE, MESLIN
" cost .... PRIX, COUT
" count .... COMTE
" country .... PAYS
" couturier .... CHANEL, DIOR,
                CARDIN
" cow .... VACHE
" cowardly .... LACHE
" credit .... FOI
" critic .... TAINE
" crude .... CRU
" cup .... TASSE
" dancer .... DANSEUSE
" dare .... OSER
" daughter .... FILLE
" dawn .... AUBE
" day .... JOUR
" dear .... CHER(E), CHERI
" decree .... ARRET

" deed .... FAIT
" defiance .... DEFI
" department .... ORNE, EURE,
       GARD, ARIEGE, AIN, AUBE,
                        AUDE
" department head .... PREFECT
" devil .... DIABLE
" dialect .... PATOIS
" doff .... OTER
" donkey .... ANE
" down .... BAS
" down with .... ABAS
" dramatist . COCTEAU, DUMAS
" dream .... REVE(R)
" drunk .... IVRE
" dry .... SEC
" dugout .... ABRI
" duke .... DUC
" dynasty ...... VALOIS, CAPET
" earth .... TERRE
" ease .... AISE
" east .... EST
" egg .... OEUF
" elder .... AINE
" empress .... EUGENIE
" enamel ware ...... LIMOGES
" enough .... ASSEZ
" equal(ity) .... EGAL(ITE)
" error .... FAUTE
" evening .... SOIR
" event .... CAS
" evil .... MAL
" exclamation .... HEIN
" explorer .... CARTIER
" eye .... OEIL
" fabric ... GROS, LAME, RAS
" faith .... FOI
" false .... FAUX, FAUSSE
" fame .... BRUIT
" farewell .... ADIEU
" fat .... GRAS
" father .... PERE
" fault .... FAUTE
" fear .... PEUR
" finally .... ENFIN
" financier .... NECKER
" finger .... DOIGT
" fire .... FEU, TIR
" floor .... ETAGE
" flower .... FLEUR
" fold .... PLI
" fool(ish) .... FOU
" forward .... AVANT
" fresh .... FRAIS(E)
" friend .... AMI(E)
" full .... PLEIN(E)
" game(s) .... JEU(X)
" gentle .... DOUX
" gilded .... DORE
" glass .... VERRE

105

"	glove .... GANT		"	mail .... POSTE
"	go .... ALLER		"	mamma .... MAMAN
"	God .... DIEU		"	man .... HOMME
"	good .... BON(NE)		"	manner .... SORTE
"	goose .... OIE		"	marshal .. FOCH, MURAT, NEY,
"	grave .... TOMBE			SAXE, PETAIN
"	gravy .... JUS		"	matin lay .... AUBADE
"	gray .... GRIS(E)		"	mayor .... MAIRE
"	green .... VERT(E)		"	meal .... REPAS
"	greeting .... SALUT		"	measure .. AUNE, ELL, TOISE,
"	grimace .... MOUE			VELTE, METRE, LITRE
"	guerilla fighters .... MAQUIS		"	merry .... GAI
"	hall .... SALLE		"	metaphysician ... DESCARTES
"	hand .... MAIN		"	method of fighting .. SAVATE
"	handle .... ANSE		"	milk .... LAIT
"	have .... AVOIR		"	mime .... MARCEAU
"	head .... TETE		"	misdemeanor .... DELIT
"	health .... SANTE		"	miser .... AVARE
"	heaven .... CIEL		"	mix .... MELER
"	heavy .... LOURD		"	month .... MOIS, MAI, MARS,
"	hell .... ENFER			JUIN, AVRIL, AOUT
"	here ICI		"	morning .... MATIN
"	high .... HAUT(E)		"	mother .... MERE
"	historian ... GUIZOT, RENAN,		"	mountains VOSGES, PYRENEES,
	THIERS			BLANC, CENIS
"	honor .... FOI		"	mountain pass .... COL
"	hot .... CHAUD(E)		"	museum .... MUSEE
"	hour .... HEURE		"	nail .... CLOU
"	house .... MAISON		"	name .... NOM
"	hunger .... FAIM		"	naval base .... LORIENT
"	husband .... MARI		"	near .... PRES
"	ill(ness) .... MAL(ADIE)		"	new .... NEUF, NEUVE
"	in .... DANS, CHEZ		"	night .... NUIT
"	income .... RENTE		"	nobleman ...... COMTE, DUC
"	ink .... ENCRE		"	noise .... BRUIT
"	iron .... FER		"	noon .... MIDI
"	island . ILE, CORSICA, OLERON		"	north .... NORD
"	lace .... CLUNY, ALENCON		"	nothing .... RIEN
"	lack .... FAUTE		"	novelist . MAURIAC, MAUROIS,
"	land .... TERRE, PAYS			BALZAC, DAUDET, LOTI, BENDA,
"	large .... GRAND(E)			SAND, PROUST
"	late .... TARD		"	nurse .... BONNE
"	laugh .... RIRE, RIS		"	painter .. MANET, DAUBIGNY,
"	law .... LOI			DEGAS, COROT, LEMOINE,
"	leather .... CUIR			MILLET, RENOIR, DERAIN
"	leave .... CONGE		"	pancake .... CREPE
"	legislature .... SENAT		"	pause .... ARRET
"	length unit .... ARPENT		"	paving brick .... DALLE
"	less .... MOINS		"	peace .... PAIX
"	level .... UNI		"	pear .... POIRE
"	light .... LEGER		"	penalty .... PEINE
"	like .... COMME		"	people .... GENS
"	liking .... GRE		"	permission .... CONGE
"	lily .... LIS		"	petticoat .... JUPE
"	liquor .... COGNAC		"	philosopher .. BAYLE, SARTRE
"	little .... PEU		"	plane .... SPAD
"	love .... AMOUR, AIMER		"	pocket .... POCHE
"	lover .... AMANT		"	poem .... VERS, DIT
"	lyric ...... DESCORT, RONDEL		"	poet .. VILLON, BAIF, MAROT,
"	maid .... BONNE			VERLAINE

"	porcelain .... SEVRES	"	son .... FILS
"	port .. BREST, CAEN, TOULON	"	soul .... AME
"	president ... LOUBET, GREVY,	"	south .... SUD, MIDI
	COTY, LEBRUN, POMPIDOU	"	spirit .... ELAN, ESPRIT
"	pretty .... JOLI(E)	"	spoken .... DIT
"	priest .... ABBE	"	square .... CARRE
"	price .... PRIX	"	stable .... ECURIE
"	promissory note .. ASSIGNAT	"	star .... ETOILE
"	pronoun .... IL(S), MOI, TOI,	"	statesman . MORNY, CARNOT,
	SOI, ELLE, EUX, LUI, NOUS,		POINCARE
	VOUS	"	stocking .... BAS
"	psychologist ... BINET, COUE	"	stoneware .... GRES
"	pupil .... ELEVE	"	storm .... ORAGE
"	purchase .... ACHAT	"	street .... RUE
"	quick .... VITE	"	stupid .... BETE
"	rabbit .... LAPIN	"	subway .... METRO
"	racecourse .... AUTEUIL	"	sum .... SOMME
"	railway station .... GARE	"	summer .... ETE
"	read .... LIRE	"	surgery, father of .... PARE
"	ready .... PRET	"	sweet .... DOUX, DOUCE
"	recruit .... BLEU	"	sweetbreads .... RIS
"	red .... ROUGE	"	thanks .... MERCI
"	remove .... OTER	"	then ... PUIS, ALORD, DONC
"	rent .... LOUER	"	there! .... VOILA
"	reputation .... BRUIT	"	thirst .... SOIF
"	resort ANTIBES, MENTON, PAU,	"	thread .... FIL
	AIX, CANNES	"	thus .... AINSI
"	revolutionist DANTON, MARAT	"	tie .... LIER
"	ridge .... VIMY	"	time .... FOIS, TEMPS
"	right .... DROIT	"	town ... AGEN, CRECY, LOOS,
"	ring .... BAGUE		NESLE, NERAC, RIOM, SETE,
"	river AIRE, AUBE, ISERE, LOIRE,		PAU, SENS
	LYS, SOMME, MARNE, MEUSE,	"	trade tax .... PATENTE
	RANCE, ORNE, SEINE, SAONE	"	tree .... ARBRE
"	roast .... ROTI	"	true .... VRAI
"	roof .... TOIT	"	uncle .... ONCLE
"	room .... SALLE	"	under .... SOUS
"	safety .... SALUT	"	underground troops . MAQUIS
"	sailor .... MARIN	"	united .... UNI
"	saw .... SCIE	"	upon .... SUR, SUS
"	saying .... DIT	"	"Upper House" ...... SENAT
"	scholar .... ABELARD	"	very .... TRES
"	school .... LYCEE, ECOLE	"	vineyard .... VIGNE, CRU
"	school of painting BARBIZON	"	wall .... MUR
"	sculptor . BARYE, RODIN, ETEX	"	warm .... CHAUD
"	see .... VOIR	"	warning .... AVIS
"	shelter ...... ABRI, COUVERT	"	water .... EAU
"	shield .... EGIDE, TARGE,	"	wave .... ONDE
	BOUCLIER	"	weapon .... ARME
"	silk .... SOIE, GROS	"	weekday ..... LUNDI, MARDI,
"	silk center .... LYON(S)		JEUDI, SAMEDI
"	skin .... PEAU	"	weight .... POIDS
"	skirt .... JUPE	"	well .... BIEN
"	sky .... CIEL	"	wheat .... BLE
"	slang .... ARGOT	"	when .... QUAND
"	slight .... LEGER(E)	"	where .... OU
"	snow .... NEIGE	"	white .... BLANC, BLANCHE
"	so much .... TANT	"	wine .... VIN
"	soap .... SAVON	"	wing(ed) .... AILE
"	soldier .... POILU	"	winter .... HIVERS

"	wolf	LOUP

" wolf .... LOUP
" wood .... BOIS, FORET
" workman .... BLOUSE
" world .... TERRE, MONDE
" worse .... PIS, PIRE
" writer .... RENAN, STAEL,
   VOLTAIRE, ZOLA, VILLON,
   FEUILLET, DAUDET
" yellow .... JAUNE
" yes .... OUI
" yesterday .... HIER
" young .... JEUNE
Frenchman . PICARD, GAUL, PARISIAN
frenzied ... BERSERK, ENRAGED, MAD,
   AMOK
frenzy .... AMUCK, FURY, MANIA,
   LUNACY, DELIRIUM
frequent .... OFT, HAUNT, HABITUAL
fresh . NEW, LUSH, NOVEL, FLIP, RAW,
   SASSY, BRASSY
" water alga .... DESMID
freshet ...... TIDE, SPATE, TORRENT
freshman NOVICE, PLEBE, TIRO, TYRO
fret .. FUME, ABRADE, NAG, ORP, VEX,
   CHAFE, IRK, RUB
Freudian term .. (SUPER)EGO, ID(S)
Freya's wife .... GERTH
friable . BRITTLE, CRISP, MEALY, FRAIL
friar .... LISTER, ABBOT, FRA, MONK,
   DOMINICAN, FRANCISCAN,
   CARMELITE, SERVITE
friar bird .... PIMLICO
fricative .... SPIRANT
friend .... AMI(E), QUAKER, DOGG,
   CHUM, KITH, BUDDY, CRONY,
   ACHATES, AMIGO
friendly .... AMICABLE
" understanding ..... ENTENTE
Friendly Island .... TONGA
frigate bird .... IWA
Frigga .... FRIDAY
Frigg's husband .... ODIN
" maid .... FULLA
" messenger .... GNAS
fright .... PANIC, FRAY, ALARM,
   FEAR, TERROR, GAST, FUNK, DISMAY
frighten ... BOH, DAUNT, SCARE, FLEY
frigid .... ARCTIC, CHILLY, GELID
frijol .... BEAN
frill RUCHE, JABOT RUFFLE, FURBELOW
fringe .... LOMA, THRUM, TASSEL
fringed .... FIMBRIATE, LACED
frisk .... HOP, ROMP, SKIP, CAPER,
   FROLIC, SEARCH, GAMBOL
fritter ...... DALLY, DAWDLE, BANGLE
frock GOWN, SOUTANE, JAM, COAT,
   KIRTLE
frog .. POLLYWOG, ANURAN, RONCO,
   RANA
froggeries .... RANARIA

frolic .. FUN, LARK, MARLOCK, PRANK,
   BINGE, CAPER, FRISK, SPREE,
   GAMBOL, SPORT, ROMP
from head to foot .... CAPAPIE
from; prefix .... APO, FRO
front ...... FACADE, OBVERSE, FORE,
   VAN, ANTEAL, ANTERO
frontiersman ...... BOONE, CARSON
frost .... ICE, HOAR, RIME
froth ... SPUME, FOAM, BOSH, SCUM,
   SUDS, LATHER, YEAST, LEVITY
frou-frou .... RUSTLE, STIR
frown LOUR, LOWER, GLOOM, SCOWL
frozen .... CHILLY, GLACE, GELID,
   FRAPPE
" dessert . ICE, MOUSSE, SHERBET,
   ALASKA
" vapor .... FROST, RIME
frugal .... ECONOMIC, CHARY, SPARE,
   THRIFTY
fruit ...... POMATO, MANGO, BERRY,
   DRUPE, PROFIT, YIELD, CROP,
   RESULT, ETAERIO, REGMA, PASA,
   POMA, HIP, SAPOTA, SAMARA,
   PEPO, SETON, ACHENE, HAW
" cordial .... RATAFIA
" , decay in .... BLET
" dots .... SORI
" flesh, part of .... PULP
" , goddess of; Rome ... POMONA
" jars, ring for packing .... LUTE
" , outer covering of ...... RIND
" , per. to .... POMONIC
" preserve .... COMPOTE
" pulp .... PAP
" , pulpy .... UVA
" , refuse of .... MARC
" , science of structure of ......
   CARPOLOGY
" skin .... EPICARP
fruiterer .... COSTER
fruitless .... STERILE
frustrate ...... DASH, FOIL, SCOTCH,
   THWART, ANIENTE
fry lightly .... SAUTE
frying pan .... SKILLET, SPIDER
Fuegian .... ONA
fuel ... ELDIN, PEAT, COAL, GAS, OIL,
   LOG, COKE, PEET
fugitive .... EXILE, FLEEING, REFUGEE,
   RUNAWAY
fugue, special passage in ... STRETTA
fulcrum .... BAIT, THOLE
fulfillment ... FRUITION, FLOWERING
full .... PLENARY, REPLETE, SATED,
   OROTUND, CLOYED
" cloth .... WALK
" house .... HAND, SRO
" of cracks .... RIMOSE
" of; suffix .... ITOUS, OSE

108

fuller's earth .... BOLE
    "   herb .... TEASEL
fullness ... SATIETY, SURFEIT, PLENUM,
                          PLETHORA
Fulton's folly .... CLERMONT
fumble .... BOTCH, BUNGLE, MUFF
fume ...... RAGE, FRET, ANGER, REEK,
                            SMOKE
fumigator .... AERATOR, SULPHUR
fuming .... AREEK, MAD, IRATE
fun .... SPORT, JOKE, PLAY
function .. OFFICE, PARTY, USE, ROLE,
    AFFAIR, FACULTY, SINE, COSINE
fundamental .... BASAL, BASILAR,
    RADICAL, ORIGINAL, PRIMAL, ABC
funeral EXEQUIES, OBSEQUIES, ARVAL,
                        ARVED
    "   attendant .... MUTE
    "   music ..... DIRGE, REQUIEM,
                        NENIA
    "   oration .... ELOGE
    "   pile .... PYRE
funereal .... EXEQUIAL, SAD
fungi ...... BOLETUS, SPORE, YEAST,
               ERYSIBE, AMANITA
fungi, parasitic .... ERGOTS, AWETO
fungoid growth .... MOLD
    "   tissue .... TRAMA
fungous .... SPONGY
fungus ..... MILDEW, MOLD, AGARIC,
             TUBER, AMADOU
    "   cells or sac .... ASCI
    "   dots .... TELIA
    " , edible .... CEPA, MOREL,
            TRUFFLE, BLEWITS
    " , growing on rye ...... ERGOT
    " , mushroom .... AMANITA
    "   plant .... UREDO
    " , poisonous .... AMANITINE
funny .... DROLL, JOCOSE, FARCICAL
fur ... FITCH, PELAGE, VAIR, MINIVER,
    HAIR, PELT(RY), SKIN, HAIR,
             NUTRIA, KID
fur-bearing animal ..... LYNX, SEAL,
    OTTER, LLAMA, BEAVER, ERMINE,
    MINK, MARTEN, GENET, SKUNK,
    WEASEL, WOMBAT, HAMSTER
    " , per. to .... PELISSE, STOLE
furbelow .... FRILL, RUFFLE
Fury(ies) .... DIRAE, ERINYES,
    EUMENIDES, ALECTO, MEGAERA,
               TISIPHONE
furl .... BUNDLE, INROLL
furlined tippet .... AMICE
furlong .... STADE, STADIUM
furnace ..... SMELTER, KILN, CRESSET,
    ETNA, CALDRON, FORGE,
    VOLCANO, STOVE, ATHANOR
    " , part of ..... BOSH, TEWEL,
             GRATE, TUYERE

furnish ..... CATER, ENDOW, ENDUE,
      EQUIP, BESTOW, PROVIDE
    "   a person with wings ... IMP
    "   with another point .... RETIP
furniture .... GRAITH, ADAM, GOODS
    " , parts of, packed together ..
                        SHOOK
furor .... FLURRY, MANIA, TUMULT
furrow .... CHAMFER, CHANNEL,
    RABBET, STRIA, SULCUS, TRACK,
           WRINKLE, GROOVE
furrowed .... SULCATE
furrowing mark .... FEER
furrows, having .... GUTTERY
furrows, notch .... SCORE
furry tail .... SCUT
fur seal .... URSAL
further .... AID, AND, MORE, YET
furtherance ... HELP, RELIEF, SUCCOR
furtive ... ARCH, COVERT, WARY, SLY,
           SKULKING, SNEAKY
fury ..... IRE, RAGE, WRATH, ERINYS
furze .... GORSE, WHIN, ULEX
fuse .... SOLDER, ANNEAL, SMELT,
    WELD, MERGE, UNITE, COALESCE
    " partially .... FRIT
fusee .... FLARE
fuss ...... ADO, FIKE, PREEN, TODO,
    BUSTLE, FANTOD, FIDGET, NIGGLE,
                  POTHER
fustet .... ZANTE
fustian BOMBASTIC, TUMID, POMPOUS
fustic coloring matter ...... MORIN
fusty .... STUFFY, FETID, PUTRID
futile .... IDLE, OTIOSE, VAIN
future .... STILL, YET, TOBE, COMING,
                    LATER
fylfot .... CROSS, EMBLEM, SWASTIKA

G

G.I. address .... APO
    " jewelry .... DOGTAG
G-man .... FBI, FED, AGENT
gabion .... BASKET
gable AILERON, PINION, WALL, CLARK
gad .... ROVE, GOAD, GALLIVANT,
            RAMBLE, PROWL
Gad, son of .... ERI
    " , tribe of .... ERITES
    " , Syrian deity .... FORTUNE
gadfly .... CLEG, BREEZE
gadget .... DOODAD, GISMO, JIMJAM
gadwall SHUTTLE, VOLANT, REDWING,
                    DUCK
Gaelic ... ERSE, SCOTCH, MANX, IRISH,
                  CELTIC

gaff ..... SPAR, GAMBLE, HOOK, SPUR, FLEECE
gag .... CHOKE, RETCH, SCOB, HOAX, JOKE, QUIP, MUFFLE
gain ..... REALIZE, LUCRE, GET, WIN, ATTAIN, APPROACH, REAP, EARN, NET, BENEFIT
gainsay ..... DENY, IMPUGN, OPPOSE
gait ... (SH)AMBLE, LOPE, RACK, STEP, WALK, PACE, STRIDE, CANTER
gaiters .... PUTTEES, SPATS, STRAD
gala .. FIESTA, FETE, POMP, FESTIVAL
Galician .... GALLEGO
" river .... STYR, SAN
Galilee, town in .. CANA, NAZARETH, TIBERIUS
galipot .... BARRAS, RESIN
gall .... BILE, SPITE, CHAFE, VEX
Gallagher's partner .... SHEEN
gallant ...... CICISBEO, HERO, SPARK, BEAU, BOLD, HEROIC
galled .... RAW, SORE, PEEVED
galleon .... CARACK, ARGOSY
gallery .... MUSEUM, LOFT, POY, SOLLAR, SALON, LOGGIA, ARCADE, VERANDA
galley ... COIN, KITCHEN, DROMOND, BIREME, TRIREME
" of retorts .... MUFFLE
" , work on .... PROOFREAD
Gallina(e) .. GROUSE, QUAIL, TURKEY, RASORES, PEAFOWL
gallinule .... HEN, RAIL
gallop .... LOPE, TANTIVY, AUBIN
"galloping dominoes" .... DICE
gallows .... GIBBET
gally .... SCARE, BOLD, BITTER
galore .... GOBS, LOTS, PLENTY
Galway island .... ARAN
gam ...... HERD, SCHOOL, VISIT, LEG
gambler ..... GAMER, DICER, PUNTER, SHARK, SHILL
gambling place .... CASINO
" , per. to .... ALEATORY
gambol ...... CAPER, CURVET, ROMP, FRISK, PRANK, DIDO
game ..... FUN, FROLIC, LAME, PLOY, MATCH, SPORT, PLAY, CONTEST, PASTIME, VALIANT, DISABLED
" bird GROUSE, GUAN, PHEASANT
" digit; anc. .... MORA
" , Greek .... AGON
" of cards .... PAM, TAROT, SKAT, GIN, RUMMY, POKER, WHIST, BRIDGE, ECARTE, GHOSTS, HEARTS, CANASTA, CASSINO
" of chance BINGO, LOTTO, KENO, ROULETTE, DICE, FARO
" of skill .. DARTS, CHESS, HALMA, MARBLES, TAW

" of sport BADMINTON, HOCKEY, RUGBY, GOLF, POLO, CRICKET, BOCCIE, SHINNY, SHINTY, SOCCER, CURLING
" , oriental .... HEI, FANTAN
" piece .... MAN, ROOK, DOMINO
" point . GOAL, RUN, SCORE, TALLY
" ragout .... SALMI
" , raisin .... SNAPDRAGON
gamecock .... STAG
gamekeeper .... RANGER
gamin ARAB, MUDLARK, URCHIN, TAD
gaming; possession of goods by finding .... TROVER
gamut .... RANGE, SCALE, SOLFA, COMPASS, REACH
gander ...... GANNET, GOOSE, STEG
Gandhi .... MAHATMA
" , place of confinement of ... POONA
gang ..... CREW, SET, BAND, NUMBER
Ganges Valley, efflorescence on . REH
gangling .... LANKY, SPINDLING
gangrenous condition ..... NECROSIS
gannet .... GOOSE, SOLAN, SULA, MARROT
gap .... CHASM, HIATUS, LACUNA, FAULT, SPLIT, SHARD, CHINK, CLEFT, CRANNY, MEUSE
gape ..... DEHISCE, OGLE, OSCITATE, YAWN, BILGE, OPE
gapes, the .... RICTUS
garab tree .... BAHAN
Garapan is. capital .... SAIPAN
garble . MUTILATE, FALSIFY, DISTORT, PERVERT
garden .... PATCH, HERBARY, VERGER, OLITORY
" of golden apples HESPERIDES
" , spacious .... PLEASANCE
" city of America ... CHICAGO
" city of England .... KENT
gardener's plague ... CUTWORM, PEST
Gardner .... STANLEY, ERLE, AVA
gargantuan ..... GIANT, HUGE, VAST
Gargantua's son .... PANTAGRUEL
garfish .... SNOOK
garish .... FLASHY, GAUDY, TAWDRY
garland ROSARY, ANADEM, FESTOON, LEI, CHAPLET, FILLET
garlic root .... MOLY, RAMSON
garment ..... KAROSS, WRAP, COTTE, ROBING, VESTMENT, WRIEL, CASSOCK, SERAPE, PONCHO
" , close fitting .... COATEE
" , Moslem .... IZAR
" like a tunic .... TABARD
" , Malay .... KABAYA, SARONG
" , outer ...... HAORI, SMOCK, COAT, PALETOT, ABA, PARKA
" , under .... SHIFT

Garner, John _____ ..... NANCE
garnet .... APLOME, PYROPE, RED,
    (H)ESSONITE, ALMANDITE,
    OLIVITE, UVAROVITE
   "   berry .... CURRANT
garnish .... (BE)DECK, TRIM, LARD
garnishment .... LIEN
garret .... ATTIC, LOFT, SOLER
garrot .... DUCK, GOLDENEYE
garvie .... SPRAT
gas NEON, ARGON, RADON, BUTANE,
    PETROL, FUEL
   " charger .... AERATOR
   ", colorless ...... KETONE, ETHANE,
    OXAN(E)
   "; comb. form .... AER(O)
   " from hot springs .... XENON
   ", marsh .... METHANE
   ", nitrogen and carbon . CYANOGEN
   ", non-inflammable .... HELIUM
gaseous .... TENUOUS, THIN
gash .... CUT, SLASH, INCISE
gasp .... CHOKE, PANT, PUFF
gastropod .... MOLLUSK, SLUG, SNAIL
   "   ; genus .... HARPA, NERITE
   "   , marine .... MUREX
gate .... SPRUE, BAB, DAR, GIT,
    PORTAL, HERSE, POSTERN, SLUICE,
    TORII, CLOW, GOOL
gateway to shrine .... TORAN
gather ..... REAP, BREW, CULL, SHIRR,
    FOLD, ACQUIRE, PUCKER, COLLATE,
    GARNER, AMASS
gathered .... MET
gathering ... MEET, HALL, PARTY, SUM
   " , social .... BEE
Gaucho knife ...... BOLO, MACHETE
gaudy ..... GARISH, GROSS, TAWDRY,
    TINSEL
gauge ... ESTIMATE, RATE, VALUE, FEE,
    MODEL, NORM, RULE, TYPE, SIZE,
    STANDARD
   " pointer .... ARM
Gaul, anc. people of .... REMI, CELT,
    AEDUI
   " , divinity of TEUTATES, TARANIS
gaunt ..... BONY, LEAN, GRIM, LANK,
    SPARE, HAGGARD, SCRAWNY
gauntlet .... GLOVE, CUFF
gauze .. MARLI, BAREGE, CREPE, LENO,
    LISSE, HAZE
gauzy film in wine .... BEESWING
Gawain's father .... LOT
gawk .... BOOBY, CUCKOO, FOOL,
    GAPE, STARE
gay .... BOON, AIRY, RORY, RIANT
   " , state of being .... RIANCY
gaze .... GAPE, PORE, REGARD, CON,
    LOOK, SCAN, OGLE
gazebo .... PAVILION

gazelle (see also "antelope") ....
    CORINNE, KUDU, MOHR, ADMI,
    CORA, ORYX, ARIEL, AHU,
    CHICARA, DAMA, KORIN,
    SPRINGBOK, GOA, KOBA
gear ... CAM, BAGGAGE, TOOLS, KIT,
    DUFFEL, PINION
Geb's consort .... NU, NUT
   " offspring .... ISIS, OSIRIS
gecko .... LIZARD, TARENTE
geese; fat .... AXUNGE
geese, flock of wild ... GAGGLE, RAFT
   " ; genus .... ANSER, CHEN
geiger tree .... SEBESTEN
gelatin JELLY, AGAR, COLLIN, GLUTEN
   " plate .... BAT
   " used as cement .... GLUE
gelid .... ICY, COLD, FROZEN
gem ... JEWEL, ICE, MUFFIN, ASTERIA,
    SARD, SCARAB, AQUAMARINE,
    LIGURE, JACINTH, BALAS
   " face .... CULET, BEZEL, FACET
   " for inlaying .... CRUSTA
   " , relief .... CAMEO
   " of conjugal happiness SARDONYX
   " of friendship .... TOPAZ
   " of good luck ...... MOONSTONE
   " of health .... AGATE
   " of immortality .... EMERALD
   " of lasting peace ...... DIAMOND
   " of love .... AMETHYST
   " of purity .... PEARL
   " State .... IDAHO
   " that warns of danger .. CATSEYE
   " of truth .... SAPPHIRE
   " of youth .... BERYL
gemmation .... BUDDING
gemsbok .... CHAMOIS, ORYX
gendarme .... POLICE, TROOPER
gender(s) .. BEGET, BREED, SEX, MALE,
    FEMALE, NEUTER
   " , common to both EPICENE
genealogy .. PEERAGE, TREE, LINEAGE,
    PEDIGREE
general ... USUAL, VAGUE, COMMON,
    GROSS, RANK
   " , famous .. SHERIDAN, BOTHA,
    SHERMAN, GRANT, BOR, ANDERS,
    HAIG, LEE, FOCH, BRAGG,
    WOLFE, ARNOLD, HODGES,
    JOFFRE, MOLTKE, PATTON,
    PERSHING, STILWELL
generate .. BREED, SPAWN, SIRE, YIELD
genesis ... NASCENCY, ORIGIN, BIRTH
genial ... WARM, CORDIAL, SOCIABLE
genipap wood .... LANA
genre ..... CATEGORY, SPECIES, KIND,
    GENUS, SORT, STYLE
gentle .... AMIABLE, TAME, BALMY,
    BLAND, DOCILE, PLACID
   " slope .... GLACIS

111

Genoese family .... DORIA
gentleman ... SIR, KNIGHT, YOUNKER,
        HERR, SENOR, SIGNOR, ROM,
                BABOO, SQUIRE
"Gentlemen Prefer Blondes" author .
                        LOOS
gentry; Eng. .... NOBLE
genuflect ...... BEND, KNEEL, CURTSY
genus ..... CLASS, ORDER, SORT, TYPE
genus of birds .... EOS, UNSER, TODI
   " " birds, the gennet ...... SULA
   " " bivalve mollusks .. ANOMIA
   " " bulbous herbs .... TULIPA
   " " burbots .... LOTA
   " " bustards .... OTIS
   " " carnivorous animals . URSUS
   " " cats .... FELIS
   " " climbing shrubs ... TECOMA
   " " crowned pigeons ... GOURA
   " " ducks ..... ANAS, HARELDA
   " " fabaceous herbs .. PSORALEA
   " " feather stars ..... ANTEDON
   " " flowering shrubs .. FUCHSIA
   " " fungi .... AMAITA
   " " fungi, fleshy ...... BOLETUS
   " " gastropods .... NERTE
   " " gastropods, per. to ... OLIVA
   " " geese .... ANSER
   " " goose barnacles ...... LEPAS
   " " grasses .. AVENA, POA, STIPA
   " " herbs ...... ACARUM, ARUM,
                        INULA, SESEL
   " " herbs; Amer. ...... LINARIA,
                          HEDEOMA
   " " hogs .... SUS
genus of lichens .... EVERNIA
   " " lily family .... BESSERA
   " " mollusks .... NERITA
   " " morays .... MURAENA
   " " nettles .... URTICA
   " " N. Amer. perennials ... IVA
   " " olives .... OLEA
   " " oysters .... OSTREA
   " " palm trees .... BACABA
   " " perennial herbs ..... IMULA
   " " plants ..... NAIAS, NOLANA,
                    LOBELIA, GRINDELIA
   " " poisonous plants .. CERBERA
   " " pond tortoise .... EMYS
   " " rats .... SPALAX, MUS
   " " sand snakes .... ERYX
   " " sheep .... BOS
   " " shrubs SABIA, TREMA, RHUS
   " " shrubs; Austral. .. ALSTONIA
   " " spider monkeys ..... ATELES
   " " spiders .... AGALENA
   " " squirrels .... SCIURUS
   " " swans .... OLOR
   " " swine .... SUS
   " " tailless amphibians ... RANA

   " " tarpon fish family ... ELOPS
   " " terns .... STERNA
   " " thistle plants ...... CARLINA
   " " ticks .... IXODES
   " " trees .. MABA, STYRAX, TREMA
   " " trop. Am. bulbs .... TARIRI
   " " tropical herbs ..... TACCA,
                        URENA, ACUAN
   " " tropical shrubs .... PISONIA,
                              IXORA
   " " whales .... INIA
   " " woody vines .... HEDERA
geode ... DRUSE, VUG, VOOG, CAVITY,
                            NODULE
geological age .... PLIOCENE,
        CENOZOIC, GLACIAL, NEOCENE,
        LIAS, MIOCENE, ARCHAEAN, ECCA,
                LYAS, DYAS, EOCENE
   "   division .. EON, ERA, EPOCH
   "   epoch .. CHAZY, DRIFT, ECCA
   "   formation ...... TERRANE,
        TERRENE, IONE, JURASSIC,
                        TRIASSIC
   "   group ..... BALA, CARADOC
   "   subdivision .... TROPIC,
                            GAULT
   "   substance .... ATANE
geometric figure ..... RHOMB, SOLID,
                    SQUARE, ELLIPSE
   "   premise ...... POSTULATE
   "   solid .. CONE, CUBE, LUNE,
                    PRISM, SPHERE
   "   term .. LOCI, SINE, LOCUS,
        TANGENT, SECANT, VERSOR,
                        THEOREM
geometry co-ordinate ...... ABSCISSA
   "   , proponent of ..... EUCLID,
                            PASCAL
   "   , proportion in ..... PORISM
George Eliot's true name ..... EVANS
Georgian .... SVAN
georgic .... RURAL, POEM
Geraint's wife .... ENID
geranial .... CITRAL, ALDEHYDE
Geranium Lake .... NACARAT
germ ...... BUD, SEED, SPORE, OVUM,
                    BACTERIA, EMBRYO,
                        MICROBE, EGG
   " elements, per. to .... GENIC
   " , fermenting .... ZYME
   " of decay .... TAINT
   " seed .... CHIT
germ-free .... ASEPTIC, ANTISEPTIC
German .... JERRY, HUN, TEUTON,
        KRAUT, BOCHE, ALMAN, ALMAIN
   " abbot .... ABT
   " about .... BEI, ETWA
   " above .... UBER, OBEN
   " across .... DURCH
   " admiral .... SPEE, TIRPITZ

"	after	NACH	"	clean	REIN, SAUBER
"	age	ALTER	"	clever	KLUG
"	air	LIED, LUFT	"	clock	UHR
"	airplane	STUKA, TAUBE	"	coal region	SAAR, RUHR
"	alas	ACH	"	coin	KRONE, MARK, T(H)ALER, GELD
"	alley	GASSE			
"	already	SCHON	"	cold	KALT
"	all	GANZ, ALLE	"	complete	GANZ
"	always	IMMER, STETS	"	composer	ABT, BACH, WAGNER, WEBER, ORFF, WEILL
"	ancestor	AHN(E)			
"	angry	BOSE			
"	animal	TIER	"	corner	ECKE
"	apple	APFEL	"	cost	PREIS
"	archbishop of Cologne	ANNO	"	cross	KREUZ
"	article	DER, DIE, DAS, EIN(E), EINES, EINER	"	count	GRAF
			"	couple	PAAR
			"	courage	MUT
"	as	ALS	"	cow	KUH
"	ass	ESEL	"	dare, to	WAGEN
"	astronomer	KEPLER	"	day	TAG
"	aunt	TANTE	"	dead	TOT
"	away	FORT, WEG	"	dear	LIEB
"	bacteriologist	KOCH	"	deep	TIEF
"	bank	UFER	"	distant	WEIT
"	beard	BART	"	district	GAU
"	beautiful	SCHON	"	doctor	ARZT
"	because	WEIL	"	dog	HUND
"	bed	BETT	"	door	TUR
"	behind	NACH	"	drinking salutation	PROSIT
"	be(ing)	SEIN	"	duck	ENTE
"	below	UNTER, UNTEN	"	dumpling	KNODEL
"	beside	NEBEN	"	ear	OHR
"	besides	NOCH	"	earl	GRAF
"	blood	BLUT	"	early	FRUH
"	blue	BLAU	"	earth	ERDE
"	boat	BOOT	"	east	OST(EN)
"	book	BUCH	"	eat	ESSEN
"	both	BEIDE	"	eel	AAL
"	bread	BROT	"	eight	ACHT
"	breath	ATEM	"	elegant	FEIN
"	breathe	ATMEN	"	eleven	ELF
"	bride	BRAUT	"	empire	REICH
"	bright	HELL	"	empty	LEER
"	broom	BESEN	"	entire	GANZ
"	but	ABER	"	evening	ABEND
"	cake	TORTE, KUCHEN	"	every	JEDE(R)
"	canal	KIEL	"	everything	ALLES
"	carriage	WAGEN	"	eye	AUGE
"	cathedral town	COLOGNE, ULM	"	far	WEIT
			"	fat	DICK, FETT
"	chair	STUHL	"	father	VATER
"	chap	KERL	"	fear	ANGST
"	cheers	PROST	"	fellow	KERL
"	cheese	KASE	"	few	WENIG(E)
"	chemist	BUNSEN	"	field	FELD, ACKER
"	chicken	HUHN	"	field marshal	ROMMEL, KEITEL, BLUCHER
"	child	KIND			
"	city	STADT, BONN, GOTHA, HALLE, ESSEN, HAMM, KASSEL, BREMEN	"	figure	BILD, ZAHL
			"	firm	FEST
			"	five	FUNF

113

"	foot	FUSS	"	lazy	FAUL
"	forest	WALD	"	leaf	BLATT
"	four	VIER	"	league	BUND
"	from	VON	"	leather	LEDER
"	fruit	OBST	"	left	LINK(S)
"	full	VOLL	"	leg	BEIN
"	game	SPIEL	"	letter	BRIEF
"	gate	TOR	"	lightning	BLITZ
"	general	MOLTKE, ZIETEN	"	little	KLEIN, WENIG
"	genuine	ECHT, WAHR	"	lord	HERR, GOTT
"	gift	GABE	"	love	LIEBE(N)
"	give	GEBEN	"	lyric poems	LIEDER
"	glad	FROH	"	man	MANN
"	gladly	GERN	"	many	VIEL(E)
"	glass mfg. city	JENA	"	mathematician	LEIBNIZ
"	glory	RUHM	"	measles	RUBELLA
"	go	GEHEN	"	mind	SINN, GEIST
"	God	GOTT	"	mister	HERR
"	good	GUT	"	money	GELD
"	gray	GRAU	"	moon	MOND
"	greatly	SEHR	"	more	MEHR
"	green	GRUN	"	mountain	EIFEL, HARZ,
"	guest	GAST			TAUNUS
"	hair	HAAR	"	mouth	MUND
"	half	HALB(E)	"	much	SEHR, VIEL
"	hall	AULA, DIELE, SAAL,	"	murder	MORD
		BURSA	"	narrow	ENG
"	halls	AULAE	"	nation	VOLK
"	harbor	HAFEN	"	naval base	EMDEN, KIEL
"	hat	HUT	"	neat	SAUBER
"	have	HABEN	"	neck	HALS
"	head	KOPF	"	never	NIE
"	heart	HERZ	"	new	NEU, NEUE, NEUES
"	hence	DAHER	"	night	NACHT
"	here	HIER	"	nine	NEUN
"	high	HOCH	"	no	NEIN
"	hill	HUGEL, BERG	"	nobility	ADEL
"	historian	NEANDER, DAHN,	"	noble	EDLE
		MOSER, MOMMSEN	"	nobleman	GRAF, BARON
"	home	HAUS, HEIM	"	noise	LARM
"	honor	EHRE	"	north	NORD
"	host	WIRT	"	nose	NASE
"	hot	HEISS	"	not	NICHT
"	house	HAUS	"	novelist	MANN, ZWEIG, HESSE,
"	hunter	JAGER			BOELL, GRASS, KIRST
"	husband	GATTE	"	number	ZAHL
"	ice	EIS	"	ocean	MEER
"	image	BILD	"	old	ALT
"	inventor	BENZ, DIESEL,	"	only	NUR
		BUNSEN, SIEMENS	"	or	ODER
"	iron	EISEN	"	orient	OSTEN
"	island	INSEL, FOHR, RUGEN,	"	over	UBER
		SYLT	"	painter	DURER, GROSZ,
"	joke	SPASS, WITZ			MENZEL, ERNST
"	knight	RITTER	"	pair	PAAR
"	lady	DAME, FRAU	"	path	GASSE, WEG
"	lake	SEE, CHIEM, WURM,	"	peace	FRIEDEN, RUHE
		BODEN	"	people	LEUTE, VOLK
"	lane	GASSE	"	philologist	BENEKE, GRIMM
"	late	SPAT			

114

"	philosopher ... KANT, HEGEL, FICHTE		"	superior .... OBER	
"	physicist .... DOPPLER, OHM, HAHN, PLANCK		"	table .... TISCH, TAFEL	
			"	tall .... HOCH	
"	picture .... BILD		"	ten .... ZEHN	
"	pietist ..... FRANCKE, SPENER		"	than .... DANN	
"	play .... SPIEL		"	thanks .... DANK(E)	
"	please .... BITTE		"	then .... DANN, DENN	
"	poor .... ARM		"	theologian ...... BAUER, ECK	
"	president EBERT, HINDENBURG		"	there .... DORT	
"	prison .... STALAG		"	thick .... DICK	
"	pronoun .. DU, ICH, SIE, UNS, WIR, IHR		"	thin .... DUNN	
			"	thing .... DING	
"	psychologist .... KOHLER		"	thirst .... DURST	
"	pure .... REIN		"	three .... DREI	
"	rain .... REGEN		"	through .... DURCH	
"	red .... ROT		"	time .... MAL, ZEIT	
"	request .... BITTE		"	tired .... MUDE	
"	rest .... RUHE		"	today .... HEUTE	
"	rich .... REICH		"	tower .... TURM	
"	rifleman ...... JAGER, YAGER		"	town .... STADT	
"	river ..... RUHR, ELBE, ODER, EGER, EDER, SAALE, WERRA, ISER, HUNTE, RHINE, ISAR, HAVEL, SPREE		"	train .... ZUG	
			"	tree .... BAUM	
			"	trousers .... HOSE(N)	
			"	true .... WAHR, ECHT	
			"	tune .... LIED	
"	ruler .... OTTO, OTHO, CONRAD(IN), HITLER		"	two .... ZWEI	
			"	upper .... OBER	
"	sea .... MEER		"	valley .... TAL	
"	seaport .... EMDEN, KIEL		"	very .... SEHR	
"	seat .... BANK		"	victory .... SIEG	
"	sentence .... SATZ		"	village .... DORF	
"	shoe .... SCHUH, STIEFEL		"	visitor .... GAST	
"	shore .... UFER		"	war .... KRIEG	
"	short .... KURZ		"	watch .... UHR	
"	silver .... ALBATA		"	watering place .... EMS	
"	silver plate .... ELECTRUM		"	well .... WOHL	
"	sir .... HERR		"	wet .... NASS	
"	six .... SECHS		"	white .... WEISS	
"	skirt .... ROCK		"	white wine .. HOCK, MOSELLE	
"	small .... KLEIN		"	whole .... GANZ	
"	society .... VEREIN		"	why .... WARUM	
"	soldier ..... SOLDAT, KRAUT		"	wide .... WEIT	
"	solid .... FEST		"	wife .... FRAU, GATTIN	
"	son .... SOHN		"	willingly .... GERN(E)	
"	song .... LIED		"	without .... OHNE	
"	space .... RAUM, PLATZ		"	woman .... FRAU, WEIB, DAME	
"	speech .... REDE				
"	spirit .... GEIST		"	world .... WELT	
"	spouse ...... GATTE, GATTIN		"	worth .... WERT	
"	star .... STERN		"	year .... JAHR	
"	state SAXONY, HESSE, BADEN, BAVARIA, PRUSSIA		"	yellow .... GELB	
			"	yet .... DOCH, NOCH	
"	steel .... STAHL		"	yonder .... DORT	
"	steel center .... RUHR, ESSEN		"	young .... JUNG	
"	steeple .... TURM		germane .. AKIN, APROPOS, COGNATE		
"	still .... DOCH, NOCH		germicide .... IODINE		
"	street ...... GASSE, STRASSE		Germany .. REICH, ALMAN, ALMAINE		
"	strife .... KRIEG		Geronimo .... APACHE		
"	submarine .... U-BOAT		Gershwin .... GEORGE, IRA		
"	sun .... SONNE		Gertrude Atherton's pen name .. LIN		

gesture NOD, WAVE, MOTION, SANNA
" dance .... SIVA
get aboard .... BERIDE
" around .... CAJOLE, OUTWIT
" away .. LAM, ELOPE, SCRAM, SCAT
Geum .... AVENS
geyser, mouth of .... CRATER
gewgaw ..... BAUBLE, GAUD, FANGLE
Ghana capital .... AKKRA
ghastly .... PALE, LURID, MACABRE,
                            GRISLY
Ghent's river .... LYS, SCHELDE
ghost .. EIDOLON, KER, LARVA, LEMUR,
        SPOOK, WRAITH, SHADE, BHUT,
        HANT, JUBA, IMAGE, TRACE,
                            SHADOW
" fish .... CHIRO
" plant .... TUMBLEWEED
" spectre .... REVENANT
ghoulish .... VAMPIRIC, EERIE
giant .... ANAK, ETEN, THURSE, OGRE,
        COTTUS, CYCLOPS, JOTUN, UTGARD,
        GOLIATH, YMER, YMIR, TITAN,
        GARGANTUA, MAMMOTH,
                        BANA, MIMIR
" ; Asterius' father .... ANAX
" , deformed .... FOMORS
" , evil .... LOKI
" , hundred-eyed .... ARGUS
" , hundred-handed .... GYGES
" mentor .... LEO
" ; Oisin's father .... FIONN
" , one-eyed ..... ARGES, BRONTES
" sea demon .... WADE
" ; Vulcan's son .... CACUS
giantess DOMNU, NATT, NORN, SKULD,
                        URTH, WYRD
giants .... EMIM, ZUMIM
gib .... GUT, SALMON, CAT
gibbet .... GALLOWS
gibbon .... APE, LAR
gibe .... HECKLE, SNEER, QUIP, FLOUT,
                            SCOFF
Gibraltar, founder of .... GEBIR
" , point opposite of .. CEUTA
gift ... ALMS, EMAM, GRANT, TALENT,
        LEGACY, LAGNIAPPE, DOW,
        LARGESS, DOLE, FEE, TIP, BONUS,
                    FAVOR, HANDSEL
gigantic ... TITAN, COLOSSEAN, HUGE
giggle ..... SNIGGER, CHUCKLE, TITTER
gila monster .... LIZARD
Gilbert island ...... MAKIN, TARAWA
gild . ADORN, AUREATE, DORE, ENRICH
gill(s) ... BRANCHIA, LUNG, STREAM,
                            WATTLE
gimcrack .... BAUBLE, TRIFLE, TRINKET
gimp .... ORRIS, TAR, TYMP
gin ...... SNARE, TRAP, SLOE, RUMMY
ginger .... PEP, ECLAT, VIM

" ; genus .... ZINGIBER
" pine .... CEDAR
" root .... COLTSFOOT
" , wild .... ASARUM
gingerbread .... PARKIN
" tree .... DOOM
ginseng .... ARALIA
Gingold, Miss .... HERMIONE
giraffe .... CAMELOPARD, DAPPLE
" , like a .... OKAPI
girasol .... OPAL
gird ... BRACE, BIND, ENCIRCLE, EQUIP
girder ... TBAR, IBEAM, TRUSS, TIMBER
girdle ... RING, OBI, CEST, CINCTURE,
            SASH, CINGLE, CESTUS,
                        KUMMERBUND
girl SIS, MINX, LASS, MISS, CHI, CHAI,
        CHIT, NYMPH, FILLY, GIGLET,
        COLLEEN, HOYDEN, TOMBOY,
        KIMMER, CUMMER, MAID(EN), SKIRT
girth .... CINCH
gist . ESSENCE, CORE, CRUX, NUB, PITH,
                        HEART, KERNEL
give IMPART, GIE, DONATE, (EN)DOW,
        DOLE, BESTOW, CONFER, IMPART
" forth .. EMIT, EXHALE, EDIT, BLAZE
" sparingly .... INCH, SHY
" up .... CEDE, FAIL, YIELD
given by word of mouth ORAL, PAROL
gizz .... WIG
gizzard trout .... GILLAROO
glacial .... ICY
" deposit .... PLACER, MORAINE,
                        DILUVIUM
" fragment .... SERAC
" ice .... FIRN, NEVE
" ridge .. ESKAR, KAME, OS(AR)
glacier, facing direction of ... STOSS
" , rel. to a .... CIRQUE
glacier mill .... MOULIN
glad .... ELATED, FAIN, MERRY
" tidings .. EVANGEL, JOY, GOSPEL
gladden ...... ELATE, SOLACE, TICKLE
glade ..... LAUND, DELL, GAP, VALLEY
" ; comb. form .... NEMO
gladiator .... FENCER, LANISTA
" , school for .... LUDI
gladly .... FREELY, FAIN, LIEF, READILY
Gladsheim .... ASGARD
glance EYE, LEER, OGLE, GLEAM, GLINT,
                        SCAN, SKIM
glance coal .... ANTHRACITE
gland .. CAROTID, PAROTID, ADRENAL,
                    PINEAL, RIS, NOIX
" secretion .. HORMONE, SALIVA,
                    INSULIN, ADRENALIN
gland-like .... ADENOID
glands, inflam. of .... ADENITIS
" , throat .... CHOKE
glandular disease .... ADENIA

116

glare ...... FROWN, GLOWER, SCOWL
glass ... STRASS, SCHMELZ(E), VERRE,
   OBSIDIAN, PANE, TALLBOY, TUMBLER,
                 GOBLET, PONY
   " beads, of .... AGGRI, AGGRY
   " handling rod .... PUNTY
   " ingredient ...... SAND, POTASH,
                     SILICA
   " in mosaic .... TESSERA
   " ; make into sheets ..... PLATTEN
   " material .... FRIT
   " , molten .... PARISON
   " scum .... CALX, GALL
glass tube for blowpipes ... MATRASS
glassmaker .... GLAZIER
   " , oven of .... TISAR, LEER
glasswort .... KALI, SALTWORT
glassy .... CRYSTAL, SANIDINE, VITRIC,
                  HYALINE
   " substance .. FELDSPAR, ENAMEL
glaster .... BAWL
Glaucus' father .... SISYPHUS
   " wife .... IONE
glaze COAT, ENAMEL, VENEER, LUSTER,
       SHEEN, VARNISH, GLOSS
   " on Chinese porcelain ... EELSKIN
glazier's diamond .... EMERY, EMERIL
glazing machine .... CALENDER
gleam .... GLINT, GLOZE, CORUSCATE,
                 FLAKE
glean .... REAP
glen .... DALE, DEN, DINGLE, VALE
gliadin .... GLUTIN
glib ... BLAND, FLUENT, VOLUBLE, OILY
glide .. SKIP, SLIP, SLIDE, SKATE, SKIM,
                 SCUD
glider-like bomb .... BAT
gliding over .... LABILE
glimmer .... BLINK, SHEEN, LEAM
glimmering .... INKLING
glitter .... CORUSCATE, GLEAM
globe .... EARTH, ORB, SPHERE, CLEW
globule .... TEAR, DROP, MINIM, BLOB,
                PILL, BEAD
glockenspiel .... LYRA, BELL
gloom .... MURK, DUMPS, BLUES
gloomy .... DIM, EERIE, DREAR, TERNE,
   WAN, LURID, SAD, DOLESOME,
      ADUST, MURKY, MOROSE
"Gloomy Dean" .... INGE
glorify ...... ADORE, BLESS, WORSHIP
glory . KUDOS, AUREOLA, FAME, HALO,
   HONOR, ECLAT, RENOWN
   " , cloud of .... NIMBUS
gloss over .. PALLIATE, EXCUSE, BLINK,
             WINK, FARD
glossary .... CLAVIS
glossy SHEENY, GLACE, NITID, SATINY,
                SLICK
   " compound .... ENAMEL

glove ...... CESTUS, GANT, CUFF, MIT,
            SUEDE, GAUNTLET
   " fabric .... KID, LISLE, NAPA
   " shape .... TRANK
   " skins, to prepare .... TAW
glower .... GLARE, GAZE, STARE
glowing .. ARDENT, LAMBENT, ASHINE,
      FLUSH, WARM, FERVENT
Gluck opera .... ARMIDE
glucose ... RUTIN, DEXTROSE, HONEY,
            SYRUP, SUGAR
   " , rel. to .... GULOSE
glucoside ... ESTEVIN, RUTIN, SALICIN
   " root .... GEIN
glue .. CEMENT, PASTE, AFFIX, FASTEN,
                STICK
glum .... DOUR, SULKY, SULLEN, SURLY
glut .... SURFEIT, SATE, CLOY, PAUNCH
glutin .... GELATIN, GLIADIN
glutinous .... SIZY, VISCID
glutton .... GOURMAND, CORMORANT,
       EPICURE, PIG, HELLUO
gluttony .... VORACITY, EDACITY
glycerose, rel. to .... FRUCTOSE
glycol .... PINACOL
glycoaldehyde .... DIOSE
gnarl ...... GROWL, KNOT, KNUR(R),
       SNARL, TWIST, NUR(R)
gnash .... GRATE, BITE, GRIND
gnaw ...... CHAMP, CORRODE, NIBBLE,
                ERODE
G-man .... FED, AGENT, HOOVER
gnome . IMP, DWARF, GOBLIN, BOGIE,
       DEEV, NIS, KOBOLD
gnomic .... DIDACTIC
gnomon .... PIN, STYLE
gnostic repesentation ..... ABRASAX,
               ABRAXAS
   " , second-century ...... SETHITE
gnu .... ANTELOPE, KOKOON, BRINDL
go GAE, GANG, SALLY, WEND, WORK,
                FARE
   " astray .... ERR, ABERRATE
   " back .... REGRESS, REVERT
   " away .... SCAT, SCRAM
   " by plane .... FLY, AERO
   " ; Latin .... VA, VADE
   " ; nautical .... TACK, WEAR
goa .... GAZELLE
Goa powder .... ARAROBA
goad .. PROD, EGG, GAD, PRICK, PROG,
           ANCUS, INCITE
goal BOURNE, META, AIM, END, HOME,
     OBJECT, IDEAL, CAGE, POST
   " , distant .... THULE, REACH
goat . PASAN, TUR, ZAC, GORAL, TAHR,
   BEDEN, SHA, SCAPE, BUCK, IBEX,
     MARKHOR, BOVID, CAPRID
   " , female .... CAPRA, NANNY
   " fish; genus .... UPENEUS

goatish ..... LEWD, CAPRINE, HIRCINE
goats; genus .... CAPRA
goat's hair cloth ...... CAMLET, TIBET
   "   "   cord .... AGAL
goatsucker ...... DORHAWK, EVEJAR,
                               SPINNER
gob .... CHOKE, GOAF, TAR
Gobi Desert .... HANHAI
   "   " , part of ...... ALASHAN
gobioid fish .... TETARD
goblet .. GLASS, BOCAL, HANAP, TASS,
              CUP, SKULL, CHALICE
goblin ... ELF, BOGIE, TROW, GNOME,
   OUPHE, BHUT, KOBOLD, NIS, TROLL,
                     PUCK, PUCA
goby .... MAPO
God . JEHOVAH, YAHWEH, DEITY, DEUS,
   JAH, ELOHIM, ALLAH, JHVH, YHVH,
            ADONAI, CREATOR
god, anc. (Babyl.) ..... UTU, ANSHAR
", anc. (Egypt.) .. CHNEMU, PTAH,
                          ANUBIS
", anc. (Gr.) .... CHAOS
", anc. (Ital.) ...... PICUS, SATURN
", answer of a .... ORACLE
", Asgard (Norse) .... AS, ASA
", chief (Assyr. Babyl.) ..... NINIB
", chief (Babyl.) .... BEL, MARDUK
", chief (Celt.) .... HAFGAN
", chief (Chinese) .... JOSS
", chief (Gr.) .. HADES, PTAH, ZEUS
", chief (Irish) .... DAGDA
", chief (Norse) ..... FENIR, ODIN,
              VALI, VANIR, YMIR
", dream (Gr.) .... ONIROS
", earth (Babyl.) .... DAGAN
", earth (Egypt.) .... GEB
", Etruscan ... TINIA, TURMS, UNI
", evil (Babyl.) .... ZU
", fish .... DAGON
", Gaelic .... LER, MIDER
", goat .... PAN
", hawk-headed (Egypt.) .... HOR
"; healer of sick (Babyl.) ..... EA
"; Hebrew name .... ELOHIM
", house (Rom.) ...... LAR, LARES
", incarnate (Egypt.) ...... MNEVIS
", Italian for .... DIO
", jackal .... ANUBIS
", Latin for .... DEUS
", Medit. (Persian) ..... MITHRAS
", moon (Assyr. Babyl.) .... SIN
", moon (Egypt.) . KHENSU, THOTH
" Odin (Ger.) .... WODAN
", patron (Rom.) .... MERCURY
", principal (Egypt.) .... MIN
", red .... MARS
", Saturday's .... SAETER
", sea (Hindu) .... VARUNA
", sea (Irish) .... LER

", supreme (Babyl.) . ANU, BEL, EA,
                            EAR
", supreme (Gr.) .... ZEUS
", supreme (Scand.) ...... ALFADIR
", supreme (Tahitian) .... TAAROA
", thunderer (Babyl.) .... LARES
", Thursday's .... THOR
", tutelary (Rom.) .... LAR
", unknown (Hindu) .... KA
", Vanir (Norse) .... FREY, NJORTH
", wise (Teut.) .... BALDER
god of agriculture ... FAUNUS, NEBO,
                   NINGIRSU, OSIRIS,
                      PISUS, THOR
" of battle (Norse) .... ODIN
" of beauty (Celt.) ...... AENGUS
" of beauty (Gr.) .... APOLLO,
                          HELIOS
" of chase (Teut.) .... ULL
" of clouds (Norse) .... YMIR
" of darkness .... FORMORIAN, SET,
                          SIN
" of dawn (Vedic) ...... ASVINS,
                         DYAUS
" of day ..... HOR, HORUS, JANUS
" of dead . ANUBIS, ORCUS, OSIRIS,
            THANATOS, PWYLL, YAMA
" of discord (Norse) .... LOKI
" of dreams .. MORPHEUS, SERAPIS
" of Earth .. DAGAN, GEB, KEB, SEB
" of evil .... TIU, NERGAL, SET, TYR,
                      VARUNA
" of faith .... COMUS
" of fertility ... DAGAN, FREY, ING,
                       OSIRIS
" of fire ..... AGNI, DYAUS, GIRRU,
                   NUSKU, VULCAN
" of fish .... DAGAN, PRIAPUS
" of force ..... MENT, PTAH, SHU
" of ghosts (Babyl.) .... ENLIL
" of Hades (Rom.) ... DIS, PLUTO
" of health .... BELI, OSIRIS
" of hearth (Etruscan) ...... LAR
" of heathen (Norse) ...... AESIR
" of Heavens (Babyl.) ...... ANU
" of Heavens (Egypt.) ...... NUT
" of herds (Rom.) .... PAN
" of house (Rom.) .... LAR
" of joy (Gr.) .... COMUS
" of justice ..... FORSETI, RAMMAN
" of law (Gr.) .... ZEUS
" of light ..... MITRA, OSIRIS, SHU
" of lightning (Hindu) .... AGNI
" of love . AENGUS, AMOR, BHAGA,
         CUPID, EROS, KAMA, POTHOS
" of marriage (Gr.) ...... HYMEN
" of mischief (Norse) ...... LOKI
" of moon (Babyl.) .... NANNAR,
                          SIN
" of music .... APOLLO, BES

"	of night (Rom.) ...... SOMNUS		"	of air (Gr.) .... AURA, HERA

" of night (Rom.) ...... SOMNUS
" of noontime (Egypt.) .... RA
" of peace .. BALDER, EIR, FORSETE,
FRET
" of pleasure (Egypt.) .... BES
" of poetry (Norse) ...... BRAGE,
ODIN
" of rain ...... AGNI, ESUS, FREY,
INDRA, JUPITER
" of science (Egypt.) ...... THOTH
" of scribes; patron (Babyl.) .....
NABU
" of seas .... AEGER, ATLAS, DYLAN,
LER, NEPTUNE, NEREUS,
PONTUS, YMIR
" of sky ...... ANU, COEL, DYAUS,
JUPITER, TYR, YMIR
" of solar disc (Egypt.) .... ATEN
" of storms (Babyl.) ... ADAD, ZU
" of sun .... AGNI, AMEN, AMON,
BAAL, BELI, FREY, HELIO,
HORUS, CHEPERA, MITHRAS,
NERGAL, NINIB, RA, SHAMASH,
SOL, TEM, UTU
" of thunder; .... DONAR, JUPITER,
TARANIS, THOR, ZEUS
" of trade (Norse) .... VANIR
" of underworld (Rom.) .... DIS,
HADES, ORCUS, PLUTO
" of vegetation .. ATTIS, BACCHUS,
ESUS
" of victory .... ODIN, ZEUS
" of war .... COEL, ER, IRA, MARS,
MENT, ARES, NERGAL, THOR,
TIU, TYR, WODEN
" of war (Gaelic) .... DAGDA
" of waters .... EA, EAR, PONTUS,
HEA, NEPTUNE, VARUNA
" of wealth .... PLUTUS
" of winds .... ADAD, AEOLUS,
BOREAS, EURUS, KAARE,
NJORD, VAYU
" of wine (Gr., Rom.) .. BACCHUS
" of wisdom .... EA, EAR, GANESA,
NEBO, ODIN, SABU, SIN, TAT,
THOTH
Godavari (B.I.) capital ..... ELLORE
goddess .... DEA
" , avenging .... FURY
" , Babylonian .... ERUA
" , Carthaginian .... TANIT
" , cat-headed (Egypt.) .. BAST,
PACHT
" , Etruscan ...... MENFRA, UNI
" , hippo-headed (Egypt.) APET
" , Panopolis (Egypt.) ... MIN
" of abundance .... SRI
" of actors .... MINERVA
" of agriculture ... CERES, ISIS,
OPS

" of air (Gr.) .... AURA, HERA
" of arts (Gr.) ...... ATHENA
" of beauty (Norse) .. FREYA
" of beauty (Rom.) ... VENUS
" of birth (Rom.) .... PARCA
" of captured arms ...... LUA
" of Carthage .... TANIT
" of chance (Gr.) ..... TYCHE
" of chase ... ARTEMIS, DIANA
" of corn .... CERES
" of crops .... OPS
" of crossroads (Gr.) . HECATE
" of crossroads (Rom.) TRIVIA
" of dawn ...... EOS, MATUTA
" of dawn (Hindu) .... USHAS
" of dawn (Rom.) .. AURORA
" of death ... DANU, HEL, HELA
" of deep (Babyl.) .... NANA,
NINA
" of destiny (Gr.) ..... MOERA
" of destiny (Norse) .. NORN
" of destruction (Gr.) ... ARA
" of destruction (Hindu) .....
KALI
" of discord (Gr.) ...... ERIS
" of doom (Norse) .... URTH,
WYRD
goddess of earth, mother (Babyl.) ..
ARURU, ISHTAR
" of earth ...... TARI, CERES,
GAEA, GE, ERDA, HERTHA,
LUA OPS, SEB, SIF
" of fare .... NORN
" of fields (Rom.) .. .... LAR,
TELLUS
" of fire (Gr.) .... HESTIA
" of fire (Hawai.) ...... PELE
" of fire (Rom.) ...... VESTA
" of flowers (Gr.) ... CHLORIS
" of flowers (Rom.) ... FLORA
" of fortune .... TYCHE
" of ghosts (Gr.) .... HECATE
" of goblins (Gr.) .... ARTEMIS
" of harvest (Rom.) .... OPS
" of healing (Babyl.) .... BAU,
GULA
" of healing (Norse) ..... EIR
" of health (Gr.) .... DAMIA,
HYGEA
" of health (Rom.) .... SALU
" of hearth (Gr.) .... HESTIA,
VESTA
" of heavens (Egypt.) ... NUT
" of history (Norse) ... SAGA
" of hope .... SPES
" of horses (Rom.) .. EPONA
" of hunting (Rom.) .. DIANA,
VACUNA
" of infatuation .... ATE
" of joy (Egypt.) .... HATHOR

119

"	of justice .... ASTRAEA, DICE, MAAT	goggler .... SCAD, AKULE

"   of justice .... ASTRAEA, DICE,
                    MAAT
"   of learning (Egypt.)   SESHAT
"   of light (Rom.) .... LUCINA
"   of love .... ASTARTE, ATHOR,
            FREYA, ISHTAR, VENUS
"   of luck (Hindu) .. LAKSHMI,
                       SHRI
"   of marriage ..... GAEA, GE,
                       HERA
"   of mischief (Gr.) ...... ATE
"   of moon BENDIS, DIANA, ISIS,
           LUCINA, LUNA, ORTHIA,
             PHOEBE, SELENE
"   of night .... LETO, NOX
"   of oceans (Babyl.) ..... NINA
"   of order .. DICE, DIKE, IRENE
"   of ovens .... FORNAX
"   of peace .... EIR, IRENE, PAX
"   of plenty (Rom.) ..... OPS
"   of rainbows (Egypt.) .. IRIS
"   of retribution (Gr.) ... ARA
"   of seas (Gr.) ... DORIS, INO
"   of seas (Norse) ...... RANA
"   of seasons (pl.) ..... HORAE
"   of sky (Egypt.) ...... NUT
"   of speech (Hindu) .... VAC
"   of state (Rom.) ..... VESTA
"   of storms .... HARPY
"   of trees (fruit) ... POMONA
"   of truth (Egypt.) .... MAAT
"   of underworld ..... ALLATU,
         FERONIA, FURY, GAEA,
         HECATE, HEL, LARUNA
"   of vegetation (Gr.) .. COTYS
"   of vegetation (Rom.) CERES,
                      FLORA
"   of vengeance (Gr.) .... ARA
"   of victory (Gr.) ...... NIKE
"   of virtue (Rom.) ..... FIDES
"   of war .... ANAHITA, ANATU,
       ATHENA, BELLONA, ENYO,
           ISHTAR, VACUNA
"   of waters (Babyl.) .... ERUA
"   of wealth (Hindu) ..... SRI
"   of weaving (Gr.) .. ERGANE
"   of wedlock (Norse) .... SIF
"   of wisdom (Gr.) .... PALLAS
"   of womanhood (Egypt.) ...
                       SATI
"   of womanhood (Theban) ..
                       MUT
"   of youth (Gr.) .... HEBE
gods, messenger of the ...... HERMES
godfather .... SPONSOR
gods, "bright land" of the .. DELOS
godwit .... PRINE, RINGTAIL
Goethe hero ....FAUST, WERTHER
Goethe's home .... WEIMAR
goggle .... STARE

goggler .... SCAD, AKULE
going .... EXIT, ULTRA
going back on .... APOSTASY
gold .. GILT, ORO, AURUM, AUR, CYME
"   braid .... ORRIS
" , cast mass of .... INGOT
"   coin (see also "coin")
"   coin of Austria ... DUCAT, KRONE
"   coin of England . GUINEA, ANGEL
"   coin of France ..... LOUIS, LUIS
"   coin of Germany .... KRONE,
                      THALER
"   coin of India .... MOHUR
"   coin of Italy .... AUREUS, SCUDO,
                      SEMIS
"   coin of Japan .... ITZEBU
"   of Persia ...... ASHRAFI, TOMAN,
                      DARIC
"   coin of Russia .... IMPERIAL
"   of Scotland .... LION
"   of Spain ...... PISTOLE, DOBLON
"   coin of Turkey .... LIRA, YUZLUK
"   coin of United States ..... EAGLE
"   colored fish .... AURATA
" , containing .... DORE
"   deposit .... PLACER
" , discoverer of .... SUTTER
"   field .... OPHIR
" , fineness of .... CARAT, KARAT
"   imitation .... ORMOLU
"   lace .... FILIGREE, ORRIS
" , like .... AUREATE, AURIC
" , magic hoard of ..... RHEINGOLD
" , seeker of .... ARGONAUT
"   sheet .... FOIL
" , symbol for .... AU, OR
" , thin plate of .... LATTEN
"   vein .... LODE
"   vessel .... CUPEL
"   washing pan .... BATEA
"Gold Bug" author .... POE
Gold Coast state .... TOGO
                TOGOLAND, GHANA
"   "   seaport .... APAM
golden ..... YELLOW, AUREATE, AURIC
"   age .... SATURNIAN
"   bough .... MISTLETOE
"   bug .... LADYBIRD
"Golden Boy" author .... ODETS
Golden Fleece ship .... ARGO
"Golden King" .... MIDAS
goldenrod ..... SOLIDAGO, BONEWORT
goldfinch ...... REDCAP, YELLOWBIRD,
                      GOWDY
goldilocks .... BUTTERCUP
gold-like alloy ...... ASEM, ORMOLU,
                      OROIDE
goldsmith's crucible .. CREVET, CRUSET
golf club .... BRASSIE, DRIVER, CLEEK,
           IRON, MASHIE, PUTTER,
          SPOON, MIDIRON, NIBLICK

```
"  club, head of ............. TOE          gospel .... EVANGEL, SPELL, SYNOPTIC
golf club .................... RYDER        gossamery .... DIAPHANOUS, GAUZY,
"  term ....... TRAP, DIVOT, SCLAFF,                          THIN, COBWEBBY
            BAFF, CHIP, PAR, PUTT,          gossip ...... EME, CAT, CHAT, CLAVER,
            TEE, SLICE, EAGLE, BIRDIE          ONDIT, NORATE, QUIDNUNC, TALK,
golfer .. JONES, SNEAD, DUBBER, TEER,          TATTLE, BUSYBODY, BLAB, GUP, PIE
            PALMER, ARNOLD                  got down ...................... ALIT
Goliath's home town ......... GATH          Gothic bard ................. RUNER
Gomer, husband of .......... HOSEA          gouge ... CHEAT, CHISEL, FRAUD, BENT
gomuti palm ................ ARENG          goulash .................... RAGOUT
gone ......... PAST, AGO, OFF, LOST         gourd ..... MELON, CALABASH, PEPO,
"  for good ............... NAPOO                          CUCURBIT, FLASK
"Gone With the Wind" char. ........         gourmand .... GLUTTON, WOLVERINE
            MELANIE, RHETT, BUTLER,         gourmet ........... EPICURE, TASTER
            SCARLETT, OHARA, ASHLEY         gout .... ARTHRITIS, DROP, PODAGRA
Goneril's sister .... REGAN, CORDELIA       goutweed ............... ASHWEED
goober .................... PEANUT          govern .... REIGN, BRIDLE, LEAD, RUN,
good ...... MORAL, BEAU, BON, WEAL                                REGULATE
"  arrangement .......... EUTAXIA           governess ............ AYA, DUENNA
"  bye .............. ADIEU, TATA           government ...... SWAY, REGIME(N),
"Good-Bye," composer of ..... TOSTI                                    POLITY
good fellow ........... BRICK, TRUMP        "     agency .. FTC, FBI, SEC,
good for nothing ..... ADDLE, MEAN,           FHA, OPA, CIA, NASA, FCC, HUD,
            SHOTTEN, CARRION                                  ICC, REA
good health, in .............. PEART        "     by ten ....... DECARCHY
Good-King-Henry ............. BLITE         "     lands; Ind. ...... AMANI
good news; good tidings .. EVANGEL,         "   , no ............ ACRACY
            GOSPEL                          governor .... DYNAST, REGENT, PILOT,
Good Queen Bess .......... ORIANA              VICEROY, WOON, DECARCH,
goods ... FEE, WARES, WRACK, BONA,                        EPARCH, NOMARCH
            SEROON, STOCK                   gown .... FROCK, SOUTANE, SULTANE,
"  in sea JETSAM, FLOTSAM, LIGAN,                          MATINEE, NEGLIGEE
            LAGAN, LAGEN                    Goya subject ........ ALBA, DUCHESS
"  , movable .............. CHATTEL         grab ............. SNATCH, COP, NAB
"  , stolen ................ CRONK          grace ......... FAVOR, ADORN, ESTE,
goon ................ ROUGH, THUG              ENHANCE, HONOR, CHARM,
goosander ................ JACKSAW             MERCY, PIETY, PARDON
goose ... GREYLAG, BARNACLE, BRANT,         graceful .. EASY, FEAT, GENT, SYLPHIC,
    SOLON, GOSLET, ANATIFA, LEPAS,                       COMELY, GAINLY, SEEMLY
    DUPE, GULL, GRAYLING, GANNET,           Graces, mother of ........... AEGLE
    GANDER, NENE, NENI, ELK, GANZA          "  , one of the ... THALIA, AGLAIA
"  , cry of ........ CACKLE, HONK           gracious ..... BENIGN, URBANE, CIVIL
"  , rel. to ............. ANSERINE         grackle ...................... DAW
"  , snow ......... WAVEY, BRANT            gradation .... ABLAUT, NUANCE, STEP,
gooseberries .......... THAPES, RIBES                            SCALE, SERIES
gopher ......... TUCOTUCO, BURGLAR          grade ..... CLASS, RANK, SORT, LEVEL,
Gopher State .......... MINNESOTA                          STEP, SLANT, MARK
gore ..... PIERCE, STAB, CRUOR, NURT,       graduate .. ALUMNUS, ALUMNA, PASS,
            GUSSET, BLOOD                                        LAUREATE
gorge .... SATE, CANYON, BOLT, GLUT,        Graeae, Gorgons' watchers ... DEINO,
            STRID, NULLAH, CLOY,                             NEYO, PEPHREDO
            CHASM, FLUME, GULLET            graft ...... IMP, CLAVE, INARCH, BUD,
gorgerin .................. NECKING                        SLIP, BRIBE, SCION
gorgons .. EURYALE, MEDUSA, STHENO          "  taker ................. BRIBEE
"  , watchers for the ... GRAEAE            grafted ..................... ENTE
gorilla .................. APE, PIGMY       grafting method .......... CUTTAGE
gormaw ................ CORMORANT           grail .... SANGREAL, SANGRAAL, AMA,
Gorme, Miss ................ EYDIE                        BOW, CHALICE
gorse ... FURZE, JUNIPER, ULEX, WHIN        "  , knight of ..... BORS, GALAHAD,
gory ......... IMBRUED, BLOODY, RED             PERCIVAL, BALAN, GARETH,
gosling .............. GOOSE, GULL              GAWAIN, LANCELOT
```

121

grain ...... CORN, OAT, ATOM, IOTA,
    WHIT, ADOR, BRAN, MEAL, MITE,
    GRIST, SPECK, CEREAL, EMMER
" beard .... AWN, ARISTA
" , black .... URD
" cradle .... CADRE
" , deriv. of .... MALT
" disease .... SMUT
" exchange .... PIT
" husk .... GLUME, BRAN
" of wood .... BATE
" , per. to .... GROATS
" , refuse of .... PUG
" shelter .... HUTCH
" , shock of .... COP
gram, molecular weight .... MOLE
gramercy .... THANKS
grammar, logic, and rhetoric ....
                     TRIVIA
grammarian .... PROSODIST
grammatical case .... DATIVE
"   construction ... SYNESIS
"   term .. GENDER, COPULA,
    MODE, PARSE, SYNTAX, TELIC
grampus .... ORC, ORCA
granary .... SILO, ELEVATOR, LATHE,
    BIN, GOLA, GUNGE, GRANGE
grand .... HOMERIC, AUGUST, EPIC
grandchild .... OYE, OY
" , great- .... IEROE
grandfather .... AIEL, PATRIARCH
"   , per. to ... AVAL, AVITAL
grandeur .... GLORY, MAJESTY
grandeval .... AGED, ATAVUS
grandmother ..... BELDAM, GRANDAM
grandson .... NEPOTE
grange ..... GRANARY, FARM, HEARTH
granilla .... COCHINEAL
granite, constituent of .. FEL(D)SPAR,
    MICA, QUARTZ
" , fine-grained .... (H)APLITE
" porphyry .... ELVAN
" , variety of .. ALASKITE, BIOTITE,
    MUSCOVITE
grant ..... CEDE, APPANAGE, APPEASE,
    ADMIT, CONFER, LOAN,
    PERMIT, ENAM, (RE)MISE,
    AWARD, DISPONE, SUBSIDY
granulite .... GRAIN, CORN, KERN
grape .... DELAWARE, CONCORD,
    ISABELLA, MALAGA, CATAWBA,
    PASA, NIAGARA
" conserve .... UVATE
" , deriv. of .... ARGOL
" disease .... ESCA, APOPLEXY,
    COLEUR
" juice ... DIBS, MUST, STUM, SAPA
" juice deposit .... TARTAR
" , pomace of .... RAPE
" refuse ... MARC, BAGASSE, MURC

" seeds .... ACINI
" sugar ...... MALTOSE, DEXTROSE
" , sun-dried .... PASA
grapefruit ...... POMELO, SHADDOCK
grape-like .... UVAL, UVIC
" fruit .... UVA
grapes, bunch of .... BOB
graph ...... CHART, LOCUS, DIAGRAM
graphic .... CLEAR, VIVID, LUCID
graphite .... LEAD, PLUMBAGO, KISH
grapple ... WRESTLE, ATTACK, FASTEN,
    KNIT, BIND, OPPOSE, TONG
grasp ..... HENT, EREPT, GRIPE, SEIZE,
    CLINCH
grasping, adapted for .... PREHENSIVE
grass .... SPART, HERB
" , Amer. ..... GAMA, RYE, SESAME
" , arrow .... ESPARTO
" , Asiatic .... COIX
" , Australian .... MARRAM
" , bamboo-like .... REED
" , barn .... ANKEE
" , Bengal .... MILLET
" , Bermuda .... DOOB
" , blade of; Anglo-Ir. ... TRANEEN
" , blue June .... POA
" , bull .... GAMA
" , Burden's .... REDTOP
" , cant-like .... SORGUM
" carpet .... SMUT
" , cat-tail .... TIMOTHY
" , cereal ... RICE, MILLET, OAT, RYE
" , cloth plant .... RAMIE
" , coarse Amer. .... GAMA
" , corn .... SEDGE, KAFIR
" , couch .... BROME
" country, So. Afr. ...... VELD(T)
" , creeping beard .... FESCUE
" , crested dogs-tail ..... TRANEEN
" , darnel .... TARE
" , devil's .... COUCH
" , dried .... HAY
" , edibles of .... GRAIN
" , esparto .... ALFA
" , feather .... STIPA
" , flyaway .... BENT
" for hay .... TIMOTHY
" , forage .... MILLET, REDTOP
" , fringed brome .... CHESS
" for thatch .... ALANG
" ; gama .... SESAME
grass, goose .... LOVEMAN, SPEAR
" , grapevine .... MESQUITE
" , Guatemala .... TEOSINTE
" , hunger .... FOXTAIL
" husk .... GLUME
" , Indian cereal .... RAGEE
" , jointed-stem .... CULM
" , Kentucky blue .... POA
" , kind of ... BARLEY, BROME, EEL,
    TAPE, GAMA, NARD

" , kind of millet .... PANIC
" , leaf of .... BLADE
" , lemon .... COCKSPUR
" , Louisiana .... BENA
" , lyme .... HASSOCK
" , marsh .... SPART
" , mesquite .... NEEDLE
" , Mexican .... TEOSINTE
" , Mexican whisk .... DEER
" , moor .... HEATH
" , oat .... AVENA
" , Philippine .... COGON
" , poison rye .... DARNEL
" , purple beard .... NEEDLE
" , quaking .... BRIZA
" , quitch .... COUCH
" , reedy, Algerian .... DISS
" , rug .... MAT
" , salt .... ALKALI
" , sedge .... BROOM
" , Seneca .... VANILLA
" , silt .... KNOT
" , Spanish .... ESPARTO
" , stiff or wiry .... BENT
" , swamp .... SEDGE
" , trampled by a stag .. ABATURE
" , tuft of .... TUSSOCK
" used in paper manufacture ALFA
" , Virginia lyme .... TERRELL
" , wiry .... BENT, POA
grasses, chaffy scales in ...... GLUME
" , genus of ...... ARUNDO, STIPA,
        POA, SETARIA, AVENA
" , imported; genus .... SORGHUM
" , meadow .... POA
grassland ...... SWARD, VELD, VELDT,
        PRAIRIE, SAVANNA, RANGE, LEA,
        PASTURE
grate ..... RASP, CHARK, RUB, SCRAPE,
        GRIDE, ABRADE
gratify PLEASE, SATE, ARRIDE, HUMOR,
        PAMPER, OBLIGE
gratinate ...... BROWN, CRISP, COOK
grating . HARSH, HOARSE, GRID, HACK,
        RASPY, LATTICE, GRILLE
gratuitous ... FREE, GRATIS, WANTON
gratuity .... TIP, FEE, DOLE, GIFT,
        LAGNIAPPE, CUMSHAW, VAIL, BOON,
        CHARITY, PILON
gravamen ...... CHARGE, GRIEVANCE,
        COMPLAINT
grave .. FOSSE, SUANT, TOMB, CARVE,
        SOBER, SEDATE, SOMBER, OSSUARY,
        SEPULCHER
" cloth .... CEREMENT
" , rel. to .... BARROW, URN
gravel ... CALCULUS, CALCULI, PUZZLE,
        GRIT, GEEST
graver .... SCULPTOR, BURIN, STYLE
gravestone ..... MARKER, STELE, SLAB

gravitate .... DROP, TUMBLE, FALL
gravure, rel. to .... ROTO
gray . ACIER, ASHEN, TAUPE, GRIS, BAT,
        GULL, HOAR, IRON
" ; comb. form .... POLIO
" matter .... BRAIN, OBEX
grayish metal .... STEEL, MANGANESE
" rock .... ANDESITE
grayling .... HERRING, UMBER
graze ...... NICK, BRUSH, RUB, SHAVE,
        AGIST, BROWSE, PASTURE, FEED
grease ... LARD, AXUNGE, FAT, MORT,
        SAIM, OIL, SUET, BRIBE
greasewood .... ORACHE, CHICO
greasy ... VOLKY, OILY, PORKY, YOLKY
great ... NOBLE, SUBLIME, BIG, MICKLE,
        HUGE, TITANIC, PLENARY, SUPER,
        EMINENT
Great Barrier island .... OTEA
" Commoner .... PITT
"Great Expectations" hero .... PIP
Great Lakes . ERIE, HURON, ONTARIO,
        MICHIGAN, SUPERIOR
great number .... LAC, LAKH, LEGION,
        GALAXY, HEAP, HOST
" spirit; Amer. Indian MANITO
greater .... LARGER, MAJOR
grebe .... DABCHICK, LOON
Greco-Egyptian deity .... SERAPIS
Greece ..... ACHAEA, ATTICA, HELLAS,
        ACHAIA
" , cape in .... MATAPAN
" , city in; anc. CHALCIS, ERETRIA,
        EUBOEA, SPARTA, SERES
" , coin .. LEPTON, OBOL, STATER
" , father of church .... ORIGEN
" , headland in .... ACTIUM
" , mountain in .... ATHOS
" , nome of .... ELIS
" , province of .... NOME
" , seaport of .... ENOS
" , subdivision of .... PHYLE
" valley of .... TEMPE
greed ... AVARICE, DESIRE, GLUTTONY,
        CUPIDITY, EDACITY, AVIDITY
greedy ..... ESURIENT, AVID, CLOSE,
        STINGY, GRIPPLE
Greek, a .... CRETE, CRETAN, EOLIAN,
        ARGIVE, HELLENE, SPARTAN
" abbess .... AMMA
" assembly .... AGORA, PNYX
" avenging spirit ERINYS, KER, ATE
" bay or inlet .... SUDA
" bondsman .... PENEST
" cape ARAXOS, ARAXUS, MALEA,
        PAPAS
" castanets .... CROTALA
" Catholic .... UNIAT(E)
" choral movement .... STROPHE
" charioteer; myth. .... PHAETON

123

"	church .... ORTHODOX
"	church sections ...... BEMATA
"	citadel .... ACROPOLIS
"	city .... SPARTA, LARISSA, ARTA, SALONIKA, MEGARA
"	city; myth. .... ARGOS
"	clan subdivision .... OBE
"	colonist .... OECIST
"	colony .... ELEA, IONIA
"	column .... DORIC, IONIC
"	commander .... NAVARCH
"	commonality .... DEMOS
"	commune, modern ..... DEME
"	contest .... AGON
"	counselor .... NESTOR
"	courtesan ... ASPASIA, THAIS, LAIS
"	cup or bowl ....DEPAS
"	Cupid .... EROS
"	dance ...... PYRRHIC, HORMOS, STROPHE
"	deity, supreme .... CRONUS
"	demon of illness ..... PYTHON
"	dialect .. AEOLIC, DORIC, IONIC
"	dirge .... LINOS
"	drama .... MIME
"	dramatist .... THESPIS
"	drinking cup . COTULA, KOTYLE
"	enchantress ..... CIRCE, MEDEA
"	entertainer .... HETAIRA
"	evil spirit .... MOMUS
"	fabulist .... (A)ESOP
"	faction .... ELAS
"	feast, religious .... TONEA
"	female worshiper ..... ORANT
"	festival .... DELIA, AGON
"	fire hero; myth. .. HEPHAISTOS
"	foot-race course .... DIAULOS, DIAULI
"	foot soldier .... HOPLITE
"	galley BIREME, TRIREME, UNIREME
"	garment . PEPLOS, FUSTANELLA, CHITON, CHLAMYS
"	geographer .... STRABO
"	ghost .... KER
"	giant .... ANTAEUS
"	gifts .... XENIA
"	god (see also "god")
"	god of Aegean Sea .... NEREUS
"	" of darkness ACRISIUS, LAIUS
"	" of flocks .... PAN
"	" of hurricane .... OTUS
"	" of love .... EROS, POTHOS
"	" of rain .... ZEUS
"	" of rivers .. AXIUS, SELINUS, SIMOIS
"	" of sky .... ARGUS, ZEUS
"	" of the heavens .. URANUS, ZEUS
"	" of the sea .... NEREUS

"	" of the setting sun .... ENDYMION
"	" of the sun ...... APOLLO, HELIOS, PHOEBUS
"	" of the underworld PYTHON
"	" of the winds ..... AEOLUS, EURUS
"	" of vegetation ... DIONYSUS
"	" of war .... ARES, ENYALIUS
"	" of youth .... APOLLO
"	goddess (see also "goddess")
"	" of agriculture ARTEMIS, DEMETER
"	" of beauty . APHRODITE
"	" of chance ..... TYCHE
"	" of chastisement ...... NEMESIS
"	" of dark night ... LETO
"	" of dawn ALCMENE, EOS
"	" of destiny, or fate .... MOERA
"	" of discord .... ERIS
"	" of earth ... GAEA, GE
"	" of fire .... HESTIA
"	" of halcyon days ..... ALCYONE
"	" of love ... APHRODITE
Greek	goddess of malicious mischief .. ATE
"	" of marriage . DEMETER, GAEA, GE, HERA
"	" of memory MNEMOSYNE
"	" of nature, wild ARTEMIS
"	" of night HECATE, LETO, NYX
"	" of peace .... IRENE
"	" of pure air .. AETHER, HERA, HERE
"	" of the chase ARTEMIS
"	" of the heavens ..... HECATE, HERA
"	" of the moon . ARTEMIS, DIANA, SELENE
"	" of the night . ARTEMIS, LEDA, LETO
"	" of the plains .. MAIA, MAJESTA
"	" of the sky ..... HERA
"	" of the violet-colored clouds IOLE, JOCASTA
"	" of twilight .... HELEN, PHAEDRA
"	" of venegeance NEMESIS
"	" of victory .... NIKE
"	" of wisdom .. ATHENA, PALLAS
"	" of youth .... HEBE
"	" ; queen of the heavens HERA
"	" , triple ...... HECATE

"	gods of the subterranean fire . TITANS	"	portico .... STOA, XYST
"	governor .... EPARCH	"	priest .... PAPAS
"	gravestone .... STELE	"	province ..... NOME, BOEOTIA
"	guerilla .... ANDART	"	river .... ARTA, LERNA, PENEUS
"	gulf . ARGOLIS, ARTA, CORINTH, LACONIA, PATRAS, SALONIKA	"	sacred inclosure .... TEMENOS, SEKOS
"	gymnasium .... XYST	"	sacred place .... ABATON
"	headband .... TAENIA	"	school, per. to a ...... ELATIC
"	hero .... NESTOR, THESEUS, ACHILLES, AJAX	"	sculptor .... PHIDIAS
"	historian .... XENOPHON	"	slave, female ... BAUBO, IAMBE
"	house, apartment in . ANDRON, THALAMOS	"	solar hero; myth. .. MELEAGER
"	huntress .... ATALANTA	"	song .... MELOS
"	immigrant, ancient ..... METIC	"	soothsayer .... CALCHAS
"	island CHIOS, CRETE, ELIS, KOS, IONIAN, MILO, NIO, SAMOS, SCIO	"	sorceress .... CIRCE, MEDEA
"		"	spirit .... KER, PNEUMA
"		"	star .... ASTER, ASTRON
"	island; myth. .... NAXOS	"	statesman . ARISTIDES, PERICLES
"	laver .... LOUTER	"	stronghold .... SULI
"	lawmaker ..... MINUS, SOLON	"	subdivision .... PHYLE
"	leather flask .... OLPE	"	symbol, music ... NETE, NEUME
"	letter ALPHA, BETA, CHI, DELTA, ETA, EPSILON, GAMMA, IOTA, KAPPA, PHI, LAMBDA, MU, NU, OMICRON, PSI, RHO, SIGMA, THETA, TAU, UPSILON, XI, ZETA, OMEGA	"	temple, part of .. CELLA, NAOS
"		"	tense of the verb ..... AORIST
"		"	theater .... ODEON
"		"	time .... CHRONOS
"		"	tongue .... ROMAIC
"		"	town .... ELIS, SERES, ARTA
"		"	township .... DEME
"	letter, discontinued . DIGAMMA	"	tragedy . RHESUS, MEDEA, ION, HECUBA
"	letter, primitive .... SAN	"	
"	love feast .... AGAPE	"	tribal division .... PHRATRY
"	lyric poet .... PINDAR	"	valley in Argolis ...... NEMEA
"	magistrate ARCHON, NOMARCH	"	vessels like wineskins ... ASCI
"	market place .... AGORA	"	village .... OBE
"	marriage song .... HYMEN	"	voting place .... PNYX
"	marsh district .... LERNA	"	war cry .... ALALA
"	mathematician .... EUCLID	Greek warrior's belt .... ZOSTER
"	measure BEMA, POUS, STADIUM	"	weight OBO, MINA, TALANTON
"	monster ..... SPHINX, CENTAUR, CHIMERA	"	word .... LOGOS
"		"	writer .... LUCIAN, AESOP
"	mountain ... PARNASSUS, IDA, OSSA, ACTIUM	green CALLOW, FRESH, RAW, VERDANT, CHLORINE, UNRIPE, LEAFY, JADE, VERT, MOSS, KELLY, NILE, VIRID
"		
"	musical note .... NETE	"	arrow .... YARROW
"	musician .... ARION, ORPHEUS	"	; comb. form .... PRASEO
"	organization . EAM, EDES, ELAS	"	copper arsenate ...... ERENITE
"	overseer .... EPHOR	"	eyed .... JEALOUS
"	painter .... GRECO	"	, grayish .... RESEDA
"	parliament .... BOULE	"	, pale sea .... CELADON
"	patriarch .... ARIUS	"	sand .... MARL
"	peninsula .... MOREA	green-back herring .... CISCO
"	people .... DEMOS	Green; famous .... GRETNA
"	philosopher ... PLATO, THALES, ZENO	greenbacks .... ONES, TENS, FIVES
"		greenery .... VERDURE
"	physician .... GALEN	greengage .... PLUM
"	pilaster .... ANTA	greenheart .... BEBEERU, TREE
"	pillar .... STELE	greenhorn ... GULL, TYRO, ROOKIE, IKONA
"	platform ..... LOGEION, BEMA	
"	poet ... ARION, HOMER, PINDAR	greening .... APPLE
"	poetess ...... ERINNA, SAPPHO	greenish yellow ..... OLIVE, CITRINE
		Greenland, base in .... ETAH

125

" , discoverer of .... ERIC
" , series of .... ATANE
Greenlander .... ITA
"Green Mansions" heroine ..... RIMA
greenroom .... FOYER
greensickness .... CHLOROSIS
green-tail fly .... GRANNOM
greet .... HALSE, ACCOST, HAIL, MEET
greeting . HOW, SALUTE, AVE, ACCOIL,
    ALOHA, WELCOME, NETOP
grego .... CLOAK, JACKET
Gregorian doxology trope .. EUOUAE
grenade .... SHELL
" bag .... GIBERNE
grenadier (fish) .... RATTAIL
Gretna Green visitor .... ELOPER
grew to be .... WAXED, BECAME
Grey; author .... ZANE
grief . DOLOR, RUE, TEEN, TRIAL, WOE,
    MISERY, ANGUISH
Grieg; composer .... EDVARD
" dancer .... ANITRA
grieve ... LAMENT, MOURN, ERME, CRY,
    COMPLAIN, AGONIZE, BEWAIL
grievous .... HEINOUS, SEVERE
griffe .... MULATTO, SPUR
griffin .... EAGLE, LION
grifter's henchman .... SHILL
grig .... CRICKET, EEL
grill .... QUIZ, GRID, GRATING
grilse .... SALMON
grimace .. MOP, MOUE, MOW, SCOWL,
    SMIRK
grimalkin .... CAT, MOLL, TOM
grime .... SMUT, SOOT, SULLY
grind . MASTICATE, BRAY, MULL, CRAM,
    CRANK, RASP, TOIL
grinder . MOLAR, TOOTH, WHEEL, MILL
grinding substance . EMERY, ABRASIVE
grindstone ... METATE, MULLER, MANO
gringo .... FOREIGNER
grip .. BAG, CONTROL, DITCH, HANDLE
gripping device .... DOG, VICE
grit NERVE, SAND, PLUCK, BRAN, GUTS
gritty part of wheat ...... SEMOLINA
grivet monkey .... TOTA
grizzly bear .... EPHRAIM
groat, half a .... DANDIPRAT
grog .... RUM, RUMBO
grommet ..... EYELET, RING, BECKET
Gromyko, Mr. .... ANDREI
groom ... STRAP, BRUSH, CURRY, TIDY,
    PAGE, SAIS, SICE, SYCE
groove .... CHASE, FLUTE, RUT, STRIA,
    RABBET, SCARF
" (cut) RIFLING, CROZE, RAGLET,
    RAGGLE
grooved .... LIRATE, SULCATE, STRIATE
grooves ....SCORES, SPLINES
grope .... FUMBLE, FEEL, PROBE

grosbeak .... FINCH, MORO
gross ..... ENTIRE, SUM, RANK, CRASS,
    CRUDE, VULGAR
grotesque BIZARRE, CLOWN, BAROQUE,
    FREAK, ODD, UNIQUE, EERIE
" figure .... MAGOT
grotto ...... CATACOMB, CAVE, VAULT
grouch CRAB, GRUDGE, GRUMBLE, SULK
ground CLOD, CLAY, GRITTED, REASON,
    SOD, TURF
" , parcel of . SOLUM, ACRE, LOT
" , piece of rising .... HURST
groundhog .... MARMOT
" day .... CANDLEMAS
groundnut .... GOBBE
grounds .... LEES, RESIDUE, DREGS
grow .... ACCRUE, RAISE, WAX
ground squirrel . CHIPMUNK, HACKEE,
    SUSLIK
group BAND, BEVY, BLOC, BODY, CREW,
    HERD, TEAM, CADRE, CLASS, CORPS,
    GENUS
" of five .... PENTAD
" of four .... QUARTET
" of modeled figures .. DIORAMA
" of nine ...... ENNEAD, NONET
" of seven ...... HEPTAD, SEPTET
" singing .... HOOTENANNY
grouped together .... AGMINATE
groups of species .... GENERA
grouse PTARMIGAN, GORHEN, POULT,
    LAGOPUS, BONASA, COMPLAIN
" courtship .... LAK
grove TOPE, PINETUM, COPSE, NEMUS
" , inhabiting a .... NEMORAL
grovel CRAWL, CRINGE, FAWN, WELTER,
    CREEP
growing in couples .... BINATE
" in waste places .... RUDERAL
" out .... ENATE
" together .... ACCRETE
" wild in fields .... AGRESTIAL
growl .... GIRN, GNAR, ROME, SNARL
growth .. ACCRETION, SHOOT, MOLE,
    CANCER
" , process of .... NASCENCY
" , retarding of ..... PARATONIC
grub LARVA, MAGGOT, MATHE, SLAVE,
    MOIL, SPUD
" ax .... MATTOCK
" clear of trees .... ASSART
grudge .... HATRED, ENVY, SPITE
grue .... SHIVER, ICE, SNOW
gruel of maize meal .... ATOLE
gruesome .... GRISLY, MACABRE
gruff .... RUDE, SURLY, CLUMSE, BLUNT
grumble .... FRET, MAUNDER, CROAK,
    HONE, REPINE, MUTTER, SNARL
grumous .... ROOTY, THICK
Grus constellation .... CRANE

guacharo .... OILBIRD
Guam, an idol in .... ANITO
  " , capital of .... AGANA
  " , port of .... APRA
guan; genus .... ORTALIS
Guana .... ARAWAKAN
guana .... LIZARD
guanaco .... LLAMA
guarantee .... BAIL, BOND, WARRANT,
                       SURETY
guarantor .. ANGEL, SURETY, VOUCHER
guarapucu .... WAHOO
guard ...... FENDER, BANTAY, PATROL,
                       PICKET
  " , freemason's .... TILER
guardhouse .... BRIG
guardian . TRUSTEE, TUTELAR, WARDEN,
    ANGEL, HELPER, ARGUS, CERBERUS
Guatemala monetary unit .. QUETZAL
  " fruit .... ANAY
gudgeon .... DUPE, GULL
Gudrun's brother .... GUNNAR
guava .... MYRTAL, ARACA
guenon .... MONKEY, GRIVET
Guiana tribesman .... BONI
  " hut .... BENAB
guess .... DIVINE, INFER, SURMISE
guide ...... PILOT, CLEW, KEY, STEER,
      COURIER, TEACH, SCOUT, PIR,
                 CICERONE
  " book .... ORDO, BAEDEKER
guiding .... DIRIGENT, POLAR
  " star ... LODESTAR, CYNOSURE
guidon .... FLAG
Guido's scale, note in .. UT, ELA, ALT,
                     ELAMI
guild .... HANSE, HUI, TONG
Guild Hall statue ..... GOG, MAGOG
guile .... FRAUD, TRAIN, DECEIT
guileless .... ARTLESS, SINCERE, NAIVE
guillemot . AUK, AWK, MURRE, MURSE,
                     QUET
guillotine, wagon to .... TUMBREL
guilt .... CULP
guilty .... WRONG, NOCENT, WICKED
guinea corn .... DURRA, MILLET
  " fowl .... KEET, PINTADO,
                   GUTTERA
  " pig . CAVIA, CAVY, BOAR, PACA
Guinea, small tree of .... AKEE
guise .... CLOAK, GARB, MIEN,
                 PRETENSE
guitar .... VINA, SITA, UKE
  " key .... DITAL
  " -like instr. ... BANDORE, ROTE,
                 SAMISEN
gulch ...... ARROYO, GORGE, RAVINE
gulf .... ABYSS, BAY, CHASM, SINE
  " , per. to .... VORTEX
  " weed .... SARGASSO

gull ..... LARID, PIRR, SEEDBIRD, SKUA,
    TEASER, XEMA, PEWEE, PEWIT,
    LARUS, JAEGER, ALLAN, COB,
         MEW, KITTIWAKE
  " , to ..... CULLY, DUPE, GUDGEON
gullet ...... MAW, CRAW, SWALLOW
Gulliver, human met by .... YAHOO
  " , flying island of ..... LAPUTA
gully ..... ARROYO, WADI, COULOIR,
         GUT, SIKE, DONGA
gum .... CONIMA, AMRA, ASA, RESIN,
    ELEMI, LATEX, LOBAN, MATTI,
         MYRRH, GALBAN
  " , a solid white .... CAMPHOR
  " arabic .... ACACIA, ACACIN
  " arabic tree .... KIKAR
  " , catechu-like ...... KINO, CHICLE
  " plant .... ULE
  " -resin narcotic .... HASHISH
  " tree ...... XYLAN, TUART, BALATA,
               NYSSA, TUPELO
gumbo .... OCRA, OKRA, SOUP
gumboil .... PARULIS
gums .... ULA
  " , of the .... ULETIC, GINGIVAL
gun .. ROD, BAZOOKA, MORTAR, ROER,
      STEN, BREN, LUGER, MAXIM,
    BARKER, MAUSER, PISTOL, CARBINE,
              GATLING
  " , caliber of .... BORE
  " chamber .... GOMER
  " case, leather .... HOLSTER
  " pointer device ... SIGHT, DOTTER,
                 BEAD
  " , swiveled .... AMUSETTE
gunboat .... TINCLAD
gun catch .... SEAR
gun cock .... NAB
gunfire .... SALVO, FUSILLADE
guns .... WEAPONS, ARMOR, ARMS
gunstock corner .... TOE
gunwale .... PORTOISE
guppy .... MINNOW, FISH
gurgling sound ..... CROOL, GUGGLE
Gurion, Mr. .... DAVID, BEN
gurnard .... CUR, ROCHET, TRIGLA
Gurth; "Ivanhoe" .... VASSAL
gush ...... POUR, STOUR, RAIN, SPURT
gust .... BLOW, GALE, PUFF
gusto ...... ELAN, ZEST, RELISH, TASTE
Guthrie .... ANSTEY
gutta .... DROP, SOH, MINIM, SIAK
gutter .. CULLIS, EAVES, DITCH, GULLY,
         CONDUIT, GROOVE
guttersnipe .... ARAB, GAMIN
guttural .. DRY, HUSKY, BURR, HOARSE,
               VELAR
guy ... BAFFLE, FOOL, EFFIGY, SHORE,
    STAY, VANG, FELLOW, JOSH

guzzle .... SWIG, SWILL, SOT, TIPPLE, TOPE, CAROUSE, TUN
gym feat .... KIP(P)
gypsum .... SELENITE, ALABASTER
gypsy ...... NOMAD, APTAL, BAZIGAR, BOHEMIAN, ZIGEUNER, ZINGANO, ZINGARO, GITANO, ZINCALO, ROAMER, ROMANY, CALE, CALO
   "   gentleman .... ROM, RYE
   "   horse .... GRI
   "   language .... ROMANY
   "   pocketbook LIL
   "   sea tribe, one of ...... SELUNG
   "   winch .... CRAB
"Gypsy Rose _____" .... LEE
gyrate .... ROTATE, SPIN, WHIRL
gyrator .... TOP, PILOT
gyre .... EDDY, CIRCLE, VORTEX, RING
gyve(s) ..... IRONS, FETTER, SHACKLE

H

H, letter .... AITCH
H-shaped .... ZYGAL
H, sound of .... ASPIRATE
habit ...... GARB, RUT, MODE, USAGE, CUSTOM, PRACTICE, WONT
habitat ...... ABODE, HAUNT, PURLIEU
habitual .... CHRONIC, WONTED, ORDERLY
habituate .. ADDICT, INURE, USE, DRILL, FREQUENT
hacienda ..... FARM, CROFT, GRANGE, PLANTATION
hack ... COUGH, GRUB, DEVIL, WRITER, DRUDGE, HORSE, NOTCH, KICK, NICK, HEW
hackle ..... COMB, HATCHEL, HAGGLE
hackneyed .... BANAL, TRITE, CLICHE, STALE, COMMONPLACE
Hades ..... ABADDON, ARALU, ORCUS, EREBUS, TARTARUS, PLUTO, LIMBO, SHEOL
   "   river .... STYX, ACHERON, LETHE
hag .... CRONE, HARRIDAN, VIXEN, BELDAME, JEZEBEL, SHREW, VIRAGO, HARPY, VECKE, FURY
Hagen; actress .... UTA
hagfish .... BORER, MYXINE
haggard ...... WAN, WORN, DRAWN, GAUNT
Haggard novel .... SHE
haggle .... CHAFFER, PALTER, PRIG
hail ..... GREET, AHOY, AVE, SIGNAL, CALL, SALUTE, WELCOME
   ", soft .... GRAUPEL

hair ... FUR, NAP, DOWN, PILE, SHAG, CRINE, THATCH, FILAMENT
   "; a molting .... ECDYSIS
   " braid .... CUE
   ", coarse rigid ..... CERDA, SETULA, SETA
   "; comb. form .... PILO
   " dresser; Fr. .... FRISEUR
   " dressing .... POMADE
   " dye .... HENNA
   ", false ..... PERUKE, FRONT, TETE
   " feeler .... PALP, PALPUS
   ", fillet for the .... SNOOD
   ", head of .... CRINE, MOP
   ", like a tuft of ... SHAG, COMOID
   ", like curly .... CIRROSE
   ", lock of .... LOVELOCK, TRESS
   ", neck .... MANE
   " net .... LINT, SNOOD
   " on end .... STARE
   " pad .... RAT
   ", part in .... LIST
   ", per. to .... LINUS, NOIL, CRINAL, PILAR
   " plant .... PILUS, PUBES
   ", remove .... EPILATE
   "; roll at back of neck .. CHIGNON
   " shirt .... CILICE
   ", strips of .. EPILATES, DEPILITATES
   " wave .... MARCEL
   ", weak .... CRINITE
   ", wisp of .... TATE
   ", wooly .... SHAG
   " worm .... GORDIUS
hairdo .... BANG, POODLE, UPDO, UPSWEEP, BRAID, BOB
hairiness .... VILLOSITY
hairless ..... GLABROUS, PELON, BALD
hairlike processes .... CILIA
hairs, beset with .... BARBATE
hairs on plants VILLI
hairy ..... PILOSE, COMATE, HIRSUTE, NAPPY, PILAR, TUFTED, COMOSE, CILIATE
Haitian bandit .... CACO
   " coin .... GOURDE
   " evil spirit ...... BAKA, BOKO
   " liberator .... TOUSSAINT
   " sorcery .... VOODOO
   " sweet potato .... BATATA
hakim .... PHYSICIAN
halberd .... AX, FRAME, GLAIVE
   " -shaped ... HASTATE, GISARME
halcyon .... KINGFISHER, CALM, TRANQUIL
Halcyone, father of .... AEOLUS
   ", husband of .... CEYX
hale .... HEARTY, WELL, ROBUST, PULL, TRAIL, TUG, DRAG
Halevy opera .... JUIVE

128

halftone picture .... DUOGRAPH, DUOTONE
half ...... HEMI, DEMI, SEMI, MOIETY
" boot .... BUSKIN, PAC
" breed .... MESTIZO, MESTEE, MULATTO, LADINO, MULE, METIS
" nelson .... HOLD
" turn .... CARACOL(E)
" witted .... IMBECILE, SILLY
" year's stipend .... ANNAT
halibut .... FLATFISH
halicore .... DUGONG
Halifax, Lord .... SAVILE
halite .... SALT, SAL
halitus .... AURA, BREATH
hall(s) . ATRIUM, AULA, FOYER, ODEON, SALA, ENTRY, LYCEUM, LOBBY, PASSAGE, ATRIA
" for athletes ... GYM, XYST(US)
" of Odin .... VALHALLA
hallow .... SANCTIFY, BLESS
hallowed .... BLEST, SACRED
hallowed spot .... HOLY, BETHEL
hallucination ...... ERROR, FANTASY, CHIMERA, MIRAGE, ILLUSION
halo .... AURA, BRUGH, NIMB(US), AUREOLE, GLORY, LIGHT, CORONA
halogen .... BROMINE, CHLORINE, FLUORINE, IODINE
halt .... CRIPPLED, END, MAIMED, HESITATE, ARREST, CEASE
halter .... HANG, NOOSE, STRAP
halved .... BISECTED, DIMIDIATED
ham .... AMATEUR, OVERACT
Hamath king .... TOI, TOU
Hamilton's birthplace .... NEVIS
Hamite ...... BERBER, KABYLE, SHILHA
Hamitic Negro ..... MASAI, SOMAL(I)
" religion .... ISLAM
hamlet ..... CASAL(E), ALDEA, DORP, THORP, MIR, BURG, DUMP
Hamlet, scene of .... ELSINORE
" , girl in .... OPHELIA
Hammerskjold, Mr. .... DAG
hammer ...... MARGE, BEETLE, PLEXOR, MAUL, MARTEL, FULLER, SLEDGE, KEVEL, BULLY, POUND
" , end or head of .. PEEN, PEIN, POLL
" , operator of trip ...... TILTER
" , pavior's .... REEL
" , presiding officer's .... GAVEL
" , to .... MALLEATE
" , trip .... OLIVER
hamper ... TRAMMEL, HOBBLE, BASKET, MAUND, SEROON, HALT, IMPEDE
hampers ... SHACKLES, IRONS, FETTERS
Hampshire district .... ROMSEY, FLEET
Ham's eldest son .... CUSH

hamstring ...... HOUGH, HOX, LAME, MAIM
hanaper .... BASKET, HAMPER
hand .. FIST, MANUS, PAW, PUD, DEAL, PART, TALENT, TENACE
" bag .... ETUI, RETICULE, SATCHEL
" ball .... FIVES, PELOTA
" , palm of .... LOOF, THENAR, GOWPEN
" , per. to .... CHIRAL, MANUAL
" used in writing Arabic ... NESKI
handbill .... DODGER
handbook .... MANUAL, CODEX, TOME
handcuffs .. MANACLES, BRACELETS, DARBIES
Handel; compo. by . LARGO, MESSIAH
handful .... GRIP, KIRN, WISP
handicap .... ODDS, RACE, EQUALIZE, HINDER
handkerchief .... MALABAR
handle .... HEFT, HELVE, ANSA, HANK, HAFT, BAIL, TOTE, TOAT, TILLER, ROUNCE, SNATH, SNEAD
" awkwardly ...... PAW, THUMB
" , to .... WIELD, TREAT
handled .... DEALT, PALMED, ANSATE
hand length .... SPAN
hand mill .... QUERN
hands off ... TABOO, INTERDICT, QUIT
" , without .... AMANOUS
handsel .... EARNEST, FAVOR, GIFT
handsome .. BONNY, COMELY, LOVELY
hand stamp .... DATER
handstone .... MANO
handwriting .... SCRIPT, PENMANSHIP
" on the wall ...... MENE, TEKEL, UPHARSIN
handy .... ADROIT, DEFT, READY, NEARBY, HEPPEN, DEXTROUS
hang .. PEND, DANGLE, DRAPE, SWAG, LAVE, PERPEND, BANGLE, LOP, IMPEND
hanger-on .... PARASITE, TOADY
hanging .... DOSSAL, DORSAL, SESSILE
hangings ... ARRAS, DOSSER, DRAPERY
hangman's noose, per. to ... HEMPEN
hangnail .... AGNAIL, WHITLOW, STEPMOTHER
hank .... RAN, SKEIN, COIL, LOOP
hanker .... CRAVE, LONG, YEARN, COVET
hanky-panky .... TRICKERY
Hannibal's father .. HAMILCAR, BARCA
haphazard .... RANDOM, CHANCE
happen ...... EVENE, BEFALL, OCCUR, FARE, BETIDE
happening . SPORADIC, TIDING, EVENT
happy .... BLEST, COSH, FAUST, GLAD
harangue ...... TIRADE, NAG, ORATE, SCREED, RANT, SPOUT, DIATRIBE

129

Haran's relative ..... MILCAH, TERAH,
LOT, ABRAHAM
harass .... CHAFE, BAIT, BESET, TEASE,
HAGRIDE, HECKLE, HECTOR, PESTER,
BADGER, HAZE
Haratin .... BERBERS
harbinger .... USHER, HERALD, OMEN,
INFORMANT, PRECURSOR
harbor . COTHON, PIER, PORT, REFUGE,
BAY, FOSTER, COVE
    "   master .... HAVENER
hard ... STEELY, STONY, DOUR, STERN,
FLINTY, ARDUOUS, CALLOUS
    "   coal .... ANTHRACITE
    "   shell .... LORICA
    "   wood .... DURA, TEAK
harden ...... GEL, ENURE, INURE, SET,
KERN, STEEL, SEAR, OSSIFY, BRACE
hardtack .... PANTILE
hard-wood tree .... MABI
hardy .... SET, HALE, LUSTY, SPARTAN,
STURDY, TOUGH, RIGID, RUGGED
Hardy character .... TESS
hare ... CONY, WAT, BAWD, LEVERET,
LEPUS, TAPETI
    " ; "Little Chief" ...... CONY, PIKA
    " , tail of .... SCUT
    " , track of .... FILE, SLOT
hare-like .... LEPORINE
    "   animal .... AGOUTI
harem .... SERAGLIO, SERAI, ZENANA
    " , room in .... ODA
    " , slave in .... ODALISQUE
harlequin ... CLOWN(ISH), BUFFOON,
DROLL, ZANY, PUNCH
    "   duck .... LADY
harm ...... DERE, MAR, SCATHE, BALE,
BANE, DAMAGE
harmful .... NOCENT, NOXIOUS,
NOISOME, ILL, SINISTER, BANEFUL
    "   influence .... NOXA, UPAS
harmless .... DOVISH, SAFE,
INNOCUOUS
harmonious .. SPHERAL, CONSONANT,
CORDIAL, DULCET
harmony ...... TONE, CHIME, CHORD,
KEY, UNION, CONCORD
harness ...... ARMOR, GEAR, GRAITH,
TAME, EQUIP
    " , part of ...... HAME, TERRET,
TUG, CRUPPER, BILLET, BLIND
Harold the Saxon's wife ...... EDITH
harp .. ITERATE, KOTO, LYRE, NANGA,
VINA
    " -guitar key .... DITAL
harpoon .... IRON, SPEAR, FISHGIG
harpsichord .... CLAVECIN, SPINET
harpy ...... AELLO, EAGLE, CELAENO,
OCYPETE
harquebusier .... CARABIN

harridan ..... HAG, JEZEBEL, VIRAGO
harrier ..... HARPY, PUTTOCK, HOUND
harrow ...... HERSE, TILL, CHIP, TEAR,
TORMENT, BREAK, DRAG, VEX
harsh .... STERN, GRIM, ACERB, DURE,
ASPER, CRUEL, RASPY, GRUFF,
AUSTERE, CAUSTIC
harshness .. RAUCITY, STRIDOR, RIGOR
hart .... DEER, SPADE, STAG
Harte; author .... BRET
hartebeest ..... ANTELOPE, BONTEBOK
    " -like animal ...... BLESBOK,
SASSABY
hartshorn, spirits of ...... AMMONIA
hartwort .... SESELI
haruspex .... SOOTHSAYER
Harvard College book prize .. DETUR
harvest .... CROP, FRUIT, REAP, YIELD,
RABI, KIRN, GLEAN, GARNER
    "   home .... HOCKEY, KIRN
    "   tick .... ACARID
Harvey char. .... RABBIT
has not .... NAS
hashish drug .... BHANG, HEMP,
CANNABIS
hassle .... FRAY, BRAWL, MELEE
Hasso; actress .... SIGNE
hassock ... BASS, DOSS, FOOTSTOOL,
PESS, TUFT
hasten .... SCUD, HIE, SCAMP(ER),
HOTFOOT, SCURRY, SPEED
hasty .... CURSORY, EAGER, RASH
hasty pudding .... MUSH, SEPON,
SUPAWN
hat .... TOQUE, BERET, FELT, TAM,
TOPPER, CHAPEAU, SHOVEL,
GIBUS, TOPEE, TOPI, TILE,
DICER, FEDORA, TRICORN
    " , ecclesiastic ...... BIRETTA, MITER
    " , fur used in .... CONEY, BEAVER
    " , hunter's .... TERAI
    " , Roman, anc. .... PETASUS
    " , soldier's .... SHAKO, BUSBY
hatch .... DEVISE, GATE, LID, SCHEME
hate .... DETEST, LOATHE, ABHOR,
DOSA, ODIUM, MALICE, RANCOR
    " ; comb. form .... MISO
hateful .... EXECRABLE, ODIOUS,
NAUSEOUS
haughty ... CAVALIER, PROUD, ALOOF
haul ...... BOUSE, DRAW, HALE, LUG,
SWAG, BOOTY
hauled up .. TRICED, ARRESTED, ROPED
haunch .... HIP, HUCK
haunt .... NEST, OBSESS, DEN, LIE,
RESORT, DIVE
hautboy .... OBOE
hauteur .... ARROGANCE, PRIDE
have .... HAE, OWN, HOLD, KEEP,
OBTAIN

```
"   effect ............ RESULT, TAKE          "   shrub ......... AKIA, POHA
"   thought of .............. IDEATE          "   silky fiber ........... PULU
haven ...... REFUGE, ASYLUM, HITHE,          "   song ............... MELE
                PORT, HARBOR, LEE            "   starchroot ............ PIA
haw .... CLOSE, EYELID, SLOE, PEGGLE         "   temple ............. HEIAU
Hawaiian .... POLYNESIAN, KANAKAN            "   tern ............... NOIO
"   breech cloth ........ MALO                "   thrush .... OMAO, OLOMAO
"   bush .............. OLONA                 "   timber tree .... KOA, OHIA
"   canoe ............. WAAPA                 "   town ............... HILO
"   city ........... HONOLULU                 "   volcano .......... KILAUEA
"   cliff ................. PALI               "   wind ............... KONA
"   cloak ............. MAMO                   "   worsted cloth ....... KAPA
"   common or profance . NOA                  "   wreath ................ LEI
"   cord ................. AEA               hawk ...... ASTUR, KARAKARA, KAHU,
"   crater ............ KILAUEA                KESTREL, PUTTOCK, FALCON,
"   dance .............. HULA                  TERCEL, EYAS, KITE, ACCIPITER, IO,
"   drink ............... KAVA                             OSPREY
"   feast ................ LUAU              "  , blind .................. SEEL
"   firm ................. HUI               "   cage ................... MEW
"   fish ................ AWA                "   fly ................. ASILUS
"   fish bait ............ HOLA              "   moth ....... SPHINGID, SPHINX
"   fish poison ....... AUHUHU               "  , sparrow ............. NISUS
"   food ..... KALO, POI, TARO              hawker . PEDDLER, CADGER, CHAPMAN,
"   fruit ................ POHA                              FALCONER
"   game ................. HEI              hawked ...................... SOLD
"   god ................. KANE              Hawkeye state ............... IOWA
"   goddess of fire ....... PELE            hawk-headed god .......... HORUS
"   goose ............... NENE              hawking leash .......... JESS, LUNE
"   gooseberry .......... POHA              hawk's nest ......... AERY, AERIE
"   governor ............ DOLE              hawkweed ................. DINDLE
"   harbor .............. PEARL             hawser frame ................ BITT
"   honey eater .......... OO               "   iron ................ CALKING
"   island ..... KAUAI, LANAI,             "   post ............ BOLLARD
                        OAHU               hawthorn ......... MAY, MAYFLOWER
"   island precipice ..... PALI            "  , fruit of ............ HAW
"   Islands ......... SANDWICH             hay bird ................ BLACKCAP
"   ", discoverer of ......                "   fever ................... ROSE
                    GAETANO                "   fodder plant .......... SAINFOIN
"   lava ................. AA              "  , kind of ............. TIMOTHY
"   line ............ CREANCE              "  , second growth ........ ROWEN
"   liquor ......... AWA, KAWA             "   spreader .............. TEDDER
"   majagua ............. HAU              haycock . RACK, COB, COIL, RICK, PIKE,
"   member of royal family ...                                GOAF
                        ALII               Hayworth; actress ............ RITA
"   mountain range ... KOOLAU              hazard ...... PERIL, BET, DARE, STAKE,
"   mulberry bark ....... KAPA                          WAGER, DANGER
"   musical instrument ... UKE,            hazardous .... CHANCY, JUMPY, RISKY
                    UKULELE                haze FILM, SMOG, MIST, FOG, VAPOR,
"   native .......... KANAKA                        GLIN, MIASMA, BRUME
"   paper cloth .. KAPA, OLONA             hazelnut ...... FILBERT, NIT, COBNUT
"   pepper ............... AVA             Hazor king ................ JABIN
"   pine ................... IE            he remains, stage direction ... MANET
"   pit, baking ........... IMU            head ....... PATE, NOB, CAPUT, TETE,
"   plant ....... OLONA, KALO                      NOODLE, BEAN, LEAD
"   porch ....... LANA, LANAI              "  , back part of .... OCCIPUT, POLL
"   president ........... DOLE             "   gear ....... BERET, WIMPLE, CAP
"   root .............. AWATI              "   on Athena's aegis ..... MEDUSA
"   salutation ......... ALOHA             "   pence ................... TAX
"   seaweed ............ LIMU              "  , rel. to ............. PARIETAL
"   shampoo ........ LOMILOMI              "  , shave the ........... TONSURE
```

headache .... CEPHALALGIA
   " , one-sided MEGRIM, MIGRAINE
headdress . ALMICE, PINNER, CAPELINE,
   WIG, TIARA, POUF, BIRETTA, MITER,
                    HENNIN
   " , military ... BUSBY, SHAKO
   " , widow's .... BANDORE
headhunter .... ITALON
headland CAPE, KOP, NESS, RAS, BLUFF,
                    NASE
headless animal .... ACEPHAL
headshaped .... CAPITATE
headline . BANNER, DISPLAY, STREAMER
headman .... HETMAN
headsman ...... EXECUTIONER, VIDAN
headwater .... UPRIVER
heal .. CURE, MEND, RESTORE, REMEDY,
                    SAIN
healer .... ASA
healing .... CURATIVE
   " , science of ...... IATROLOGY
health; comb. form .... SANI
health-drinking word . SKOAL, SALUTE,
                  PROSIT
healthy .... SANE, HALE, HEARTY
heap SORITE, STACK, COP, PILE, TUMP,
     AMASS, GOBS, RAFT, SHOCK
   " , per. to .... ACERVAL
hearer .... AUDIENT, LISTENER
hearing .. OYER, TRIAL, AUDIT, PROBE
   " , defective .... OTOSIS
   " , of .... AURAL, OTIC
hearsay . REPORT, RUMOR, TALK, BRUIT,
                  GOSSIP
hear ye .... OYES, OYEZ
hearse .... FRAME, RAKE, BIER
heart ...... CARDIA, COR, GIST, PITH,
            KERNEL, TICKER
   "   action, denoting too-active ....
                  STHENIC
   "   ailment .... ANGINA
   "   bleeding .... DICENTRA
   "   cavities .... ATRIA
   "   contraction .... SYSTOLE
   " , Egyptian .... AB, HATI
   " , innermost .... CORE
heart, per. to .... CARDIAC
   "   stimulant .... DIGITALIS
heartburn .... PYROSIS
hearth .... BRAZIER, FIRESIDE, INGLE
   " , chamber of .... CAMERA
heart-shaped .... CORDATE
heartwood of a tree .... DURAMEN
hearty .... HALE, LUSTY, ROBUST
heat . CALOR(IC), ARDOR, FIRE, ZEAL,
     TEPOR, CAUMA, FEVER, FERMENT
   " -resistant alloy CERAMAL, CERMET
   "   unit .... THERM, CALORIE
heater ...... ETNA, TISAR, RADIATOR
heath MOOR, BENT, GRIG, PLAIN, ERICA

heathberry .... BILBERRY
heathbird .... GROUSE
heathen .. GENTILE, GODLESS, PAGAN,
       PAYNIM, INFIDEL, ETHNIC
heating vessel .... RETORT
heave ... SCEND, THROW, FLING, HURL
heaven ...... ETHER, ARCADIA, EDEN,
     ELYSIUM, CIEL, SKY, VALHALLA,
   PARADISE, NIRVANA, ECSTASY, ZION
   " ; comb. form .... URANO
heavenly ...... SUPERNAL, URANIAN,
     CELESTIAL, EDENIC, EMPYREAN,
                SERAPHIC
   "   being ..... ANGEL, CHERUB,
              SERAPH, AFA
   "   body COMET, MOON, STAR,
                    SUN
   "   path .... ORBIT
heavens, per. to .... ORRERY, URANIC
heavy . LEADEN, GLOOMY, HARD, SAD,
        DULL, GRAVE, INERT
   "   blow .... ONER
Heber's wife .... JAEL
Hebrew .... ZION, SEMITE
   "   acrostic .... AGLA
   "   alien resident .... GER
   "   allies .... HABIRI
   "   alphabet ..... ALEPH (ALEF),
     BETH, GIMEL, DALETH, HE, VAU
   (WAW), ZAYIN, CHETH, TETH, JOD
     (YOD, YODH), CAPH (KAPH),
     LAMED (LAMEDH), MEM, NUN,
     SAMEKH, AIN (AYIN), PE, SADHE,
     KOPH, RESH, SIN (SHIN), TAV
                  (TAW)
   "   ancestor .... EBER
   "   brotherhood ...... ESSENE
   "   canonical law book . TALMUD
   "   doctrine .... KARAISM
   "   dry measure (see "measure")
   "   excommun. .... HEREM
   "   festival .... PURIM, SEDER
   "   flute .... NEHILOTH
   "   food inspector ..... SHOMER
   "   for Hades .... SHEOL
   "   healer .... ASA
   "   herdsman .... AMOS
   "   high priest AARON, ELI, EZRA
   "   king of demons .. ASMODEUS
   "   "Law of Moses" TORA, TORAH
Hebrew marriage custom ... LEVIRATE
   "   measure .. KES, OMER, EPHAH
   "   month ...... TISHRI, HESHVAN
     (BUL), KISLEV, TEBET, SHEBAT
     (SEBAT), ADAR, VEADAR,
     NISAN (ABIB), IYAR(ZIV),
     SIVAN, TAMMUZ, AB, ELUL
   "   name for God ..... ADONAI,
                  ELOHIM

"   name (place) of Old
          Testament MISPEH, MIZPAH
"   next of kin .... GOEL
"   order .... ESSENE
"   Passover month .... ABIB
"   psalms of praise .. HALLEL
"   priest's helper .... LEVITE
"   prophet DANIEL, AMOS, NASI
"   prophet, suppositious ....
                          MALACHI
"   prophetess .... DEBORAH
"   proselyte .... GER
"   quarter .... GHETTO
"   scarf .... ABNET, TALLITH
"   scholar .... SABORA
"   seer BALAAM, ISAAC, MOSES
"   unclean .... TREF
"   songs of praise ...... HALLEL
"   stringed inst. .... ASOR
"   teacher .... RAB
"   tribe .... DAN, LEVITES
"   universe .... OLAM
"   vowel point .... SEGO, TSERE
"   weight .... GERAH
"   word .... SELAH
"   word for city ...... KIRJATH
Hebrides Is. .. IONA, RUM, SKYE, UIST
Hector's father .... PRIAM
"   wife .... ANDROMACHE
Hecuba's husband .... PRIAM
heddle .... CAAM, CORD, GUIDE
hedgehog .... ECHINUS, URCHIN
"   -like animal .... TENREC
hedge .... BOMA, HAW, HAY, RADDLE
"   trimmer ... PLASHER, TOPIARIST
Hedin; explorer .... SVEN
heed NOTE, LISTEN, MIND, RECK, CARE,
                          NOTICE, OBEY
heedful .... VIGILANT, ALERT
heedless .... LAX, RASH, REMISS
heel .... BOUNDER, CAD
"   bone .... CALCANEUM, FIBULA(R)
Heflin; actor .... VAN
hegira .... EXODUS, FLIGHT
heifer .... COW, STIRK
height ...... ALT, APEX, TOP, SUMMIT,
        STATURE, HEYDEY, PINNACLE, ACME
"   of drama action .. CATASTASIS
heir .. LEGATEE, HERITOR, PARCENER,
                    SCION, POSTERITY
Hejaz, holy city in .. MECCA, MEDINA
held; mus. .... TENUTO
Helen of Troy, mother of ...... LEDA
"   , son of .... DORUS
Helena's husband; Shak. ... BERTRAM
helical .... SPIRAL, TORSE
helicopter landing place ... HELIPORT
Heliopolis .... MATARIYA, ON
Helios .... SOL, APOLLO
"   , sister of .... ARTEMIS

heliotrope .... GIRASOL
hell PIT, ABYSS, HADES, ORCUS, SHEOL,
        TOPHET, ABADDON, AVERNUS,
        AVICI, GEHENNA, INFERNO
hellbender .... DEBAUCH, TWEEG,
                          SALAMANDER
Hellene .... GREEK
Helles' mother .... NEPHELE
helix simple .... UNISPIRAL
Hellespont, city on .... ABYDOS
Heloise's husband .... ABELARD
helm .... RUDDER, TILLER, TIMON
helmet .... ARMET, GALEA, MORION,
        HEAUME, ELME, SALLET, TOPI,
        TOPEE, BASINET, CASQUE
"   bird .... TURACOU
"   flower ..... ACONITE, ORCHID
"   , lower part of .... BEAVER
"   , nose guard of .... NASAL
"   -shaped .... GALEATE
"   "   part .... GALEA
"   , upper part of . VISOR, VIZOR
helminth .... WORM
helmsman . CONNER, PILOT, TILLER,
                          COXSWAIN
helot .... ESNE, SERF, SLAVE
help STEAD, ABET, AID, CURE, SUCCOR,
                REMEDY, SECOND, BOTE
helper ..... AID, ASSIST(ANT), ANSAR
helpless .... LIMP, SPINELESS
Hel's watchdog .... GARM
Helvetic .... SWISS
hem .... EDGE, BORDER, SEW, FOLD
"   in .... BEBAY, BESET, FENCE
hematite .... LIMONITE, ORE
Hemingway; author .... ERNEST, PAPA
hemlock .... TSUGA, CONIUM
hemorrhage .... HEMOPHILIA
hemp .... CORDILLA, PITA, TOW, IFE,
        LHIAMBA, SUNN, SABZI, BHANG,
        OAKUM, ABACA, BANG, BENG,
                          CARL, RINE
"   as a narcotic .... HASHISH
"   dried leaves .... KEF, KIEF
"   fabric .... BURLAP
"   fiber .... AGAVE, SISAL
"   , flowering heads of ... GANJA
"   resin .... CHARAS
hen .... PARTLET, PULLET, BIDDY
"   harrier .... HAWK
"   hawk .... REDTAIL
"   , large water .... GALLINULE
"   , mud .... RAIL
"   roost .... PERCH
henbane .... HYOSCINE
henbit .... LAMIUM
hence ...... ERGO, OFF, AWAY, THEN
Hengest's brother .... HORSA
henna .... ALCANA, ORCHANET
henpeck .... NAG

133

Henry .... HAL
Henry II, wife of .... ELEANOR
Henry IV, birthplace of .... PAU
"Henry VI" character .. CADE, VAUX
Henry VIII; wives .. ANNE, BOLEYN,
   CATHERINE, PARR, JANE, SEYMOUR,
                    HOWARD
hen's bill .... SAINFOIN
Hera, husband of .... ZEUS
  " , mother of .... RHEA
  " , rival of .... LETO
  " , son of .... ARES
herald .. MESSENGER, CRIER, PRECURSE,
        BLAZON, USHER, PAGE
  " , coat of .... TABARD
heraldic design .... RUSTRE
  "   fillet .... ORLE
  "   shield, border in a; .. ORLE,
                  BORDURE
  "   shield, boss in a ..... UMBO
  "   shield, broad vertical stripe
      in .... PALE
  "   shield, concealed half of ...
                  SINISTER
  "   shield, division of .... ENTE
  "   shield, horizontal band across
                  FESS
  "   shield, rectangular division of
                  CANTON
  "   shield-shaped ...... PELTATE
  "   shield, two circular segments
      at sides .... FLANCH
  "   shield, upper third of CHIEF
  "   shield, vertical position of .
                  PALY
  "   shields, series of small VAIR
  "   term . FRACTED, PATTE, SEME,
                  URDE
  "   wreath .... TORSE
heraldry, an ordinary in ...... BEND
  " ; back to back .... ADDORSED
  " ; balls or plates ... ROUNDELS
  " ; barnacle .... BREY
  " ; bastardy mark ..... BATON
  " ; beakless and footless bird in
                  MARTLET
  " ; bear .... GRICE, GRISE
  " ; bearing .... TRESSURE, ORLE
  " ; bearing of two curved lines
    .   GORE
  " ; beast partly visible . ISSUANT
  "   bend, small .... COTISE
  " ; blind .... SEEL
  " ; black .... SABLE
  " ; blue .... AZURE
  " ; body bent or folded .....
                 DEBRUISED
  " ; broken .... ROMPU

  " ; chaplet .... ORLE
  " ; checkered ... VAIR, CHECKY
  " ; cherub .... SERAPH
  " ; cross .... NOWY, SALTIRE
  " ; cross-like CLECHE, PATONCE
heraldry; depicting animal's head ...
                 CABOSHED
  " ; divided by bars ..... BARRY
  " ; divided into squares ......
                COMPONY
  "   duck, footless and beakless
                CANNET
  " ; either of two barrulets .....
                GEMEL
  " ; facing each other AFFRONTE
  " ; factor .... GENE
  " ; figure like Y .... PALL
  " ; fillet .... ORLE
  " ; foreleg of a beast ... GAMB
  " ; fountain .... SYKE
  " ; fur .... PEAN, POTENT, VAIR
  " ; gold in .... AU, OR
  " ; grafted .... ENTE
  " ; green .... VERT
  " ; head of dart or javelin
      bearing .... PHEON
  " ; horizontal band .. BAR, FESS,
                  FILL
  " ; left side .... SINISTER
  " ; lozenge (voided) ... MASCLE
  " ; metal end of a sheath ....
                 BOTEROL
  " ; notched .... RAGULY
  " ; one of the honorable
      ordinaries ..... CHEVRON
  " ; ordinary .... SALTIRE
  " ; ornament of headpiece CREST
  " ; partly swallowed ENGOULED
  " ; pointed .... URDE
  " ; purple .... PURPURE
  " ; red tincture .... GULES
  " ; running, as of a beast .....
                COURANT
  " ; scattered .... SEME
  " ; sheaf of grain GARBE, GARB
  " ; sitting, as a lion .... SEJANT
  " ; sitting down .... ASSIS
  " ; sky blue .... AZURE
  " ; snake .... BISSE
  " ; springing up ...... JESSANT
  " ; squirrel skin .... VAIR
  " ; standing position . STATANT
  " ; strewing .... SEME
  " ; swimming .... NAIANT
  " ; symbol of the Am. savage ..
                 TATTOO
  " ; symbol of the Danes RAVEN
  " ; symbol of the tribe of Judah
                LION
  " ; tincture, bright brown TENNE

" ; to describe a coat of arms BLAZON
" ; triangular form ... GYRON
heraldry; turned to show the back .. AVERSANT
" ; turning head toward spectator GARDANT, GAZE
" ; vertical division ..... PALY
" ; wavy ... ENTE, ONDE, UNDE
" ; wickerwork trap ..... WEEL
" ; winged .... AILE
" ; wreath .... ORLE, TORSE
" ; yellow .... OR
herb CARAWAY, PARSLEY, SAGE, THYME, TELLIMA, SEDGE
" , aromatic ANET, ANISE, BASIL, DILL
" , Asiatic .... HEMP
" ; bitter GENTIAN, ALOE, RUE, TANSY
" ; buckwheat family ...... SORREL
" , climbing .... LENS
" , coarse weedy ..... ERYNGO, IVA
" ; dill .... ANET
" dish .... SALAD
" , edible .... PARSNIP
" , Eurasian weedy ...... GOSMORE
" , European ..... RUTA, TARRAGON
" , eve .... IVA
" , fabulous .... MOLY
" , flowering; genus ..... HEPATICA
" , fragrant .... BALM
" , ginger .... ALPINIA
" , kind of . WORT, BLITE, COMFRAY, NEP
" , Malayalam .... ENTADA
" , medicinal .. CORIANDER, SENNA, BONESET, TANSY
" ; mint family ...... BALM, BASIL, HYSSOP
" ; nightshade family .... HENBANE
" of grace .... RUE
" of the goosefoot order . QUINOA
" , onion-like .... CHIVE
" ; parsley family . FENNEL, ERYNGO
" ; parsley family, Old World; ..... CHERVIL
" , perennial . BALM, DIGITALIS, PIA, SEGO
" , perennial rocaceous; genus GEUM
" ; poisonous hemlock ... CONIUM
" , pot .... CYCLAMEN, WORT
" , small tropical .. LUFFA, LOOFAH
" , sweet aromatic .... CICELY
" tonic .... BONESET
" yielding starch .... PIA
herbage ...... TURF, PASTURE, GRASS, FOLIAGE
herbs; genus .... APIOS, CICER, ARUM, TOVARIA, HEDEOMA, SAGINA
Hercules, captor of .... IOLE
" , mother of ...... ALCMENE

" , wife of .... DEIANIRA, HEBE
herd ... DROVE, GREGAL, MOB, RABBLE
herdsman ..... COWBOY, RANCHERO, SENN, VACHER, VAQUERO, GAUCHO, DAMOETAS
here; Fr. ICI
here and there ...... ABOUT, THINLY, PASSIM
heretofore .... ERENOW
hereditary ...... ANCESTRAL, LINEAL, INNATE, INBORN, INBRED
" factor .... GENE, DNA, RNA
" right .... UDAL, ODAL
heretic ... ARIAN, SCEPTIC, DISSENTER
heritage . ESTATE, LEGACY, PATRIMONY
Hermes .... MERCURY
" , father of .... ZEUS
" , footgear of .... TALARIA
" , mother of .... MAIA
" , personification of .... WIND
hermetic .... HERMANIC
hermit RECLUSE, ANCHORITE, EREMITE, SANTON, STYLITE, NUN, MONK, FRIAR, CRAB, ASCETIC, CENOBITE
Hernando de .... SOTO
hero ... IDOL, STAR, DEMIGOD, LION
" , legendary ... ETANA RUSTUM, AMADIS, PALADIN, TRISTAN
Hero, lover of .... LEANDER
hero of the first crusade ... TANCRED
heroic .. BOLD, BRAVE, EPIC, GALLANT, VALIANT
heroic poem ..... EPOS, EPIC, EPOPEE
Herodias' daughter .... SALOME
heroine, d'Urberville .... TESS
" of "Last Days of Pompeii" ... IONE
Herold opera .... ZAMPA
heron ... AIGRET, EGRET, HERLE, HERN, ARDEA, CRANE, POKE, QUA(WK), SOCO, BOATBILL, BITTERN
" , flock of .... SEDGE
heroner .... HAWK
herpes .... SHINGLES
herpetic .... REPTILIAN
herring ...... RAUN, SPRAT, ALEWIFE, ALOSA, CISCO, MATIE, BRIT, COB, SILE
" measure .... CRAN
" pond .... OCEAN
" sauce .... ALEC
" tub .... CADE
Hertha .... ERDA, NERTHUS
hesitate ..... DEMUR, HAW, HEM, ERS, PAUSE, WAVER, BOGGLE, PALTER, TEETER
hesperian .... BUTTERFLY
Hesperides ...... ATLANTIDES, AEGLE, HESPERA, HESTIA

135

Hesperus' daughter .... ERYTHEA
    "   father .... ASTRAEUS
    "   mother .... EOS
hessonite .... GARNET
Hestia's father .... CRONOS
    "   mother .... RHEA
hetaera .... LAIS, ASPASIA, THAIS
hetero- .... OTHER
heterodoxy .... HERESY
hetman .... ATAMAN
hew .... CHIP, FELL, FORM, HACK
hex ...... BEWITCH, JINX, HAG, SPELL
hexapod .... INSECT
hiatus .... COL, GAP, LACUNA, BREAK,
    FISSURE, PAUSE, CHASM, INTERVAL
hibernate .... SHACK, WINTER
Hibernia .... ERIN, IRELAND
hibertia .... ROCKROSE
hickory .... PECAN
    "   nut .... KISKATOM
    "   wattle .... ACACIA
hidden .... LATENT, ARCANE, COVERT,
    CRYPTIC, PERDU, SECRE
hide .... HOOD, WRAP, CACHE, SKULK,
    ENSCONCE
    " , a .... KIP, PELT
hideous .... GRIM, SCABROUS
hides, remove hair from .... MOON,
    SLATE
hiding place .... MEW, LATIBULUM
hie .... URGE, SCUD, SPEED, GO
hieroglyphics, key to .... ROSETTA
hi-fi enthusiast .... AUDIOPHILE
    "   loudspeaker .... MONITOR
high .... ALOFT, GAMY, LOFTY, TALL,
    SERENE, ELA, ALT, DEAR,
    SHRILL, DRUNK
    "   blood pressure .. HYPERTENSION
    "   -flown diction .... EUPHUISM
    "   mountain .... ALP
    "   -strung .... TAUT, TENSE
highest; comb. form .... ACRO
    "   number of a die .. SICE, SISE
    "   point .. NOONTIME, APOGEE,
    ACME, APEX, ZENITH
highland of Central Asia ..... PAMIR
Highlander ..... TARTAN, GAEL, SCOT
    "   , pouch of .... SPORRAN
highway .... ITER, PIKE, TOBY, ALCAN,
    ROUTE, AUTOBAHN
highwayman .... PAD, LADRONE
hilarity .... GLEE, GAIETY, MIRTH
hill .... BRAE, COPPLE, KOP, LOMA,
    LOMITA, BUTTE, MORRO,
    KAME, DOWN, DUNE
    " , fortified .... RATH
    " , top of a .... PAHA, COP, TOR
hillock .... HURST, KNOLL, COPSE,
    TERTRE

hills, chain of .... AAS, RIDGE
    " , steep rocky .... SCARS
hilum of an organ .... PORTA
    " , per. to the .... HILAR
Himalayan animal ..... KAIL, OUNCE,
    GORAL, PANDA
    "   dweller .... NEPALESE
    "   goat .. KRAS, TAHR, GORAL
    "   grassy tract . TERAI, TARAI
    "   peak .... API, AKU, NEPAL,
    SIKKIM, EVEREST, HUMP,
    ANAPURNA
    "   pheasant .... MONAL
    "   sheep .... NAHOOR
    "   subranges ...... SIWALIKS
    "   tableland .... TIBET
    "   tea plant .... AUCUBA
    "   trees . DEODAR, SAL, TOON
    "   walnut .... CORYLUS
himself; Lat. .... IPSE
himyarite .... AXUMITE, SABAEAN
hind .... ROE, HEARST, BACK, REAR
    "   bow of saddle .... CANTLE
    " , red .... CABRILLA, GROUPER
hinder . BALK, CRAMP, CUMBER, DETER,
    EMBAR, HAMPER, IMPEDE, THWART
hindrance .... RUB, CLOG
Hindu .... KOLI, SER, TAMIL, SIKH,
    JAIN(A), BABU, AGHORI
    "   acrobat .... NAT
    "   age of world .... YUGA
    "   alkali plants .... USAR
    "   ancestor of man ...... MANU
    "   ascetic ..... YATI, YOGI, FAKIR
    "   atheist .... NASTIKA
    "   bandit .... DACOIT
    "   betel nut .... SUPARI
    "   bird .... MUNIA
    "   blacksmith .... LOHAR
    "   caravansary .... CHOULTRY
    "   carriage ..... GHARRI, GHARRY
    "   caste ... SUDRA, JAT, MAL, TELI,
    GOLA, KORI, KULI, PARIAH,
    PASI
    "   cavalry troop .... RISALA
    "   ceremonial gift .. KHILAT, LEPA
    "   charitable gift .... ENAM
    "   city, any .... ABAD
    "   city, holy .... BENARES
    "   class member .... MAL
    "   congregation .... SAMAJ
    "   convent .... MATH
    "   court officer .... AMALA
    "   cottage .... BARI
    "   custom of incremating widows
    SATI, SUTTEE, SUTEE
    "   cymbals .... TAL
    "   dancing girl .... BAYADERE
    "   deity ... DEVA, KAMA, VISHNU,
    MANU, SIVA

"	deity, eighth avatar of Vishnu KRISHNA		"	loincloth .... DHOTI	
"	demon .... ASURA		"	lord .... SWAMI	
"	dependency .... TALUK		"	lord of the world .... JAGANNATH(A)	
"	deposit; law .... ADHI		"	magic .... JADU, MAYA	
"	disciple .... SIKH		"	mantra .... OM	
"	discount .... BATTA		"	margosa .... NEEM	
"	doctrine .... DHARMA		"	master ...... SAHIB, MIAN	
"	drinking pot .... LOTA		"	meal .... ATA	
"	dye, morindin ... AL, AAL, AWL		"	measure .... HATH, KOS	
"	ejaculation or mantra .... OM		"	medicant .... NAGA	
"	elephant-headed god GANESA, GANESHA		"	merchant ...... BANIAN, TELI	
"	essence .... AMRITA, RASA		"	military .... SIK(H)	
"	estate .... TALUK		"	money of account ..... ANNA, RUPEE	
"	evil spirit ...... ASURA, MARA		"	month . BAISAKH, JATH, ASARH, SAWAN (SARAWAN),	
"	exchange rate .... BATTA			BHADON, KATIK (KARTIK), ASIN	
"	fabled mountain .... MERU			(KUAR), AGHAN, PUS, MAGH,	
"	fair .... MELA			PHAGUN (PHALGUN), CHAIT	
"	farmer .... HAMAL		"	mountaineer .... BHIL	
"	female slave .... DASI		"	mountain pass .. GHAT, GHAUT	
"	festival ... DASAHARA, DEWALI, HOLI		"	musical instr. ... SAROD, SITAR, VINA	
"	flying beings .... GARUDAS		"	nobleman .... RAJA(H)	
"	garment for female ..... SARI		"	of Aryan speech .... SWAT	
"	gentleman ...... BABOO, BABU		"	Olympus .... MERU	
"	god (see also "god")		"	patriarch .... PITRI	
"	god ..... DEVI, BRAHMA, SIVA		"	peasant .... RYOT	
"	god of fire .... AGNI		"	philosophy .... YOGA	
"	god of love .... KAMA		"	poet .... TAGORE	
"	god of nature .... DEVA		"	poison .... BIKH	
"	god of the dead .... YAMA		"	prince ... MAHARAJ(A), RANA, RAJA(H)	
"	god of the sky .... DYAUS		"	princess .. (MAHA)RANI, RANEE	
"	god of the triad .... SIVA		"	principle of existence PRANA, TATTVA	
"	god of waters .... VARUNA		"	private apartment .... MAHAL	
"	god of wisdom .... GANESA		"	pundit .... SWAMI	
"	goddess . UMA, DEVI, VAC, SHRI		"	queen .... RANI, RANEE	
"	goddess of destruction ... KALI		"	rainy .... VARSHA	
"	godling .... DEVATA		"	reign .... RAJ	
"	goldsmith .... SONAR		"	religion .... JAINISM, SIVAISM	
"	grant of land ... ENAM, INAM, SASAN		"	religious ascetic .... MUNI	
"	groom .... SYCE		"	" book .... SASTRA	
"	guitar .... SITAR		"	" devotee .... MUNI	
"	hillbilly .... BHIL		"	" fair .... MELA	
"	holy books . SASTRA, SHASTRA, VEDA		"	" rite .... SRADDHA	
"	idol .... PAGODA, SWAMI		"	" sect .... JAINA	
"	ignorance, philosophy of ..... TAMAS		"	" teacher ... GURU, PIR	
"	incarnation .... AVATAR		"	rice .... BORO	
"	jackal .... KOLA		"	rite .... ACHAR	
"	kala .... BULBUL		"	robe .... JAMA	
"	lady .... DEVI		"	rule .... RAJ	
"	language ..... SANSKRIT, URDU		"	sacred literature .... VEDA	
"	law books .... MANU		"	sage ..... GAUTAMA, MAHATMA	
"	leader GANDHI, SIRDAR, NEHRU		"	scarf .... SAREE	
"	lease .... PATTA, POTTAH		"	school of philosophy .... MIMANSA, MIMAMSA	
"	life principle .. PRANA, ATMAN		"	school, Skr. .... TOL	
"	literature, sacred . SRUTI, VEDA				

"	scriptures ... TANTRA, SASTRA
"	scriptures, per. to ... TANTRIC, AGAMA
"	sect, one of a .... SADH
"	serpent .... NAGA
"	silversmith .... SONAR
"	soldier .... SEPOY
"	spirit of evil .... MARA
"	spiritual darkness .... TAMAS
"	stele .... LAT
"	storeroom .... GOLA
"	summer residence .... MAHAL
"	supreme deity .... VISHNU
"	swan; myth. .... HANSA
"	temple tower SIKARA, SIKHARA, SIKHRA, VIMANA
"	title ... MIR, SIDI, NAIK, SAHIB, MIAN, SRI, SREE
"	trader .... BANIAN, YAN
"	trinity, member of .. BRAHMA, SIVA, VISHNU
"	trinity, the .... TRIMURTI
"	twenty .... CORGE
"	veranda .... PYAL
"	village .... ABADI
"	viol .... RUANA, SARINDA
"	weaver .... TANTI
"	weight .... MAUND
"	widow .... SATI, SUTTEE
"	worshiper of Siva ...... SAIVA
"	worst of the four ages ... KALI
"	writer .... SIRCAR

Hinduism .... ANIMISM
" essence .... ATMAN
Hindu Dravidian .... TODA
Hindu Nepalese .... MURMIS
Hindustan rice crop ...... AGHANEE
Hindustani .... HINDI, URDU
hinge JOINT, PIVOT, KNEE, AXIS, BUTT
hint ..... ALLUDE, EYEWINK, GLANCE, INKLE, CUE, REFER, POINTER
hinterland .... GRASSROOTS
hip .... COXA, HUCK(LE)
" bones .... ILIA
" , per. to the .... SCIATIC
hippo, bib. .... BEHEMOTH
" ; thong of hide ...... CHICOTE
Hippocrates, drug of .... MECON (OPIUM)
Hiram .... GRANT
hircine .... GOATISH, LEWD
hire ... CHARTER, HACK, SIGN, TICCA, FEE, SALARY, STIPEND, ENGAGE
hirsute .... HAIRY
hispid .... STRIGOSE, STRIGOUS
hissing .... TST, FIZZ, SIBILANT, SHISH
historian ...... ANNALIST, BOSWELL, BEDE, GIBBON, PLUTARCH, SALLUST
history .. DRAMA, ERA, PAST, MEMOIR, RECORD, ANNALS, LORE

" , muse of .... CLIO
" of indiv. development ONTOGENY
hit ... BOP, SLOG, BUFFET, ACE, BUNT, FLICK, SRO, STRIKE, CLOUT, POMMEL, LARRUP, SWAT, SMITE, IMPACT
hitch .... ATTACH, CATCH, FASTEN
Hittites' ancestor .... HETH
" capital .... PTERIA
hive ..... SWARM, BOX, GUM, APIARY
hives .... UREDO, URTICARIA
hoatzin .... ANNA
hoard . AMASS, GARNER, SUPPLY, PILE, STORE
hoarder .... MISER, NIGGARD
hoarfrost .... RAG, RIME
hoarse ..... HARSH, HUSKY, RAUCOUS
hoary ..... GRAY, OLD, CANESCENT
hoax ...... BAM, BILK, CANARD, GULL
hobbled .... PASTERNED, LIMPED
hobby .. FAD, DOLLY, GARRAN, WHIM
hobgoblin .... ELF, BOGEY, IMP, PUG, SPRITE, SCRAT
hock .... HAM, PAWN, GAMBREL
hockey ..... HURLEY, SHINDY, SHINNY
" term .... SIX, CAGE, PUCK, CAMAN, STANLEY
hocus DRUG, DECEIVE, FRAUD, CHEAT
hodgepodge MESS, MELANGE, OLIO, CENTO, MEDLEY, STEW
Hodgins; author .... ERIC
hoe .... LARRY, PADLE
hog food MAST, ACORN, SLOP, SWILL
" , ground .... MARMOT
" , salted side of .... FLITCH
" shears .... SNOUTER
" ; S. Amer. .... TAPIR
" weed .... AMBROSIA
" , wild; N.Z. .... BENE
" , young .... SHOAT, SHOTE
hogfish .... CAPITAN
hoggerel .... SHEEP, BOAR
hogs; genus .... SUS
hogshead ...... CASK, MEASURE, PIPE
hoi polloi .... MASSES
hoiden .... ROMP, RUDE, TOMBOY
hoist ...... HEAVE, LIFT, REAR, JACK
hoisted up, as sails .... ATRIP
hoisting device .... GIN, PARBUCKLE, DAVIT, CAPSTAN
hoity-toity .... ROMP, SNOOTY
hokum .... BUNK, NONSENSE
hold . GRIP, KEEP, STAY, BELAY, HATCH, THINK
" back .... DAM, INHIBIT
" for nails .... NOG
" ; naut. .... AVAST, HOWE
" off .... AVERT, REFRAIN

holder ..... OWNER, TENANT, PAYEE, DOP(P)
holding .... TENURE, SEAT
hole ... DEN, SLOT, PIT, BORE, GEAT, GIME, VOID, CHASM, CAVITY
" for ship's cables .... HAWSE
" in garment for sleeves ... SCYE
holiday .FERIA, FERIE, FIESTA, RECESS
" take .... LAKE
holla .... CEASE, STOP
Holland ... NETHERLANDS, FRIESLAND
" aborigine .... CELT
" anatomist .... RAU
" badger .... DAS
" botanist .... DEVRIES
" capital .... AMSTERDAM
" , city in . ARNHEIM, HAGUE, LEYDEN, UTRECHT, HAARLEM
" colonist .... BOER
" commune .... EDE, EPE
" coin .. RYDER, DOIT, FLORIN, GULDEN, GUILDER, DAALDER
" cupboard .... KAS
" dialect FRISIAN, SAXON, TAAL
" early political party HOEKST
" gin .... SCHNAPS
" measure .. DUIM, VOET, KOP, BUNDER, AUM, STREEP
" painter .. BOSCH, DOU, EYCK, HALS, HOET, LELY, LIS
" pileworm .... TEREDO
" poet .... DECKER
" political party .... GEUZEN
" province DRENTHE, ZEELAND
" river .... EMS, LEK, SCHELDT, YSSEL, SCHELDE, WAAL
" scholar .... ERASMUS
" ship .... GALLIOT, KOFF
" town .... BREDA, EDE
" uncle .... EME
" woman .... FROW
" writer .... CATS
hollow .. CAVERNOUS, FALSE, GORE, PIT, BOWL, DENT, VOID, EMPTY, SCOOP, BASIN
" , circular .... CORRIE
" in tile .... KEY
" , narrow .... DINGLE
" spindle .... TRIBLET
holly .... HULL, HOLM, ILEX, TOYON, DAHOON
" ; genus .... OLEARIA
" , Indian tea .... YAPON
" , per. to ILICIC
hollyhocks .... ALTHEA
Hollywood prize .... OSCAR
holm .... AIT, EYOT, ISLET, ILEX
" thrush .... MISSEL
Holmes's word .... ELEMENTARY
holt .... COPSE, WOODS

holy CHASTE, NUN, VESTAL, DEVOUT, DIVINE, PIOUS, SACRED
Holy Grail ... SANGREAL, SANGRAAL
" " , achiever of .... GALAHAD
holy oil .... CHRISM
" -water font ..... CRUET, STOUP
homburg .... FELT, HAT
home .. NEST, ASTRE, HABITAT, KERN, ABODE, HEARTH
" base .... PLATE
" of gods .... OLYMPUS, ASGARD
" of Golden Fleece .... COLCHIS
"Home, Sweet Home" composer .. PAYNE
homely .... PLAIN, RUDE, SIMPLE
Homeric .... EPIC
" saga .... ILIAD, ODYSSEY
homeland; myth. .... HAVAIKI
Homer; artist .... WINSLOW
Homer's birthplace .... CYME
" burial place .... IOS
" instrument .... LYRE
" legendary parent ..... MELES
homesickness .... NOSTALGIA
homespun .... RUSSET
homestead .. GARTH, FARMERY, TREF, ONSTEAD, STEADING, TOFT
homicide; Teu. .... MORTH
homily .... SERMON, ORATION
hominy .... SAMP
homo .... MAN
hone .... GRUMBLE, PINE, STROP, SHARPEN
honest ...... CANDID, JUST, UPRIGHT
honey .... DEAR, MEL, DARLING
" bear .... KINKAJOU, MELURSUS
" bee .... DESERET, DINGAR
" buzzard .... KITE, PERN
" eater .... IAO, MOHO
" ; fermented drink ...... MEAD, MORAT
" ; med. preparation ... MELLITE
" , per. to .... MELISSIC
" , source of .... NECTAR
" tube .... NECTARY
" weasel .... RATEL
honeycombed .. ALVEOLATE, FAVOSE, RIDDLED
honeydew .... MELON, NECTAR
honeysuckle .. VINE, WIDBIN, WEIGLA
Hong Kong bay .... MIRS
Honolulu, cliff in .... PALI
" suburb .... EWA
honor . ATHEL, PROW, REPUTE, REVERE, ESTEEM, VIRTUE
honoraria .... DOUCEURS
honors .... DIGNITIES, GREE, TITLES
hood .... BONNET, GANGSTER, COIF, BABUSHKA, AMICE, CAPUCHE, COWL, BASHLYK

```
"  , cloak  .... BURNOOSE, CAPOTE          "  rudder ....... HYDROFOIL
"  , part of a .......... CAMAIL           "  timber ............ LINTEL
hooded ................. CUCULLATE      hormone .... CORTISONE, ESTROGEN,
"  seal ..... BLADDERNOSE, WIG                    ESTRONE, PROLACTIN
hoodoo ................. JINX, JYNX      horn . DAG, CUSP, PALP, TINE, BOCAL,
hoodwink ..... BLEAR, DUPE, COZEN,             BUGLE, CORNU, PRONG, ANTLER,
             CHEAT, WILE, SEEL                  CROCHE, FEELER, BUCCINA,
hoof . PASTERN, CLEE, CLUVE, DANCE,                    SHOPHAR
     TRAMP, UNGULA, UNGUIS, CLOOF        "  of an insect ........ ANTENNA
"  -paring tool ........ BUTTERIS         "  on beak of a bird . EPITHEM(A)
"  print .. PIST(E), SPOOR, TRACK         "  , pierce with a .......... GORE
"  -shaped ........... UNGULATE         hornbill .................... TOCK
hook HAMULE, CROCK, DECOY, SNARE,       horned viper ....... ASP, CERASTES,
     TRAP, GAFF, HANGLE                                    WAMPUM
"  dagger ................. CHAPE       hornet ........... VESPID, STINGER
"  money .................. LARI        hornless . POLLED, ACEROUS, DODDED,
"  , stretcher ............ TENTER                          POLEY
hookah ........... PIPE, NARGHILE        "  cow ....... MULEY, MULLEY
hooked .. ADUNC, HAMATE, HAMOSE,       hornpipe ............... MATELOTE
             CLEEKED, ANCONAL          horny ................... CERATOSE
"  prong .......... PEW, PUGH            "  scale ............ NAIL, SCUTE
"  -shaped .......... HAMULATE           "  tissue ........ CERATIN, SCUR
hook-like ....... FALCATE, UNCINAL,     horrible ................ DIRE, GRIM
             UNCINATE                   Horsa, brother of ........ HENGIST
hooks ...................... HAMI       horse ........ BLOCK, FRAME, HARASS,
hoop ... BAIL, EMBRACE, RING, FRETTE               STAND, BIDET, ARAB,
"  skirt . CRINOLINE, FARTHINGALE               PACER, STEED, CANUCK,
hooper ............. SWAN, COOPER                          BEAST
hoosegow ...... JAIL, CLINK, PRISON      "  , ankle of a ......... HOCK
Hoosier State ............ INDIANA       "  , Austral. .. WARRAGAL, WALER
hoot ..... BOO, WHOO, CRY, HONK,         "  , Barbary .............. BARB
             ULULATE                     "  blanket .............. MANTA
hop ... CAPER, FRISK, GAMBOL, HIP,       "  , British; slang .......... PRAD
             TRIP, VINE, BINE            "  buyer ............ KNACKER
"  bush ..................... AKE         "  , check back of ..... SACCADE
"  disease .................. FEN         "  chestnut ........... BUCKEYE
"  flea ................. (H)ALTICA       "  , color of a PIED, PINTO, ROAN
"  kiln ................ OAST, OST        "  ; comb. form ........... HIPPO
"  marjoram ............. DITTANY         "  dealer; Eng. .......... COPER
"  trees ................... PTELEA       "  disease SPAVIN, SURRA, LAMPAS
hope SPES, ASPIRE, OPTIMISM, EXPECT,     "  , easy-paced .............. PAD
             OPAL, LONG, PANT            "  eyelid inflammation .... HAW
hoped for ............... SPERATE        "  family, of the ..... ASS, ZEBRA
hopeless ... FORLORN, FUTILE, GLUM,      "  , female ............... MARE
             LOST, VAIN                  "  fennel ................ SESELI
hop-o'-my-thumb .......... DWARF         "  ; genus .............. EQUUS
Hophni's brother .......... PHINEAS      "  , guide rope for ...... LONGE
"  father ............... ELI            "  , half-wild .......... MUSTANG
hops between two and four years old      "  , leap of a ............ CURVET
             OLDS                        "  mackerel . SCAD, ATULE, TUNNY
"  , narcotic in ......... HUMULENE       "  , male ..... GELDING, STALLION
hopscotch stone ........... PEEVER       "  of different colors ... CREAM,
Horae, one of the ..... DIKE, EIRENE,                  TAN, PALOMINO
             EUNOMIA                     "  , old .. PLUG, AVER, ROSINANTE
horde ................. TRIBE, TROOP     "  , position of a ....... PESANTE
horizon, appear above ........ RISE      "  , prehistoric Am. TIT, EOHIPPUS
"  , arc of the ...... AZIMUTH            "  -race board ............ TOTE
"  glass ............. SEXTANT            "  , race (inferior) ........ PLATER
horizontal .... FLUSH, LEVEL, PLANE,     "  , rearing of a .......... PESADE
             PRONE                       "  , resembling a ........ EQUOID
```

140

" round-up .... RODEO
" shoe, calk on ...... CALTROP
" , small . BRONCO, GENET, NAG,
TIT
" , spirited ..... STEED, COURSER
" , swift .... PACOLET
" -track slope .... CALADE
" -training place ...... LONGE
" , trotting ...... COB, MORGAN
" , wheel .... POLER
" , work; British .... GARRAN
" , worthless ..... JADE, CROCK,
SHACK
Horse Mesa dam river .... SALT
horsemanship, art of ..... MANEGE
horseradish tree .... BEHEN, BEN
horses, famous .. NASHUA, NEEDLES,
MANOWAR, SECRETARIAT
horse's forehead .... CHANFRIN
" cry .... NEIGH, NIE, WHINNY
" hoof, part of ...... PASTERN
" leg, part of . FETLOCK, INSTEP
horses, per. to .. CABALLINE, EQUINE
horsewhip .... CHAB(O)UK, FLOG
Horus .... RA
" , father of .... OSIRIS
hospice .... MARET, IMARET
hospital ...... MALADERY, INFIRMARY
host .... SERVER, ARMY, SUM, PATEN,
WAFER, PYX, LEGION
hostel ..... INN, TAVERN, MANSION,
MOTEL, LODGE
hostess .... PERLE, MESTA
hostility ... ANIMUS, RANCOR, FEUD,
ENMITY, WAR
hostler .... GROOM
hot; Span. .... CALIDO
" iron .... CAUTER
" spring .... GEYSER
" -tempered .... IRACUND
hotel . TAVERN, FONDA, HOSTEL, INN,
IMARET
" keeper .... BONIFACE
hothouse .... STOVE, STEW
Hottentot .... NAMA, NAMAQUA
" cloak .... CAROSS
" encampment ...... KRAAL
" tobacco .. DACCHA, DAGGA
hound ..... CERBERUS, TREER, TUFTER,
LEASH, SLEUTH, LIMER, HARRIER,
SETTER, BASSET, BEAGLE,
SKIRTER
" , to .... HUNT, BEDOG
" , wolf .... ALAN
hour(s) .... HORA(E), TIME
houri .... NYMPH
hourly .... FREQUENT, HORAL
house .. COTE, CASA, GRANGE, PENT,
HOME, FIRM, HUT, COTTAGE,
MANSION, PALACE, BOARD, SHACK

" ; comb. form .... ECO
" , oriental .... TEMBE, SERAI
" , per. to .... DOMAL
" , ranch .... CASITA, HACIENDA
" , Russ. log .... ISBA
" , summer GAZEBO, VILLA, RANCH
" , timber-and-plaster CALAMANCO
household ...... MENAGE, MAINPOST
" fairy .... PUCK
" tutelaries .. LARES, PENATES
housel .... EUCHARIST
houses, buyer of old ...... KNACKER
housewarming .... INFARE
housing .... PAD
Houston college .... RICE
hovel .... HUT, SHACK, STACK, CABIN,
DEN, DUGOUT, HUTCH, SHANTY,
LEANTO
hover ...... FLUTTER, POISE, WAVER
Howe; inventor .... ELIAS
however .... FAR, MUCH, YET
howitzer .... GUN, SKODA
howler monkey .... ARABA
hoyden .... TOMBOY
Hoyle; writer .... EDMUND
Hreidmar's son .... REGINN
hub ... NAVE, PITH, BOSTON, CENTER,
KERNEL
hubble-bubble .... PIPE
"Hudibras" author .... BUTLER
hue CRY, TINT, TONE, ALARM, COLOR,
SHADE, TINGE
huge .... TITANIC, VAST, ENORM,
COLOSSAL
Huguenot leader .... ADRETS
hugger-mugger .... SLY
huisache ... POPINAC, CASSIE, WABI,
AROMO
hull POD, HUSK, PEEL, SHELL, CASING,
SHUCK
hum . WHIZZ, DRONE, CROON, TUNE,
BOMBINATE
human .... MAN, ADAMITE, MORTAL,
HOMO, PERSON
" frailty .... ADAM
hummeling machine .... AWNER
humble ..... ABASE, CHASTISE, DEMIT,
LOW, MEEK, SHAME, DEGRADE
humboldtine .... OXALITE
humbug ... PAH, BOSH, CHEAT, FLAM,
HOAX
humdinger .... ONER, CORKER
humdrum . PROSY, ROUTINE, TEDIOUS
humid .. DANK, MOIST, DAMP, SULTRY
humiliate .... SHAME, ABASH, NITHER
humility .... MODESTY
hummingbird COLIBRI, BLUET, SAPPHO,
STAR, SYLPH, RACKETTAIL, RUBY,
RAINBOW

141

humor . CAPRICE, QUIRK, MOOD, CUE, WIT, WHIM, CATER, BABY, FLUID, INDULGE
" , ill .... IRE, SPLEEN, TIFF, TID
humorist ... ADE, CARD, JESTER, NYE
humus .... MULCH, MOLD, SOIL
Hun .... GERMAN, VANDAL, MAGYAR, BOCHE
" leader ...... ETZEL, ATTILA, ATLI
" race .... AVARS, TARTAR
Hunan river .... YUEN
hundred .... CRORE
" ; comb. form .... HECTO
" -fold .... CENTUPLE
" -weight .... CENTNER, CENTAL
"Hundred Years' War" battle CRESSY
hundredth of a right angle ... GRAD
Hungarian .... MAGYAR
" composer ...... BARTOK, KODALY, LEHAR
" conductor . REINER, SZELL, DORATI
" county .... ARVA
" dynasty .... ARPAD
" legislature .... FELSOHAZ
" measure ..... AKA, JOCH, METZE
" money . GULDEN, PENGO
" mountains ... ALPS, TATRA
" physicist .... TELLER
" river . RAAB, UNA, DRAVE, THEISS
" town .... PECS, VAC
" violinist .... SZIGETI
" wine .... TOKAY
" wine measure ITCZE, ANTAL
hunger ITCH, YEN, CLEM, PINE, COVET, ACORIA
" , causing .... ESURINE
hungry ...... AVID, BARREN, EAGER, STARVED, YAP, FAMISHED
Hungry Horse _____ ...... DAM
Hunky .... EVEN, RIGHT, WELL
hunt . DIG, CHASE, SEEK, SCOUT, TRAP, POACH, STALK, TRAIL
hunter .... ACTAEON, JA(E)GER, CHASSEUR, NIMROD, ORION, TRAPPER, SHIKARI
hunting coyote .... WOLFING
" dog .... BASSET, BEAGLE
" expedition .. SHIKAR, SAFARI
" , fond of .... VENATIC
" ; French .... CHASSE
" leopard .... CHEETAH
" weasel .... FERRET
huntress . DIANA, ARTEMIS, ATALANTA
hurdy-gurdy ... ROTA, LIRA, ORGAN
hurly .... CONFUSION, UPROAR
hurly-burly .... TUMULT
hurrah .... VIVA, CHEER, OLE, ROOT

hurried; mus. .... AGITATO
hurry .... CHASE, SESSA, SPEED, HIE, DASH, RUSH
hurt .... DERE, HARM, HARRY, PANG, SORE, IMPAIR
hurtful . MALEFIC, NOCENT, NOISOME
husband STORE, SANNUP, GOODMAN, GROOM, OLDMAN, SPOUSE
" , brother of .... LEVIR
husbandman .... FARMER, GRANGER, TILLER
hush .. ALLAY, STILL, CALM, ASSUAGE
husk ... SHOOD, BRAN, LEAM, SHUCK
husky ... ESKIMO, BRAWNY, RAUCOUS
Huss; martyr .... JOHN
hussy BAG, CASE, MINX, QUEAN, SLUT
hut ... ISBA, COT(E), SHACK, HOVEL, HUMPY, SHANTY, SHED, LEANTO, JACAL, SKEO
" , portable .... NISSEN
hutch .... PEN, COOP, WARREN
Huxley; essayist .... ALDOUS
hyacinth .... LILY, HAREBELL, CAMAS
" gem .... ZIRCON
Hyades, star in the ..... ALDEBARAN
hybrid CATALO, CROSS, MULE, HINNY, MONGREL
" citrus tree .... TANGELO
hydra .... POLYP, SERPENT
hydrate, ethyl .... ALCOHOL, SLAKE
hydraulic brake .... CATARACT
" device .... TREMIE
hydrocarbon ... CARANE, CHRYSENE, PYRENE, CETANE
" , gaseous .... FLUORINE
" , inflammable ... BUTANE
" , liquid CUMOL, NONANE, TOLUOL
" , oily .... ETHERINE, VIRIDINE
" radical .... AMYL
" , unsaturated .. OLEFINE
" , volatile ...... TETROL, BENZENE
" , white crysalline.......
TOLANE, DITOLYL, RETENE
hydrogen atoms, having two BIBASIC
" compound .... IMINE
hydrophobia .... LYSSA, RABIES
hydrous silicate ..... STEATITE, TALC
" sodium carbonate .. TRONA, URAO
" wool fat .... LANOLIN
hyena-like animal ...... AARDWOLF
hymenopter .... BEE, WASP, ANT
hymn book ...... PSALTER, HYMNAL
" , non-metrical .... CANTICLE
" , sacred .. ANTHEM, TRISAGION
" sung in unison ..... CHORALE
hyperbole .... ELA, AUXESIS

142

hyperbolic function .... COSH
Hyperion's daughter .... EOS
hyphen .... DASH
    " , without a .... SOLID
hypnotic condition ...... LETHARGY,
                    TRANCE, COMA
hypnotism, founder of ..... MESMER
hypnotize .... CHARM, ENDORM
hypochondria .... NOSOMANIA
hypocrisy ..... CANT, DECEIT, GUILE
hypocrite ... PRETENDER, TARTUF(F)E
hypothecate .... PLEDGE
hypothesis . GUESS, SURMISE, THEORY,
                        THEOREM
hypothetical force . IDANT, OD, BIOD,
                        ELOD
hydrax CONY, DAMAN, DAS, SHAPHAN,
                        BADGER
hyson .... TEA
hyssop .... MINT
hysteria .... NERVES

I

I .... EGO, IOTA, SELF
I, letter .... EYE
I, excessive use of letter I IOTACISM
I love; Lat. .... AMO
I have found .... EUREKA
Iago, wife of .... EMILIA
iambic trimeter .... SENARIUS
Iberia .... SPAIN
ibex ZAC, SAKEEN, BOUQUETIN, DAAL,
                    KAIL, BEDEN
ibid. .... SAME, MONITOR
Ibsen character . ASE, NORA, ANITRA
    " , native land of ..... NORWAY
Icarus' daughter .... ERIGONE
ice . FLOE, GEM, RINE, SISH, GLACIAL,
                    SHERBET, GRUE
ice, mass of .. GLACIER, BERG, CALF,
                        GROWLER
    " performer .... HENIE
iced .... GELID, GLACE, FROSTED
Iceland bay .... FAXA
    " , bronze coin of .... EYRIR
    " legislature .... ALTHING
    " volcano .... ASKJA, HEKLA
Icelandic chief gods ... ASIR, BALDER,
        FORSETI, ODIN (WODEN),
    HEIMDALL, LOKI, THOR (DONAR),
                    TYR (TIU)
    " language .... NORSE
    " literature ...... EDDA, SAGA
    " measure .... FET, LINA, ALEN

    " musician and poet .. SKALD
icteric .... JAUNDICED
Idaho capital .... BOISE
idant .... CHROMOSOME
ide .... ORFE
idea .. EIDOS, SCHEME, PLAN, FANCY,
        MODEL, NOTION, CONCEPT
ideal . UNREAL, UTOPIAN, HERO, IDOL,
            COMPLETE, FAULTLESS
    " , remote .... THULE
    " state .. EDEN, OCEANA, UTOPIA
ideate .... CONCEIVE, THINK
identical .... ALIKE, SAME, ONE
ideology ...... ISM, DOGMA, THEORY
ides day .... NONES
idiocy .. AMENTIA, ANOESIA, FATUITY
idiom CANT, DICTION, ARGOT, STYLE,
                        LOCUTION
idiot MORON, CRETIN, NATURAL, OAF,
        BOOBY, DUNCE, IMBECILE
idle .. SORN, DRONE, LOAF, OTIOSE,
    TIFFLE, LAZY, MOON, VAIN, INERT,
                LOITER, GAMMER
idleness .... SLOTH, OTIOSITY
idler . LOUNGER, DAWDLER, FANIENTE
idling .... MOONING, OTIOSE
idocrase .... VESUVIANITE
idol ... ZEMI, FETISH, DEITY, SYMBOL,
                        TERAPH
    " , social .... LION
idolator . BAALITE, PAGAN, HEATHEN
Idumean .... EDOMITE
Idun .... ITHUN(N)
idyl ...... IMAGE, POEM, PASTORAL
"Idyls of the King," lady in ETTARRE
i.e. .... IDEST
if ever .... AND, ONCE
if not .... ELSE, NISI, UNLESS
iffy .... DOUBTFUL
igneous rock . DACITE, BOSS, DIABASE
ignited .... AFIRE, KINDLED, LIT
ignoble . HUMBLE, LOW, BASE, MEAN,
                    VILE, ABJECT
ignoramus ... DOLT, DUNCE, NITWIT,
                        SCIOLIST
ignorance ..... INERUDITION, TAMAS
ignorant ..... LAY, NESCIENT, GREEN
ignore .... ELIDE, CUT, OMIT, SNUB,
                SLIGHT, OVERLOOK
iguana ..... GUANA, LIZARD, EGUAN,
                        WANA
ileus .... COLIC
ilex .... HOLLY, OAK
Iliad, herald in the .... STENTOR
    " hero .... ACHILLES, AJAX, HECTOR
ilk .... CLASS, TYPE, SORT, STRIPE
ill ... AILING, BAD, SICK, EVIL, ABED,
                FAULTY, UNWELL
    " temper ... SPLEEN, ANIMUS, TOUT

143

" will .... SPITE, MALICE, RANCOR, GRUDGE, ENMITY
illegal .. CONTRABAND, FOUL, ILLICIT
" toll .... MALTOLTE, MALETOLT
Illinois county .. BOND, CASS, CLAY, COOK, FORD, KNOX, KANE, LAKE, LEE, OGLE, PIKE, POLL, WILL
" , native of .... SUCKER
" river .... SPOON
" town .... ZION, PANA, KARMI DIXON, GALVA
illiterate .... UNREAD, INERUDITE
illuminate ...... (IM)BLAZE, MINIATE, MYSTIC, CHEER, LIGHT, LIMN
illumination in eclipse ... PENUMBRA
" unit .... LUX, PHOT
illusion CHIMERA, FALLACY, FANTASY
illustrate ..... CITE, DESIGN, EXPLAIN, PICTURE, ELUCIDATE
illustration ...... INSTANCE, EXAMPLE, SIMILE, SPECIMEN, CASE, DIAGRAM
image .... (E)IKON, ICON, IDOL, EIDOLON, IDOLUM, EFFIGY, PHOTO, SHAPE, FORM, RECEPT, REPLICA
imagination .... DREAM, FANTASY
imaginative .... POETICAL
imagine ... CONCEIVE, IDEATE, WEEN, FANCY, SUPPOSE, SURMISE, GUESS
imbecile ... WITLESS, ANILE, MORON, CRETIN, AMENT, DOTARD, FATUOUS
imbroglio .... CABAL, INTRIGUE, PLOT
imbrue ...... MACERATE, SOAK, STEEP
imbue .... TINCT, DYE, INGRAIN, LEAVEN, SATURATE, TINGE
imitate ..... MIMIC, APE, MIME, COPY, MOCK, ECHO, FEIGN
imitation ... MIMESIS, PARODY, APISM, COPY, SHAM, PARODY
" pearl .... OLIVET
imitative in color or form APATETIC
immature .. YOUNG, CRUDE, CALLOW, RAW, GREEN, UNRIPE, NEANIC
immaturity ..... NONAGE, INFANCY
immense .... VAST(Y), ENORM, TITANIC, INFINITE
immerse ..... DOUSE, ENGROSS, DIP, DUNK, INFUSE, BAPTIZE
immigrant .... METIC, GUINEA
immobile .... FIXED, SET, FIRM, RIGID
immoderate .... UNDUE
immortal ..... UNDYING, AMBROSIAL, GLORIOUS, PERPETUAL
immortality .... ATHANASIA, AMRITA
immune body .... DESMON
" , render .... VASTATE
immure .... CONFINE, WALL, ENTOMB
immutable .... ETERNAL, STABLE
imp .... FAIRY, FAY, SPRITE, BRAT, ELF, GREMLIN
impact .... FORCE, CRAM, STROKE, CEMENT, CONTACT, JAR, SLAM

impair ... MAR, RUIN, VITIATE, HARM, WARP, SPOIL
impale ... GORE, PIERCE, SPIT, STING
impalpable ...... FINE, INTANGIBLE
impart .... GIVE, LEND, TELL, CONFER
impartial ..... EQUITABLE, FAIR, JUST
imparting motion .... KINETIC
impasse ...... CULDESAC, STALEMATE, DEADLOCK, HITCH
impatient .... EAGER, RESTIVE, ITCHING, FRETFUL
impeach .. ACCUSE, ARRAIGN, INDICT
impede ...... BLOCK, CLOG, RETARD, STYMIE, ESTOP, (DE)BAR
impediment ... BARRIER, HITCH, SNAG
impel .... DRIVE, URGE, GOAD
impelling forces .... MOMENTA
imperfect ... FALLIBLE, FRAIL, ERRATIC, WANTING
" goods .... FENT
" , prefix for .... MAL
imperial .... AUGUST, REGAL, STATELY
impersonate ... COPY, EMBODY, MIMIC
impetus ... BENSEL, BIRR, MOMENTUM
impious .... GODLESS, PROFANE, UNGODLY
impish .... ELVAN, ELVISH, PERT
implant .. (EN)ROOT, (EN)FIX, IMBUE
implement .... KIT, TOOL, GEAR, GRAITH, TACKLE, DEVICE, ENGINE, ENFORCE, UTENSIL
" , early flint .... EOLITH
" , to deprive of an RATTEN
implied .... INFERENTIAL, TACIT
implore ...... ASK, BEG, PRAY, PLEAD, ADJURE, BESEECH
imply ..... SUPPOSE, ARGUE, INDUCE, CONNOTE, ALLUDE, INFER
impolite .... RUDE, INSOLENT
import .. DRIFT, VALUE, INTENT, SENSE
importance ..... MOMENT, PRESTIGE, STRESS
impose .... INFLICT, ENTAIL, LEVY, PALM, FOIST, TAX, DUPE
imposing REGAL, AUGUST, POMPOUS
impost ... TAX, TOLL, TRIBUTE, ABWAB
impostor SHAM, CHEAT, FAKER, FRAUD, QUACK, CHARLATAN
impregnate .... TINCT, FECUNDATE
imprecation CURSE, OATH, MALISON, ANATHEMA
impress ... PRINT, DENT, STAMP, AWE
impression ...... IDEA, MARK, EFFECT
imprison ... CAGE, IMMURE, CONFINE
improper AMISS, PAW, EVIL, WRONG
improve ..... AMEND, BETTER, RECTIFY
improvise ...... PONG, VAMP, ADLIB, FLASH, HUNCH, INVENT, CONTRIVE
impudent ... MALAPERT, BRASSY, PERT, SAUCY, CHEEKY, BOLD

144

impugn ...... ASPERSE, BLAME, DENY
impulse ... ESTRO, FORCE, ATE, RUSH,
               SPUR, MOTIVE, IMPETUS
impunity ...... EXEMPTION, FREEDOM
impure form of flint .... CHERT
   "   metallic product ..... ALLOY,
               MATTE
   "   ore .... SPEISS
impute ...... ARET, ASCRIBE, CHARGE
in .... ATHOME
   "   a line .... AROW
   "   a row .... SERIAL, ALINE
   "   accordance with ...... PURSUANT
   "   addition .... ALSO, FURTHER, TOO
   "   as much as .. SINCE, SEEING, FOR,
               QUA
   "   case of .... LEST, INRE
   "   respect to .... ANENT
   "   spite of .... MALGRE
in the same place ...... IBID, IBIDEM
   "   the presence of .... CORAM
Ina; actress .... CLAIRE
inability to chew .... AMASESIS
   "   to execute movements ......
               APRAXIA
   "   to read aloud .... ALEXIA
   "   to stand erect ..... ASTASIA
Inachus, daughter of .... IO
inaction .... INERTIA, TORPOR
inactive IDLE, INERT, OTIOSE, SUPINE,
               DORMANT, PASSIVE
inane ...... PUERILE, FATUOUS, SILLY,
               VOID, JEJUNE
inapt .... CLUMSY, GAUCHE, UNFIT
inarticulate ... DUMB, APHONIC, MUTE
inauspicious ..... ADVERSE, MALIGN,
           UNTIMELY, HOSTILE, OMINOUS
inborn ... INNATE, NATIVE, INHERENT
   "   desire .... CONATUS
incarnation ... EMBODIMENT, AVATAR
   "   of Vishnu .... RAMA
incense .... MYRRH, JOSS, OLIBANUM,
             STACTE, ENRAGE
   "   , to burn .... THURIFY
   "   tree .... BURSERA, ICICA
incensed ...... ANGRY, IRATE, STUNG,
             WROTH, FIRED
incentive .... MOTIVE, STIMULUS,
            BROD, SPUR, GOAD
inch .... CREEP, EDGE, WORM
inch of twelve seconds .... PRIME
   "   , part of an .... LINE, MIL
inches, nine .... SPAN
incident .... EPISODE, EVENT
incidental .... BYE, EPISODIC, CASUAL
incidentally ...... OBITER, APROPOS
incinerator .. CREMATORIUM, FURNACE
incision ...... CUT, GASH, SLIT, SCAR
incite .... EGG, AGITATE, SPUR, ABET,
        BUZZ, STING, SUBORN, IMPEL,
        PROVOKE, FOMENT, (A)ROUSE

inclination .. GRADE, NOD, CONATUS,
            TASTE, SLANT, BIAS
incline .... TEND, LEAN, RAMP, SLOPE,
            SLANT, CANT, VERGE
inclined ...... PROPENSE, APT, LEANT,
          PRONE, PRONATE, BENT
   "   to eat .... ESURIENT
inclining ..... DISPOSED, ALIST, BENT
inclose .. EMBAR, ENCLAVE, PIN, COOP
inclosure .... CORRAL, SEPT
income ...... USANCE, RENTE, WAGES
   "   , rel. to ... TONTINE, ANNUITY
incorrect ... BASE, WRONG, SOLECIST
   "   naming of objects ....
             PARANOMIA
increase ... AUGMENT, ACCRETE, EKE,
          WAX, RISE, DILATE
incredulity, cry of .... WALKER
increment .... ACCRUAL
incubate .... HATCH, SIT, CLOCK,
          CONCOCT, SCHEME
incubus DEMON, NIGHTMARE, BURDEN
incumbrance ... CLAIM, LIEN, BURDEN
incursion ...... FORAY, RAID, INFLUX
incus .... ANVIL, HAMMER
indecisive .... SEESAW, TEETERY
indeclinable noun .... APTOTE
indeed .... ARU, AROO, AROON
indefinite .... BLURRED, VAGUE,
          AMBIGUOUS
indentation ... DINGE, CRENELET, JAB,
          NOTCH, NICK
   "   on a blade .... CHOIL
indented .. EROSE, CRENATE, SERRATED
indeterminate, the .... APEIRON
index .... GNOMON, PIP, NEEDLE,
          POINTER
   "   mark .... FIST
India .... SILK, PAPER, INK
   "   ; air conditioner .... TATTY
   "   , anc. emperor of ...... ASOKA
   "   , bean of .... URD
   "   , city in .. AGAR, DHAR, AGRA,
         BARODA, GAYA, BIHAR,
         AMBUR, DELHI
   "   , coin of ANNA, PICE, RUPEE, PIE
   "   , covered litter of ..... DOOLEE
         DOLY
   "   , European in .... SAHIB
   "   , gold piece for bride .... TALIS
   "   , inland mail of .... DAK
   "   , native state of ..... ALWAR,
       BARODA, MANIPUR, POONCH,
       MYSORE, GWALIOR
   "   ; a hundred lakhs ...... CRORE
   "   , people of northwestern .. JATS
   "   , region of ... ASSAM, MALABAR
   "   , religious community in ......
         PARSEE, PARSI
   "   , river in ..... IRAWADI, INDUS,
         RAPTI, GANGES

"	, robber of .... DACOIT	"	dialect ..... PRAKRIT, PUSHTU
"	, sacred city of NASIK, BENARES	"	dill .... SOYA
"	, shrine in ... DEWAL, DAGOBA	"	disciple .... CHELA
"	; sixteen annas .... RUPEE	"	district ...... AGRA, MALABAR
"	, spinning wheel of ... CHARKA	"	dog .... DHOLE, KOLSUN
"	, state ceremony in ... DURBAR	"	drama .... NATAKA
"	; Sudra caste, one of ..... MAL	"	drink .... SOMA
"	, summer capital of ..... SIMLA	"	drug .... BHANG
"	, tower of .... MINAR	"	dust storm .... PEESASH
"	, wild dog of .... DHOLE	"	dye stuff .... AAL, AL
"	wild sheep of ...... NAHOOR,	"	elephant .... HATHI
	OORIAL, SHA	"	elk .... SAMBAR
Indian (East) abuse .... GALI, GALEE		"	estate .... TALUK
"	acrobat .... NAT	"	falcon .. BES(A)RA, SHAHEEN,
"	animal .... ZEBU, DHOLE		SHAHIN
"	antelope SASIN, NILGAI, CHIRU	"	fan .... PUNKAH
"	army officer .... JEMADAR,	"	festival .... DEWALI
	TANADAR	"	fiber plant .... AMBARY
"	assembly hall .... KIVA	"	fig tree .... PIPAL
"	astrologer .... JOSHI	"	fish .... DORAB
"	attendant, female .... AYAH	"	flute .... BIN, PUNGI
"	bail .... ANDI	"	footprint .... PUG
"	banker .... SHROFF	"	footstool .... MORA
"	bear .... BALOO, BALU	"	fruit .... BEL
"	bearer .... SIRDAR	"	gateway .... TORAN(A)
"	bed of a stream ...... NULLAH	"	gazelle .... CHIKARA
"	bill of exchange ...... HUNDI	"	glorious .... SHRI, SRI
"	bison .... GAUR	"	goat .... MARKHOR, TAHR
"	black wood .... BITI	"	gorge .... TANGI
"	boat .... DONGA, DUNGA	"	government estates .... AMANI
"	bodice .... CHOLI	"	granary GOLAH, GUNGE, GUNJ
"	Brit. rule .... RAJ	"	grant .... ENAM
"	buffalo .... ARNA, ARNEE	"	grass .. DOORBA, GLAGAKUSHA,
"	bulbul .... KALA		MANO, RAGI
"	butter .... GHEE	"	groom .... SYCE
"	cape .... DIVI	"	handkerchief .... MALABAR
"	capital .... DELHI, SIMLA	"	harem .... ZENANA, SERAI
"	carriage .... RATH, GHARRY	"	harvest .... RABI
"	caste .... LOHANA, RAJPUT,	"	hawk .... SHIKRA
	MALI, MEO	"	headman of village ..... PATEL
"	cavalryman .... SOWAR	"	helmet .... TOPI
"	charm .... OBI	"	herb .... PIA, SESAME, SOLA
"	chief .... RAJAH, SIRDAR	"	hill dweller .... DOGRA
"	church .... SAMAJ	"	hills .... GARO
"	cigarette .... BIRI	"	hog deer .... ATLAS
"	city .... BENARES, SURAT	"	holy man ...... FAKIR, SADHU
"	civet cat .... ZIBET(H)	"	horse disease .... SURRA
"	cloak .... CHOGA	"	hunting expedition .... SHIKAR
"	cloth ... SALU, SAL(L)OO, TAT,	"	hut .... TOLDO
	SURAT	"	invader .... SACAE
"	cloth strip .... PATA	"	jacket .... KOLA
"	comb. form .... INDO	"	king .... RAJA(H)
"	coconut .... NARGIL	"	king; myth ...... NALA, SESHA
"	corn .... SAMP, ZEA	"	laborer .... PALLI
"	crocodile .... GAVIAL	"	lace .... GOTA
"	cuckoo .... KOEL	"	lady .... BEGUM, BIBI
"	custom .... DASTUR	"	land between two rivers DOAB
"	dancing .... NAUTCH	"	land grant .... SASAN
"	deer .... AXIS, CERVUS, CHITAL	"	landing place .... GHAT
"	, designating an .... KUSAN		

"	language ..... SANSKRIT, URDU, PALI, HINDUSTANI, TAMIL	"	reception .... DURBAR
"	leader .... GANDHI, NEHRU	"	religious sect .... SAMAJ
"	levee .... DURBAR	"	resort for invalids SIMLA, ABU
"	licorice, poison .... ABRIN	"	rice .... BORO
"	lieutenant governor ..... NAIB	"	rifle pit .... SANGAR
"	low class .... BHAT	"	road .... PRAYA
"	macaque .... RHESUS	"	root .... ATIS
"	madder .... AAL, AL	"	ruler ..... RAO, NAWAB, RAJA, NABOB, NIZAM
"	mahogany .... TOON	"	ruminant .... ZEBU
"	mail .... DAK	"	sacred city .... BENARES
"	master .... SAHIB	"	sacred word .... OM
"	matting .... TATTA, TATTY	"	sailor .... LASCAR
"	meal .... ATA, ATTA	"	savant .... BHAT, PUNDIT
"	measure ... KOB, ADOULIE, GUZ	"	score .... CORGE
"	medicinal nut ...... MALABAR	"	sect .... BALI
"	medicine man ...... SHAMAN	"	servant .... AMAH, MATY
"	merchant .... SITH, SOUDAGUR	"	shed .... PANDAL
"	midwife .... DHAY	"	sheep .... OORIAL, SHA
"	millet .... DHOOR, DURRA	"	shrine .... DAGOBA
"	minor native official .. AMEEN, AMIN	"	shrub .... ARUSA, MADAR, MUDAR, ODAL
"	minstrel .... BHAT	"	skipper .... SERANG
"	monetary unit .... CRORE, LAC, LAKH	"	snake .... CRAIT, BONGAR, KATUKA, COBRA
"	mountain pass .... GHAT	"	soldier .... SEPOY, PEON
"	mountains .... VINDHYA	"	sorghum .... CUSH
"	mulberry .... AAL, AL	"	spinning wheel ... CHARK(H)A
"	musket ball .... GOLI	"	sugar .... GUR
"	mus. instrument .. BINA, VINA, RUANA, SAROD, SARON, SITAR	"	surety .... ANDI
"	narcotic .... BHANG, HASHISH	"	symbol, phallic ...... LINGAM
"	nation, anc. .... TAMIL	"	tax district .... TAHSIL
"	; Nilgiri, one of tribe BADAGA	"	tax-free land .... ENAM
"	nurse .... AMAH, AYAH	"	teacher .... GURU
"	Ocean island .... CEYLON, MALDIVE, MINICOY, MAURITIUS	"	title .... NAWAB, SAHIB, RAJA(H), MIAN, SRI
"	officer ...... DEWAN, JEMADAR	"	tower .... MINAR
"	ox .... GAUR	"	tracker .... PUGGI
"	pageant .... TAMASHA	"	tree .... BEL, GORAN, PIPAL, POON, TEAK, DAR, SAL
"	palanquin .... PALKEE	"	turban .... PUGREE
"	palm .... NIPA	"	twilled cotton ... SALOO, SALU
"	panda .... WAH	"	vehicle .... EKKA, GHARRY, TONGA, RATH
"	partridge .... KYAH	"	veranda .... PYAL
"	peasant .... RYOT	"	vessel .... LOTA(H), PATAMAR
"	pepper .... BETEL	"	viceroy ...... NABOB, NAWAB
"	philosopher .... YOGI	"	village .... ABADI
"	physicist .... RAMAN	"	vine .... ODAL, SOMA
"	pigeon .... TRERON	"	viol .... RUANA
"	pillar .... LAT	"	violin .... SAROD, SAROH
"	plum .... AMRA	"	warrior .... SINGH
"	police station .... THANA	"	watchman .... MINA
"	powder .... ABIR	"	whaler .... HOH, QUILEUTE
"	priest .... SHAMAN	"	weight ...... CHITTAK, MASHA, MAUND, PICE, RATTI, RATI, SER, SEER, TANK, TOLA, VIS(E), MAGELIN, CATTY
"	priest's garment .... DHOTI		
"	prime minister .... DEWAN		
"	prince .... RANA		
"	princess ...... RANI, RANEE		
"	property .... DHAN	"	window screen .... TATTY
"	queen .... BEGUM, RANI	"	wine .... SHRAB

"   wood ..... KOKRA, SAL, TOON
"   xylophone .... SARON
Indian (Amer.) .... CHIPPEWA, CREE,
        SAC, UTE, INCA, MIRANHA,
        PONCA, AMERIND
" , Aht confederacy, one of .....
        NOOTKA
" , Alabama .... CREEK
" , Alaska .... ALEUT
" , Algonquian .. ARAPAHO, CREE,
        MOHICAN, NIANTIC, SAC,
        SAUK, WEA
" , Arizona ...... APACHE, HOPI,
        PIMA, YUMA
"   blanket .... STROUD
" , bloodthirsty .... KIOWA
" , Bolivian ...... CHARCA, ITEN,
        MOXO
"   bread .... TUCKAHOE
" , Caddoan ...... REES, ARIKARA
" , Cal. YUKI, PERICUI, SERI, YUROK
"   ceremonial pipe ..... CALUMET
Indian chief .. LOGAN, SACHEM, TYEE,
        SAGAMORE, SANNUP
"   chief of Seminoles .. OSCEOLA
" , Creek .... ALABAMA
" , Dakota .... SIOUX
" , Dakota (N.) ... ARIKAREE, REE
" , Delaware .... LENAPE
" , Ecuadorian .... CANELO
" , female of the .... MAHALY,
        SQUAW
" , Florida .... SEMINOLE
" , Georgia .... CREEK
"   great spirit .... MANITOU
"   group of So. Amer. ...... GES
" , Guatemala .... XINCA
"   hamlet .... RANCHERIA
" , Iroquois .... ONEIDA, ERIE,
        HURON, SENECA
" , Kansas .... PANI, PAWNEE
"   linguistic group ..... TINNEH
"   linguistic stock ...... SASTEAN
"   memorial post .... TOTEM, XAT
" , mestizo ..... GRIFFE, LADINO
" , Mexican .. SERI, YAQUI, AZTEC
" ; Miami tribe .... WEA
" , Miss. river MANDAN, TONIKAN
"   money ..... PEAG, SE(A)WAN,
        WAMPUM
" , Nebraska .... OMAHA, PONCA
" , New Mexico ... PUEBLO, ZUNI,
        TANO
" , New York IROQUOIS, SENECA
" , nomad .... APACHE
"   of mixed blood ...... METISSE
"   of the Iroquois tribe .. MINGO
"   of the Pacific ...... CHINOOK,
        NOOTKA
" , Oklahoma .... ARAPAHOE

" , Oregon .... YANAN
"   ornament .... RUNTEE
"   people .... POMOS
" , Peru ...... BORO, INCA, CANA
"   pole .... TOTEM
"   pony .... CAYUSE
"   pueblo .... HOPI, ZUNI
" , Salishan .... TULALIP
" , Seowan .. SIOUAN, OTO, OTOE
" , Shoshone dial. .... MOQUI
" , Shoshonean .... BANAK,
        BANNOCK, PIUTE, UTE
" , Sioux .... KAW, OTOE, OSAGE,
        TETON
" , So. Amer. AYMARA, GES, ONA
" , Sonoran .... SERI
" , Tanoan .... ISLETA
"   unit of money .... PIMAN
"   village .... PUEBLO
"   wampum .... SEAWAN
" , Washington or Vancouver AHT
Indian, western .... HOPI, OTO, UTE
"   wigwam .... TEPEE
Indiana model city .... GARY
Indiana river .... MAUMEE
Indiana, state nickname ... HOOSIER
Indiana, town in .... PAOLI, GARY
Indians (miscellaneous)
" , Antilles .... CARIB
" , Arikara .... REES
" , Athapascan .... DENE
" , Bolivia ..... MAROPA, MOXO,
        OTUKE
" , Brazil; .... ARAUA, CARIB,
        GUARANI, INCA, ACROA, TUPI
" , Canada .... DENE, HAIDA
" , Chile .... ARAUCA
" , Keresan .... SIA
" , Manitoba .... CREE
" ; Mayan tribe .... QUICHE
" , Mexico .... AZTEC, CORA,
        OPATA, OTOMI
" , Panama .... CUNA
" , Peru CANA, CHANGOS, PANO
" , S. Amer. ..... ANETO, CARIB,
        ONA, OTA, TUPI
" ; S. Amer. group .... GES
" , Tierra del Fuego ... FUEGIAN,
        ONA
" , Vera Cruz .... TOTONAC
" , Wakashan .... AHT
" , Yucatan .... MAYA
Indian's "yes" .... UGH
indicate ..... SIGNIFY, BETOKEN, CITE
indicator ...... ARROW, DIAL, VANE,
        TABLE, GNOMON, FIST, POINTER
indict ..... ARRAIGN, ACCUSE, PANEL,
        CHARGE, (IM)PEACH
indifferent .... BLASE, NEUTRAL,
        DETACHED

148

indigence ..... NEED, WANT, PENURY
indigenous .... ENDEMIC, INNATE,
             EDAPHIC, NATIVE
indigent .... POOR, VOID, DESTITUTE,
             NEEDY
indigestion .... DYSPEPSIA
indignant .... ANGRY, HOT, IRATE
indignation .... IRE, CHOLER, WRATH
indignity .... AFFRONT, DUDGEON,
             OUTRAGE
indigo .... BLUE, ANIL, WOAD
   "   and zinc .... INDOL
   "   , bale of .... SEROON
   "   berry .... RANDIA
   "   , Chinese .... ISATIS
   "   , commercial ...... INDIGOTIN
   "   derivative .... KETOLE
   "   , source of ...... ANIL, ISATIN
   "   , wild .... BAPTISIA
indisposition .... MALAISE
indite .... PEN, WRITE, (IN)SCRIBE
indistinct .... VAGUE, DIM, HAZY
individual SINGLE, SOLE, SELF, BION
   "   ; comb. form .... IDIO
   "   of a compound animal ...
             ZOON
individuality ... EGOHOOD, NATURE,
             SEITY
Indo-Aryan ..... JAT, KHATRI, RAJPUT
Indo-China, part of .... ANNAM,
             VIETNAM, CAMBODIA, LAOS
Indo-Chinese aborigines . HOS, KHAS,
             MEOS, THAI, YAOS
   "   bull .... ZEBU
   "   delta .... MEKONG
   "   native rock .... TRIASSIC
   "   tongue ...... AO, AKA, TAI
indoctrinate COACH, EDIFY, INSTRUCT
Indo-European .. ARYAN, CROAT, LETT
indolence INERTIA, SLOTH, LETHARGY
indolent .... OTIOSE, IDLE, SUPINE
Indonesian DYAK, BUGI, IBAN, MALAY,
             DAYAK, IGOROT, LAMPONG, ATA
   "   island .... BALI, BORNEO,
             CERAM, CELEBES, SUMATRA, TIMOR
   "   lake .... TOBA
   "   president ...... SUKARNO
Indo-Persian measure .... GUZ
indorse .... ATTEST, RATIFY, VISA
indubitable .... EVIDENT, SURE
inductance, unit of .... HENRY
indulge .... PAMPER, YIELD, BABY,
             HUMOR, CODDLE, COSSET, PETTLE
Indus tribesman .... GOR
industrious ...... DEEDY, ASSIDUOUS,
             SEDULOUS
indweller .... DENIZEN, INDIGENE
inebriate .... DRUNKARD, SOT, TOPER,
             TIPSY, SQUIFFY
inept .... PUERILE, SILLY, UNFIT

inert ... LATENT, DEAD, TORPID, DULL,
             SUPINE, STOLID
inevitable result .... NEMESIS
infamy ... ODIUM, SHAME, IGNOMINY
infant .. MINOR, WEAN, BABY, CHILD,
             BRAT, TOT, CHIT, PAPOOSE
infantryman ...... ASKAR, DOGFACE,
             DOUGHBOY
infatuate .... CHARM, ENAMOR, BESOT
infatuation .... ATE
infect .... IMPURE, TAINTED, SMIT
infer .... PRESUME, DERIVE, IMPLY
inference ..... COROLLARY, ILLATION
inferior ...... LOWER, POOR, DICKY,
             SUBALTERN, LESS, MENIAL, MINOR,
             PETTY
   "   lawyer .... LEGULEIAN,
             PETTIFOGGER, SHYSTER
   "   ; said of judges ...... PUISNE
infernal .... TARTAREAN, HELLISH,
             STYGIAN
inferno .... ABYSS, HADES, GEHENNA,
             NARAKA, SHEOL, AVERNUS, LIMBO
   "   , ferry to the .... STYX
infested .... HAUNTED, OVERRAN
infidel .... ATHEIST, SARACEN,
             AGNOSTIC, HERETIC, HEATHEN
infirm ...... ANILE, SENILE, DECREPIT
inflame .... FAN, RILE, INCITE, KINDLE
inflammable ... ACCENDIBLE, PICEOUS
   "   gas .... ETHANE
   "   liquid .... ACETONE
   "   substance PUNK, TINDER,
             AMADOU
inflammation .... IRITIS, UVEITIS
   "   of bone ..... OSTEITIS
inflated .... BOLLEN, DISTENDED,
             TURGID, BOMBASTIC
inflection ... ACCENT, CROOK, TENOR
inflexible .... IRON, RIGID, STIFF
inflict .... IMPOSE, DEAL, WREAK
inflorescence, axial circle of   WHORL
   "   , cluster .. CYME, RACEME
influence . PULL, IMPEL, SWAY, INFLUX
influenza .... FLU, GRIP(PE)
inform .... APPRISE, SQUEAL, ADVISE,
             NOTIFY, RAT
information ...... NEWS, AIR, AVISO,
             LORE, DATA, DOPE, FACT
informed .... HEP, ONTO
informer AFFIRMER, DELATOR, STOOL,
             NARK
infringement of copyright ... PIRACY
infundibulum, orifice of .... LURA
infusion .... TEA, DECOCTION
   "   of malt .... WORT
infusoria .... VORTICEL(LA), ACINETA
Inge play .... PICNIC
ingenious ...... DEDAL, FINE, ADROIT
ingenuous .... FRANK, NAIVE

ingest .... EAT, SWALLOW, CONSUME
ingot .... SYCEE, GAD, PIG
  " workers .... BARMEN
ingress ...... ENTRY, ACCESS, PORTAL
inhabitant .. CIT(IZEN), DENIZEN, ITE
inhabiting an island .... NESIOTE
inhale .... RESPIRE, SNIFF, SMELL
inhere ...... CLEAVE, CONSIST, LODGE
inherent INBORN, INTRINSIC, INNATE,
                       BASIC, NATIVE
inheritance .... LEGACY, BEQUEST,
                      PATRIMONY
inheritor ... HEIR, LEGATEE, PARCENER
inhibit RESTRAIN, BAN, BAR, ENJOIN
inhuman .... BESTIAL, CRUEL, FELL
inimical .... ADVERSE, HOSTILE
initial .... PARAPH, FAC
initiate .. OPEN, EPOPT, HAZE, FOUND
inject ..... IMMIT, INSERT, INTROMIT
injection .... CLYSTER, ENEMA
injure ..... GRIEVE, MAR, TEEN, LAME
  " by scorching .... SCATHE
injurious .... NOXIOUS, NUSANT
injury .... DAMAGE, EVIL, LESION,
        HARM, WOUND, TRAUMA,
          MAYHEM, BLEMISH
  " , causing .... MALEFIC
  " , sense of .... UMBRAGE
ink .... BLACK, DAUB
  " bag .... SAC
  " berry ...... HOLLY, INDIGO
  " fish .... CUTTLE
  " spreader .... BRAYER
inker .... PAD, BRAYER, DABBER,
            TOMPION, ROLLER
inkling .... CLUE, NOTION, HINT, CUE
inky fluid .... MELENA
inlaid work .... MOSAIC, NIELLO,
              TARSIA, BUHL
in-law .... MESNE
inleague .... ALLY
in league .... PARTNERS
(in)league .... CAHOOTS
inlet ... PORE, ARM, FIORD, RAE, RIA,
     SUMP, STRAIT, BIGHT, VOE, ZEE,
             COVE, BAYOU
inn .... ABODE, TAVERN, FONDA,
   HOTEL, MOTEL, LOCANDA, OSTERIA,
        SERAI, IMARET, KHAN
innkeeper .... HOTE, BONIFACE,
             PUBLICAN
innate .... NATIVE, NATURAL
inner .... ESOTERIC, ENTAL, OBSCURE
  " ; comb. form ...... ENTO, ESO
innermost lining of a lymphatic ....
                      INTIMA
Innisfail .... EIRE, IRELAND, ERIN
innocent .... FREE, PURE, CHASTE,
              NAIVE, ARTLESS
innuendo ..... ALLUSION, HINT, SLUR

inordinate .... FABULOUS, UNDUE
inquest .... ASSIZE, SEARCH
inquiry PROBE, QUEST, TRIAL, EXAMEN
inquisitive ... PEERING, PRYING, NOSY
insane .... BATTY, FRANTIC, MAD,
              CRAZY, LUNATIC
  " asylum ... BEDLAM, MADHOUSE
  " , make .... DEMENT, DEMONIZE
insanity .. AMENTIA, VESANIA, MANIA
inscribe .. ENGRAVE, ENROL, RECORD
inscription at book end COLOPHON
inscrutable ... ABSTRUSE, MYSTERIOUS
insect ...... NIT, APHID, LERP, SPIDER,
     ANTLION, ERIA, GNAT, MITE,
     TICK, BUG, LOUSE, CHINCH,
     GRIG, ROACH, EARWIG, LOCUST,
      MANTIS, MOTH, EGGER, FLY
  " , an order of .. ACARID, DIPTERA
  " antenna, end of .... CLAVA
  " , back of .... NOTUM
  " , dipterous .... MOSQUITO
  " , eyes of an .... OCELLI
  " , four-winged .... BEETLE
  " genus .. CICADA, NEPA, TERMES,
        EMESA, CICALA, THRIPS
  " , hard covering of ..... CHITIN
  " , immature .... LARVA
  " larva .... GRUB, MAGGOT
  " leg .... PROLEG
  " , lepidopterous .... MOTH
  " -like .... ENTOMOID
  " , mature .... IMAGO
  " , middle division of ... THORAX
  " , migratory .... LOCUST
  " , molting of .... ECDYSIS
  " , order of .... DIPTERA
  " , parisitic; Mex. ...... TURICATA
insect, a simple eye of ..... STEMMA
  " resin .... LAC
  " , slender grotesque ..... EMESA,
                 MANTIS
  " , small .... BUG, APHID
  " , social .... ANT, BEE
  " sound .... STRIDOR
  " stage in life .... INSTAR, PUPA,
       NYMPH, EGG, LARVA,
         COCOON, IMAGO
  " sting .... ICTUS
  " , stinging .... GADFLY
  " , winged .... WASP
  " , wingless; order ...... APTERA
  " with tail forceps .... EARWIG
insecticide .... DDT
insectivorous mammal . HEDGEHOG,
                 DESMAN
insect's feeler .... PALP
insects, genus of aquatic .. RANATRA
  " , morbid plant excrescence
      caused by .... GALL
  " , per. to .... ENTOMIC

" , plant-feeding ...... THRIPS
insecure ... RICKETY, ASEA, DUBIOUS
inseminate .... IMPLANT, SOW
insensibility ..... ANALGESIA, COMA
insert PANEL, IMMIT, INGRAFT, INLAY,
                        GODET, GOSSET
" wrongly .... FOIST
insertion of letter . EPENTHESIS, INSET
" of cords .... SHIRR
inset .... PANEL, INFLUX
inside out, turn .... EVERT
insight .... ACUMEN, KEN, APERCU
insidious ...... ARCH, FOXY, SNAKY,
                        CUNNING
insignia ...... BAR, REGALIA, BADGE
insignificant ... PETTY, PETIT, MINOR,
                        PUNY
insinuate .. HINT, INTIMATE, SUGGEST
insipid ..... DRY, FLAT, STALE, VAPID
insist .... (AF)FIRM, URGE, PRESS
inspect .. PRY, EXAMINE, TEST, SCAN,
                        AUDIT, PROBE
inspiration AFFLATUS, SPUR, STIMULUS
inspire .... ANIMATE, INHALE, IMBUE
install ...... INDUCT, ORDAIN, INVEST
instance .... EXAMPLE, CASE
instant .... TIME, TRICE, POP, POINT,
                        MOMENT, JIFFY, FLASH
instead .... ELSE, LIEU, RATHER
instigate ABET, SPUR, INCITE, SUBORN,
              PROVOKE, TEMPT, EGG, IMPEL
instruction TUITION, LORE, TUTORAGE,
                        NURTURE
" , art of ..... PAIDEUTICS,
                        PEDAGOGY
instructor .. TUTOR, COACH, DOCENT,
              LECTOR, MASTER, LECTURER
instrument .... AGENT, BOND, DEED,
              TOOL, WILL, LEASE, MEANS,
       MEDIUM, ORGAN, DEVICE, GADGET
" , astronomical ..... ARMIL
" , boring .... JUMPER
" ; comb. form ...... LABE
" for copying . PANTOGRAPH
" for expanding ... DILATER
" for finding latitude .. ABA
" for measuring eggs.......
                        OOMETER
" for measuring elec. current
                        RHEOMETER
" for striking grain STRICKLE
" , hooked .... BILL
" of knowledge .. ORGANON
" , sharp .... STYLUS
insular .... NARROW, NESIOTE
insulate ... SEGREGATE, ISOLATE, ISLE
insulating material . KERITE, OKONITE
insulin discoverer ... BANTING, BEST
insult . CAG, FIF, SLUR, FLOUT, RUFFLE,
              CHEEK, ABUSE, AFFRONT

insurance applicant .... RISK
insurgent MUTINEER, REVOLTER, REBEL
intaglio .. DIAGLYPH, MATRIX, MOULD
integer .... GNOMON, NORM
integral .... ALL, SUM, INNER, WHOLE
integrity .... ENTIRETY, VIRTUE
integument ARIL, TESTA, COAT, DERM,
                        SKIN
intellect .... MIND, INWIT, NOUS,
              MENTALITY, BRAINS, NOESIS,
                        SENSE
intellectual .... SOPHIC, MENTAL,
                        EGGHEAD
intelligence .... NEWS, ACUMEN,
              CAPACITY, MIND, NOESIS
intelligent ...... APT, BRIGHT, ASTUTE,
              BRAINY, KEEN, GASH
" animal .... CHIMP
intensity . DEPTH, VIGOR, VEHEMENCE
intent AIM, GOAL, RAPT, WILL, EAGER,
              ETTLE, VOLITION
inter . BURY, ENTOMB, INHUME, INURN
inter _____ .... ALIA
intercalary month; Heb. .... VEADAR
intercalate ..... INSERT, INTERPOLATE
intercept .. BLOCK, CATCH, NAB, SEIZE
intercessor ...... BISHOP, MEDIATOR
interdiction BAN, TABU, VETO, DECREE
interest BEHALF, SHARE, USURY, WEAL,
                        CLAIM, STAKE
interfere .. CLASH, MOLEST, CONFLICT
interim .... DIASTEM, INTERVAL,
                        MEANTIME
interference .... STATIC
interjection . BAM, EH, EGAD, OUTCRY
interlude ...... STASIMON, EPISODE,
              VERSICLE, VERSET, GAP, REST,
                        BREAK
intermediate .... MESNE, MEDIAN
intermission . ENTRACTE, LULL, PAUSE,
                        RECESS, RESPITE
intermitter .... RESTER
internal .... ESOTERIC, INNER
international business comb. .. CARTEL
" language .... IDO, OD,
              ESPERANTO, RO, VOLAPUK
interpolate .. FARSE, CORRUPT, FOIST
interpose .... MEDIATE, DISAFFECT
interpret . OPEN, SCAN, REDE, RENDER,
                        CONSTRUE
interpretation . EXEGESIS, DITTOLOGY,
              VERSION, MEANING
interpreter .... DRAGOMAN, EXEGETE,
                        LATINER
" of Koran .... ULEMA
interrogation ...... INQUEST, PROBE,
              QUERY, QUIZ, TEST
interrogator ...... PUMPER, INQUIRER
interred .... INEARTHED
intersect .... DECUSSATE, MEET, CROSS

151

intersection, of .... NODAL, SECANT
interstice ..... PORE, CRACK, CREVICE
    " , per. to .... AREOLAR
intersticed . CHINKY, CLEFTED, RIMOSE
interval .... GAP, INTERIM, REST,
    CAESURA, HIATUS, LAPSE, PITCH
intervening .... INTERJACENT, MESNE
interweave .... PLASH, PLAT, RADDLE,
    SPLICE
interwoven .... NETTED, RETIARY
    "   fabric .... TISSUE
    "   rods .... WATTLE
intestine .... COLON, THARM
    "   coating .... CAUL
    "   part; comb. form ... ILEO
    "   , part of small ..... ILEUM
    "   , per. to .... ENTERIC
intimate ... CRONY, SIB, HINT, IMPLY,
    CHUMMY, REFER, ALLUDE, FAMILIAR
intimation ... CUE, HINT, INNUENDO
intimidate .. DAUNT, ABASH, COW,
    AWE, COERCE, BULLY, BROWBEAT
into .... AMONG, UNTIL
intolerance .. BIGOTRY, DOGMATISM,
    BIAS
intonation ...... SONANCE, CADENCE
intone .... CHANT, CROON
intort .... CURL, TWIST
intoxicant ... SOMA, GIN, WHISK(E)Y
intoxicated .. SOSH, SOT, HEADY, LIT,
    STEWED, BOOZY, TIPSY
intracellular .... HISTONAL
intractable . UNRULY, SULLEN, ORNERY
intricate . D(A)EDAL, GORDIAN, MAZY
intrigue .... AMOUR, BRIGUE, CABAL,
    PLOT, RUSE
intrinsic . REAL, IMMANENT, INHERENT
introduce ..... IMMIT, INFUSE, USHER
introducing new word .... NEOLOGY
introduction .... PREFACE, PROEM,
    ISAGOGE, PREAMBLE
introductory cry .... HEAR, OYEZ
intuitive .... SEEING, NOETIC,
    PERCEIVING
inulase .... ENZYME
inulic acid, salt of .... INULATE
inulin .... ALANTIN
inundation FRESHET, DELUGE, FLOOD,
    SPATE
inure ... BENEFIT, HARDEN, TOUGHEN
inurn .... BURY, ENTOMB, INTER
invade .... RAID, TRESPASS, INTRUDE
invalid .... NULL, VOID, SICK, WEAK,
    FALSE, FEEBLE, DISABLED
invalidate .... QUASH, VITIATE
invasion . BREACH, IRRUPTION, FORAY,
    INROAD, RAID
invective .... CURSE, ABUSE, DIATRIBE
inveigh .... CENSURE, ASSAIL, CHIDE

inveigle .. SNARE, SEDUCE, WHEEDLE,
    COAX, ENTICE, LURE
invent .... COIN, CONCOCT, SCHEME
invention .... FIGMENT
inventor ..... BELL, COLT, DAVY, TAIT,
    MORSE, NOBEL, TESLA, BUNSEN,
    DIESEL, EDISON, FULTON, SPERRY,
    WRIGHT, EASTMAN
inventory .... CATALOG(UE), LIST
invertebrate ...... INSECT, MOLLUSK,
    SPINELESS
invest . EDUE, SPEND, CLOTHE, FEOFF,
    DON, ORDAIN
investigate ...... SIFT, PROBE, TRACE
investigation .. SCRUTINY, INQUEST,
    TEST, AUDIT, ZETETIC
inveterate ...... CHRONIC, ADDICTED,
    HABITUAL
invigorate .. RENEW, BRACE, FORTIFY,
    ENERGIZE
invite . BEG, SUE, ASK, WOO, COURT,
    SUMMON
invoke . BEG, PRAY, IMPLORE, ENTREAT
involve .... ENTAIL, LAP, WRAP
inward .... ENTAD
inwards, in general INMEATS, UMBLES
inwick .... INRING
inwrap .... ABSORB, ENVELOP, ROLL
iodine source .... KELP
ion, negative .... ANION
    " , positive .... CATION
Ionian city .... MYUS, TEOS
    "   gulf .... PATRAS
    "   island ... KAI, LAUT, LET(T)I,
    PAXOS, ZANTE
iota .... ACE, JOT, WHIT, ATOM
Iowa college .... COE
    "   college town .... AMES
    "   county .. CASS, CLAY, IDA, LEE,
    LINN, LYON, PAGE, POLK, SAC,
    TAMA
    "   society .... AMANA
ipecacs; genus .... EVEA
iracund .... CHOLERIC
Iran .... PERSIA
    " , anc. people of .... TAT, MEDES
    " , capital of .... TEHERAN
    " , city in .... AMOL, AMUL
Iranian .... IRANIC
Iranian angel .... MAH
    "   bird .... BULBUL
    "   carpet ...... HAMADAN, KALI
    "   civil officer .... KHAN
    "   dyestuff .... INDIGO
    "   evil spirit .... AHRIMAN
    "   fairy .... PERI
    "   fire worshiper . PARSEE, PARSI
    "   gate .... DAR
    "   gazelle .... CORA
    "   governor .... SATRAP

" grass .... MILLET	" county .. CAVAN, CORK, KERRY,
" hero .... RUSTAM, YIMA	MAYO, MEATH, SLIGO, CLARE
" moon .... MAHI	" dialect .... OGHAM
" mystic .... SUFI	" district .... BIRR
" oil center .... ABADAN	" doctor .... OLLAH, OLLAY
" river ...... KARUN, TAB, ZAB	" double-edged dagger ... SKENE,
" rug .... SENNA	SKEANE
" sacred cord .... KUSTI	" dramatist ..... BEHAN, SHAW,
" screen .... PURDAH	SYNGE, YEATS
" seaport .... BASRA	" early kingdom ...... MUNSTER
" sir .... AZAM	" endearment term ... ALANNAH
" tiara .... CIDARIS	" exclamation ..... ARRA, ARRAH
" tile .... KAS(H)I	" foot soldier .... KERN
" trading center ...... ISPAHA	" fortification .... LIS
" water vessel .... AFTABA	" Free State, county in ..... LEIX
" water wheel .... NORIA	" freebooter .... RAPPAREE
" writings .... AVESTA	" freeman .... AIRE
Iraq, city in ...... BAGHDAD, BASRA	" frock .... INAR
irascibility .... CHOLER, IRE	" general .... SHEA
irascible ...... BRASH, TESTY, EDGY	" girl .... COLLEEN
irate .... ANGRY, HOT, WROTH	" goblin .... LEPRECHAUN
Ireland .. IERNE, EIRE, ERIN, HIBERNIA	" groggery .... SHEBEEN
" , alphabet of ...... OGHAM	" island .... ACHILL, BEAR, CLEAR
" , county in ... CLARE, KERRY,	" island group .... ARAN
MAYO	" laborer, class of .... AIRE
" , Danish, settlers in .. OSTMEN	" lake .... CONN, CORRIB, DERG,
" , island group of ..... ARAN	ERNE, LOCH, MASK, REE, NEAGH
" ; lake ... LOCH, ERNE, LOUGH	" landholding system .. RUNDALE
" , people of .... IRISHRY	" legislature .... DAIL (EIREANN)
" , personified .... IRENA	" lighthouse rock ...... FASTNET
" , poetic name ..... INVERNIA,	" limestone .... CALP
INNISFAIL	" love .... GRA
" , revolutionary of ... FENIAN	" luck .... CESS
" , river in ... SHANNON, ERNE	" militia .... FENIAN
" , song of .... RANN	" monk's cell .... KIL, KILL
" , symb. for .... DEIRDRE	" moss .... CARRAGEEN
" , system of landholding......	" mountain .. COMERAGH, ERRIGAL,
RUNDALE	DONEGAL, SPERRIN, WICKLOW
" ; town .. TARA, CORK, COBH,	" mus. festival .... FEIS
KILKENNY, SLIGO	" mus. inst. . CRUT, LYRE, TYMPAN,
Ireland's saint .... PATRICK	TIMPAN, CROWD
irenic .... HENOTIC	" novelist .... ASHE, REID, SHAW
iridescent ...... OPALINE, NACREOUS	" patriot .... EMMET
iridic acid, salt of .... IRIDATE	" peasant .... KERNE
iris .... IXIA, ORRIS, RAINBOW, IRID,	" poet .... YEATS
TILEROOT, FLAG, SEG	" princess .... YSEULT
" ; comb. form .... IRIDO	" proprietor; law .... TANIST
" , inflammation of pigment of....	" river ... BOYNE, CAVAN, ERNE,
UVEITIS	FOYLE, SHANNON, SUIR
" , layer of .... UVEA	" saint .... AIDAN
Irish accent .... BLAS, BROGUE	" sea god .... LER
" anc. capital .... TARA	" seaport .... DUBLIN, TRALEE
" anc. mus. inst. .. CRUT, CROWD	" society .... SINNFEIN
" bay .... CLEW, GALWAY	" soldier KERN, ASHE, GALLOGLASS
" borrowed stock .... DAER	" song .... RANN
" cape .... CLEAR	" statesman .. BRISCOE, DEVALERA
" castle .... TARA	" steward .... ERENACH
" chisel .... CELT	" surgeon .... COLLES
" clan .... SEPT, SIOL	" tenant .... SAER, FUIDHIR
" clansman .... AIRE	" tribe .... CINEL

153

"	verse .... RANN	Islamite .... MOSLEM
"	violin-like inst. ...... CROWD	island ...... ILOT, HOLM, EYOT, AIT,
"	wandering harvester . SPALPEEN	ATOLL, KEY, CAY, KAY, ISLET
"	whiskey .... POTEEN	island, Alaskan ATTU, PRIBILOF, ALEUT
"	white .... BAWN	", Aegean Sea ...... LEROS, SCID
Irishman .... MILESIAN, PADDY, PAT,	", Baltic Sea .... OSSEL
TEAGUE, AIRE, CELT, MICK	", Caroline; N. Pac. .... YAP
irk .... BORE, NETTLE, VEX, FRET	", coral .... ATOLL
iron .. MITIS, MANGLE, PRESS, HORSE	", Cycladean .... MELOS, NAXOS
" block in battery .... VOL	", Danish .... AERO
" lamp .... CRESSET	", enchanted .... BALI
" molders' tool .... LIFTER	", Dutch E. Indies .... NIAS
" ore .... FERRIC, HEMATITE	", E. Africa .... ZANZIBAR
" -ore sand .... ISERINE	", Grecian .... SAMOS
", per. to .... FERRIC, FERROUS	" group in S. W. Pac. .. SAMOA
" pin in quoits .... HOB	" group in N. Pac. ...... KURIL
" protector for boot heel .. SHOD	" in New York harbor ... ELLIS
" sheet .... PLATE, TERNE	", inhabiting an ...... NESIOTE
" weed; genus .... VERNONIA	", Italian .... ELBA
" wood .... ACLE	", Leeward .... BARBUDA
ironclad .... MONITOR	", low .... KEY
iron .... GYVE	", Mediterranean .. CAPRI, CRETE,
", meteoric .... SIDERITE	MALTA
", native .... ORE	", of an; prefix .... NESO
ironstone .... EAGLESTONE	" of Odysseus .... ITHACA
irony ... LAMPOON, SATIRE, SARCASM	of Scotland . SHETLAND, ARRAN
Iroquois demon .... OTKON	of the Nile .... RODA
irrational number .... SURD	of the Pacific .. BONIN, GUAM
irregular .... ATACTIC, ATYPIC, ODD,	off Jutland coast ..... ALSEN
ERRATIC, SPOTTY	off N. Norway ...... SEILAND
" standard .... ABERRANT	on Gulf of Riga .... OSEL
irregularly toothed .... EROSE	", Philippine .... PANAY
irreligious .... GODLESS, PAGAN	", small AIT, CAY, KEY, OE, QUAY
irrepressible, as laughter .. HOMERIC	", small, near a larger .... CALF
irrevocable .... FINAL	", small river ..... EYOT, HOLM
irritability; med. .... ERETHISM	", Society group ...... TAHITI
irritable .. IRACUND, SPLEENY, TECHY,	S.E. of Celebes MOENA, MUNA
CRABBY, HUFFY, TESTY	", W. Indies; Brit. .... NEVIS
irritable one .... TARTAR	" west of Dutch New Guinea ARU
irritant . POISON, PTOMAINE, VENOM	islands in Pacific .... ELLICE, SAMOAN
", susceptible to ..... ALLERGIC	" Indian and Pacific Ocean....
irritate . RILE, CHAFE, IRE, VEX, GALL,	OCEANIA
PEEVE, NEEDLE, NETTLE, RANKLE,	" off coast of Asia Minor......
PROVOKE, ROIL	IONIAN
irritated .... GRATED, AFRET	Isle of Man officer .... DEEMSTER
irruption .... INVASION, INROAD	Isle of Wight borough .... RYDE
is ..... EXISTS, LIVES, NOW, NONCE	islet .... CAY, KAY, KEY
is not .... AINT, NYS, NIS	isolate .... ENISLE
Iseult's husband .... MARK	isomer .... METAMER
" love .... TRISTRAM	isomeric hydrocarbon ..... OCTANE,
Isaac's son .... JACOB, GAD, ESAU	TERPENE
Ishmael, mother of .... HAGAR	isometric . CUBIC, REGULAR, PARALLEL
", son of .... KEDAR	Israel .... JACOB, ZION, SCION
isinglass .... AGAR, MICA	" ancient city of ...... BETHEL,
Isis, brother and husband of . OSIRIS	SAMARIA, TIRZAH
", mother of .... NUT	" city or town .... RAMLE
", shrine of .... ISEUM	" desert .... NEGEV
", son of .... SEPT	" parliament .... KNESSET
Islam convert .... ANSAR	" plain .... SHARON
" teacher .. MULLAH, ALIM, AGA	" port ..... HAIFA, JAFFA, ACRE

Israeli diplomat . EBAN, BEN GURION, MEIR
Israelite .... HEBREW, JEW, SION
" scribe .... EZRA
issue ... EMANATE, EMIT, END, ARISE, EDITION, EMERGE, DOLE, ENSUE, FLUX, MET, VENT, PROGENY
Istanbul caravansary . SERAI, IMARET
" quarter ...... PERA, FANAR
isthmus .. BALK, LAND, NECK, STRAIT
" , Malay and Siam ...... KRA
it is silent; mus. .... TACET
it is so; Lat. .... SIC
Ita .... NEGRITO
Itala .... VULGATE
Italian ..... LATIN, ROMAN, SABINE, PICENE
" actress .. MAGNANI, ANGELI, LOREN, DUSE
" airplane .... CAPRONI
" art center .... SIENA
" astronomer ... AMICI, GALILEI
" author .... DANTE, PETRARCH
" bandit .... CACO
" bowl .... TAZZA
" breed of cattle ..... MODICA, PADOLIAN
" canals .... CANALI, RII
" Celtic tribe ...... SENONES
" cheese .. GRANA, PARMESAN, FONTINA
" chest .... CASSONE
" city .... ASTI, TRENT, UDINE, PISA, SPEZIA, PARMA
" coastal region ..... LIGURIA
" coins .... LIRE, SOLDI
" commune ... ATESSA, DEGO, MASSA, NOLA, ATRI, ASOLA, ALBA, URBINO
" composer .... ROSSINI, VERDI PUCCINI, MENOTTI, GUIDO, BELLINI
" condiment .... TAMARA
" conductor ...... TOSCANINI, MANTOVANI
" country .... CAMPAGNA
" culture, fourteenth-cent...... TRECENTO
" dance .... CORANTE, VOLTA, TARANTELLA
" dear .... CARO, CARA
" dessert .. SPUMONI, TORTONI
" dome .... CIMA
" dramatist .... ALFIERI
" dynasty .... SAVOY
" faction ...... BIANI, NERI
" family .... ASTI, CENCI, ESTE, COLONNA, DONATI, DORIA, MEDICI, BORGIA
" festival .... RIDOTTO

" flower .... FIORE
" game .... BOCCE
" god (see also "god") FERRUS, JANUS, PICUS, TIBER
" goddess ...... CERES, DIANA, MINERVA, OPS, POMONA, VENUS, SALUS
" gulf ...... GENOA, SALERNO, TARANTO, VENICE
" hamlet ... BORGO, CASAL(E)
" hand .... MANO
" harp .... ARPA
" health resort ...... AGNONE
" historian .... CANTU
" house .... CASA
" inlay .... TARSIA
" innkeeper .... PADRONE
" island PIANOSA, CAPRI, ISCHIA, LIDO, LIPARI, SARDINIA, SICILY
" lady ..... DONNA, SIGNORA
" lake .... AVERNO
" language ... TUSCAN, OSCAN
" magistrate . PODESTA, SYNDIC
" marble .... CIPOLIN
" measure .. BRACCIO, CANNA, PALMA, PUNTO, TAVOLA, STAIO
" meat balls .... RAVIOLI
" millet .... BUDA, MOHA
" movie director ... ROSSELINI, FELLINI, PONTI
" naval base .... TARANTO
" noblewoman .... MARCHESA
" nothing .... NULLA
" opera house .... SCALA
" painter ..... CANALE, RENI, GIOTTO, TITIAN, LIPPI, LUINI, ROSSI, SARTO, SPADA, CRESPI, DAVINCI
" paste .... LASAGNA
" patriot .. FOSCOLO, GARIBALDI
" peak .... CIMA
" peasant .... CONTADINO
" people ...... OSCAN, VOLSCI, SABINES
" philosopher .... VERA, DION, DANTE
" physicist ...... ROSSI, VOLTA
" pie .... PIZZA
" plague .... PELLAGRA
" poet .... REDI, TASSO
" polemical writer .... GIOBERTI
" police officer .... SBIRRO
" political party .. BIANCI, NERI
" political writer ..... GIUSTI
" porridge .... POLENTA
" port ... BARI, GENOA, FIUME, POLA, TRANI
" pottery .... FAENZA
" , pre-Latin .... OSCAN

" primadonna .... DIVA
" province CUNEO, ESTE, UDINE
" public entertainment RIDOTTO
" region CALABRIA, CAMPAGNA,
LAZIO, LIGURIA, MARCHE,
PIEMONTE, PUGLIA, SARDEGNA,
SICILIA, TOSCANA, VENETO
" resort ... LIDO, CAPRI, COMO
" restaurant .... PIZZERIA
" river ... PIAVE, ADIGE, ARNO,
PO, ADDA, TIBER
" ruler, barbarian ... ODOACER
" satirist .... ARETINO
" sausage .... SALAME
" sculptor .... LEONI, DUPRE
" secret society .... MAFIA,
CAMORRA
" sheep .... MERINO
" singer ...... CARUSO, GIGLI,
PINZA, ALBANESE, TEBALDI,
CORELLI, MARTINELLI, SCHIPA
" spa .... AGNONE
" title .... CONTE, SER
" town ATRI, ESTE, ELEA, POLA
" under .... SOTTO
" violinmaker .... AMATI
" volcano ... ETNA, STROMBOLI,
VESUVIUS
" weight LIBRA, ONCIA, DENARO,
GANDUM, LIBBRA, OTTAVA
" wind .... SIROC(CO)
" writer ..... DANTE, MANZONI
Italy, anc. country of .... TUSCANY,
ETRURIA
" , anc. name of .... AUSONIA
" , Celts of .... SENONES
" , Greek colony in .... ELEA
" , marshy lands in .... MAREMMA
itch ...... PRURITUS, PSORA, SCABIES,
RIFF, CRAVE, MANGE
" , barbers' .... SYCOSIS
" , salt rheum .... ECZEMA
item .... ASSET, AGENDUM, ENTRY,
FACTOR, ARTICLE, DETAIL,
OBJECT, SCRAP
itineration .... CIRCUIT, EYRE,
JOURNEY, ROVING
"Ivanhoe" author .... SCOTT
" char. ..... BOEUF, CEDRIC,
ROWENA, ULRICA
Ives; singer .... BURL
ivories .... DICE, TEETH, KEYS
ivorine .... WHITE
ivory; bone black .... ABAISER
" dust and cement ...... EBURITE,
EBURIN
" ; Lat. .... EBUR
" -like DENTINE, TUSK, EBURNEAN
" nut .... TAGUA, ANTA
" , synthetic .... IVORIDE

Ivory Coast capital .... ABIDJAN
ivy, crowned .... HEDERATED
" , ground .... HOVE(A)
" , poison; genus .... RHUS
I.W.W. emblem .... SABCAT
ixtle .... ISTLE, PITA
Izmir; former name .... SMYRNA

J

J, letter .... JAY
jaal goat .... BEDEN, IBEX
jab ..... PUNCH, THRUST, DIG, POKE
jabber .... BABBLE, GABBLE, PRATE
jabberwocky .... RIGMAROLE
" word .... BRILLIG
jacinth .... ZIRCON, IRIS
jack .... JUG, TANKARD, KNAVE,
BOWER, HOIST, MULE, CARD, FLAG,
SAWHORSE, PUMP
" -in-the-pulpit ... DRAGON, AROID
" of clubs in loo .... PAM
"Jack Pudding" ..... BUFFOON, ZANY
jackal .... JOLA, DIEB
" god .... APUAT
jackass .... DONKEY, DOLT, FOOL,
WITLING, ONO
jacket ... BIETLE, ETON, REEFER, RIND,
SKIN
" , Arctic hooded ...... ANORAK
" , Eskimo .... TEMIAK
" , knitted ...... JERSEY, SONTAG
" , light loose .... BLOUSE, JUMP
" , Scottish .... CLEADING
" , short .... JERKIN, SPENCER
" , sleeveless ... VEST, PENELOPE,
BOLERO
" , steel-plated . ACTON, AKETOUN
" with short flaps ...... COATEE
" , women's .... JUPE, JUPON
" worn in the Levant ... GREGO
jacket-like .... CAMISOLE
Jack Ketch .... HANGMAN
jackstays .... HORSES
jacksnipe . SANDPIPER, PECTORAL, PERT
Jacob's brother .... EDOM, ESAU
" daughter .... DINAH
" eldest son .... REUBEN
" father-in-law .... LABAN
" ladder .... PHLOX
" son .... JUDAH, ASHER, GAD,
DAN, LEVI
" wife .... LEAH, RACHEL
jaconet .... NAINSOOK
jade .... HUSSY, TIT, TIRE, NEPHRITE,
NAG, PLUG, CLOY, FAG, WEARY
" -like stone .... MURRA

jaeger	ALLAN, SHOOL, SKUA	" dancing girl	GEISHA
jag	BARB, CLEFT, NOTCH, DAG	" deer	SIKA
jagged	CLEFT, EROSE, SERRATED	" diplomat	ITO, TANAKA
Jagannath, home of the	PURI	" door	FUSUMA
jaguar	PANTHER, OUNCE, TIGER	" drama	NO, KABUKI,
jai alai	PELOTA		NOGAKU
" ", player of	PELOTARI	" emperor	MIKADO
" " term	CESTA, FRONTON,	" Empire, former name	EDO
	REBOTE	" family crest	MON
jail	COOLER, BRIDEWELL, LIMBO,	" festival	BON
	JUG, PEN, BRIG, CAGE, COOP,	" fish, poisonous	FUGU
	GAOL, STIR, CLINK, BASTILLE	" garment	HAORI, KIMONO
jam	BLOCK, BRUISE, CRAM, CROWD,	" gateway	TORII
	JELLY, PICKLE	" gentry	SHIZOKU
Jamaica bitter wood	QUASSIA	" gold coin	OBAN
" cobnut	OUABE	" "great ruler"	TAIKUN,
Jamshid, realm of	PERIS		TYCOON
jangling	CLASHING, HARSH	" harp	KOTO
janitor	PORTER, SEXTON, SUPER	" herb	UDO
Janizarian chief	DEY	" immigrant	ISSEI, NISEI
Japan	NIPPON, CIPANGO	" island	HONDO, HONSHU,
Japanese	AINO, AINU		IZU, KURIL, KYUSHO, SADO
" administrative division	FU	" lake	BIWA, SUWA
" admiral	ITO	" language	AINU
" American	NISEI, ISSEI,	" legislature	DIET
	SANSEI	" litter, covered	NORIMON
" apricot	UME	" loquat	BIWA
" army reserve	HOJU	" measure	BOO, CHO, RIN,
" art with paper	ORIGAMI		SUN, HIRO, SHAKU, KOKU
" art of self-defense	JUJITSU,	" mile	RI
	KARATE	" military governor	SHOGUN
" badge of nobility	MON	" monastery	TERA
" baron	HAN	" mountain	FUJI
" battle cry	BANZAI	" musical inst.	SAMISEN
" bay	ISE, YEDO	" naval base	KURE
" boxes, set of	INRO	" news service	DOMEI
" Buddha	AMITA, AMIDA	" nobility	SAMURAI, DAIMIO,
" Buddhism	ZEN		KUGE
" cape	DAIO, IRO, JIZO, MELA,	" ornament	NETSUKE
	MINO, NOMO, OKI, OMA,	" outcast	ETA, RONIN
	SADA, SAWA, SUZU, TOI	" overcoat	MINO
" carp	KOY	" pagoda	TAA
" carriage	SADOS	" palanquin	KAGO, NORIMON
" case	INRO	" painting school	KANO
" cedar	SUGI	" people of the North	AINUS
" cherry	FUJI	" persimmon	KAKI
" city	SENDAI, NARA, KOBE,	" pine	MATSU
	YEDO, OSAKA, EDO, UBE, KOFU,	" plum	KELSEI
	KURE, OTSU	" porgy	TAI
" clogs	GETA	" pottery	AWATA
" clover	HAGI	" prefecture	OITA, OWARI
" coin	RIN, SEN, TEMPO, YEN	" premier	TOJO, SATO,
" commoner	HEIMIN		KISHI, KONOYE, TANAKA
" commune	DESSA	" quince	JAPONICA
" composition	HAIKAI	" radish	DAIKON
" confection	AME	" receptacle	INRO
" conveyance	KAGO	" religion, early	SHINTO
" court	DAIRI	" religious dance	NO
" crash pilot	KAMIKAZE	" revolving storm	TYPHOON
" crest	MON	" rice drink	SAKE

" robe .... KIMONO	" village community ... DESSA
" salad plant .... UDO	" volcano .... SEMERU, SLAMET

" robe .... KIMONO
" salad plant .... UDO
" salmon .... MASU
" saltwater fish .... AYU
" sash .... OBI
" sauce .... UDO
" seaport ...... TAKATA, TSU,
  KOBE, MOYI, OITA, UBE
" seaweed .... NORI
" ship .... MARU
" shrub .... GOUMI
" sliding door ...... FUSUMA
" song .... UTA
" statesman GENRO, MORI, ITO
" stomach-cutting .. HARAKIRI
" storm .... MONSOON,
       TYPHOON
" suicide .. SEPPUKU, HARAKIRI
" sword ..... CATAN, CATTAN
" vegetable .... UDO
" verse ..... HOKKU, TANKA
" vine .... KUDZU
" volcano .... ASO(SAN)
" wasp .... TIPHIA
" weight ...... FUN, MO, RIN
" wisteria .... FUJI
" writing .... KANA
Japan's Pittsburgh .... YAWATA
Japetus .... SATURN
Japheth, father of .... NOAH
 ", son of .. MESCHECH, JAVAN
japonica.................. QUINCE
jar .. TERRINE, BANGA, KALPIS, CROCK,
  GOGLET, GURGLET, OLLA, CADUS,
  DOLIUM, BOWL, EWER, CRUSE,
  PELIKE, AMPHORA, JOLT, BOCAL
jardiniere .... POT, SOUP, VASE
jargon .. LINGO, CANT, RANE, ARGOT,
  DRIVEL, PATOIS, FLASH, SPEECH,
       ABRACADABRA
Jason, lady deserted by ..... MEDEA
 ", father of .... AESON
 ", ship of .... ARGO
jasper .... BIOTITE, MICA, MURRA,
        MORLOP
jaundice .... ICTERUS
jaundiced .... BIASED, JEALOUS
jaunt ...... JOLT, SALLY, SHAKE, TREK
jaunty .... AIRY, PERKY, SPRUCE
Java capital .... JAKARTA
 ", island east of .... BALI
 ", pepper .... CUBEB
Javanese .... MADURESE, SUNDANESE
 " badger ...... RATEL, TELEDU
 " climbing civet .... RASSE
 " dumb show .... TOPENG
 " language .... KAVI, KAWI
 " port .... TEGAL
 " squirrel .... JELERANG
 " tree .... UPAS

" village community ... DESSA
" volcano .... SEMERU, SLAMET
" weight .... TALI, POND
javelin .. LANCE, DART, ASSAGAI, PILE
 " game .... JERID, JEREED
"Javert," creator of .... HUGO
jaw .... MAW, CHAP, CHOKE, GONIA,
        WANG
 "; comb. form .... GNATHO
 ", lower .... MANDIBLE
 " muscle .... MASSETER
 ", per. to .... GNATHIC
 ", upper .... MAXILLA
jawless .... AGNATHIC
jayhawker .... KANSAN, GUERILLA
jazz musician .... MONK, BRUBECK
jeans .... OVERALLS, TROUSERS
jeer . TAUNT, DERIDE, JAPE, JIBE, MOCK
Jeeter Lester's vegetable ..... TURNIP
Jeeves, to play .... BUTTLE
Jefferson's home .... MONTICELLO
Jehiel's son .... NER
Jehoahaz's mother .... HAMUTAL
jejune ... MEAGER, ARID, BANAL, DRY,
     FLAT, STALE, INSIPID
jelly .. GELATINE, SAPA, ASPIC, PECTIN
jellyfish .. ACALEPH, MEDUSA, QUARL,
      AURELIA, CARVEL
 "; comb. form .... CTEN(O)
 ", stinging .... SEANETTLE
 ", umbrella of a .... PILEUS
jelly-like ..... GELATINOUS, COLLOID
jennet .... ASS, DONKEY, HORSE
Jenny   ; "Swedish
 Nightingale" .... LIND
jeopardy .... HAZARD, PERIL, RISK
jeremiad .... TALE, LAMENT, WOE
jerk ..... TWITCH, NIDGE, TIC, TWEAK
jerked beef .... CHARQUI
Jerusalem; anc. name .... SALEM
 " thorn .... RETAMA
Jespersen's language .... IDO
jess .... RIBBON, STRAP
Jesse's father .... OBED
 " son .... DAVID
jessur .... DABOIA, SNAKE
jest ... JAPE, MOT, QUIP, TRIFLE, WIT
jester ... CLOWN, MINE, WAG, ZANY
 ", roving student ..... GOLIARD
Jesuit founder .... LOYOLA
 " saint .... REGIS
Jesus ...... ANOINTED, IHS, MESSIAH
jet ...... SPURT, COAL, EBONY, SPRAY,
  STREAM, NOZZLE, SCORPION
jetty ...... MOLE, PIER, WHARF, WALL
jewel .... BRILLIANT, GEM, JOY, NAIF,
      PRIZE, BIJOU
 " setting BEZEL, OUCH, DOP, PAVE
jeweler's glass .... LOUPE
 " weight .... KARAT

jewelry .... LOGIES, BIJOUTRY, QUOIN
"   alloy .... OROIDE
" , set of .... PARURE
" , cheap .... PASTE, STRASS
jewelweed .... CELANDINE
"Jewels of the Madonna" character ..
                                   STELLA
Jewett; writer .... (SARAH)ORNE
Jewish (see "Hebrew") ...... SEMITIC
"   skullcap .... YAMILKE
Jews, dispersion of .... DIASPORA
jew's-harp .... CREMBALUM, TRUMP
Jezebel's husband .... AHAB
"   victim .... NABOTH
jib .. CHORE, BALK, BOOM, SPAR, ARM,
                         CRANE, DERRICK
jibe .. AGREE, HARMONIZE, FIT, TACK
jiffy .... INSTANT, SECOND, TRICE
jiggle .... DANCE, SHAKE, JERK, ROCK
jinn .... EBLIS
jinni .... GENIE, DEMON
jinx .... HOODOO, HEX, WHAMMY
jitters .... DITHERS, NERVES
jittery .... EDGY, JUMPY
jivatma .... ATMAN, EGO
"Joan of Arc," name for .... PUCELLE
Joan's spouse .... DARBY
job ...... TASK, CHORE, STINT, CHAR
" , soft .... SNAP, SINECURE
jockey ..... CAVALIER, DISC, TURFITE,
              CHEAT, ARCARO, SHOEMAKER
jocose .... MERRY, DROLL, DRY, LEPID,
                       WAGGISH
"_____ Joey" .... PAL
jog ... REMIND, DUNCH, TROT, NUDGE,
                     HOD, WARN
John .. IAN, EOIN, SEAN, IVAN, JUAN,
                        JEAN
"John Brown's Body" author .. BENET
Johnnie .... LOTHARIO
Johnson .... LYNDON, CLAUDIA,
              LADYBIRD, ANDREW
join .... LOCK, COALESCE, MEET,
      SOLDER, PIN, MERGE, UNITE, MITER
joint ..... TENON, HIP, HINGE, SEAM,
     ELBOW, NODE, SUTURE, MORTISE
" cavity .... BURSA
" lubricator .... SYNOVIA
" , make tight .... STEM
" of plant stem ...... PHYTOMER,
                        PHYTON
" , right-angle .... ELL, KNEE
" , to put out of .... LUXATE
jointed stem of grass .... CULM
joke .. GAG, QUIO, SALLY, JEST, JAPE,
                     PRANK, JOSH
joker .... MISTIGRIS, CARD, WAG,
     CLOWN, FARCEUR, BUFFOON, DOR
jolly .... CHEER, CROUSE, BLITHE
" boat .... YAWL

Joloano .... MORO
Jolson, Al .... ASA
jolt .... SHAKE, JAR, JOUNCE, JUT
Jonah .... JINX
Jonathan's father .... SAUL
jonquil ..... NARCISSUS, LILY, LILIUM
Jordan, part of .... MOAB
Jose _____; dancer ...... GRECO
Joseph's wife .... ASENATH
josh .... BANTER, KID, CHAFF, GUY
Joshua's burial place .... GAASH
"   father .... NUN
Josip Broz .... TITO
jostle .. ELBOW, RUSH, SHOCK, SHOVE
jot ..... ITEM, ACE, BIT, IOTA, MINIM,
     ATOM, MITE, POINT, TITTLE, WHIT
jotting .... MEMO, ENTRY, NOTE
joule, part of a .... ERG
jabiru .... STORK
jasmine .... BELA, JESSAMY
Jerry .... KRAUT
journal ... RECORD, DIARY, REGISTER,
                    PAPER, LOG
journey ..... TREK, TOUR, FARE, RUN,
              TRIP, HADJ, JAUNT
" in circuit .... EYRE
" , per. to .. ITINERANT, VIATIC
joust ...... COMBAT, TILT, BOUT, SPAR
Jove .... JUPITER
jowl .... CHAP, HEAD, JAW, CHEEK
joy ..... BLISS, ECSTASY, GLEE, MIRTH
joyous .... MERRY, ELATED, BUOYANT
Judah, ancient city of .... AMAM
Judah's son .... SHELAH
Judaism, convert to .... GER
Judas .... BETRAYER, TRAITOR
Judean king .... ASA, HEROD
judge .. DEEM, ALCALDE, OPINE, TRIER,
      KADI, CADI, HAKIM, CRITIC,
      ARBITER, UMP(IRE), REFEREE
" ; Isle of Man .... DEEMSTER
" , aide of .... ASSESSOR
" , per. to chamber of ... CAMERAL
" , entry after verdict of .. POSTEA
" , seat of .... BANC
judgment .. DOOM, ARRAY, OPINION
" , lack of .... ACRISY
judicious .... WISE, POLITIC, PRUDENT
judo .... JUJITSU
jug .... BUIRE, CRUSE, EWER, FLAGON,
            OLPE, TOBY, PRISON
Juggernaut .... KRISHNA
jugs, room for .... EWRY
jujube .... BER, ELB, LOZENGE
juice .... SAP, MUST, RHOB, STUM
Juliana's house .... ORANGE
Juliet's betrothed .... PARIS
" father .... CAPULET
"Julius Caesar" char. BRUTUS, CASCA,
       CINNA, CASSIUS, CICERO

jumble .... MEDLEY, MIX, PI(E), RAFF, ROG, BLEND, HASH
jump .... HOP, LEAP, START, LOUP
" in Greek game .... HALMA
jumping .... SALTANT
" rodent .... JERBOA
" stick .... POGO
junco .... FINCH, SNOWBIRD
juncture .... CRISIS, STRAIT, SEAM
June bug .... DOR
junior .... CADET, PUISNE, PUNY, FILS
juniper .. CEDAR, RETEM, SAVIN, CADE
junk .... TRASH, WASTE, SLOUGH
Junker; Ger. .... SQUIRE
junket .... BANQUET, FEAST, DISH, PICNIC, OUTING
Juno .... UNI, HERA
" , messenger of .... IRIS
junta .... COUNCIL, MEETING
junto ..... CLIQUE, FACTION, CABAL, COTERIE
Jupiter, consort of .... JUNO
" , daughter of ...... MINERVA
" , son of .... ARCAS
jural .... LEGAL, JURISTIC
Jurassic division .... LIAS
jurisdiction .. SOKE, SEE, SOC, VENUE
jury .... VENIRE, ASSIZE, PANEL
juryman .... ASSIZER, JUROR, DICAST
jus .... JUICE, LAW(S)
just ..... DUE, FAIR, MORAL, ALMOST, PROPER, ETHICAL
justice ...... EQUITY, RIGHT, PENALTY
" of the peace .... SQUIRE
justice of Supreme Court .... CHASE, FULLER, HUGHES, TAFT, STONE, JAY, VINSON, WARREN, WHITE, BURGER
justification ...... EXCUSE, WARRANT, DEFENSE
justify .... CLEAR, DEFEND, ABSOLVE
jut .... PROJECT, PROTRUDE
" out .... ABUT, BEETLE
jute ...... BURLAP, GUNNY, TAT, DESI
Jutlander .... DANE
jutting rock .... TOR, CRAG, BRAE
juvenile killings .... TEENICIDE
Juventas .... HEBE
juxtaposition .... CONTIGUITY, TOUCH

K

Kaffir .... INFIDEL
" corn .... MILLET
" language .... XOSA
" , rel. to .... MATABELE
" warriors .... IMPI
kaiak .... CANOE

kale . BORECOLE, BROCCOLI, COLLARD, COLE
kali .... GLASSWORT
Kalinite .... ALUM
Kalmuck .... ELEUT(H)
Kandh .... KONDH, KUI
kangaroo .. MACROPODIAN, WALLABY, FORESTER, FLIER
" , female .... DOE, GIN
" , male ...... BILBI, BOOMER
" , rat .... POTOROO
" , young .... JOEY
Kansas, city in .. IOLA, PAOLA, ARMA, WEIR, CANEY, COLBY
kapok tree .... CEIBA
kaput .... DOOMED, RUINED
Karachi is its capital SIND, PAKISTAN
Karaism, believer in .... ANANITE
karakul .... LLAMA, SHEEP
Karelian lake .... SEG
Karenina, Miss .... ANNA
Karloff; actor .... BORIS
karma .... DESTINY, FATE
Kartvelian .... SVAN(E)
karyotin .... CHROMATIN
Kashmir alphabet .... SARADA
" town .... LEH
kat shrub .... KAFTA, CAFTA
Kava .... AVA
Kay _____; writer .... BOYLE
Kazan, Mr. .... ELIA
Keats poem .... LAMIA
keel ..... CAPSIZE, LIST, TILT, CAREEN
" , part of ...... CARINA, FIN, SKEG
" , without a .... RATITE
keel-like .... CARINAL, CARINATED
keen .... ASTUTE, GARE, SNELL, TART, SHARP, CRY
keenness .... EDGE, ACIES, ARDOR
keep .... CASE, SAVE, RETAIN, HIDE, HUSBAND, MANAGE, TEND
" out ..... EXCEPT, EXCLUDE, BAR
" under .... MORTIFY
keeper .... RISP, STANG, TILER, NABRANGER, MAHOUT
" of the golden apples ITHUN
" of the marches ... MARGRAVE
_____ keepers .... FINDERS
keepsake ... RELIC, TOKEN, SOUVENIR, BIBELOT, MEMENTO
keeve .... KIER, TUB, VAT
Kefauver, Mr. .... ESTES
keg ... CADE, CASK, FIRKIN, TUN, VAT
" , open a .... UNHEAD
kegler .... BOWLER
Kelly, Mr. .... EMMETT, GENE
kelp . WRACK, WARE, ASH, SEAWEED, VAREC
ken .. LORE, DESCRY, INSIGHT, RANGE
Kent district .... ERITH

Kentish freeman .... LAET
Kentuckian .... CORNCRACKER
Kentucky college .... BEREA
   " county .. BATH, BELL, BOYD,
     CLAY, HART, KNOX, LEE, LYON,
     OWEN, PIKE, TODD
   " town ... CORONA, PADUCAH
Kenya's capital .... NAIROBI
kerchief ... CURCH, PEPLUM, MADRAS,
     ANALAV, RUMAL
Keresan Indian .... SIA
kernel ..... GIST, SEED, NUT, GRAIN,
     CAUSE, CORE, HEART, PITH,
     ESSENCE
   " , having a .... NUCLEATE
ketch .... SAIC, JACK, SHIP
kethib .... KERE, KRI
ketone .... ACETONE, BUTYRONE
kettle .... CAULDRON, POTHOLE
kettledrum NAKER, TIMPANO, ATABAL
   " , cavalry .... ANACARA
key .... COTTER, ISLET, CLAVIS, CLEW,
     CRIB, PONY, CODE
" , false .... GLUT
" filler .... ULLER
" fruit .... SAMARA
" in music .... TASTO
" of instrument .... MANUAL
" , part of ..... BIT, BOW, PIN, WEB
" , per. to .... TONAL
" , telegraph .... TAPPER
keyboard ...... DIGITORIUM, CLAVIER
   " instrument .... CELESTA
keyed up .... AGOG, EAGER
Keyserling, Mr. .... LEON
keystone .. SAGITTA, SUPPORT, WEDGE
Keystone State, founder of .... PENN
khan .... INN
Khan .... ALY, AGHA
Khedive estate .... DAIRA
Khrushchev, Mr. .... NIKITA
kibe .... CHILBLAIN
kibitzer .... SPECTATOR
kick .... BOOT, FUNK, KEVEL, GRIPE,
     PUNT, RECOIL, RESIST
kickshaw .... BAUBLE, TOY
kid .... GUY, LAD, RIB, TOT, JOSH,
     SUEDE, TAUNT, BANTER
kiddy .... OUTWIT, HOAX
kidnap ...... ABDUCT, SEIZE, SNATCH,
     STEAL, SHANGHAI
kidney bean .... FASEL
   " , per. to .... RENAL
   " stone .... NEPHRITE, JADE
kidney-shaped .... RENIFORM
Kienzl, opera by .... URVASI
Kilauea, goddess of .... PELE
Kilimanjaro peak .... KIBO
kill ..... BLAST, BURKE, SLAY, CANCEL,
     FINISH, GARROTE, RUIN, VETO,
     MASSACRE

" by stoning .... LAPIDATE
killer whale .... ORCA
killing .... HOMICIDE, CARNAGE
killing of a wolf .... LUPICIDE
" of old men .... SENICIDE
" of royalty .... REGICIDE
Kilmer poem .... TREES
kiln ... OAST, OST, LEHR, LEER, TILER,
     STOVE
kilt .... FILIBEG, PHILIBEG, PLEAT
kin ..... GERMANE, FOLKS, COGNATE
kind ...... CLASS, STRAIN, SORT, ILK,
     GENUS, SEELY, GENRE, BENIGN,
     HUMANE, GENIAL, TENDER,
     SPECIES, VARIETY
kindle .... BURN, FIRE, ROUSE, WHET,
     FOMENT, IGNITE, INCITE
kindly .... GAIN, BENIGN
kindness ...... GRACE, MERCY, LENITY
kindred COGNATE, ALLIED, AKIN, KITH,
     SIB
king ...... SOVEREIGN, ROI, REX, REY,
     RANK, KRAL, REGULUS
king, Albanian .... ZOG
King Arthur, death place of CAMLAN
" " , father of ...... UTHER
" " , foster brother of KAY
" " , knights of .. GALAHAD,
     GARETH
" " , resting place of ....
     AVALON
" " , wife of .... GUINEVER
King Arthur's capital ..... CAMELOT
" " clown ..... DAGONET
King Arthur's court, lady in .. ENID
" " fairy sister ....
     MORGANLEFAY
" " lance .... RON, RONE
" " magic sword EXCALIBUR
" " mother .... IGRAINE,
     YGERNE
" " nephew ... GAWAIN,
     MODRED
" " shield, name of .....
     PRIDWIN
King Canute's consort .... EMMA
King Cole .... NAT
King David's cave .... ADULLAM
King David's faithful friend ... ITTAI
King David's father .... JESSE
King David's son . ABSALOM, AMNON
"King Henry IV" char. .. BLUNT, HAL,
     PERCY, SCROOP, POINS
King Lear's daughter ...... GONERIL
" " dog .... TRAY
" " favorite daughter........
     CORDELIA
" " second daughter .. REGAN
king, legendary .... MIDAS
king, Midian .... EVI, REBA

king of Amalek .... AGAG
   " of Arcadia; Gr. leg. ... LYCAON
   " of Assyria .... PUL
   " of Bashan .... OG
   " of Belgium .. BAUDOUIN, ALBERT
   " of birds .... EAGLE
   " of Britain; leg. ..... ARTEGAL,
         BLADUD, ELIDURE, LEAR, LUD
   " of Bulgaria .... BORIS
   " of Corinth .... POLYBUS
   " of Damascus .... ARETUS
   " of dwarfs .... ALBERICH
   " of Egypt .... FUAD, FAROUK
   " of England .... STEPHEN
   " of England and Denmark . KNUT
   " of Fomorians .... BALOR
   " of Gerar .... ABIMELECH
   " of Hamath .... TOI, TOU
   " of Hazor .... JABIN
   " of herrings .... OPAH
   " of Huns; myth. .... ATLI
   " of Iran .... XERXES
   " of Iraq .... FEISAL
   " of Israel AHAB, BAASHA, ELAH,
         OMRI, PEKAH
   " of Israel, last .... HOSHEA
   " of Judah ABIJAH, AHAZ, AMON,
         ASA
   " of Judea .... ASA, HEROD
   " of Langobards .... ALBOIN
   " of Moab .... EGLON
   " of Naples; nineteenth cent. ...
         MURAT
   " of Norway .... OLAF, OLAV
   " of Persia .... CYRUS, XERXES
   " of Phrygia; myth. .... MIDAS
   " of Pylus; anc. Gr. ...... NESTOR
   " of serpent race .... SESHA
   " of Sodom .... BERA
   " of Syria .... HAZAEL, REZIN
   " of the Ammonites ..... HANUN
   " of the Amorites .... SIHON
   " of the Devas .... INDRA
   " of the fairies .... OBERON
   " of the Fomors .... BALOR
   " of the Lapithae; myth. .. IXION
   " of the mullets .... BASS
king of Thebes, wife of .... DIRCE
   " of Troy, in the "Aeneid" PRIAM
   " of Tyre .... HIRAM
   " of waters .... AMAZON
   " , petty .... REGULUS
   " , Scottish .... ROBERT, BRUCE
   " , Spanish .... REY
   " , Spartan .... MENELAUS
   " , steward to a .... DAPIFER
   " , the greedy .... MIDAS
   " ; third of India .... ASA
   " ; Volsunga saga .... ATLI

king crab .... LIMULUS
kingdom ..... REALM, EMPIRE, ESTATE
"Kingdom by the Sea" dweller ......
         ANNABEL
kingdom near Babylon .... ELAM
   " north of India ..... NEPAL,
         BHUTAN, SIKKIM
   " of Nimrod .... BABEL
kingfish BARB, OPAH, HAKE, TOMCOD
king-geld .... ESCUAGE
kingly .... LEONINE, REGAL, AUGUST
king's bodyguard .... THANE
   " chamber .... CAMARILLA
   " clover .... MELILOT
   " evil .... SCROFULA
   " servant .... DAPIFER
kingship .... ROYALTY
kink .... KNOT, TWIST, SNARL, WHIM,
         BURL, SPASM, QUIRK
kinkajou .... POTTO
kinship ...... AGNATION, ENATION,
         NASAB
kinsman .... RELATIVE, SIB
kiosk .... PAVILION
Kipling's "Shere Khan" .... TIGER
Kish's father .... NER
   " son .... SAUL
kismet .... DESTINY, FATE, DOOM
kiss ...... OSCULATE, BUSS, CARESS,
         SMACK, PECK
   " in Italy .... BACIO
   " of peace ..... PAX, CALUMET
"Kiss," sculptor of .... RODIN
kitchen COOKERY, CUISINE, SCULLERY,
         GALLEY
kite .. ELANET, GLEDE, CHIL, DRAGON
Kitt; singer .... EARTHA
kitty .... POT, ANTE, POOL, CAT
kiwi; genus .... APTERYX
kleptomaniac .... THIEF, FILCHER
knack ...... HANG, SKILL, ART, FEAT,
         EASE, TRINKET
knarl ... GNARL, KNAG, KNURL, NODE
knave ...... ROGUE, LOREL, LOSEL,
         BOWER, CHURL, SCAMP, RASCAL
   " in cribbage .... NOB
   " of clubs .... PAM
knead . ELT, MALAXATE, RUB, MASSAGE
knee .... FLEXURA, GENU
   " , inflammation of ..... GONITIS
   " joint .... HOCK
   " , rel. to the .... HAM
   " , to bend the .... GENUFLECT
kneecap .... PATELLA
   " -like .... ROTULAR
kneeling desk .... PRIEDIEU
knew .... KENNED, WIST
knickknack .... GIMCRACK, TRIFLE
knife .... SNY, SNEE, STAB, BLADE,
         WOUND, BARLOW, MACHETE

" , Burmese .... DAH
" , curved Hindu .... KUKRI
" , Irish .... SKEAN
" , large pocket ...... BOLO, SNEE
" , Malay .... KRIS, CREESE
" , Maori .... PATU
" , Moro .... BARONG
" , plaster-and-paint ..... SPATULA
knife-like dagger .... DIRK
knight ...... SIR, GALLANT, EQUITE,
    EQUES, LOVER, TEMPLAR, RITTER,
        DUB, ARMIGER, HORSEMAN
" errant .... PALADIN
" of the Red Eagle .... KRE
" of the "Round Table" BOHORT,
    BORT, YWAIN(E), BALAN, BALIN,
        GALAHAD, GAWAIN
knighthood .... CHIVALRY
knight's cloak .... TABARD
" fight .... JOUST
knit ...... COUPLE, JOIN, SEAM, PURL
knitting . UNION, BROCADE, CROCHET
" term .... PURL, GAUGE,
        STITCH, CABLE
knitting-machine guide .... SLEY
knob .... KNURL, NODE, UMBO, BOSS,
        STUD, FINIAL
" , morbid .... TUBERCLE
knobby .. NODOSE, NODAL, TOROSE,
        LUMPY, HILLY
knobkerrie .... KIRI
knock ..... BLAME, BOX, BUFFET, CUFF
knock out .... BASH, KAYO
knock-knee .... INKNEE, XLEG
knoll .... HILLOCK, KNAP, MOUND
knot .. SNAG, JOINT, NODE, TIE, NEP
" in wood .... KNAR, NURL, BURL,
        KNAG
" of hair or silk .... NOIL
" , running .... NOOSE
" , tree .... GNARL, NUR
" weed .... ALLSEEDS
knots, free from ENODATE, UNRAVEL,
        ENODE
know REGARD, REVEAL, KEN, WIS(T),
    WOT, HEP, AWARE, GNOSTIC
know-all ...... WISEACRE, QUIDNUNC
knowledge KEN, KITH, LORE, OLOGY,
        SCIENTIA, NOESIS
" , an object of ..... SCIBILE
" , mean to ...... ORGANON
" , superficial .... SCIOLISM
" , universal .. PANTOLOGY
" , without .... ATECHNIC
known ...... COUTH, FAMED, NOTED
knuckle .... SUBMIT, YIELD, STRIKE
" bone .... DIB
knurl .... MILL, RIDGE
kobold .... GNOME, HOBGOBLIN,
        BROWNIE, NIS

Kohinoor .... DIAMOND
Kol dialect .... HO, MUNDARI
Koran, division of ... ALCORAN, SURA
" scholar .... ULEMA
" , teacher of .... ALFAQUI
Korea .... CHOSEN
" , capital of .... SEOUL
" , city in ...... PUSAN, FUSAN
Korean leader .... RHEE
" meeting place .... KAESONG
" port ...... GENSAN, INCHON
" river .... YALU
" soldier .... ROK
" weight .... KON
Korzeniowski .... CONRAD
kosher .... CLEAN, FIT, PURE
" meat, maker of ..... PORGER
" , opposed to .... TREF(A)
krimmer .... LAMBSKIN
Kronos' wife .... RHEA
kulak .... FIST, PEASANT
Kulanapan .... POMO
kumiss-like .... KEFIR(IC)
Kuomintang dept. .... YUAN
Kurile is. .... ITURUP
Kyushu base .... SASEBO
" volcano .... ASO

L

L, letter .... EL, ELL
Laban's daughter ..... LEAH, RACHEL
label ...... TAG, FLAP, NAME, LAPPET,
        TASSEL, STICKER
labile .... UNSTABLE
"La Boheme" char. MIMI, RODOLFO,
        MUSETTA
labor ..... DRAG, MOIL, WORK, TASK,
        TRAVAIL, DRUDGE, STRIVE
" leader .. LEWIS, MEANY, REUTHER
" union .... AFL, CIO, ILGWU, ILA
labored .... OPEROSE, STIFF
laborer .. FELLAH, PEON, TOTY, HAND,
        NAVVY, COOLIE
Labrador tea .... LEDUM
labyrinth .... MAZE, MEANDER
lace ...... GIN, NET, NOOSE, SNARE,
    BEAT, LASH, TRIM, ORRIS, EDGING,
    GRILLE, ALENCON, POTLACE, FILET,
    ENTWINE, WEAVE, TAT(TING)
" cape .... MANTILLA
" , frilled .... RUCHE
" , fringed work of .... CREPINE
" front .... JABOT
" , Mechlin .... MALINES
" opening .... EYELET
" (string) .... THONG

lacerate . RIP, CUT, REND, TEAR, CLAW
lacerated .... RENT, TORN
lachrymose .... TEARFUL
lacing .... THRASHING
lack .... REQUIRE, WANT, NEED, FAIL,
                    DEARTH, ABSENCE
" of power .... ATONY
lackey .. FOOTMAN, FLUNKEY, TOADY
lacking .... DEVOID, SHY, SHORT
Laconian capital .... SPARTA
" subdivision .... OBE
laconic ..... CONCISE, TERSE, BRIEF,
                        PERT, PITHY
lacquer ... ENAMEL, VARNISH, JAPAN
lacuna .... BREAK, GAP, HIATUS
ladder ..... RUN, STEE, STY, SCALADO
" , attack with ..... (ES)CALADE
" , part of .... RUNG
ladder-like .... SCALAR
lading of ships ... CARGO(ES), LOAD
ladle .... DIP, SCOOP, BAIL, GEAT
ladrone .... ROGUE, THIEF, ROBBER
Ladrone island GUAM, SAIPAN, ROTA,
                              TINIAN
lady .... BURD, FEMALE, WOMAN,
            DONNA, MADAM, BEGUM, FRAU,
            DAME, MATRON, SPOUSE, SENORA
Lady Churchill .... CLEMENTINE
"Lady of Lyons" heroine ... PAULINE
"Lady of the Lake" .. ELLEN, VIVIAN,
                              NIMUE
ladybird .... BEETLE, VEDALIA
ladyfish .... PUDIANO
ladylove .... DELIA
lady's slipper .... ORCHID
lady's thumb PEACHWORT, PERSICARY
lag DELAY, IDLE, LOITER, DRAG, TARRY
"La Gioconda" .... MONALISA
" " char. .... LAURA
lagoon .... HAFF, LEMAN
Lahr; comedian .... BERT
laic .... CIVIL, SECULAR, TEMPORAL
lair .... CAVE, CAVERN, DEN, TRAP
Laius, son of .... OEDIPUS
" , wife of .... JOCASTA
lake .. LOCH, MERE, POND, SHAT, LIN,
            TARN, LOUGH, SHOTT, LAGOON
" , African .... NYASSA, CHAD,
                            VICTORIA
" , Asian ..... BAIKAL, URMIA, VAN
" at Geneva .... LEMAN
" , Australian .... EYRE, FROME
Lake George .... HORICON
" , Great .... ERIE, HURON,
            ONTARIO, MICHIGAN, SUPERIOR
lake, Hoover Dam .... MEAD
" in California .... MONO, SODA,
                        TAHOE, GOOSE
" in Ethiopia .. DEMBEA, T(S)ANA
" in Finland ... SAIMA(A), ENARE

" in Iran .... URMIA
" in Italy .... ALBANO, BOLSENA,
                    COMO, GARDA, NEMI
" in New York GEORGE, ONEIDA,
                    OTSEGO, PLACID
" in Panama .... GATUN
" in Russia ..... ARAL, BAIKAL,
            BALKASH, ILMEN, LACHA,
            LADOGA, ONEGA, SEG
" in Switzerland BIENNE, LEMAN,
            LUCERNE, MORATH, THUN, ZUG
" in Wales .... BALA
" , man-made .... MEAD
" of Hades .... AVERNUS
" , outlet of a .... BAYOU
" , per. to a .... LACUSTRAL
" , third-largest .... ARAL
"Lake of the Cat" .... ERIE
lama .... MONK, PRIEST
——— Lama ...... DALAI, TESHU
lamb ...... EANLING, CADE, COSSET,
                        AGNUS, EWE
" , breast of .... CARRE
" , bring forth .... YEAN
Lamb, Chas.; pen name .... ELIA
lame .... CRIPPLE, HALT, MAIM, COJO,
                    HOBBLING, FEEBLE
Lamech's wife .... ADAH
lamelia .... PLATE, SCALE
lament .... HONE, MOAN, PLANGOR,
            RUE, WEY, KEEN, DIRGE, (RE)PINE
lamentation .... SIGH, ELEGIAC,
            JEREMIAD, TANGI, LINOS
lamina .... LAYER, OBEX, SHEET
laminated .. SPATHIC, TABULAR, FLAKY
" rock SHAUL, SHALE, FISSILE
lamp CRUSIE, ETNA, LUCERN, LUCIGEN,
            DAVY, ARATI, GEORDIE, ALADDIN
" black .... SOOT
" condensing ring .... CRIC
lamplighter .... SPILL
lampoon .. SATIRE, SQUIB, SKIT, LIBEL
Lancashire, section of .... ECCLES
Lancaster, Mr. .... BURT
lance .... JAVELIN, SPEAR, DART, CUT
" head .... MORNE
Lancelot's love .... ELAINE
lancer .... UHLAN, HUSSAR, TROOPER
lancet, point of .... NEB
Lanchester, Miss .... ELSA
lancinate ...... STAB, LACERATE, TEAR
land .... REALM, TRACT, EARTH, TILTH,
                    REGION, TERRAIN
" , a cleared .. FIELD, ASSART, ACRE
" , barren .... DESERT, WASTE
" , border of .... RAND
" connection .. NEK, NECK, REACH
" , cultivated .... ARADO, TILLAGE,
                            ARADA
" east of Eden .... NOD

" ; ecclesiastical benefice ... GLEBE
" , fallow .... LEA
" held in fee .. ALOD, ODAL, UDAL
" in return for service .... FEOFF
" left fallow .... ARDER
" , low, near a stream .... HOLM
" -mark, west U.S. .... SENAL
Land o' Cakes .... SCOTLAND
" of the Midnight Sun .. NORWAY
land of Nod .... SLEEP
Land of promise CANAAN, PALESTINE
Land of the Rising Sun ..... JAPAN
" of the Rose .... ENGLAND
" of the Shamrock ..... IRELAND,
EIRE, ERIN
" of the Thistle .... SCOTLAND
land, piled-up .... CAIRN
" , plowed .... ARADA, ARADO
" , point of low .... SPIT
" ; prepare for seed .... TILL
" reverting to state ..... ESCHEAT
" , Scottish .... ERD
" , small triangle of ..... GORE
" , snow-covered ...... SAVANNA
" , strip of .... RAP
" tenure .... LEASEHOLD
" , to .... DEBARK, ALIGHT
" , tongue of; Ind. .... DOAB
" , treeless .... SAVANNA
" , triangular piece of ..... DELTA
" valued for taxes .... CADASTRE
landing .... JETTY
" place .... KEY, DOCK, GAUT,
GHAT, PIER, PORT, QUAY, LEVEE,
WHARF
landlord ... HOST, OWNER, BONIFACE
landmark .. BOUNDARY, COPA, SENAL
Landolphia fruit .... ABOLI
Landowska, Mme. .... WANDA
landscape .... PAYSAGE, SCENERY
Landtag .... DIET, LEGISLATURE
Langobard king .... ALBOIN
language LIP, IDIOM, LINGO, SLANG,
PATOIS, SPEECH, DICTION
" , artificial ESPERANTO, RO,
VOLAPUK, IDO
" , Buddhist .... PALI
" , French slang ...... ARGOT
" of the Caucas .... ANDI
" , ordinary .... PROSE
" , thieves' .... ARGOT
languages, knowing all .. POLYGLOT,
PANTOGLOT
languish ...... DROOP, WASTE, PINE,
FLAG
languor .... LASSITUDE, KEF, KIEF
lantern light .... GLIM
Lanterns, Feast of .... BON
Lanza, Mr. .... MARIO
Laodamia, father of .... ACASTUS

Laomedon, son of .... TITHONUS
Laos tribesman .... YUN
Lao Tse concept .... TAO
lapdog .... PET, POM
lapel .... REVERS, FACING, FLAP
Lapetus' son .... PROMETHEUS
" wife .... GAEA, GE
lapidation, act of PELTING, STONING
lapin .... RABBIT
Lapithae, king of the .... IXION
Lapland city .... KOLA
" sled .... PULK(A)
lappet .... LOBE, WATTLE, FLAP
lapwing ... PLOVER, HOOPOE, PEWIT,
PEEWEE, TEWIT, TERUTERU
larch .... TAMARACK, LARIX
lard ...... BEDECK, ENARM, GARNISH,
SUET, TALLOW, AXUNGE
" and wax .... CERATES
larder ..... PANTRY, SPENCE, BUTTERY
large amount .... SCADS, OODLES
lariat .. NOOSE, LASSO, REATA, ROPE
" ; eye .... HONDA, HONDO,
HONDOO
lark .. ADVENTURE, PRANK, ALOUETTE
" -like bird .... PIPIT
larva; early stage ...... PUPA, REDIA
" ; final stage .... CHRYSALIS
" , footless .... MAGGOT
" of a beetle .... GRUB
" of eye .... LOA
" of horsefly .... BOT
" , wingless .... CREEPER
lascar .... SERANG
lash .... QUIRT, SPLICE, TIE, RATE,
SCOLD, SCOURGE, WALE, KNOUT
lassie .... COLLEEN
lasso .... LARIAT, CABESTRO, REATA,
LASH, ROPE, NOOSE
last LOWEST, UTMOST, OMEGA, CODA,
HOLD, ABIDE, FINAL(E), DERNIER
" but one .... PENULT(IMATE)
"Last Days of Pompeii" char. .. IONE
Last of the Goths .... RODERICK
" of the Mohicans .... UNCAS
last person in a contest .... MELL
Last Supper .... CENA
last syllable of a word ...... ULTIMA
latch .... SNECK, BELAY, HOOK, LOCK
latchet on a shoe .... TAP
late RECENT, TARDY, NEW, DEAD, NEO
" at school .... SERO
later ...... POSTERIOR, AFTER, PUISNE
lateral .... SEAM, RAPHE
laterite .... CABOOK
latex of a plant .... MILK
lathe ... TURRET, SLAT, SPALE, SPLINT,
BLANCHARD
lather .... SOAP, FOAM, FROTH,
FRENZY, SCUM, SUDS, SPUME

Latin ..... ROMANIC, ROMAN, CUBAN, ITALIAN, SPANIARD
" alas .... VAE
" another .... ALIA, ALIUS
" born .... NATUS
" both .... AMBI
" brother .... FRATER
" bug .... CIMEX
" but .... SED
" copper .... CUPRUM
" custom .... RITUS, MOS
" day .... DIES, DIEM
" deities .... DEI, DEAE
" deny .... NEGO, NEGARE
" divination .... SORS
" dog .... CANIS
" door .... JANUA
" earth .... TERRA
" equal .... PAR
" eternity .... AEVO, AEVUM
" evil .... MALUM, MALA
" field .... AGER
" force or power .... VIS
" from .... DE
" gentle .... LENIS
" go .... IRE, VADO
" himself .... IPSE
" historian .... JUSTIN
" holidays .... FERIA
" hope .... SPES
" lamb .... AGNUS
" law .... JUS, LEX
" learned .... DOCTUS
" man .... HOMO, VIR
" mind .... MENS
" mine .... MEUM, MEA, MEUS
" mountain .... MONS
" needle .... ACUS
" nobody .... NEMO
" noun case ... DATIVE, VOCATIVE
" observe .... NOTA
" old .... VETUS
" order .... ORDO
" other(s) .... ALIA, ALIUS, ALTER
" our .... NOSTER
" poet .... HORACE, OVID
" prison .... CARCER
" pronoun ...... HIC, HAEC, HOC, MEA, ILLE, TUA, SUI, SUA
" same .... IDEM
" ship .... NAVIS
" side .... LATUS
" sister .... SOROR
" skin .... CUTIS
" stone .... LAPIS
" there .... IBI(DEM)
" thus .... ITA, SIC
" toad .... BUFO
" total .... OMNIS, SUMMA
" unless .... NISI

" version of the Bible ..... ITALA
" water .... AQUA
" where .... UBI
" wool .... LANA
latria .... (HYPER)DULIA
Latter-day Saint . MORMON, IRVINGITE
lattice ..... GRILLE, TRELLIS, CANCELLI
" -work .... ESPALIER
Latvian .... LETT
" capital .... RIGA
" monetary unit .... LAT, LATU
laud .... SING, EXTOL, PRAISE, PSALM
laudation .... PANEGYRIC
laugh .... CHORTLE, CHUCKLE, DERIDE, FLEER, GUFFAW, ROAR, TITTER, SNICKER, GIGGLE, HAWHAW, HAHA
laughable .... COMIC, DROLL, RISIBLE
laughing .... MERRY, RIANT
laughter .... RISUS
" , provoking ..... GELOGENIC, GELASTIC
launch .... HURL, START, DESCANT, LANCE, BEGIN, FLOAT
laurel BAY, DAPHNE, IVY, MAGNOLIA, KALMIA, MADRONA
" wreath .... IRESINE
lava .... ASH, LATITE, SCORIA, TAXITE
" field .... PEDREGAL
" , fragment of .... LAPILLUS
" , round lump of .... BOMB
" , solidified .... COULEE
lavaliere .... PENDANT
lave .... ABSTERGE, BATHE, WASH
lavender .... ASPIC
lavish .. FREE, PRODIGAL, GIVE, LUSH, FEE, TIP, BESTOW, PROFUSE
law .. CANON, CODE, DROT, STATUTE, JUS, LEGE, LEX, JURE, RULE
" -breaker .... FELON, SINNER
" ; decree .... NISI, EDICT
" degree .... LLB
" , fictitious name in .... DOE
" for fourth offenders .... BAUMES
" , German .... SALIC
" ; like for like .... TALION
" , Mosaic ... TORA(H), PENTATEUCH
" , opposing .... ANTINOMY
" , per. to .... FORENSIC, LEGAL
" , points in .... RES, GONIA
" student .... STAGIARY
" term .... TROVER, CONSTAT, NISI
" usage .... USANCE
" volume .... CODEX
lawful ...... ENNOMIC, LICIT, LEGAL
lawlessness ..... ANARCHY, LICENSE, VICE, MUTINY, RIOT
lawmaker ...... LEGISLATOR, SOLON, MOSES, MINOS, DRACO, SENATOR
Lawrence, Miss .... GERTRUDE
" , T. E. .... SHAW

laws of Manu .... SUTRA
lawsuit ... ACTION, LITIGATION, CASE
lawyer .... BARRISTER, JURIST, LEGIST,
    COUNSEL(OR), ADVOCATE,
    SOLICITOR, HIRST, ABOGADO,
    PORTIA
lax .... FLABBY, LIMP, SLACK
laxative .... APERIENT, PURGATIVE
lay .... DITTY, PAVE, PUT, PLACE,
    LAIC(AL), TUNE, ASCRIBE
" up .... HEAP, REST, STORE
layer ...... COAT, STRATUM, LAMINA,
    TIER, SLAB, PROVINE, PLY
" of stone ...... DESS, DASS, SIAL
layman .... LAIC, AMATEUR
lazy (one) ...... BUM, DRONE, IDLER,
    LUSK, INERT, OTIOSE, SUPINE
Lazy Susan .... TURNTABLE
lea .... MEADOW, LAY, MEAD
lead .... HEAD, PILOT, EXCEL, PRECEDE
" astray .... MANG
" , black .... GRAPHITE, PLUMBAGO,
    WAD
" glass for gem making ... STRASS
" , mock .... BLENDE, PLUMMET
" monoxide .... LITHARGE
" ore (sulphide) .... GALENA
" tellurite .... ALTAITE
" , white .... CERUSE
leader .. ETHNARCH, CHIEF, DUX, VAN,
    DUCE, HEAD, GUIDE, SCOUT,
    SNELL, HETMAN, EDITORIAL
" , bib. .... MOSES
" , chorus .. CANTOR, CORYPHEUS
" of the Argonauts ...... JASON
" of thieves .... ALI
" of sheep .... SHEPHERD,
    BELLWETHER
leading ..... MAIN, CHIEF, FIRST, VAN
leaf .... GEMMA, OLE, OLLA
" disease .... ERINEA
" , hinged .... FLAP
" , large .... FROND
" manna .... LERP
" midrib .... PEN
" , modified .... BRACT
" network .... AREOLA
" of grasses .... BLADE
" , one side of a .... PAGE
" , part of a ...... VEIN, RIB, STIPEL
" , pore of a .... STOMA
" , small gland on .... LENTICEL
" stalk, per. to .... PETIOLAR
" , vein of a .... COSTA
leafless .... APHYLLOUS
leaflet ..... PINNA, TRACT, PAMPHLET
" , per. to ... FOLIOUS, FOLIOSE
league . COMBINE, UNION, ALLY, BLOC,
    BUND, HANSE, COVENANT,
    LENGTH
" , of a .... FEDERAL

lean . BARE, TILT, LANK, POOR, SPARE,
    RELY, SLIM
" animal .... RIBE
" , make .... MACERATE
" , making; as a fever ..... MARCID
" , to .... SLOPE
" ; to incline .... CAREEN
" to one side .... HEEL
" toward .... TEND
Leander's love .... HERO
leaning to one side .... ALOP
lean-to .... SHACK, LINTER, SHED
leap SPANG, CAPRIOLE, CURVET, DIVE,
    LUNGE, SALTO, BOUND, CAPER,
    SKIP
leaping .... SALIENCE, SALTANT
Lear, daughter of .. GONERIL, REGAN,
    CORDELIA
learned .. ERUDITE, LETTERED, LITERATE
" man PUNDIT, SAGE, SAVANT,
    SCHOLAR
learning ... LORE, CULTURE, KEN, LEAR
lease DEMISE, LET, CHARTER, CONVEY,
    HIRE
leash ...... CURB, LUNE, JESS, THREE
leather ..... ELK, BOCK, CALF, NAPA,
    ROAN, YUFT, ALUTA, SUEDE,
    CHAMOIS, VELLUM, CAPESKIN,
    CANEPIN, KIP
" , convert into .... TAW
" flask .... OLPE, MATARA
" hamper .... BUFFALO
" , inspector of .... SEALER
" strip .... RAND, WELT
" , to moisten .... SAM
leather-like cloth .... KERATOL
leatherneck .... MARINE, SEASOLDIER
leave BOW, EXIT, QUIT, ADIEU, CONGE,
    DEMISE, DESERT, VACATE, STAY,
    WILL, ABANDON, VAMOOSE,
    DESIST
" of absence .... EXEAT
leaven ..... BARM, YEAST, (EN)ZYME,
    INFUSE, IMBUE, FERMENT
leaves .... PAGES
" , having ..... FOLIAR, PETALED
" of a calyx .... SEPALS
" , secretion on .... LERP
" , vegetable .... SHAWS
leavings .... REFUSE, WASTE, CHAFF,
    DREGS, LEFT, REST, ORTS, DRAFF,
    RELICS, RESIDUE
Lebanon capital .... BEIRUT
" city .... HERMEL, SAIDA, SUR,
    ZAHLE
Lebens _____ .... RAUM
"Le Misanthrope" char. .... ALCESTE
lectern .... AMBO, DESK, PULPIT
lecture ... JOBE, RATE, SCOLD, REBUKE
lecturer .... DOCENT, PRELECTOR

Leda's lover .... SWAN
    " son .... CASTOR, POLLUX
ledge .. SHELF, APRON, CAY, BERM(E),
                       REEF, SILL
ledger item .... DEBIT, CREDIT
lee ....COVER, SHELTER
", opposed to .... STOSS
leech .. PARASITE, BDELLOID, ANNELID
leek; genus .... ALLIUM
leer ..... OVEN, SCOFF, OGLE, STARE
lees DRAFF, DREGS, SEDIMENT, DROSS
Lee's men .... REBS
Leeward is. .... BARBUDA, NEVIS,
                       ANTIGUA
left PORT, KAY, LARBOARD, DEPARTED,
             SINISTRAL, HAW, WENT
" aground .... NEAPED
" by mother .... CADE
" -hand page .... LEVO, VERSO
" -hand pitcher .... SOUTHPAW
" over .... ORT, MORSEL
leg, bone of the FIBULA, TIBIA, FEMUR
" armor .... GREAVE
", fleshy part of .... CALF
", forepart of .... SHIN
" from knee to ankle CRUS, SHANK
" in heraldry .... GAM
" joint covering .... KNEELET
", per. to .... CRURAL, SURAL
", rel. to knee of .... HOCK
leg armor, part of .... JAMB
leg of lamb cooked .... GIGOT
legal ... LAWFUL, LEAL, VALID, JURAL,
                        LICIT
" abstract .... PRECIS
" action .... RES, CASE, SUIT
" claim .... LIEN
" contestant .... LITIGANT
" defense .... ALIBI
" delays .... MORAE
" hearing .... OYER
" offense .... DELICT
" plea .... ABATER
" possession .... SEIZIN
" process .... CAVEAT, DETINET
" profession .... BAR, LAW
" record .... ESTREAT
" site .... VENUE
" summons .... SUBPOENA
" wrong .... TORT, MALUM
legally competent .... CAPAX
legend .... EDDA, FABLE, TALE, MYTH,
           SAGA, CAPTION, MOTTO
legging, furnished with .... OCREATE
leggings .. COCKERS, GAMBADO, STRAD
legislate .... ENACT
legislative assembly .... ASSIZE
    " body .... DIET, SENATE
legislature (two branches), per. to
                   BICAMERAL

legislator .... SOLON, SENATOR
legitimate ...... LAWFUL, LICIT, LEGAL
legume .... POD, PEA, BEAN, UVA
leguminous seeds ... LOMENTS, PULSE
Lehár; composer .... FRANZ
Leigh; actress .... VIVIEN
leipoa .... LOWAN, MALLEE
leisure .... EASE, TIME, TOOM, OTIUM,
                   REPOSE, REST
lemon .... CITRUS
" -like fruit .... LIME
lemur ... AYEAYE, MONKEY, SEMIAPE,
     LORIS, COLUGO, GALAGO, INDRI,
     MONGOOSE, MACACO, MAKI, VARI
lemuroid .... POTTO
length unit .... DHA, MICRON
lengthy .. PROLIX, TIRESOME, VERBOSE
lenient CLEMENT, MILD, SOFT, BALMY
lens .... ADON, GLASS, TORIC
" inflammation .... GLENITIS
Lenten season .... CAREME
lenticular .... PHACOID
lentigo .... FRECKLE
lentil meal .... REVALENTA
Leoncavallo opera .... (I)PAGLIACCI
leopard .... OCELOT, PARD, JAGUAR,
               CHEETAH, OUNCE
lepadidae .... BARNACLES, LEPAS
leper ...... LAZAR, OUTCAST, PARIAH
lepidopter .... MOTH
Lepontine _____ .... ALPS
leprechaun ELF, GOBLIN, PIGMY, SPRITE
leprous .... UNCLEAN
lepus .... HARE
"Les Miserables" char. ..... FANTINE
Lesbian .... SAPPHO, ARION
less ...... MINOR, MINUS, FEW
lessees, body of .... TENANTRY
lessen ABATE, PALLIATE, MINCE, WANE,
                   MINIFY
lesson .... TASK, REBUFF, CENSURE
let ..... ALLOW, LEASE, PERMIT, RENT
" go .... UNHAND
" it be given .... DETUR
" it stand .... STET
" up .... CEASE
lethargic .. INERT, TORPID, COMATOSE
lethargy .... SOPOR, STUPOR, COMA,
       APATHY, LANGUOR, TORPOR
lethe .... OBLIVION, DEATH
Leto .... LATONA
", child of ...... APOLLO, ARTEMIS
letter ... CHAIN, ELL, ESS, TEE, BREVE,
     BILLET, AITCH, RUNE, EFF, ZED,
     EDH, MISSIVE, CHIT(TY), EPISTLE,
                   MISSIVE
", cross stroke of .... SERIF
", cut off last .... APOCOPE
" designating a star .... BETA
" for letter .... LITERATIM

" from the pope .... BULL
" , initial .... FAC
" of challenge .... CARTEL
" opener .... CENSOR, SIR
letters, illuminate with ..... MINIATE
" , man of .... LITERATUS
lettuce ..... MINION, COS, ROMAINE,
LACTUCA, BOSTON, ICEBERG
" , sea ..... LAVER, ULVA, ALGA
leucite .... LENAD
Levant, madder of the ...... ALIZARI
Levantine garment .... CAFTAN
" ketch .. XEBEC, SAIC, SETTEE
" valley .... WADI
levee .... DIKE, DURBAR, QUAY
level RAZE, RASE, EVEN, GRADE, AIM,
FLUSH, PLANE, STEADY
" ; comb. form .... PLANI
" plot .... PARTERRE, TERRACE
" sandy ridge .... LANDE
leveling slip .... SHIM
lever .... CRANK, TAPPET, PEAVY, BAR,
PRISE, PRY, PEEVY, CANT
" for crossbow .... GARROT
" in lumbering .... SAMSON
leveret .... HARE
Levi's son .... GERSHOM, MERARI
levitate .... FLOAT, RISE
Levite mus. composer .... ASAPH
levy ... COLLECT, ESTREAT, TAX, CESS,
DUTY, ASSESS, IMPOSE
Lewis Carroll char. ALICE, MADHATTER
Lewis' Gantry .... ELMER
Leyte capital .... TACLOBAN
" city .... DULAG
liability .... OBLIGATION, DEBT, DUTY,
ARREAR, DEBIT
" , halting of .... CESSER
liable .... APT, BOUND, SUBJECT
liana .... CIPO
liar .... CHEAT, FIBBER, ANANIAS,
WERNARD, FAKER
Lias system, division of .... JURASSIC
libel .... ABUSE, DEFAME, MALIGN,
SLANDER, ROORBACK
liberal ..... ECLECTIC, FRANK, AMPLE,
LAVISH, TOLERANT
liberate ..... FREE, REDEEM, RANSOM
Liberian coast .... KRU
" native .... VAI, VEI
" town .... SINO
libretto .... BOOK, TEXT, WORDS
Libyan gulf .... SIDRA
" measure .... DRA, PIK
" oasis .... SEBHA
" queen loved by Zeus .. LAMIA
" town .... DERNA
license .... RIGHT, ABANDON, LAXITY,
PATENT, GRANT

lichen PARELLA, MOSS, ARCHIL, PERSIS,
LITMUS
" ; genus .... EVERNIA, USNEA
licit ...... LAWFUL, LEGAL, JUST, DUE
lick .... BAFFLE, DEFEAT, MOISTEN
licorice .... ABRIN, JEQUIRITY
lid ... CAP, CASE, ROOF, COVER, TILT,
CURB, HAT
" -like part .... OPERCULUM
lie ... FIB, MENDACITY, REST, DECEIVE,
RECLINE
" face downward FELL, PROSTRATE,
PRONATE
" in wait .... LURK, SKULK
Liechtenstein capital .... VADUZ
" monetary unit .. RAPPEN
lieu .... PLACE, STEAD
life HOURS, VIE, DAYS, ENERGY, BIOS,
SPIRIT, SPARK, VITALITY
" , animal .... BIOTA, FAUNA
" , past middle .... AUTUMNAL
" ; prefix .... BIO
" principle .. JIVA, ATMAN, PRANA
" prolonger .... ELIXIR
" , rel. to .... BIOTIC
" , without .... AZOIC
"Life with Father" author ..... DAY
lifebelt .... MAEWEST
" filling .... KAPOK
lifeless ... DEAD, FLAT, AMORT, INERT
lift .... AID, PERK, HELP, RAISE
lifting muscle .... ERECTOR, LEVATOR
ligament .... BOND, TAENIA
" ; comb. form .... DESMO
ligan, rel. to ...... FLOTSAM, JETSAM
light ...... LUMEN, FINE, LAMP, LEGER,
SLEAZY, ILLUM(IN)E, FACILE,
MATCH, KLIEG
" , a burning ..... TORCH, CRESSET
" anchor .... KEDGE
" beacon .... FANAL
" , celestial .... LUMINARY
" , circle of ..... AUREOLA, HALO,
NIMBUS, CORONA
" ; comb. form .... PHOT
" , faint .... GLIM
" flux .... HEFNER
" -headed ... GIDDY, DIZZY, FAINT
" images .... SPECTRA
" , spirit of; Persia .... ORMAZD
" , standard of .... CARCEL
" unit ....LUX, RAD
" , without .... APHOTIC
lighter .... SCOW, BARGE, BOAT
" , make .... LEAVEN
" -than-air craft ...... AEROSTAT
"Lighthorse Harry" .... LEE
lighthouse ... PHARE, FANAL, PHAROS,
BEACON
lightning .... LAIT, FLASH, LEVIN

169

"   rod .... ARRESTER
ligneous .... WOODY, XYLOID
"lights out" .... TAPS
ligulate .... LORATE
like SIMILAR, AS, EQUAL, AKIN, DOTE,
                                 ALLIED
" ; suffix .... INE, OID
likely .. COMELY, SEEMLY, APT, PRONE
likeness EFFIGY, IMAGE, GUISE, ICON,
                       ANALOGY, PORTRAIT
likewise ..... ALSO, DITTO, EKE, TOO
likewise not .... NOR
Lilith's successor .... EVE
Lilliputian .... MIDGET, TINY
lily .... WOKAS, ALOE, IXIA, LIS
" , butterfly ..... MARIPOSA, SEGO
" daffodil; genus ...... NARCISSUS
" family .. BESSERA, CAMAS, SQUILL
" , palm .... TI
" , sand .... SOAPROOT
" , shaped like a .... CRINOID
" , "The Turk's Cap" .. MARTAGON
" , water ...... NYMPHAEA, LOTUS,
                              CASTALIA
"Lily Maid of Astolat" ...... ELAINE
limacine .... SLUG, SNAIL
limax .... SLUG
limb BRANCH, LEG, BOUGH, MEMBER,
                            FIN, WING
" adapted for swimming ....
                            NECTOPOD
limber .... PLIANT, AGILE, LITHE
limbo .... HELL, PRISON, JAIL
limbs, destitute of AMELIA, ACOLOUS
lime .... CALX, CITRON, CEDRA
" bush .... SNARE
" , deriv. of .... APATITE
" hound .... LYAM
" , per. to .... CALCIC
" powder .... CONITE, KONITE
" tree .... BASS, LINDEN, TEIL
limestone ...... MALM, LIAS, MARBLE,
                OOLITE, CALP, CAEN, CHALK
limewort .... DIANTHUS
limit .. FIX, BOURN, SPAN, TERM, PALE,
                EDGE, STINT, CONFINE
" ; comb. form .... ORI
limited .. FEW, FINITE, LOCAL, SCANT,
                              TOPICAL
limn .... DEPICT, DRAW, PAINT
limp ... FLABBY, FLACCID, HALT, FAIL,
                SOFT, LAX, FLIMSY, WILTED
limpid .... CLEAR, PELLUCID
Lincoln .... ABE
" , portrayer of .... MASSEY
" , slayer of .... BOOTH
" , War Secretary of .. STANTON
" , wife of .... TODD
Lind; singer .... JENNY
linden; genus .... LIN, TEIL, TILIA

line .. ROUTE, CORD, GRY, ROW, CUE,
                        WAD, STRIA(E)
" ; as a ball of thread ...... CLEW
" for fastening sail .... EARING
" in trigonometry .. SECANT, SINE
" joining barometric points ISOBAR
" not meeting curve ... ASYMPTOTE
" of color .... STREAK
" of junction .... SEAM
" of no magnetic declination .....
                              AGONIC
" of soldiers CORDON, FILE, RANK
" the inside .... CEIL
" with bricks .... REVET
lineage .. LINE, RACE, STOCK, STRAIN,
                KINDRED, TRENE, PEDIGREE
linen GULIX, BARRAS, CRASH, DOWLAS,
                LINGERIE, CREA, LOCKRAM,
                CAMBRIC, DAMASK, LAWN, SCRIM
" for window shades ... HOLLAND
" , officer in charge of ... NAPERER
" room .... EWERY
" , sail .... DUCK
" tape .... INKLE
" , table .... NAPERY
liner .... SHIP, SHIM
ling .... BURBOT, HEATHER
linger ... DELAY, DWELL, HOVER, LAG,
                LENG, SAUNTER, LOITER, DALLY
lingo CANT, JARGON, PATTER, PATOIS,
                                 ARGOT
lingua .... TONGUE
linguist ...... POLYGLOT, CLASSICIST
links; connect in series ... CATENATE
link .... NEXUS, YOKE, CHAIN, MARRY
lint .... TENT, FLAX, FLUFF, HEMP, NAP
lion .... LEO, SIMBA
" , monster, half eagle .... GRIFFIN
" , mountain ...... PUMA, COUGAR
" whelp .... LIONET
lion-headed consort of Ra ... MUT
lip .... LABRUM, GEAT
" ornament .... PELELE, LABRET
" , swollen .... BLOBBER
" , tumid upper .... CHILOMA
" , under .... JIB
lip-formed .... EDGED, LABIAL
lipide .... CERIDE, STERIDE
lipoma .... TUMOR
liquefied by heat .... FUSILE
liqueur .. MARC, RATAFIA, CURACAO,
                CREME, GENEPI, NOYAU, KUMMEL
" , add flavoring to .... TUN
" , aromatic .... ABSINTHE
liquid SPIRIT, LIMPID, FLUID, WATER(Y)
" fatty oil .... ELAIN, FURFURAL,
                                 OLEIN
" for cooling cylinders COOLANT
" , having no .... ANEROID
" , light colorless .... TRIDECANE

" soap .... NAPALM
" , thick ..... DOPE, GRAITH, TAR
" , weak .... BLASH
liquidate .... AMORTIZE, KILL, PURGE,
SETTLE
liquor .... RUM, RYE, TIPPLE, ELIXIR
" -bottle case .... CELLARET
" from must .... ARROPE
" , fruit .... RATAFIA, GIN
" , intoxicating .... LUSH
" , malt .... STOUT, ALE
" , oriental .... ARRACK
" , rice .... SAKE
" to remove taste of coffee .....
CHASSE
liripipe .... TIPPET
lissome LITHE, LIMBER, SUPPLE, AGILE,
SVELTE
list CATALOG, AGENDA, TABLE, NAME,
HEEL, CAN, TIP, CAREEN
" ; as a council .... ROTA
" of candidates .... LEET, SLATE
" of officers .... ROSTER
" , writing .... SCRIP
listen EAVESDROP, BUG, HEAR, HARK,
HEED, OBEY
listening .... AUDIENT
" post .... ECOUTE
listlessness .... ACEDIA, ENNUI
Liszt; pianist .... FRANZ
litany .. EKTENE, ORISON, ROGATION,
COLLECT
literary ...... LETTERED, VERSED, BLUE
" criticism .... EPICRISIS
" fragments ..... ANA(LECTA)
" hack .... GRUB
" productions .... OPERA
" style, affectation in PURISM
" style, descriptive of . PROSE,
PEDANTIC
lithe .... AGILE, SLIM, LISSOME, BAIN,
SVELTE
Lithuanian capital KAUNAS, KOVNO
" coin .... LITAS, LIT
" seaport MEMEL, KLAIPEDA
litter .. BIER, CABIN, COFFIN, DOOLER,
DOOLY, DOOLI, JUMBLE, MESS
" of pigs .... FAR, FARROW
" , to .... STREW, MULCH
little .... PALTRY, TRIVIAL, PUNY, TINY,
WEE, POCO, MINUTE
" flag .... BANDEROLE
"Little Henry" .... HAL
little ring .... ANNULET
Little Russia ...... UKRAINE, POLAND
little toe .... MINIMUS
litus .... COLONUS, SERF
live .... BREATHE, DWELL, EXIST, ARE,
ABIDE, VITAL, RESIDE, SUBSIST

liveliness ... ACTIVITY, VIVACITY, PEP,
SPIRIT
lively ... SPRY, AGILE, GAY, GRIG, VIF,
PERK(Y), PERT, BRISK, VIVID, NIMBLE,
BUOYANT, YARE, TITTUPY
" air .... LILT
" ; mus. .... ANIMATO
liven .... CHEER, ROUSE
liver, disease of the ...... HEPATITIS,
CIRRHOSIS
" , per. to .... HEPATIC
liverwort .... HEPATICA, RICCIA
livid .... WAN, ASHEN, PALLID, PALE
living .... BEING, LIVE, EXTANT
" again .... REDIVIVUS
" , capable of .... VIABLE
" dead GHOST, PHANTOM, ZOMBI
" in deep sea .... BATHYBIC
" in seclusion .... EREMITISM
" in tents .... SCENITE
" in water .... LOTIC, LENITIC
Livistona palm .... FAN
Livonian .... ESTH, LETT, LIV
lixiviate .... ALKALI, LEACH
lixivium .... LYE
lizard NEWT, EFT, MONITOR, SAURIAN,
MOLOCH, SALAMANDER, GILA,
IGUANA, ADDA, BASILISK, URAN,
VARAN, CHAMELEON, AGAMA, UTA,
SKINK
" , fabled .... DRAGON
" , Philippine .... IBID
" , serpent .... SEPS
" , spiny .... DABB
" , starred .... HARDIM
" , wall .... TARENTE, GECKO
llama ... GUANACO, VICUNA, ALPACA
llano .... PLAIN
lo .... BEHOLD, ECCE, SEE
loach; genus .... COBITIS
load .... FREIGHT, DOPE, CARK, ONUS,
JAG, CARGO, BURDEN
" .... ONERATE, ENCUMBER
loader .... STEVEDORE
loaf ..... IDLE, LOUNGE, MASS, MIKE,
DRONE, LOLL
loam .... LOESS, REGUR
" , constituent of ... CHALK, CLAY,
SOIL, LIME
loath .... AVERSE, HOSTILE
loathe ABHOR, DETEST, HATE, SCORN
loathsome ...... CLOYING, FOUL, VILE,
ODIOUS, NAUSEOUS
lob ..... THROW, PITCH, DROP, STRIKE
lobby CORRIDOR, HALL, FOYER, SOLICIT
lobe of the wing .... ALULA
loblolly .... PINE
lobster .... MACRURAN, POLYPOD
" claw .... NIPPER, CHELA
" eggs .... CORAL, ROE

" ; floating trap .... POT, CORF, CREEL
" ; last segment .... TELSON
" , part of a .... THORAX
" , rel. of .... CRAB, SHRIMP, BARNACLE
local .... CHAPTER, EDAPHIC, TOPICAL
" court .... GEMOT
" irritant .... ARNICA
locale .... SCENE, VENUE
locality ... AREA, PLACE, SITUS, SPOT, ZONE, LOCUS, PURLIEU
" , of a particular .... ENDEMIC
loch .... BAY, CREEK, INLET, POND
lock .... HASP, DETENT, COTTER
" of hair .... BERGER, CURL, DAG, TRESS
locker for bow and arrow .. ASCHAM
lockjaw .... TETANUS, TRISMUS
lock-up CALABOOSE, LIMBO, JUG, JAIL
Locrine's daughter .... SABRINA
" father .... BRUT
locomotive MOGUL, BIGBOY, PRAIRIE, MIKADO, SWITCHER
" cowcatcher .... PILOT
locust .... WETA, CICADA, CICALA
" creak .... STRIDULATE
" tree . ACACIA, CAROB, CLAMMY, HONEY
locust-like insect .... MANTIS
lode ..... VUG, VEIN, LEDGE, DEPOSIT
lodge .. DORM, STOW, BOARD, CABIN, ROOST, BILLET, ENCAMP, QUARTER
lodging cars .... DOLLIES
" place; Fr. .... GITE
lofty ..... AERIE, ANDEAN, EMINENT, HAUGHTY, ALPINE, DISTANT, IMPOSING
" abode .... EYRIE, AERIE
log measure .... SCALAGE
" roller .... BIRLER, DECKER
" , spin floating .... BIRL
" , split .... PUNCHEON
logarithm inventor .... NAPIER
logarithmic unit .... BEL
logger's boots .... PACS
logging, evade work in .... SNIB
" sled .... TODE, TRAVOIS
" wheels, a pair of ... KATYDID
logic .... PONENT, SALTUS, ORGANON
" , Baconian .... INDUCTIVE
" , fallacy in .... IDOLUM
" , premise of .... LEMMA
logs, men who nose .... SNIPERS
Lohengrin's bride .... ELSA
loin of mutton .... CHUMP, RACK
loincloth DHOTI, MARD, MALO, PERGU
loins .... REINS
Loire, city on .... ORLEANS
" ; old name .... LIGER

" tributary .... INDRE
loiter ... LAG, POKE, DALLY, DAWDLE, LINGER, SAUNTER
loiterer .... IDLER, LAGGER
Loki, daughter of .... HEL, HELA
" , wife of .... SIGYN
Lollobrigida .... GINA
Lolo .... NOSU
Lombardy king .... ALBOIN
lomboy .... PLUM
London art gallery .... TATE
" hawker .... COSTER, MUN
" prison .... NEWGATE
" quarter ..... SOHO, MAYFAIR, ADELPHI, CHELSEA, HOLBORN, LAMBETH
" suburb .... EALING
" subway .... TUBE
Londoner .... COCKNEY
Lone Ranger's companion ... TONTO
Lone-Star State .... TEXAS
lonely ... DESOLATE, LORN, SOLITARY
long .. HONE, WORDY, YEARN, PROLIX, HANKER, PANT, PINE
" ago .... ELD, YORE
" discourse .... DESCANT
" jump .... HALMO
" -legged bird .... STILT
" -legged bug .... EMESA
" life .... LONGEVITY
" -limbed .... RANGY, LEGGY
" story .... RIGMAROLE
longing .... YEN
longshoreman .. DOCKER, STEVEDORE, STOWER
loo .... PAM
look .... FACE, GAZE, EYE, CON, KEN, PORE, PRY
" obliquely .... SKEW
" pryingly ...... PEEK, KEEK, PEEP
" slyly GLANCE, LEER, GLY, OGLE
" steadily .... GAZE, SCAN
looked for .... SOUGHT
lookout .. CONNER, CUPOLA, GUARD, SCOUT, SENTINEL, TURRET
loom .. APPEAR, SEEM, TOOL, WEAVE
" bar .... EASER
" harness .... LEAF
" , heddles of a .... CAAM
" , lower level of a .... LAM
" reed .... SLEY
loon .... DIVER, WABBY
loop . TAB, ANSA, BRIDE, TERRY, PICOT, HONDO, BIGHT, NOOSE, EYE, AMBIT, CURVE
loophole ..... MUSE, MEUSE, PRETEXT
loose(n) . (RE)LAX, EASE, FREE, LEWD, LIMP, UNDO, BAGGY, UNTIE, VAGUE, FLABBY, REMISS, UNLOCK, WANTON

172

" robe for women .. PEIGNOIR, SIMAR, BANIAN
loot . PLUNDER, SACK, SPOILS, PILLAGE, BOOTY, RIFLE, PRIZE
lop .... SNIP, SNED, PRUNE, OCHE
lopsided .... ALOP, ALIST
loquacious, be .... PRATE
loquacity .... GARRULITY
lord ... GRANDEE, LIEGE, PEER, EARL, KHAN, KAAN, LAIRD, NOBLEMAN
" of a sanjak .... BEY
" , wife of a ....LADY
"Lord High Executioner" ..... KOKO
Lord's Prayer, The .... PATERNOSTER
lordly .... DESPOTIC, UPPISH
lore ...... WISDOM, ERUDITION, LEAR
Lorelei .... SIREN
loris .... LEMUR
Lortzing opera .... UNDINE
lose ...... MISS, FORFEIT, AMIT, SPILL, ESTRANGE, MISLAY, FAIL, SQUANDER
" interest .... FAG, FLAG, TIRE
loss .... FORFEITURE, LEAK, DEATH, DEFEAT, DAMAGE
" of eyelashes .... MADAROSIS
" of feeling .... ANAESTHESIA
" of hair .... ALOPECIA
" of memory .... AMNESIA
" of reason .... AMENTIA
" of sense of smell ..... ANOSMIA
" of speech ..... APHASIA, ALALIA
" of voice .... APHONIA
" of will power .... ABULIA
lost .... MISLAID, GONE, LORN, ASEA
" color .... FADED, PALED
lot SCAD, SHARE, DOOM, FATE, MUCH, LUCK, LAND, HAP, SUM, CHANCE, HAZARD
Lot's father .... HARAN
" sister .... MILCAH
lots, divination by ...... SORTILEGE
lottery .... CHANCE, RAFFLE, TERNO, BINGO, LOTTO
lotus .... CHINQUAPIN, NELUMBO
" tree .... SADR
loudmouthed .... THERSITICAL
loudspeaker ...... WOOFER, TWEETER
Louis XVI nickname .... VETO
Louis Viaud, pen name of ..... LOTI
Louise de la Rame, pen name of.... OUIDA
Louisiana .... PELICANSTATE
" acc't book .... BILAN
" county .... PARISH
" parish .... ACADIA, ALLEN, CADDO, GRANT, SABINE, TENSAS, WINN
" town ...... HOUMA, PELLA, ALGONA

lounge ..... LAZE, LOLL, SOFA, DIVAN
louse .... NIT, APHID
lout .... BEND, BOW, GAWK, LOOBY, CUIF, GOOF
love WOO, AMO, AMARE, FANCY, GRA, ADORE, ARDOR, FLAME, (EN)AMOR, DOTE, CHARITY, DARLING
" affair .... AMOUR
" feast, early Christian ... AGAPE
" , full of ..... EROTIC, AMATIVE, DOTING
" ; Ger. .... MINNE
" , god of ... AMOR, BHAGA, CUPID, EROS, KAMA
" goddess of .... (H)ATHOR, FREYA, VENUS
" knot .... AMORET
" of fine arts .... VIRTU
" , parental .... STORGE
" potion .... PHILTER
lovebird .... PARROT, PARAKEET
Lovelace heroine .... LUCASTA
lover . BEAU, MINION, ROMEO, FLAME, LEMAN, SWAIN, ADMIRER, PARAMOUR, RATO
Lover's Leap promontory ... DUCATO
"Love's Labours Lost" char. .. BIRON, COSTARD, BOYET, MARIA
loving . AMOROUS, AMATIVE, EROTIC, ARDENT, FOND
" ; comb. form .... PHIL
" cup .... TIG
low . SNEAKY, BAS, MOO, ORRA, VILE, BLUE, ABJECT, COMMON, MEAN
" dividing wall .... SPINA
lowan .... LEIPOA, MALLEE
lower ..... DIP, DIM, DEMIT, RESIGN, NETHER, DEMOTE, VAIL, ABASE
lowest class of animal life AMOEBA, AMEBA
" point ... NADIR, NETHERMOST, PERIGEE
" -ranked peer .... BARON
lowland .... HOLM, SPIT
loyal .... LEAL, STANCH, TRUE, LIEGE
loyalty ... FIDELITY, FEALTY, HOMAGE, PIETAS
Loyalty island .... LIFU, UVEA
lozenge .. PASTILLE, TROCHE, ROTULA
lubber .... BOOR, CHURL, GAWK
lubricate .... ANOINT, OIL, WAX
lubricator ... OILER, DOPER, OILCAN
lucerne .... FODDER, ALFALFA
lucid .... BRIGHT, SANE, CLEAR, VIVID
lucidity .... SANITY, CLARITY
lucifer . DEVIL, MATCH, SATAN, VENUS
Lucius Domitius Ahenobarbus . NERO
luck . FORTUITY, LOT, BREAK, CHANCE
" , bad .... CESS, DEUCE
" , stroke of .... FLUKE, STRIKE

lucky stone .... ALECTORIA
lucrative .... FAT, PAYING
lucre ...... PELF, EMOLUMENT, PROFIT
ludicrous .... RISIBLE, ABSURD, DROLL
Ludolphian number .... PI
lug .... EAR, LOOP, PULL, TUG, HALE,
   HAUL, TOTE, DRAG, CARRY
lugworm .... ANNELID, LOB
lukewarm .... TEPID
 " , make .... TEPIFY
lull ...... HUSH, STILL, ROCK, ALLAY
lumberman ...... GIRDLER, SAWYER,
      LOGGER, TOPPER
 " , shoe of .. LARIGAN, PAC
 " , sled of . WYNN, TRAVOIS
luminary ...... RADIANT, STAR, SUN
luminous impression .... PHOSPHENE
lump .. CLOT, MASS, LOB, NUB, WAD,
   BURL, HUNK, NODE, NODULE
lumpish .... DULL, STOLID, INERT
lunacy ... MADNESS, MANIA, MOON
lunar mission .... APOLLO
lunatic asylum .. BETHLEHEM, BEDLAM
lunch room .... CAFE, DINER
luncheon ... SNACK, TIFFIN, UNDERN
lung ailment .... CHALICOSIS
 " sound .... RATTLE, RALE
lungs .... LIGHTS
Lupino, Miss .... IDA
lurch ...... ROLL, SWAG, BILK, JOLT,
     CAREEN, PITCH
lure ... BAIT, DECOY, ATTRACT, COAX,
    TEMPT, SEDUCE
lurer .... ENTICER, SIREN
lurid .... GHASTLY, GRISLY, DARK
lurk .... SKULK, SNEAK, PROWL
lush ...... DRINK, JUICY, SUCCULENT
luster .. NAIF, SHEEN, GLOSS, GLORY,
     SCHILLER
lusterless .... DULL, MAT, DIM
lustrous ... BRIGHT, SILVERY, RISING,
    SILKY, NAIF, NITID
lusty .... ROBUST, STURDY
lute; mus. ...... ASOR, PANDORE,
   THEORBO, GUITAR, UKULELE
luxuriant ...... RANK, FERTILE, LUSH,
   LAVISH, ORNATE, OPULENT
luxurious .... PLUSH
Luzon people .... ITANEG, TINGUIAN,
   ITNEG, TINGGIAN, TAGALAS,
     IGOROT
 " Negrito .... AETA, ATA
Lydia capital .... SARDIS
Lydian .... EFFEMINATE
 " king .... CROESUS, GYGES
lye .... LIXIVIUM
lying ...... DECUMBENT, FALSE, ABED
 " prone .... PASSIVE, SUPINE
lymphatic .... AQUATIC, PLASMIC
Lynette's knight .... GARETH

lynx ... CARACAL, LOSS(E), LUCERN,
   BOBCAT, CATAMOUNT
lynxlike .... WILDCAT
lyre .... ASOR, ARP, SHELL, TRIGON,
    CITHARA, SACKBUT
lyrebird .... MENURA
lyre-shaped .... LYRATE
lyric .. ALBA, EP(ODE), POEM, MELIC
 " poem of thirteen lines RONDEAU
 " poet .... ODIST
 ———————— -Lytton; novelist .. BULWER

M

macabre ...... GHASTLY, GRIM, LURID
Macao, coin of .... AVO
macaque .... KRA, RHESUS
Macaulay; novelist .... ROSE
Macbeth char. ..... ANGUS, BANQUO,
   HECATE, LENNOX, MACDUFF, ROSS
mace .. GAVEL, STAFF, STICK, SCEPTER
 " beadle .... BEADLE, MACER
 " of a nutmeg .... ARIL
 " , reed .... DOD
Macedonia, ancient capital of . PELLA
 " , city of ... BEREA, VEROIA,
    PYDNA, EDESSA
 " , king of .... ABGAR
macerate .... RET, SOAK, STEEP
machete .... KNIFE, BOLO, CUTLAS(S)
Machiavellian .. DECEITFUL, CUNNING,
    CRAFTY
machinate ..... CABAL, PLOT, SCHEME
machine ...... AUTOMATON, SYSTEM,
  DEVICE, GADGET, PARTY, ENGINE
 " for glazing ...... CALENDER
 " for maturing cloth ... AGER
 " for separating ore . VANNER
 " for shaping objects EXTRUDER
 " for softening clay ....
    MALAXATOR
 " gun .. GATLING, HOTCHKISS,
    MAXIM
 " -gun party, hidden ... NEST
 " , pile driving .... GIN
Mackenzie, Miss .... GISELE
mackerel ... TINKER, SCOMBER, CERO,
   PETO, SIERRA, SPIKE
 " , horse . JUREL, SAUREL, TUNNY
 " net .... SPILLER
mackerel-like fish .... SCAD, BONITO
mad .. MANIACAL, FRENETIC, INSANE,
  WILD, RABID, LUNATIC, RAVING
Madagascar fiber palm .... RAFFIA
 " lemur .... INDRIS
 " mammal .... TENREC

" , tribe of .... HOVA, MALAGASY
madam ...... SENORA, FRAU, MILADY, DONNA
Madame Chiang's maiden name ..... SOONG
Madame Butterfly ..... CHOCHO(SAN)
madcap ... HOTSPUR, RASH, RECKLESS
madden .... INCENSE, GRAZE, VEX
madder RUBIA, AAL, GARANCE, LIZARY
Madeira Island capital ..... FUNCHAL
" wine .... TINTA
madhouse .. ASYLUM, BEDLAM, CHAOS
madman .... ALIENE, LUNATIC
madness FRENZY, RAGE, FOLLY, MANIA, FURY, DELIRIUM
Madras town .... ADONI
" weight .... POLLAM
madrepore .... CORAL, GLASS
Madrid museum .... PRADO
madrigal .... GLEE, ODE, LYRIC
Madrileño .... SENOR, DON
maelstrom .... EDDY, SWIRL, TURMOIL
Mae West .... LIFEBELT
magazine .... ARMOR, ARSENAL, CHAMBER, DEPOT
" rifle .... MAUSER
maggot .... GENTLE, GRUB, MATHE, MAWK
Magi . GASPAR, MELCHIOR, BALTHASAR
magic ... JADU, MAYA, RUNE, OBEAH, VOODOO, THEURGY, GOETY
" , act of .... CONJURATION
" , goddess of .... CIRCE
" lant. color glass .... TINTER
" seals .... SIGILLA
" symbol ..... PENTACLE, CARACT
" wand .... CADUCEUS
" word ..... PRESTO, SESAME
magical . CHARMING, GOETIC, OCCULT
magician .. MAGE, WIZARD, SORCERER, MAGUS, CONJURER, MERLIN, MANDRAKE, WIZARD, WITCH, HOUDINI, BLACKSTONE, THURSTON
" , assistant of .... FAMULUS
magistrate .. EPHOR, ALCALDE, BAILIE, SYNDIC, PUISNE, EDILE, MAYOR, PREFECT, CONSUL, DOGE, JUDGE
" of ancient Athens .... ARCHON
Magnani; actress .... ANNA
magnate ..... BARON, LORD, BIGWIG, NABOB, VIP, PASHA, BASHAW, MOGUL, SHOGUN, TYCOON
magnesium .. SELLAITE, TALC, LOWEITE
magnet .. LOADSTONE, LODE(STONE), ADAMANT, BAR
" , electro- .... SOLENOID
" , per. to ..... ARMATURE, RED

magnetized steel sphere ..... TERELLA
magnify .... ENLARGE, DILATE, SWELL
magnolia .... YULAN, BIGBLOOM
magpie .... MADGE, PICA, PIE(T), TALKER, PIANET
" diver .... SMEW
" shrike .... TANAGER
Magyar .... HUNGARIAN
mahogany .... RATTEEN, ACAJOU, CAOBA, TOON, TOTARA
" , streak in .... ROE
Mahomet (see "Mohammed") ...... MACON
Mahomet's tomb, location of MEDINA
" uncle .... ABBAS
mahua ..... BUTTER, FULWA, PHULWA
Mahatma .... ARHAT, ARAHT, ARAHAT, GANDHI
maid .... ABIGAIL, AMA(H), EYAH, BONNE, SLAVEY, WENCH, ANCILLA, MATRANEE
" of Athens .... MACRI
maiden .. LASS(IE), MISS(Y), DAMSEL, UNUSED, VIRGIN, COLLEEN, GAL
" turned into a spider .... ARACHNE
mail .... DAK, DAWK, POST, CONSIGN
" boat .... PACKET
" , coat of .... ARMOR, BRINIE, HAUBERK
maim .... MAR, INJURE, MAYHEM, MAIHEM, MANGLE, SPOIL
main ... POTENT, CONDUIT, PIPE, SEA, CHIEF, OCEAN, PRIME, VITAL
" action of drama ...... EPITASIS
" beam .... WALKING
" point ...... JET, NUB, GIST, PITH
Maine bay .... CASCO
" college .... COLBY, BATES
" county ... KNOX, WALDO, YORK
" island .... ORRS
" motto .... DIRIGO
" promontory .... KINEO
" symbol .... PINE
" town .... BATH, MILO
maintain .... AVOW, CLAIM, UPHOLD, ASSERT, KEEP, AFFIRM
maintenance .... ALIMONY, UPKEEP
maize .... ZEA, CORN, MEALIES
majagua .... BALO, GUANA
major .... DUR, DITONE
major-domo ... SENESCHAL, STEWARD
majority ...... AGE, MOST, SENIORITY
Majorca city .... PALMA
" island .... IBIZA, IVIZA
make ... FORM, GAIN, BRAND, CAUSE, SHAPE, MO(U)LD, CREATE, DEVISE
" believe .... FEINT, FICTION, FEIGN, SHAM, PRETENSE
" fast .... BELAY

175

" level .... EVEN, TRUE
" over ... REDO, REPAIR, REVAMP,
                              RENOVATE
" public ...... AIR, BRUIT, NOISE,
                              DELATE
" smooth .... SLEEK, SLICK
makeshift .... STOPGAP
Malabar measure .... ADY
" people .... NAIR
malachite green .... BICE
malady . AILMENT, DISEASE, DISORDER
malapert .... BOLD, SAUCY
malaria .... MIASMA, MIASM
" carrier .... ANOPHELES
Malay .... MORO, ILOKANO, SAKAI
" boat .... TOUP
" canoe .... PRAH, PROA
" chief .... DATO, DATU
" city .... IPOH
" cloth .... BATIK
" coin .... TAMPANG, TRA
" condition .... LATA
" dagger .... CREESE, KRIS
" dress .... SARONG
" feather palm .... ARENG
" fiber tree .... TERAP
" gibbon .... LAR
" island(s) .... BALI, JAVA,
                     PENANG, SUMATRA,
                     BORNEO, TIMOR, CELEBES
" isthmus .... KRA
" jacket .... BAJU
" knife .... KRIS
" law .... ADAT
" malady to kill .... AMOK
" measure .... PAU
" mountain .... TAHAN
" Negrito .... ATA, ATTA
" neuralgia .... LATA
" of Luzon .... ITALONE
" palm .... ARENG, TARA
" race, one of .. TAGAL, VISAYAN
" seacoast town .... MALACCA
" state .... KEDAH, PERAK
" title of respect .... TUAN
" tree .... DURIAN, UPAS
" wild ox .... BANTENG
Maldive Islands capital .... MALE
male . HE, MANLY, VIRILE, MAN, HAND
" , gelded .... GALT
malediction ...... ANATHEMA, CURSE,
                     BAN, THREAT, MALISON
malefactor .... CRIMINAL, FELON
malevolence .... GRUDGE, SPITE, EVIL
malevolent .... ENVIOUS, HATING,
                              SPITEFUL
malice ...... ENVY, RANCOR, VENOM,
                              PIQUE
malign ..... DEFAME, VILIFY, ASPERSE
malignant .... ILL, EVIL, VICIOUS

malignity .... VENOM, VIOLENCE
malison .... CURSE, TORMENT
mallard .... DUCK, ANAS
malleable ..... TENSILE, DOCILE, SOFT
malle bird .... LEIPOA, LOWAN
mallet .... TUP, MACE, BEATER, GAVEL,
                     BEETLE, MADGE, MAUL
mallow ..... SIA, ALTEA, HOCK, MAW
malodorous ..... FETID, FUSTY, PUTRID
malt froth .... BARM
" infusion .... WORT
" , tasting of .... CORNY
" vinegar ...... ALEGAR, WORT
Malta island .... GOZO, MELITA
" wind ...... GREGALE, LEVANTER
Maltese ...... LACE, CAT, DOG, CROSS
malty .... ALISH
Mamie's town ...... BOONE, DENVER
mammal .... APE, MAN, WHALE,
                              PRIMATE
" , aquatic .... DUGONG,
                     MANATEE, ORCA, OTARY,
                     BELUGA, WALRUS,
                     DOLPHIN, SEAL
" , Australian .... KANGAROO
" , cat-family .... LION, PARD,
                     PUMA, TIGER, GENET,
                     OUNCE, ANGORA, EYRA
" ; cetacean . DOLPHIN, WHALE
" , flight .... BAT
" , gnawing .... MOUSE, RAT,
                     CAVY, CONY, HARE, MOLE,
                     PACA, PICA, AGOUTI
" , Indian ...... OUNCE, ZEBU
" , insectivorous .... BAT
" , lower order of . MARSUPIAL
" , marsupial ...... OPOSSUM,
                     KANGAROO, JOEY,
                     KOALA, JERBOA
" , nocturnal ... LEMUR, RATEL
" , swine-family .. BOAR, GALT,
                     HOG, PECORA, PECCARY
" , So. American .... TAPIR,
                     TAYRA, COATI
mammals, gnawing order of ....
                              RODENTIA
man .. HOMO, BAING, BIPED, FORTIFY,
                     PERSON, SOMEONE, VIR, WER,
                     HUMAN, VALET, VASSAL, HUSBAND,
                              SERVANT
" bound to single life ... CELIBATE
" , elderly .. SIRE, SENILE, CODGER,
                     CRONE, FOGY, GAFFER, DOTARD,
                              DODO, GEEZER
" , handsome ...... BEAU, ADONIS
" , iron .... TALUS
" , newly married .... BENEDICT
" of all work .... FACTOTUM
man of letters ... LITERATUS, SAVANT
Man, Isle of; capital .... DOUGLAS

"Man Without a Country" author .. HALE
"   "   "   " char. ..... NOLAN
man-like .... ANDROID
manage TEND, DIGHT, WIELD, WANGLE,
    RUN, HANDLE, CONDUCT
manageable .... DOCILE, YARE
management .... GESTION, CONDUCT
manager DIRECTOR, GRIEVE, OPERATOR,
    GERENT, OVERSEER, BOSS
manakin ...... DWARF, MODEL, PIPRA
mañana .... TOMORROW
Manchu tribe .... DAUR, DAURY
Manchurian town ..... AIGUN, PENKI
mandarin's home .... YAMEN, YAMUN
mandate . EDICT, ORDER, BEHEST, WRIT
mandible .... BEAK, JAW, CHOPS
mandrake .... MANDRAGORA
mandrel . ARBOR, LATHE, BOBBIN, PICK
mandrill .... BABOON
manducate .... CHEW
mane ... JUBA, ROACH, BRUSH, SHAG,
    STUBBLE
maned .... JUBATE
maneuver ...... ARTIFICE, RUSE, TRICK
mange .... FODDER, ITCH
"   , cause of ...... ACARID, MITE
"   , sheep .... SCAB
manger ..... BIN, CRIB, CRECHE, RACK
mangle ... MAR, CALENDER, BRUISE,
    PRESS, BOTCH
mango .... BAUNO
"   bird .... ORIOLE
"   fruit .... AMINI, DRUPE
"   grove .... TOPE
mangrove .... GORAN
"   pole .... BORITY
mangy .... SCURVY, RONION
maniacal .... DEMONIAC, MAD, CRAZY
manifest .... OPEN, OVERT, PATENT,
    ARRANT, PUBLIC, EVINCE, REVEAL,
    SHOW
manifestation .... AURA, AVATAR
manifested ..... TOKENED, DISCLOSED
manifesto ... EDICT, RESCRIPT, OSTENT
manikin ... PHANTOM, DWARF, MODEL
Manila airfield .... CLARK
"   Bay boat .... BILALO
"   Bay hero .... DEWEY
maniple ..... FANON, ORALE, FANUM
manipulate .... HANDLE, RIG, USE
mankind .... HUMANITY, ADAM, FOLK
manner(s) ... AIR, MIEN, SORT, STYLE,
    MOS, WAY, MODE, WONT, MODUS,
    ASPECT, CUSTOM, MORES
manor .. MANSION, ESTATE, DEMESNE,
    BURY
mantel ... BEAM, LEDGE, LINTEL, SLAB,
    SHELF

mantelet .... SHELTER, GALAPAGO
mantis crab .... SQUILLA
mantle . CLOAK, CAPE, PALLIUM, FOAM,
    ROBE, SPREAD, PALL, COPE, OCREA
"Mantuan Swan" .... VIRGIL
Manu, laws of .... SUTRA
manual .... PORTAS(S), TUTOR, VADY
"   training SLOYD, SLOID, CRAFT
manumission .... FREEING
manumit ... FREE, LIBERATE, RELEASE
manuscript(s) . FOLIO, CODEX, MS(S),
    CODICES
"   marks, old .... OBELI,
    DORSO
"   , unpublished .. INEDITA
Manxman .... CELT, GAEL
many .... GOBS, LOTS, SCADS, DIVERS
" -colored ... PIED, PINTO, MOTLEY
Maori Adam .... TIKI
"   canoe .... WAKA
"   clan ... RINGATU, ATI, HAPU
"   fuel tree .... MAPAU
"   hand weapon .... PATU
"   hero .... MAUI
"   parrot bird .... TUI
"   raft .... MOGUEY, MOKI
"   rootstock .... ROI
"   wages .... UTU
"   war club .... MERE
map .... CHART, PLAT, CARTE, SKETCH,
    ATLAS, GRAPH
maple cup .... MAZER
"   , flowering .... ABUTILON
"   seed .... SAMARA
" -sugar spout .... SPILE
"   tree .... ACER
mar .. BLEMISH, DEFACE, SCAR, IMPAIR
marabou .... ARGALA, STORK
maraud ...... PLUNDER, ROB, PILLAGE
marauder .... CATERAN
marble ...... AGATE, MIB, TAW, MIG,
    BASALT, DOLOMITE, RANCE, CIPOLIN,
    AGGIE, MARMOR, CARRARA,
    BROCATEL
"Marble Faun" char. .... HILDA
Marceau, Mr. .... MARCEL
march .... FILE, PARADE, HIKE, TRAMP,
    TREAD, ETAPE
March sisters ... AMY, MEG, BETH, JO
Marco Polo's title .... MESSER
Mardi Gras king .... REX
mare .... JADE, YOUD, HORSE
Margaret of Anjou's father .... RENE
margarine .... OLEO
margin FRINGE, BRIM, EDGE, RIM, SIDE,
    BRINK, TURN, VERGE
marginal note ... APOSTIL, SCHOLIUM
"   reading ..... KRI, KERE, KERI
Marianas base .... SAIPAN
"   island .... ROTA

177

marigold ... CAPER, COWSLIP, TAGETES
marihuana cigarette .... REEFER
marine . NAVAL, OCEANIC, NAUTICAL,
 NERTICAL, SEASCAPE, PELAGIC,
 SEAAPE, SEADEVIL, SEADOG,
 LEATHERNECK, TAR
 " : benthonic plant ..... ENALID
 " calcareous skeleton ... CORAL
 " , English .... JOLLY
 " individuals .... MERPEOPLE
 " plant group .... BENTHOS
 " : whale food .... BRIT
mariner .... JACKY, SALT, WATERMAN,
 TAR, GOB, SEAMAN, SAILOR
mariner's compass card .... ROSE
 " compass, points of RHUMBS
marjoram .... MINT, ORIGAN
mark ..... TRAIT, BRAND, DOT, LABEL,
 TARGET, SIGN, STAMP, CATCHET
 " , critical .... OBELUS
 " , diacritic .... BREVE, TILDE
 " for identification .... DAGGER,
 EARMARK
 " for omission .... DELE
 " in curling .... TEE
 " of disgrace .... STIGMA
 " of omission .... CARET
 " over a vowel .... MACRON
 " , printer's ...... DIESIS, OBELISK
 " with a pointed instrument ....
 SCRIVE
 " with scars .... ENSEAM
Mark Twain .... CLEMENS, SAM
marked with rounded sables ....
 PELLETED
 " with spots .... NOTATE
marker ... PYLON, CHIP, META, STELA,
 STELE, SCORER, MONITOR
market(s) ..... MART, FORUM, FORA,
 RIALTO, AGORA, EMPORIUM, SOUK,
 BAZA(A)R, TRADE
marksman ..... SHOT, AIMER, SNIPER
marl .... GREENSAND, MALM
marlinspike .... FID
marmalade .... CONFECTION
 " tree .... ACHRAS, SAPOTEA
marmoset .. SAGOIN, MONKEY, MICO,
 TAMARIN
marmot ..... BOBAC, RODENT, PAHMI,
 SUSLIK
marmota .... ARCTOMYS
maroon ... ABANDON, SLAVE, ISOLATE
Marpessa's abductor .... IDAS
Marquand's detective .... MOTO
marquee ... SHELTER, TENT, AWNING,
 CANOPY
marquetry material .... NACRE
marriage ...... ESPOUSAL, WEDLOCK,
 NUPTIALS, MOTA, MUTA
 " , absence of .... AGAMY

 " broker .... SCHATCHEN
 " contract .... KETUBA
 " , hater of ..... MISOGAMIST
 " notice .... BANS
 " outside the tribe . EXOGAMY
 " , second DIGAMY, DIGAMOUS
marriage settlement DOS, DOT, MAHR,
 DOWRY, DOWERY
 " vows .... TROTH
marriageable .... NUBILE
marrow MEDULLA, PITH, ESSENCE, SAP,
 SUET, KEEST
marry .... WED, WIVE
Mars .... ARES
 " , green belt on .... LIBYA
 " , per. to ..... AREAN, MARTIAN
 " , priests of .... SALII
 " red .... COLCOTHAR, TOTEM
 " , spot on .... OASIS
"Marseillaise" author .. ROUGET, LISLE
Marseilles soap .... CASTILE
marsh ..... LERNA, QUAG, BOG, FEN,
 MORASS, MIRE, SLUE, SWALE,
 MAREMMA
 " bird .... SORA, STILT, SNIPE
 " crocodile .... GOA
 " , drained .... DAM
 " fever ... TRAIDENUM, HELODES
 " gas ...... FIREDAMP, METHANE
 " grass .... SEDGE
 " harrier .... HARPY
 " hawk .... HARRIER
 " plant ..... BULRUSH, IVA, TULE
 " rosemary .... MOORWORT
marshal GUIDE, RANGE, USHER, ALINE,
 ARRAY
Marshal of France NEY, PETAIN, MURAT
Marshall island .. EBON, MILI, NAMUR,
 RALIK, RATAK
marshmallow .... ALTEA
marshy ...... BOGGY, FENNY, WET,
 PALUDINE, PALUDAL
marsupial .... KOALA, OPOSSUM,
 KANGAROO, TAPOA, TAFA, WOMBAT
marten .... FISHER, SABLE
Martinique volcano .... PELEE
marvel .... PRODIGY, WONDER
Maryland county ... ANNEARUNDEL,
 CECIL, HOWARD, KENT, TALBOT
Marx CHICO, GROUCHO, HARPO, KARL
masculine .... MANLY, MAS, VIRILE
Masefield poem .... CARGOES
mask . VISOR, CLOAK, DOMINO, VEIL,
 LOUP, BLIND, ONKOS, SCREEN
masked .... HIDDEN, LARVATE
 " comedy .... SCAPINO
masker .... MUMMER, DOMINO
Masonic doorkeeper .... TILER
mason's mixing rod .... RAB
masquerade . (DIS)GUISE, MUMM(ERY)

mass . WAD, BULK, LUMP, NODE, PILE, BOLUS, TUMOR, GATHER, COLLECT
Mass book .... MISSAL
mass, confused .... GOB
Mass directory .... ORDO
mass of coal .... JUD(D)
   " , per. to a .. MOLAR, MISSATICAL
Mass vestment .... AMICE
Massachusetts city ..... LYNN, SALEM, WARE
   " county BRISTOL, DUKES, ESSEX, SUFFOLK
   " state flower .. ARBUTUS
massacre CARNAGE, HAVOC, POGROM, DECIMATE
massage .... KNEAD, RUB
massager .... MASSEUR, MASSEUSE
Massenet opera .... MANON, SAPPHO, THAIS
Massey, Miss .... ILONA
mast ACORNS, NUTS, SPAR, BIBB, POON
   " supports .... STEPS
master .... BAAS, BOSS, HEAD, LORD, MIAN, RAB(B)I, CHIEF, SAHIB, ARTIST, EXPERT
   " of ceremonies .... MC, EMCEE
   " of Syracuse .... DION
   " , per. to.............. HERILE
   " stroke .... COUP
   " , to ...... CONQUER, SUBDUE, SUBJECT, MANAGE
mastery . SKILL, VICTORY, GREE, SWAY, ASCENDANCY
mastic .... RESIN, GUM
mastodon .... GIANT, MAMMOTH
mat ... SNARL, TWIST, BOLSTER, YAPA, BANIG
Mata Hari .... SPY
Mataco .... APAR, INDIAN
matador's garment .... CAPE
   " staff .... MULETA
   " sword .... ESTOQUE
match ... TALLY, COPY, MATE, LUCIFER, FUSEE, PEER, PIT, VESTA, RIVAL, CONTEST
   " in politics ..... LOCOFOCO
   " or class .... SORT, EQUAL
matchless .... ALONE, PEERLESS
mate ... PAIR, FERE, MARRY, CONSORT
materia medica .... ACOLOGY
_____ mater .... ALMA, DURA, PIA
material ...... HYLIC, PLASMA, STUFF, SWATCH, REAL, VITAL
   " for embroidery ... ARRASENE
   " for glassmaking ...... FRIT
   " , silk ... SATIN, TULLE, FAILLE,
   " , upholstery ..SCRIM, LAMPAS
maternal relationship ...... ENATION
matgrass .... MARRAM, NARD
math .... MOWING

mathe .... GRUB, MAGGOT
mathematical constant ... PARAMETER
   " diagram .... GRAPH
   " function .... (CO)SINE, TANGENT
   " instr. .. NABLA, VERNIER
   " line .. VECTOR, SECANT
   " number .. RADIX, SURD, SCALAR
   " surface .... NAPPE
   " symbol DIGIT, FACIEND, OPERAND
   " term .... PLUS, MINUS, COSH, TANH
mathematician .... EUCLID, ALBIRUNI, CREMONA, KELVIN, VIETA, LAPLACE, NEWTON, GAUSS, RUSSELL, FERMAT, NAPIER, PASCAL, EULER
matinee LEVEE, SALON, SOIREE, PARTY
matrass .... BOLTHEAD
matriculate .... ENROL, ENTER, ADMIT
matrix ..... BED, MOULD, CAST, FORM
matrix ores, bed in .... GANGUE
matter ...... BODY, PITH, PUS, GEAR, ELEMENTS, ATOMS, HYLE, THEME, IMPORT
matthiola .... STOCK
mattock-like ...... ADZ, AXE, PICKAX
mature .... PERFECT, AGE, DIGEST, RIPE(N), SEASON, COMPLETE, MELLOW
maturing early .... RATHRIPE
Mau Mau land .... KENYA
maudlin .... BEERY, TIPSY, WEEPY
   " state ...... TEARFUL, FUDDLED
Maugham heroine .... SADIE
   " play .... RAIN
maul .. BEETLE, MALLET, MOTH, GAVEL, DAMAGE, DEFORM, MANGLE
Mauna _____ .... LOA
mauve .... VIOLET, MALLOW
maverick .... CALF, DOGIE, STRAY
maw .... CRAW, CROP, STOMACH
mawkish .... SICKLY, STALE, VAPID
maxilla .... JAW(BONE)
maxim .. MOTTO, GNOME, RULE, SAW, AXIOM, ADAGE, APHORISM, LOGIA, TRUISM
Maxwell, Miss .... ELSA
May apple .... MANDRAKE
May first .... BELTANE
   " fly .... DUN, EPHEMERID
   " tree .... HAWTHORN
Mayan Indian .... MAM
   " year .... HAAB
   " year-end day of calendar .... UAYEB
Mayence, Count of ...... GAN(ELON)
mayfish .... KILLFISH
mayflower .... ARBUTUS, HAWTHORN

179

mayor .... ALCALDE, ALCADE
mazed .... MEANDERED, LOST
Mazo de la Roche work ..... JALNA
McCambridge, Miss ..... MERCEDES
McLaglen's role .... INFORMER
mead .... HYDROMEL, METHEGLIN
meadow .. SWALE, BAAN, LEA, VEGA,
         WANG, WONG
 "   mice .... ARVICOLA
 "   mouse .... VOLE
 "   sweet; genus .... SPIREA
Meadows, Miss .... JAYNE
meager .... ARID, BARE, SCANT, SLIM,
       PUNY, JEJUNE
meal MESS, POWDER, REPAST, RATION,
    TIFFIN, BRAN, MASA, AT(T)A,
     CENA, TEA, SNACK
mealy .... FARINACEOUS, PALE
mean . SNIDE, MEDIAL, AVERAGE, BASE,
   SMALL, LOW, PAR, AGENT, IMPLY,
   MODUS, CONVEY, IMPORT
meaning .... PURPORT, SENSE
meaningless refrain .... DERRY
means .... AGENT, AGENCY, REVENUE,
       PROPERTY
meantime ....INTERVAL, INTERIM
measles .... MORBILLIN, RUBEOLA
measure .. DOSE, GAGE, METE, SCAN,
   SIZE, GAUGE, EXTENT, COMPUTE,
   STANDARD, METER, TIME, STEP,
       ROTL
 " , Annam .... SAO, TAC, MAU
 " , Argentine .... VARA
 " , biblical . CAB, CUBIT, EPHAH,
      HIN, HOMER, SPAN
 " , Brazil .... PE, LEGOA, MILHA
 " , Chinese CHANG, CHIH, TSUN,
         TU
 " , Chinese; rood LI
 " , cloth, of length ..... ELL
 " , Cuban .... TAREA
 " , dry; Egypt .... ARDEB
 " , dry; Heb. .... CAB, EPHA(H),
       OMER, KOR
 " , dry; Tunisian ... SAA, SAH
 " , Dutch .... AAM, ANKER
 " , Dutch E. Ind. . DEPA, PARAH
 " , Eng. land .... MANENT
 " , foot .... ANAPEST
 " for vibrations .... SIRENE
 " , French (old) . MINOT, TOISE
 " , herring; British ..... CRAN
 " , Indian ...... ADOULIE, GUZ
 " , Indo-Persian ..... GAZ, GUZ
 " , Japanese ... MO, RI, RIN, SE,
        SHO
 " , Javanese ...... PAAL, PALEN
 " , land ... ACRE, AR, ARE, MILE
 " , land; Swiss ...... IMI, IMMI
 " , Libyan .... DRA

 " , liquid .... CARGA, TIERCE
 " , liquid, bib. DRAM, HIN, LOG
 " , liquid; Phil. I. ..... APATAN
 " , Malacca .... ASTA
 " , medicinal .... HEMINA
 " : meter cube .... STERE
 " , metric .... ARE, MICRON
 " , music .... CODA
 " , nautical .... KNOT
 " , Netherlands KAN, STREEP, EL
 " of capacity .... CASK, CRAN,
       ORNA
 " of distance; Ind. var. . COSS,
       KOS
 " of Earth .... GEODESY
 " of length ... CUBIT, MIKRON,
    PACE, METER, ROD, PERCH
 " of length; anc. .... TOISE
 " of length; Russian .... VERST
 " of length; Turkey .. DRA, PIK
 " of length: ¾ of an inch DIGIT
 " of length: 2¼ inches . NAIL
 " of magnetism .... GAUSS
 " of Rangoon .... LAN
 " of sounds .... DECIBEL
 " of two metrical feet . DIPODY
 " of weight ... GRAM, METAGE,
       BALE
 " of wine in cask .... BUTT
 " ; 160 perches .... ACRE
 " , Persian .... PARASANG
 " , Scandinavian .... ALEN
 " , Siamese .... SESTI
 " , Spanish .... VARA, LINEA
 " , Tunisian ...... SAA, SAAH
 " , Turkish ALMUD, DJERIB, OKA
 " , wire .... MIL
"Measure for Measure" char. . LUCIO,
   ANGELO, ELBOW, FROTH, JULIET
measurement ... METAGE, SUBSTANCE
measuring instrument .... ALIDAD(E),
    STADIA, SCALE, TAPE, RULE
 " rod .... CALIPER
meat .... FLESH, KERNEL, SOD, FRIGO
 " balls .... RAVIOLI
 " , cut of . FILET, BRISKET, ICEBONE
 " , dried and cured HAM, BILTONG,
       PEMMICAN
 " eaters .... CARNIVORA
 " , fat .... SPECK
 " jelly .... ASPIC
 " , minced ..... SANDERS, RISSOLE
 " pie .... PASTY
 " , piece of .. COLP, COLLOP, RAND
 " , preserve .... CORN
 " , ragout of ..... HARICOT, SALMI
 " roasted on a stick ..... CABOB,
      KABOB, KEBAB
meatless .... MAIGRE, LENTEN
meatus .. CANAL, OPENING, PASSAGE

Mecca, pilgrimage to .... HADJ
   " pilgrim's dress .... IHRAM
   " , shrine at .... KAABA
mechanical INVOLUNTARY, AUTOMATIC
   " man .... GOLEM, ROBOT,
                 AUTOMATON
mechanism .. RIGGING, TACKLE, GEAR
medal .... BADGE, CAMEO, PLAQUE,
           TABLET, MEDALLION
meddle .. TEMPER, OBTRUDE, FUSS,
               SNOOP, PRY
Medea's father .... AEETES
median ..... MEAN, MESNE, AVERAGE
   " line of valve .... RAPHE
   " plane .... MESIAL
Median prince .... REBA
mediant .... THIRD, MODE
mediate .... CHEW, OPINE, HALVE
mediator .... ARBITER, REFEREE,
                 UMP(IRE)
medic .... DOC
medical .... CURATIVE, IATRIC
   " compound .... HEPAR
   " drug .... SENNA
   " group .... AMA
   " monster .... TERAS
   " officer .... CORONER
   " science, div. of .... THERAPY
   " suffix ..... ITIS, OSIS, OMA
   " treatment; comb. form IATRY,
                 IATRIA
medicate ... CURE, DOSE, DRUG, HEAL
medicated fluid .... LOTION
medicinal herb .... BONESET, CHIRATA
   " plant COHOSH, RUE, SPURGE
   " remedy .... ANTIDOTE
   " root JENA, JALAP, ARTAR
   " tea .... TISANE
medicine administrator ...... DOSER
   " man ...... PRIEST, SHAMAN,
       KAHUNA, PEAI, BASIR, PIAY,
                 PIACHE
   " , quack .... NOSTRUM
   " , science of .. PHYSICS, IATRY
   " , universal .... PANACEA
medicine-like .... PILULAR
mediety; law .... MOIETY
medieval helmet .... ARMET
   " hooked weapon .... ONCIN
   " monster .... WEREWOLF
   " prayer book ..... PORTASS
   " shield .... ECU
Medina citizen converted to Islam ...
                 ANSAR
mediocre .... FAIR, MIDDLING, SOSO
meditate ...... MUSE, PORE, PONDER,
           REFLECT, COGITATE
meditation .... RUMINATION
Mediterranean fruit .... AZAROLE

   " galley .... GALIOT
   " grass .... DISS
   " gulf .... TUNIS
   " island .. GOZO, CRETE,
      CAPRI, MALTA, CORSICA,
      CYPRUS, ELBA, SICILY
   " resort . NICE, CANNES,
              MENTONE
   " , river to . AUDE, EBRO,
      JUCAR, NILE, RHONE
   " ship ... XEBEC, KEBEC,
        SETTEE, ZEBEC
   " storm .... BORASCO
   " tree ..... CAROB, OLEA
   " volcanic is. .... LIPARI
   " wind .... LEVANTER,
        SOLANO, SIROCCO
medium .... MEAN, PSYCHIC, ORACLE,
    PAR, SOSO, AGENT, CHANNEL
medley ... FARRAGO, MELANGE, OLIO,
      POTPOURRI, PASTICHE,
           SALMAGUNDI
   " ; music .... FANTASIA
   " race .... RELAY
medulla .... MARROW, PITH
Medusa .... GORGON
   " , sister of .... STHENO
   " , slayer of .... PERSEUS
meerschaum .... SEAFOAM, SEPIOLITE
meet ..... EQUAL, FIT, MATCH, SEEMLY
meeting .. RALLY, MALL, SYNOD, TRYST,
      JUNCTION, SESSION,
      INDABA, GAM, CAUCUS
   " of Big Three ...... POTSDAM
megalithic chamber .... DOLMEN
megapode .... MALEO
   " , mound-building .. LEIPOA
megrim .... CAPRICE, WHIM
megrims .... HEADACHE, BLUES
Mehitabel .... CAT
"Mein Kampf" author .... HITLER
melancholy ...... TRISTFUL, ATRABILE,
      DREAR, SAD, BLUES, DUMPS,
    GLOOMY, MISERY, SOMBRE, VAPORS
   " , make .... HYP
Melanesian native .... FIJI
   " super-being ...... ADARO
melanous .... BRUNETTE
melee ...... (AF)FRAY RIOT, BRAWL,
         SCRAP, SETTO
melicocca .... GENIP
Melissa .... MINT
melilotus .... CLOVER
melli- .... HONEY
mellow ..... MALM, RIPE, OLD, SOFT,
         DULCET, GENIAL
melodic flourish .... MELISMA
melodious .. ARIOSE, DULCET, ORPHIC,
        ARIOSO, ORPHEAN

melody ... CAVATINA, CHARM, CHIME,
RHYTHM, ROUND, STRAIN, UNISON,
ROSALIA, THEME, ARIA, RAGA
" , per. to .... PLAGAL
meloid .... BEETLE
melon .... PEPO, GOURD, DUDAIM
" -pear .... PEPINO
melt .... RUN, FUSE, SWALE, THAW
" down .... LIQUEFY, RENDER
" ore .... SMELT, CONVERT
Melville char. .... AHAB, MOBY(DICK)
" novel .... TYPEE, OMOO
member .... ORGAN, PART, LIMB
membrane ..... PIA, SKIN, WEB, FILM,
FOLD, TELA, VELA
" , a fold of .... PLICA
" covering brain ....
MENINGES, MATER
" , diffusion through OSMOSIS
membranous fringe .... LOMA
memento .. RELIC, KEEPSAKE, BIBELOT,
CURIO, SOUVENIR
memorabilia .... ANA
memorandum ... CHIT, NOTE, MINUTE
" book ..... NOTANDUM,
TICKLER
memorial .... EBENEZER, RECORD,
TROPHY, TOTEM
memorist .... PROMPTER
memory .... MIND, ROTE
" , loss of ..... AMNESIA, LETHE
" , per. to .... MNESIC,
MNEMONIC
Memphis god .... PTAH
mend ... COBBLE, PATCH, DARN, HEAL,
REPAIR, BETTER
mendacity .... DECEIT, FIB, LIE
mender .... TINKER, COBBLER
mendicant ... FAKIR, BEGGAR, NAGA,
EUCHITE
meniscus .... LENS
Mennonite sect .... AMISH
meno .... LESS
Menotti .... GIANCARLO
men's underwear .... SKIVVIES
mental .... PHRENIC, CEREBRAL
" disorder .. PARANOIA, DEMENTIA
" state .... DOLDRUM, MORALE
mentality .... SANITY, SENSE
mention ... CITE, REFER, MIND, NAME,
ALLUDE
Mentum .... CHIN
menu .... CARTE, FARE, DIET
Menuhin .... YEHUDI
mercenary ... HESSIAN, HACK, HIRED,
VENAL, HIRELING,
MYRMIDON
merchandise .... WARES, GOODS,
STOCK
" , per. to .... EMPOREUTIC

merchant .... TRADER, MONGER,
DEALER, SELLER, VENDOR, SETH
" guild .... HANSE
" vessel .... INDIAMAN
"Merchant of Venice" ..... ANTONIO
" " " char. .. NERISSA,
JESSICA, LORENZO, PORTIA,
SHYLOCK, TUBAL
merciless .... CRUEL, FELL, FERAL,
SAVAGE
Mercury .... HERMES
" , son of .... ELEUSIS
" , staff of .... CADUCEUS
" , winged cup of ..... PETASUS
" , winged shoes of ... TALARIA
mercy .... GRACE, PITY, LENITY, RUTH,
PARDON, QUARTER
" killing .... EUTHANASIA
merely .... ONLY, BARELY, SOLELY
merganser ..... HARLE, HERALD, NUN,
SMEE, SMEW, GOOSANDER
merge ...... WED, FUSE, JOIN, BLEND
merger .... FUSION, UNION
meridian ...... APEX, ZENITH, NOON,
ACME
merino....................... WOOL
merit .... EARN, MEED, WORTH
Merkel, Miss .... UNA
merry .. BLITHE, JOCOSE, JOYFUL, GAI
merry-andrew .... JOKER, ANTIC,
JESTER, ACROBAT, MIME
merry-go-round .... CAROUSEL
merry-making .... REVEL
merrythought .... WISHBONE
"Merry Widow" composer .... LEHAR
"Merry Wives of Windsor" char. ....
SLENDER, CAIUS, FENTON, FORD,
NYM, PAGE, PISTOL, ROBIN, RUGBY
mescal ...... CACTUS, PEYOTE, SOTOL
mesh .... NET, MITOME, TISSUE
mesial plane, toward .... MESAD
mesmeric force .... OD
Mesopotamia .... IRAQ, IRAK
" city .... EDESSA
" northwest wind . SHAMAL
mesquite .... ALGAROBA, PACAY,
PROSOPIS
" bean flour .... PINGLE
mess .... CHOW, BOTCH, BUNGLE,
LITTER, POTTER, CONFUSE
message .... BODE, BREVET, EVANGEL,
MEMO, TIDINGS
messenger .... APOSTLE, NUNCIO,
SAND, TOTY, ENVOY, IRIS, HERALD,
MERCURY, COURIER
" , mounted . ESTAFET, REVERE
Messina rock .... SCYLLA
met ...... AGREED, EQUALED, TRYSTED
metal bar on door .... RISP
" , bar of .... INGOT

"	clippings	SCISSEL
"	, coarse	MATTE
"	coat	PATINA
"	filings	LEMEL
"	fissure	LODE
"	, heavy	LEAD
"	, impure	REGULUS
"	ingot	GAD
"	, lightest	LITHIUM
"	, lump of	PIG
"	plates, thin .	FOIL, SHIM, LAMES
"	refuse	SLAG
"	shaper	SWAGE
"	, silver-white	CALCIUM
"	, to ornament	DAMASKEEN
"	-ware	REVERE, TOLE
"	-worker	WELDER, SMITH, VULCAN
"	zinc blende	GALLIUM

metallic alloy .... SOLDER
" chemical element ...... COBALT,
TERBIUM
" content, having .... ORY
" element ..... LUTECIUM, ERBIUM,
YTTRIUM
" oxide .... OCHRE
metamere ...... SOMATOME, SOMITE
metamorphosis .. CHANGE, MUTATION
" , stage of .... PUPA
metaphor ...... SIMILE, TRALATITION,
TROPE, IMAGE, ANALOGY
meteor ..... BIELID, LEONID, FIREBALL,
BOLIDE, BOLIS
" , mark of .... CRATER
meteors, shower of ..... ANDROMEDE
meter ...... RHYTHM, CADENCE, TIME,
VERSE, GAUGE
" , cubic .... STERE
" , gas .... WET
" , millionth of a .... MICRON
" unit .... MORA
meters, one hundred sq. .... AR, ARE
methane .... PARAFFIN
metheglin .... MEAD
method .. SYSTEM, WAY, MODE, PLAN
" of aircraft navigation NAVAR
methylbenzene .... TOLUENE
methyl ketols .... ACETOLS
meticulous one .... PURIST
métier .... WORK, TRADE
metis .... MULATTO
metric measure ...... ARE, CENTARE,
TONNE, LITRE, STERE, DECARE
metric-system comb. form ..... DECI,
CENTI
metric weight .... GRAM, KILO
metrical foot ...... ANAPEST, IAMB,
IAMBUS, ARSIS, CHORIAMB,
TROCHEE, IONIC
stress of voice .... ICTUS
metropolitan .... (ARCH)BISHOP

Metz's river .... MOSELLE
Meuse river .... MAAS
mew .... STABLE, CAGE, DEN, GARAGE
" , a ...... COB, GULL, SEAGULL
" ; as a cat .... MIAOW, MIAUL
" , in the .... MOLT
mewl .... WHIMPER
Mexican American .... GRINGO
" basket grass .... OTATE
" beverage .... PULQUE
" bird .... TINAMOU
" blanket .... SERAPE
" brigand .... LADRONE
" cactus .... MESCAL
" cat .... MARGAY, EYRA
" city .... JALAPA, OAXACA,
ORIZABA, TEPIC
" clover .... COCA
" coin .... TLAC, TLACO
" composer .... CHAVEZ
" coral drops .... BESSERA
" dish .... TAMALE, TORTILLA
" dollar .... PESO
" drug .... DAMIANA
" early dweller ... AZTEC, MAYA
" fiber plant .. .. DATIL, ISTLE,
PITA, SISAL, IXTLE
" foodfish .... SALEMA
" foot covering .... HUARACHO
" gopher .... TUCOTUCO
" gruel .... ATOLE
" hut .... JACAL
" Indian OTOMI, AZTEC, OPATA,
SERI, LIPAN, TOLTEC, MAYAN
" intoxicating drink ... MESCAL
" laborer .... PEON
" lake .... CHAPALA
" landmark .... SENAL
" masonry .... ADOBE
" mat .... PETATE
" money .... CUARTO
" noble .... HIDALGO
" octoroon .... ALBINO
" of mixed blood ..... MESTIZO
" painter .... OROZCO, RIVERA,
SIQUEIROS
" persimmon .... CHAPOTE
" pine .... OCOTE
" plant .... AGAVE
" plant, soap .... AMOLE
" plantation .... HACIENDA
" policeman .... RURAL
" porridge .... ATOLE
" president .... MADERO, ORTIZ,
ALEMAN, CALLES, DIAZ, HUERTA,
JUAREZ
" proprietor .... RANCHERO
" pyramid .... TEOCALLI
" race .... TOLTEC
" reed .... OTATE

"	resort .... ACAPULCO	migratory worker .... OKIE, JOAD
"	river ..... CONCHOS, FUERTE, SALADO, TONTO, YAQUI	Mikado, court of .... DAIRI
"	saloon .... CANTINA	Milan opera house .... SCALA
"	sauce .... TABASCO	mild .. BLAND, MEEK, BENEDICT, SOFT, MOY, SHY, SUAVE, GENTLE
"	scarf .... TAPALO	" offense .... DELIT
"	seaport .... TAMPICO	mildew ..... BLIGHT, MO(U)LD, MUST, FUNGUS, ROT
"	shawl .... SERAPE	mile, nautical, per hour .... KNOT
"	state .... COLIMA, DURANGO, JALISCO, SONORA, MORELOS, TABASCO, YUCATAN, SINALOA, HIDALGO	Miled's son .... IR
"	stirrup cover ...... TAPADERA	milestone .... STELE, MARKER
"	sugar .... PANOCHA	milfoil .... YARROW
"	thong .... ROMAL	milieu ENVIRON, MEDIUM, BET, SETTING
"	throwing stick .... ATLATL	military .. SOLDIERY, MARTIAL, MILITIA
"	town ...... MORELIA, AMECA, TORREON	" cap ...... BUSBY, KEPI, SHAKO
"	volcano .. COLIMA, JORULLO	" cloak .... SAGUM

migratory worker .... OKIE, JOAD
Mikado, court of .... DAIRI
Milan opera house .... SCALA
mild .. BLAND, MEEK, BENEDICT, SOFT,
          MOY, SHY, SUAVE, GENTLE
   " offense .... DELIT
mildew ..... BLIGHT, MO(U)LD, MUST,
               FUNGUS, ROT
mile, nautical, per hour .... KNOT
Miled's son .... IR
milestone .... STELE, MARKER
milfoil .... YARROW
milieu ENVIRON, MEDIUM, BET, SETTING
military .. SOLDIERY, MARTIAL, MILITIA
   " cap ...... BUSBY, KEPI, SHAKO
   " cloak .... SAGUM
   " craft .... LST
   " device .... CROC
   " division .... UNIT, CORPS
   " engine .... ONAGER, ROBINET
   " force .... ARMY, LEGION
   " landing pt. ...... BEACHHEAD
   " messenger .... ESTAFET
   " rank .... BANNER, COLONELCY
   " salute .... SALVO
   " signal .... CHAMADE
   " storehouse ETAPE, ARSENAL, PX
   " truck .... CAMION
militate .... FIGHT
milk . LAC(TOSE), CURD, WHEY, WHIG,
    CLABBER, KOUMISS, LEGAN, TAYIR
   " coagulator .... RENNET
   " , curd from .... CASEIN
   " fish .... AWA, SABALO
   " food .... LACTICINIA
   " pail .... ESHIN
   " , per. to .... LACTIC
   " -weed fluid .... LATEX
   " whey .... SERUM
Milky Way .... GALAXY
mill .... (K)NURL, QUERN, ARRASTRA,
            GRIND(ER), PRESS
millepore .... CORAL
miller .... MOTH, FLY
millet ...... PEARL, HIRSE, CHENA
millimeter, thousandth part of ......
                 MICRON
million deaths .... MEGADEATH
   " , thousand .... MILLIARD
   " tons .... MEGATON
millionth part of an ohm .. MICROHM
millpond .... DAM, DIKE, DITCH
millstone, part of .... RYND, INK
mill-wheel float .... LADE
Milquetoast, Mr. .... CASPAR
Milton's "Regent of the Sun" . URIEL
mime ... APER, ACTOR, IMITATE, COPY
mimic ..... APE, MOCK, SHAM, FEIGN
mimicry .... PARROTRY, APISM, ECHO,
               MIMESIS

Meyerbeer opera .... AFRICAINE
mezereon .... DAPHNE
mezzanine .... ENTRESOL
Miami's county .... DADE
miasma .... MALARIA
mica BIOTITE, GLIST, ISINGLASS, TALC
   " : chlorite .... RIPIDOLITE
   " , lithia .... LEPIDOLITE
mice; genus .... MUS
   " of India .... METADS
Michigan county .. ALGER, BAY, CASS,
    CLARE, DELTA, IONIA, IOSCO,
    IRON, KENT, LAKE, LUCE, WAYNE
   " river .... CASS
   " state capital ...... LANSING
   " town .. ECORSE, HOLT, FLINT
microbe .... BACTERIUM, GERM, VIRUS
microcosm .... WORLD, MONAD
microscopic alga .... DIATOM
   " organism ..... AMOEBA, AMEBA
microspores .... POLLEN
middle ...... CENTRY, MESIAL, MESNE,
    MEDIAL, FOCUS, WAIST, HUB, CORE
   " -class .... MIDDLEBROW
   " ; comb. form ...... MEDI, MES
   " , toward the .... MESAD
middling ...... AVERAGE, SOSO, FAIR
midge ..... FLY, GNAT, PUNKIE, STOUT
Midianite prince REBA, HUR, EVI, ZUR
mid-Lent Sunday .... LAETARE
midriff .... DIAPHRAGM
midshipman .... REEFER, CADET, PLEBE
"Midsummer Night's Dream" char. ..
    EGEUS, HERMIA, OBERON, PUCK,
    QUINCE, SNOUT, SNUG, THESEUS,
               THISBE
midwife .... DHAI, HEBAMME
mien ..... GUISE, LOOK, AIR, OSTENT
mighty . POTENT, VALIANT, FELL, VAST
mignonette .... RESEDA
migration .... TREK, EXODUS

184

mince .... CUT, HASH, SLASH, DICE
minced meat .... RISSOLE
    "   oath .. BEGAD, DRAT, EGAD,
                                    ODS
mind ..... NOUS, MOOD, RECK, CARE,
              HEED, OBEY, TEND, MENS
    " , peace of .... ATARAXIA
Mindanao language .... ATA
    "   town .... DAVAO
    "   volcano .... APO
mine BONANZA, PIT, SAP, LODE, VEIN
    " coal .... ROB
    " : deviate from vertical ... HADE
    " entrance .... ADIT
    " horizontal passage ..... STULM
    " ; Lat. .... MEUM
    " partition .... SOLLAR
    " prop .... STULL, SPRAG
    " rubbish .... GOAF, GOB
    " shaft, place in for water ......
                           STANDAGE
    " shaft, step in .... STEMPEL
    " : stepwise excavation ... STOPE
    " -sweeper .... PARAVANE
    " -tender of air doors .... TRAPPER
    " tub .... CORF
    " unsystematically ...... GOPHER
    " ; Welsh .... BAL
    " -worker COLLIER, CAGER, SAPPER
mineral .... ORE
    " , amorphous .... PINITE
    " , black . URANINITE, GRAPHITE
    " : carbonate of lime . CALCITE
    " caoutchouc ...... ELATERITE
    " , crystalline .... FELSPAR
    " deposit ...... LODE, SINTER
    " deposit (not a vein) . PLACER
    " , gray-white .... TRONA
    " , hard ...... ALALITE, SPINEL
    " jelly .... VASELINE
    " matter: mix .... MAGMA
    " oil .... COLZA
    " , pale-yellow . EPIDOTE, PYRITE
    " : phosphate of lime . APATITE
    " : pitch .... ASPHALT
    " : plaster of paris .... GYPSUM
    " : pulp .... TALC
    " , rare brittle THORITE, EUCLASE
    " salt .... ALUM
    " silicate .... MICA
    " tar .... MALTHA
    " water ...... VITCHY, SELTZER
    " , whitish ..... BARITE, SPALT
    " , yellow-green ...... EPIDOTE
miner's basket .... DAN, CORF
    " chisel .... GAD
    " mandrel .... PICK
    " safety lamp .... DAVY
    " surveying inst. .... DIAL

Minerva .... ATHENA, AZALEA
    " shield of .... EGIS
mines, guardian of .... GNOME
mingle ...... ADMIX, COALESCE, MELL,
               WEAVE, MERGE, MIX
miniate .... RUBRICATE
minimum .... JOT, LEAST, TITTLE
mining surveyor .... DIALER
minim JOT, DROP, TITTLE, WHIT, DASH,
                     MITE, TAWNY
minion .. FAVORITE, IDOL, HANGERON
minister CURATE, TEND, SERVE, ENVOY,
            DOMINIE, NUNCIO, NURSE
Minnesota Centre .... SAUK
Minnesota county CASS, CLAY, COOK,
    LAKE, LYON, PINE, POLK, POPE,
       RICE, ROCK, SCOTT, TODD
minor .. SMALLER, LESS, YOUTH, MOLL
minorate .... CURTAIL
minoress .... CLARE
minority . NONAGE, PUPILAGE, TEENS
Minos' daughter .... ARIADNE
minstrel ..... BARD, GLEEMAN, POET,
   RIMER, HARPER, PIERROT, GOLIARD,
         SKALD, BHAT, AREOI
mint . CHIA, COIN, HYSSOP, RAMONA,
        STAMP, FRESH, INVENT
    " charge .... BRASSAGE
    " family .... CALAMINT
    " ; genus .... MENTHA
    " , mountain .... BASIL
    " , rel. to; Sp. .... YERBA
    " sauce .... MONEY
    " -seasoned .... SAGY
minuet's replacement ...... SCHERZO
minuscule .... PETTU, LETTER
minute TRIFLING, ITEM, NOTE, ACTUM,
    MEMO, TINY, MOMENT, INSTANT
minx ... GIRL, JADE, COLLEEN, DOLL,
                    MISS
miracle ...... ANOMY, MARVEL, PLAY,
           PRODIGY, WONDER
    " scene ...... CANA, LOURDES
    " -worker ...... THAUMATURGE
mirage ...... SERAB, ILLUSION, VISION
Miranda's father .... PROSPERO
Miranda; actress .... CARMEN, ISA
mire .... GLAR, ADDLE, MOIL, SLUDGE,
              OOZE, MUD, FEN
mirror CRYSTAL, SPECULUM, REFLECTOR,
                   IMAGE
    " , per. to a .... CATOPTRIC
mirth .... FUN, GLEE, SPLEEN
miry ... OOZY, SLIMY, BOGGY, LUTOSE
misanthrope ... HATER, TIMON, CYNIC
miscellany .... ANA, SUNDRIES
mischief .... ATE, ILL, WRACK
misdemeanor .. OFFENSE, SIN, CRIME,
       TORT, FAULT, MISDEED
misdirect ...... PERVERT, LIE, MYSTIFY

miser ..... HUNKS, NABAL, NIGGARD, SCROOGE, SKINFLINT
miserly . CLOSE, SORDID, NEAR, TIGHT, GNEDE, STINGY
misery . GRIEF, HEARTACHE, CHAGRIN, WOE, DOLOR, PENURY
misfortune .... HARM, ILLS, CALAMITY, TRIAL
mishmash ...... OLIO, HASH, JUMBLE
Mishna festivals .... MOED
" section .... ABOT(H)
mislead .... DELUDE, DECEIVE
mismanage .... BUNGLE, BLUNK
mispronunciation .... CACOLOGY
miss .... ESCAPE, FAIL, LACK
missile ...... LANCE, ARROW, BULLET, OUTCAST, GRENADE, NIKE, THOR, ATLAS
missing .... ABSENT, LOST, WANTING, TRUANT
Mississippi county PONTOTOC, LAMAR, CLAY, HINDS, LEE, PIKE, TATE, YAZOO
" fish ...... CRAPET, CRAPPIE
" nickname .... BAYOU
" resort .... BILOXI
Missouri county .. ADAIR, CASS, CLAY, COLE, DADE, DENT, HOLT, IRON, KNOX, LYNN, PIKE, POLK, RALLS, RAY, OZARK
" river Indian .... SAC
misspelling .... CACOGRAPHY
mist . SMUR, HARR, BRUME, DIM, MISLE, SEREIN, FOG, DROW, HAZE
mistake ...... BONER, BARNEY, BULL
" in date ...... ANACHRONISM
" in writing .... ERRATUM
" of syntax .... SOLECISM
mister .... SIR, DON, GOODMAN, MONSIEUR, SENOR, HERR, BABU
mistress DOXY, BEEBEE, DULCINEA, MRS
Mitchell, Helen Porter ...... MELBA
mite .... ATOM, MOTE, SPECK, ACARID
miter .. FILLET, GUSSET, TIARA, TIMBRE
miterworts .... TIARELLA
mites .... ACARI, ACARINA
mithridate .... ANTIDOTE
mitigate . TEMPER, EASE, ABATE, ALLAY, PACIFY, ASSUAGE
mix .. STIR, CONSORT, JUMBLE, KNEAD
" clay .... PUG
" wine .... PART
" with water .... SLAKE
" with yeast .... BARM
" up .... SNAFU
mixable .... MISCIBLE
mixed-blood person .. METIS, GRIFFE, MESTEE, MUSTEE, MESTIZO, MULATTO, OCTAROON
mixed type .... PI

mixer .... RAB
mixture .... AMALGAM, HASH, SALAD, MELANGE, OLIO, MONG, FARRAGO
Mizar, small star near ..... LACOR
mizzle .... MIST, DRIZZLE
moa .... DINORNIS, RATITE
" , relative of the .... APTERYX
Moab people .... EMIMS
moan . GROAN, CRY, LAMENT, BEWAIL, COMPLAIN
moat ... FOSS, GRAFFE, CANAL, DITCH, TRENCH
mob ROUT, THRONG, CANAILLE, HERD, DROVE, GANG, PRESS, RUCK, RABBLE
"mobile" sculpture .... CALDER
mobster's girl .... MOLL
"Moby Dick" author ...... MELVILLE
" " pursuer .... AHAB
moccasin .... PAC, LARRIGAN
mock ...... GIBE, DERIDE, APE, FLOUT, MIMIC, SCOFF, FLEER, JEER
" blow .... FEINT
" jewelry ..... LOGIE, IMITATION
mockery .... FARCE, SHAM, TRAVESTY, DELUSION, RIDICULE
" , evil spirit of ...... MOMUS
mockingbird .... MOWER
" ; genus .... MIMUS
mock orange ..... SERINGA, SYRINGA
mode ..... FAD, VOGUE, STYLE, FLAIR, TENOR, DRIFT, TREND
model . SITTER, GAUGE, NORM, SHAPE, MANIKIN, PARADIGM, PARAGON, ARCHETYPE, STANDARD, POSE
moderate ...... BATE, SOME, FRUGAL, LESSEN, TEMPER(ATE), CALM, PRESIDE
modern ...... NEO(TERIC), LATE, NEW, NOVEL
" school of art .... DADA
modest ..... CIVIL, COY, SHY, DEMURE
modified leaf .... BRACT
modify ...... ALTER, TEMPER, MASTER, AMEND, REVISE, VARY
modulate .... INFLECT, ADAPT, ATTUNE
mogul ... LORD, NABOB, MONGOLIAN
Mohammed ... MAHOMET, MAHOUND
" , adopted son of .... ALI
" , birthplace of ..... MECCA
" , burial place of .. MEDINA
" , daughter of ...... FATIMA
" , supporters of .... ANSAR
" , wife of .... AISHA
Mohammed-Malay law .... ADAT
Mohammed's flight from Mecca ... HEGIRA
" successor .... CALIF
Mohammedan ablution .... WUDU
" Angel of Death AZRAEL
" annual fast .. RAMADAN

"	antenuptial settlement . MAHR	"	salutation ...... SALAM

" antenuptial settlement . MAHR
" ascetic .... FAKIR
" bible KORAN, ALCORAN
" bier or tomb .... TABUT
" blood relationship ..... NASAB
" body of interpreters ... ULEMA
" calif, capturer of Jerusalem .... OMAR
" cap .... TAJ
" caravansary ... IMARET
" chief . SAYID, DAT(T)O
" court officer ..... AGA
" creed .... SUNNAH
" crusade . JEHAD, JIHAD
" deity .... ALLAH
" demon .... JINNIE
" devil ... EBLIS, SHAITAN
" drinking cup ... LOTAH
" fast .... RAMADAN
" festival ... BAIRAM, EED
" garment .... ISAR, IZAR
" guide .... PIR
" hierarchy ...... ULEMA
" hospice ...,..... IMARET
" house ...... SELAMLIK
" infidel .... KAFIR
" judge ...... CADI, RAZI
" lord .... SAYID
" magistrate .. KADI, CADI
" Malay .... SASSAK
" Messiah .... MAHDI
" minister of finance .... DIWAN
Mohammedan month JUMADA, RABIA, RAJAB, RAMADAN, SAFAR, SHABAN, SHAWWAL
" mystic .... SUFI
" noble ...... AMIR, EMIR
" , non- .... KAFFIR
" nymph .... HOURI
" , orthodox ...... HANIF, SUNNITE
" pantheist .... SUFI
" paradise, nymph of .... HOURI
" platform .... MASTABA
" potentate ...... CALIPH
" prayer .. SALAT, NAMAZ
" prayer, hour of .. AZAN
" priest ... IMAM, WAHABI
" prince ... AMEER, EMIR, SEID
" religion .... ISLAM
" ruler .... SULTAN
" sacred book . ALCORAN, KORAN
" saint ..... PIR, SANTON

" salutation ...... SALAM
" seminary ..... MADRAS
" shirt ... CAMISE, KAMIS
" slave .... MAMELUKE
" spirit ..... JINN, GENIE
" stringed instrument .... REBAB
" student .... SOFTA
" teacher ... ALIM, IMAM, MULLAH
" title . AMIR, CALIF, AGA, NAWAB, NUWAB, SAYID
" unbeliever ...... KAFIR
" veil .... YASHMAK
" widow, non-marrying, period of .... IDDAT
" woman's outer wrap ... IZAR
Mohammedans, messiah expected by the .... MAHDI
Mohicans, last of .... UNCAS
moil .... TAINT, TOIL, DAUB, WET
moist DEWY, UVID, DANK, HUMID, WET, DAMP
moisten .... ANOINT, DAMPEN, IMBUE, MOIL, SOAK, SPARGE
" skins .... SAM
moisture, exposed to .... RET
" : swollen plant condition ... EDEMA
molar .... GRINDER, CHOPPER, TOOTH
molasses ...... TREACLE, THERIAC(A)
mold .... KNEAD, CAST, MUST, PLASM, MATRIX, SOIL, MOULAGE, MATRICE
" , core of a .... AME, NOWEL
" , pouring hole in .... SPRUE
Moldavian .... RUMANIAN
" city .. BALTA, IASI, JASSY
molded building material ...... PISE
molder's tool .... FLANGE
molding(s) . ASTRAGAL, CYMA, OGEE, GULA, TORI, LISTEL, SCOTIA, REEDING, REGLET, TORUS, OVOLO, OVOLI, SPLAY
" , concave .... COVING
" , curved .... NEBULE
" edge .... ARIS, ARRIS
" , egg-shaped ..... OVOLO, OVOLI
" ornamented with disks .. BEZANT(EE)
moldy .... FUSTY, MUSTY, MUCID
mole .. BLES, PIER, TALPA, QUAY, TAPE, TAUPE, NEVUS, STARNOSE
" rat .... NESOKIA
molecule .... MONAD, PARTICLE
" component ..... ATOM, ION, ANION
mole-like animal ..... DESMAN, TAPE

187

Molière char. ...... DAMIS, TARTUFFE, DORANTE, SCAPIN
mollify (A)BATE, SOFTEN, CONCILIATE, SLEEK, PACIFY, APPEASE, RELAX, TEMPER, ALLAY
Mollusca ... MUREX, MURICES, OCTOPI
mollusk CLAM, OYSTER, SNAIL, UMBO, SHELL, OYSTER, VOLUTE, SCALLOP
" , bivalve .... LEDA, VENERIDA, CHAMA
" , double-shell .... LIMPET
" , edible .... ASI, MUSSEL
" , eight-armed ...... OCTOPUS
" , fresh-water CHITON, ETHERIA
" , gastropod ... ABALONE, SLUG
" ; genus .... MUREX, ASTARTE, BUCCINUM
" gills .... CERATA
" , large part of .... MANTLE
" , larval .... VELIGER
" , sea .... ABALONE, SALP
" , shell of a univalve COWRY, COWRIE
" teeth .... RADULA
" , ten-armed .... SQUID
" , type of .... WHELK, CONCH
" used for fish bait .... LIMPET
" , wrinkled-shell ...... COCKLE
" , young .... SPAT
Molotov cocktail .... BOMB
molt .... MEW, MUTE, CAST, EXUVIATE, SHED, SLOUGH
molten rock .... LAVA, MAGMA
Molucca island .. CERAM, SOELA, OBI, KAI
moment .... SEC, FLASH, POINT, TRICE
monad . ATOM, PARTICLE, UNIT, ENTITY
monarch .... DYNAST, CZAR, TSAR, SACHEM, CHIEF, DICTATOR, EMPEROR, POTENTATE, KAISER, KING, RULER, SHAH, SULTAN
" , greedy .... MIDAS
monastery ... FRIARY, ABBEY, HOSPICE, MATH, TERA, VIHARA
monastic MONK(LY), OBLATE, RECLUSE
" haircut .... TONSURE
" visitor .... DEFINITOR
monetary .... PECUNIARY, FINANCIAL, BURSAL, FISCAL
" unit (see "coin"; also "money")
money CASH, COIN, CUSH, DUST, GELT, JACK, KALE, MOSS, PELF, DOUGH, FUNDS, LUCRE, MAZUMA, TENDER, WAMPUM, CABBAGE, LETTUCE, BREAD, GRIG, TALENT, WAD, COWRY, SHEKELS, UHLLO
" , Anglo-Saxon ...... ORE, ORA
" box .... ARCA, TILL

" changer ..... CAMBIST, SARAF, SERAF
" -changing .... AGIO
" , coined .... SPECIE
" , found .... TROVE
" gift .... ALMS
" manual .... CAMBIST
" : 1/60th talent .... MINA
" premium .... AGIO
" roll of .... ROULEAU
" , Scotch .... SILLER
" ; slang ...... BOODLE, RHINO, WAMPUM, GILT
" sorter .... SHROFF
" standard .... BANCO
" , to coin .... MINT
monger ..... TRADER, VENDER, MERCER
Mongol . TARTAR, TAMERLANE, ASIAN, BURIAT, ELEUT, HU, KALMUCK, SHARRA
" dynasty .... YUAN
" , Siberian .... TATAR
" tribe .... SHAN
Mongolia, capital of .... URGA, ULAN BATOR
" , river of .... PEI
" , silver coin of ...... TUGRIK
Mongolian conjurer .... SHAMAN
" people of Siberia . YAKUTS
Mongoloid people of Nepal RAIS, LAI
mongoose ICHNEUMON, CIVET, MUNGO
mongrel . CUR, MUT(T), HYBRID, MIXED
monition .... ADVICE, WARNING
monitor ...... PREPOSITOR, MENTOR, ADVISER, WARN
" lizard .... URAN, VARAN
monk ..... ABBE, PADRE, RECLUSE, FRA
" , ascetic .... FAKIR, DERVISH
" , community . CENOBITE, SCETE, SKETE
" , early English ..... BEDA, BEDE
" , Franciscan .... CAPUCHIN
" , hermit .... ANCHORET
" hood .... AMICE, COWL
" , monastic-order .... FRIAR
" of the Eastern church CALOYER
" , oriental ...... BONZE, YAHAN, LOHAN, LAMA
monkey ... MONA, NISNAS, QUAKARI, TOTA, MIMIC, PRIMATE, SIME, SIMIAN, VITOE, TOTA
" , arboreal; W. Afr. ... POTTO
" , Asiatic .... MACAQUE
" , bearded .... ENTELLUS
" , Brazilian .... TEETER, SAI
" bread .... BAOBAB
" , Capuchin .... SAPAJOU, SAI
" , Ceylonese .... MAHA, TOQUE
" , Diana .... ROLOWAY

"   flower .... FIGWORT
"   flower; genus ...... MIMULUS
"   : grivet .... TOTA
"   house .... APERY
"   , howler ..... ARABA, MONO,
                            STENTOR
"   , long-tailed, Asiatic . LANGUR
"   , long-tailed, W. Afr., . PATAS
"   , Malabar .... WANDEROO
"   , proboscis .. KAHA, NOSEAPE
"   puzzle .... PINON
"   , sacred, of India .... RHESUS
"   , small; So. Am. . MARMOSET,
                                TITI
"   , S. Afr. ..... MONA, VERVET,
                    TAMARIN, TEETEE
"   , S. Amer. . ALOUATTE, ACARI,
                                SAKI
"   , small, arboreal .... GRIVET,
             SIME, TARSIER, TITI, TOTO
"   , spider; genus .... ATELES
"   , squirrel .... SAMIRI
"   , tufted or bonnet ...... ZATI
monkey-cup; genus .... NEPENTHE
monkey-like animal . NCHEGA, LEMUR
monkshood ... ATEES, ATIS, ACONITE
monkey puzzle .... PINON
monkish .... MONASTIC
monolith ... MENHIR, PILLAR, OBELISK
monopoly ..... CARTEL, POOL, TRUST,
                    CORNER, GAME
monosaccharide .... OSE
monotonous .. SAMELY, DRONE, DULL,
             TEDIOUS, HUMDRUM, DRAB
monster ...... GILA, CERBERUS, FIEND,
                            GHOUL
"   ; comb. form. ...... TERATO
"   , fabled SPHINX, BUCENTAUR,
                    HARPY, KRAKEN
"   , female . GORGON, MEDUSA
"   , fire-breathing ... CHIMERA
"   , giant .... OGRE
"   in classical myth MINOTAUR
"   , medical .... TERAS
"   serpent .. ALLOPS, DRAGON
monster-like .... TERATOID
monstrous .... ENORM(OUS), ABSURD,
                        COLOSSAL
Montana city .... HELENA, BUTTE
"   county BLAINE, CARTER, HILL,
             LAKE, PARK, TETON, TOOLE
"   mountain .... KIPP
"   river .... TETON
Monte Cristo author .... DUMAS
"   "   hero .... DANTES
month .... ULTIMO, INSTANT
"   , excess of calendar over lunar
                            EPACT
"   ; Fr. Rev. ....NIVOSE, FLOREAL,
             MESSIDOR, THERMIDOR

"   ; Sp. .... MES, ENERO, AGOSTO
monument .. TOMB, DOLMEN, RECORD,
        ARCH, OBELISK, PILLAR, STATUE,
                            MENHIR
mood TOD, TONE, VEIN, WHIM, SPIRIT,
                            HUMOR
moon ...... CYNTHIA, LUNA, PHOEBE,
        CRESCENT, GAZE, SATELLITE, STARE
"   , area on .... MARE
"   calf .... DUNCE, IMBECILE,
                        MONSTER
"   : crescent point ... CUSP, HORN
"   goddess; Egypt. .... ISIS
"   goddess; Greek HECATE, ORTHIA,
                            SELENE
"   goddess; Lybian . TANITH, TANIT
"   goddess; Rom. .. LUCINA, LUNA,
                            PHOEBE
"   goddess; Syrian .... ASTARTE
"   , imaginary inhabitants of .....
                            SELENITES
"   , of the .... SELENIC
"   , picture of ..... SELENOGRAPH
"   : point farthest from Earth ...
                            APOGEE
"   , position of .... OCTANT
"   , valley on .... RILLE
moon's age at beginning of year ....
                            EPACT
moon's apogee or perigee ..... APSIS
moonshine .... WHISKEY
moonstone .... FELDSPAR, HECATOLITE
Moor .... ALGERINE, BERBER, SARACEN
moor ..... HEATH, PLAIN, FEN, LANDE
"   buzzard .... HARPY
"   , to .... DOCK, FASTEN, ANCHOR
moor cock .... GROUSE
Moorish .... MORISCAN
"   palace .... ALCAZAR
"   tabor .... ATABAL
moose ... ALCE, ELAND, ELK, ORIGNAL
"   ; genus .... ALCES
mop SWAB, MERKIN, POUT, TUFT, WIPE,
                            SCOVEL
moppet .... CHILD, DOLL, TOT
mora tree .... FUSTIC
moral ..... ETHICAL, GOOD, EPIMYTH,
        ALLEGORY, APOLOG, LESSON
"   law .... DECALOGUE
"   poem .... DIT
morally strengthen .... EDIFY
morass .... BOG, FEN, MARSH
Moravia capital .... BRNO
moray .... CONGER(EE), EEL, HAMLET
"   ; genus .... MURAENA
morbid displacement of an organ ...
                            ECTOPIA
more .... AGAIN, PIU, PLUS, BIS, TOO,
             ANEW, EXTRA, ENCORE

More's island .... UTOPIA
morello .... CHERRY
moreover .... BESIDES, ALSO, AND,
                                THERETO
morepork .... RURU, PEHO
Morgan's raiders .... REBS
moribund .... DYING, SICK
moringa tree .... BEN
morion .... HELMET
    " , variety of .... QUARTZ
Mormon ... DANITE, SMITH, YOUNG,
                        LAMAN, ELDER
morning ...... EOS, AURORA, MATIN,
                       UMAGA, DAWN
    " concert .... AUBADE
    " glory .... NIL
    " , per. to .... MATUTINAL
    " reception .... LEVEE
    " song .... MATIN
    " star . JUPITER, LUCIFER, MARS,
                    SATURN, VENUS
Moro chief .... DATO
    " high priest .... SARIP
    " island .... MINDANAO
    " prince .... CACHIL
    " tribe .... ILANO, SULU
Moroccan ..... BERBER, MOOR, RIFF
    " coin .. DIRHAM, RIAL, OKIA,
                      OUNCE
    " general .... KAID
    " hat .... FEZ
    " infantryman .... ASKAR
    " land .... GISH
    " seaport .... AGADIR, CEUTA,
                   RABAT, TETUAN
    " town .... FEZ, TANGIER
    " tribesman .... KABYLE
morocco, imitation .... ROAN
Morocco, ruler of .... SULTAN
moron .... AMENT, IDIOT
morose GLUM, GRUM, SOUR, SPLENETIC,
                  SULKY, CRABBY
morphon, opposed to .... BION
Morro Castle site .... HAVANA
morsel . SOP, BITE, SCRAP, ORT, SNACK
morsure .... BITING
mortal .... DEADLY, FATAL, LETHAL,
                HUMAN, TERRENE
mortar CANNON, COEHORN, HELMOS,
                PERRIER, SWISH
    " mixer .... RAB
    " , relative of ..... BRAY, PESTLE
mortarboard .... CAP, HAWK
"Morte d'Arthur" author ... MALORY
mortician .... UNDERTAKER
mortification .. CHAGRIN, GANGRENE,
                SHAME, PENANCE
mortify ..... ABASE, DENY, HUMILIATE
mortise, to .... AMORTIZE

" , machine to .... SLOTTER
mortuary ..... CINERARIUM, MORGUE,
                CHARNEL, CEMETERY
    " car .... HEARSE
    " roll .... OBIT
morvin .... MALLEIN
mosaic ... MUSIVE, TESSERA, ORMOLU
    " , apply .... INCRUST
Mosaic law .... TORA, TORAH
Moscow citadel .... KREMLIN
    " 3rd International . COMINTERN
Moses, elder brother of .... AARON
    " , father-in-law of ...... JETHRO
    " , sister of .... MIRIAM
    " , wife of .... ZIPPORAH
Moslem .... ISLAMIC, SARACEN, MORO
    " cap .... TAJ
    " chief .... RAIS
    " devil .... EBLIS
    " devotee .... DERVISH
    " dignitary .... SHERIF
    " headgear .... FEZ
    " in Turkestan .... SALAR
    " judge .... CADI
    " lawyer .... MUFTI
    " leader .... AGA
    " learned teacher .... ALIM
    " minister of finance .. DEWAN
    " orthodox .... HANIF
    " pilgrimage to Mecca ... HADJ
    " priest .... IMAM
    " religion .... ISLAM
    " religious college ...... ULEMA
    " sage .... ULEMA
    " saint .... PIR, SANTON
    " school .... MADRASAH
    " sect of Alexandria .. SENUSSI
    " shrine .... KAABA
    " state .... MUSCAT, OMAN
    " tribe, Kartvelian ....LAZ
    " viceroy .... NAWAB
mosque .... JAMI, OMAR, MASJID
    " tower .... MINARET
mosquito ...... CULICID, GALLINIPPER,
                  SKEETER
    " -bite preventive .... CULICIDE
    " ; genus .... CULEX
moss .... WEEPER, AGAR, TORTULA
    " -like .... MNIOID
mossback .... FOGY
mossbunker .... MENHADEN
Mossi language .... MO, MOLE
motel .... STOPOVER, INN
moth CRININE, FOOTMAN, PUG, MILLER,
          IMAGO, EGGER, FORESTER
    " spots; med. .... CHLOASMA
mother .. MATER, AMMA, DAM, ABBESS
    " of day and night.... NOX, NYX
    " of pearl ..... NACRE, ABALONE

" of presidents .... VIRGINIA
" of the gods ... CYBELE, FRIGGA, RHEA
" : related on her side . ENATIC, ENATE
" ; Tag. .... INA
Mother Carey's chicken ...... PETREL
"Mother of the Gracchi" .. CORNELIA
moths, suborder of ..... HEREROCERA
" , wing spot of .... FENESTRA
motion AESTUS, GAIT, REQUEST, FLUX, IMPETUS, MOVE
" , imparting .... KINETIC
" , jerky .... BOB, LIPE
" picture .... CINEMA, FLICK
" -picture arc light ...... KLIEG
motionless .. INERT, STAGNANT, FIXED
motive ..... REASON, PRESS, PRETEXT, CAUSE, THEME, IMPULSE
motor part .... ROTOR, CYLINDER
" , speed up .... REV
mottled . PIED, PINTO, MARBLED, ROEY
motto BYWORD, ADAGE, MOT, REASON, MAXIM, SLOGAN, APOTHEGM
moue .... GRIMACE
mouflon .... SHEEP
mound .... DUNE, HILL, TEE, TUMULUS, KNOLL, HAMMOCK, TERP, STUPA
mount .... SCALE, ESCALADE, ASCEND, SOAR, SEAT, HORSE
Mount of Olives .... OLIVET
mountain .. ALP, BERG, MESA, RANGE, MONS, BEN
" ; Babylonian .... ARARAT
" ; comb. form .... ORO
" crest (spur) ...... ARETE
" formation .... OROGENY
" from which Moses saw Canaan .... NEBO
" gap .... GATE, CORRIE
" , high .... ALP
" , highest .... EVEREST
" in Africa .... ATLAS, PARE
" in Asia .... ALTAI, URAL
" in Asia Minor .... IDA
" in California .... MUIR
" in India .... GHAUT
" in Thessaly .. OSSA, PELION
" in Tibet .... NANSHAN
" in W. Hemisphere ....
ACONCAGUA
" in W. United States . SHASTA
" lake, small .... TARN
" , legendary ...... KAF, MERU
" , low .... BUTTE
" mint .... BASIL
" pass ..... DEFILE, COL, GHAT
" peak .... CONE
" ridge ..... SAWBACK, SIERRA

" , rocky .... TETON
" shelter; Fr. .... GITE
" spinach .... ORACH
Mountain State .... MONTANA
mountain sunsets, reflection of ......
ALPENGLOW
" , the muses' ...... HELICON
" trail marker .... KARN
" under Pelion .... OSSA
" , Wyoming .... MORAN
mountaineer .... TIERSMAN
mountaineering peg .... PITON
mountains, science of .... OROLOGY
" , study of ..... OROGRAPHY
mountebank .... EMPIRIC, QUACK, CHARLATAN
mourn .... RUE, SIGH, WAIL, ERME
mourner .... MUTE, DISMAL
mournful ..... THRENODIC, SAD, DIRE
mourning dress ALMA, SABLES, WEEDS
mouse RODENT, CRABER, VOLE, JERBOA
" bird .... COLY
" , shrew .... ERD
" , tiny .... HARVEST
mouth LORRIKER, MUN, OS, ABRA, GOB
" , away from the ...... ABORAL
" of furnace .... BOCCA
" open .... AGAPE
" organ HARMONICA, CREMBALUM, PANDEAN
" , part of the .. PHARYNX, UVULA
" , per. to ...... RICTAL, STOMAL, STOMATIC
" , per. to glands of ... SALIVARY
" , river ... LADE, ESTUARY, DELTA
" ; Sp. .... BOCA
" , through the .... PERORAL
" , toward the .... ORAD
" , uttered through the ... PAROL, ORAL
" , wide .... RICTUS
mouthful .... SIP, SUP
mouthpiece .... REED, BOCAL
mouths .... ORA
movable parts .... MOBILES
move . KELTER, GEE, MOG, SKIRR, STIR, BUDGE, GOAD, SPUR
" along .... MOSEY
" back .... EBB, RECEDE
" furtively . SKULK, SLINK, SNEAK
" heavily .... LUG, FIDGET
" in circles .... PURL, WRITHE
" noisily .... BUSTLE
" over .... JOLL
" quickly HURTLE, SPEED, HASTEN, RUN, SPANK, FLIT, CAREEN
" slowly ... INCH, EDGE, WORM
" to and fro SHUTTLE, WAG, FLAP, SWAY

191

moved sidewise .... SIDLED, SLUED
     " swiftly .... FLEW
movement .... MOTO, TAXIS, RHYTHM,
    TEMPO, THEME, DRIVE, MOMENTUM
movie .... FLICK, TALKIE
    " ; comb. form .... CINE
    " fare .... POPCORN
    " process .... TECHNICOLOR
    " script .... SCENARIO
moving .. NOMADIC, MOTILE, MOBILE,
             PATHETIC, PITIFUL
    " -picture award .... OSCAR
mow .. MATH, DESS, SHORTEN, GOAF,
           PUCKER, HAYRICK
Mowgli's bear friend ... BALOO, BALU
Mozambique native .... YAO
Mozart opera .... SERAGLIO
much MOLTO, FELE, LOT, MANY, GOBS,
            SCADS
"Much Ado About Nothing" char. ..
      ANTONIO, CLAUDIO, HERO,
         LEONATO, URSULA
mucilage ...... GUM, PASTE, MUCAGO
mud SLUDGE, MIRE, SILT, SLIME, OOZE,
       MUCK, SULLAGE, GLAIR
    " batch .... ILLUTATION
    " eel .... SIREN
    ", fix in .... BEMIRE
    ", living in .... LIMICOLOUS
    " volcano .... SALSE
mudar fiber .... YERCUM
muddle .. ADDLE, MESS, SOSS, SNAFU,
         JUMBLE, FOG
muddled SLIMED, BURBLED, MUZZY, REE
muddy . ROILY, SLAKY, MOIST, TURBID,
           SLIMY
muezzin's call to prayer ...... AZAN
muffin .... GEM, COB
muffle .. MUTE, DEADEN, STIFLE, WRAP
mug .... NOG, POT, TOBY, CUP, FACE,
        STEIN, SEIDEL, FOOL
mugger .... GOA, CROCODILE
mulatto .... METIS
mulberry bark .... TAPA
    " beverage .... MORAT
    " Indian AAL, AWL, ACH, AUTE
    " trees; genus .... MORUS
mulch .... STRAW
mulct .... AMERCE, FINE, PUNISH,
         FORFEIT
mule MUTE, HINNY, HYBRID, HARDTAIL
mules, drove of .... ATAJO
mull PONDER, THINK, SWEETEN, GRIND
mullet .. GOATFISH, SUCKER, HARDER,
         BOBO
multitude GALAXY, HOST, MOB, SHOAL,
      CROWD, THRONG, LEGION,
         MYRIAD
mumble ..... CHAVEL, MUMP, MUTTER
mummer .... GUISER

mummy .... CADAVER, RELIC, CORPSE
    " , spirit of .... KA
munch .... CHAMP
mundane TERRENE, SECULAR, TEMPORAL,
           WORLDLY
mungo .... BEAN
munia .... PADDA
municipal .... CIVIC, BOND
Munro, H. H. .... SAKI
muntjac .... RATWA
murder ..... BURKE, HOMICIDE, SLAY,
         MASSACRE
    " fine .... CRO
    " of a king .... REGICIDE
    " of a prophet .... VATICIDE
murderous ...... FELL, GORY, DEADLY
murk .... GLOOM
murmur .... HUM, COO, PURL
"Musa Dagh _____ Days of" ..
         FORTY
Mus, former member of ...... RAT
Muscat native .... OSMANI
muscle BRAWN, LACERT, TERES, SINEW
    " , derived from .... INOSIC
    " , lack of .... ATAXIA
    " , like .... MYOID
    " , outward-turning ... EVERTOR
    " sugar .... INOSITE
    " , type of .... ROTATOR
muscular .. BRAWNY, THEWY, TOROSE,
         MIGHTY
    " contraction, spasm of TONUS
    " inability to walk .... ABASIA
muse . PONDER, MULL, REVE, MEDITATE,
         RUMINATE
    " of astronomy .... URANIA
    " of comedy .... THALIA
    " of dancing .... TERPSICHORE
    " of epic poetry .... CALLIOPE
    " of history .... CLIO
    " of lyric poetry and love . ERATO
    " of music .... EUTERPE
    " of sacred song .... POLYMNIA
    " of tragedy .... MELPOMENE
muses, rel. to the .... PIERIAN
muses, sacred place of PIERIA, AONIA
muses, the .... PIERIDES
museum ..... PRADO, METROPOLITAN
    " head .... CURATOR
mush . SAGAMITE, ATOLE, PAP, SEPON,
        SUPAWN, PUDDING
mushroom . FUNGUS, AGARIC, TRUFFLE,
        MITRA, LEPIOTA
    " cap .... PILEUS
    " disease .... FLOCK
    " , parts of a .... GILLS
    " , superior .... MOREL
mushy .... GOOEY, THICK
Musial, Mr. .... STAN

music ... HARMONY, MELODY, MOTET, RHYTHM, STRAIN, SYMPHONY
" , a lead in .... PRESA
" , a skip in .... SALTO
" aftersong .... EPODE
" , Anglo-Ind. melody ..... RAGA
" bells, set of .... PEAL
" canto .... PASSUS
" , character in .... KEY, CLEF
" ; half major tone .... SEMITONE
" hall . ODEUM, ALHAMBRA, BIJOU, WINDMILL, MET, SCALA, ODEON, ODEA, CARNEGIE
" in major .... DUR
" , leap in .... SALTO
" , major scale in .... GAMUT
" , major thirds in Gr. .. DITONES
" , mark in .... SLUR
" , measured beat in ..... MOTO, PULSE
" , melodic phrase in .. LEITMOTIF
" , melodious in .... ARIOSO
" , metrical compo. in ..... POEM
" , nine-piece compo. in .. NONET
" , ninth in .... NONA
" , non-concerted .... SOLO
" ; note in Guido's scale; .... ALT, ELA, ELAMI, UT
" played on a set of bells CHIMB
" , set of verses in .... DERRY
" sextuplet .... SESTOLET
" ; short song .... ODE
" , sign in .... SEGNO
" ; simple song ... AIR, TUNE, LAY
" , slowly in .. ADAGIO, LARGO, LENTO, TARDO
" ; smooth ....LEGATO
" : so much .... TANTO
" , soprano in .... CANTO
" , three, thrice in .... TER, TRIAD
" , time in .... TEMPO
" , twice in .... BIS
musical DULCET, LYRIC(AL), OROTUND, TONAL
" ballad .... DERRY
" comedy .... REVUE
" compo. ...... FUGUE, MOTET, SONATA, CONCERTO
" direction .... STA, SOLI
" direction for silence . TACET, CEASE
" interlude, short ..... VERSET
" interval ... TRITONE, OCTAVE
" medley RONDO, CENTO, OLIO
" nocturne .... SERENADE
" passage, brilliantly executed . CODA, BRAVURA
" performance .... REVUE

" rattle .... SISTRUM
" scale, degree .... GRADO
" score .... NOTATOR
" sign .... ISON
" suite; It. .... PARTITA
" theme .... ETUDE, TEMA
" third .... TIERCE
" work ORATORIO, OPUS, OPERA
mus. instrument ... REED, ASOR, OAT, ROCTA, KAZOO, BUGLE, UKE
" " , African .... NANGA
" " , anc. stringed ...... BANDORE, DULCIMER, PANDURA
" " , bass wind . SERPENT
" " , biblical ... SABECA, TABRET
" " , brass ..... CORNET, TROMBA
" " , E. Ind. BINA, RUANA, VINA
" " , flute-like FLAGEOLET
" " , guitar-like ... LUTE, ROTE, UKULELE
" " , keyed ..... CLAVIER, SPINET
" " , old .... REBEC, CELESTA, GITTERN, MARIMBA
" " ; saxhorn family .... ALTHORN
" " , six-string .. GUITAR, BANJO
" " , small CITOLE, SITOL
" " , Spanish . CASTANET, ATABAL
" " , string ASOR, AMATI, CELLO, CROWD, VIOLA, STRAD, KIT, HARP, LUTE, VINA, FIDDLE
" " , terracotta OCARINA
" " , trumpet-like ...... CLARION, TUBA, SAX
" " , used to play .... PLECTRUM
" " , wind FLUTE, ORGAN, BUGLE, SHOFAR, HORN, OBOE, REED
musk cat .... CIVET
musket .... HAKE, FUSIL
musket ball .... GOLI
Musketeer . ARAMIS, ATHOS, PORTHOS
muskmelon ...... ATIMON, CASABA
muslin TARLATAN, ADATI, SHELA, MULL, NAINSOOK, SEERHAND, BAN, JAMLANEE, GURRAH, BROTH, DORIA
muss ...... DISHEVEL, LITTER, RUMPLE, MESS, MUDDLE
mussel NAIAD, UNIO, MYTILUS, HORSE, NERITA, PALOUR, MOUGAR
" , part of a .... BYSSUS
Mussolini's son-in-law .... CIANO

Mussulman .... MOSLEM, SARACEN
must .... SAPA, JUICE, MILDEW, STUM
mustard .. SENVY, WOAD, CHARLOCK,
                  CADLOCK, SINAPSIS
" , black .... NIGRA
" gas .... YPERITE
" , per. to ... BRASSICA, SINAPIC
" plaster . SINAPISM, CAPSICUM
musteline carnivore MARTEN, WEASEL
muster ...... GATHER, LEVY, MARSHAL,
                  SUMMON
" out .... DISBAND
musty .... RANCID, FUSTY, RAFTY, BAD,
       FETID, RANK, MOLDY, TRITE
Mut .... MOTHER
" , husband of .... AMON
mutable ...... FICKLE, ERRATIC, FITFUL
mutate .... ALTER, SPORT, VARY
mute .... LENE, MUM, TACITURN, SURD,
             DEADEN, MUFFLE
mutilate .. GARBLE, GELD, MAIM, MAR,
       DEFORM, INJURE, DEFACE
mutiny ...... PUTSCH, REVOLT, COUP,
               SEDITION
mutter .... MAUNDER, PATTER, MUMBLE
mutton ...... KABOB, CABOB, SHEEP
" -bird .... OIL
" -fish .. EELPOUT, PORGY, SAMA
mutual .... JOINT, COMMON
muzzle ... NOSE, SNOUT, GAG, BIND,
           CENSURE, SILENCE
muzzy .... DAZED, CONFUSED
My Gal _____ .... SAL
myopic .... NEARSIGHTED
myriapod .... CENTIPEDE
myrmicid .... ANT
myrtle ...... PERIWINKLE, RAMARAMA,
                CAJUPUT
myself; Scot. .... MASEL
mysterious .. CRYPTIC, MYSTIC, SECRET,
     ARCANE, OCCULT, ESOTERIC,
          WEIRD, OBSCURE
mystery .. RUNE, ARCANUM, ESOTERY,
              ENIGMA
" story .... WHODUNIT
mystic .. EPOPTIC, ASCETIC, GNOSTIC,
     SUFI, TAOIST, RUNIC, OCCULT
" art .... CABALA
" cry .... EVOE
" doctrine .... ESOTERIC
" ejaculation .... OM
" secret word .... ABRAXAS
mystical character .... ECKHARDT
" significance ...... ANAGOGE
" word .... ABRACADABRA
mystify .. BEFOG, OBFUSCATE, BAFFLE,
          PERPLEX, RATTLE
myth .. LEGEND, FIGMENT, ALLEGORY,
           SAGA, FABLE
mythical island in the west ATLANTIS

mythological matricide ..... ORESTES
" monster .... OGRE, ARGUS,
     HARPY, HYDRA, LAMIA,
   GORGON, CENTAUR, CHIMERA,
      GRIFFIN, UNICORN
" serpent .... APEPI

N

nab .... GRAB, ARREST
Nabal's wife .... ABIGAIL
nabob .... DIVES, PLUTOCRAT, MIDAS
nacelle .... CAR, CHASSIS
nacre .... PEARL
nadir, opposed to .... ZENITH
naevus .... FRECKLE
nag . HENPECK, HECTOR, SCOLD, TWIT,
      PLAGUE, TEASE, HORSE
Naha is capital of _____ OKINAWA
nahoor .... BHARAL, SHEEP
Nahor's wife .... MILCAH
naiad .... NYMPH
nail .. SPAD, BRAD, STUD, DRIVE, HOB,
             SINKER
" : driven slantingly .... TOED
" , headless .... SPRIG
" , ingrowing .... ACRONYX
" , marking on the ...... LUNULE
" or claw .... TOE, UNGUIS
" , shoemaker's .... SPARABLE
" size .... TENPENNY
naïve .... INGENUE, ARTLESS, FRANK
naked .... BARE, EXACT, LITERAL
namaycush .... TROUT, LAKER, LUNGE
_____ Nam _____ ... VIET
"Namby-Pamby" author ..... PHILIPS
namby-pamby . INSIPID, SILLY, VAPID
name . DUB, TERM, COGNOMEN, TITLE,
   ENUMERATE, CALL, CITE, REPUTE,
        NOMINATE
" , assumed .... ALIAS, PEN
" , bad .... CACONYM
" , first .. PRAENOMEN, FORENAME
" of a thing .... NOUN
" or call .... CLEPE
" tablet .... FACIA
" , to ...... NEVEN, CHRISTEN
" written backward ...... ANANYM
named ...... CITED, YCLEPT, YCLEPED
namely .... SCILICET, TOWIT, VIZ
namesake ...... HOMONYM, EPONYM
nanny .... NURSE, GOAT
Naomi .... MARA
naos .... TEMPLE, CELLA
nap SNOOZE, DOZE, PILE, RAS, SIESTA,
       WINK, TEASEL, SHAG
nape SCRUFF, NIDDICK, SCURF, TURNIP,
       NUQUE, NUCHA

" of sheep's neck .... SCRAG
napery .... LINEN
Naphtalite .... ENAN
napkin .... DIAPER, DOILY
Naples .... NAPOLI
" king .... MURAT
" secret society .... CAMORRA
nap-like woolen cloth .... DUFFEL
Napoleon's battle .. ACRE, JENA, ULM,
                    WATERLOO, BORODINO
"   brother-in-law .... MURAT
"   isle ...... ELBA, CORSICA,
                    HELENA
Napoleon's (III) mother .. HORTENSE
nappy .... WOOLLY, DOWNY
nap raiser .... TEASEL, TEAZEL
narcissus ...... EGOIST, NANCY, LILY,
                    CRINUM
narcosis .... DROWSINESS, SLEEP
narcotic ... HEMP, ANODYNE, BHANG,
            CODEINE, ETHER, COCAINE,
            FAGINE, GANJA, POT, SNOW,
            DRUG, DOPE, OPIATE, REEFER
narcotic plant .... POPPY, COCA, KAT,
            KAAT, KHAT, DUTRA, MANDRAKE
nardoo .... CLOVER
nares .... NOSTRILS
narghile .... HOOKAH
narial .... RHINAL
nark .... SPY
narrate .. RECITE, RELATE, BRUIT, SPIN,
                    TELL
narrative CONTE, FABLE, TALE, RECITAL
"   poem .... EPIC, EPOS
narrow .. CLOSE, ANGUST, LIMITED,
            SCANT, MEAGER, BIGOTED, LINEAL
"   ; comb. form .... STEN
"   opening, per. to .. STENOPAIC
narrowly incised .... LACINIATE
narrow-mindedness .. BIGOTRY, BIAS
narrows .... SOUND, STRAIT
nasal ...... RHINIAL, NARINE, NARIAL
nascency ...... GENESIS, BEGINNING
Nash; humorist .... OGDEN
", Richard .... BEAU
nasty . NAUSEOUS, OBSCENE, ODIOUS,
                    RIBALD
Nata's wife .... NANA
native INDIGENOUS, ITE, NATAL, SON,
            RAW, BORN, INNATE, ENDEMIC,
            ABORIGINAL, ABORIGINE
"   agent .... COMPRADOR(E)
"   ; of mineral .... LIVE
"   , original .... PRIMEVAL
"   plant .... INDIGENE
natty ..... CHIC, NEAT, JAUNTY, TRIM,
            DAPPER, POSH, SPRUCE
natural .. UNFEIGNED, BORN, INNATE,
                    NAIVE, REAL
"   condition .... NORM

"   group .... ETHNIC, RACE
"   location .... SITUS
"   luster .... NAIF
"   philosophy .... PHYSICS
"   voice .... DIPETTO
naturalist ...... ANIMIST, BIOLOGIST,
            AUDUBON, BREHM, MENDEL,
            BURBANK, LINNE, DARWIN, CARVER,
            PLINY, THOREAU
naturalization .... DENIZATION
naturalize .... ADAPT, ACCLIMATE
nature .... ESSENCE
", per. to .... COSMIC
"   quality .... GUNA
", spirit of .... NAT
nausea .... PALL, QUALM
nauseous ...... FULSOME, OFFENSIVE
nautical .. OCEANIC, MARINE, NAVAL,
                    MARITIME
"   hook .... BECKET
"   instr. ... SEXTANT, COMPASS,
                    PELORUS
"   line ...... BOBSTAY, MARLINE,
                    EARING
"   mile per hour .... KNOT
"   term .. ANEAD, ATRY, ABEAM,
            AFORE, AHOY, AVAST, ATRIP,
                    ABAFT
nautilus .... ARGONAUT
"Nautilus" commander .... NEMO
Navaho hut .... HOGAN
naval .... NAUTICAL, MARINE
"   air base .... ALAMEDA
"   reserve girl .... WAVE
"   safe-conduct pass .... NAVCERT
"   station; Fr. .... BREST
nave .... HUB, HOB, NEF
navigate .... AVIATE, KEEL, SAIL
navigation system ... LORAN, SONAR
navy task force .... ARMADA
nawab .... NABOB
Nazi concentration camp ... DACHAU
"   symbol ...... SWASTIKA, FYLFOT
Nazimova; actress .... ALLA
near ...... CLOSE, AT, WITHIN, DEAR,
            ADJACENT, INTIMATE, ABOUT
Near East .... LEVANT
"   "   native ... ARAB, TURK, KURD,
            IRAKI, OMANI, AFGHAN,
                    YEMINI
nearsighted .... MYOPIC, PURBLIND
nearby .... ANENT, GIN, NIGH
neat ..... ADROIT, NATTY, NICE, TRIG,
            TRIM, DAINTY, PRECISE
neatherd .... COWHERD
neater .... PRIMMER
neb .... BEAK, BILL
Nebraskan city .... OMAHA, WAHOO
"   county ... BOYD, BURT, CASS,
            CLAY, GAGE, HALL, HOLT,
            KNOX, LOUP, POLK, ROCK, YORK

195

"   Indian ..... RONCA, OTOE,
PAWNEE
nebulous .... HAZY, VAGUE
"   envelope ...... CHEVELURE,
COMA
necessary REQUISITE, VITAL, ESSENTIAL
necessitate .. COMPEL, FORCE, ENTAIL,
OBLIGE
necessity .. NEED, COMPULSION, MUST
"   of life .... ALIMENT
neck . SWIRE, CRANE, CERVIX, COLLUM,
ISTHMUS
"   , a part of the .... GULA
"   , armor for the .... GORGET
"   , back of the .... NAPE, NUCHA,
SCRUFF
"   , chief artery of ...... CAROTID
"   cloth .... BARCELONA, CRAVAT
"   frill .... JABOT, RUCHE
"   of land .... STRAKE
"   part of a coat .... GORGET
"   , part of a horse's .... WITHERS
"   , per. to .... CERVICAL
"   piece .... BOA, FICHU
"   scarf .... ASCOT
"   , thin .... SCRAG
─────── Necker; Fr. statesman ....
JACQUES
neckerchief .... BELCHER
necklace .... BEADS, BALDRIC, RIVIERE,
CHOKER, TORQUE
necking .... GORGERIN
necktie .. CRAVAT, SCARF, TIE, ASCOT
necromancer ..... DIVINER, EXORCIST
necromancy .... GOETY, MAGIC
nectar .... HONEYDEW, AMBROSIA
need .. LACK, STRAIT, WANT, CRAVE,
PENURY, POVERTY
needle BODKIN, OBELISK, STYLO, SEW,
POINTER, HECKLE
"   bug .... NEPA, RANATRA
"   case .... ETUI, ETWEE
"   finisher .... EYER
"   gun .... DREYSE
"   hole under skin ...... SETON
"   , Latin for .... ACUS
"   , pointed .. ACERATE, ACEROSE
"   , sea .... GARFISH
needlefish .... GAR
needle-shaped .. ACICULAR, SPICULAR,
ACUATE
needlework, piece of .... SAMPLER
negate .... NULLIFY, DENY, REFUTE
negation . NULLITY, VETO, NEIN, NYET,
NON
negative .. NAY, NOR, DENIAL, DINNA
"   ion .... ANION
"   pole .... CATHODE
neglect . OMIT, SHIRK, IGNORE, SLIGHT
negligent .... LASH, LAX, REMISS

negotiate ...... DEAL, TREAT, PARLAY,
BARGAIN, SELL, DICKER
Negrito .... ATA, ATTA, AETA, TAPIRO,
BAMBUTE, BATWA, SEMANG, KARON
Negro .. BLACK, DARKIE, HUBSHI, LURI,
EWE, BINI, SAMBO
"   , African ... DAHOMAN, JUR, VEI
"   , cant name applied to a ....
CUFFEE, CUFFY, QUASHEE
"   dance .... JUBA
Negro, Egyptian .... NUBIAN
"   from Benin .... EBOE
"   , Gold Coast .... GA
"   , Liberian ... GREBO, KROO, KRU
"   magico-religious belief........
FETISHISM
"   , Niger .... EFIK, IBO, NUPE
"   , offstring of a mulatto and....
SAMBO
"   , offspring of white and ......
MESTEE, SACATRA
"   people of the Soudan HAUSAS
"   , Sudan .... EGBA
"   tribe of Cape Verde ... SERER
"   magic .... VOODOO
Negroes of Nigeria .... BENI
Negroes of S. Afr. .... BASUTOS
Negroid, Medit. .... HAMITE
"   race, Afr. .... BANTU, KAFFIR
"   race of pigmies .... AKKA
"   , S. Kordofan .... NUBA
"   tribe of Afr. PONDO, TEMBU,
XOSA
neighborhood .... PURLIEU, VENUE,
VICINITY
neighboring ... ACCOLENT, ADJACENT
Neleus, son of .... NESTOR
nelumbo .... LOTUS
nemesis .... AVENGER, AGENT
neophyte .... CONVERT, CATECHUMEN,
TYRO, NOVICE
neoplasm .... TUMOR
Nepal capital .... KATMANDU
"   coin .... MOHAR
"   district .... TERAI
"   mongoloid .... RAIS
"   mountain .... EVEREST, LHOTSE
"   native .... KHA, GURKHA
"   tribesman .... AUL
Nephele's daughter .... HELLE
nephew .... NEPOTE, NEVE, VASU
nephrite .... JADE
Neptune, Celtic .... LER
"   , discoverer of .... GALLE
"   , scepter of .... TRIDENT
"   , son of .... TRITON
Nereid chief .... THETIS
Nereus' wife .... DORIS
Nero .... TYRANT, FIDDLER
"   , mother of .... AGRIPPINA

196

" , successor to .... GALBA
" , victims of ..... SENECA, LUCAN
" , wife of .... OCTAVIA
nerol .... ALCOHOL
nerve cell .... NEURON
" -cell extension .... AXON
" connective tissue .. NEUROGLIA
" element .... NEURONE
" layers .... ALVEI
" network ... PLEXUS, RETIA, RETE
" passage .... HILUM
" process .... NEURITE
" , sensory .... AFFERENT
" ; slang .... CRUST
nerves, substance found in the ......
                              LECITHIN
" ; comb. form .... NEURO
" , tumor of the .... GLIOMA
nervous ...... JITTERY, EDGY, TOUCHY,
                    UNEASY, RESTLESS
" malady .. APHASIA, NEURITIS
" seizure . ANEURIA, AMOK, TIC
Ness .... CAPE
nest .. DEN, NIDE, NIDUS, AERIE, AERY,
                              EYRIE
" , build a .... NIDIFY
" of boxes .... INRO
" of squirrels .... DRAY
nestle ..... SNUGGLE, CUDDLE, PETTLE
nestling .... BIRD, EYAS
" place .... JUG
Nestor .... SAGE, SOLON
net . GIN, TOIL, TRAP, SNARE, SAGENE,
    SNOOD, SEINE, TRAMMEL, MALINES,
        RETICLE, MESH, WEB, CATCH
nether .... DOWN, INFERNAL
Netherlands (see "Holland")
netted . INTERWOVEN, RETIARY, MESHY
nettle .. URTICA, STINGER, PIQUE, VEX
" rash . URTICARIA, HIVES, UREDO
network(s) ..... FRET, MOKE, PLEXUS,
    RETICULUM, WEB, PLEXA, VAS, MESH
neume .... PNEUMA, VIRGULA
neurad, opposed to .... HEMAD
neural .... NERVAL, DORSAL
" , opposed to.......... HEMAL
neurite .... AXON(E)
neuter .... GENDER
neutral body chemical ...... TAURIN
" color .... BEIGE
" equilibrium .... ASTATIC
Nevada city .... ELKO, RENO
" county ... LYON, NYE, STOREY,
                              WASHOE
neve .... ICE, SNOW, FIRN
never .... NARY
nevertheless .... YET, HOWEVER
new ... LATE, NEO, MODERN, RECENT,
              NOVEL, FRESH, NEOTERIC
New Caledonia bird .... KAGU

New Deal agency CCC, NRA, TVA, NYA
New Englander .... YANK
New Britain capital .... RABAUL
New Guinea city .... LAE
" " , export of ...... COPRA
" " gulf ...... HUON, PAPUA
" " , native of ...... PAPUAN
" " port of entry ..... DARU
" " river .... FLY
" " victory .... GONA
" " , wild hog of ...... BENE
New Hampshire county ...... COOS
" " mountain .... FLUME
" " state flower .. LILAC
New Hebrides island .... EFATE, EPI,
                    VATE, TANA, TANNA
" " port .... VILA
New Jersey city . NEWARK, TRENTON,
                    NUTLEY, HOBOKEN
" " county ... BERGEN, ESSEX,
    HUDSON, MERCER, MORRIS,
    OCEAN, PASSAIC, SALEM,
                    SUSSEX, UNION
" " river ... TOMS, RAMAPO
New Mexico county . OTERO, TAOS,
                EDDY, LEA, LUNA, MORA
" " river .... GILA
" " state flower .... YUCCA
" " town .... RATON
" " turpentine tree . TARATA
new word .... NEOLOGISM
New York baseball team ...... METS
" " city . OLEAN, ALBANY, RYE,
    ELMIRA, TROY, ITHACA,
                              DEPEW
" " county ...... ULSTER, ERIE,
    ONEIDA, GREENE, ESSEX,
    LEWIS, TIOGA, YATES
" " mountain(s) . BEAR, SLIDE,
                    CATSKILLS
" " university or college .....
    ALFRED, ELMIRA, HOBART,
    VASSAR, CORNELL, COLGATE
New York City .... GOTHAM
" " " borough MANHATTAN,
    BRONX, BROOKLYN, QUEENS
" " " college ..... HUNTER
" " " river . HUDSON, EAST
" " " subway BMT, IRT, IND
New Zealand bell bird .... MAKO
" " caterpillar .... AWETO,
                              WERI
" " cattail .... RAUPO
" " compensation .... UTU
" " corn .... KANGA
" " , extinct bird of ...MOA
" " evergreen tree TARATAH
" " fern root .... ROI
" " fish .... HIKU, IHI
" " fort .... PA, PAH

197

"   "   fuel tree ...... MAPAU
"   "   harbor .... OTAGO
"   "   island .... OTEA, NIUE
"   "   lake .... TAUPA
"   "   morepork .... RURU
"   "   native ... MAORI, MORI
"   "   owl .... RURU
"   "   palm .... NIKAU
"   "   parrot .... KAKA, KEA
"   "   pigeon .... KUKU
"   "   plant .... KARO
"   "   raft .... MOKI
"   "   railbird .. KOKO, WEKA
"   "   red pine .... RIMU
"   "   reptile .... TUATERA
"   "   shark .... MAKO
"   "   shrub RAMARAMA, KARO
"   "   tree . AKE, KAURI, MIRO,
     RATA, PUKA, TARATA, RIMU,
                    TITOKI, TOTARA
"   "   tribe .... RINGATU, ATI
"   "   vine .... AKA
"   "   volcano .... RUAPEHU
"   "   wages .... UTU
"   "   war club .. MERE, MERI
"   "   wingless bird ... WEKA,
                    APTERYX, KIWI
"   "   wood robin ..... MIRO
Newfoundland cape .... RACE
     "   capital ... SAINTJOHNS
news .... TIDINGS, WORD, EVANGEL
news beat .... SCOOP
news commentator .... CRONKITE,
     BRINKLEY, SEVAREID, REASONER
newspaper official EDITOR, REDACTOR
news service . ANETA, TASS, REUTERS,
               DOMEI, INS, UPI
news stand .... KIOSK
newt EFT, EVET, SALAMANDER, TRITON
" -like animal .... LIZARD, ESK,
                    AXOLOTL
next .... NEIST, THEN, IMMEDIATE
nexus .... LINK, TIE
nibble . PECK, BROWSE, GNAW, KNAB,
                    BITE, CHAMP, NIP
Nicaragua city ... LEON, MANAGUA
nice .... FINE, NEAT
niche . RECESS, APSE, NOOK, ALCOVE,
                    BAY
nick DINT, SCORE, DENT, MAR, NOTCH
nickel alloy .... INVAR, KONEL
nickel; slang .... JIT
nickname MONICKER, MONICA, ALIAS
nicotinic acid .... NIACIN
nictitate .... BLINK, WINK
nidor .... AROMA, SAVOR, SCENT
nidi .... NESTS
nidus .... NEST, REPOSITORY
niepa bark .... NIOTA
Niger, mouth of .... NUN

Nigeria capital .... LAGOS
"   state .... NUPE
"   town .... EDE, ISA
Nigerian region ...... BENIN, BINUE
"   river .... BENUE, NIGER
"   tribe ..... EFIK, EBOE, BENIN,
                    EDO, ARO
niggard .... MISER, SKINFLINT, PIKER,
               CLOSE, STINGY, TIGHT
nigh .... ANEAR, AT
night . DEATH, NOX, NYX, EVE, NOTT,
                    NATT
" ; comb. form .... NYCTI
nightfall, occurring at .. ACRONICAL
nighthawk ....BULLBAT, PISK
nightingale . PHILOMEL, THRUSH, LIND
nightjar .... POTOO
nightmare .... ALP, INCUBUS, MARA,
                    DREAM
nightshade .... DATURA, MOREL,
                    BELLADONNA
nightwatchman .... SERENO
nihil .... NOTHING
Nile bird .... IBIS
" boat .... BARIS, CANGIA
" catfish .... BAGRE
" city .. ABRI, ARGO, ASYUT, IDFU,
                    ISNA
" , falls of the .... RIPON
" , floating vegetable in ..... SUDD
" , island in the .... RODA
" native .... NILOT
" Negro .... JUR, LUO, SUK
" region .... NUBIA
" , per. to .... NILOTIC
" River city .... ROSETTA
" ship's captain .... RAIS, REIS
" , source of .... TSANA
" , tributary of the .... KAGERA
" Valley depression .... KORE
nimble DEFT, FLIT, GLEG, LISH, AGILE,
                    VOLANT, SPRY
nimbus ... AUREOLA, GLORIA, HALO,
                    AURA
nimrod .... HUNTER
"Nina Leeds" by .... ONEILL
nincompoop ... DOLT, WITLING, ASS,
                    NINNY
nine days' devotion ...... NOVENA
" -headed monster .... HYDRA
" inches .... SPAN
" , number .... ENNEA, ENNEAD
" -sided figure .... NONAGON
ninepins .... KEELS, SKITTLES, KAYLES
ninny BLOCKHEAD, DOLT, LOUT, FOOL,
                    SIMPLETON, SAMMY
ninth .... NONUS, ENNEATIC
" , day before the ides ... NONES
" day, recurring each .. NONANE
Niobe's brother .... PELOPS

198

"   father .... TANTALUS
"   husband .... AMPHION
niobic .... COLUMBIC
nip BLAST, CHILL, CUT, JIBE, SARCASM,
                    CHIP, PECK, TANG
nipa palm .... ATAP, ATTAP
nisus .... EFFORT, IMPULSE
niter .... POTASH
niton .... RADON
nitrite .... AZOTITE
nitrobenzene .... MIRBANE
nitrogen; comb. form .... AZO
"   ; old name .... AZOTE
nitroglycerin .... GLONOIN
nitrous acid, salt of .... NITRITE
nitwit .... BOOB, DUNCE, FOOL
niveous .... SNOWY, WHITE
nix ... SPIRIT, NO, NOTHING, DENIAL,
                    NEIN, NON, NYET
Nixon ...... DICK, PAT, TRICIA, JULIE
no one .... NEMO, NIX, NOBODY
Noah's father .... LAMECH
"   grandson .... ARAM
"   son .... JAPHETH, SHEM, HAM
nob .... HEAD, NAVE
Nobel Prize winner ORR, MOTT, PIRE,
        ASSER, BALCH, GOBAT, LIBBY,
        LAMAS, HAHN, UREY, CURIE,
        CORI, BOHR, RABI, MANN,
        CAMUS, TAGORE, UNDSET
nobility GENTRY, YEOMANRY, DIGNITY,
        ELITE, GRANDEUR, PEERAGE
noble .... EDEL, EPIC, GRAND, SUPERB,
        IMPERIAL, HIGHBORN, LOFTY, MORAL
nobleman . EARL, THANE, LORD, PEER,
        DUKE, BARON, MARQUIS, RITTER
nobleness of birth .... EUGENY
noblewoman .. CONTESSA, MARQUESA
nobody ... JACKSTRAW, NONENTITY
noctuid .... MOTH, WORM
nocturne .... LULLABY, SERENADE
nod ... NIP, BECK, BOW, WINK, DOZE
nodding .... ANNUENT, NUTANT
node .... PLOT, JOINT
nodular bone .... SESAMOID
nodule .... AUGE, GEODE
noggin .... GILL, MUG, PATE
noise CLAMOR, BLARE, CHANG, ROAR,
        STRIDOR, STREPOR, DIN, BOOM,
        SCANDAL, BABEL, UPROAR
"   abroad .... BRUIT, AIR, PEAL
"   ; dial. Eng. .... LEDEN
"   ghost .... POLTERGEIST
noisily, go .... LARUM
noisome FETID, NOXIOUS, FOUL, RANK
noisy .... CREAKY, BLATANT, RIOTOUS
nomad ...... LURI, ARAB, SARACEN,
        SCENITE, GYPSY, ROVER,
        WANDERER, BEDOUIN
nomenclature ..... ONYMY, NAMING

nominal ...... PAR, TITULAR, TRIVIAL
nonage .... MINORITY, PUPILAGE
nonchalant .. ALOOF, CASUAL, COOL
nonconformist ... HERETIC, SECTARY,
        BEATNIK, DISSENTER, BOHEMIAN,
                            REBEL
nonconformity .... RECUSANCE
none .... NARY, NAE, NIN
nonentity .... NOBODY, CIPHER, NIL
nonessential .... ADVENTITIOUS
non-gypsy .... GAJO
non-Jew .... GOY, GOI
non-Moslem .... RAYA, RAIA
nonmetallic element BORON, BROMIN,
                    SILICON, IODIN
"   mineral .... SPAR
nonpareil .... TYPE, APPLE
nonplus .... MYSTIFY, PUZZLE, STUMP
nonplused ...... PERPLEXED, PUZZLED
nonprofessional .... LAY, LAIC
nonsense .... ROT, BLAH, FOLDEROL,
        BLATHER, STITE, BALDERDASH, PISH,
        POOH, HOKUM, TRASH, TRIVIA,
                            HOOEY
"   creature .... GOOP, SNARK,
                            SMOO
noodle dish .... RAVIOLI
nook .. HERNE, CANT, COVE, RECESS,
                    BAY, CORNER
noon .... MIDDAY, MERIDIAN
noonday rest .... SIESTA
nootka .... AHT
noose .... LOOP, LEASH
norm ...... MODEL, RULE, STANDARD
norma .... SQUARE, PATTERN, GAUGE
normal .. NATURAL, JUST, MEAN, PAR
Normandy capital .... ROUEN
"   cheese .... ANGELOT
"   department ... CALVADOS,
                    EURE, MANCHE, ORNE
"   , early conqueror of ROLLO
Norn .... SKULD, URTH, WYRD
Norris; novelist .... FRANK
Norse Adam .... ASK(R), BURE, BURI
"   bard .... SAGAMAN, SCALD
"   chieftain .... JARL
"   deity . ODIN, RAN, THOR, VAN
"   epic .... EDDA
"   explorer .... ERIC, LEIF
"   giant .. FAFNIR, JOTUN, MIMIR,
                    LOKI, YMIR, YMER
"   giantess .. NATT, NOTT, NORN
"   god .... AS, ASA, DONAR, ULL,
                            VALI
"   god of discord and evil . LOKI
"   god of fruitfulness ...... FREY
"   god of light .... BALDER
"   god of peace ... FORSETI, FREY
"   god of poetry ... BRAGI, ODIN

199

"	god of sea .... AEGER, NJORD, YMIR	northwest highway .... ALCAN	
"	god of sun .... BALDER	northern .... BOREAL, ARCTIC, POLAR	
"	god of thunder .... THOR	northern constellation . ANDROMEDA	
"	god of war .. ER, ODIN, THOR, TYR	northern bear .... RUSSIA, USSR	
"	god of watchfulness . HEIMDALL	Norway .... NORGE	
"	goddess, giant ... NORN, URTH	" , coin of ..... KRONA, ORA	
"	goddess of beauty ...... FREYA	" mountain range ... KJOLEN	
"	goddess of death .. HEL, HELA	" ruler .... HAAKON	
"	goddess of destiny .... NORN	" river ...... NAMSEN, TANA	
"	goddess of earth .... SIF	" , saint of ..... OLAF, ODES	
"	goddess of healing .... EIR	" ter. division .... AMT	
"	goddess of history ...... SAGA	" , whirlpool of ... MAELSTROM	
"	goddess of love FREYA, FREYJA	Norwegian composer .... GRIEG	
"	goddess of peace .... EIR	" counties .... AMTER	
"	goddess of the seas RAN, RANA	" county .... FINNMARK, TROMS(O)	
"	goddess of the sky .... FRIGG	" eruptive rocks .... GABRO, NORITE	
"	gods .... AESIR, ASA, FORSETI, LOKI, THOR, VANIR, YMIR	" explorer .... NANSEN	
"	gods, abode of the .. ASGARD	" game bird .... RYPE	
"	gods, king of .... WODEN	" governor .... AMTMAN	
"	guardian of Asgard . HEIMDALL	" inlet of sea . FIORD, FJORD	
"	king; myth. .... ATLI	" needlework ... HARDANGER	
"	navigator .... ERIC	" parliament ..... LAGTHING, STORTHING	
"	nobleman .... JARL	" soprano .... FLAGSTAD	
"	plateau .... FJELD	" statesman .... LIE, DAG	
"	poem .... RUNE	" town .... BERGEN, NARVIK, OSLO	
"	poet .... SCALD	" writer .... IBSEN, HAMSUN	
"	poetry .... RUNE, RUNIC	nose .... NASUS, CONK, NEB, SCENT, SNOUT, PROW, SNUFF, SNIFF	
"	queen of the underworld . HEL, HELA	" ailment .... CORYZA	
"	saint .... OLAF	" , bee's .... LOR	
"	serpent; myth. ..... MIDGARD	" , cartilage of the ...... SEPTUM	
"	tale .... SAGA	" , elongated .... PROBOSCIS	
"	: Viking .... ROLLO	" , having large ...... NASUTE	
"	warrior; myth. .... BERSERKER	" , inflammation of ..... RHINITIS	
"	watchdog; myth. ...... GARM	" , openings in .... NARES	
"	wolf; myth. .... FENRIR	" , partition in .... VOMER	
"	world tree; myth. .. YGDRASIL	" , per. to . RHINAL, NARIAL, NASAL	
North Carolina cape . FEAR, HATTERAS		" , rare word for ..... OLFACTOR	
"	" county .. ASHE, CLAY, DARE, HOKE, HYDE, LEE, NASH, PIT, POLK, WAKE	" , snub, having a .... SIMOUS	
		nosebleeding .... EPISTAXIS	
"	" river .... PEEDEE, TAR, NEUSE	nosegay .... POSY, TUTTY	
"	" sound .... CORE	nostalgia .... HOMESICKNESS	
"	" university ..... DUKE	nostology .... GERIATRICS	
North Caucasian language ... AVAR UDI(SH)		Nostradamus .... PROPHET, SEER	
North Dakota city ... MINOT, FARGO		nostril ...... NARE(S), NARIS, THRILL	
"	" county .. TRAILL, CASS, DUNN, EDDY	not any .... NARY, NUL, NONE	
		not; Fr. .... PAS	
North Pole discoverer .... PERRY		" ; Ger. .... NICHT	
North Sea port EMDEN, BERGEN, HULL, BREMEN		" in style .... OUT, PASSE	
		notch .. (IN)DENT, JAB, NICK, SCORE, DINT, NOCK, CRENA, GROOVE	
"	" , river to ALLER, DEE, EIDER, ELBE, EMS, MEUSE, RHINE, TEES, TYNE	notched .... EROSE, SERRATED, CRENELATED	
		notches .... HILA	
North Star ...... LODESTAR, POLARIS		note ... MINUTE, BILLET, IOU, MEMO, LOAN	

" , double whole .... BREVE
" , explain by .... GLOSS
" , explanatory .... SCHOLIUM
" , half .... MINIM
" , marginal .... POSTIL
" , musical .... PUNCTUS
" , of .... FAMED
" , promissory .... GOOD
" , short .... CHIT, CHITTY
" sounded at kill .... MORT
" , tail of a .... FILUM
" , visible .... MARK
notebook .... DIARY, JOURNAL, LOG
notes in Guido scale ... ALT, ELA, UT
" , succession of . STRAIN, TIRALEE
nothing . NIHIL, LUKE, NIL, ZERO, NIX,
BLANK, CIPHER, NAUGHT
" but .... MERE
notice .... MARK, QUOTE, SEE,
BULLETIN, POSTER, ORDER, (E)SPY
notify .. APPRISE, CITE, INFORM, TELL,
PUBLISH
notion .. IDEA, VIEW, WARES, WHIM,
GADGET, BEE, FREIT
notoriety ..... ECLAT, FAME, RENOWN
notorious .... ARRANT
notwithstanding . NATHLESS, YET, THO
nougat .... CONFECTION, NUT
noumenal .... ONTAL
noun . APTOTE, GERUND, NAME, ANA,
EPICENE
" , per. to .... CASAL
" suffix . ERY, IER, ION, FER, ISE,
IST, ENCE
nourish FEED, FOSTER, NURSE, SUCCOR
nourishing .. RICH, ALIBLE, NUTRITIVE
nourishment ..... MANNA, ALIMENT,
PABULUM, DIET
nous .... MIND, INTELLECT
nouveau riche .... UPSTART, PARVENU
nova; astron.: new _____ . STAR
Nova Scotia .... ACADIA, ACADIE
"   "   bay .... FUNDY
"   "   cape .. CANSO, BRETON,
GEORGE, SABLE
"   "   lake .... BRAS D'OR
"   "   native ...... BLUENOSE
Novarro; actor .... RAMON
novel ...... FRESH, RARE, ROMANCE
novelty .... FAD, NEWNESS
novice .... TYRO, TIRO, AMATEUR,
NEOPHYTE, HAM, GOYIN
novitiate .... PROBATION
now HERE, YET, TODAY, NOO, EXTANT,
PRESENT, INSTANT
Nox (Rom.) .... NYX
" , brother of .... EREBUS
" , husband of .... CHAOS
noxious .... EVIL, BANEFUL, NOCENT,
NOISOME

nozzle NOSE, SNOUT, TUYERE, SPOUT,
VENT, GIANT
nub .... JAG, KNOB, SNAG, PITH
Nubian mus. instrument .... SISTRUM
nucha .... NAPE
nuclear chemist .... SEABORG
" element .... PROTON
" network fiber .... LININ
" physics .... NUCLEONICS
" pile .... REACTOR
nucleus .... CADRE, UMBRA
nudge ..... PROD, KNUB, POKE, NOG,
GOAD, PUSH, JOG
nugget .... LUMP, MASS, SLUG
nuisance ... BANE, PEST, PAIN, BORE,
STING, PLAGUE
" remover .... ABATOR
nullify ... CANCEL, VOID, ABROGATE,
NEGATE, UNDO, VETO, OFFSET,
REPEAL
numb ... DAZED, DEADEN, HEBETATE,
DULL, TORPID
number SURD, COUNT, DIGIT, SCALAR,
UNIT, AMOUNT, COMPUTE,
INTEGER, ORDINAL, CARDINAL
" four .... TETRAD
" nine .... ENNEAD
numbered; bib. .... MENE
numerous ...... LOTS, MANY, DIVERS,
GALORE, MYRIAD, COPIOUS, SUNDRY
Numidian city .... HIPPO
" crane .... DEMOISELLE
numskull .... DOLT, LACKWIT,
LOGGERHEAD
nun ..... TERESA, SISTER, MINORESS,
CLARE, MONASA, VOTARESS
nuncio .... MESSENGER, LEGATE
nun moth .... TUSSOCK
nunnery .... CLOISTER
nunni .... BLESBOK
nun's headgear .... WIMPLES
nuptial .. HYMENEAL, BRIDAL, MARITAL
nurse . AMAH, AYAH, BONNE, NORICE,
BABA
" , to . FOSTER, SUCKLE, CHERISH,
FEED, REAR, TEND, CARE
nurse shark .... GATA
nursery .... CRECHE
" furniture .... PLAYPEN
nut BEN, BETEL, BRAZIL, KOLA, PECAN,
FOOL, KERNEL, PITH, PROBLEM
" confection MARZIPAN, MARCHPANE
", per. to .... NUCAL
Nut, son of .... RA
nuthatch .... TITMOUSE
" ; genus .... SITTA
nutlet .... PYRENE
nutmeg .... SEED, SPICE
" -like fruit .... CAMARA(N)
nutria-producing animal .... COYPU

201

nutriment .... FOOD, ALIMENT
nutritive .... ALIBLE
nuts .... MAST, SHACK
nutty FOOLISH, GAGA, QUEER, RACY,
    ZANY, ZESTFUL, SPICY
nuzzle .... BURROW, ROOT
nymph ... SYLPH, ECHO, MAIA, MUSE,
    NAIS
" abducted by Idas .. MARPESSA
" beloved by Pan ..... SYRINX
" changed into laurel tree.....
    DAPHNE
" , fountain ..... NAIAD, EGERIA
" , Hesperid .... AEGLE
" , mountain .... OREAD
" of Moham. Paradise .. HOURI
" , sea .. NEREID, SCYLLA, SIREN
" , tree .... DRYAD, HAMADRYAD
" , water .... UNDINE
" , wood of Elis, ... ARETHUSA
" , woods .... DRYAD
nyroca .... AYTHYA
nyssa .... TUPELO
Nyx .... NOX, NIGHT
" , daughter of .... ERIS
" , husband of .... CHAOS
Nzambi, relatives of ...... BAKONGO

O

oaf BOOR, DOLT, DUNCE, LOUT, IDIOT
oak . AIK, ROBUR, DURMAST, QUERCUS,
    ILEX, AMBROSE, CERRIS, ROBLE
" bark .... CRUT, EMORY, MILL
" , fruit of . CAMATA, MAST, ACORN,
    BELLOTE
" thicket .... CHAPARRAL
oakum, seal with .... CALK
oar ...... PADDLE, SPOON, SCULL, PLY,
    POLE, BLADE, PROPEL
" fulcrum .... THOLE
" part .. PEEL, WASH, PALM, LOOM,
    ROWLOCK
" -shaped ...... REMIPED, REMIFORM
oars; collec. .... OARAGE
oars, having one bank of .. UNIREME
oarsman .... REMEX
oasis .. WADI, MERV, DAKHLA, GAFSA
oast .... KILN, OVEN
oatcake .... CAPER
oatear .... WAGTAIL
oath .. VOW, BEDAD, SERMENT, AITH,
    DRAT, GOSH, CURSE, PLEDGE
oatmeal cake .... PONE, SCONE
oats; genus .... AVENA
" paid as rent .... AVENAGE

obdurate ..... HARD, MULISH, STONY
obedient .... AMENABLE, DUTEOUS
obeisance .... HOMAGE, FEALTY
" , to make ..... CONGEE,
    SALAAM, BOW, CURTSY
obelisk ..... NEEDLE, PYLON, GUGLIA,
    DAGGER
Oberon .... FAIRY
" ; movie star .... MERLE
" , wife of .... TITANIA
obese FAT, FLESHY, LIPAROUS, TURGID,
    PUFFY, PURSY, PORTLY
obey . MIND, EAR, HEAR, YIELD, HEED,
    DEFER, COMPLY, SUBMIT
obfuscate .... CONFUSE, DARKEN
obi .... CHARM, FETISH, SASH
object AIM, END, GOAL, THING, CARP,
    CAVIL, DEMUR, BAR
" of art .... BIBELOT, CURIO
" set up to be tilted at.........
    QUINTAIN
objects, bib. .... URIM, THUMMIM
objurgate ...... CHIDE, REPROVE, JAW
oblate, opposed to .... PROLATE
obligation ... TIE, DEBT, BOND, DUTY,
    ONUS, OBSTRICTION, IOU, MUST
oblique ..... AGLEY, ASKANCE, AWRY
obliterate . SPONGE, ERASE, EXPUNGE,
    BLOT, ANNUL, EFFACE, DELE,
    ABOLISH
obliteration .... ERASURE
oblivion producer .... NEPENTHE
" , stream of . SILENCE, LETHE,
    NIRVANA
obnoxious HATEFUL, RANCID, ODIOUS,
    VILE
oboe ...... HAUTBOY, REED, MUSETTE,
    PIFERO, PIPE
obscuration .... ECLIPSE
obscure ..... NAMELESS, DIM, MIRKY,
    ECLIPSE, VAGUE, REMOTE, MURKY,
    DARKLE, CRYPTIC, CONCEAL,
    DELUDE, OVERSILE
obscurity .. DARKNESS, FOG, GLOOM
obsequies .... FUNERAL, PYRE, WAKE
obsequious ..... SERVILE, OBEDIENT,
    DUTIFUL
observation .... PROEM, ESPIAL,
    ASSERTION, IDEA, REMARK
observatory LICK, PALOMAR, HOOKER,
    HALE, YERKES
observe .... NOTICE, EYE, MARK, SEE,
    BEHOLD, MENTION, ADHERE
observed, matter to be .. NOTANDUM
obsidian .... LAVA, ITZLE, LAPIS
obsolete . DISUSED, ARCHAIC, EFFETE
obstacle .. BAR, DAM, SNAG, BARRIER,
    DRAWBACK
obstinate . DOUR, SET, MULISH, SULKY,
    DOGGED, UNRULY, RENITENT

obstruct .... DAM, BAR, CLOG, FOIL, IMPEDE, OCCLUDE, HAMPER, STAY
obtain ..... EARN, GET, WIN, FANG, SECURE, PROCURE
obverse .... COUNTERPART, FRONT
obvious ... GROSS, PATENT, EVIDENT, MANIFEST, VISIBLE
oca .... OXALIS, SORREL
occasion ...... EVENT, NONCE, SELE, INCIDENT, FUNCTION, CAUSE
occasional .... ODD, ORRA, CASUAL, SPORADIC
occident .... WEST, SUNSET
occidental ...... HESPERIAN, PONENT
occult .... CRYPTIC, HIDDEN, MYSTIC, ARCANE, ESOTERIC
occultism .. CABALA, MYSTERY, MAGIC
occupation .... CALL, NOTE, PURSUIT, JOB, CRAFT, TRADE, TENURE, WORK
occupy INTEREST, FILL, TAKE, ENGAGE, INHABIT, POSSESS
occur BEFALL, COME, BETIDE, CHANCE, HAPPEN
occurring at nightfall ... ACRONICAL
    "   at regular intervals . HORAL
    "   at eight-day intervals......
                                OCTAN
ocean BRIM, BRINE, DEEP, MAIN, POND
    " , on the .... ASEA
    " route .... LANE
Oceania, part of .... POLYNESIA
oceanic .. PELAGIC, MARINE, DIPS(E)Y
Oceanus, wife of .... TETHYS
ocellus .... EYE
ocelot .... CAT, TIGER, CHATI
ocher .... ALMAGRA
    " , red .... TIVER
    " , yellow .... SIL
ocilli, one of the .... STEMMA
octahedrite .... ANATASE
octave .... EIGHT
    " of a feast .... UTIS, UTAS
Octavia's brother .... AUGUSTUS
    "   husband .... ANTONY
octopus ...... POLYP, POULP, SQUID
octoroon .... METIS, MESTEE, MUSTEE
ocular ...... OPTIC, ORBITAL, VISUAL
oculi .... EYES
odd ... AZYGOUS, EXTRA, ORRA, LEFT, DROLL, QUEER, UNIQUE
oddity .... IDIOSYNCRASY
odds ..... DISCORD, EDGE, HANDICAP
Oder tributary .... NEISSE
odic electrical force .... ELOD
    " force .... OD
Odin .... WODEN, WOTAN
    " , brother of .... VILE, VILI
    " , son of ..... BALDER, TYR, VALI
Odinic Olympus .... ASGARD

Odin's horse .... SLEIPNER
    " wife ...... RIND, FRIA, FRIGG
odium .... AVERSION, DISLIKE, HATRED
odor .. AROMA, FETOR, NIDOR, NOSE, SCENT
    " of cooking meat ..... FUME(T)
odorous ...... REDOLENT, AROMATIC, BALMY, FRAGRANT, PERFUMED, OLENT
Odysseus .... ULYSSES
    " , dog of .... ARGOS
    " , father of .... LAERTES
    " , wife of .... PENELOPE
Odyssey author .... HOMER
Oedipus' brother-in-law ..... CREON
    " daughter ...... ANTIGONE
    " father .... LAIUS
oestrid fly larva .... BOT
oeuvre .... WORK
off ... AGEE, ASIDE, AWAY, BEGONE, DOFF, REMOTE, DISTANT
offend ..... RASP, PIQUE, CAG, MIFF, MORTIFY, ANNOY, NETTLE, INSULT, VEX
offense ...... FELONY, GRIEF, MALUM, DELICT, SIN, TORT, VICE, WRONG, AFFRONT, UMBRAGE
offer .. HAND, BID, PROPINE, PROFFER, PRESENT, PROPOSAL
offering .... CORBAN
    " resistance to force RENITENT
offhand .... EXTEMPORE, CASUAL, IMPROMPTU, CURT, ADLIB
office .... POST, FUNCTION, STATION, WIKE, BUREAU, METIER, TASK
    " -holder .... PLACEMAN
    " of a cardinal .... DATARIA
    " , relinquish .... DEMIT
officer .. COP, ENS, NCO, SGT, AMIN, EXON, DEWAN, DIWAN, BAILIE, BEADLE, DEPUTY, LICTOR, PARNAS, TINDAL, CONSTABLE
    " , assistant of ... AIDE, ADJUNCT, ADJUTANT
official .... BASHAW, HAJIB, KUAN, KWAN, (A)EDILE, SATRAP, TRIBUNE
    " approval .... VISA, VISE
    " decree .... UKASE
    " , government ..... BUREAUCRAT
    " order .... RESCRIPT
    " sent by king .... MISSUS
offshoot . SPRIG, BRANCH, ISSUE, ROD, SON, SCION
O'Flaherty; novelist .... LIAM
ogee molding .. TALON, CYMA, GULA
Ogier .... NORSEMAN, DANE
"Ogier le Danois," island in AVALON
ogle ...... EYE, LEAR, LEER, MARLOCK
oh; Scot. .... OCH

203

Ohio county . DARKE, HARDIN, LOGAN,
MEIGS, PREBLE, SCIOTO
" town ..... BEREA, CLYDE, LIMA,
MINGO, XENIA, AKRON
oil ... ASARUM, BEN, GREASE, OLEUM,
LUBE, FAT, LARD, ANOINT, CETENE
" beetle; genus .... MELOE
" ; comb. form .... OLEO
" flask .... OLPE
" , fragrant .... ATTAR
" lamp .... LUCIGEN
" made from butter .... GHEE
" maker .... TELI
" obtained from coal .. PHOTOGEN
" of orange .... NEROLI
" port .... ABADAN, HAIFA
" -producing tree .... BEN
" skin .... SEBUM
" tree ..... MAHUA, EBOE, MAHWA
" tubes, destitute of ..... EVITATE
" , unproductive boring for . DUSTER
" well gone wrong .... GASSER
oilbird .... GUACHARO
oilet .... EYELET
oilseed .... SESAME, TIL
oilstone .... HONE
oily . OLEIC, GREASY, GLIB, OLEOSE,
UNCTUOUS, SLIPPERY, BLAND
" beach-tar compound ... CRESSOL
" ketone .... CARONE, IRONE
" liniment .... OLEANDER
" liquid .. PICAMAR, TAR, ANILINE,
OCTANE
" substitute in fats .... OLEIN
ointment BALSAM, CEROMA, UNGUENT,
GREASE, SALVE, POMADE, NARD
" ; bib. .... SPIKENARD
" oil ...... CERATE, CARRON
Oise tributary .... AISNE
O.K. .... RIGHT, ROGER
Okie .... MIGRANT
Okinawa capital .... NAHA
Oklahoma city . ENID, HUGO, MAUD,
RYAN
" county .. GARVIN, ADAIR,
ATOKA, KIOWA
" Indian . CHEROKEE, CREEK,
PAWNEE, PONCA
" mountain .... OZARK
" river .... RED
" state flower ... MISTLETOE
" state name ...... SOONER
okra . BENDY, GUMBO, GOBO, GUBBO
old ...... SENESCENT, SENILE, GRAY,
OGYGIAN, DATED, ARCHAIC,
FEEBLE, WORN, HOARY, ELD
" cloth measure .... ELL
" -fashioned .... QUAINT, FOGRAM
" -fashioned word ..... ARCHAISM

" man ...... ALTE, GAFFER, GEEZER,
NESTOR
" refrain .... FALA
" sailor .... SALT
" saying .... ADAGE, MAXIM, SAW
" ; Sp. .... VIEJO
" squaw .... DUCK
" time ..... ELD, QUONDAM, YORE
" woman .. CRONE, HAG, GAMMER
" -womanish .... ANILE
"old sod" .... ERIN, EIRE
Oldcastle, John .... COBHAM
older .... SENIOR, STALER
oldest geologic division of Europe . .
JURASSIC, LIAS
oleander . NERIUM, LAUREL, DOGBANE
oleic acid .... OLEATE
oleoresin ...... ANIME, ELEMI, TOLU
olfaction .... OSMESIS
olio .... CHOWCHOW
Oliphant; novelist .... MARGARET
olive .... OLEA, OXHORN
" , fruit of the .... DRUPE
" -shaped .... OLIVARY
" , stuffed .... PIMOLA
" , wild .... OLEASTER
olive oil; comb. form ...... ELAIO
ollapodrida .... HASH
Olympic cupbearer ...... GANYMEDE
" game site .... ELIS
Olympus of Hindus .... MERU
Omar Khayyám .... TENTMAKER
" " , country of ......
PERSIA, IRAN
omber, card in .... BASTO
omen .... PORTENT, TOKEN, AUSPICE,
AUGURY, PRESAGE, (FOR)BODE
omers, ten .... EPHA
omicron .... CETI
omission .. CARET, ELISION, SYNCOPE,
OVERSIGHT, DEFAULT, ERROR,
FAILURE
omit .... BATE, IGNORE, DELE(TE), SKIP
omnivorous animal .... HOG
on dit .... RUMOR
"On the Banks of the Wabash" writer
DRESSER
on the ocean .... ASEA
"On the Town," by ..... BERNSTEIN,
LENNIE
on the windward side .. AWEATHER,
ALEE
on this side; Lat. .... CIS
onager .... ASS
once .... ANES
one ITE, UNO, ACE, AN, UNIT, YIN,
ONLY, SAME
" after the other .... SERIATIM
" against .... ANTI
" ; comb. form .... MONO, UNI

204

" hundred thousand .... LAC
" -sided .... UNILATERAL
" -spot .... ACE
" third of an inch .. BARLEYCORN
" thousand sq. meters .... DECARE
one-footed .... UNIPED
one's own; comb. form .... IDIO
" self alone, belief in . SOLIPSISM
onion .... BOLL, CEPA, CIBOL, INGAN
" bulb .... SET
" ; genus .... ALLIUM
" , small .. ESCHALOT, SCALLION
" , young .... SHALLOT
onion-like herb .... CHIVE
" plant .... LEEK
only ..... LONE, MERE, SOLE, SIMPLY,
SOLITARY, SAVE, BUT
onslaught .... ATTACK, BRUNT
onus .. BURDEN, LOAD, WEIGHT, DUTY
onward .... AHEAD, FORTH
onyx ..... NICOLO, ONICOLO, TECALI
oopak .... TEA
oorial .... SHA
ooze ...... EXUDE, SLIME, LEAK, SEEP,
FILTER, SYPE, SIPE
" through pores ...... TRANSUDE
oozing moisture .... ADRIP
opah .... CRAVA, SUNFISH, KINGFISH
opal .. HYALITE, NOBLE, CACHOLONG,
MENILITE
" , fire .... GIRASOL
" , reddish .... HARLEQUIN
opalescent .... IRISATED
opaque .... DARK, OBSCURE, DULL,
CLOUDED, DIM, VAGUE, OBTUSE
open OVERT, PATENT, UNDO, UNSEAL,
APERT, AJAR, AGAPE, CANDID,
PUBLIC, VACANT
" air, in the .... ALFRESCO
" country .... WEALD, VELDT
" for discussion .... MOOT
" passage in the woods ... GLADE
" shelf cabinet .... ETAGERE
" , to gape .... DEHISCE
opening .. LOOP, BAY, HIATUS, SINUS,
EYELET, FENESTRA, FORAMEN,
SLOT, RIMA, VENT, CLEFT, GAP,
CAVITY, FISSURE
" from a ventricle ..... PYLAE
" in a mold .... INGATE
" in chess .... GAMBIT
" of ear .... BURR
openings; zool. .... STOMATA
openwork .... FILIGREE
opera .. AIDA, MONA, FAUST, TOSCA,
NORMA, MARTHA, OTELLO,
RIENZI, LAKME
" by day .... SOAP
" executive .... BING
" glass .... BINOCLE, LORGNETTE

" hat .... GIBUS, TOPPER
" house .... LASCALA,
MET(ROPOLITAN)
operated ...... RAN, RUN, MANAGED
operatic role .... BUFFO, TENOR,
SOPRANO, BASSO
operator .... DEALER, MAKER, AGENT,
ACTOR, DENTIST, SURGEON, DOER,
PILOT
ophidian ... SNAKE, REPTILE, SERPENT
opiate ..... DOPE, ANODYNE, HEMP,
NARCOTIC, SOPORIFIC, SEDATIVE,
DRUG
opine .... DEEM, THINK
opinion . VIEW, WENE, DOXY, TENET,
BELIEF, CONCEPT, NOTION
opium alkaloid .... CODEINE
" , derivative of ...... MECONIC
" , Egypt. .... THEBAINE
" , extract of ...... CHANDOO
" seed .... MAW
" , source of .... POPPY
oppidan .... URBAN
opossum . MARMOSE, QUICA, SARIGUE,
YAPOK
opponent .. ENEMY, FOE, RIVAL, ANTI
opportune .... APROPOS, APT, READY,
TIMELY, FITTING
opportunity ..... TIDE, HENT, BREAK,
CHANCE
opposed ANTI, COPED, FRONTED, MET,
DEFIED
" (with "against") .... PITTED
" to entad .... ECTAD
" to science .... ART
" to stoss .... LEE
" to zenith .... NADIR
opposite .. OTHER, CONVERSE, POLAR,
CONTRA, HOSTILE, COUNTER,
ANTI(PODAL)
opposition, in .... WITHER
oppress ...... RACK, SWAY, WEIGHT,
MACERATE, ABUSE, SUBDUE, CRUSH
opprobrium .... INFAMY, ODIUM
oppugn .... DISPUTE
Ops, consort of .... SATURN
" , early associate of ... CONSUS
" , festival of .... OPALIA
opt .... CHOOSE, WISH
optic .... EYE, OCULAR, VISUAL
optical instrument .... ALIDADE,
ERIOMETER, LANTERN
" illusion .... MIRAGE
" lens .... CONTACT
optimistic ..... HOPEFUL, SANGUINE,
ROSEATE, EXPECTANT, HELPFUL,
ROSY
opulent ... ABUNDANT, FLUSH, LAVISH,
(P)LUSH, RICH
opus .... ETUDE, STUDY, WORK

oquassa .... TROUT
oracle .. SIBYL, SEER, AUGUR, DELOS,
                    DELPHI, PROPHET
" , per. to an .... PYTHONIC
oracular .. VATIC, WISE, AMBIGUOUS
oral ..... PAROL(E), ALOUD, VOCAL,
                    VERBAL, SPOKEN
orange ..... TANGELO, GENIP, CHINO
"Orange Bowl" site .... MIAMI
orange, Chinese .... MANDARIN
" flower oil .... NEROLI
" ; genus .... CITRUS
" , kind of ..... HEDGE, MOCK,
                    OSAGE
" peel .... ZEST
" -red .... CORAL
" -red dyestuff . CORALLINE, ALGA
orange seed .... PIP
orange, seedless .... NAVEL
" , spring .... STYRAX
" tincture .... TENNE
orange-like fruit ... BEL, TANGERINE
orangewood tree .... OSAGE
orangutan ...... APE, MIAS, PONGO,
                    WOODMAN
orator .... RHETOR, SPEAKER, BRYAN,
             CATO, CICERO, HENRY
oratorical .... ELOQUENT
oratorio, coda in .... STRETTO
" , Handel .... MESSIAH, ACIS
" , Haydn .... SEASONS
oratory .. CHAPEL, BETHEL, CHANTRY,
                    ORIEL
orbed .... LUNAR
orbit . EYE, ELLIPSE, PATH, KEN, SCOPE
" point .... APSIS, APOGEE
orchestra circle .... PARTERRE
" conductor .... STOKOWSKI,
TOSCANINI, KARAJAN, BERNSTEIN,
       WALTER, SZELL, MAESTRO
orchid ..... POGONIA, FAHAM, FAAM,
            DUFOIL, DISA, LISTERA
" appendage .... CAUDICLE
" , part of .... ANTHER
" -plant drugs .... SALOOPS
" pods, derivative of .. VANILLA
orchids, dried tubers of ...... SALEP
" , male .... PURPLE, CULLION
Orcus .... HADES
ordain ... CALL, WILL, DECREE, ENACT,
          INVEST, FROCK, APPOINT
ordained ..... PRESCRIPT, LEGAL, DUE
ordeal ... GAFF, CRUCIBLE, TEST, TRIAL
order .... MANDATE, ARRAY, BID,
     COMMAND, DIRECT, CLASS, WILL,
TAXIS, WRIT, FIAT, SYSTEM, KELTER,
          DICTATE, GENUS
" of merit ...... BATH, CROWN,
     ALBERT, LEOPOLD, SWORD, VASA
" , put in .... TIDY, SETTLE

ordinal _____ .... NUMBER
ordinance .... ASSIZE, LAW, RITE,
     STATUTE, DECREE, CANON, ROBINET
ordinances; Lat. .... DECRETA
ordinary .... VULGATE, AVERAGE,
    NORMAL, NOMIC, PROSAIC, USUAL,
          BANAL, COMMON
ordinary's court .... PROBATE
ordnance ... ARMOR, GUNS, PETARDS,
                    MATERIEL
_____ ore . IRON, METAL, MINERAL,
                    TIN
" , earthy-looking .... PACO
" -fusing establishment SMELTERY
" ; horizontal layer ..... STOPE
" , impure .... SPEISS
" , iron, used as a pigment ...
              OCHER, OCHRE
" -loading platform ...... PLAT
" , method of cleansing ....
              VANNING
" mill roller ...... EDGESTONE
" , small bunch of NEST, SQUAT
" , trough for washing . STRAKE
" vein .... STOPE, LODE, SCRIN
" , worthless .... MATTE
oread .... NYMPH, PERI, SEAMAID
Oregon capital .... SALEM
" city ..... EUNICE, PORTLAND,
              EUGENE
" county COOS, GILLIAM, LINN,
          UMATILLA, WASCO
" , first explorer of ..... FENO
" mountain .. CASCADE, COAST
" , site of university in EUGENE
orellin, relative of .... BIXIN
Orestes, friend of .... PYLADES
" , sister of .... ELECTRA
" , wife of .... HERMIONE
organ ...... AGENT, MEANS, MEDIUM
" interlude .... VERSET
" ; mus. .... REGAL, ACCORDION,
       MELODEON, MELODION
" of speech .... TONGUE
" , original .... SYRINX
" , pipe of an .... FLUE, REED
" -pipe voicer .... TONER
" stop .. DULCIANA, OBOE, VIOLA,
   CELESTA, SEXT, DOLCAN, MELODIA
organ stops, adjust ...... REGISTRATE
organic .... INHERENT, VITAL
" body .... ZOOID
" compound .... AMINE, KETOL
" radical .... ETHYL
" remains, without .... AZOIC
organism . AM(O)EBA, ANIMAL, PLANT,
      MONAD, MONAS, BODY
" in certain plants .... SPORE
" , potential .... IDORGAN

"   of surface of sea   NEKTON, PLANKTON
organization .... UNIT, SETUP, CADRE, FIRM, OUTFIT, COMPANY, SOCIETY
organize ..... ARRANGE, FORM, PLAN
organized body of persons ... CORPS, POSSE
orgy .... BINGE, REVEL
oribi .... ANTELOPE, PALEBUCK
oriel .... BAY, WINDOW
Orient .... ASIA, EAST, LEVANT
oriental . LEVANTINE, BRIGHT, ORTIVE, EASTERN
"   beverage .... ARRACK
"   caravansary .... IMARET
"   carpet .... KALI
"   cart .... ARABA
"   Christian .... UNIAT
"   destiny .... KISMET
"   dish .... PILAU, PILAW
"   dwelling .... DAR
"   gate; Ind. ....DAR
"   hospice ..... MARET, IMARET
"   inn .... SERAI
"   kettledrum .... ANACARA
"   laborer .... COOLIE
"   man servant .... HAMAL
"   note .... CHIT
"   nurse .... AMAH, AYAH
"   palanquin .... DOOLEE
"   patent .... BERAT
"   people, anc. .... SERES
"   ruler .. KHAN, SHAH, SULTAN
?   salute ...... SAHEB, SALAAM
"   skipper .... RAIS, REIS
"   tamarisk .... ATLEE
"   tambourine .... DAIRA
"   taxi .... RICKSHA(W)
"   vessel .... SAIC
orifice .... PORE, OSTIOLE, HOLE, OPENING, MOUTH, CAVITY, VENT, STOMA, PORULE, SPIRACLE
"   in the brain .... LURA
origan .... MARJORAM
origin ROOT, BIRTH, GENESIS, NATURE, ALPHA, SEED, PROVENANCE, PARENTAGE, RISE, OUTSET, FONT, SOURCE
original ... NATIVE, INITIAL, PRISTINE, CREATIVE, PRIMARY, UNIQUE, FONTAL
originally .... FIRST
original sin .... ADAM
originate .... ARISE, COIN, EMANATE, INVENT, STEM, CREATE
oriole .... LORIOT, PIROL, HANGBIRD, ICTERUS
Orion, seen in BETELGEUX, BETELGEUSE
orison .... PRAYER, REQUEST
Orkney Islands capital .... KIRKWALL

"   "   fishing bank ... HAAF
"   "   freehold . ODAL, UDAL
"   "   , largest of .. POMONA
"   "   tower .... BROCH
Orlando's friend .... ADAM
ormer; genus .... HALIOTIS
ormolu .... ALLOY, GOLD
ornament ... SPANG, AMULET, GUTTA, OUCH, DECOR, SEME, ROSETTE, BROCADE, (BE)DECK, EPI, GAUD, STUD, SEQUIN
ornamental belt .... CINCHER
"   button .... STUD
"   edge on lace ..... PICOT
"   vessel .... VASE
ornamented, as a book cover TOOLED
ornaments, set of jeweled ... PARURE
ornate .... FANCY, FLORID, GAY
ort .... END, LEFTOVER, SCRAP
orthorhombic mineral .... IOLITE
ortolan .... BUNTING
Osaka Bay port .... KOBE
oscillate . ROCK, SWAY, WAG, WAVER, VIBRATE
oscillating .... VIBRATORY
oscillation transformer .... TESLA
osculate .... BUSS, KISS
osier ... SALLOW, WAND, WILLOW
"   band .... WITHE
Osiris' brother .... SET
"   father .... SEB
"   mother .... NUT
"   sister .... ISIS
"   son .... ANUBIS, HORUS
"   wife .... ISIS
osprey .... FEATHER, HAWK, GLED(E)
osseous .... BONY, LITHIC, SPINY
Osset division .... DIGOR
ossicle .... BONE
ostentation .... POMP, ECLAT, FLARE, PARADE, GLOSS, STRUT, PAGEANT
ostracize EXPATRIATE, BANISH, TABOO
ostracism .... BAN, EXILE, EXPULSION
ostrich .... NANDU, RHEA
"   -like bird .. EMU, EMEU, RATITE
"   tail feathers .... BOOS
otalgia .... EARACHE
Othello's wife .... DESDEMONA
other; comb. form .... ALLO
others .... ETAL, RESIDUE, REST
otherwise .... ALIAS, ELSE, OR
"   ; mus. .... OSSIA
otic .... AURAL
otiose .... FUTILE, INDOLENT, IDLE
Otis; patriot .... JAMES
otter .... HURON, MUSTELID, LUTRA
Ottoman .... TURK
ottoman .. POUF, SEAT, (FOOT)STOOL, COUCH
Ottoman court .... PORTE

"	Empire non-Moslem subject RAIA	ouzel ...... BLACKBIRD, PIET, WHISTLER	
"	Empire province .. VILAYET	oven .. UMU, KILN, OAST, LEER, TISAR, LEHR	
"	high official .... PASHA	" mop .... SCOVEL	
"	leader .... OSMAN, AHMED	over .... ACROSS, ALSO, TOO, ANEW,	

"   Empire non-Moslem subject
                RAIA
"   Empire province .. VILAYET
"   high official .... PASHA
"   leader .... OSMAN, AHMED
ought BOOD, CIPHER, MOTE, NOUGHT,
                MUST
ouija board .... PLANCHETTE
ounce, half of an .... DRAM
oust ... EVICT, EXPEL, CASHIER, SLACK
out .. FROM, AWAY, EX, EXIT, EGRESS,
           ARRANT, UIT, PASSE
" of; foreign to .... DEHORS
" of sorts .... NOHOW
outbreak .... EMEUTE, RASH, RIOT,
              ERUPTION
outburst GERE, ACCESS, FLARE, GALE,
            STORM, SPATE
outcast ... LEPER, PARIAH, CHANDALA,
        (Y)ETA, ISHMAEL, RONIN
outcome .... DENOUEMENT, ISSUE,
           UPSHOT, RESULT
outcry .... GAFF, CLAMOR
outdo .... EXCEL, SURPASS, BEST, TOP
outdoor theater .... DRIVEIN
outer .... ECTAL, FOREIGN
" coat of grain ... TESTA, EXTINE
" garment .... PALETOT, WRAP
" layer of roots ...... EXODERM
Outer Mongolia, capital of ... URGA,
           ULANBATOR
outer, opposed to .... ENTAL
" portion of earth .... SIAL
" shell of oyster .... TEST
outfit REGALIA, KIT, EQUIP, RIG, GEAR,
               UNIT
outlandish BIZARRE, STRANGE, EXOTIC,
       OUTRE, ODD, UNCOUTH
outlaw .. BANDIT, PROSCRIBE, RONIN,
       ROBROY, DACOIT, DHU
outlet .... ISSUE, EGRESS, EXIT, VENT,
          FAUCET, SOCKET
" , water .... BAYOU
outline ... TRACE, SKETCH, CONTOUR,
         PROFILE, SUMMARY
outlook ... FRONTAGE, SCOPE, VIEW,
       PURVIEW, VISTA, WATCH
outmoded ... OUTMODED, OLD, USED,
        DATED, OBSOLETE
output .... TURNOUT, YIELD, CROP
outrigger .... PROA
outspoken ..... BLUNT, ROUND, FREE,
         CANDID, FRANK
outrival ..... ECLIPSE, EXCEL, OUTVIE
outstrip .... BEST, EXCEL, OUTDO
outward .. ECTAD, EXTRINSIC, FORMAL
" , turn .... EVERT
outwit .... EUCHRE, BALK, BEST, FOIL,
        DUPE, COZEN, GULL
outwork .. TENAIL, RAVELIN, LUNETTE

ouzel ...... BLACKBIRD, PIET, WHISTLER
oven .. UMU, KILN, OAST, LEER, TISAR,
              LEHR
" mop .... SCOVEL
over .... ACROSS, ALSO, TOO, ANEW,
       ATOP, DEAD, DONE, ABOVE,
        AGAIN, ENDED, ENCORE
" ; prefix .... SUR
overact .... HAM, OUTDO, EMOTE
overawe ...... COW, DAUNT, SUBDUE
overbearing .. CAVALIER, ARROGANT,
        HAUGHTY, LORDLY
overcoat .... BENNY, CAPOTE, ULSTER,
      SURTOUT, RAGLAN, PALETOT,
           INVERNESS
overcome . BEAT, HURDLE, AWE, BEST,
     LICK, PREVAIL, SUBDUE, ROUT,
           DISCOMFIT
overdue .... LATE, TARDY, REMISS
overfeed .... AGROTE, PAMPER
overflow ...... DELUGE, SPATE, TEEM,
       SURPLUS, INUNDATE
overhang .... BEETLE, EAVES
overhead .... UPKEEP, ALOFT
overjoy .... ELATE, JUBILANT
overlapping .... IMBRICATE
overlay ... LAP, CEIL, HIDE, SMOTHER
overloaded .... PLETHORIC
overlook .. SCAN, IGNORE, MISS, SKIP,
        SURVEY, PARDON
overplus .... EXCESS, REST
overpower ...... AWE, MASTER, BEAT
overreach .... NOBBLE, STRAIN
override .... ABROGATE, VETO
overrun .... INFEST, SWARM, RAVAGE
overscrupulous person .... PRUDE
overseer INSPECTOR, BAILIFF, STEWARD
overshadow .... ECLIPSE, OBSCURE
overshoe .... ARCTIC, GALOSH, GUM
oversight .... LAPSE, SLIP, FAULT, GAP
overt .... OPEN, PATENT, PUBLIC
overtake .... REACH, REJOIN, PASS
overthrow DOWN, UNHORSE, TOPPLE,
           WORST
overture .... OFFER, PROPOSAL
overturn ... SUBVERT, CAPSIZE, UPSET,
           THROW
Ovid's burial place .... TOMI
ovine . GOAT, SHEEP, LAMB, EWE, TUP
ovule .... EGG, EMBRYO, SEED
" , outer integument of . PRIMINE
ovum .... EGG
owl ...... LULU, RURU, UTUM, HULLET,
    WAPACUT, MADGE, POUIE, MOMO,
      HOWLET, AZIOLA, KAKAPO
" genus .... SYRNIUM, STRIX
" -like .... STRIGINE
" , plumed eye area of .... DISC
" , to hoot as an .... ULULATE
" , wail of an .... ULULU, HOOT

own ..... NAIN, ADMIT, HAVE, HOLD, ALLOW, POSSESS, CONCEDE
ox . NOWT, BEEF, BEEVE, BISON, NEAT
" , extinct .... URUS
" , fierce Indian . TSINE, GAUR, GOUR
" , forest .... ANOA
" , grunting .... YAK
" , Indian .... GAYAL, ZEBU
" , Java .... BANTENG
" meat, cured .... BILTONG
" stomach .... TRIPE
" , wild horned .... REEM
" , working .... AVER
oxford .... SHOE
oxidize .... CALCIDE, RUST
ox-like .... BOVINE
oxter .... ARM, ARMPIT
oxtongue .... BUGLOSS
oxygen .... OZONE, OXIDE
oyez .... ATTEND, HEAR
oyster ...... BIVALVE, HUITRE, SHELL, MOLLUSC, SET, SPAT
" bed .... LAYER, STEW
" -bed material .... CULCH(ES)
" catcher .... OLIVE, TIRMA
" farm ..... CLAIRE, PARC, PARK
" gatherer .... TONGMAN
" , outer shell of .... TEST
" ova .... SPAWN
" rake .... TONG
" shell .... HUSK, SHUCK
oyster-fish .... TAUTOG
oyster-grass .... KELP
oyster-plant .... SALSIFY
Ozanna .... ANTELOPE
Ozark resort .... IRONTON

P

paca .... LABBA, AGOUTI, CAVY
pace . TROT, GAIT, LOPE, STEP, TRACE, AMBLE, RUN, TEMPO, GALLOP
pachyderm . ELEPHANT, RHINO(CEROS), HIPPO
Pacific island   YAP, UEA, ANAA, ATIU, BIAK, EBON, GUAM, MAULI, MILI, NIUE, OAHU, RAPA, SAVO, TRUK, EFATE, KAUAI
pacifier .... NIPPLE, RING, SOP
pacifist .... BOLO
pacify ... APPEASE, CALM, ALLAY, LULL
pack .. CRAM, EMBALE, STOW, STEEVE, GANG, SHOOK, TRUSS, BALE, TAMP, STUFF
" animal .... BURRO, LLAMA
" horse .... SUMTER, SOMER

package BALE, PACK, PARCEL, CEROON, ROBBIN, FADGE
packing ring .... LUTE
pact .... TREATY, ENTENTE
pad ...... MAT, QUILT, TABLET, TRAMP
" , collar .... HOUSING
" , harness .... TERRET
paddle ... SCULL, SPOON, OAR, ROW, FLIPPER, BLADE
paddock ..... GARSTON, PARK, FIELD
Paderewski; composer ...... IGNACE
" opera .... MANON
padre .... FATHER, MONK, PRIEST
paean .... HYMN, SONG
pagan .... HEATHEN, ETHNIC, PAYNIM
" , relative of .... GNOSTIC
page ..... BOY, LEAF, CAHIER, VERSO, FOLIO, RECTO, RUBRIC
Page; songstress .... PATTI
pageantry ... PARADE, POMP, SHOW
pages, number the .... PAGINATE
Paget; actress .... DEBRA
"Pagliacci" char. ..... TONIO, BEPPO, SILVIO, NEDDA, CANIO
pagoda ..... TAA, TAE, TEMPLE, PON
" , finial on .... TEE
pagurian .... CRAB
Pahlevi's countrymen ..... IRANIANS
paid out .... SPENT
paillasse .... MATTRESS
paillette .... SPANGLE
pain ...... AIL, PANG, ACHE, AGONY, THROE, MISERY, ANGUISH, DISTRESS, SMART
" , be in .... THROB, THRAW
paint .. LIMN, ROUGE, STAIN, COLOR, DEPICT, PORTRAY
" face .... FARD, PARGET
" spreader .... SPATULA
" with vermilion .... MINIATE
painting .... GENRE, MURAL, SECCO, IMPASTO
" method .... GRISAILLE
" technique .... TEMPERA
pair SPAN, TEAM, YOKE, BRACE, DUAD, DUET
" of units .... DYAD, TWO
paired; her. .... GEMEL
palace ... COURT, PRETORIUM, STEAD, SERAGLIO
Palamon, rival of .... ARCITE
palanquin bearer .... SIRDAR, HAMAL
" , oriental .. DOOLEE, KAGO
palatable ...... TASTY, SAPID, SAVORY
palate .. UVULA, VELUM, RELISH, TASTE
pale ..... MEALY, ASHY, BLANCH, DIM, WAN, SALLOW, WAXY, PASTEL, HAGGARD
" , a .... STAKE
" , become .... ETIOLATE

"   buck .... ORIBI
", to .... FENCE
", yellow .... FLAXEN
Palestine .... PHILISTIA, ERETZ, ISRAEL
"   battle site .... ELTEKEH
", conquerors of .... TURKS
", lake of .... MEROM
"   mountain ...... EBAL, NEBO
", part of .... CANAAN
Palestinian, anc. .... AMORITE
palisades .... CLIFF, PALES, RIMER,
                    HURDIS, ESPALIER
pall CLOAK, MANTLE, SATE, FAIL, JADE,
                            GORGE
pallet ...... BLANKET, PAWL, QUILT,
                            PLANCHER
palliate EXCUSE, TEMPER, LESSEN, EASE,
                            MITIGATE
pallid .... PALE, THIN, WAN
palm .... FANLEAF, ERYTHEA, CYCAD,
        PRIZE, THENAR, CONCEAL, IMPOSE
", Arabian .... DOUM
", areng .... GOMUTI
", Asiatic .. NIPA, NYPA, PALMYRA
", betel .... ARECA, BONGA
", book .... TARA, TALIERA
", Brazilian ...... ASSAI, BACABA,
                    TUCUM, URUCURI
", Bussu .... TROOLIE
", cabbage .... PALMETTO
", Ceylon .... TALIPOT
", civet; East Ind. ...... MUSANG
", drink ...... SURA, ASSAI, NIPA
", dwarf fan; genus ...... SABAL
", East Indian .... TALA, TOKOPAT
", edible fruit of .... NIPA
", fan-leaf ... PALMETTO, TALIPOT
", fiber .... BURI, TAL, RAFFIA
", Florida .... ROYAL
", fruit .... COCONUT
", gingerbread .... DOOM, DOUM
", leaf .. OLAY, FROND, OLA, OLLA
", lily .... TOI, TI
", Malayan ..... GEBANG, ARENG,
                            GOMUTI
" -leaf mat .... PETATE
", nipa .... ATAP, ATTAP
" of Asia .... ASSAI, CALAMI
" of the hand .... THENAR
" of the hand, belonging to .....
                    VOLAR, PALMAR
", off .... FOB, FOIST
", Palmyra .... BRAB, TAL
", pith .... SAGO
", reed-like stem of .... RATTAN
", sago .... ARENG, GOMUTI, IROK
", South American .... DATIL, ITA,
                            NIKAU
", starch .... SAGO
", stem of .... CANE, RATAN

"   sugar .... JAGGERY
"   tree; genus .... DOUM
"   wine .... TODDY
palmate .... WEBBED, ANTLER
palmetto .... SERENOA, THRINAX
palmistry .... CHIROMANCY
palms; genus ...... ARECA, ATTALEA,
                            BACABA
palp .... FEELER
palpable .... EVIDENT, MANIFEST,
                            OBVIOUS
palpitation .... BEAT, PULSE, PALMUS,
                            THROB
paltry ... LACKING, PICAYUNE, PUNY,
                            SORRY
pampas .... PLAIN
pamper ... HUMOR, COSHER, COSSET,
        POSSET, DANDLE, SPOIL, PET
pamphlet BROCHURE, TREATISE, TRACT
Pan, relative of .... FAUNUS
", son of .... SILENUS
pan .... FACE, LAPPET, TAB, ROAST
panacea .... ELIXIR, CATHOLICON,
        CUREALL, NEPENTHE, SOLACE
panache .... PLUME, TUFT, CREPE,
                            FLAPJACK
Panama Canal lake .... GATUN
"   currency .... BALBOA
Panay capital .... ILOILO
pancake .... FRITTER, FROISE
panda .... BEARCAT, WAH
pander .... DAWD, PIMP, CATER
panegyric .... ELOGE, ENCOMIUM
panel ... PANE, JURY, INSERT, TABLET,
                            VENIRE
pang ... ACHE, RACK, PRONG, THROE,
                            SPASM
pangolin .... ANTEATER, MANIS
panhandle .... BEG
panic .... SCARE, FEAR, FRAY, TERROR,
                            FUNK
pannier .... BASKET, DOSSER, CORBEIL
Panopolis, chief deity of .... MIN
panorama ...... VIEW, SCENE, VISTA,
                            SWEEP
Pan's pipes .... SYRINX
pant .... GASP, HEAVE, THROB, HUFF,
                    PUFF, YEARN
pantheon, chief Teutonic god of ....
                            AESIR
"   , chief Hawaiian god of ....
                            KANE
panther ... COUGAR, LEOPARD, PARD,
                    PUMA, PAINTER
" -like animal . JAGUAR, OCELOT
pantry .... AMBRY, SPENCER, CLOSET,
                    BATTERY, LARDER
papal book of edicts ...... DECRETAL
"   chancery .... DATARY
"   court .... SEE, CURIA

210

" envoy .... ABLEGATE, NUNCIO
" reformer .... GREGORY
" scarf or veil .. FANON, ORALE
" sign on letter .... BULLA
papaya .... CARICA, PAPAW
paper .. PAPIER, PAPYRUS, ESSAY, SPILL,
THEME
" , cloth-like ..... TAPA, PAPYRUS
" , crisp thin .... PELURE
" cutter .... SLITTER
" , damaged ...... RETREE, CASSE
" lighter .... SPILL
" measure .... REAM, QUIRE
" , official .... TARGE
" once-folded .... FOLIO
" size .... ATLAS, COPY, CROWN,
DOUBLE, DEMI, POTT, IMPERIAL,
OCTAVO, (FOOLS)CAP
" , untrimmed edge of ... DECKLE
papillae .... CERATA, PIMPLES
Papua bay .... MILNE
papyrus .... REED
par _____: by air .... AVION
parable .... FABLE, APOLOGUE, TALE,
MYTH, ALLEGORY, MORAL
parabola .... CURVE, SIMILITUDE
parachute strap .... RISER
" surface .... CANOPY
parade .. MARCH, FLAUNT, FILE, ARRAY,
STRUT, WALK
" of cars .... MOTORCADE,
AUTOCADE
paradise ... NIRVANA, UTOPIA, EDEN,
ELYSIUM, HEAVEN
paradisiac .... EDENIC
paragon .... TYPE, IDEAL, MODEL,
PALADIN, NONPAREIL, RIVAL,
NONESUCH
paragraph .. SECTION, ITEM, PILCROW,
CLAUSE, INDENT
Paraguay city .... LUQUE, ASUNCION
" tea .... MATE, YERBA
parakeet .... ROSELLA, CONURE
parallelogram .... RHOMB(US)
paralysis .... PALSY, PARESIS
paralyze .... NUMB, SCRAM
paramorphine .... THEBAINE
paramour .... LEMAN, LOVER
parapet .... BERM, PODIUM, RAMPART,
REDAN
" portion .... MERLON
parasite .. APHID, DRONE, SYCOPHANT,
TOADY, BINE, FAWNER
" of trout .... SUG
" , relative of .... FLUNKY
" plant .... ENTOPHYTE
parasites, internal .... ENTOZOA
parasitic fungus .... LICHEN
" worm .... TRICHINA
parcel ...... LOT, DOLE, PLAT, PACKET

parch . TORREFY, BRISTLE, ROAST, SEAR,
SCORCH
parchment .... DEED, FOREL, PELL,
VELLUM, DIPLOMA
" used more than once ....
PALIMPSEST
pardon ..... REMIT, AMNESTY, MERCY,
SPARE, REPRIEVE
pardonable .... VENIAL
pare .... RESECT, CURRY, SKIN, SLICE,
REDUCE, FLAY
parent ... DAD, SIRE, GENITOR, PATER,
MATER
parentage, per. to .... GERMANE
parental affection .... STORGE
parhelion .... SUN, SUNDOG
pariah .... OUTCAST
Paris .... PAREE
" airport .... ORLY
" district .... AUTEUIL
" , Roman name for .... LUTETIA
" subway .... METRO
parish head .... RECTOR
Parisian designer ..... DIOR, CARDIN,
CHANEL
" thug .... APACHE
Parks of TV .... BERT
parley .. POWWOW, CONVERSE, TALK,
CHAT, CONFER
parlor .... SALON, SALLE, BEN
parnassian .... POET
parody ...... SATIRE, SKIT, TRAVESTY,
TAKEOFF
parol .... ORAL, PLEADINGS
Paros, native of .... PARIAN
paroxysm . THROE, ANGER, EMOTION,
AGONY, SPASM, FIT
parrot ...... LORY, ARA, COCKATOO,
TIRIBA, POLLY, CORELLA, CAGIT,
MACAW, LORO, LORIKEET, KARA,
KEA
" fish .. LABROID, SCAR, SHANNY
" ; genus .... PSITTACUS, NESTOR
" , small ..... LORILET, PARAKEET
" , to ..... ECHO, REPEAT, MIMIC
parry .... FEND, ELUDE, AVERT, EVADE,
SHIFT, REPARTEE
parsley ...... UMBEL, ACHE, CONIUM
parsley, deriv. of ...... APIOL, APIIN
parsnips; genus .... SIUM
parson bird .... TUI
parsonage BENEFICE, MANSE, RECTORY
part .. ROLE, SEGMENT, SHARE, BREAK,
SECTOR, ELEMENT
" of a flower .... PETAL
" of a measure .... ALIDADE
" of a step . NOSING, RISER, TREAD
" of a turtle .... CALIPEE
" of an ear .... TRAGUS
" of speech .... NOUN, VERB
" that's kept .... RETENT

211

parted ...... CLOVEN, CLEFT, PARTITE
participate .. SHARE, DIVIDE, PARTAKE
particle ..... IOTA, GEN, ATOM, JOT,
TITTLE, GRAIN, GRANULE, BIT,
MESON, SHRED, SPECK
particolored .... PIEBALD, PIED
particular .... SOLE, SINGLE, ITEM,
UNIQUE, FUSSY, FINICAL, ODD
partisan .... SIDE, ZEALOT, GUERILLA,
ADHERENT, CHAMPION
" groups .... CAMPS
partition ... SCANTLE, ALLOT, SEPTUM,
BARRIER, DIVIDE
" , imperfect ...... SEPTULATE
partlet .... HEN
partnership CAHOOTS, COMATES, HUI,
HOEY, UNION
partridge .... GROUSE, QUAIL, TETUR,
TINAMOU
" food .... PUPAE
party ..... SQUAD, DRUM, GAID, SECT,
SHINDIG, TEA, CLIQUE, SIDE,
LABOR, SOCIAL, PROM, TORY,
WHIG, GOP
parvenue .. ARRIVISTE, UPSTART, SNOB
pass . SPEND, GHAT, MOVE, COL, GAP,
SKIP, ELIDE, HAPPEN
" a rope through .... REEVE
" , a sudden .... LUNGE
" , Alpine ...... SIMPLON, BRENNER,
GOTTHARD
" by .... ELAPSE, IGNORE, OMIT
" , dangerous .... PLIGHT
" lightly along .... FOIST, SKITTER
passage ADIT, ATRIUM, GANG, TRAVEL,
AVENUE, DUCT, ITER, AISLE,
CLAUSE, TRANSIT
" between two walls .... SLYPE
" , covered .... PAWN
" in a mine .... STOPE
" ; one end closed .... IMPASSE
passageway ...... ALLEY, RAMP, HALL
passenger ... PILGRIM, TOURIST, FARE,
TRAVELER, VOYAGER
passe . FADED, AGED, OBSOLETE, OUT,
WORN, OUTMODED
passion PAIN, IRE, YEN, ANGER, RAGA,
FERVOR, RAPTURE, URGE, EMOTION
passer of bad checks .... KITER
passing by, a .... PRETERITION
passion flower .. MAYPOP, MARACOCK
passive .... QUIET, INERT, STOIC
Passover festival .. SEDER, PASCH(A),
SEDAR
" , per to .... HALLEL, PASCHAL
passport .... VISA, VISE, CONGEE
passus .... CANTO
password .... COUNTERSIGN
past AGONE, DEAD, SINCE, AGO, YORE,
AFTER, OVER, ENDED, ELD, BYGONE

" tense .... PRETERITE, AORIST
paste .. GLUE, PAP, STICK(UM), BOND,
GUM
" -up art work .... COLLAGE
pastoral ... RURAL, COUNTRY, IDYLLIC,
RUSTIC, AGRESTIC, SHEPHERD
" cantata .... SERENATA
" crook .... PEDUM
" god .... PAN
" pipe .... REED, OAT
" poem ..... ECLOGUE, BUCOLIC
pastry ...... ECLAIR, PIE, TART, TUCK,
STRUDEL
pasture ...... AGIST, GRASS, GRAZE,
SHIELING
" grass .... GRAMA
" land .... HAM, ING, LEA
pasty mixture .... MAGMA
pat .. CARESS, FIT, PALP, BUTTER, DAB,
APT
Patagonian cattle .... NIATAS
" deity .... SETEBOS
" rodent .... CAVY
patch .... PARCEL, PLOT, TRACT, FIELD
" of woods .... MOTTE
" , to ..... BODGE, CLOUT, VAMP,
REPAIR, DARN
patcher ..... SARTOR, MENDER, SEWER
patella .... KNEECAP, PAN
paten .... DISC, PLATE
patent ...... BERAT, GRANT, SALIENT,
LICENSE
path ..... LANE, ROUTE, TRAIL, BERM,
ORBIT, RODDIN, TRACK, COMINO
patois .... ARGOT, JARGON, SPEECH,
CANT, CREOLE, LINGO, SLANG
patriarch . FATHER, SIRE, PATER, NASI,
PITRI
patriot ... ALLEN, REVERE, OTIS, HALE
patron ... ANGEL, BACKER, SPONSOR,
CLIENT
patron saint (female) .... CECILIA
" " of beggars ...... GILES
" " of boys .... NICHOLAS
" " of England .... ANNE,
GEORGE
" " of lawyers .... IVES
" " of sailors .... ELMO
patronage .... FAVOR, (A)EGIS
pattern .... BYSEN, NORM, SEME,
TEMPLATE, PARADIGM, MODEL,
FORMAT, STENCIL, PARAGON,
DAMIER, TYPE
" of flower beds ..... PARTERRE
Patti; singer .... ADELINA
paucity .... DEARTH, FEWNESS
Paul's companion .. SILAS, TYCHICUS
" city of birth .... TARSUS
paunch .... BELLY, RUMEN, ABDOMEN
pause . STAND, CEASE, SELAH, STANCE

212

pave .... TILE, PATH, COVER
paver .... TUP
pavilion MARQUEE, TABERNACLE, TENT,
ARBOR, GAZEBO
paving stone ..... PAVER, SETT, FLAG
Pavlova; dancer .... ANNA
paw .... GAUM, PATTE, PUD, CLAW
pawl ...... CLICK, DETENT, TONGUE,
RATCHET
" in gunlock .... SEAR
pawn . GAGE, HOOK, WAGER, PLEDGE,
HOSTAGE
pay FEE, REWARD, TIP, REMIT, DEFRAY,
WAGE
" dirt .... ORE
" the penalty of .... ABY
paying attention .... AUDIENT
paymaster ... PURSER, BAKSHI, BUXY
payment .... CRO, MAIL, TAC, FEE,
LOBOLA, MENSE, ERIC
paynim .... HEATHEN, PAGAN
pea ..... CICER, GRAM, CARMELE, DAL
peace PAX, SERENITY, NIRVANA, CALM
peaceful . IRENIC, HENOTIC, HALCYON,
SOLOMON
peach .... CRAWFORD, ELBERTA,
NECTARINE, MELOCOTON
" , native country of ..... PERSIA
" .... BETRAY
" -stone .... PUTAMEN
peacock ...... PAVONE, PAVO, PAWN
" blue .... PAON
" butterfly .... IO
" fan .... FLABELLUM
" , female .... PEAHEN
" fish .... WRASSE
" , like a .... VAIN, PAVONINE
peak ALP, CONE, CUSP, APEX, CROWN,
TOP, FINIAL, CLIMAX, ZENITH,
CREST, EPI, CRAG
peaked .... THIN, WAN, WORN
peal .... ECHO, BOOM, CLAP
peanut ...... GOOBER, MANI, PINDA,
ARACHIS
pear .. COMICE, SICKLE, SECKEL, BOSC,
ANJOU, NOPAL, PYRUS, OPUNTIA
" cider .... PERRY
" -shaped .... PYRIFORM
pear-like fruit .... AVOCADO
pearl .... GEM, ONION, MARGARITE,
OLIVET
" eye .... CATARACT
" of great luster .... ORIENT
Pearl Buck heroine .... OLAN
pearlweed .... SEALWORT
pearlwort .... SAGINA
pearly .... NACREOUS, ROSETAN,
OPALINE
Peary; explorer .... ROBERT

peasant COTTAR, HIND, RUSTIC, BOOR,
CARL(OT), CEORL, CHURL, TILLER,
KULAK, PAISANO, PEON, RYOT,
FELLAH, KERN
" farmhold .... COTLAND
pease; coll. Lat. .... PISUM
" crow .... TERN
peaseweep .... LAPWING, PEWIT
pea-shaped .... PISIFORM
peat .... MOOR, TURF, VAG, GOR
" bog .... CESS, MOSS
" spade .... SLANE
peavey .... CANTHOOK
pebble .... SCREE
peccary .... TAGASSU
peck ...... DAB, NAG, TWIT, (K)NIP,
PEGGLE
pectinoid bivalve .... SCALLOP
peculiar ..... ODD, PROPER, UNIQUE,
ERRATIC, QUEER
" ; comb. form .... IDIO
peculiarity ...... KINK, QUIRK, TRAIT
pedal ...... TREADLE, LEVER, CELESTE
pedant . BLUESTOCKING, PRIG, TUTOR,
PURIST
peddle .... HAWK, SELL, VEND, TRANT
peddler .... COSTER, HAWKER
" , accomplice of .... SHILL
" , pack of .... WALLET
pedicel .... RAY, STALK, STEM
pedestal, part of DADO, DIE, SURBASE,
ORLO, PLINTH, SOLLE
pedometer .... ODOGRAPH
peduncle .... SCAPE
" , not raised upon a SESSILE
peel .. RIND, SKIN, SLIPE, STRIP, BARK,
FLAY, FLAKE
" off .... DECORTICATE, HARL, PARE
peep .. CHEEP, PRY, PULE, SKEG, VIEW
peephole .... APERTURE, EYELET
peepshow .... RAREE, SPECTACLE
Peer Gynt, mother of .... ASE
" " , lady friend of ... ANITRA
peer .... PRY, MATCH, NOBLE
peer's residence .... BARONY
peevish .. PENSY, SULKY, TESTY, SOUR,
CROSS, PETULANT, GRUFF, TOUCHY
peewee .... LAPWING, LARK
Pee Wee; baseball .... REESE
peg HOB, NOB, PIN, TEE, LEG, KNAG,
SPIKE, SPILL, DOWEL
pega .... REMORA
Pegasus' rider .... BELLEROPHON
Pegotty's niece .... EMILY
Pegu native .... MON
pelagic .... MARINE, OCEANIC
Pelias' son .... ACASTUS
pellet . GRANULE, PALLION, PILL, GOLI
pellicle .... FILM, SKIN, LAYER, SCUM
Pelops' son ...... ATREUS, THYESTES

pelota, relative of .... CESTA
pelt .. FELL, HIDE, STONE, RIND, PEPPER
pelvic bone .... ILIAC
pen ..... QUILL, COOP, COAT, HUTCH,
    SCRIPT, STY, WRITE, JAIL, BARN,
    CORRAL, SWAN
   " point .... NEB, NIB
penalize .... PUNISH, MULCT, FINE,
    AMERCE
penalty . CAIN, RONCE, NEMESIS, FINE,
    DEDIT
pencil, belonging to a ...... DESMIC
   " points .... APICULA
pendant ... TASSEL, TAG, AGLET, BOB,
    EARRING
"Pendennis" heroine .... LAURA
pendent ornament .... LAVALIERE
Penelope's father .... ICARUS
   "   husband .... ODYSSEUS
penetrate .... DELVE, PIERCE, IMBUE,
    IMPALE, REACH, BORE, GORE
penetrating ... INTRANT, SHRILL, DEEP
penguin .... JOHNNY, AIRPLANE, AUK,
    DIVER, DIPPER
   "   breeding place .... ROOKERY
   " ; genus .... EUDYPTES
peninsula ...... NECK, PENILE, IBERIA
penitent .... CONTRITE, SORRY
penman .... SCRIBE, WRITER
penmanship .... HAND, CALLIGRAPHY
pennant ..... BANNER, ENSIGN, FLAG,
    BURGEE, AWARD, GUIDON, JACK
penny ..... COPPER, GROAT, SALTEE
   " ; New Testament .... DENARIUS
penny-a-liner .... HACK
pension .... ANNUITY, STIPEND
pentacle .... STAR, SYMBOL
Pentateuch ...... TORA(H), LAW
Pentheus' (grand)parent .. CADMUS,
    AGAVE
penthouse .... AERIE, PENTICE
peon ...... SOLDIER, SERF, PAWN
peony .... MOUTAN, PINY
people ..... FOLK, DEMOS, KIN, RACE,
    ETHOS, CLAN, VOLK, GENTE,
    CROWD, NATION
   " , lowest order of ... CANAILLE,
    RABBLE
peopled village .... ABADI
pepper (K)AVA, PIMIENTO, CAPSICUM,
    CAYENNE, PAPRIKA, BETEL, CUBEB
   " -and-salt .... GRAY
   " , betel .... SIRI
   " , to .... PELT, SEASON
peppermint camphor .... MENTHOL
   " , synthetic .... ANISYL
pepper-picker .... PIPER
peppery .. CHOLERIC, PUNGENT, FIERY,
    HOT
perambulator .... PRAM

perceive ... SENSATE, NOTICE, DESCRY,
    ESPY, SPOT
perception ACUMEN, TACT, SENSE, ESP
perch . AERIE, ROOST, POLE, BAR, SIT,
    BARSE, POPE
perched .... LIT, SAT
percolate .. EXUDE, MELT, OOZE, SEEP,
    STRAIN, FILTER, BREW, DRIP, LEACH,
    SILT, TRANSUDE
percussion inst. .. TRAP, GONG, TAAR,
    BELLS, BONGO, TABOR, CYMBAL,
    TAMTAM, TOMTOM, TYMPAN,
    DRONE, KETTLE
perdition .... WRECK, RUIN
peregrine .. ALIEN, FOREIGN, FALCON
perennial; genus ..... GEUM, ARNICA
perfect ... INVIOLATE, SPHERAL, SOLE,
    COMPLETE, FLAWLESS, PURE
   " ; comb. form .... TELEO
perfection .... ACME, IDEAL
perfidy .... APOSTASY, TREASON
perforate ...... TREPAN, GRID, DOCK,
    POUNCE, PIERCE, RIDDLE, BORE,
    DRILL, PUNCH
perforated block .... NUT
   "   marker .... STENCIL
   "   nozzle .... ROSE
   "   sphere .... BEAD
perforation...... BORE, EYELET, HOLE
perform ..... (EN)ACT, PLAY, RENDER,
    ACHIEVE, WORK
   "   again .... REDO
performer .... ACTOR, DOER
   " , inferior .... SHINE
perfume ... AT(T)AR, ESSENCE, ESTER,
    NOSE, FRANGIPANI, BOUQUET,
    OTTO, AROMATA, ODOR,
    (IN)CENSE
   " , medicated .... PASTIL
   " , musky .... CIVET
   " , oriental .... MYRRH
   " , pad .... SACHET
   " , strong-scented .... MUSK
perhaps .. PERCHANCE, HAPLY, BELIKE,
    MAYBE, ABLINS
peril .... HAZARD, JEOPARDY, RISK
perilous .... ICARIAN, RISKY
perimeter .... CIRCUIT, BORDER, AMBIT
period .. .. POINT, DOT, TRACK, TERM
   " of race's apex .... HEMERA
   " of time .... (A)EON, AGE, ERA,
    CYCLE, SPAN
periodic ......ERAL, ANNUAL, ETESIAN
periodical .... PAPER, JOURNAL,
    MAGAZINE, RECURRING
peripatetic ..... WALKER, NOMAD(IC),
    VAGRANT
peripheral .... DISTAL
periphery ... LIP, AMBIT, LIMIT, EDGE,
    END, RIM

perish ...... DECAY, DIE, ROT, WITHER
peritoneum, fold of ...... OMENTUM
periwinkle .... MUSSEL, MYRTLE
Perle of society .... MESTA
permeate IMBUE, INSINUATE, PERVADE,
                      STEEP, SOAK
permission ... GRACE, LEAVE, LICENSE,
                      WARRANT
permit .... ALLOW, SUFFER, LET, LEVE
pernicious . NOISOME, VICIOUS, EVIL,
                  MALIGN, SINISTER
Perón .... JUAN, EVA, EVITA
perpendicular . VERTICAL, SINE, ERECT,
                    STEEP
perpetuity .... ETERNITY, SERIAL
perplex .. BESET, ELUDE, STUMP, CRUX,
           NONPLUS, MYSTIFY, BAFFLE
perplexing ..... KNOTTY, CARKING
perplexity .... STALEMATE, FOG, WERE
perquisite .... APPANAGE, FEE, PROFIT
persecute .... BESET, OPPRESS, PURSUE,
                ANNOY, BAIT
Persephone .... KORE
    "   , mother of ...... DEMETER
Perseus, mother of .... DANAE
    " , star of .... ALGOL, ATIK
Persia .... IRAN
    " , anc. people of ...... ELAMITES,
                    MEDES
    " , conqueror of .... CYRUS
Persian .... LUR, IRANIAN
    "   book of scriptures .. KORAN
    "   carpet HAMADAN, KALI, SENNA
    "   city ... OMOL, TABRIZ, SHIRAZ,
                    TEHERAN, NIRIZ
    "   civil officer .... KHAN
    "   coin ..... ASAR, BISTI, DARIC,
                DINAR, RIAL, KRAN, STATER
    "   copper coin .... PUL, PAL
    "   demi-god .... YIMA
    "   dyestuff .... INDIGO
    "   dynasty, anc. .... SELJUK
    "   dynasty, founder .. PAHLAVI
    "   evergreen .... OLAX
    "   evil spirit . ARIMAN, AHRIMAN
    "   fairy .... ELF, PERI, FAY
    "   fire worshiper .... PARSI
    "   gate .... BAR, DAR
    "   gazelle .... CORA
    "   gold coin .... TOMAN
    "   governor .... SATRAP
    "   hook money .... LARI
    "   language; anc. ZEND, PAHLAVI,
                    AVESTAN
    "   lynx .... CARACAL
    "   meas. of length ... PARASANG
    "   mystic .... SUFI
    "   myth .... MAH
    "   oil center .... ABADAN
    "   pantheist .... BABIST

    "   plant .... OPIUM, POPPY
    "   poet ..... HAFIZ, OMAR, SADI
    "   port .... BUSHIRE
    "   priest .... MAGI, NADAB
    "   river .... KARUN, TAB
    "   rose .... GUL
    "   ruler .... MIR, ATABEK, SHAH,
                    SULTAN
    "   salt lake .... URMIA
    "   salt swamp .... KAVIR
    "   sect .... SHIITE, SUNNI
    "   screen .... PURDAH
    "   shah ... ISMAIL, REZA, RIZA
    "   song bird .... BULBUL
    "   spirit of light ...... ORMAZO
    "   sun god .... MITHRAS
    "   tiara .... CIDARIS
    "   title ...... MIR, MIRZA, SHAH
    "   town dwellers ..... LUR, SART
    "   trading center ...... ISPAHAN
    "   twenty dinars .... BISTI
    "   viceroy, anc. .... SATRAP
    "   water vessel .... AFTABA
    "   water wheel .... NORIA
    "   weight .... ABBAS, MISKAL, SIR
    "   writings .... AVESTA
persiflage .... BANTER, BADINAGE
persimmon family .... EBONY
persimmon; Mex. .... CHAPOTE
persist ... LAST, STICK, ENDURE, TORE
person ... BEING, ONE, WIGHT, BODY,
                      MAN
    "   accused .... APPELLEE
    "   assigned to serve writ . ELISOR
    "   held as a pledge ... HOSTAGE
    "   of distinction ..BIGWIG, LION,
                  NOTABLE, VIP
    " , private; law ...... RELATOR
    " , small .... POPPET
personal; comb. form .... IDIO
personify .... INCARNATE
personnel ..... CREW, HANDS, STAFF,
           SQUAD, STABLE, TROUPE
perspective ..... VIEW, SLANT, VISTA,
                   SCOPE
perspicacious .... ACUTE, KEEN
perspicacity .... ACUMEN
perspiration .... SWEAT, SUDOR
persuade ..... ENTICE, INDUCE, URGE
pert .. BRASH, DAPPER, NIMBLE, SASSY,
             SAUCY, FLIPPANT
    "   girl .... BOLD, MINX
pertain .... BELONG, RELATE, FIT
pertaining to ..... ANENT, APROPOS
per. to a hypothetical force ... ODIC
    " " a seam .... SUTURAL
    " " animals .... ZOOID
    " " antimony .... STIBIAL
    " " debtors' joint obligation .....
                  CORREAL

" " dissenters' chapel .... PANTILE
" " earth .. GEAL, TELLURIC, TERRA
" " fat .... SEBACIC
" " gambling .... ALEATORY
" " gulls .... LARINE
" " insects ...... ENTOMOLOGIC
" " meaning in language SEMANTIC
" " medicine .... IATRIC
" " old age .... GERATIC
" " oscine birds ...... TIMALINE
" " room of state ...... CAMERAL
" " sculpture .... GLYPHIC
" " sea .... THALASSIC
per. to skin .... DERIC
" " skull .... INIAL
" " sole of feet .... PLANTAR
" " the deer .... CERVINE
" " tibia .... CNEMIAL
" " vascular system ...... HEMAL
" " vowel sounds ...... VOCALIC
" " wife .... UXORIAL
pertinent ..... PAT, RELEVANT, ANENT
perturb . AGITATE, TROUBLE, DERANGE
Peru; early empire of _____
                        INCAS, YNCAS
peruke .... HAIR, PERIWIG, WIG
peruse ... SURVEY, CON, READ, SCAN,
                        STUDY
Peruvian, ancient .... INCA
"   bark .... CINCHONA
"   city ...... ICA, LIMA, CUZCO,
                CALLAO, PUNO, PISCA
"   coin ... DINERO, SOL, LIBRO,
                        PESETA
"   creeper .... PITO
"   deer .... ALPACA
"   department .. CUZCO, PIURA,
                        TACNA
"   goddess .... MAMA
"   inn .... TAMBO
"   king .... INCA
"   llama .... ALPACA, PACO
"   mark of nobility .... LLAUTU
"   partridge .... YUTU
"   relic .... HUACO
"   river ..... ICA, RIMAC, SAMA
"   seaport ... CALLAO, ILO, YLO
"   singer .... SUMAC
"   shrub .. MATICO, RATANHIA,
                RATANY, RHATANY
"   tree .... ALGARROBO
"   tribe .... INCA, ANTI, CAMPA
"   volcano .... MISTI
pervade .... PERMEATE, IMBRUE
perverse .... AWK, FROWARD, WOGH
perversely .... AWRY
perversion of taste .... MALACIA
Pesach .... PASSOVER
peso, silver .... DURO
pessimist .... WORRYCARL

pessimistic .... FOREBODING
pest .... BANE, PLAGUE, SCOURGE
pester .... BADGER, RIB, HARASS, NAG,
                ANNOY, TEASE, VEX
pestilence ...... PLAGUE, SCOURGE
pestle ...... MASHER, MULLER, BRAYER,
                PILUM, PISTIL
"   vessel ...... MORTAR, POUNDER
pet .... CODDLE, DANDLE, FONDLE
"   lamb .... CADE, COSSET
", in a .... TOUCHY, HUFFY
petal .... LABELLUM
", relative of a .. ALA, COROLLA,
                        WHORL
petals, without .... APETALOUS
"Peter Pan" figure ...... NANA, SNEE
peter out ..... DWINDLE, FADE, WANE
petiole .... STEM, STALK, STIPE
petition .... ASK, BEG, PRAY, SUE
petrify . DAZE, STUN, FREEZE, HARDEN,
                        PARALYZE
Petrograd .... LENINGRAD
petrol .... GAS(OLINE)
", deriv. of .. BUTANE, NAPHTHA,
                COKE, ASPHALT
petticoat ... BALMORAL, JUPON, KIRTLE
pettish .... FRETFUL, PEEVISH
petty .... MINUSCULE, SMALL, TRIVIAL,
                PALTRY, PICAYUNE
"   fault .... PECCADILLO
petulant .. PERT, WANTON, CAPTIOUS,
                HUFFY, SURLY, TESTY
pewit .... LAPWING
peyote .... CACTUS, MESCAL
Phaidos school .... ELIAN
phalanger . TAPOA, CUSCUS, OPOSSUM
phantasm .... EIDOLON, IDOLUM
phantom .... EIDOLON
pharaoh .... RAMESES, KHUFU, MENES,
                        PTOLEMY
pharos .... BEACON, LIGHTHOUSE
pheasant ...... CHEER, CHIR, MONAL,
                PURKAS, PURKUS, TRAGOPAN,
                        LEIPOA
"   , brood of .... NIDE, NYE
phase ASPECT, FACET, STAGE, CHAPTER,
                        SIDE
phenol deriv. . ANOL, BALOL, THYMOL,
                ORCIN, CRESOL
phenomenon .... EVENT, SIGHT
phenyl .... ARYL
philabeg .... KILT
philippic .. TIRADE, SCREED, JOBATION
Philippine aborigine . IFIL, AETA, ATA
"   ant, white .... ANA, ANAY
"   breadfruit . CAMANSI, RIMA
"   buffalo .... TIMARAU
"   canoe .... BANCO
"   century plant .... MAGUEY
"   child .... BATA

216

"	Christianized tribe BISCOL, TAGALOG, VISAYAN	"	soldiers' barrack . CUARTEL

"   Christianized tribe BISCOL,
     TAGALOG, VISAYAN
"   city ...... ALBAY, CAVITE,
     DAGUPAN, BOAC, MANILA,
     BONTOC, IBA, NAGA, BASCO
"   coconut deriv. ..... COPRA
"   coin .... PESO
"   dagger .... ITAC
"   dialect ... IBANAG, TAGAL
"   district .... LEPANTO
"   dogwood tree .... TUA
"   drink, alcoholic .... BENO
"   dwarf race NEGRITO, AETA
"   evergreen tree ..... KAPOK
"   farmer .... TAO
"   fern .... NITO
"   fetish .... ANITO
"   food staple .... TARO
"   governor general ..... IDE
"   grass, coarse ..... COGAN
"   hardwood .... NARRA
"   headman .... DATTO
"   hemp .... ABACA
"   house .... BAHAY
"   idol .... ANITO
"   island SAMAR, CEBU, PANAY,
     TICAO
"   island group .... SULU
"   island, largest .... LUZON,
     MINDANAO
"   Island wide stream .. ILOG
Philippine Islands, discoverer of ....
     MAGELLAN
"   knife .... BOLO
"   language .... TAGALA,
     TAGALOG
"   lighter .... CASCO
"   litter .... TALABON
"   mountain peak . APO, IBA,
     MAYON
"   native .... ITA, MORO
"   Negrito .... AETA, ATA, ITA
"   oil liquid .... CEBUR
"   palm ...... ANAHAU, NIPA
"   peasant .... TAO
"   pepper .... BETEL
"   plum ..... LANSA, LANSEH
"   port .... ILOILO, CEBU
"   province . ILOILO, ISABELA,
     SAMAR, TARLAC, ABRA,
     BATAAN, LAN, LANAO, LEYTE
"   rice .... PAGA
"   river .... ABRA, PASIG
"   sash .... TAPIS
"   sea .... SULU
"   shrub .... NABO
"   skirt .... SAYA
"   slave .... ALIPIN
"   soldier or brigand ....
     LADRONE

"   soldiers' barrack . CUARTEL
"   summer capital ... BAGUIO
"   sweetsop .... ATES
"   thatch .... NIPA
"   tree ACLE, DAO, DITA, IPIL,
     TUA
"   tree, large .... IBA, ANAM,
     LIGAS
"   tribe .... MUNDO, IGALOT,
     IGOROT, IGORROTE
"   volcano . ALBAY, APO, TAAL
"   water buffalo ... CARABAO
"   weapon .... BOLO
"   wood ..... NARRA, EBONY,
     SANDAL, TEAK
Philippine-Malay .... ITALON
philomel .... NIGHTINGALE
Philomela, sister of .... PROCNE
philosopher CYNIC, ELEATIC, SKEPTIC,
     ZETETIC, ERISTIC, STOIC, KANT,
     PLATO, ZENO, THALES, SOCRATES,
     HEGEL, FICHTE, HUME, SPENCER,
     LOCKE, SARTRE, RUSSELL
philosopher's stone .... ELIXIR
philosophical .... ERUDITE, SAPIENT
"   theory .... MONISM
philosophy .... YOGA
phlegmatic . COLD, DULL, INERT, SLOW
phloem .... TISSUE, BARK, BAST
Phoebe; moon personified .... SELENE
Phoebus .... SOL, APOLLO
Phoenician capital .... TYRE
"   god .... BAAL
"   goddess . ASTARTE, BALTIS
"   seaport .... SIDON
phonetic sound .... PALATAL
"   system .... ROMIC
phonograph record .... PLATTER, DISC
phosphate .... PALAITE, APATITE
photo .... STAT, MUG, SHOT, PIC, PIX,
     SNAP
"   copy, make .... TINTYPE
"   developer .... ADUROL, ORTOL,
     TONER
"   powder .... AMIDOL, METOL
"   solution .... HYPO
"   unit ..... LUX, PYR, RAD, LUMEN
photography, early producer of .....
     NIEPCE
"   , inventor of .. TALBOT,
     DAGUERRE
photology .... OPTICS
phrase .... EPIGRAM, IDIOM
"   , style of .. DICTION, SLOGAN
phratry .... CLAN, CURIA, PHYLE
Phryxos' mother .... NEPHELE
Phrygian Christianizer .. MONTANIST
"   god of vegetation .... ATTIS
"   king .... MIDAS
"   river .... MEANDER

physical .... SOMATIC, BODILY, EXAM
physician ... CURER, MEDIC, DOCTOR,
      SURGEON, DOC
  " , famous . GALEN, LAVERAN,
     MAYO, LISTER, MORTON,
     OSLER, PAGET, REED, DOOLEY,
     HARVEY, MESMER, SALK
  " , ignorant .... MEDICASTER,
        QUACK
physicians' group .... AMA
  " , per. to .... IATRIC
  " symbol .... CADUCEUS
physicist .... GALVANI, FARADAY,
    MARCONI, AMPERE, BUNSEN,
   ERMAN, RABI, FERMI, TELLER, HAHN,
   MACH, ROSSI, OHM, VOLTA, CURIE,
    BRAUN, BOHR, BORN, HERTZ,
      PAULI, PLANCK
physics, branch of ...... PNEUMATICS
physiognomy ..... FACE, MUG, MIEN
physostigmine .... ESERINE
pian .... FRAMBOESIA, YAWS
pianist CLYBURN, ITURBI, SERKIN, HESS,
    KEMPF, RUBINSTEIN, BORGE,
       LIBERACE
piano .... GRAND, DIGITORIA, SPINET,
       CLAVIER
piaster, one twentieth of ..... ASPER
picaroon .... ROGUE, THIEF
Picasso .... PABLO
Piccard, Auguste .... AERONAUT
pick . CHOOSE, CULL, ELITE, PLECTRUM
picket .. SENTRY, GUARD, STAKE, POST,
     TETHER, PALE
pickle ... MESS, ACHAR, ALEC, BRINE,
   VITRIOL, MARINADE, CORN, CURE,
     GHERKIN, VINEGAR
  " salt .... SOUSE
pickpocket .... DIP, THIEF, WIRE
picnic .... GIPSY, JUNKET, OUTING
"Picnic" dramatist .... INGE
picture ..... IMAGE, PASTEL, PORTURE,
    PROFILE, TABLEAU, SCENERY,
    MOVIE, DRAW, PORTRAIT
  " award .... OSCAR
  " , composite .... MONTAGE
  " , moving ... CINEMA, FILM, TV,
       FLICK
  " tube .... KINESCOPE
piebald ... PINTADO, DAPPLED, PIED,
    PINTO, CALICO, MOTTLED
piece . BIT, HUNK, CHUNK, FRAGMENT,
     PATCH, SHRED
  " out .... EKE, CANTLE
pier ...... STILT, SOCLE, ANTA, MOLE,
   PILLAR, POST, COB(B), PILASTER,
     QUAY, WHARF
pierce ... GORE, STICK, LANCE, ENTER,
    STAB, GRIDE, GOUGE
piercer .... BORER, SPEARER

piercing .... KEEN, SHRILL, TART
Pierre .... CURIE, LAVAL, PETER
pig .... BACON, SLOB, COCHON
  " deer .... BARBIRUSA
  " dialect .... ELT
  " , female .... SOW
  " -iron ballast .... KENTLEDGE
  " , male .... BOAR
  " , metal .... INGOT
  " , young ...... GRICE, SHOAT, GILT
pig-like animal .... PECCARY
pigpen .... STY, REEVE, FRANK
pigs, litter of .... FARROW
  " , per. to .... PORCINE
pigeon ...... PIPER, GOURA, POUTER,
    CUSHAT, CULVER, FANTAIL,
    WONGA, NUN, RUFF, TUMBLER,
       BARB
  " call .... COO
  " , carrier .... HOMER, HOMING
  " , dwarfed .... RUNT
  " , extinct .... DODO
  " , fruit .... LUPE
  " genus .... COLUMBA
pigeon house .... COLUMBARY
pigeons, food for .... SALTCAT
pigment .... DYE, TINT, PAINT, STAIN
  " , anthracene .... ALIZARIN
  " , arsenic yellow ... ORPIMENT
  " , black .... TAR, MELANIN
  " , blue .... SMALT
  " board .... PALETTE
  " , brown ...... BISTER, AMBER
  " , calico-printing ... CANARINE
  " , coal-tar .... ANILINE
  " , cuttlefish .... SEPIA
  " , lake .... MADDER
  " , orange .... REALGAR
  " , oxide-of-lead .... MASSICOT
  " , pale-yellow .... ETIOLIN
  " , white .... BARYTA
  " , without .... ALBINO,
      ACHROMATIC
  " , yellow ..... OCHER, SIENA
pigmy .... DWARF, MINIM, SHORT
pigtail ..... CUE, BRAID, QUEUE, PLAIT
pike .... DORE, GED, PICK, POULAINE
  " -like fish ...... ARAPAIMA, LUCE,
      ROBALO
pilaster .... ANTA, ALETTE
pilchard .... SARDINE
pilcher .... PILCHARD, SCABBARD
pile HEAP, STACK, SHAG, NAP, CAIRN,
     SCREE, GATHER
  " driver OLIVER, RAM, TUP, FISTUCA,
       GIN
piles, defense work of ..... ESTACADE
pilewort .... FIGWORT, GRAIN
  " fiber .... ADAD

pilgrim . WAYFARER, CRUSADER, HADJI, PALMER
" , garb of .... IHRAM
"Pilgrim's Progress" char. .... DEMAS
pill BALL, BOLUS, PELLET, TABLET, GOLI
pillage ... FORAY, RIFLE, FLAY, HARRY, SACK, RAPINE, LOOT, BOOTY
pillar .... STELE, LAT, JAMB, SHAFT, OBELISK, OSIRIDE
pillory STOCK, CANGUE, YOKE, TRONE
pillow .... COD, BOLSTER
pilose .... HAIRY
pilot ... AVIATE, FLYER, GUIDE, LEAD, STEER
" fish ...... JACKFISH, ROMERO
" , plane without .... DRONE
pilous .... HAIRLIKE
Piman Indian .... OPATA
pimento .... ALLSPICE
pimp in "Beggar's Opera" PEACHUM
pimple .... PAPULE, QUAT
pin .... ACUS, BROOCH, FIBULA, NOG, DOWEL, FID, PEG, LILL, STYLE
" ; fulcrum for oar .... THOLE
" ; jackstraw .... SPILIKIN
" to fasten meat .... SKEWER
" with a looped head ... EYEBOLT
pinafore .... SLIP, APRON, TIER
pincers .... TONGS, TEW, PLIERS
pinch .... PUGIL, SNAPE, CRAMP, NIP, TWEAK, RUB, GRIPE, STRAIT, STEAL, CRISIS
pinched ... NABBED, ARRESTED, CHITTY
pine . HONE, ARAR, KAURI, LANGUISH, FRET, YEARN, CHIR
" -tar extract .... RETENE
" , textile screw .... PANDAN
pineapple .... ANANAS, PINA
"Pine Tree" State ....MAINE
pink .... CORAL, PAW, STAB
Pinkerton's wife .... KATE
pinks; genus .... SILENE
pinkster flower .... AZALEA
pinna .... AURICLE, FEATHER
pinnacle .... CREST, EPI, ZENITH
" of glacial ice .... SERAC
" , rocky .... TOR
pinniped .... SEAL, WALRUS
pinochle term ... DIX, MELD, WIDOW
pinpoint .... DOT
pintado .... CHINTZ, SIER, CERO
pinto . SPOTTED, PIEBALD, PONY, BEAN
Pinza, Mr. .... EZIO
pip ACE, HIT, SEED, SPECK, PAIP, SPOT, ROUP
pipe . HOOKA(H), REED, TUBE, OFFLET, SLUICE, SUCKER, CANAL, FILLER, DUCT
" caking .... DOTTLE
" fitting .... CROSS, TEE

" , flanged end of .... TAFT
" , form of .... TUBULAR, TUBAL
" of peace .... CALUMET
" , oriental .... NARGHILE
" player .... FIFER
" , shepherd's ...... OAT, LARIGOT
" , short .... DUDEEN
" , small .... TUBULE
" , smoke .... TEWEL
piper's son .... TOM
pipette .... TUBE, TASTER
pipit .... TITLARK
"Pippa _____" .... PASSES
picturesque .. SCENIC, VIVID, GRAPHIC
pie .... JUMBLE, PATTY
" dish .... COBBLER, COFFIN
piquancy SPICE, RACINESS, SALT, ZEST, TARTNESS
pique .... VEX, PEEVE, STING
piquet term ... PIC, RUBICON, CAPOT
pirate ...... PICAROON, FREEBOOTER, CORSAIR, LAFITTE, ROVER, STEEL
" flag .... ROGER
" , gallows of .... YARDARM
" , weapon of .... SNEE
Pisgah's summit .... NEBO
pismire .... ANT
pistol . DAG, DERRINGER, ROD, BARKER, BULL(DOG), IRON, REPORTER, DRAGON
" case .... HOLSTER
piston .... PLUNGER
pit ...... CAVE, SLUIG, SUMP, BONE, ENDOCARP, RUA, HOLE, SEED, LACUNA
" in theater .... PARQUET
" of a peach .... PUTAMEN
pitch .. KEY, REEL, CODE, TONE, TOSS, RESIN
" inst. .... TONOMETER
pitchblende deriv. . RADIUM, URANIUM
pitcher . CROCK, EWER, GORGE, OLLA, TOSSER, JAR, JUG
" , lefthand........ SOUTHPAW
" plant .. FLYTRAP, NEPENTHE
" -shaped .... URCEOLATE
" -shaped vessel ...... AIGUIERE
pitches, as a vessel .. SENDS, PLUNGES
pitfall ..... TRAP, DECOY, GIN, SNARE
pith .. GIST, JET, PULP, MARROW, NUB, MEDULLA
" , full of .... MEATY, CORKY
" helmet .... TOPEE
" of the Nile .... AMBASH
pithy ..... LACONIC, TERSE, CONCISE
pittance .... SONG, DOLE, MITE, ALMS
pitted .... FOVEATE, STONED, ETCHED
pity .... MERCY, RUTH, YEARN
pivot .... AXLE, FOCUS, HINGE
pivotal .... POLAR

219

pivoted .... SWUNG, SWIVELED
pixy ...... ELF, GOBLIN, FAIRY, SPRITE
placard ..... AFFICHE, POST(ER), BILL
place ... BOUND, STEAD, SPOT, POSIT,
    SITUS, LIEU, STATUS, ASSIGN, NICHE
"   apart .... ENISLE
"   before .... APPOSE
"   beneath .... INFRAPOSE
"   ; comb. form .... TOPO
"   for trade .... MART
"   from which jury is taken ....
                    VENUE
"   , hiding .... MEW
"   in a row .... ALINE
"   in; rare .... INNEST
"   , intermediate .... LIMBO
"   , meeting .... TRYST
"   of nether darkness .... EREBUS
"   , to .... PUT, SET
placed .... LAIN, SITUATED, PUT
places .... LOCI, POSTS
placid .... CALM, SUANT, SERENE
plagiarism .... CRIB, PIRACY
plagiarist .... THIEF, BORROWER
plague . TEASE, HARRY, HECTOR, TWIT,
    DUN, PEST, TORMENT, BADGER
plaid cloth .... MAUD, TARTAN
plain ...... CHOL, EVEN, FLAT, BLUNT,
    FRANK, HEATH, LEVEL, HOMELY,
    WOLD, MERE, MOOR, LOWLAND
"   dweller .... LLANERO
"   , elevated .... MESA
"   , grassy .... CAMAS, SAVANNAH
"   , Italian .... CAMPAGNA
"   , Olympic games .... ELIS
"   , Russian ...... STEPPE, TUNDRA
"   , salt-covered .... SALADA
"   , S. Afr. .... VELD(T)
"   , Span.-Amer. .... LLANO, VEGA
"   , treeless .... PAMPAS, BARE
plains .... DOWNS
plaintiff .... SUER, ACCUSER
plaintive ..... SAD, ELEGIAC, WISTFUL,
    DOLEFUL, PITEOUS
plait ...... MILAN, PLEX, WIMPLE, PLY
plaited .... KILTED
"   helmet .... BASINET
"   rope .... SENNIT
plan ... DRAFT, ETTLE, PLOT, SCHEME,
    STRATEGY, DEVISE, LAYOUT
"   , architectural .... EPURE
plane .... AERO, EVEN, FLUSH
"   chart .... MERCATOR
"   handle .... TOAT, TOTE
"   , inclined .... RAMP, CHUTE
"   , iron .... BIT
"   part .. FLAP, NOSE, TAIL, WING
"   propulsion system . JET, ATOM
"   tree .... CHINAR, PLATANUS

planet .... MOON, URANUS, STAR,
    WANDERER, EARTH, NEPTUNE,
    SATURN, MARS, MERCURY, PLUTO,
    VENUS, JUPITER
planetarium .... ORRERY
planetary aspect .... CUSP, TRINE
planisphere .... ASTROLABE
plank .... SHOLE, SHORE, DICK, SLATE,
    TICKET
"   down .... PAY, ADVANCE
"   of bridge .... CHESS
planking, breath of .... STRAKE
plant (see also "shrub") . SOW, MILL,
    SEED, FLORA, PLACE, INSERT,
    FACTORY
"   , aconite .... BIKH
"   adapted to dry climate ......
                  XEROPHYTE
"   , African .... ARGEL
"   , agave .... PITA
"   , algae; genus .... NOSTOC
"   , Alpine .... EDELWEISS
"   , ambrosia .... RAGWEED
"   , anise .... DILL
"   , any climbing .... LIANA
"   , apiaceous .... PARSLEY
"   , apiaceous-dwarf .... CUMIN
plant, apoplexy .... ESCA
"   appendage .... STIPULE
"   , aralia .... FATSIA
"   , aromatic . ANISE, MINT, NARD,
    LAVENDER, TANSY, THYME
"   , aromatic, flavoring TARRAGON
"   , aromatic gum .... ARALIA
"   , aromatic seed .... ANET
"   , arrow-root; Bermuda ARARAO
"   , arum-family .... AROID, TARO
"   , Asiatic fiber .... RAMIE
"   , Asiatic oil .... ODAL
"   , Assam .... TEA
"   , aster-family .... DAISY
"   , astringent, an .... MATICO
"   , auricula .... PRIMROSE
"   , Austral. .... CORREA, FUCHSIA,
    HAKEA
"   , Austral.; genus ..... ALSTONIA
"   , berry, acid .... CURRANT
"   , betel-pepper, leaf of .... BUYO
"   , bitter .... RUE
"   , bitter-vetch .... ERS
"   bodies without stems .. THALLI
"   , bog .... ABAMA
"   , box .... BUXUS
"   , bramble .... GORSE
"   , brassica ... COLE, RAPE, TURNIP
"   , broom CYTISUS, GENISTA, SPART
"   , bud of .... CION
"   , burning-bush .... WAHOO
"   , burdock .... CLITE

      " , cactus CEREUS, DILDO, PEYOTE,
                     MESCAL, SAGUARO
      " of cactus kind .... XEROPHYTE
      " , cactus; Mex. .... CHAUTE
      " , calyx-leaf .... SEPAL
      " , Canna .... ACHIRA
      " capsule .... POD
      " , catchfly .... SILENE
      " , catnip-family .... NEP, NEPETA
      " cells .... GAMETES
      " , cellular flowerless .... LICHEN
      " , century AGAVE, ALOE, MAGUEY,
                     PITA
      " , chaffy scale .... PALEA
      " , cherry-laurel .... CERASUS
      " , Chinese .... RAMIE
      " lacking chlorophyll ... ALBINO
      " , climbing .... LIANA, LIANE
      " , clover .... MEDIC
      " clusters, flat-top .... CYME
      " , cruciferous ... ALYSSUM, CRESS
      " , cryptogamous .... MOSS
      " cuticle .... CUTIN
      " , dill .... ANET
      " , Dipsacus .... TEASEL
      " disease BLISTER, ERINOSE, SMUT,
             APHID, AECIUM, BLET, BUNT,
             ESCA, GALL, RUST
      " , dogwood .... CORNUS
plant, dye-yielding .. MADDER, WOAD
      " dyers'-medium .... WELD
      " , E. Ind. BENNE, DEUTZIA, MADAR,
             CREAT, REA, SESAME, SOLA,
             SUNN
      " , Egypt. aromatic ..... CUMIN
      " , embryo of .... PLANTULE
      " , Erica .... HEATH
      " , Euphorbia .... SPURGE
      " , European .... AZAROLE,
                   SNEEZEWORT
      " , everlasting .... ORPINE
      " , exudation .... RESIN
      " fabaceous .... ERS
      " , fern; N. Z. .... TARA
      " fiber . ISTLE, PITA, RAMIE, SISAL,
                     SIDA
      " , floating .... FROGBIT
      " , flower-pot .... CINERARIA
      " , flowering ...... ACANTHUS,
             BARRETA, CALLA, ORPIN,
             RHODORA, TAMARIX
      " , flowerless ..... FERN, LICHEN,
                   THALOGEN
      " for tanning .... SUMAC
      " , fragrant .... ANISE, ANGELICA
      " , fragrant-root .... ORRIS
      " , fruit-yielding-dye ...... MUSA
      " , furze .... GORSE, ULEX
      " , garden .... ASTER, LETTUCE
      " , garlic, wild .... MOLY

      " ; genus ..... TIA, AGAVE, ARUM,
                     ERINGO
      " , genus Isatis .... WOAD
      " , genus Ulex .... FURZE
      " , grass .... AVENA
      " growing from inside ENDOGEN
      " growing on sea bottom ENALID
      " growing wild ...... AGRESTIAL
      " , growth on a .... GALL
      " habitat adjustment .... ECESIS
      " having astringent bark . ALDER
      " having grape-like leaves ......
                     SALAL
      " , haw, black .... SLOE
      " , Hawaiian .... OLONA
      " , hawthorn, kind of ... AZAROLE
      " , healing .... SANICLE
      " , heath; genus .... ERICA
      " , holly .... YAPON
      " hop-vine-stem .... BINE
      " hybridization .... XENIA
      " indigo .... ANIL
      " , interior chaff of . PALEA, PALET
      " , ipecac .... EVEA
      " , iris family .... IRID, IXIA
      " , Japanese .... AUCUBA, TEA
      " , Jap. quince .... CYDONIA
      " juice .... MILK, SAP
      " , leguminous .... LENTIL, MEDIC,
                     SENNA
      " lice; genus .... APHIS
      " , lilac .... SYRINGA
      " , liliaceous . LEEK, ONION, SEGO,
                   TULIP, SOTOL
      " , lily-like .... ALOE, LOTUS,
          ASPHODEL, SABADILLA, SQUILL,
                     YUCCA
      " louse .... APHID
      " ; genus Lychnis ...... CAMPION
      " , main axis of .... STALK
      " , malvaceous ... ALTEA, ESCOBA
      " , manioc ... CASSAVA, TAPIOCA
      " , marine .... ENALID
      " , marine-skeleton ...... CORAL
      " , medicinal; .... ARNICA, ALOE,
           BONESET, ANISE, GENTIAN,
                   LOBELIA
      " , menthaceous .... CATNIP
      " , Mexican .. DATIL, CHIA, SALVIA
      " , mignonette-like . WELD, WOAD
      " , millet, broom-corn ..... HIRSE
      " , mint; Eur. .... LAVENDER
      " , mint family ... BASIL, CATNIP,
                     SAGE
      " , modified .... ECAD
      " , monkshood .... ATIS, ACONITE
      " , moss-like .... HEPATICA
      " , mushroom .... ACARIC, MOREL
      " , mustard-family .... CRESS
      " , nep .... CATNIP

" ; genus Nepeta ...... CATMINT
" , N. Amer. .... GARRYA
" , noxious .... WEED
" of cabbage family ...... RAPE
" of the heath order .... LING
" of the lily family ... IRID, IRIS
" of vegetable kindgom EXOGEN
" , family Olacaceae .... OLACAD
" on a heath .... ERICOPHYTE
" organs .... STOMATA
" painful to skin ... SMARTWEED
" , pansy .... HEARTSEASE
" , parsley, annual of ANISE, DILL
" , parsley, wild; Eng. .... ELTROT
" , part of .... AXIL, STIPEL
" , pepper .... ITMO, IKMO
" , perennial ...... CAREX, SEDUM
" , Peru .... OCA, RHATANY
" , Philippine .... ALEM
" , pitcher .... DARLINGTONIA
" , poisonous; genus .... DATURA
" poisonous to cattle .... LOCO
" poisonous to fowls . HENBANE
" , pore of a .... LENTICEL
" , prickly BRIER, CACTUS, NETTLE,
                              TEASEL
" , primrose .... AURICULA
" , rat-poison .... OLEANDER
" , receptable .... TORUS
" , rock .... LICHEN
" root .... RADIX
" , rose-family .... AVENS
" , rye fungus .... ERGOT
" , sage, aromatic .... SALVIA
" , sap of .... MILK
" , satin-flower .... HONESTY
" scales ...... PALEAE, RAMENTA
" , sea .... ENALID, ALIMON
" , seaweed, leaf of ..... FROND
plant secretion .... LERP
" , sedge; genus .... CAREX
" seed organ .... PISTIL
" , seedless, per. to ..... AGAMIC
" , sensitive .... MIMOSA
" shoot .... CION, STOLO
" shrubbery .... BETEL
" shrubs; genus ..... ITEA, RIBES
" ; genus Silenne ...... CAMPION
" , snake-bite remedy; Mex.
                              GUACO
" , snake-root ... SENECA, SENEGA
" , snow-drop .... HALESIA
" , S. African .... ALOE
" , soap .... AMOLE, MO
" , soft-wooded ...... FUCHSIA
" , spring .... GORSE
" stalk .... HAULM
" , starch-yielding ..... PIA, TARO
" stem .... BINE, CAULIS
" stem joint .... NODE

" , strawberry .... FRASIER
" , summer .... SAVORY
" , sun-rose .... CISTUS
" , sweet bay .... LAURUS
" , sweet-scented .... YERBA
" ; symbol of Ireland . SHAMROCK
" , tansy .... TANACETUM
" , tapicoa .... CASSAVA
" , taro-root .... EDDO
" , taro-root, food from ..... POI
" that bears fruit but once .....
                              MONOCARP
" , thorny .... BRIAR
" tissue, per. to .... TAPETAL
" , trifoliate .... SHAMROCK
" , tropical ..... ALTEA, BACCHAR,
     HAMELIA, MANGROVE, MUSA,
                    PALM, TARO, UDO
" , trumpet .... BIGNONIA
" used to flavor vinegar ....
                              TARRAGON
" used in perfumery .... MYRTLE
" , valerian .... NARD
" , vine .... VITIS
" , water-side .... SEDGE
" weed, kind of ... DOCK, WHIN
" , W. Ind. climbing ... REDWITHE
" , winter-flowering ..... EPACRIS
" with bitter leaves ...... TANSY
" with scale-like leaves .. SAVIN
" yielding a cosmetic dye HENNA
" yielding an astringent . AVENS
plantation .... HOLT, FINCA
     " of cacti .... NOPALRY
planter ..... SOWER, FARMER, SEEDER
plants .... SEEDS, FLORA
" , per. to .... VEGETAL
plaque ...... BROOCH, MEDAL, TABLET
plash PLEACH, POOL, PUDDLE, LIP, PLOP
plasma .... QUARTZ, WHEY, LATEX
plaster .... GROUT, PARGET
     of Paris ..... GESSO, STUCCO
     " , wax .... CERATE
plastic .... FICTILE, PLIANT, SUPPLE
" material . PUG, LIGNIN, LUCITE,
     BAKELITE, VINYL(ITE), ACETATE,
                    FORMICA, ACRYLIC
" repair paste .... SLURRY
plate(s) . PATERA(E), URIM, BASE, DISC
" of a storage battery ... GRID
" of soap frame .... SESS
" shaped like ship .... NEF
" , thin ..... LAMELLA, LAMINA,
                              PATEN
plateau ... MESA, TABLELAND, KAROO,
                              PARAMO
platform . PERRON, ROSTRUM, ESTRADE,
                    KANG, DAIS
" in a fort .... BARBETTE
" , mining ..... SOLLAR, SOLLER

222

" , nautical .... MAINTOP	plover .... SANDY, KILLDEER, PIPING,	
" , raised ...... SOLEA, TRIBUNE	DOTTEREL, LAPWING	
platoon .... SQUAD	" crab .... DROME	
Plato's school .... ACADEME	plow .... ROVE, SCAUT, TILL, FURROW	
" work APOLOGY, CRITO, REPUBLIC,	" blade .... SHARE	
PHAEDO, TIMAEUS	" , crosspiece of .... BUCK	
platter ..... LANX, TRENCHER, SALVER	" handle .... HALE, STILT	
plausible excuse .... ALIBI	" knife .... COLTER	
play ...... DRAMA, FROLIC, (EN)ACT,	" , man's first .... STICK	
MELODRAMA, ROMP, SPORT, FARCE,	" , sole of a .... SLADE	
SPIEL, FUN, COMEDY, TRAGEDY	" subsoil .... MOLE	
" badly ...... STRUM, THRUM, ERR	" , type of .... SULKY	
" , exhibit a .... STAGE	plowed land . ARADO, ARADA, ARATA,	
" mean trick .... SHAB	ERD	
" on words .... PUN	plowland .... CARUCATE	
" part .... ACT, BIT, ROLE, SCENA,	plowman .... TILLER	
STANZA, WALKON, EXODUS,	pluck off .... AVULSE, PUG	
FINALE	plucky .... NERVY, GAME	
" , silent .... PANTOMIME	plug .... ESTOP, BUNG, TAP, SPILE,	
" truant .... MICHE	TAMPON, BOTT, STOPPER, BOOST,	
player DUB, HAM, ACTOR, DIVA, STAR,	CORK	
THESPIAN, BARNSTORMER, TROOPER,	" for a cannon .... TAMPION	
MUMMER, MIME	" ; med. .... CLOT, EMBOLUS	
playground ....PARC, PARK	" , to .... CALK, CAULK	
plaything .... DIE, BAUBLE, TOY	plug-ugly .... ROWDY	
playwright . MILLER, SHAW, WILLIAMS,	plum ... AMRA, DAMSON, PERSIMMON,	
MOLNAR, IBSEN, ODETS, INGE	LOMBOY, SLOE, GAGE, BULLACE,	
plea . SUIT, ENTREATY, ABATER, NOLO,	JAMBOOL	
APOLOGY	" cake .... BABA	
pleasant GENIAL, WINSOME, LEESOME	" , sapodilla .... LANSON, LANSEH	
pleasantness .... AMENITY	plumage .... ROBE	
please .... ARRIDE, ELATE, FANCY	plumbago .... GRAPHITE, LEAD	
pleased .... GAME, GLAD, SUITED	plumber .... PIPER	
pleasure .... GREE, WILL, GRACE	plume .... FEATHER, EGRET, CREST,	
" ground .... PLEASANCE	PANACHE, QUILL, AIGRET	
" , per. to .... HEDONIC	plummet .... FATHOM	
plebiscite .... REFERENDUM, VOTE	plump .... FAT, BLUNT, PLOP, BUXOM,	
pledge ... SWEAR, BET, GAGE, PLIGHT,	CHUBBY	
WAGE, TOAST, VAS, VOW, OATH,	plunder .. REAVE, RIFLE, BOOTY, LOOT,	
PAWN	SPOIL, PILLAGE, RANSACK, ROB,	
pledget .... SWAB	SACK, POACH, STRIP, RAPE,	
Pleiad ...... MAIA, STEROPE, MEROPE,	RAVAGE, RAVEN	
ALCYONE, ELECTRA, CELAENO,	plundered .... RAPINED, REFT	
TAYGETA	plunderer FREEBOOTER, PREYER, RAIDER	
Pleiades .... ATLANTIDES	plunge .... DIP, DOUSE, PLUNK	
plentiful . COPIOUS, AMPLE, FULL, RIFE,	" into a liquid ..... CLAP, DIVE,	
BOUNTIFUL	LUNGE, (IM)MERSE	
plenty .... UBERTY, GALORE	plunk .... BLOW, PLUMP, TWANG	
plenum .... ABUNDANT, FULL	Plutarch's opus .... LIVES	
plexus .... RETE, NETWORK	Pluto .... DIS	
pliable .... LITHE, SUPPLE, DUCTILE	" , kingdom of .... HADES	
plight .... CASE, SITUATION	plutocrat .... CROESUS, NABOB	
plinth .... BASE, BLOCK, ORLO, DADO	pluvial .... RAINY	
plod .... DIG, TORE, TRUDGE, SLOG	ply FOLD, HANDLE, URGE, BENT, LAYER,	
plot ...... CABAL, BREW, PACK, TRICK,	SAIL, WORK	
INTRIGUE, AREA, ACRE, PLAN,	pneuma ...... BREEZING, SOUL, SPIRIT	
SCHEME	pneumonia .... LOBAR, CROUPOUS	
" of a play .... NODE	poach .... MIX, SHIRR, TRESPASS	
ploughshare . COLTER, COULTER, REEST	poacher .... LURCHER, STALKER	

pocket ... SAC, LODE, POCHE, POUCH
pocketbook .... LIL, FOB, PURSE
pod .. ARIL, BOLL, CAROS, KID, SHUCK,
           CAPSULE, PEEPEE, CHILI
Poe heroine .... LENORE
" work .... RAVEN, GOLDBUG
poem .... ODE, EPODE, EPOPEE, EPOS,
     ECLOGUE, IDYL, LAI, LAY, VERSE,
           SONNET, GEORGIC
" , division of a .... CANTO
" of eight lines .... TRIOLET
" , French .... DIT
" , Icelandic .... EDDA
" , irregular, wild .... DITHYRAMB
" , mournful .... ELEGY
" of six stanzas .... SESTINA
" , old Norse .... RUNE
" , per. to .... ODIC, ELEGIAC
"Poems of Ossian" hero .... FINGAL
Poe's bird .... RAVEN
poesy .... SONGCRAFT, VERSE
poet .... IDYLIST, BARD, ODIST, LYRIST,
       METRIST, RIMER, SCALD
" , British KEATS, TENNYSON, POPE,
           BURNS
" , French .... PROUST
" , German GOETHE, HEINE, UHLAND
poetaster ..... ASTER, BAVIAN, RIMER,
       RHYMESTER, VERSIFIER
poetic foot DACTYL, IAMBUS, SPONDEE,
           ANAPEST
poetry, line of .... STICH
" , muse of .... CALLIOPE, THALIA,
           ERATO
poets, inspiring to .... HELICON
poi source .... TARO
poignant .... KEEN, ACUTE
poignard .... DAGGER
point .. DOT, GIST, JOT, PERIOD, AIM,
     APEX, PRICKLE, NODE, GOAL,
           PUNTO
" , conical .... UNODE
" , geometric, relating to a curve
           ACNODE
" , highest .... ZENITH
" in curve of tangents . CRUNODE
" in law .... RES
" , lowest .... NADIR
pointed CONICAL, PIKED, AIMED, TERSE
" arch, like a .... OGIVAL
" ; as a leaf .... APICULATE
" mining tool .... GAD
" stick .... GOAD
pointer .... FESCUE, CLUE, ROD, HINT,
           WAND
pointless ...... INANE, SILLY, INSIPID
points .... FOCI
" of leaves .... APICULI
poise .... BALANCE, LIBRATE

poison TOXIN, ATTER, ETTER, ARSENIC,
     BANE, INEE, UPAS, CURARI, CURARE,
     TAINT, URALI, BIKH, VENIN,
           VENENE, VIRUS
" ivy .... RHUS, SUMAC
" , rat .... SQUILL
" , snake .... VENOM
" with a weed, to .... LOCO
poisoned arrow .... SUMPIT
poisoning, food .... BOTULISM
poisonous ... LOCO, VENOUS, VIROSE,
           TOXIC, VIRULENT
" alcohol .... TREMETOL
" alkaloid .... CONINE
" fish of Japan .... FUGU
" fungus .... AMANITA
" gas ...... STRIBINE, ARSINE
" herb .. MANDRAKE, HENBANE
" juice .... HEBENON
" liquid .... URUSHIOL
" lizard .... GILA
" protein ..... ARBIN, RICIN
poke ... GORE, HOOK, PROD, DAWDLE
poker counter .... CHIP
" stake .... ANTE, POT, KITTY
" , to call in .... SEE
pokeweed ... POCAN, GARGET, SCOKE
Poland, anc. name of ..... SARMATIA
" , city of ..... LODZ, WARSAW,
           LUBLIN, RADOM
" , coin of .... GROSZ, ZLOTY
" , port of .... GDYNIA
" , president of ...... PILSUDSKI
" , weight of LUT, FUNT, KAMIAN
pole .... MAST, ROD, AXIS, CABER
" as a symbol .... TOTEM
" ; lure for birds .... STOOL
" , memorial .... XAT
" of a vehicle .... THILL
" , positive .... ANODE
" , rope dancer's .... POY
" , Sp.-Amer. .... PALO
" used in handling fish GAFF, PEW
polecat .. ZORIL(LA), WEASEL, FERRET,
     SKUNK, FITCHEW, FITCHET,
           MUSANG, PUTORIUS
polestar .... POLARIS, LODESTAR
pole-to-pole .... AXIAL, AXAL
police organization .... PAL
policeman . BOBBY, PEELER, DICK, COP,
       BULL, ZARP, MOUNTIE
" , club of BILLY, TRUNCHEON
" station .. BARRACKS, TANA,
           THANA
polish LUSTER, LEVIGATE, WAX, GRAZE,
     PLANISH, SHINE, GLAZE, BUFF
polished ...... SHINY, SLEEK, GLOSSY
polishing material .... RABAT, ROUGE
Polish commander .... BOR
" pianist .... RUBINSTEIN

" dance ...... KRAKOWIAK, POLKA
" nobleman .... STAROST
" scientist .... CURIE
polite .. GENTEEL, DEBONAIR, URBANE,
CIVIL, SUAVE
political division . COUNTY, HUNDRED,
NOME, SHIRE, STATE, WARD,
PALATINATE
" faction .. BLOC, JUNTA, CLAN,
PARTY, TORY, WHIG
polled .... HORNLESS
pollen-bearing . STAMINATE, ANTHERAL
" brush of bee .... SCOPA
pollex .... THUMB
———— polloi .... HOI
Pollux or Castor .... ANAX, TWIN
polo stick .... MALLET
Polonius' daughter .... OPHELIA
poltroon ..... CRAVEN, SCARAMOUCH
polygon .... ISAGON, NONAGON,
HEXAGON, PENTAGON, NGON
Polynesian butterfly .... IO
" chestnut .... RATA
" divine hero .... MAUI
" dragon .... ATI
" dress .... MALO
" god ...... ATUA, PELE, TANE
" Hawaiian .... KANAKA
" herb .... TARO, PIA
" island .... SAMOA, FIJI,
PHOENIX, TOKELAU, COOK,
ELLIS, TONGA, EASTER
" mulberry bark ...... TAPA
" myth .... AVAIKI
" native ..... MALAY, MAORI
" pine .... HALA
polyp CORAL, HYDRA, TUMOR, SEAPEN
polyphonic school, exponent of BYRD
pome fruit ..... APPLE, PEAR, QUINCE
Pomerania, island of RUGEN, USEDOM
" , river of .... ODER
pommel .... FLAP, FLAT, KNOB
" bag................ CANTINA
pomp .... RIALTY, BOBANCE, GALA
pompano .. ALEWIFE, ALLICE, SAUREL
pompous . AUGUST, PODSNAP, STILTY,
TURGID, FUSTIAN, VAIN
Ponce de León .... JUAN
Ponchielli opera .... GIOCONDA
pond ... LAGOON, POOL, AQUARIUM,
TARN, MERE, LOCHAN
ponder .... BROOD, MUSE, PORE,
RUMINATE, WEIGH
ponderous .... BULKY, HEFTY, VAST
poniard .... STYLET, DIRK, DAGGER
Ponselle, Miss .... ROSA
pontiff ...... BISHOP, POPE, PONTIFEX
pony ... SHELTY, BRONCO, CAB, NAG,
TATTOO, PIEBALD, PINTO, TAT,
DRAM, TROT

poodle ...... BARBET, BEAGLE, SHOCK
pooh-pooh ...... DERIDE, BAH, HOOT
pool ..... CARR, LINN, MERE, PLASHET,
PUDDLE, TANK, TARN
" ball .... RINGER
" , game in .... PIN
poon tree KEENA, DILO, PUNA, DOMBA
poor . SOSO, NEEDY, SEELY, INFERIOR
Poor John .... FISH, HAKE
pop ..... CRACK, SNAP, SODA, BURST
pope .... RUFF, WEEVIL
pope; family name of RATTI, MONTINI,
PACELLI, RONCALLI, ANGELO
popes .... LEO, PIUS, ADRIAN, URBAN,
CONON, DONUS, LANDO, PETER
pope's cathedral .... LATERAN
" collar .... ORALE
" court officer .... DATARY
" crown .... TIARA, MITRE
" palace .... VATICAN, PAPACY
Pope, the .... PAPA
Popeye's sweetheart .... OYL
popinjay .... PARROT, FOP
poplar .. ABELE, ALAMO, ASPEN, TULIP,
GARAB, BAHAN
poppy .... FOXGLOVE, PAPAVER
poppycock .... BOSH, ROT
poppy corn ...... PONCEAU, RHOEAS
" field .... CANKER
" ; genus .... PAPAVER
" seed .... MAW
populace ...... DEMOS, PEOPLE, MOB,
HOIPOLLOI, RABBLE
popular DEMOTIC, EPIDEMIC, COMMON
popularity .... FAME, VOGUE
" poll .... GALLUP, HOOPER,
HARRIS
porcelain .... CHINA, KAOLIN, DERBY,
MING, MURRA, SPODE, MEISSEN,
LIMOGES, SEVRES
" mold .... RAMEKIN
porch PORTICO, DINGLE, LANAI, STOA,
VERANDA(H), STOOP
" toward west .... GALILEE
porcupine ...... HEDGEHOG, URSON,
PORKPEN
" grass .... STIPA
" spine .... QUILL
pore .... CON, STUDY, PONDER
" , minute OSTIOLE, STOMA, PORUS
" of plant .... LENTICEL
pores, without .... APOROSE
porgy .... PAGRUS, SCUP, TAI, BREAM
pork chop .... GRISKIN
" fish .... SISI
porpoise ... DOLPHIN, INIA, HOGFISH,
PELLOCK, PHOCAENA
porridge ..... BROSE, ATOLE, GROUT,
POLENTA, GRUEL, SAMP
port ..... LARBOARD, HAVEN, HARBOR

225

portable bridge .... BAILEY
     "   hut .... QUONSET
     "   rocket launcher .. BAZOOKA
portal .... DOOR, GATE, ENTRY
     " , at the .... ADOOR
portend ...... BODE, AUGUR, PRESAGE
portent ..... OMEN, TOKEN, AUGURY,
                         OSTENT
porter ... ALE, JANITOR, BEER, HAMAL,
                  REDCAP, OSTIARY
Porter; composer .... COLE
portia tree .... BENDY
Portia's maid .... NERISSA
portico ...... ARCADE, PORCH, STOA,
         VERANDA, XYST(US), ATRIUM
     " , enclosed space of .. PTEROMA
portion ... DOLE, DUNT, SHARE, PART,
        SUM, ALLOT, PARCEL, SEGMENT
portoise .... GUNWALE
portrait statue .... ICON, IKON
     "   " , per. to .... ICONIC
portray . DESCRIBE, ACT, FORM, DEPICT,
     LIMN, PICTURE, DELINEATE
Portsmouth dock .... PORTSEA
Portugal monetary unit .... ESCUDO
     " , premier of .... SALAZAR
Portuguese city .... LISBON, OPORTO,
        FARO, BRAGA, EVORE
     "   coin PECA, DOBRA, PATACA,
               REI, MOIDORE
     "   colony .... MACAO, TIMOR,
               GOA, DIU
     "   islands .... AZORES
     "   king; anc. .... NINIZ
     "   lady .... DONA
     "   legislature .... CORTES
     "   measure SELAMIN, PE, VARA
     "   navigator ..... MAGELLAN,
               GAMA
     "   province . ALGARVE, EVORA
     "   river DUERO, MINHO, TAGUS
     "   title .... DOM
     "   weight ...... LIBRA, ONCA
pose .... MODEL, FEIGN, SIT, MIEN
poser .... FACER, STICKER, RIDDLE
Poseidon, wife of .... AMPHITRITE
positing .... PONENT
position . UBIETY, COIGN, SITU, LOCUS,
             STANCE, RANK
positive .... CONSTANT, PLUS, THETIC,
         EMPHATIC, EXPLICIT
     "   pole .... ANODE
     "   saying .... DICTA
possess .. OWN, HAVE, HOLD, OCCUPY
possessing feeling .... SOULED
     "   landed property ... ACRED
possession, assume, again .... REVEST
possum .... FEIGN
post DAK, MAIL, NEWEL, XAT, MARKER,
        PILLAR, STAKE, FORT

     " , turning; Rom. .... META
     " -chaise .... JACK, COACH
poster BILL, BULLETIN, CARD, PLACARD,
               STICKER, AFFICHE
postpone ADJOURN, TABLE, PROROGUE,
               SHELVE, DEFER
postponed law case .... REMANET
postscript .... ENVOY
postulate ...... POSIT, ASK, DEMAND,
               PREMISE
posture .... POSE, STANCE, STAND
posy .. BOUQUET, NOSEGAY, CORSAGE
pot ... LOTHA, OLLA, ALUDEL, BIGGIN,
               MARMIT, DIXIE
potassium ..... ALUM, NITER, POTASH
potato SPUD, TUBER, OKA, YAM, TATER
     "   beetle .... HARDBACK
     "   disease .... CURL, POX
     "   flower .... FLOW
     "   oil .... OTTO
     " , sweet .... PATATA
potency . EFFICACY, STRENGTH, POWER,
               ELAN, VIS
potent .... COGENT, MIGHTY
potential energy .... ERGAL
pother .... STIR, WORRY, ADO, BUSTLE
potherb, relative of . OLITORY, WORT
potion .... DOSE, DRAM, DRAUGHT
potpourri .... MEDLEY, OLIO, FARRAGO
potsherd .... SHARD, TEST
potter ... MESS, PRY, TRIFLE, DAWDLE
potter's clay .... ARGIL
     "   wheel .... DISK, LATHE, THROW
pound ...... BRAY, TAMP, THUMP, RAM
pottery ...... BLANC, DELFT, CERAMIC,
               CELADON
     " , Arezzo .... ARETINE
     "   clay .... KAOLIN
     " ; decorated .... SIGILLATE
     " ; enameled .... MAJOLICA
     " , fragment of .. SHARD, SHERD
     " ; glass-like .... VITREOUS
     " ; glazing term .... SLIP
     " ; mineral .... FELDSPAR
     " ; vessel for firing .... SAGGER
pouch .... BURSA, POD, SAC, BAG
     " , girdle .... GIPSER
     " , highlander's .... SPORRAN
pouch-shaped .... SACC(UL)ATE
poultry breed ... ANCONA, DORKING
     "   disease .... PIP, ROUP
     " , dish of .... GALANTINE
     "   farm .... HENNERY
Pound; poet .... EZRA
pour forth .... VENT, WELL, GUSH
     "   melted glass in water . DRAGADE
     "   molten steel .... TEEM
     "   off .... DECANT
     "   to the gods .... LIBATE
pouring hole in a mold .... SPRUE

pourpoint .... GIPON, JUPON
pout .... PIQUE, MOUE, MOP, SULK
poverty DEARTH, LACK, ILLTH, PAUCITY,
NEED, INDIGENCE
powder .... TALC, BIR, CORDITE, DUST,
ARISTOL, RACHEL, BORAL, ABIR
" beater .... SINTERER
" , stamping .... POUNCE
powdered; her. .... SEME
power CAN, DINT, GIFT, SWAY, STEAM,
JET, CONTROL, FORCE
" , degree of .... POTENCE
" device .... TELEMOTOR
" of attorney .... AGENT,
PROCURATORY
" ; theoretical .... ODYL(E)
powerful .. LEONINE, POTENT, STURDY,
DRASTIC
practical .... PRAGMATIC, UTILE
" joke .... HOAX, HUMBUG
practice . DRILL, USE, PRAXIS, METHOD,
HABIT
Prague .... PRAHA
prairie . BAY, CAMAS, MEADOW, MESA
" chicken .... GROUSE
" mud .... GUMBO
" plant .... CAMASS
" wolf .... COYOTE
praise KUDOS, EXTOL, EULOGIZE, EXULT,
LAUD, TRIBUTE
" of another's facility MACARISM
praline .... CONFECTION
prance .... SPRING, CAVORT, STIR
prandial ...... REPAST, DINNER, MEAL
prank .... ANTIC, CAPER, JIG, SHINE,
FROLIC, DIDO, LEAP
prase .... CHALCEDONY
prate ..... CHATTER, GAB, RANT, BUKH
prattle .... CLACK, GAB, BLATHER
pray BESEECH, ENTREAT, IMPLORE, SUE
prayer .... AVE, BENE, ORISON, PLEA,
BEAD, SUIT, GRACE
" bead .... ROSARY, AVE
" book BREVIARY, MISSAL, RITUAL
" , hour of, Moham. ..... AZAN
" , last, of day ..... COMPLIN(E)
" stick .... BAHO, PAHO, PAJO
praying figure .... ORANT
preacher .... HOMOLIST, PULPITEER
preachment .... SERMON
preceded .. FORERAN, LED, PREVENTED
precedence ...... LEAD, PAS, PRIORITY
preceding ABOVE, PREVIOUS, ANTERIOR
precept .... MAXIM, RULE, WRIT
precious .... DEAR, RARE, COSTLY
" stone ..... AGATE, NAIF, OPAL,
JEWEL, RUBY, SARD, TOPAZ,
EMERALD, LASK(E)
precipice .. BLUFF, CRAG, LYNN, CLIFF,
PALI

precipitate HURRY, FLOC, HEADY, RASH,
HEADLONG, ABRUPT
precipitous ...... SHEER, HASTY, RASH
" rock .... SCAR, STEEP
precise .... FORMAL, EVEN, PRIM
preclude ..... DEBAR, ESTOP, PREVENT
preconceive .... IDEATE, SCHEME
precursor .... CRIER, HERALD
predatory bird .. OWL, HAWK, HARPY,
FALCON, EAGLE, VULTURE
predicament .... PASS, FIX, PLIGHT
predict . BODE, OMEN, WEIRD, AUGUR,
DIVINE, PROPHESY
predisposed ... BIASED, PARTIAL, SOLD
pre-eminent .... PALMARY
preen .... PERK, PLUME, DRESS
preface .... PREAMBLE, FRONT, PRAYER,
HERALD, PROEM, PROLOG
prefer .... CHOOSE, ELECT
preference ..... FAVOR, OPTION, PICK
prefix .... AFFIX, TITLE
" for against .... ANTI
" for appearing as .... QUASI
" for before .... PRAE, PRE
" for between .... META
" for distance .... TELE
" for earnest .... SERIO
" for false .... PSEUDO
" many .... MULTI, POLY
" for twice .... BI
" for with .... CON, COL
" for wrong .... MIS
" used in physics .... STAT
prejudice . BIAS, HARM, HURT, DAMAGE
prelate ..... POPE, BISHOP, CARDINAL,
INGE, PONTIFF, CLERIC
preliminary .... PROEMIAL
prelude PREFACE, PROEM, RITORNEL(LE)
premises ..... GROUNDS, LAND, DATA
premium ...... BONUS, AGIO, STAKE,
GUERDON, MEED
preoccupied .... ENGROSSED, LOST
preparation .... FITTING
prepare ...... FIT, FIX, PAVE, TRAIN
" for boiling .... DECOCT
" for the press .... EDIT
" skins for gloves .... TAW
preposition BY, TO, AT, IN, FORM, ON,
OUT, OF, WITH, AFTER, UNTO,
ONTO, INTO, UPON
presage .. BODE, OMEN, OSSE, DIVINE,
PORTENT, SIGN, OSTENT, TOKEN
prescribe .... ALLOT, DICTATE, ORDAIN
prescribed .... THETIC
present ...... BESTOW, BOON, NOW,
LAGNIAPPE, TODAY
" from pupil .... MINERVAL
" time ...... NONCE, CURRENT
presently .... ANON, NOW
preservative ..... VINEGAR, MEDICINE

227

preserve . CURE, CAN, CORN, TIN, JAM, KEEP, SAVE
" in oil .... MARINATE
preserved human in the twilight of the gods .... LIF
press . WEDGE, CRAM, CROWD, FORCE, THRONG, IRON, URGE, COMPEL
" , famous .... ALDINE
" in ranks .... SERRY
presser .... IRONER, SADIRON
pressing .... URGENT, EXIGENT
pressure INSTANCY, DURESS, URGENCY
" unit MESOBAR, BARIE, BARAD
prestige .... SWAY, FACE
presumptuous ..... BRASH, INSOLENT, SASSY, SAUCY
pretend .. CLAIM, FEIGN, SHAM, FAKE
pretended omission ..... PARALEPSIS
pretense .... ACT, RUSE, CANT, FEINT, CLAIM, EXCUSE, POSTICHE
pretty .... COMELY, FAIR, JOLI
"Pretty Worm of Nilus" .... ASP
prevail .... EXIST, DOMINATE, OBTAIN, WIN, SWAY
prevalent ..... GENERAL, WIDESPREAD, RAMPANT, CURRENT, POPULAR, EXTANT, RIFE
prevaricate ... QUIBBLE, SHUFFLE, LIE
prevent AVERT, DETER, THWART, WARN, OBVIATE, BALK
" legally ... ESTOP, FORECLOSE
preventive medicine .... ANTIBIOTIC, ANTIHISTAMINE
previously .... ERST, PRIOR, DONE
prey .. LOOT, SPOIL, VICTIM, QUARRY, BOOTY, PLUNDER, PRIZE, ROB
" upon .... FEED, RAVIN, RAVEN
Priam's daughter .... CASSANDRA
" grandfather .... ILUS
" son .. HECTOR, PARIS, TROILUS
" wife .... HECUBA
price .. RATE, COST, SUM, FARE, TOLL, OUTLAY
prick ... GAD, PIERCE, QUALM, SPUR, URGE, GOAD
pricket .... BUCK, CANDLE
prickle .... BRIAR, SPICULA, ACULEUS, SETA, BARB, THORN
prickly MURICATE, ECHINATE, SPINY, THORNY
" heat .... LICHEN
" pear .... NOPAL
" shrub .... LOASA, BRIAR
pride ...... CONCEIT, VANITY, PLUME
"Pride and Prejudice" author AUSTEN
" " " , char. in DARCY
priest .... CURE, DRUID, FLAMEN, ORATORIAN, OBLATE, PADRE, ABBE, IMAM, LAMA, PASTOR, SHAMAN

" , high .... ELI, PONTIFF, AARON, SARIP
priestess .... AUGE, VESTAL
priestly .... SACERDOTAL
" cap .... BIRETTA
" vestment ALB, EPHOD, ORALE, SCAPULAR
priest's assistant .... ACOLYTE
" mantle .... COPE
" neckpiece ...... AMICE, STOLE
" ornament .... URIM
" scarf .... MANIPLE, RABAT
" surplice .... EPHOD
"Priests of the Oratory," founder of . NERI
prig .... PRUDE, THIEF
prim .. PRUDISH, SMUG, FORMAL, STIFF
prima donna .... DIVA, LEAD
primate . APE, ELDER, PRELATE, LEMUR, EXARCH, MAN
prime of life .... BLOOM, HEYDEY
primeval .... OLD, EARLY, NATIVE, PRISTINE
primer .... HORNBOOK, TYPE
primitive QUAINT, PRISCAN, PRISTINE, NAIVE, BASIC, CRUDE
primrose . COWSLIP, OXSLIP, PRIMULA, PIMPERNEL, SPINK
primp .... DRESS, PREEN, PRINK
prince ... DAUPHIN, HAMLET, MIRZA, KHAN
Prince of Darkness .... AHRIMAN
" of Liars .... PINTO
" of Poets .... RONSARD
" of the Sonnet .... BELLAY
" of Spanish Poetry .... VEGA
prince, petty .... SATRAP
Prince of Monaco .... RAINIER
" Philip .... MOUNTBATTEN
princess of Argos .... DANAE
" of Tyre .... DIDO
" or lady; Ind. .. BEGUM, RANI, RANEE
Princess Anne's husband ...... MARK, PHILLIPS
" Margaret's husband ...... ANTHONY, SNOWDON
principal ... CAPITAL, ARCH, CAPTAIN, TOP, MAIN, FIRST, CHIEF
principality, independent .. MONACO
principle .. AXIOM, THEOREM, CAUSE, PRANA, TENET, LOGOS
print .. FABRIC, MARK, PHOTO, STAMP
printer . TYPE, DAY, PLANTIN, CAXTON, FUST, JENSON
printer's helper .... AID, DEVIL
" ink pad .... DABBER
" mark .... SERIF, CARET, STET, TILDE

" measure .... EM, EN
" type .... PI(E)
printing form .... DIE
" frame .... FRISKET, CHASE
" hand inst. .... BRAYER
" mark ... DELE, ELLIPSE, DIESIS
" metal block .... QUAD
" mistake(s) ERRATUM, ERRATA
" press, part of .... PLATEN,
ROUNCE
" process .... OFFSET
" system for the blind ....
BRAILLE
prior .... ERE, LEAD, FORMER
Priscilla's husband .... ALDEN
prisms, pair of .... PORRO
prison BRIDEWELL, CLINK, GAOL, JUG,
JAIL, QUOD, CAGE, STIR, COOP,
HOOSEGOW, CAN, BARS
" , French .... BASTILLE
" in London .... NEWGATE
" , Latin for .... CARCER
" , naval ... HULK, BRIG, BAGNIO
prissy .. NICE, PRECISE, PRIM, FINICKY,
SISSIFIED
pristine .... EARLY, PRIMITIVE
private ... COVERT, ESOTERIC, SOLDIER
" ; comb. form .... IDIO
" eye ... DETECTIVE, SLEUTH, TEC
privateer .... CAP, CAPER, KIDD
privet .... IBOTA, IBOLIUM
privilege ..... SOC, PATENT, CHARTER,
LIBERTY, OCTROI, LICENSE
privy seal .... SIGNET
prize ... STAKE, ESTEEM, VALUE, MEED,
PALM, TROPHY, CUP, LAURELS,
PLUME
probability . ODDS, VANTAGE, CHANCE
probation ...... TRIAL, PAROLE, TEST
probe ..... SEARCH, INQUEST, SEARCH
" or tracer .... SEEKER, EXPLORER
" , surgical .... STYLET, TENT
probity .... HONESTY, INTEGRITY
problem .... NUT, CRUX, KNOT, POSER
proboscide section .... LORE, LORUM
proboscis SNOUT, TRUNK, NOSE, BEAK
" monkey .... NOSEAPE
proceed .... WEND, PLOW, ARISE, GO
proceedings .... ACTA, DOINGS
proceeds ... MARCHES, GOES, INCOME
process in organisms .... MIOSIS
" in steelmaking .... BESSEMER
procession ... CORTEGE, FILE, LITANY
proclaim .. ENOUNCE, HERALD, KNELL
proclamation . BANDO, EDICT, NOTICE
Procne, husband of .... TEREUS
prod .... GOAD, URGE, POKE, EGG
prodigal LAVISH, SPENDER, RECKLESS
produce ... CAUSE, CARRY, ENGENDER,
WAGE, GENERATE, BEGET, BREED

produced in a garden ...... OLITORY
product ..... CROP, FRUIT, SUM, HEIR,
EFFECT, OPUS, YIELD
proem .... PREAMBLE, PREFACE
profession . JOB, LINE, CAREER, METIER
proficient APT, ADEPT, SKILLED, VERSED
profit ...... AVAIL, BOOT, MEND, NET
profitable .... UTILE, PAYING, FAT
profits .... RETURNS, BENEFITS
profound .... RECONDITE, INTENSE
progenitor .... SIRE, PARENT
progeny ..... SEED, ISSUE, OFFSPRING
prognosticate .. BODE, OMEN, PREDICT
prognosticator .... DIVINER, SEER
program ... AGENDA, CATALOG, PLAN
progress ... TELESIA, TELESIS, GROWTH
prohibit . ESTOP, DEBAR, TABOO, TABU,
VETO
prohibited .... ILLICITED, TABOO
prohibiting .... VETITIVE
prohibition BAN, ESTOPPAL, EMBARGO
project ... PROTRUDE, BEETLE, JET, JUT,
PLAN, SCHEME, PLOT, IDEA
projectile .... BOMB, MISSILE, ROCKET,
ARROW, SHELL
projecting pedestal .... SOCLE
" piece .. ARM, FLANGE, RIM
projection .. BULGE, FIN, LOBE, LEDGE,
CAM, KNOP, PRONG, HOB(B)
prolific, to be .... TEEM, FECUND
prolix . PLEONASTIC, WORDY, VERBOSE
prolocutor ..... ORATOR, CHAIRMAN
prolong .... SPIN, EXTEND
Prome, native of .... BURMESE
promenade . ALAMEDA, MALL, MARINA,
GALLERY, PASEAR
prominence SALIENCE, CUSP, PRESTIGE,
CLOUD, SIGNAL
promise . OATH, VOW, PAROLE, WORD,
PLEDGE, AVOW, IOU
promontory .... CAPE, MOUNT, NESS,
SKAW, LAND, SPIT, NOUP, NASE
promote .... AVAIL, NURSE, INCREASE
promotion ...... PREFERMENT, BREVET
" of Christianity .... IRENICS
prompt ...... ANIMATE, SOON, YARE,
ADVISE, EARLY, TELL, URGE
prompter .... READIER, READER, CUER
prone; face down ... FELL, PROSTRATE
" ; face up .... SUPINE
prong .. FORK, NIB, TANG, PEG, FOLD,
TINE, ANTLER, FANG
pronoun . ITS, YOU, HER(S), HIM, HIS,
ONE, OUR(S), MINE, THAT, THEE,
THOU, THEIR, THOSE
pronounce BURR, SLUR, ASSERT, STRESS,
DECLAIM, SPECIFY
pronunciation mark .... CEDILLA
proof TRIAL, EVIDENCE, GALLEY, REVISE
proofreaders' mark DELE, CARET, STET

prop .... BRACE, GIB, NOG, STAFF,
    SPRAG, SHORE, TRUSS, BOLSTER,
                   STILT
propeller . FAN, DRIVER, VANE, SCREW,
            ROTOR, PADDLE
proper .... MEET, PRIM, FIT, DUE
property .... ATTRIBUTE, ASSET, TRAIT,
    ALODIUM, GOODS, DHAN
    " , act to regain ..... REPLEVIN
    " ; bride's gift to husband ....
              COURTESY, DOS
    " , hold on .... LIEN
    " in law .... BONA
    " in physics .... INERTIA
    " , of landed ESTATE, CADASTRAL
    " , personal .... CHATTEL
    " , receiver of .... ALIENEE
    " , wanton destruction of ....
              SABOTAGE
prophesy ..... AUGUR, OSSE, PRESAGE
prophet ...... ORACLE, MANTIS, SEER,
    AUGUR, VATIS, MOHAMMED
    " ; bib. . AMOS, HOSEA, MICAH,
    NAHUM, MOSES, DANIEL
prophetess .... SEERESS, PYTHIA,
    CASSANDRA, SIBYL
prophetic ..... VATIC(AL), ORACULAR
propinquity ...... NEARNESS, KINSHIP
propitious .... BENIGN, ROSY, TIMELY,
              LUCKY
proportion . PRORATE, RATIO, QUOTA,
    SHARE, DEGREE
proposal ... MOVE, BID, FEELER, OFFER
proposition ..... COROLLARY, THESIS,
    PORISM, LEMMA
proscribe .... FORBID, BAN, CONDEMN
proscription .... OUTLAWRY, EXILE
prose form .... ROMANCE
prosecute ...... INDICT, INTEND, SUE
proselyte to Judaism .... GER
Proserpina's mother .... CERES
prosody .... METER, VERSE, SCANSION
prospect .. SCENE, VIEW, VISTA, HOPE,
    SURVEY, MINE
prospectus ..... PROGRAM, CATALOG
prosper .... CHEVE, SPEED, THRIVE
prosperity ...... WEALTH, FORTUNE,
    WELFARE, HAP, UPS, WEAL
    " symbol .... TURQUOISE
Prospero's sprite .... ARIEL
prosperous .. PALMY, SONSY, (F)LUSH,
    PLUSH, BOOMING
prostrate . FELL, FLAT, PRONE, FALLEN,
    REPENT, BOW, SUPINE
prosy .... DULL, DRY, JEJUNE
protecting influence ... (A)EGIS, SHIELD
protection . APRON, BIB, LEE, DEFENSE,
    BULWARK, SHELTER, UMBRELLA
    " right .... MUND
protector of vineyards ...... PRIAPUS

Proteidae family .... NECTURUS
proteids .... AMINES
protein .... ALEURONE, PROLAMIN,
    CASEIN, FIBRIN, GLOBULIN,
    ALBUMIN, RICIN, HISTON,
    LEGUMIN, GLIADIN
    " particle .... RIBOSOME
    " , source of .... EGG, SOY
    " substance .... RENIN
proteles .... AARDWOLF
protest .... DENY, OPPOSE, REFUSAL
Protestant sect .... AMISH
Proteus .... OLM
protoplasm .... SPORE
protozoan . LOBE, AM(O)EBA, MONER
protract ..... STRETCH, DEFER, EXTEND
protuberance ... HUNCH, LOBE, SNAG,
    NODE, GNARL, TORUS
    " , occipital .... INION
    " , rounded . HUMP, UMBO
prove .... EVINCE, TRY, TEST, VERIFY
proverb .. AXIOM, ADAGE, APHORISM,
    SAW, SAYING, BYWORD, PARABLE
provide SUPPLY, CATER, AFFORD, YIELD,
    PURVEY, ENDOW, ENDUE
provided .... BODEN, SOBEIT
providing that .... IF, PROVISO
province .... BEAT, CIRCUIT, NOME
provincial speech .... PATOIS
provisions .... LARDER, CATES, CHOW,
    ANNONA
    " , search for .... FORAGE
proviso .... CLAUSE, SALVO
provisory .... IFFY
provoke .... BAIT, SPUR, STIR, RILE,
    NEEDLE, ANGER, NETTLE
prow .... BOW, NOSE, PROA, STEM
proximal, opposed to .... DISTAL
proxy AGENT, DEPUTY, PROCTOR, VICAR
prude .... PRIG
prune . FROG, PLUM, SNED, LOP, THIN,
             TRIM
pruritus .... ITCHING
Prussian lancer JUNKER, ULAN, UHLAN
    " legislature .... LANDTAG
    " seaport .... EMDEN
    " watering place .... EMS
prussic acid, discoverer of . SCHEELE
pry PEER, LEVER, NOSE, SNOOP, RAISE,
             PEEP
psalm .... ODE, CANTATE, LAUDS,
    CANTICLE, MISERERE, PRAISE,
             HALLEL
pseudo .... BOGUS, SHAM, FALSE,
    SPURIOUS, FAKE
pseudonym .... ALIAS, ANONYM,
    SOBRIQUET, NOM
pshaw .... POOH
psyche .... MIND, SOUL, SPIRIT

psychiatrist ALIENIST, ANALYST, FREUD,
JUNG, ADLER, HORNEY, BRILL,
RANK, REIK
psychic emanation .... AURA(E)
psychologist . SIMON, BINET, PAVLOV,
MESMER, WUNDT
pteric .... ALAR
pteris rootstock .... ROI
pteropod .... CLIONE, MOLLUSK
public .... OVERT
" council, per. to ...... CAMERAL
" land .... AGER
" , make .... AIR, DELATE
" notices .... ADS
publicist .... WRITER, SOLON
publish . DELATE, BLAZON, EDIT, VENT,
RADIO, REVEAL, PRINT, DIVULGE,
SPREAD, AIR, ISSUE
publisher's announcement ..... BLURB
Puccini; composer .... GIACOMO
" opera ...... BOHEME, TOSCA,
BUTTERFLY, LESCAUT, MANON
puck .... RUBBER, SPORT, DISK
puckered .... BULLATE
pudding ... SAGO, DICK, DUFF, MUSH,
HOY
puddle ... DUB, PLASHET, PLUD, POOL
Pueblo assembly room .... KIVA
" Indian ... ACOMA, HOPI, PIRO
puerile ... BOYISH, FEEBLE, INFANTINE
Puerto Principe .... CAMAGUEY
Puerto Rico beverage .... MABI
" " , conqueror of ..... MILES
" " porkfish .... SISI
" " , territory of ... CULEBRA,
VIEQUES
puff .... BLOW, FLAM, PANT, WAFF
" attached to headdress .... POUF
" up .... BLUB, ELATE
puffbird .... BARBET
pugilist .... BOXER
pugilistic .... PUGNACIOUS, FISTIC
pulchritude .... BEAUTY
pule .... WHIMPER, WHINE
pulex .... FLEA
pull .... PLUCK, TOW, YANK, WRENCH,
DRAG, BOUSE, HALE
pulldevil .... SCRODGILL
pulley FUSEE, GORGE, SHEAVE, TACKLE
Pullman .... SLEEPER
pulp CHYME, FLESH, PITH, PAP, SLIME,
POMACE
pulpit . ROSTRUM, AMBO, BEMA, DESK
pulpy dregs .... MAGMA
" fruit .... FIG, POME, UVA
" state ... MASH, FLESHY, SOFT
pulque liquor .... MESCAL
pulsate .... BEAT, THROB, VIBRATE
pulsatory .... RHYTHMIC, SYSTOLIC
pulse .... BEAT, RHYTHM

pulverize . ATOMIZE, MULL, TRITURATE,
BRAY, MEAL, COMMINUTE,
LEVIGATE
puma .... PAINTER, COUGAR, FUR
pump .. QUIZ, SLIPPER, CHAIN, FORCE,
LIFT
" handle .... SWIPE
" plunger .... RAM
pumpkin .... PEPO(N)
pun .... NICK, PARAGRAM
punch ... PRITCHEL, DOUSE, GAD, JAB,
PASTE, CLOWN, MATTOIR, STAMP,
NEGUS
"Punch and Judy," dog in ..... TOBY
puncheon .... CASK, POST
punctilious ...... EXACT, NICE, STRICT
punctuation mark .... DASH, COLON,
HYPHEN, PERIOD
puncture .... HOLE, PERFORATE, PRICK,
BORE, PINK
pundit .... SCHOLAR, NESTOR
pungent .... PEPPERY, PIQUANT, ACRID
Punic .... CARTHAGINIAN
" warrior .... SCIPIO, HANNIBAL
punish ..... FRAP, CHASTEN, WREAK,
AMERCE, MULCT, WHIP
punishment BASTINADO, FINE, WRACK,
FERULE
punitive .... PENAL
Punjab town .... LAHORE, SIMLA
" warrior .... SIKH
punt .... KENT, POLE, POY, KICK
punty .... POINTEL
pupa .... CHRYSALIS
pupil ..... NEOPHYTE, TYRO, ECOLIER,
ELEVE, TRAINEE, MURID
pupilage .... NONAGE
puppet .. DOLL, MARIONETTE, MAUMET,
GUY, JUDY, PUNCH
puppeteer .... SARK
puppy .... WHELP, DOG
purchase of office .... BARRATRY
pure .. CANDID, CLEAN, NEAT, SIMON,
MERE, INVIOLATE, CHASTE, KOSHER,
ABSOLUTE, HOLY
purgative drug .... JALAP
purgatory .... LIMBO, EREBUS
purge ..... PHYSIC, ABSTERGE, CLEAR,
PARDON, SHRIVE
purification .... CATHARSIS
purify .... EPURATE, LUSTRATE, SPURGE
purl .... EDDY, FRILL, MURMUR, SWIRL
purloined .... FINGERED, STOLE
purple dye .... CASSIUS
Purple Heart .... MEDAL
purple ragwort .... JACOBY
" , shade of LILAC, PUCE, TYRIAN,
AMARANTH
purport .... FECK, GIST, TENOR
purpose ...... AIM, END, SAKE, ARTHA

231

purposive .... TELIC
purse .... CRUMENAL, PUCKER, STAKE
purser .... BOUCHER, BURSAR
pursue .. CHASE, PLOD, FOLLOW, TAG,
                          HAUNT, STALK
pursuit .... SCENT, QUEST, TRADE
pursy ..... FAT, OBESE, PUFFY, STOUT
purvey .... CATER, PANDER
push IMPEL, NUB, PING, PROD, NUDGE,
                                 SHOVE
put away .... KEEP, BANK
  " forth ...... APPLY, EXERT, SPROUT
  " off .... DOFF, HAFT
  " on . ADORN, STAGE, DON, ENDUE,
                        FEIGN, PRODUCE
  " on the alert .... ALARUM
  " out .... RETIRE, EVICT
putrefaction .... ROT, DECAY
putrid .... BAD, FOUL, SEPTIC
puttee .... GAITER
puzzle POSE, CAP, CRUX, GRIPH, REBUS,
    PERPLEX, TANGRAM, AMAZE, BAFFLE,
                     CONFUSE, MYSTIFY
pygarg .... ADDAX
Pygmalion's sister .... DIDO
    " statue .... GALATEA
pygmy .... DOKO, MANIKIN, ATOMY,
        SHORT, DWARF, RUNT, MINIM
pygostyle .... VOMER
pylon .... MARKER, META, POST
pyramid .. KHUFU, CHEOPS, CHOLULA
  " , site near .... GIZEH
Pyrenees, highest point of . ANETHOU
  " , pass of the PERCHE, SOMPORT
  " , resort of .... PAU
pyre .... TOPHET, BALE
pyrol .... URD
pyromaniac ...... ARSONIST, FIREBUG
pyroxene mineral ...... SALITE, JADE
Pythagoras, birthplace of .... SAMOS
    " , daughter of ...... CAMO
python ..... BOA, SNAKE, ANACONDA
    " slayer .... APOLLO
pythonic .... ORACULAR
pyx .... BINNACLE, CIBORIUM

Q

Q; letter .... CUE
Q.E.D., part of .... QUOD, ERAT
qua .... AS
quack ... MOUNTEBANK, CHARLATAN,
                CROCUS, HUMBUG, FAKER
  " grass .... COUCH
  " ; med. ...... NOSTRUM, EMPIRIC
quad .... QUOD, TYPE
quadragesimal .... FORTY, LENT

quadrangle .. COURTYARD, TETRAGON
quadrant .... ARC, FOURTH, SECTION
quadrate .... AGREE, SQUARE, ADAPT,
                     CONFORM, QUARTER
quadriga .... CHARIOT
quadrilaterals .... TESSARA
quadrille .... CARDS, DANCE
quadroon .... MULATTO
quadruped .... MAMMAL
quare .... ASK, INQUIRE
quaff .... DRINK, SWILL
quagga-like animal .... ZEBRA
quagmire ..... BOG, FEN, LAIR, HAG
quahog .... CLAM, VENUS, BULLNOSE
quail .. BOBWHITE, COLLIN, MASSENA
  " , flock of .... COVEY, BEVY
  " genus .... COTURNIX
  " , to ... BLENCH, COWER, FLINCH,
                                 CRINGE
quaint .... DROLL, QUEER, ODD
quake .... QUIVER, TREMBLE, TREMOR,
                     SHIVER, SHUDDER
quaker .... HERON, MOTH
Quaker FRIEND, HICKS, FOX, CANNON
quaking .... ASPEN, TREPID
qualify .... LIMIT, VARY, TEMPER, FIT,
                    MODIFY, NAME, ADAPT
quality ...... NATURE, STRAIN, TRAIT,
                     CALIBER, FEATURE
  " according to Sankhya system
        GUNA, SATTVA, RAJAS, TAMAS
  " , high .... STATE, TASTE
  " of tone .... TIMBRE
qualm .... NAUSEA, PALL, REGRET
quamash .... CAMASS
quandary ... DILEMMA, STRAIT, PICKLE
quantity .... DOSE, ANY, KITTY, LOT,
                    SCAD, SPATE, MASS
  " , irrational .... SURD
Quapaw Indian .... OZARK
quarantine .... ISOLATE
Quarles; poet .... FRANCIS
quarrel .. SPAT, BICKER, FLITE, SCENE,
        TIFF, MIFF, WRANGLE, BRAWL,
                                 MELEE
quarrelsome ... LITIGIOUS, CHOLERIC
quarry .... CHASE, DELF, GAME, PREY
quarrying term .... TIRR
quarter note .... CROTCHET
quarters ..... BILLET, BIVOUAC, DIGS
quartic curve .... LIMACON
Quartodeciman .... PASCHITE
quartz ONYX, RUBASSE, SILEX, PLASMA,
                     PRASE, SARD, SILICA
  " , variety of AGATE, AMETHYST,
        CITRINE, FLINT, JASPER, TOPAZ
quash ... CRUSH, ANNUL, CASS, VOID
quaternion .... TETRAD
  " , turning factor of VERSOR
quaver ..... TREMOLO, TRILL, SHAKE

232

quay .... PIER, LEVEE, WHARF
queachy ... SWAMPY, BOGGY, FENNY
queasy ... DELICATE, NAUSEOUS, SICK
queen .. BEGUM, REINE, RANI, RANEE
    " of Greek gods .... HERA
Queen of Hearts .... ELIZABETH
    " of Isles .... ALBION
queen of Roman gods .... JUNO
    " of Sheba .... BALKIS
Queen of the Antilles .... CUBA
    " of the East .... ZENOBIA
queen of the fairies .. TITANIA, MAB
Queen Elizabeth's name .... ORIANA
queens, miscell. .. ANNE, BESS, DIDO,
    MARY, MARIE, VICTORIA, (EL)ENA
queenly .... REGINAL, REGAL
Queensland capital .... BRISBANE
queer ..... FUNNY, FAINT, ODD, RUM
quell .. ALLAY, END, SUBDUE, CRUSH,
    CALM, PACIFY
quench .. COOL, SLAKE, STIFLE, SATE,
    SUBDUE
Quercus .... OAKS
querulous .... PEEVISH, PETULANT,
    TOUCHY
question . DOUBT, QUERY, POSE, QUIZ,
    ASK, NUT, GRILL
    " , mark indicating a EROTEME
questionable .... MOOT, DUBIOUS
questioning .... GRILLING, HECKLING
questionnaire . FORM, FEELER, STRAW
quetzal .... TROGON
queue ...... LINE, PIGTAIL, FILE, CUE
quib .... GIBE, QUIP
quibble .... CARP, CAVIL, EVADE,
    SOPHISM, PUN
quick .... YARE, AGILE, ACTIVE, LISH,
    RAPID, FAST, FLEET
quicken .... ANIMATE, ROUSE, SPEED
quickly ..... APACE, PRESTO, ANON,
    PRONTO, FLIT
quickness, mental .. NOUS, DISPATCH
quicksand .... TRAP, SYRT(IS)
quickset .... HEDGE, THICKET
quicksilver .... MERCURY
quid .... CUD, FID, CHEW, WAD
quidnunc .... GOSSIP, FRUMP
quiddity .... WHAT, CAVIL
quiescent ... STATIC, SLEEPING, INERT
quiet .... EASE, MUM, TUT, HALCYON,
    PEACE, PACIFIC, SILENCE, PST, TST,
    CALM, LULL, SOOTHE, HUSHED
quietus .... DEATH, MORT, OBIT
quill feather(s) .... REMEX, REMIGES
    " for playing a spinet ..... SPINA
    " for winding silk .... COP
    " , porcupine .... PEN
quillai .... SOAPBARK
quilt . CADDOW, DUVET, PATCHWORK,
    EIDER, THROW

quilted silk .... MATELASSE
quip .... JEST, JIBE, MOT, TAUNT
quirt .... ROMAL, WHIP
Quisling .... RAT
quit .. FREE, CLEAR, RID, STOP, CEASE,
    DESIST, ABANDON
quiver ... FLUTTER, SHUDDER, TREMOR,
    SHAKE, CASE
quivering .... ASPEN, QUAKING
quixotic ...... UTOPIAN, ROMANTIC
quiz ..... EXAM, POSER, TEST, COACH
quodlibet; mus. .... FANTASIA
quoits term DISC, DISCUS, HOB, MOT,
    TEE
    " : stone cover of a _____ ..
    CROMLECH
quondam .. ONETIME, FORMER, ONCE
quota .... CITE, SHARE, WHO
quotation .... CHRIA, EXCERPT, CITAL
quote .... CITE, ADDUCE, REPEAT
quotidian .... DAILY, ORDINARY
quotient .... RESULT

R

R, letter .... ARE
Ra, bull form of .... BACIS
    " , sun god . ATEN, CHEPERA, HORUS,
    SOKARI(S), TUM
rabato .... RUFF
rabbi ...... AMORA, GAON, HAKAM
rabbit . LAPIN, ADAPIS, HARE, BUNNY,
    LEPUS, TAPETI
    " burrow .... CLAPPER
    " ears .... ANTENNA
    " fever .... TULAREMIA
    " fur .... CONEY, CONY
    " net .... HAY
    " shelter .... HUTCH
    " , skin of .... RACK
rabbit-eared .... OARLOP
    " -like animal PERAMELES, MARMOT,
    PIKA
rabbitry .... WARREN
rabbit's foot .... CLOVER
    " tail .... FUD, SCUT
rabble .. CROWD, MOB, RAFF, DREGS,
    SCUM
rabid ...... MAD, RAMPANT, VIOLENT
rabies .... LYSSA, LYTTA, RAGE
raccoon .... PANDA, COON, WASHER
    " -like .... COATI, MAPACH
race .. PEOPLE, CASTE, STRAIN, BREED,
    LINE(AGE)
    " , an undivided .... HOLETHNOS
    " , channel .... FLUME
    " ; family .... ILK, STIRPS

233

" , gait in a long .... LOPE
" hatred .... RACISM
" mill .. LADE, CHANNEL, CURRENT
" , science of ...... ETHNOLOGY
" , short .... BICKER
" , to .... HIE, HASTEN
" , water .... ARROYO
racecourse LAP, CIRCUS, HEATS, OVAL,
　　　　TURF, ASCOT, DOWNS, EPSOM,
　　　　　　　HIALEAH, PIMLICO
" 　　marker .... META
racehorse .... KELSO, NASHUA,
　　　　　MANOWAR, CITATION,
　　　　　　　SECRETARIAT
" 　, inferior .... PLATER
raceme .... CLUSTER, SPIKE
racetrack tipster .... TOUT
Rachel's father .... LABAN
rachis .... STRIG, SPINDLE
Rachmaninoff; comp. .... SERGEI
racing colors .... SILKS
" 　forecaster .. TIPSTER, DOPESTER
rack . GIN, SKIN, AGONY, PAIN, CRIB,
　　　　　JIB, CREEL, TORMENT
racket .... BAT, CROSSE, DIN, REVEL,
　　　　BABEL, HUBBUB, UPROAR
racy FRESH, RICH, PIQUANT, PUNGENT,
　　　　　BRISK, STRONG, SPICY
Radames' love .... AIDA
radar housing .... RADOME
" 　image .... BLIP, PIP
" 　screen .... SCOPE
" 　signal .... IFF, RACON
radian .... ARC
radiant .. AGLOW, BEAMY, LAMBENT,
　　　　　SHEEN, GLORIOUS
radiate .... BEAM, GLEAM, EMIT, SHED
radiating .... EMANANT, CASTING
radical ... EXTREME, LEFT, ULTRA, RED,
　　　　　　FULL, WHOLE
radicel ...... ETYMON, RADIX, ROOT
radio .... SEND, BROADCAST
" 　beacon .... CONSOL
" 　channel .... AIRWAY
" 　gear .... ANTENNA
" 　interference .... STATIC
" 　operator, amateur .... HAM
" 　program rating ..... HOOPER,
　　　　　　　NIELSEN
" 　response .... ROGER
" , small .... TRANSISTOR
" 　tube .... GRID
radioactive element .... CURIUM,
　　FERMIUM, NOBELIUM, PLUTONIUM
radium container .... RADIODE
" , discoverer of .... CURIE
" , emanation of .... NITON
" 　F .... POLONIUM
" , source of ...... CARNOTITE,
　　　　　　　URANITE

radius SPOKE, EXTENT, RANGE, SWEEP
radix ...... ROOT, RADICAL, ETYMON
raffish .... LOW, INFAMOUS, VULGAR
raffle .... CHANCE, LOTTERY, TANGLE
raft CATAMARAN, FLOAT, GOBS, BALSA
rage ..... RAVE, FUROR, MODE, RESE,
　　　　　VOGUE, DESIRE, FURY
ragged .. SCOURY, SHREDDED, SHABBY
raging .... GRIM, RAMPANT
ragout ... GOULASH, HARICOT, HASH,
　　　　　　CIVET, SALMI
ragweed .... IVA
raid .. FORAGE, SIEGE, FORAY, TALA,
　　　RAZZIA, COMMANDO, INROAD
rail BAR, COOT, COURLAN, ORTOLAN,
　　　　　　CRAKE, SORA
" , altar .... SEPTUM
" 　at ..... RANT, RATE, SCOFF, JAW
railing .... GRATE, PARAPET
raillery .... ASTEISM, BANTER,
　　　　　　　PERSIFLAGE
railroad .... LINE, RUSH, TRACK
" 　car .... DINER, SLEEPER,
　　　　　PULLMAN, TENDER
" 　flare .... FUSEE
" 　switch .... FROG
" 　timber .... TIE, SLEEPER
rails, per. to the .... RALLINE
rain .... BANGE, DAG, MISLE, SEREIN,
　　　　MIST, DRIZZLE, POUR
" , per. to .... PLUVIAL
rainbow .... ARC, IRIS, ARCH
" , per. to .... IRIDAL
raincoat .... SLICKER, MINO
rain gauge .. UDOMETER, HYETOMETER
Rainier (Mt.): Ind. name .. TACOMA
rain spout .... RONE
rain tree SAMAN, GENISARO, ZAMAN
rainy .... WET, MISTY, SHOWERY
raise ... EXALT, REAR, TRICE, UPLIFT,
　　BOOST, EXCITE, MUSTER, ELEVATE,
　　　　　　　HOIST
raised aloft .... HEFTED, HOVE
" 　to the third power .... CUBED
" 　with a bar .... LEVERED
rajah's wife .... RANI, RANEE
Rajmahal creeper .... JITI, CHITI
rake .... LECHER, SATYR, RAFF, ROUE
" 　with gunfire .. ENFILADE, PEPPER
rally .... COLLECT, JOKE, BANTER
ram ...... CRAM, STUFF, BUCK, TUP,
　　　WETHER, BUTT, TAMP, ARIES
ram-headed god .... AMMON
ramble PROWL, SPROGUE, GAD, ROVE,
　　　　　ROAM, SAUNTER
ramentum .... PALEA, PALET
ramification .... BRANCHING, RAMUS
ram-like .... ARIETINE
"Ramona," writer of ...... JACKSON

234

ramp .. EASING, GRADING, RUN, SLIP, PLATFORM, SLOPE
rampart ..... PARAPET, ESCARP, LINE, BULWARK, RAVELIN, BRAY, AGGER, VALLUM, REDAN
    " -like .... WALL, DEFILADE
    " , part of .... SPUR
ram's horn; Heb. .... SHOPHAR
ramus .... BRANCH
ran .... HARED, SPED
ranch .... CASA, ESTANCIA, FARM, HACIENDA
rancid STALE, FROWZY, MUSTY, RANK, FETID
rancor .... GALL, HATRED, SPITE
rand .... MARGIN, BORDER, EDGE
range .. AREA, GAMUT, ORBIT, SIERRA
    " -finder .... MEKOMETER
ranged .... FORAYED, ROAMED
rank . CLASS, GRADE, FILE, ROW, TIER, DEGREE, ARRANT, ESTATE
rankle .... FESTER, IRRITATE
ransack .... RAKE, RIFLE
ransom ...... RESCUE, REDEEM, RAIM
rant .... RAVE, STEVEN, BOAST
rap ... KNOCK, THWACK, KNAP, TIRL, BOP, BOX, CENSURE
rapacious .... AVARICIOUS, LEONINE
rapacity ... VORACITY, RAVIN, GREED
raphe .... SEAM, SUTURE
rapid .... FAST, QUICK, SWIFT
rapids, narrow .... DALLES, RIFT
rapier ...... BILBO, SWORD, VERDUN
    " -blade heel .... RICASSO
rapt .... ABSORBED, ECSTATIC
rare metallic element ..... THORITE, YTTRIUM
Ra's mother .... NUT
    " wife .... MUT
rascal .... LOON, VARLET
rash . WANTON, ICARIAN, MAD, WILD, GIDDY
    " man .... HOTSPUR
    " , skin .... ERUPTION, ECZEMA
rashness .... TEMERITY, ACRISY
rasp .... GRATE, FILE, OFFEND
raspberry; genus .... RUBUS
raspings .... SCOBS
rat .... DESERTER, SNOB, APOSTATE, GNAWER, MURINE, VOLE, RODENT, TRAITOR
    " -like animal ...... MOLE, ROTTAN, HAMSTER
    " poison .... ANTU
ratafia .... CURACAO, NOYAU
ratchet .... CLICK, DETENT, PAWL
rate . AGIO, BATTA, CESS, TAX, ASSESS, ESTIMATE, REVILE
Rathbone; actor .... BASIL
rather ...... THAN, ERE, ERER, ASTITE

ratify .. PASS, SEAL, CONSENT, AMEN
ratio .... RATE, QUOTA, DEGREE
rational ...... SANE, SOUND, WISE, NORMAL, PROPER, LOGICAL
rations ...... DIET, FOOD, QUANTITY
ratite bird .... MOA, EMU, EMEU
rattan .. WHIP, LASH, THONG, CANE, PALM
    " ; genus .... CALAMUS
ratten .... STEAL, CRIB, FILCH, POACH
rattle .... RALE, CLACK, RICK, NOISE, PRATTLE, TIRL
    " , crier's .... CLAPPER
rattlesnake .. SIDEWINDER, CROTALUS
    " plantain .... NETWORT
ratwa .... MUNTJAC
raucous .... HARSH, HOARSE, DRY
ravage .... RAVEN, SACK, EAT
ravaged .... OVERRAN, WASTE
rave .... RAGE, STORM, RANT
ravel .... FRAY, SLEAVE
ravelin .... OUTWORK, DEMILUNE
ravelings, fine .... LINT
raven ALALA, CORBEL, CORVIN, RALPH
"Raven God" .... ODIN
ravine . CLOUGH, GULCH, LINN, DELL, NULLAH, WADI, ARROYO
    " , narrow .... STRID, CHINE
raw .... CRUDE, RUDE, SORE, UNRIPE, BLEAK, GREEN
rawboned ..... GAUNT, SCRAG, LEAN
rawhide whip .... SJAMBOK, KNOUT, QUIRT, THONG
raw meat, eating of ... OMOPHAGIA
raw sugar .... CASSONADE
ray .... BEAM, SKATE, GLEAM, ALPHA, BETA, GAMMA
    " , eagle .... OBISPO
    " , thornback ...... DORN, FLAIR, TORPEDO, ROKER
Ray; actor .... ALDO
Rayburn, Mr. .... SAM, SPEAKER
rayed badge .... STAR
rayon .. ACETATE, VISCOSE, CELANESE
rays, like .... RADIAL
    " , sun's .... ACTINIC
raze DEMOLISH, LEVEL, EFFACE, ERASE, WRECK
razor ...... SHAVE, SCRAPE, RATTLER
    " -billed auk FALK, MURRE, NODDY
    " clam .... SOLEN
    " , to .... HONE, STROP
razorback ... HOG, FINBACK, WHALE, RORQUAL
razz .... DERIDE, RIDICULE
razzle-dazzle .... CONFUSE
re .... ANENT, ABOUT, CONCERNING
rea .... TURMERIC
reach . ADVENE, GAIN, SPAN, ATTAIN, STRETCH, SCOPE

reaching after applause . CAPTATION
reaction .... TROPISM, TAXIS
read . SKIM, COUNSEL, RELATE, SCAN,
PRELECT, PERUSE, CON
reader .... LECTOR, LISTER, TEACHER,
ANAGNOST, PRIMER
readiness ... ALACRITY, ART, FACILITY
reading .. LECTION, VARIATION, KERE,
KERI
    " desk .. ESCRITOIRE, LECTERN,
AMBO
    " inability .... ALEXIA
ready .... PROMPT, BAIN, HERE, YARE,
APERT, PRET
reality .... FACT, BEING, MCCOY
realize ... GAIN, KNOW, SENSE, WIN
really .. FANCY, INDEED, ARU, LITERAL
realm ..... DOMAIN, EMPIRE, SPHERE,
RICHE
    " of Jamshid .... PERIS
reamer ... WIDENER, BORER, CHERRY,
SPUD
reanimate ...... RALLY, RESUSCITATE
rear, toward the . (A)BAFT, (A)STERN
rearhorse .... MANTIS
rearing .... PESADE, STEND
reason . ARGUE, CAUSE, LOGIC, SENSE,
NOUS, MOTIVE
    " , deprive of .... DEMENT
    " , want of .... AMENTIA
reata .... LARIAT, LASSO, ROPE
reave .... BREAK, REND, TEAR
rebec .. LYRE, VIOLIN, FIDDLE, SAROD
Rebecca's brother .... LABAN
    " son .... ESAU
rebel .. RED, TURNCOAT, RESIST, DEFY
rebellion . TREASON, MUTINY, PUTSCH,
REVOLT, SEDITION
rebound .. RICOCHET, STOT, CAROM,
ECHO, RESILE
rebounding .... SPRINGY, RECOILING
rebuff ... CHIDE, LESSON, SLAP, SNUB
rebuke . ADMONISH, SLAP, TUT, SCOLD
recalcitrant .... RENITENT, RESISTANT
recall ...... REPEAL, ANNUL, ENCORE
recant .... ADJURE, RETRACT, REVOKE
recapitulate ... SUM, REPEAT, REVIEW
recede .... WITHDRAW, EBB, REGRESS
receive .. ADMIT, FANG, HOLD, GREET
receiver of property in trust . BAILEE
    " of stolen goods ..... FENCE
recent . LATE, NEW, MODERN, NOVEL,
NEO(TERIC)
receptacle .... HANAPER, CONTAINER,
BAG, BIN, SACK, URN
    " for corporal cloth .. BURSE
    " for holy water .... STOUP
    " for oil and wine ... CYST
    " for scent and water SEBILLA

reception . OVATION, INFARE, LEVEE,
SOIREE, SALON, TEA
recess ALA, BAY, CRYPT, NICHE, SINUS,
APSE, ALCOVE
recidive .... RELAPSE
recipe ...... FORMULA, DISH, REMEDY
recipient .... CONFEREE, DONEE, HEIR
reciprocate ..... BANDY, EXCHANGE
recital . NARRATIVE, SAGA, CONCERT,
MUSICALE
recitative; mus. .... SCENA
recite .. REPEAT, SPEAK, SCAN, QUOTE
reckless ... MADCAP, HOTSPUR, PERDU
recklessly .... RAMSTAM
reckon .... IMPUTE, COMPUTE, OPINE,
GUESS, TALLY
reckoning ... TAB, TALE, DATE, POST,
SHOT, COUNT, TABLE
    " table .... ABACUS
reclaim .... RENEW, RESTORE, REDEEM
reclaimed land .... POLDER
reclining ...... ABED, PRONE, SUPINE
recluse . ANCHORET, EREMITE, HERMIT,
MONK, ASCETIC, NUN
recoil .... RESILE, SHY, WINCE, KICK
recollection .... ANAMNESIS
recompense . REPAY, MEAD, GUERDON,
REWARD, ERIC, WAGE
reconcile .... ATONE, SETTLE, PACIFY,
WEAN, ADJUST, SQUARE
reconnoiter ... SCOUT, SCAN, SURVEY
record .... ENTRY, ESTREAT, LEGEND,
POSTEA, FILE, NOTATE, LOG, TAB,
TAPE, DIARY, ENTER
    " , formal .... NOTE, MINUTE,
REGISTER
    " of events; Lat. .... FASTI
recorded proceeding(s) ACTUM, ACTA
recorder ...... REGISTRAR, CARTULARY
records .... ANNALS, ARCHIVE
recount .... RELATE, NARRATE, DETAIL
recover .... RALLY, RETRIEVE, RECOUP,
REDEEM, CURE
recovery .... TROVER
rectify .... AMEND, CORRECT, ADJUST
recuperation(s) .... LYSIS, LYSES
red .. CERISE, CORAL, ERIC, NACARAT,
FLEA, GOYA, HEBE, LAKE, PUCE
    " cedar .... JUNIPER, SAVIN
    " cherry gum .... CERASIN
    " clay, tropical .... LATERITE
    " corpuscles .... HEMATID
    " cosmetic .... HENNA
    " dye . AURINE, AAL, CHAY, EOSIN,
LAC
    " , glowing .... RUTILANT
    " grouse .... PTARMIGAN
    " gum .... STROPHULUS
    " iron oxide .... RUBIGO
    " Madeira wine .... TINTO

" ochre .... TIVER
" paint pigment .... CHICA, ROSET
" stone .... RUBY, SARD
" translucent mineral .... GARNET
" -yellow . PEACHBLOW, BARK, BOLE
Red, the .... ERIC
redact ..... REVISE, EDIT, DRAFT, PEN
redbird .... TANAGER
Redcross Knight, wife of ...... UNA
reddish brown .... AUBURN, RUSSET,
                                SORREL
" -brown mineralite ..... RULITE
" red-yellow .... AGATE
" yellow .... OLD GOLD
" -yellow dyestuff .... ALIZARINE
redeem ...... FREE, RANSOM, ATONE
redeemer ... MESSIAH, SAVIOR, GOEL
redeye .... RUDD
redfaced .... BLOWZED
redmouth fish .... GRUNT
redolent . AROMATIC, SCENTED, BALMY
redouble .... ECHO, REPEAT
reduce .. DERATE, LOWER, PARE, PULL,
    THIN, SLIM, DIET, SHRINK, CURTAIL,
                            DIMIDIATE
redundant ... PLEONASTIC, PLETHORIC
reed ..... ARROW, GRASS, PIPE, STEM
" loom .... SLEY
" mace .... MATREED
" pipe .... KAZOO, MIRLITON
reedbuck .... BOHOR, NAGOR
reef .... CAY(O), KEY, LEDGE, ATOLL,
                        SANDBAR, SHOAL
" (a sail) .. SWIFT, SHORTEN, FURL
" , mining ..... LODE, RIDGE, VEIN
reek ..... FUME, SMOKE, FUG, SMELL
reel . TEETER, DANCE, ROCK, STAGGER,
                          TOTTER, SWAY
" off a story .... SCRIEVE
" used in dyeing .... WINCE
" , yarn .... SWIFT
reem; bib. .... UNICORN
Reese; nickname .... PEEWEE
refectory .... FRATER
refer .. ASCRIBE, IMPUTE, ALLUDE, CITE,
                            HARP, SEND
referee ...... MODERATOR, UMP(IRE),
                        ARBITER, JUDGE
refined spirit .... ELIXIR
reformer .... AMENDER, LUTHER,
    ZWINGLI, HUSS, CALVIN, WAHABI
refraction, per. to ..... ANACLASTIC
refractor ... PRISM, TELESCOPE, LENS
refractory .... INDOCILE, REBEL
refrain .... BOYCOTT, DESIST
" in music . DERRY, EPODE, BOB,
                                LALA
refuge(s) ROCK, ARK, ASYLUM, ASYLA,
    HAVEN, RETREAT, DOORN, SHELTER
refugee .... EMIGREE

refund .... REBATE
refuse .... COOM(B), CULM, DROSS,
    MARC, ORT, NAYSAY, DENY, SCUM,
        SLAG, CHAFF, DRAFF, OFFAL,
                        TRASH, SCORIA
" from coffee beans ... TRIAGE
refute .... REBUT
regale .... DIVERT, FEAST, TREAT
regard ...... DEEM, ESTEEM, HONOR
regarding .... ANENT, INRE
Regent diamond .... PITT
"Regent of the Sun" .... URIEL
regimen .... DIET, SYSTEM
regiment; framework .... CADRE
region .. AREA, REALM, NELT, SPACE,
                        LOCALE, SECTOR
" ; comb. form .... NESIA
register .. ENROL(L), LIST, ROLL, ROTA,
        CARTULARY, ROTULET, DOCKET
" of death .... NECROLOGY
regret .... REW, RUE, RUTH, REPENT,
        DEPLORE, PENITENCE, WOE
regulate . ADJUST, CONTROL, FIX, TIME,
                                DIRECT
rehearsal garment .... LEOTARD
rehearse ...... COACH, DRILL, TRAIN
reign .... RAJ, SWAY, TERM
" , per. to .... REGNAL, REGNANT
Reims, former name .... REMI
reins ..... HAUNCHES, LEASH, LOINS
reinstate . REVEST, ESTABLISH, RESTORE
reiterate .... DRUM, HARP, REPEAT
reject .. REPEL, SPURN, JILT, DISCARD,
                              CASHIER
rejoice ..... ELATE, EXALT, GLADDEN
relate .... PERTAIN, TELL, RECITE
related .. GERMANE, INHERENT, TOLD,
        AKIN, INLAW, SEPTAL
" by blood . AGNATE, COGNATE,
                                SIB
" on the mother's side .. ENATE
relation .... ACCOUNT, RECITAL,
                          KIN(DRED)
relational .... CASAL, NOTIONAL
relative ... GRANNY, SIB, EME, AUNT,
                        NIECE, PARENT
" , favor to a ...... NEPOTISM
" pronoun . WHO, THAT, WHAT
relax .. LOOSEN, EASE, OPEN, REMIT,
                            SLACKEN
relay .... DAK, DAWK, REMUDA
release FREE, UNDO, RELET, TRIP, REST,
                        LOOSE, PAROLE
" ; as a claim .... REMISE
reliance .... TRUST, HOPE, FAITH
relic ... CURIO, HUACA(O), MEMORIAL
" box .... CHASSE
relief . SPELL, SOTE, SUCCOR, REDRESS,
        DOLE, RELIEVO, FRET

237

religion ... PIETY, FAITH, TRUST, CULT,
    BUDDHISM, ISLAM, SIKHISM,
    TAOISM, SHINTO
religious art work PIETA, ICON, IKON
    "   belief .... DEISM, CREED
    "   brotherhood ...... SODALITY
    "   devotee .... FAKIR
    "   devotion .... NOVENA
    "   doctrine, system of .... RITE,
    CULT(US)
    "   fair .... MELA
    "   jurist .... GAIUS
    "   mendicant .... SERVITE
    "   observance ..... FAST, PURIM
    "   offering OBLATION, DEODATE
    "   order, one of a ..... ESSENE,
    MARIST, TEMPLAR, BABIST,
    OBLATE
    "   -service directories ORDINES
    "   sect .... AMISH, CENOBY
relinquish .... LEAVE, YIELD, LET
reliquary .... APSE, ARCA, CHEST
relish ... GUSTO, ZEST, SAUCE, TANG,
    FLAVOR
reluctant ..... AVERSE, LOATH, THRO,
    WARY, CHARY
rely .. BANK, DEPEND, LIPPEN, COUNT,
    TRUST, LEAN
remain .... LEAVE, BIDE, LAST, STAND
remainder .. ARREAR, REST, RESIDUUM,
    SCRAPS, BALANCE
remains ...... ASHES, CORPSE, RUINS
remark ... NOTE, SAY, SEE, COMMENT
remedy .. ANTACID, CURE, AID, BOTE,
    GAIN, BALM, ELIXIR, PANACEA,
    ARCANUM, NOSTRUM, BALSAM
remembrance ...... MINNIE, TROPHY,
    MEMENTO
remex .... FEATHER, OARSMAN
remnant RAG, SCRAG, RESIDUE, DREG,
    ODDMENT, PIECE
remora .... PEGA, STOPSHIP
remorse ...... REGRET, PITY, SORROW
remote .. ELENGE, FORANE, ULTERIOR,
    SLIGHT
    "   goal .... THULE
remove AVOID, DELE, BALE, ELOIGN,
    ELOIN, DOFF, STRIP, OUST,
    DEPOSE, DISBAR
    "   impurities .... PASSIVATE
remuneration . EMOLUMENT, BOUNTY,
    FEE
Remus' brother .... ROMULUS
rend . CHOP, RIP, RIVE, SUNDER, TEAR,
    RUPTURE
render .... CONSTRUE, TRY, YIELD
    "   harsh .... HOARSEN
    "   knotty .... GNARL
    "   unstable .... UNHINGE
rendezvous ... DATE, TRYST, MEETING

renegade ..... APOSTATE, RAT, REBEL,
    DESERTER, TURNCOAT
renew .... MEND, REFORM, REVIVE
    "   wine .... STUM
rennet .... APPLE, LAB
renounce ... REJECT, ABJURE, RENEGE,
    RENAY, WAIVE, SPURN, CEDE
renovate .... RENEW, REPAIR
rent . RIP, HIRE, TAC, LEASE, LET, TEAR,
    SPLIT, AVENAGE, ONSTAND
rental .... LOAN, KAIN
repair .... BOTE, MEND, DARN
reparation .... REDRESS, AMENDS
repartee ..... RIPOSTE, RETORT, SALLY
repast ...... PRANDIAL, LUNCH(EON),
    TIFFIN, TREAT, MEAL, SNACK,
    COLLATION
repay . QUIT, ANSWER, AVENGE, MEED,
    REFUND
repeal .... ABROGATE, RESCIND
repeat . RECUR, RETELL, ITERATE, RAME,
    BIS, ECHO, TWICE
repent .... ATONE, GRIEVE
repeater .... HOLDOVER, FIREARM
repentance .... RUE, RUTH, SHAME
repetition .. ROTE, ANAPHORA, ECHO,
    MERISM, TAUTOLOGY
replace .... REPONE, STEAD, STET
replate .... RETIN, RESILVER
replete .... FULL, SATED, GORGED
replica .... COPY, IMAGE, BIS, ECTYPE,
    CARBON
reply ...... RETORT, ANSWER, REJOIN
report .. DILATE, CANARD, BRUIT, POP,
    RUMOR, BULLETIN, BANG, NOISE,
    CRY, GOSSIP, RADIO, HANSARD
    "   , legislative .... CAHIER
repose .... SIT, EASE, RELY, REST
represent .. ENACT, EXHIBIT, PORTRAY,
    TYPIFY
representative . AGENT, ENVOY, PROXY
repress .... CRUSH, CURB, REIN, STIFLE
repression ... INHIBITION, REJECTION
reprimand .... SCOLD, SLATE, REBUKE
reproach CHIDE, ODIUM, RACA, BALME,
    TAUNT, CENSURE
reproductive body .... GAMETE
reproof .... CENSURE, SNUB
reptile ... LIZARD, TOAD, TURTLE, ASP,
    BOA, ADDER, COBRA, NAGA, ADDA,
    MAMBA, GECKO, SLIDER, SAURIAN,
    OPHIDIAN
    "   , Nile .... CROC
    "   , scale of a .... SCUTE
"Republic" author .... PLATO
repudiate .... RECANT, REJECT
repulsion .... AVERSION, DISGUST
repulsive . REVOLTING, LOATHLY, UGLY
reputation ...... NAME, FAME, ECLAT
repute .... ODOR, CREDIT, WORD

reputed DEEMED, SUPPOSED, PUTATIVE, RENOWNED
request ASK, BEG, SUIT, PRAY, SOLICIT, BESEECH, PLEA, ROGATION
requiem masses .... TRENTAL
require .... LACK, NEED
requite ...... ATONE, PAY, RETALIATE
rescind RECALL, RECANT, REPEAL, VOID, ANNUL, VACATE
rescue .... RANSOM, SAVE, AID
resemblance .... RINGER, BLUSH
resembling a comb .... PECTINAL
resentment .... DUDGEON, UMBRAGE, CHOLER, PIQUE, IRE
reserve ...... BACKLOG, FUND, STOCK
reserved . ALOOF, DISTANT, KEPT, COY, SHY
reservoir ..... STORE, SUMP, PISCINA, BASIN, CISTERN
reside .... BIDE, DWELL, LODGE
residence ... DWELLING, ABODE, SEAT, MANSE, MANSION, YAMEN
resident CIT, BURGESS, LESSEE, TENANT
residue ORT, REMANET, ASHES, DREGS, DOTTLE, OVER
resign .. DEMIT, ABDICATE, ABANDON
resiliency .... TONE, ELASTICITY
resin .... GUM, EXUDATE, ROSIN
" alkaloid in beans .... ESERINE
" as a varnish .... ANIME
" , balsam gum .... BDELLIUM
" , fragrant .... ELEMI
" , fragrant inflammable .... FRANKINCENSE
" ; genus .... MYRRH
" gum DAMMAR, GUGAL, COPAL, MASTIC
" incense .... SANDARAC(IN)
" , medicinal .... ELATERITE
" of S.A. tree .... ACOUCHI
" of Chian turpentine ...... ALK
" of the agalloch .... ALOE
" substance .... LAC
" , yellowish .. GAMBOGE, AMBER
resist .. STEM, FEND, WITHER, OPPOSE, REBEL, DISOBEY
resisting ... OPPUGNANT, TENACIOUS
" power .... WIRY
" pressure .... RENITENT
resolute ...... GRITTY, LEAL, STAUNCH
resort .... PURLIEU, DIVE, SPA, USE
resound .... ECHO, PEAL, CLANG, PLANGENT, RING
resource .... MEANS, ASSETS, FUNDS, MONEY, CAPITAL, DEVICE
resourceful .... FERTILE, SHARP
respiration .... EUPNOEA
respire .... BREATHE, EXHALE, INHALE
respite, give .... FRIST, DELAY
resplendent .... AUREATE, GRAND

respond .... REACT, FEEL
response .... ANTIPHON, ECHO, REPLY
responsibility .. CHARGE, ONUS, DUTY, TRUST
rest .. SIT, LEAN, RELY, SEAT, RECLINE, PERCH, BASE, SIESTA
" in reading .... CESURA
" , musket .... GAFFLE
restaurant CAFETERIA, AUTOMAT, CAFE, DINER, BISTRO, EATERY
rested .... LAIRED, SLEPT
restharrow .... WHIN
restless; mus. .... AGITATO
restore . FIX, HEEL, MEND, SET, RENEW
restrain .. FETTER, BRIDLE, REIN, STINT, DETER, TETHER
restraint .... CURB, BIT, TRAMMEL
restrict ... LIMIT, TIE, CRAMP, CENSOR
result .... EFFECT, END, ISSUE, TOTAL, PROCEED
résumé .... ABSTRACT
resume .... RENEW, REOPEN
ret .... ROT, SOAK, STEEP
retailer of wine .... COOPER
retained .... HELD, KEPT, OWNED
retaliation TALION, REPRISAL, REVENGE
retard . LATEN, DELAY, IMPEDE, BRAKE, CHECK, DEFER
retardant .... OBSTACLE, REMORA
retch .... VOMIT, GAG
rete .... NETWORK
retiary .... NETLIKE, SPIDER, TELAR
reticulum .... MITOME
retinue . CREW, ESCORT, TRAIN, SUITE, CORTEGE
retired .... ABED, LONE, WITHDRAWN
" from service .... EMERITUS
retort REPARTEE, REPLY, QUIP, RIPOSTE, ALEMBIC, SALLY
retract .. DISAVOW, RECANT, ABJURE, DISOWN, RECEDE
retreat .... ROUT, ASYLUM, DEN, LAIR, NOOK, RETIRE, SANCTUM, PRIVACY, ABRI
retrench .... CURTAIL, DECREASE
retribution .... REQUITAL, NEMESIS
" , law of .... KARMA
retributive .... VENGEFUL
retrieve .. RECOVER, AMEND, REGAIN, FIND, RECOUP
retrograde .. RETRAL, SLOW, DECLINE, RECEDE, (RE)LAPSE
return .... RECUR, YIELD, ANSWER
" thrust .... RIPOSTE
reveal .... EXHIBIT, TELL, WRAY, BARE, UNVEIL, IMPART, EXPOSE
reveille ... DIAN, CALL, LEVET, SIGNAL
revel . RIOT, CAROUSAL, ORGY, FEAST, LARK, SPREE

revelation ...... ORACLE, DISCLOSURE, GOSPEL
revenant .... EIDOLON
revenue ..... INCOME, YIELD, RENTAL, TITHES, PROFIT, BENEFICE
   " of a bishop .... ANNAT
reverberating .. ECHOING, REBOANT, RINGING
reverence .. WORSHIP, AWE, HOMAGE
reverie .... DREAM, FANTASY
revers .... LAPEL
reversion .... ESCHEAT, ATAVISM, (RE)LAPSE
revile . ASPERSE, VILIFY, MALIGN, RAIL, ABUSE
revise .... AMEND, EDIT, UPDATE
revision .... RECENSION
revive .... RALLY, RELIVE, RESPIRE
revoke ..... ABJURE, RENEGE, REPEAL
   " ; as a legacy .... ADEEM
revolution .. CYCLE, GYRE, TURN, COUP
   " ; essayist .... PAINE
revolutionist ... ANARCH, MARAT, REB, FENIAN, TROTSKY, DANTON, LENIN
revolve .. ROLL, GYRATE, WHEEL, SPIN, TWIRL, ROTATE, BIRL
revolver . PISTOL, REPEATER, GAT, ROD, STICK, COLT
revolving chimney cover ..... COWL
   " part ... CAM, ORBY, ROTOR
reward . GUERDON, MEED, UTU, TONY, YIELD, BONUS, OSCAR, EMMY
   " to a dog .... HALLOW
rhea ... AVESTRUZ, EMU, OPS, NANDU
rhetoric, repetition in .... PLOCE
rhetorical .... ORATORIC
   " figure .... LITOTES
rheum .... CATARRH, COLD
rhinal .... NASAL
rhinoceros . ABADA, BORELE, KEITOLA, REEM
rhizoid .... ROOTLIKE
rhoda .... ROSE
rhoeadine .... POPPY
rhombus .... LOZENGE
rhonchus .... SNORING, RALE
Rhône tributary . ARVE, ISERE, SAONE
rhubarb . PIEPLANT, YAWWEED, RHEUM
rhus, kind of .... SUMAC
rhyming scheme .... TERCET
rhythm .... MEASURE, LILT, CADENCE, METER, PULSE, ICTUS, BEAT, SWING
ria .... INLET
rialto ..... BRIDGE, EXCHANGE, MART
riant .... AIRY, BLITHE, GAY
ribald .... ATELLAN, LOW, COARSE
rib .... BONE, COSTA, TEASE, WIFE
ribbed .... COSTATE, RIDGED
ribbon . CORDON, TAPE, CORSE, TASTE
   " , binding .... LISERE

   " -shaped .... TAENIOID
   " worm .... NEMERTINE
ribs, per. to the .... COSTAL
ribwort .. PLANTAIN, KLOPS, RATTAIL
rice ..... PALAY, DARAC, PADDY, PADI
   " boiled with meat .. PILAU, PILAF
   " of inferior grade .... CHITS
   " , wild .... REED
rich .. COPIOUS, FECUND, FAT, OPIME
   " man NABOB, PLUTOCRAT, MIDAS, CROESUS, DIVES, PLUTO
Richelieu's successor ...... MAZARIN
riches LUCRE, OPULENCE, WEALTH, PELF
   " , demon of .... MAMMON
rickety .... SENILE, FRAIL, SHAKY
riddle .... REBUS, ENIGMA, PUN, CRUX
   " , to .... PIERCE, SIFT, REE
ridge .... RIDEAU, SIERRA
   " , anatomical .... SPINE, STRIA, JUGUM
   " between two furrows PORCATE
   " , circular, in shells ...... PILAE
   " , low ... PARMA, RAND, CUESTA
   " of a drift .... KAME, OSAR
   " of a glacial drift OESAR, ESKER, ARETE
   " of stubble .... MANE
   " or mark .... WALE, WELT
   " , relative of a .... CARINA
   " , sand .... AS(AR), OSAR
   " , shell .... VARIX, VARICES
   " , to .... CHINE
ridicule .... ROAST, ASTEISM, BANTER, PAN, MOCK, JEER, DERIDE, RAZZ
ridiculous .... ABSURD, FUNNY, GROTESQUE, FARCICAL
riding breeches .... JODHPURS
   " school .... MANEGE
   " whip .... QUIRT
rifle .... CARBINE, MAUSER, STRIP, GARAND, ROB, MARTINI, ESCOPET
   " ; Fr. .... CHASSEPOT
   " pin .... TIGE
rift .... CLEFT, GAP, LAG, RIMA, SPLIT
rig ... EQUIP, LATEEN, BEDIZEN, GEAR, CHEAT, OUTFIT
Riga, native of ...... LATVIAN, LETT
rigging, part of .. SPAR, GEAR, ROPES
right ...... EMEND, TITLE, DROIT, PAT
   " hand .... DEXTER
   " -handed page .... RECTO
   " of precedence .... PAS
   " time; Scot. .... TID
   " , turn to .... GEE
righteously .... GODLILY, WELL
rigid ... STRINGENT, AUSTERE, STRICT
Rigoletto's daughter .... GILDA
rigorous ...... DRASTIC, STIFF, STERN
Riis; writer .... JACOB
rile ...... ANGER, OFFEND, ROIL, VEX

rim ... EDGE, LIP, BRIM, BRINK, VERGE,
　　　　　ORLE, FELLY, WEB
rime .... ICE, HOAR(FROST)
"Rime-cold Giant" ...... YMER, YMIR
Rinaldo's steed .... BAJARDO
rind ... BARK, CRUST, EPICARP, HUSK,
　　　　　PEEL, SKIN
ring .... ANNULET, ARENA, BAGUE,
　　　　COTERIE, SET, GIMMAL, SIGNET,
　　　　HOOP, LOOP, TOLL, CIRCLET
" ; as a bell . CLANK, CHIME, KNELL,
　　　　　PEAL
" -dove .... CUSHAT
" in a setting .... BEZEL, CHATON
" , metal .... BEE
" of a harness pad .... TERRET
" of rope .... GROMMET
" , ornamental .... LEGLET
" , packing .... LUTE
ringing .... CLAM, OROTUND
ringlet ..... CRISP, CURL, LOCK, TRESS
ring-shaped .... ANNULAR, CIRCULAR,
　　　　　CIRCINATE
ring-tailed animal .... COON
ringworm .... SERPIGO
" infection .... TINEA
rinse .. SLUICE, ABSTERGE, LAVE, SIND
Rio de _____ .... ORO, JANEIRO
Rio de Janeiro native ...... CARIOCA
riot .... MELEE, FRACAS, FRAY
riotous .... WANTON, PROFLIGATE
riotously .... ARIOT
rip .... CUT, RENT, TEAR, CLEAVE
ripen .... AGE, MATURE
ripe .. MELLOW, ADULT, MATURE, AGE
ripened stalk .... STRAW
ripple EAGRE, PURL, ACKER, FRET, RIFF,
　　　　LAP, WAVE, DIMPLE, BILLOW
ris de veau .... SWEETBREAD
rise ... GROW, REBEL, SOAR, ASCEND,
　　　　　EMERGE, TOWER
" again .... REAR, RESURGE
" from liquid .... EMERSE
risible .. ABSURD, LAUGHABLE, FUNNY,
　　　　　DROLL, GELASTIC
rising .. MONTANT, ORTIVE, SURGENT
risk ... DARE, DANGER, PERIL, PLIGHT,
　　　　　HAZARD, JEOPARDY
rite, ritual CEREMONY, NOVENA, CULT,
　　　　LITURGY, PRAYER, SALAT, ABDEST,
　　　　MARRIAGE, LAVABO, MASS,
　　　　BAPTISM, SACRAMENT
rival ... EMULATE, EVEN, FOE, MATCH,
　　　　　PEER, COMPETE, VIE
riven .... CLEFT, RENT, SPLIT
river ...... REE, RIO, CREEK, STREAM,
　　　　　TORRENT
" bank .... LEVEE, RAND, RIPA
" bank, per. to a .... RIPARIAN
" , Bavarian ..... LECH, EGER, ISAR

" , Belgian .... LYS, DYLE, YZER
" , Bohemian .... ELBS, ISER
" , Bolivian .... BENI, PIRAY
" bottom land .... HOLM
" , British-Afr. .... TANA
" Caesar crossed .... RUBICON
" channels .... ALVEI
" , Chilean .... BIOBIO, LOA
" dragon .... CROCODILE
" duck .... TEAL
" , Dutch .... EMS, MAAS
" gauge .... NILOMETER
" horse; short form .... HIPPO
" in Arizona .... GILA
" in Armenia .... ARAS
" in Austria ... ACH, DRAVE, ISER,
　　　　　SAVE
" in Brazil ...... DOCE, APA, RIO
" in Burma .... IRAWADI
" in Chile .... ITATA
" in China .... HWANG, WEI
" in Colorado .... LARAMIE
" in Czech. .... VAH, IPOLY, OHRE
" in England . ALN, ESK, TEES, EXE,
　　　　　USK, TRENT
" in France ..... AIRE, AA, ISERE,
　　　　MEUSE, AISNE, CHER, LYS, ORNE,
　　　　OISE, RHONE, VESLE
" in Germany .. ALLE, ELBE, ODER,
　　　　　HUNTE
" in Hades . ACHERON, LETHE, STYX
" in India . INDUS, GUMTI, KISTNA
" in Indo-China ... MEKONG, HUE
" in Italy ADDA, ARNO, NERA, PO,
　　　　　TIBER
" in Louisiana .... AMITE
" in Luxemburg .. ALZETTE, SAUER
" in Moravia .... ODER
" in Nebraska .... NEMAHA
" in N. Carolina .... NEUSE
" in Peru .... MARANON
" in Portugal .... TAGUS
" in Poland .. BUG, VISTULA, SAN,
　　　　　SERET
" in Romania .... SERETH
" in Russia . ILI, NEVA, OREL, OKA
" in Scotland .... AYR, DEE
" in Siam .... MENAM
" in Siberia AMUR, LENA, OB, OBI
" in South America ... ORINOCO,
　　　　　APA
" in S. Carolina .. SALUDA, PEEDEE
" in Spain .... ARGA, TAGUS,
　　　　　DOURO, RIO
" in Switzerland ..... AAR, REUSS
" in the Levant ..... WADI, WADY
" in Turkey .... SARUS, ZAB
" in Tuscany ...... ARNO, ORCIA
" in Umbria; It. .... TEVERE
" in Venezuela ..... ARO, CARONI

" in Yorkshire .... URE
" inlet .... SLEW, SLOUGH
" , inlet from a .... BAYOU
" , isle in .... HOLM, AIT
" , mouth of a ... BOCA, ESTUARY, LADE, DELTA
" nymph .... NAIS
" of the underworld .... STYX
" passage .... FORD
" , per. to a ..... AMNIC, RIVERINE
" siren .... LORELEI
" Thames at Oxford .... ISIS
river to Danube ... RAAB, ISAR, ILLER, INN, LECH
Rivera; muralist .... DIEGO
resonant .... SONOROUS, REECHOING
rivulet ..... BROOK, STREAM, RUNNEL, BURN, RILL
roach .... CYPRINID, BRAISE
Roach, Mr. .... HAL
road . ESTRADA, AGGER, DRANG, ITER, COURSE, HIGHWAY, LANE, PATH, PIKE, VIA
" , cul-de-sac .... IMPASSE
" paving .... TARMAC
" runner ..... PAISANO, CUCKOO
roadster .... RUNABOUT, AUTO
roam .... ERR, GAD, RANGE, ROVE, RAMBLE, MEANDER, STRAY
roar ...... BELL, STEVEN, BROOL, DIN, FREAM
" of sea .... ROTE
roast .... ASSATE, BANTER, PARCH
" by fire .... TORREFY
" meat .... CABOB
roasting stick .... (TURN)SPIT
rob .... DESPOIL, LOOT, PELF, TOUCH, RIFLE
Rob Roy, a .... CANOE
robbed; mus. .... RUBATO
robber .. THIEF, PIRATE, REAVER, PAD, YEGG, LADRONE, LARON, CATERAN, DACOIT, CORSAIR
robbery ...... PIRACY, REIF, LARCENY, PILLAGE, THEFT
robe ... CHIMER, ABA, CAMIS, CAMUS, DOLMAN, TALAR, SYRMA, CYMAR, SIMAR, STOLE
Robin Goodfellow ...... FAIRY, PUCK
Robin Hood .... BANDIT
" " , foe of .... SHERIFF
" " , forest of .... SHERWOOD
" " , love of .... MARIAN
"Robinson Crusoe" author ... DEFOE
" " char. ..... FRIDAY
Robinson, Ray .... SUGAR
robot ..... AUTOMATON, GOLEM, RUR
" bomb .... DOODLEBUG
robust SOUND, HALE, WALLY, BRAWNY, HARDY, HUSKY

roc, the .... SIMURG(H), BIRD
rock SHAKE, TEETER, TRASS, TOR, CRAG, SWAY, WHIN, KLIP, GNEISS, REEL
rock and gravel .... MORAINE
" beds, per. to .... STRATAL
" , black igneous .... BASALT
" -boring tool .... TREPAN
" cavity .... DRUSE
" , cavity in bedded ...... GEODE
" clay .... SLATE, GANISTER
" ; comb. form .... PETRO
" concretions cemented together OOLITE
" crystal ingredient ...... SILICA
" decay .... GEEST, LATERITE
" , discarded broken .... ATTLE
" , finely broken .... SAND
" fish; Cal. .... REINA, RENA
" , fissile .... SHALE
" formed by geyser deposit SINTER
" , fragmental .... PSEPHITE
" , granite-like ... GNEISS, DIORITE
" hopper ... MACARONI, PENGUIN
" , igneous . BASALT, PERIDOT, BOSS
" , intrusive .... DACITE
" , jutting .... CRAG, TOR
" , laminated; Eng. . SHALE, SHAUL
" of quartz and albite .. ADINOLE
" oil .... NAPHTHA, NAPTHA
" or roll .... TITUBATE
" pinnacle .... NEEDLE, SCAR
" , porous .... TUFA, TUFF
" , schistose .... EPIDOSITE
" , siliceous igneous .... SIAL
" stratum .... LENTICLE
" ; suffix .... ITE, YTE
" that splits .... SCHIST
" , volcanic .. LAVA, DACITE, LATITE
" weed .... TANG
rocket . (A)RISE, SOAR, MISSILE, NIKE, THOR, TITAN
" , antisubmarine . ASROC, ASTOR
" , balloon .... ROCKOON
" ; detachable part .... CAPSULE
" engineer .... BRAUN, LEY
" fuel .... LOX
" , Navy .... ARCON
" section .... (NOSE)CONE
" , sounding .... ARCAS
rockling .... GADE, WHISTLER
rocks .... MONEY
" , per. to .... SAXATILE
rocky .. CLIFFY, SHAKY, DIZZY, WEAK, HARD
" crag .... NUNATAK
" decay .... GEEST, SAPROLITE
" pinnacle .... SCAR, TOR
rod EYEBAR, GAD, WAND, LYTTA, TROLL, PLET, GUN, CANE, POLE, BATON, SCEPTER, FERULE, PISTON

" ; 16½ feet .... PERCH, POLE
rodent .... PIKA, UTIA, CAVY, JERBOA,
    GOPHER, MOUSE, RAT, VOLE, CONY,
    CONEY, LEROT, MOLE, AGOUTI,
    DEGU, PACA, COYPU
   " , aquatic ... BEAVER, MUSKRAT,
    COYPU
   " , bushy-tailed .... MARMOT
   " ; genus .... MUS
   " , jumping; genus .... DIPUS
   " , nocturnal .... SEWELLEL
rodents' disease .... TULAREMIA
rods, 160 square .... ACRE
roe ..... OVA, EGGS, SPAWN, CAVIAR
rogation ...... SUPPLICATION, LITANY
   " flower .... MILKWORT
Rogers, Mr. .... ROY, WILL
rogue ...... IMP, KITE, WAG, KNAVE,
    RASCAL, PICARO, SCAMP
roguish .. ARCH, ESPIEGLE, PAWKY, SLY
roisterer .... MUN
Roland's destroyer GAN(ELON), GANO
role .. CHARACTER, PART, PERSON, BIT,
    INGENUE, HEAVY, WALKON
roll .. BUN, LIST, ROTA, FURL, TATTOO,
    CAROTTE, RUNNER, ROSTER,
    SCROLL, CADRE
   " along .... TRUNDLE
   " of coins .... ROULEAU
   " of hair .... CHIGNON
roller ... SIRGANG, BILLOW, BREAKER,
    CASTER, WAVE
romaine lettuce .... COS
Roman .... LATIN, ITALIAN
   " apostle .... NERI
   " arch abutment .... ALETTE
   " assembly .... FORUM
   " author .... VARRO
   " awning .... VELARIUM
   " basilica .... LATERAN
   " bishop .... POPE
   " boxing glove .... CESTUS
   " bronze .... AES
   " calendar .... CALENDS
   " chariot .... ESSED
   " chest .... CIST
   " circus; the barrier .... SPINA
   " citizen; anc. ...... AERARIAN
   " clan .... GENS
   " cloak; anc. . ABOLLA, PLANETA
   " coat .... PAENULA
Roman coin; anc. .. AUREUS, DINDER,
    SEMIS
   " coin, copper .... AS, AES
   " comic afterpiece ..... EXODE
   " comic poet .... TERENCE
   " concert halls .... ODEA
   " consul .... SCIPIO
   " court of the pope ...... CURIA
   " court, open .... ATRIUM

   " cupid .... EROS
   " late .... NONES, IDES
   " deity .... LAR
   " dictator .... SULLA
   " dish .... PATERA
   " divine law; Lat. .... FAS
   " diviner .... AUSPEX
   " domestic gods .... LARES
   " earthwork .... AGGER
   " emperor . OTTO, TITUS, GALBA,
    NERVA, GALLUS, SEVERUS,
    HADRIAN
   " empress .... EUDOCIA
   " entrance .... ATRIUM
   " fates .... PARCAE
   " festival days .... FERIAE
   " galley .... BIREME
   " gambling cube .... TESSERA
   " garment . PALLA, STOLE, TOGA,
    TUNIC
   " general .. MARIUS, SULLA, TITUS
   " ghosts ...... LEMURES, MANES
   " gladiator .. RETIARIUS, SAMNITE
   " goal post .... META
   " god (see also "god")
   " god, chief .... JOVE, JUPITER
   " god(s), household ..... LAR,
    PENATES
   " god of festive joy ... COMUS
   " god of fire .... VULCAN
   " god of Hades .... DIS, ORCUS,
    PLUTO
   " god of lightning .... JUPITER
   " god of love ... AMOR, CUPID
   " god of seas .... NEPTUNE
   " god of sky .... JUPITER
   " god of sleep .... MORPHEUS,
    SOMNUS
   " god of thieves ...... MERCURY
   " god of underworld DIS, ORCUS,
    PLUTO
   " god of woods .... SYLVANUS
   " god of war .. MARS, QUIRINUS
   " goddess (see also "goddess") .
    DEA
   " goddess of agriculture .. OPS
   " goddess of birth .... PARCA
   " goddess of childbirth LUCINA
   " goddess of corpse .. LIBITINA
   " goddess of dawn ... AURORA
   " goddess of death PROSERPINE
   " goddess of earth ...... TELLUS
   " goddess of fertility .. ANNONA,
    FAUNA
   " goddess of fountains FERONIA
   " goddess of harvest ..... OPS
   " goddess of love ...... VENUS
   " goddess of moon .... LUNA
   " goddess of night ...... NOX

"	goddess of peace ...... PAX, MINERVA		"	province .... DACIA
"	goddess of seas .... SALACIA		"	road .... ITER, VIA
"	goddess of war ... BELLONA, MINERVA, VACUNA		"	road, famous .... APPIAN
"	goddess of womanhood JUNO		"	roads .... ITINERA
"	governor .... PROCONSUL		"	room .... ALA, ATRIUM, TABLINUM
"	guard .... LICTOR		"	sacrificial plate .... PATERA
"	hairpin .... ACUS		"	seat .... SELLA
"	highway .... ITER		"	senate house .... CURIA
"	hill .... AVENTINE, CAELIAN, PALATINE, QUIRINAL, CAPITOLINE, ESQUILINE, VIMINAL		"	senator .... CATO
			"	serf, female ...... COLONA
			"	serf, male .... COLONUS
			"	shields ..... SCUTA, ANCILES
"	historian . SALLUST, LIVY, NEPOS		"	shop .... TABERNA
"	holiday .... IDES, FERIA		"	spirits of the dead .. LEMURES, MANES
"	javelin .... PILUM, PILE		"	sports official ...... ASIARCH
"	judge .... AEDILE, EDILE		"	street .... CORSO
"	judges, one of three TRIUMVIR		"	tax .... ANNONA
"	jurist .... GAIUS		"	term .... GAINE
"	king .... ALARIC		"	treasurer .... QUAESTOR
"	lands acquired in war . AGER		"	turning post .... META
"	law .... CERN, MOS, LEX		"	vessel .... AMPHORA
"	leader .... DUX		"	vestment .... TOGA
"	legendary nymph .... EGERIA		"	virgin warrior ..... CAMILLA
"	legendary king ...... NUMA		"	war machine; anc. .... TEREBRA
"	libation vessel ...... PATERA		"	weight; anc. .... AS, BES, DODRANS, LIBRA
"	libra .... AS		"	world of the dead ... ORCUS
"	magistrate .. CENSOR, EDILE, PRETOR, PRAETOR, TRIBUNE		"	writing table ...... DIPTYCH
			romance ...... WOO, GESTE, AFFAIR
"	maiden who opened the citadel to the Sabines....... TARPEIA		"	verse, form of ... SESTINA
			Romance language .... CATALAN
"	malarial plain .... CAMPANA		Romanian city ... GALAT, LASI, IASI, JASSY, ARAD
"	matron's garment .... STOLA		"	coin .... LEY, LEU
"	measure .... URNA		"	conservative ..... BOJAR
"	measure; a foot .... PES		"	dramatist ..... IONESCO
"	midday meal .... CENA		"	king .... CAROL
"	military cloak ...... SAGUM		"	king's wife ...... MAGDA
"	military insignia ... PHALERA		"	river .. ALUTA, ARGES, JIU, OLT, ALT
"	money .... SEMIS		"	river port ...... GALATZ
"	month .... MARTIUS, APRILIS, MAIUS, JUNIUS, QUINTILIS		"	title .... DOM
			"	unit of currency BANI, BAN
"	month, first day of .. CALENDS		Rome, conqueror of .... ALARIC
"	naturalist .... PLINY		" , lake near .... NEMI
"	official ...... EDILE, LICTOR		" , legendary founder of ROMULUS
"	official in Judea ...... FELIX		" , public land in anc. .... AGER
"	orator .... CATO, CICERO		romp .... PLAY, SPORT, TOMBOY
"	ornament .... BULLA		romping .... RAW, RANTIPOLE
"	palace .... LATERAN		Roncesvalles .... ROLAND
"	patriot .... CINNA, CATO		rood .... CROSS, CRUCIFIX
"	people, early ...... SABINES		roof .. CUPOLA, DOME, FIG, GAMBREL
"	philosopher .... SENECA		"	angle .... HIP
"	poet .... VERGIL, JUVENAL, LUCAN, CINNA, OVID		" , overhanging edge of .... EAVE
			" ; raised border ...... COAMING
"	port; anc. .... OSTIA		"	support .... CRUCK
"	pound .... AS, LIBRA		" , thatched .... CHOPPER
"	praenomen .... TITUS		"	with thin boards .... SARK
"	priest of pagan deity FLAMEN	
"	priests of the cult .. LUPERCI	
"	priestly official ...... AUGUR	

244

roofing ..... PANTILE, RAG, SHINGLE, THATCH
rook .. CASTLE, CHEAT, CUB, SHARPER
room .... SALA, AULA, SCOPE, LODGE, QUARTER, DEN, EWERY, SUITE, ATRIUM
" in harem .... ODA
" used in Indian rites ..... KIVA
Roosevelt, Mrs. .... ANNA, ELEANOR, SARAH
roost .... SIT, JOUK, PERCH, POLE
root ...... BASE, GRUB, IMBED, STEM
", edible ... POTATO, YAM, TARO
" -footed .... RHIZOPOD
" form of word RADICAL, ETYMON
" in cough mixture .... SENEGA, SENEKA
" out .... EVERSE, ERADICATE
" stock, pungent ...... GINGER
" used in a tonic .... ATIS
rootlet .... RADICEL, RADICLE
rope ..... JEFF, CORD, LASSO, RIATA, LARIAT, TETHER, SNOTTER, MARLIN
" fiber .... ISTLE, IXTLE
", guiding .... LONGE
", guy .... CABLE, VANG
", make a turn with ...... BELAY
", nautical FRAP, PARREL, HAWSER, FOX, TYE, STAY, RATLIN(E), LANYARD
", ship's . RODE, SHROUD, PAINTER
", slack .... SLATCH
" splicer's tools .... FIDS
" threaded through block ... REEVE
" walker .... FUNAMBULIST
Roper, Mr. .... ELMO
rorqual .... WHALE, FINBACK
rosary . BEADS, CHAPLET, AVE, GAUDY
rose .. RHODA, ALTHEA, ACAENA, GUL
" apple .... POMAROSA
" bush, false fruit of .... HIP
", dog .... CANKER
" family .... ROSACEAE
" -petal oil .... ATTAR, OTTO
" -red dye ...... EOSIN, RHODAMINE
rosette-like .... ROSULAR
roster ...... LIST, ROLL, ROTA, SLATE
rostrum ...... DAIS, STAGE, TRIBUNE
rosy .... AURORAL, PINK, ROSACEOUS
rot ...... DECAY, NONSENSE, WASTE
rota .... LIST, COURT
rotate .... BIRL, GYRATE, SLUE, ROLL, WHIRL, SPIN, REVOLVE
rotating piece .... CAM, ROTOR
rotche .... DOVEKIE, BULL
rotten .... FETID, RANK, CARIOUS
roué .... RAKE
rough ... SCABROUS, HOARSE, RASPY, SEAMY, AGRESTIC, CURT, (C)RUDE, COARSE, HARSH

" cloth .... TERRY
" hair .... SHAG
roughen .... FRET, NURL, CHAP, FRAY, GNAW
roughshod, go .... TRAMPLE
roughneck .... GOON
roulette term .. BAS, NOIRE, ROUGE, MILIEU, MANQUE
round . ORBED, BOUT, CURVE, ROTUND, PERIOD
" country dance .... HAY
" ; mus. .... TROLL
" protuberance .... UMBO
" timber .... SPAR
" -up .... RODEO
Round Table knight .... KAY, BALAN, BALIN, BOHORT, GARETH, PELLAS, GALAHAD, GAWAIN
roundabout ..... INDIRECT, AMBIENT, DEVIOUS, JACKET
rounded .... RETUSE
rouse ... KINDLE, STIR, WAKE, EXCITE, ROUST
Rousseau hero .... EMILE
rout .... SCATTER, DEBACLE, BEAT
route .... LANE, PATH, TRIP, WAY
routine ... EVERYDAY, REGULAR, HABIT, GROOVE, RUT
rove .... RANGE, GAD, SWERVE
rover PILGRIM, WAIF, NOMAD, PIRATE
row .. FILE, BROIL, OAR, TIER, FIGHT, SCULL
" boat ..... CANOE, GIG, RANDAN
", form in a .... ALIGN, ALINE
" -lock support .... POPPET, THOLE, FULCRUM
rowan cloak .... PLANETA
rowdy THUG, BULLY, RUFFIAN, ROUGH, HOODLUM
rowel .... PRICK, URGE, SPUR, WHEEL
rowen .. CROP, AFTERMATH, EDGREW
rowing match .... REGATTA
royal .... AUGUST, KINGLY, IMPERIAL, REGAL
" bay .... LAUREL
" blue .... SMALT
" court, of .... AULIC
" crown .... TIARA
" house ...... STEWART, TUDOR, WINDSOR, YORK, HANOVER
" mace .... SCEPTER
" title .... SIRE, REGENT
rub .... MASSAGE, SMEAR, TRITURATE, BUFF, CHAFE
" away .... ABRADE
" out OBLITERATE, EXPUNGE, ERASE, SCRAPE
" together .... RAKE
"Rubaiyat" author .... OMAR

rubber .... CAUCHO, ELASTIC, LATEX, CEARA, GUM, EBONITE
" compound .. ERASER, FACTICE, KERITE
" lining .... LUTE, GASKET
" sheeting .... PLIOFILM
" shoe .... GALOSH
" , synthetic .... NOREPOL
" tree .... PARA, SERINGA, ULE
"   " ; genus .... FICUS
rubbers; sheep disease ... RAY, SCAB, SHAB
rubbery .... ELASTIC, TOUGH
rubbish .. ATTLE, DROSS, ROT, GOAF, JUNK, SCREE, SCORIA
" , mining .... STENT
rubeola .... MEASLES
Rubinstein opera .... DEMONIO
"   ; pianist .... ARTUR
rubrics, book of .... ORDO
ruby ...... SPINEL, RUBASSE, BALAS
rudder HELM, TIMON, STEER(ER), STERN
rude .... CALLOW
rudiment ... ANLAGE, EMBRYO, FIRST
rudiments .... ABC, ELEMENTS
rue .... DEPLORE, REGRET, GRIEF
" ; herb .... RUTA
ruff, female ..... REE, REEVE, TIPPET
" , support for a .... RABATO
ruffer .... NAPPER
ruffle . DERANGE, MUSS, CRIMP, RUCHE
rufous .... REDDISH
rug .... MAT, PETATE, MAUD, SENNA, RUNNER, KIRMAN, HERAT, WILTON, USHAK
rugby term .... FIVES
Rugen is. cape .... ARKONA
rugged ...... ASPER, CRAGGY, HARDY
Ruhr city .... ESSEN, HAMM
ruin .... SPOIL, WRACK, BANE
ruins ASHES, HAVOC, WRECK, DEBRIS, REMAINS
rule .... PRECEPT, LEAD, LAW, NORM, SWAY, MAXIM, REGIMEN, DOMINEER, HABIT, CANON
ruler .... GERENT, EMIR, MIN, PRINCE, DYNAST, DESPOT, CALIF, MONARCH, NEGUS, NIZAM, SHAH, ARCHON, REIGNER, SWEEP
" of a religious body .. HIERARCH
" , wife of a EMPRESS, QUEEN, RANI
rum .... TAFIA
rumba king .... CUGAT
rumen .... GULLET, CUD, POUCH
ruminant ... ALPACA, GOAT, LLAMA, YAK, BISON, DEER, SHEEP
" , second stomach of........ RETICULUM
" , third stomach of OMASSUM

ruminants are a division of _____ UNGULATA
ruminate .... CHEW, REFLECT, MUSE, PONDER, MILL
rummy .... ODD, QUEER, SOT
rumor BRUIT, FAMA, HEARSAY, NOISE, REPORT
rump .... BREECH, BUTTOCKS
rumple ...... CREASE, MUSS, TOUSLE
rumpus .... FRACAS, ROW
run ... HIE, SCUD, TROT, GAD, FLOW, LOPE, RACE, SPRINT, OPERATE, PANIC
" away ..... DECAMP, ELOPE, FLEE
" out .... PETER
runnel .. BROOK, CHANNEL, RIVULET
runner . COURIER, RACER, MILER, MAT, TOUTER
running .... EASY, CURSIVE
runt ...... DWARF, PYGMY, CHIT, ELF
" of a brood .... WRIG
runway ... RAMP, AIRSTRIP, TARMAC
rupee ..... ANNA, CRORE, LAC, LAKH
rupture ..... RENT, RHEXIS, QUARREL
rural . BUCOLIC, GEORGIC, PASTORAL, RUSTIC(AL), AGRESTIC
" game .... DIBS
" poem .... ECLOGUE
rush .... SPATE, PRESS, SURGE, SPURT, SPEED, HURTLE
" , kind of .... SPRAT
Russell, Miss ..... LILLIAN, ROSALIND
Russia .... SOVIET, MUSCOVY
" , founder of .... IVAN
Russian ...... RED, RUSS, MUSCOVITE, MOSCOVITE
" astronaut ..... COSMONAUT, LEONOV, TITOV, GAGARIN
" carriage . TARANTAS(S), TROIKA
" cathedral .... SOBOR
" cereal grain .... EMMER
" chess champion .. ALEKHINE, SPASSKY
" choreographer ..... MASSINE
" city .. OMSK, OREL, KIEV, UFA, KEM, BISK, BALTA, AYAN
" coal area .... DONETS
" coin .. POLTINA, KOPEK, ALTIN, RUBLE
" community .... MIR
" composer .. CUI, PROKOFIEV, STRAVINSKY
" convict shelter ...... ETAPE
" co-operative society .. ARTEL
" cossack .... TATAR
" council DUMA, SOVIET, RADA
" dance .... ZIGANKA
" dancer . DANILOVA, PAVLOVA
" desert .... TUNDRA
" dog .... OWTCHAH

"	edict	UKASE
"	empress	TSARINA, CZARINA, CATHERINE
"	for yes	DA
"	fur	KARAKUL, CARACUL
"	guild	ARTEL
"	inland sea	ARAL, AZOV, AZOF
"	instrument; mus.	GUSLE
"	lake	NEVA, ARAL, ONEGA
"	landed proprietor	BOYAR
"	leather	SHAGREEN, BULGAR
"	legal assembly	RADA
"	log hut	ISBA, ISPA
"	massacre	POGROM
"	measure	LOF, SAGENE, VERST, DUIM, CHARKA
"	monetary unit	RUBLE
"	mountains	ALAI, URAL
"	musical inst.	BALALAIKA
"	negative	NYET
"	novelist	TOLSTOI
"	oil center	BAKU
"	painter	CHAGALL
"	parliament	DUMA
"	peasant	KULAK
"	people	SLAVS
"	plane	MIG
"	poet	PUSHKIN, YEVTUSHENKO
"	pound	POOD
"	prince	KNEZ, KNYAZ, IGOR
"	province	AMUR, TULA
"	republic	KARELIA, ARMENIA, UKRAINE, UZBEK, KIRGIZ
"	river	NEVA, ONEGA, OREL, ROS, LENA, RHA, URAL, KARA, VOLGA, DVINA, UFA, DON
"	ruler	IVAN, PETER, ALEXANDER, NICHOLAS
"	sea	BAIKAL, ARAL, BLACK
"	secret service	CHEKA, OGPU
"	soup	BORSCHT
"	state airline	AEROFLOT
"	statesman	MOLOTOV, GROMYKO, STALIN, LENIN, KOSYGIN
"	tea urn	SAMOVAR
"	teacher	STARETS
"	trade union	ARTEL
"	villa	DACHA
"	violinist	ELMAN, OISTRAKH, ZIMBALIST
"	wagon	TELEGA
"	weight	POOD, PUD, LOT, DOLA, FUNT
"	wheat	EMMER
"	whip	PLET, KNOUT
"	wolfhound	ALAN, BORZOI
rust		CORRODE, EAT, AERUGO, ERODE, VERDIGRIS, PATINA, BLIGHT, FERRUGO

Rustam's father		ZAL
rustic		GEOPONIC, BUCOLIC, RUBE, PLAIN, DORIC, RURAL, CLOWN, SYLVAN, YOKEL, PEASANT
"	lover	CORYDON, SILVESTER, SWAIN
"	peasant	AGRESTIAN, CLOD, BOOR
"	pipe	REED, CORN
"	; poet.	CARL
rustle		SWISH, FROUFROU, STEAL, STIR, SCROOP
Rustum's son		SOHRAB
rut		ROUTINE, GROOVE, IMPASSE
rutabaga		TURNIP
Ruthenia, county in		UNG
Ruth's mother-in-law		NAOMI
Ruy Díaz de Bivar		CID
rye disease		ERGOT
" ; genus		SECALE
Ryukyu island		OKINAWA

S

S, letter		ESS
S-curve		OGEE
S-shaped		SIGMATE, SIGMOID
sable		BLACK, EBON, PELLET, SKUNK, MARTEN, LEMMING, MUSTELA, TATAR
Sabrina River		SEVERN
sac		ASCUS, BURSA, CYST, VESICLE
saccharine		SWEET, HONEYED
"	source	TAR
Sacco, Mr.		NICOLA
sacerdotal		PRIESTLY, CLERICAL
sachet		PAD, SAC, BAG, PERFUME
sack		POUCH, LOOT, POKE, GUNNY
sackbut		TROMBONE
sacred		HOLY, PIOUS, DIVINE, HALLOWED
"	bull	APIS, ZEBU
"	cantata	MOTET
"	casket	CYST, PYX
"	; comb. form	HIERO
"	disease	EPILEPSY
"	Egyptian bird	IBIS
"	fig tree	PIPAL
"	grove	ALTIS
"	image	PIETA, ICON, IKON
"	instrument, Mormon	URIM
"	interdiction	TABOO
"	language of Buddhist literature	PALI
"	, not	PROFANE
"	object	ZOGO

247

```
"       place ALTIS, ABATON, HIERON,        ", furl a ................. REEF
                          SHRINE            "  line ................... EARING
"       scriptures KORAN, BIBLE, VEDA,      ", slack part of ........... SLAB
                          AVESTA            ", tie a .................. TRICE
"       things, traffic in .... SIMONY      sailboard used to tack ...... RATCH
"       wine vessel ............ AMA         sailing race term ............ LEG
"       word .................. OM           saint .... CANONIZE, HOLY, ANGEL,
sacrament ......... BAPTISM, HOST,                     HALLOW, PIR, STE, ALVAR
                  COVENANT, RITE             ", inferior worship of a ... DULIA
sacrifice ...... FOREGO, IMMOLATE,           ", memorial of a ........ RELIC
OBLATION, LIBATION, HOLOCAUST,               ", painted ................ ICON
LOSS, ATONEMENT, HECATOMB                    ", patron, of cripples .... GILES
sacrificial fire ............... IGNI        ", per. to a .......... FERETORY
"       offering .... SOMA, HIERA            ", Roman ................. NERI
sacristy, per. to a ....... VESTRAL          Saint Andrew's Cross ....... SALTIRE
sad .. BAD, DIRE, SORRY, BLUE, WAN,          St. Catherine's home ........ SIENA
TRISTE, DOLENT, SOMBER                       Saint Elmo's fire ...... CORPOSANT
saddle ..... PIGSKIN, PILCH, PILLION,        Saint John's bread CAROB, ALGAROBA
                          APAREJO            Saint-Louis is its capital ... SENEGAL
"       blanket ...... CORONA, TILPAH        Saint Paul's birthplace ...... TARSUS
"       boot ............. GAMBADO           Saint Philip ................. NERI
"       bow ........ ARSON, POMMEL           Saint-Saens, opera by ...... DALILA
"       cloth ...... PANEL, SHABRACK         Saint Vitus's dance ........ CHOREA
"       corn crusher ......... QUERN         saints, biographies of HAGIOGRAPHY
"       girth ................ CINCH         saints, catalogue of ....... DIPTYCH
"       horses .... REMUDA, PALFREYS         saint's tomb ............... SHRINE
"       pad ................. PANEL          sailing raft ................ BALSA
", place behind ...... CROUP                 "       vessel .... BUCKEYE, BUGEYE,
"       pommel ..... CRUTCH, TORE                    SETEE, SAIC, DHOW, CAT,
", rear part of ....... CANTLE                       BRIG, JUNK, PRAM, YAWL
"       strap ......... GIRTH, LATIGO        sailor ... MARINER, MIDDY, SHIPMAN,
saddler .................... LORIMER         TOTY, MATELOT, SEABEE, SEADOG,
sadness ......... PATHOS, DOLOR              TARPOT, GOB, TAR, SALT, JACKY
safari ............. JOURNEY, TREK           ", cable ................. TIERER
safe ......... PETE, VAULT, SECURE           ", E. Ind. ............. LASCAR
"   conduct CONVOY, COWLE, PASS              ", female ............. WAVE
safeblower ............... PETERMAN          "  song ................ CHANTY
safeguard against shortage STOCKPILE         sailor's amusement ..... SCRIMSHAW
safekeeping ............... CUSTODY          "       baked dish ......... SCOUSE
safety lamp ................. DAVY           "       choice ...... GRUNT, PINFISH
saffron .................... YELLOW          "       furlough ............ LEAVE
"       plant ............. CROCUS           "       meeting ............ GAM
sag ...... BEND, SINK, WILT, DROOP           "       mess tub ............. KID
"   in a timber ............. SNY            "       patron saint ........ ELMO
saga ..... EPIC, TALE, LEGEND, EDDA          "       potion ............ GROG
sagacious .... WISE, SAPIENT, WITTY,         "       quarters ......... FOCSLE
ARGUTE, KEEN, ASTUTE                         "       wages ........... PORTAGE
sagacity .... ACUMEN, KEN, WISDOM            sails furled and helm lashed . AHULL
sage ......... SALVIA, WISE, SOLON           "   laid back ............. ABOX
"   hen .................. GROUSE            ", storm .............. TRYSAILS
"Sage of Emporia" .......... WHITE           sake ........ BEHALF, BENEFIT, SCORE
sage of Pylus ............. NESTOR           Sakhalin Gulf river .......... AMUR
Sagebrush State .......... NEVADA            salaam .......... BOW, BEND, NOD
sagitta .......... ARROW, KEYSTONE           salable ........ VENDABLE, SUITABLE
saguaro ................... CACTUS           salad ..... ENDIVES, CRESS, LETTUCE,
sail ..... JIB, LUFF, LATEEN, MIZZEN,                  SLAW, ROMAINE
SPANKER, VELA, KITE, LUG                     salamander OLM, EFT, NEWT, LIZARD,
", center of ................ BUNT           TRITON, HELLBENDER, CRAWLER,
", corner of .............. CLEW             DOGFISH, URODELA, AXOLOTL
", edge of a square ....... LEECH            salame .................. SAUSAGE
```

salary .... WAGES, STIPEND
sale AUCTION, DEAL, VEND, HANDSEL,
BARTER
salicylic acid deriv. .... ASPIRIN
salientia .... ANURA
saliferous .... SALINE
salin .... POTASH
saline solution .... BRINE
saliva ... PTYALISM, RHEUM, SPITTLE
salivary gland .... RACEMOSE
    "   " , per. to .... PAROTID
salix .... ITEA, OSIER, WILLOW
sallow .... PASTY, ADUST, GREY
sally ISSUE, JEST, LEAP, SORTIE, START,
ESCAPADE
salmagundi . HASH, POTPOURRI, OLIO,
MEDLEY
salmon ... GILLING, LAX, LOX, SMOLT
    " , dog .... CHUM, KETA
    " , female ...... BAGGIT, RAUN
    " herring .... MILKFISH
    " , kind of ..... DOG, QUINNAT
    " , landlocked .... QUANANICHE
    " , male ..... GIB, KIPPER, COCK
    " net .... YARE
    " of Asia .... TAIMEN
    " , one-year-old .... BLUECAP
    " , per. to .... GRILSE
    " pool .... STELL
    " , quinnat .... TYEE
    " shark .... PORBEAGLE
    " , silver .... COHO
    " trout-like; Brit. .... SEWEN
    " , third-year .... MORT, PUG
    " , two-year-old . SMOLT, HEPPER
    " , young ALEVIN, JERKIN, PARR,
ESSLING, GRILSE, PINK, SAMLET,
SPRAG
salmonoid fish .... POWAN
salon .... PARTY, HALL, LEVEE
saloon .. BAR, DRAMSHOP, GROGGERY,
PUB, TAVERN, INN
salt .. FLAVOR, HUMOR, SAVOR, TASTE,
WIT, SAILOR, MARINER, SEAMAN,
BRINE, TAR
" , acid .... FORMATE
" , alkaline .... BORAX
" beds .... VATS
" , chemical .... ESTER, LACTATE,
OXANILATE
" , crystalline .... ANALGENE
" developer .... AMIDOL
" in chemistry .... SAL
" lake .... CHOTT
" marsh .... SALINA
" mineral astringent .... ALUM
" , rock .... HALITE
" , soluble .... ALKALI
" spring .... LICK, SALINE
" , tartaric acid .... TARTRATE

" tax .... GABELLE
" , to .... KERN
" tree .... ATLE
salt-like .... HALOID
saltworks .... SALTERY, SALINA
saltworks pond .... SUMP
saltwort .... KALI
saltant LEAPING, DANCING, JUMPING
salted .... ALAT, MARINATED
saltpeter .... NITER, NITRE
salts .... CORNS, SEASONS
salty mixture .... REH
salutary ...... HEALTHY, SALUBRIOUS,
USEFUL, TONIC
salutation ...... ALOHA, AVE, PROSIT,
SALAM
salute .. CURTSY, HALE, HALSE, GREET,
KISS, SALVO, BOW, HAIL, TOAST
salvage ...... RESCUE, SAVE, RECLAIM
salve .. CURE, BALM, PLASTER, LOTION,
UNGUENT, CERATE
salver .. TRAY, SAVE, SERVER, WAITER
salvia .... CHIA
samara fruit .... ELM
Sambal language .... TINO
sambar deer ..... MAHA, RUSA, SABIR
same ... ONE, COGNATE, DITTO, ILK
" place, in the .... IBID
" , the .... IDEM
sameness ANALOGY, IDENTITY, PARITY,
MONOTONY
samlet .... PARR
Samoan .... POLYNESIAN
" barn owl .... LULU
" cloth .... TAPA
" clothes .... PAREUS
" council .... FONO
" island .... MANUA
" mountain .... VAEA
" seaport .... APIA
" warrior .... TOA
samovar .... TEAPOT, URN
sample ... PATTERN, SWATCH, TASTER,
SPECIMEN, TASTE
Samson's city .... ZORAH
" father .... MANOAH
Samuel's father .... ELKANAH
" mother .... HANNAH
" teacher .... ELI
samurai .... RONIN
Sancho Panza's wife .... TERESA
Sana is its capital .... YEMEN
San Antonio in 1836 .... ALAMO
San Francisco resort ..... TAMALPAIS
sanction .. AMEN, FIAT, ABET, RATIFY,
ENDORSE
sanctuary HAVEN, FANE, TEMPLE, ARK,
HOME, REFUGE, ASYLUM, CELLA,
BAMAH
" ; inner part ... PENETRALIA

249

sanctum of a temple .... ADYTUM
sand .... GRIT, GRAVEL, PAAR
" bank .... HURST, SHOAL, REEF,
BEACH, SPLIT
" , dry bed of .... ESKER
" dune .... DENE, MEDANO
" eel .... GRIG, LAUNCE
" flea .... CHIGOE
" grouse .... ATTAGEN, GANGA
" hill(s) .... AREG, DUNE
" launce .... HORNEL, LANT
" mineral .... ISERINE
" particle .... SILT
" , quick- .... BOG, SYRT
" ridge ..... ASAR, KAME, OS(AR)
" -stone .. BEREA, MEDINA, SARSEN
" -storm .... SAMUM, HABOOB
" -sucker .... DAB
" tableland .... KAROO
" verbena; genus .... ABRONIA
sandal . BUSKIN, SOCK, SHOE, SCUFFER,
TEGUA
sandals, winged .... TALARIA
sandalwood .... BUCIDA, SANTAL,
CHANDAM
" , coloring matter from ...
SANTALIN
" , relative of .. BARWOOD,
CAMWOOD
sandarac .... REALGAR
" resin .... TEARS
" tree .... LIGNUM, ARAR
" wood ...... ALERCE, ALERSE
sand bar .... SPIT
sandbox tree capsule .... REGMA
sandpiper ..... STIB, DUNLIN, TATTLER,
KNOT, RUFF, TEREK, PECTORAL,
SANDERLING, TILTUP, TEETER,
PEETWEET
" , female of the ... REE(VE)
" ; genus .... TRINGA
Sandwich Islands native .... KANAKA,
HAWAIIAN
sandworts; genus .... ARENARIA
sandy ... ARENOSE, SABULOUS, GRITTY
" drift .... DENE, ESKER
" region .... LANDE
sangfroid ...... COOL, INSOUCIANCE
sanguine .... RED, ARDENT, WARM
sanity .... REASON
Sanskrit .... HINDU, VEDIC
" , analogous phenomena in ...
SANDHI
" college .... TOL
" deity .... ADITI
" dialect .... PALI
" epic character .... SITA
" god ... ADITYA, INDRA, KAMA,
VAYU
" goddess .... DEVI, UMA

" language of W. India MARATHI
" metrical unit .... MATRA
" poem .... RHAGUVAMSHA
" vernacular; Hindu .. PRAKRIT
" writer .... KALIDASA
Santa Maria tree .... CALABA
sap DRAIN, JUICE, LYMPH, MINE, SAPOR,
SEVE
sapajou .... MONKEY, VARINE
saphead .... DOLT, SIMPLETON
sapid .... ZESTFUL, SAVORY, TASTY
sapience .... SENSE, WISDOM
———— sapiens .... HOMO
sapodilla ... CHICO, NISPERO, SAPOTE
sapor ... GOUT, GUSTO, RELISH, TASTE
Sappho's home .... LESBOS
sappy .... JUICE, SUCCULENT, LUSH
sapwood .... BLEA, ALBURNUM
Saracen ..... MOOR, MOSLEM, ARAB
" leader .... SALADIN
Sarah's handmaid .... HAGAR
sarcastic .... MORDANT, IRONICAL
sardine ..... BANG, PILCHARD, SARDEL
Sardinian city .... SASSARI
" structure ...... NURAGH(E)
sardonic ..... MOROSE, CYNICAL, DRY
Sardou, drama by .... FEDORA
sargassum .... GULFWEED
sartor .... TAILOR
sash ..... CUMMERBUND, GIRDLE, OBI,
CASING
sash weight .... MOUSE
Saskatchewan capital .... REGINA
sassafras, oil of .... SAFROL
" tea .... SALOOP
Satan LUCIFER, TEMPTER, BELIAL, EBLIS,
AZAZEL, ASMODEUS, ABADDON,
ARCHFIEND, APOLLYON, DEIL
satchel ETUI, CABAS, ETWEE, BAG, SACK
sate .... GLUT, SURFEIT
sated .... BLASE, FULL
satellite .. LUNA, MOON, COMPANION
" of Jupiter . HESTIA, PAN, HERA
" of Mars .... DEIMOS, PHOBOS
" of Neptune ... NEREID, TRITON
" of Saturn RHEA, DIONE, MIMAS
" of Uranus .. OBERON, TITANIA
satiate .... CLOY, GLUT, GORGE, PALL,
SATISFY
satin fabric ..... ETOILE, RAYON, SILK
satire .... IRONY, WIT, SKIT
satirical .. ABUSIVE, CAUSTIC, IRONIC,
DRY, WRY, BITING
satirize ...... GRIND, LAMPOON, LASH
satisfaction AMENDS, COMFORT, TREAT,
DUEL, PAYMENT, CRO, UTU
satisfy ..... PAY, ATONE, MEET, CLOY
saturate ...SEETHE, SOG, STEEP, WET,
SOAK, DRENCH
Saturnalia .... ORGY, REVELS

Saturnalian friendship token .. XENIA
Saturn's moon .... IAPETUS
   " rings ...... MOONLETS, ANSA
   " wife .... OPS
satyr BUTTERFLY, DEITY, SILENUS, FAUN,
                   PANISC
Sault Ste. Marie .... SOO
sauce .... CURRY, FLAVOR, GRAVY,
                INSOLENCE
   " for fish .... ALEC
   " for meat ... DAUBE, TABASCO
   ", garlic .... GANSEL
   ", syrupy .... CREME
   ", velouté-and-onion ... SOUBISE
saucepan .... POSNET, SKILLET, HORN,
                SPIDER
saucy . MALAPERT, RASH, COCKY, PERT,
              PIET, SASSY
Saul's army leader .... ABNER
   " father .... KISH
   " herdsman .... DOEG
saunter .. LOITER, LAG, MOG, POTTER,
         STREEL, STROLL, AMBLE
saurel .... XUREL, SCAD, POMPANO
saurian .... LIZARD, REPTILE
sausage SALAME, BOLOGNA, CERVELAT,
           SAVELOY, FRANK
   " -shaped .... ALLANTOID,
             BOTULIFORM
sauté .... FRY
Sava tributary .... DRINA
savage ... YAHOO, FELL, CRUEL, FERAL,
              BRUTAL
Savage Island language .... NIUE
save .... KEEP, HOARD, REDEEM
savin .... CEDAR, JUNIPER
saving .... CHARY, FRUGAL, RESCUE
savoir-faire .... TACT
savor .... SMACK, ODOR
savory .... GUSTIBLE, SAPID, TASTY
saw .... REDE, ADAGE, SPOKE, MAXIM,
           MOTTO, EPIGRAM
   ", a cross-cut .... BRIAR
   " of a sawfish .... SERRA
   ", surgical .... TREPAN
sawbuck .... TENSPOT
sawdust ..... COOM, SCOBS, FILLINGS
sawfish .... RAY
sawhorse .... BUCK, JACK
sawmill gate .... SASH
saw palmetto .... SCRUB
saxhorn .... ALTHORN, TUBA
saxifrage .... SESELI
Saxon .... SASSENACH
   " coin .... SCEAT
   " king .... INE, INA
   " swineherd .... GURTH
say .... AVER, CITE, UTTER
saying ADAGE, SAW, DIT, MOT, AXIOM,
         APHORISM, MAXIM

sayings .... LOGIA, ANA
scab .... ESCHAR, RAT, CRUST
scabbard .... SHEATH, PILCHER, CHAPE
scabies .... ITCH
scads .... OODLES, GOBS, LOTS
scale CLIMB, RUSTRE, FILM, RULE, BRACT,
     FLAKE, GAMUT, GAUGE, LIBRA,
     PALET, RATIO, LAMINA, SCUTUM,
            BALANCE
   " ; comb. form .... LEPIS
   ", measuring .... VERNIER
   " of colors .... TINTOMETER
scale-like .... LEPROSE
scales .... RAMENTA
   " on fern stems .... CHAFF
   ", pair of .... LIBRA
scallop CRENA, QUIN, NOTCH, MOLLUSK
scalloped .... CRENATE, PINKED
scalpel .... BISTOURI, LANCET, KNIFE
scaly ...... TEGULAR, SCUTATE, FLAKY
scamp .... SCALAWAG, CHEAT, ROGUE
scamper .... BRATTLE, HIE, SCUD
scandalize ... MALIGN, REVILE, VILIFY
scandalmonger .... CLAT
Scandinavian ... NORSE(MAN), LAPP,
    DANE, SWEDE, ROS, RUS, VIKING
   " goblin .... NIS
   " god of strife ...... LOKI
   " god of thunder ... THOR
   " heaven .... ASGARD
   " heritable land .. ODAL,
               ODEL
   " hors d'oeuvres ....
         SMORGASBORD
   " legend ..... EDDA, SAGA
   " musician and poet .....
              SCALD
   " name .. NILS, OLE, OLAF
   " narrator ..... SAGAMAN
   " navigator .... ERIC
   " sea monster ... KRAKEN
   " terr. division ...... AMT
   " weight LOD, VOG, PUND,
              STEN
scant ... CHARY, STINT, FEW, MEAGER,
    SPARING, NIGGARDLY, NARROW
scar .. CICATRICE, BLEMISH, ARR, CLIFF,
    SHORE, CATFACE, CRAG, MAR
   ", resembling a .... ULOID
scarcity .... WANT, PAUCITY
scare .. DAUNT, FRIGHT, PANIC, COW,
           ALARM, SHOO
scarecrow .... EFFIGY, GUY, MALKIN,
    DUDMAN, SHAIL, JACKSTRAW
scaremonger ... ALARMIST, TERRORIST
scarf . ASCOT, PENDENT, TIPPET, RABAT,
    STOLE, FANON, ORALE, SASH,
      BOA, NUBIA, MANIPLE
   " bird .... CORMORANT
   " -like head covering . RIGOLETTE

scarfskin .... CUTICLE, EPIDERMIS
Scarlett's home .... TARA
scary .... EERIE, SPOOKY
scatter LITTER, SPRAY, (BE)STREW, TAD,
    DISPEL, ROUT, DISPERSE, BEGONE,
                           SKAIL
scattered ..... SCARCE, DIFFUSE, SEME,
                      SPORADIC
scattering .... DIASPORA
scenario .... LIBRETTO, SCRIPT
scene .. VIEW, VISTA, SCAPE, TABLEAU
scenery .... DIORAMA, PROPS, SET
scent .... FLAIR, NIDOR, NOSE, ODOR,
                AURA, TRAIL
   "   bag .... SACHET, PERFUMER
scented (RED)OLENT, AROMATIC, SPICY
schedule . CARD, LIST, TABLE, AGENDA,
                PROGRAM
scheme . PLAN, AIM, CABAL, COMPLOT,
             CHART, PROJECT
schism DESCENT, RENT, SPLIT, DISCORD
schismatic ...... HERETIC, SECTARIAN
schizocarp .... REGMA
Schnozzola .... DURANTE
scholar .... PUNDIT, PEDANT, SABORA,
         SAVANT, ULEMA, SAGE
scholarly .... ACADEMIC, PHILOMATH,
         ERUDITE, LEARNED
scholars .... APOSTLES, LITERATI
scholarship . STIPEND, BURSE, BURSARY
school ... BEVY, HERD, FLOCK, SHOAL,
    ETON, ECOLE, LUCEE, ACADEMY,
      PREP, DROVE, OXFORD
   "   grounds .... CAMPUS
   "   group .... PTA
   "   of medicine CLINIC, INFIRMARY
   "   of philosophers ELEATIC, STOIC
   " , religious ... SECT, PAROCHIAL
   " , riding .... MANEGE
schooner . PRAIRIE, TERN, CONESTOGA
schottische .... POLKA
science .... ART, SKILL, STUDY
   "   of character .... ETHOLOGY
   "   of dining .... ARISTOLOGY
   "   of healing .... IATROLOGY
   "   of motion .... KINETICS
   "   of self-defense . JUDO, KARATE
   "   of words .... SEMANTICS
   "   writer .... CARSON, LEY
scilicet .... VIDELICET
scimitar .... SEAX, SAX, SWORD, TURK
scintilla ..... BIT, IOTA, TRACE, WHIT
scion ... GRAFT, IMP, SLIP, SON, HEIR,
              SPRIG, ROD
Scipio .... AFRICANUS
scoff RAIL, FLEER, GIBE, DERIDE, FLOUT,
               TAUNT
scold ..... RAIL, RANT, BERATE, CHIDE,
    SHREW, REPROVE, VIXEN, NAG
sconce ..... HEAD, TOP, CANDLESTICK

scoop .... GOUGE, CHISEL, DREG, DIG
scope .. TETHER, AREA, RANGE, SPAN,
                LEEWAY
scopoline .... OSCINE
scorch ... SEAR, CHAR, PARCH, SINGE,
                BLISTER
scorched .... ADUST
score . TALLY, CHALK, TICK, TAB, MARK,
           MUSIC, TWENTY
scoria .... LAVA, SLAG, DROSS
scorn ... GECK, SLIGHT, SPURN, MOCK
scorpine .... HOGFISH
Scorpio, star in .... ANTARES
scorpion .... LIZARD, WHIP, STINGER,
              SCOURGE
   "   senna, deriv. of ... INDIGO
   " , water; genus .... NEPA
Scot .... CALEDONIAN, GAEL, PICT,
                BLUENOSE
scoter .. COOT, FULICA, DIVER, DUCKER
Scots; coll. .... SAWNEE
Scotland .. CALEDONIA, ALBA, ECOSSE,
                SCOTIA
   " , district of .... KYLE
Scottish accent .... BIRR
   " , arrange in .... ETTLE
   " , ask in .... SPERE
   " , askew in .... AGEE
   "   attendant ..... GILLIE, GILLY
   "   bailiff .... REEVE
   "   bank .... BRAE
   "   boundary .... MEAR
   "   brandy .... ATHOLE
   "   broadsword ..... CLAYMORE
   "   brook .... SIKE
   "   brownie .... NIS
   "   cake .... SCONE
   "   chest .... KIST
   "   child .... BAIRN
   "   city .... AYR
   "   clothe .... CLEAD
   "   cold mist .... DROW
   "   counsel .... REDE, REED
   "   court officer .... MACER
   "   cup .... TASS
   "   curlew .... WHAUP
   "   dagger .... SKEAN
   "   daisy .... GOWAN
   "   dance .... FLING, STRATHSPEY
   "   dirge .... CORONACH
   "   dog .... SEALYHAM
   "   earnest money ...... ARLES
   " ; to empty .... TOOM
   "   explorer .... RAE
   "   faithful .... LEAL
   "   farmer .... CROFTER
   "   fireplace .... INGLE
   "   game .... SHINTY
   "   godmother CUMMER, KIMMER
   "   haul of fish .... DRAVE

"	Highlander	GAEL
"	hillside	BRAE
"	historian	HUME, SKENE
"	ill-humored	CROUSE
"	, keen in	SNELL
"	kilt	FILIBEG
"	kindred	SIB
"	, lake in ..	LIN, LOCH, LOUGH
"	landholder ...	LAIRD, THANE
"	land tax	CESS
"	list of candidates	LEET
"	low rich river land	CARSE
"	lowlander	SASSENACH
"	magistrate	BAILIE
"	marauder	CATERAN
"	martial music of the bagpipe	PIBROCH
"	, mate in	FERE
"	measure	CRAN
"	, mismanage in	BLUNK
"	mud rake	CLAUT
"	muddled	REE
"	negative	DINNA, NAE
"	, nephew in	NEPOTE
"	, nimble in	GLEG
"	, own in	AWN
"	ox	NOWT
"	pay for a killing	CRO
"	peasant	COTTAR
"	plaid	TARTAN
"	plan	ETTLE
"	poet	MOIR, HOGG
"	pole	CABER
"	porridge	BROSE
"	pouch	SPORRAN
"	prefix to names	MAC
"	pudding	HAGGIS
"	race	ILK
"	river TEVIOT, AFTON, AYR, DEE,	TAY
"	rivulet	RINDLE
"	robbery	REIF
"	rope	WANTY
Scottish	rosin	ROZET
"	scythe handle	SNEAD
"	servant	GILLY
"	shawl	MAUD
"	, shivering in ..	OORIE, OURIE
"	soldier	CATERAN
"	tartan pattern	SET, SETT
"	, taste in	PREE
"	tenant	CROFT
"	to	TAE
"	town	BURGH
"	tribal payment	CRO
"	tuyere	TEW
"	uncle, per. to	EME
"	, undergo in	DREE
"	unroof	TIRR
"	vigor	VIR

"	water sprite	KELPIE
"	weighing machine ..	TRONE
"	weight	TRONE, DROP
"	, whine in	YIRN
"	, world in	WARL
scoundrel		CAD, KNAVE, ROGUE, VARLET, RASCAL, HEEL, SCAMP
scour		BURNISH, POLISH, SAND
scourge ...	BANE, FLOG, SWINGE, LASH
"Scourge of God"		ATTILA
scout		SPY, FELLOW, GUIDE, SEEK
" unit		DEN, PACK, TROOP
scow		GARVEY, ACON
scowl		GLOWER, FROWN, MOUE
scram		DECAMP, VAMOOSE, ELOPE
scramble ...	MUSS, STRIVE, HASTE, MIX
scrap ..	MORSEL, ORT, END, MELEE, BIT
scrape		ABRADE, RUB, GALL, RAKE, SCLAFF, GRAZE
scraped linen		LINT
scrapings RAMENTA, SHAVINGS, CHAFF
scratch	GRATE, MAR, RIT, SCARIFY
scratching ground for food	RASORIAL
scrawl		POTHOOK, SCRIBBLE
screech		SCREAK, SHRIEK
screed ..	TIRADE, DIATRIBE, HARANGUE
screen ..	BLIND, CLOAK, GRILLE, PAVIS, RIDDLE, SIEVE, SHOJI, TATTY, PURDAH, HIDE, SIFT
" , canvas		PAVISADE
" , chancel		JUBE, REREDOS
" , ecclesiastical		PARCLOSE
" , hall		SPIER
" mesh		LAUN
screw		HELIX, SPIRAL
" pine		ARA
scribble		SCRAWL, MARKS
scribe		SCRIVENER, AMANUENSIS
scrimmage		FIGHT, ROW, TUSSLE
scrip		MONEY, SCRAP
script		RONDE, SERTA, PESHITO
scriptural interpreter		EXEGETE
scripture	TEST, WRIT, BIBLE, VEDA, KORAN, TORAH, AGAMA, AVESTA, ALCORAN
" version		ITALA, VULGATE, DOUAY
scrive		SCRIBE, WRITE, SCORE
scroll		LIST, ROLL, VOLUTE
scrounge		PILFER
scruff		NAPE, SCUFF
scruple, one half		OBOLE
scrutinize	AUDIT, PROBE, EYE, PRY, SCAN, SIFT, EXAMINE, CON
scryer		SEER
scuffle	TUSSLE, HOE, FIGHT, FRAY
scull		PADDLE, SPOON, OAR
scullion ..	SERVANT, WRETCH, MENIAL, GIPPO

253

sculptor .. IMAGER, PHIDIAS, ANGELO, RODIN
    " , tool of . EBAUCHOIR, GRAVER
scup .... BREAM, FISH, PORGY
scurry .... HIE, SKELTER, SCUTTLE
scutage .... ESCUAGE
scuttle ..... HOD, SINK, RUN, SWAMP
scuttlebutt .... RUMOR
scythe handle ...... SNATH, SNEAD
    " sweep .... SWATH
Scythian lamb .... BAROMETZ
sea . MAIN, LAKE, OCEAN, BRINE, DEEP, SURF, SURGE, BAHR
" anemone .... ACTINIA, POLYP
" animal ..... ROSMARINE, PELAGIAN
" , arm of the .. SINUS, FIORD, FRITH
" bird ..... ERN(E), CAHOW, KESTREL, PUFFIN, SULA, TERN
" cow .... DUGONG, MANATEE
" cow, the Steller's .... RYTINA
" deity, daughter of a . DEINO, ENYO
" demigod .... TRITON
" dog .... GOB, TAR
" duck .... SCOTER, COOT
" ear .... ABALONE
" , French for .... MER
" god; Gaelic .... LIR, LER
" holly root .... ERYNGO
" inlet .... FIORD, FJORD
" lemon .... DORIS
" mile .... KNOT, NAUT
" monster .... CETE, KRAAKEN
" needle .... GARFISH
" nettle ...... MEDUSA, ACALEPH
" nymph .... GALATEA, NEREID
" , per. to the .. PELAGIC, THALASSIC
" ; rise and fall, as the ...... LOOM
" -salt producer .... HALOGEN
" slug .... TREPANG
" spray .... SPINDRIFT
" swimming organisms; per. to ..... NEKTERIC
" unicorn .... NARWHAL
" urchin, fossil .... ECHINI, ECHINITE
sea-green color .... CELADON
seal .... STAMP, BULLA, SICCA, SIGIL, WAFER, CACHET, RATIFY, SECURE, SIGNET, SIGILLATE
seal (animal) .. OTARY, PINNIGRADE, URSUK, SADDLER, HOPPER, PUP, SWILE
" fur .... URSAL
" ; genus .. OTARIA, PHOCA, MATKA
" , per. to .... PHOCINE
seam .... RAPHE, JOINT
" , per. to ...... SUTURAL, JOINING
sea-maid .... SIREN, MERMAID, NYMPH
seaman . JACKIE, NAUTILUS, SALT, TAR, GOB, MARINER, SAILOR
seamen's chapel .... BETHEL, CHURCH

sea-mew .... GULL
sea-onion .... SQUILL
seaplane projection .... SPONSON
" , type of .... FLOATPLANE
sear ...... FRY, SERE, BRAISE, CAUTER
search ... FERRET, HUNT, COMB, RAKE, RANSACK, GROPE, FRISK, DELVE, DOWSE
" for game .... GHOOM
" for political victims WITCHHUNT
searing .... BURNING
seashore, per. to .... LITTORAL
seasickness ... NAUPATHIA, MALDEMER
season SPICE, TIME, BEEK, INURE, DEVIL, CORN, CURE, AGE
" ; Scot. .... SELE
seasoning GARLIC, FORCE, SALT, THYME, CONDIMENT, SPICE, RELISH
seasons, the .... HORAE
seat .. MASTABA, SELLA, SITE, PEWAGE, ASANA, POST, HOWDAH
" cloth ...... DORSAL, DOSSEL
" , coach .... DICKY
" in a chancel .... SEDILE
" of honor .... CURULE
" of justice .... BANC
seats, tier of .... GRADIN
sea water .... BRINE
seaweed .. WRACK, AGAR, ORE, ALGA, KELP, CARRAGEEN, DULSE, LAVER, NORI
" ; genus ..... ALARIA, NOSTOC
" , leaf of .... FROND
" , product of ... AGAR, GELOSE
seaweeds .... CONFERVAE
" , ashes of ...... VAREC, KELP
" , deriv. of .... BARILLA
" , per. to .... ALGOUS
" , substance found on ALGIN
" , tough leathery ..... FUCUS
seaworm .... LURG
Seb's children .... ISIS, OSIRIS
" consort .... NUT
sec, opposed to .... BRUT
secluded .... ISOLATED, CLOISTRAL, COVERT, LONELY
seclusion PRIVACY, SOLITUDE, RETIRACY
second ... JIFFY, ASSISTANT, MOMENT
" lieutenant .... SHAVETAIL
" preparation .... HASH
" , to ..... BACK, SUPPORT, ABET
secondary MINOR, LESS, BYE, INFERIOR
secrecy, bind to .... TILE
secret .... COVERT, MYSTIC, DERN, ESOTERIC, CRYPTIC, RETIRED, PRIVY, HIDDEN, ARCANUM
" council .... JUNTO
" , keep .... ENSEAL
" place ...... ADYTUM, SANCTUM

    "   police . OGPU, GESTAPO, CHEKA, NKVD
    "   society . BLACKHAND, CAMORRA, TONG, MAFFIA
secretly .... SUBROSA, SLY, INLY
secrets .... ARCANA, BYENDS
sectarian ..... HERETIC, HETERODOX
section . PART, SEGMENT, PANEL, AREA
    "   of three folio sheets TERNION
sector .... ARC, AREA
secular .... LAIC, LAY
secure .... GET, MOOR, FIX, BIND, ANCHOR, RIVET, NAIL, ROPE
security ..... BOND, PLEDGE, GAGE, VADIUM, SHELTER, SAFETY, BAIL
sedate .... QUIET, STAID, STILL, CALM, DOUCE, PLACID, SERENE
sedative ...... ANODYNE, BROMIDE, NERVINE, ALDOL, OPIATE
sedge . TUSSOCK, TOITOI, SEG, CHUFA, LING
    " ; genus CAREX, XYPRIS, CARICES
sediment .... MAGMA, GREAVES, LEES, SILT, DREGS, FAEX, FEGULA
seditious ... FACTIOUS, TREASONABLE, RIOTOUS
seducer .... ENTICER, LOTHARIO
see . ESPY, VIDE, VIEW, DISCERN, LO, LOOK, GRAZE, DESCRY, DIOCESE
seed ANISE, SOW, PIT, KERNEL, SPERM, PIP, GERM
    " , apple .... PIP
    " -bearing organ in flower .. PISTIL
    " coating ...... POP, APRIL, TESTA
    " fluid .... LATEX
    " , food .... PEA, LENTIL
    " germ ...... BEGINNING, CHIT
    " , immature .... OVULE
    " , naked .... ACHENE
    " of a tropical tree .... BEN
    " of canary grass .... ALPIST
    " , one-celled .... CARPEL
    " plant, bitter .... CUMIN
    " plant, cooking ...... CARAWAY
    " pod, gaping .. DEHISCENCE, KID
    " , primitive .... SPORE
    " scars .... HILA
    " , two-valved .... LEGUME
    " vessel .... BUR, POD, SILICLE
    " weevil; genus .... APION
seedcake .... WIG
seed coat .... BUR(R), TEGMEN, TEGUMEN, HULL
    "   " , broken .... BRAN
seedless plant .... FERN
seedy .. SHABBY, DINGY, TACKY, FADED
seeing .... SIGHT, ESPIAL
seek ... EXPLORE, SEARCH, TRY, ENSUE, ASPIRE, FISH, HUNT
seeking .... ZETETIC

seeming .... GUISE, LIKELY, QUASI
seemly PROPER, BECOMING, MEET, NICE
seep .... PERCOLATE, OOZE, DRIP
seer .... DIVINER, GAZER, ORACLE, PROPHET, SCRYER
seeress ...... PHOEBAD, SAGA, SIBYL, CASSANDRA, PYTHIA
seesaw .... TEETER, TILT, WAVER
    " -like .... BASCULE
seethe ...... BOIL, STEW, COOK, SOB
seething .... ABOIL, BULLER
segment ... TELSON, CANTLE, SECTOR, CHAPTER
    " ; biol. ... LACINIA, METAMERE
    " of an animal ... SOMATOME
    " -shaped .... TORIC
seine ..... FARE, NET, SAGENE, TRAWL
Seine tributary .... EURE, OISE
seism .... EARTHQUAKE
seismic, vertical .... EPICENTER
seize ... CLUTCH, USURP, REAVE, NAB, YOKE, GRIP, ANNEX, COLLAR, SNATCH
    " for debt CONFISCATE, DISTRAIN, EMBARGO
Selassie .... HAILE
select .. CULL, ELITE, CHOOSE, GOOD, TAKE, OPT, VOTE, RARE
self .... EGO, PERSON, ENTITY, SEITY, SAME, VERY
    " ; comb. form .... AUTO, AUT
    " -defense ... JUJUTSU, JUDO, KARATE
    " -deification .... AUTOTHEISM
    " -denial .... ASCETICISM
    " -fear .... AUTOPHOBY
    " -knowledge .... AUTOLOGY
    " -murderer .... FELODESE
    " , own .... NAINSEL
self-assertion ...... EGOISM, VANITY
    " -centered ..... EGOCENTRIC, SMUG
    " -confidence ..... APLOMB, BALANCE
    " -contradiction .... PARADOX
    " -esteem .. EGOTISM, PRIDE, VANITY, VAINGLORY
sell .... VEND, BARTER, CANT, MARKET, AUCTION, CONVINCE
    " over official rate .... SCALP
    " .... CHEAT, TRICK
seller ...... COSTER, DEALER, VENDOR, PEDDLER
selvage of cloth .... LIST
selvedge .... LISTING
Semele's sister .... INO
semester .... BIANNUAL, TERM
semicircular tart .... TURNOVER
Seminole chief .... OSCEOLA
Semiramis, husband of ...... NINUS
Semite .... HEBREW, ARAB, JEW
Semitic language ..... GEEZ, HARARI
    " weight .... GERAH, MINA

semolina .... SUJI
senatorship ...... TOGA, CHAIR, SEAT
send ... DRIVE, HURL, MAIL, TRANSFER
  "   back .... REMIT, REMAND
  "   out .... EMIT, ISSUE, RADIATE
senescent .... AGED, OLD
senility .... CADUCITY, DOTAGE
senior .... AINE, DEAN, ELDER
sensational .... LURID
sense .. FLAIR, SAPIENT, VIEW, INTUIT,
             SIGHT, SMELL, TASTE
  "   organ .... SENSILLA
senseless .... FATUOUS, INEPT, FUTILE,
                 STUPID
sentence ..... FUTWA, ADAGE, JUDGE,
               CONDEMN
  "   ; analyze .... PARSE
  "   balance .... PARISON
  "   , concluding ..... EPILOG(UE)
  "   construction .... SYNTAX
  "   , latter clause in a APODOSIS
  "   part ... CLAUSE, NOUN, VERB
sententious .... PITHY, TERSE
sentiment, strong EMOTION, PASSION
sentinel ..... GUARD, PICKET, VIDETTE,
              SENTRY, VIGIL
sentry .... KITE, WATCH, SOLDIER
separate ... DISCRETE, ISOLATE, REND,
             SIDE, PART, SORT
separated .... FREE, SHREDDED, ALONE
separatist .... PILGRIM, HERETIC
sepia .... DUN, INK, CUTTLEFISH
sepiolite .... MEERSCHAUM
septa in corals .... TABULA
septic poisoning .... PY(A)EMIA
septule .... SEVENFOLD
sepulchral .... URNAL, CHARNAL
  "   chest .... CIST
  "   mounds .... TUMULI
  "   vault .... CATACOMB
sequence ... SERIES, STRAIGHT, CHAIN
sequester .... ISOLATE, CLOISTER
sequin .... SPANGLE, DISK, VENETIAN
sequoia .... REDWOOD, TREE
seraglio .... HAREM, SERAI
serai .... CARAVANSARY
seraph .... ANGEL, CHERUB
Serb .... SLAV
sere .. SLAW, DRIED, WORN, WITHERED
serenade ..... NOCTURNE, CHARIVARI
serene ...... LITHE, PLACID, HALCYON
serf ..... ESNE, ETA, PEON, THRALL,
           VILLEIN, HELOT, COLONA
  "   , female .... NEIF
  "   , per. to .... BOND
seric .... SILKEN
series .... SET, SEQUENCE, STRING,
          CATENA, GAMUT, TALLY
  "   , graded .... NEST
  "   , in a .... SERIATIM

  "   of discussions .... SYMPOSIUM
  "   of events .... EPOS
  "   of piles .... DRIFT
  "   of steps .... SCALE
  "   of six .... HEXAD
serious GRAVE, STAID, SOBER, SEDATE,
            DEMURE, EARNEST
sermon .... DISCOURSE, HOMILY
serow ..... ANTELOPE, GORAL, JAGLA
serpent . ASP, NAGA, BASILISK, SNAKE,
       SEPS, APEPI, VIPER, ADDER,
          (A)BOMA, RACER
  "   of Borneo .... BOIGA
  "   of India ...... KRAIT, COBRA
  "   , Vedic sky .... AHI
  "   worship .... OPHISM
serpentine . SINUOUS, ZIGZAG, SUBTLE,
         TINEA, OPHITE, HERPES
serpent-like .... ANGUINE
serrano .... PERCOID
servant ... BATA, BILDAR, CHELA, GYP,
    COISTRIL, FLUNKY, EQUERRY, AMAH,
    BUTLER, MENIAL, PAGE, HAMAL,
              SCULLION
serve ...... BESTEAD, DEAL, DO, WAIT,
        BENEFIT, SUCCOR, LADLE
  "   as an escort .... SQUIRE
service ... RITUAL, RITE, USE, WAGE
  "   for the dead ... DIRGE, SONG
  "   in R.C. church ....TENEBRAE
servile ...... ABJECT, BASE, SLAVISH,
        SYCOPHANTIC, MENIAL
  "   agent .... MINION
servite .... MENDICANT
sesame grass .... GAMA
  "   plant .. TIL, BENI, BENNE, TEEL
  "   seed .... GINGILI
session ... SEANCE, COUNCIL, VESTRY
  "   , hold ..... SIT, MEET, CONFER
set . LAY, POST, PUT, SERIES, GEL, JELL,
          CLIQUE, COTERIE
  " apart .... TABOO, DEFER
  " back .... REVERSE
  " firmly .... POSIT, PLANT
  " in order .... FILE, POST
  " of opinions .... CREDO
  " of rules .... CODE
  " on fire ..... TIND, KINDLE, ABLAZE
  " thickly .... STUD
  " up .... RIG, CIRCLE, PUT
seta .... BRISTLE, HAIR, SPINE
Seth's father .... ADAM
  "   son .... ENOS
Seton .... ERNEST THOMPSON
sets of three horses .... RANDEMS
setting SCENE, LOCALE, MILIEU, BEZEL,
              CHATON
settlings .... LEES, SEDIMENT
set-to ...... BOUT, CONTEST, COMBAT
Sevareid, Mr. .... ERIC

seven, group of . HEPTAD, HEBDOMAD,
SEPTET
" ; comb. form .... HEPTA
" gods of happiness ...... EBISU
" languages .... HEPTAGLOT
"Seven Against Thebes," one of the
TYDEUS
sevenfold .... SEPTUPLE
severe .. ACUTE, DRASTIC, DURE, GRIM,
AUSTERE, STERN
" critic .... SLATER
sew .... BASTE, PREEN, SUTURE
" with gathers .... FULL
sewing-machine inventor ..... HOWE
sewer .... CLOACA, SINK, DRINK
sexes, common to both ..... EPICENE
sexton ..... JANITOR, BEETLE, SACRIST
Sforza, Mr. .... CARLO
shabby . SCURVY, SEEDY, TACKY, RATTY,
WORN
shack .... CABIN, HUT
shackle ...... GYVE, FETTER, TRAMMEL
shackler .... SLOTTER
shad .. ALEWIFE, ALLICE, ALLIS, ALOSE
shaddock .... POMELO
shade TINGE, VISOR, NUANCE, SWALE,
TONE, BLIND, COLOR, TINT,
SCREEN, GHOST, PHANTOM
shades of the departed MANES, SPIRITS
shadow . DOG, SCUG, SHEPHERD, TAIL,
SPECTER, UMBRA
" forth .... ADUMBRATE
" , man without .... ASCIAN
" ; people throwing it opposite
ways .... ANTISCIANS
shadows, fight with ..... SCIAMACHY
" , projecting of .. SCIAGRAPHY
shady ..... ADUMBRAL, ELMY, HIDDEN
shaft ARROW, GROOVE, VERGE, SPIRE,
COLUMN, PILLAR, SPINDLE
" , convex swelling of ... ENTASIS
" handle .... HELVE
" , Hindu .... LAT
" of a cart .... THILL
" of a column FUST, SCAPE, TIGE
" of a feather .... SCAPE
" of a plant .... AXIS
shaggy .... HIRSUTE, BUSHY, NAPPY
shake .... AGITATE, JAR, JOLT
" off .... DOFF, SHED
Shakers, founder of .... LEE
Shakespeare's wife .... ANNE
shale .... FISSILE, ROCK
shall .... CAN, MUN, MUST
shallot . ONION, SCALLION, ESCHALOT
shallow .... CURSORY, EMPTY, TRIVIAL
sham .... DUMMY, FAKE, FEIGN, HOAX
Shamash attendant .... BUNENE
shameful .... GROSS, VILE, INDECENT
shampoo ... MASSAGE, TRIPSIS, WASH

Shan .... TAI
shanghai .... DRUG, SHIP
shank .... CRUS, GAMB, SHIN
" , green-legged .... KNOT
" , per. to .... CRURAL
" , yellow .... TATTLER
shanny .... BLENNY
shantung .... TUSSAH
shanty .... HOVEL, HUT, SHACK, SHED
shape ... MOLD, CUT, MODEL, DESIGN,
FORM, PLAN, GUISE, PATTERN
" , without .. AMORPHOUS, CRUDE
shaping machine .... EDGER
shard .... FRAGMENT, SCAR
share ...... DOLE, LOT, PART, QUOTA
shark .... GATA, LAMIA, TOPE, RHINA,
MAKO
" adherent ...... REMORA, PEGA
" ; genus .... GALEUS
" ; order .... SELACHII
sharp . SNELL, SLY, ACID, KEEN, ACUTE,
ACUATE, BITING, EDGY
" ; comb. form .... ACET(O)
" fragments of bone ... SPICULAE
" -sighted .... LYNCEAN
" ; Sp. .... AGUDO
" to the taste .... ACERB, ACRID
sharpen .. CACUMINATE, KEEN, HONE
sharpened slightly .... ACUTATE
sharper ... CUTER, GYP, CHEAT, KNAVE
sharpshooter .... SNIPER, MARKSMAN,
JAGER
shatter .... DASH, SMASH
shave .... CUTE, PARE, STRIP, SCRAPE
shaveling .... FRIAR, MONK, PRIEST
shavetail . ENSIGN, MULE, LIEUTENANT
Shaw; author .... IRWIN
shawl MANTA, SERAPE, NUBIA, TAPALO,
LAMBA
sheaf ... KERN, GERB, OMER, HATTOCK
shear .... CLIP, NIP, TRIM, FLEECE
shears, cloth .... LEWIS
sheatfish .... DORAD, WELS
sheath . SLEEVE, CASE, OCREA, THECA,
SCABBARD, FOREL, LORICA
sheathe .... INCASE, COVER
Sheba .... SABA
Shechem's father .... HAMOR
shed . CAST, COTE, DOFF, MOLT, SPILL,
EFFUSE
" ; shelter; dugout .... ABRI
sheen ..... GLOSS, LUSTRE, SPLENDOR
sheep ... WOOLLY, BLEATER, AOUDAD,
ARGALI, OVINE, MUTTON
" , cry of .... BAA, BLAT
" disease ANTHRAX, BANE, BLAST,
BRAXY, COE, CORE, GID, RESP,
ROT, SCRAPIE
" , female .... EWE
" fly .... FAG

257

" ; genus .... OVIS
" , hardy kind of .... KARAKUL
" head .... JIMMY
" keeper .... ABEL
" laurel .... KALMIA
" , kind of .... MERINO
" , leader of a flock of ....
                              BELLWETHER
" leather .... ROAN
" , leg hair of .... GARE
" , male .. BUCK, HEDER, RAM, TUP,
                              WETHER
" mange .... SCAB
" mountain .... IBEX
" of Eng. ..... CHEVIOT, DISHLEY
" of Tibet . SHA, SHABO, OORIAL,
                              URIAL
sheep pen .... FANK
" , per. to .... OVINE
" , pet .... COSSET
" pox .... OVINIA, WILDFIRE
" skin for tanning BASAN, BASIL,
                              DONGOLA
" , species of wild ...... BHARAL,
                              MOUFFLON
" , theft of .... ABIGEAT
" tic .... KEB, KED
" , two-year-old ...... HOB, TEG
" , W. Afr. .... ZENU
" , wild .. AOUDAD, ARGAL, URIAL
" , wool-producing ...... MERINO
" , yearling .... HOGGET, TAG
" , young .... LAMB, EANLING
sheepfold ... COTE, KRAAL, OVIL, PEN,
                              REEVE, REE
sheeplike .... MEEK, OVINE
sheep's-bit .... HERB, IRONFLOWER
sheepshead .... SALEMA
sheepskin . PELT, WOOLFELL, DIPLOMA,
                              BOCK, ROAN, SKIVER
sheer .... BRANT, PURE, THIN, ABRUPT
sheet .... LATTEN, DUEDECIMO
sheeting .... PERCALE, CANVAS
shekel, one twentieth of a ... GERAH
sheldrake .. MERGANSER, BARGOOSE
shelf ..... LEDGE, BINK, REEF, SHOAL
" , embankment .... BERM(E)
shell CARAPACE, COWRY, SHARD, POD,
                              BURR
" , covered with a ...... LORICATE
" ear .... ORMER, ABALONE
" , explosive .... BOMB, DUD,
                              SHRAPNEL, GRENADE
" -fish ..... BARNACLE, PIPI, NACRE,
                              COCKLE
" , gastropod .... CHANK
" groove .... LIRA
" , marine .... CONCH
" mechanism .... SPALTER
" , mollusk .... WHELK

" money .. COLCOL, PEAG, SEWAN
" ridges .... VARICES
" shank .... SANKHA
" , spiral .... CARACOL(E)
" tribal money; Afr. .... COWRIE
Shelley drama .... CENCI
shelly covering of mollusk .... TESTA
shelter .. COVERT, (EN)SCONCE, ABRI,
    DUGOUT, HAVEN, ASYLUM, SCUG,
    SKUG, ARK, HOSTEL, SHEAL, SAFETY
" , cattle .... STELL
" ; movable roof ..... MANTELET
" ; naut. .... LEE
" , toward; naut. . ALEE, LEEWARD
Shem's descendant .... SEMITE
" son .... ELAM, ARAM, LUD
shepherd god .... PAN
shepherdess .... AMARYLLIS, BERGERE
shepherd's club .... MULLEIN
" pipe .... LARIGOT, OAT
" rod .... TEASEL
" staff .... CANT, CROOK
Sheridan play .... RIVALS
sheriff SHRIEVE, JAILER, REEVE, ELISOR
"Sherlock Holmes" author .... DOYLE
sherry wine OLOROSO, XERES, SOLERA
Shetland fishing grounds ...... HAAF
shibboleth ..... SLOGAN, PASSWORD
shield ... ECU, PAVIS, SCUTE, SCUTUM,
    TESTUDO, TARGE, APRON, (A)EGIS,
              GUARD, DEFEND, PROTECT
" around base of petiole . OCREA
" , band across .... FESS
" , border in a .. BORDURE, ORLE
" , boss in a .... UMBO
" , division of a .... ENTE
" , fillet around a .... ORLE
" ; heraldry .... ESCUTCHEON
" , sacred .... ANCILE
" -shaped ...... SCUTATE, PELTATE,
                              CLYPEATE
shift .... STIR, VEER, DEVIATE, DODGE,
    GANG, GYBE, SPELL, TOUR, SWERVE
shifts ...... SHUNTS, CAMISE, SMOCK
shill .... ACCOMPLICE
Shillong's cap .... ASSAM
shilly-shally .... VACILLATE
shin .... SHANK, CLIMB
" , per. to .... TIBIAL
shine ...... BEAM, RADIATE, GLISTEN,
    GLITTER, RUTILATE, GLOW, SPARKLE,
                              GLOSS
shiner . MINNOW, CHUB, BREAM, DACE
shingle ..... FACIA, CLIP, SHIM, ZONA
shingles .... HERPES, SIGNBOARDS
shining GLARY, AGLOW, LUCID, NITID,
                              GLOSSY
Shinto .... SINTU
" gods .... KAMI

258

"	temple	SHA
"	temple gateway PAILOU, TORII	
"	war god	HACHIMAN
ship	MAIL, POOP, SEND, BOAT, CRAFT, FERRY, LINER, RACER, YACHT, CUTTER, PACKET, TANKER, VESSEL, WHALER	
"	, ancient	NEF, GALLEON
"	, body of a	HULK
"	, curved timber of	APRON, STEMSON
"	employee ... ABLE, HAND, MATE, PURSER, STEWARD	
"	fender	SKID
"	fraud	BARRATRY
"	, left side of	PORT
"	mortgage	BOTTOMRY
"	of desert	CAMEL
"	, part of .. BOW, RIB, SNY, DECK, DOCK, HELM, KEEL, MAST, PROW, ORLOP, SNAPE, STRAKE	
"	, square-rigged	BRIG
"	table frame	FIDDLE
"	timber .... KEELSON, BITT	
"	, title of captain of a . RAIS, RAS, REIS	
"	, to stave in bottom of ...	BILGE
"	worm .... BORER, TEREDO	
ship's	ballast	LASTAGE
"	beam, top of ..... TIMBERHEAD	
"	bottom, to clean	BREAM
"	carpenter	CHIPS
"	crew leader	BOSUN
"	daily record	LOG
"	galley	CABOOSE
"	jail .... HULK, BRIG	
"	lifting device ... CAMEL, DAVIT	
"	permit to enter port . PRATIQUE	
"	prow	PRORE
"	rope	SHROUD
"	stern rail	TAFFRAIL
ships	of fame ... NINA, PINTA, ARGO, MARIA, MAINE, BOUNTY, TITANIC, LUSITANIA, MAYFLOWER, MONITOR, MERRIMAC, CLERMONT	

shipwreck, goods lost in a . FLOTSAM
shirk .. SLACK, MALINGER, GOLDBRICK
shirker .... RUNAWAY, TRUANT
shirt CAMISE, KAMIS, SARK, CHEMISE, HEMD, SHIFT, DICK(E)Y
" bosom .... PLASTRON
shiver ..... QUAKE, SHUDDER, TOTTER, TREMBLE
shoal .... REEF, BAR, DRAVE
shock .. JAR, STARTLE, BRUNT, IMPACT, TRAUMA, BLOW
" absorber .... SNUBBER
" ; to set up as sheaves .. STOOK
shod .... CALCED, SOLED

shoe	..... BALMORAL, BLUCHER, BOOT, CLOG, OXFORD, BROGAN, STOGY, SOLLERET, SNEAKER, BUSKIN, MOYLE, MULE, PUMP, SANDAL, SLIPPER, CHOPIN	
"	cleat	CALK
"	covering .... PRUNELLA, GAITER	
"	lace .... LATCHET, WANG	
"	, margin of	RAND
"	, part of .. INSOLE, EYELET, HEEL, LAST, WELT, VAMP	
"	, wooden SABOT, PATTEN, SECQUE	
shoe	holder .... HORN, TREE	

shoelace tag .... AGLET
shoemaker .. SOUTER, CRISPIN, SUTOR, BOTCHER, COBBLER, ZAPATERO
shoemaker's nail .... SPARABLE
" oilstone .... SLIP
" patron saint ... CRISPIN
shogun .... TYCOON, CHIEF
Scholem; author .... ASCH
shoot .. RATOON, CHIT, TILLER, TWIG, ROD, SCION, STOLON, VIMEN, BINE, GEMMA, HURRY, BAG
" from cover .... DART, SNIPE
shooting iron ..... PISTOL, REVOLVER
" match .. TIR, SKEET, SHOOT
" star .... LEONID, COWSLIP, PRIMWORT, METEOR
shoots, stripper of small .... BRUTTER
shop ... MART, ATELIER, BURSE, TOKO, FACTORY, TABERNA
shore .. COAST, PROP, MARGE, PLAYA, SAND, BEACH, RIPA
" bird .... AVOCET, CURLEW
" of the sea ..... BRINK, STRAND
" , per. to .... LITTORAL
short . BRIEF, SCANTY, LACONIC, CURT, CRISP, CONCISE
" and fat .... PODGY
" essay .... TRACT
" forms .... ABBRS
" -legged .... BREVIPED
" -lived .... EPHEMERAL
" of breath ..... DYSPNEIC, PURSY
" -sighted .... MYOPIC
shortage ...... DEFICIT, LACK, ULLAGE
shorten . DOCK, LOP, LESSEN, CURTAIL, DELE, ELIDE
shortened .... CURTATE
shortening of syllables ..... SYSTOLE
shorthand system ... GREGG, PITMAN, STENOTYPE
Shoshonean .... OTOE, PIUTE, UTE
shot ... PELLET, CHARGE, DRINK, SHELL
" : one under par .... BIRDIE
shoulder .... BERM, EPAULE
" badge .... EPAULET
" belt .... BALDRIC
" blade .. OMOPLATE, SCAPULA

"   , gout in the ...... OMAGRA
"   inflammation ... OMALGIA,
                                    OMITIS
"   muscle .... DELTOID
"   of a bastion .... EPAULE
"   of a road .... BERM
"   , per. to .. ALAR, HUMERAL
"   ; yoke pail .... COWL, SOE
shovel .... SCOOP, SPADE
show .. LEGIT, EVINCE, RAREE, EXPOSE,
                                    DIVULGE
"   as false .... BELIE
"   off .... DISPLAY, FLAUNT
"Show Boat" authoress . EDNA FERBER
"   "   composer .... KERN
showcase .... VITRINE
shower ... SCAT, DROW, MISLE, RASH,
                        PARTY, SPRAY, SPATE
"   of meteors .... ANDROMID
showy ... GARISH, ARTY, GAY, TINSEL,
                            GAUDY, SPORTY
shrapnel .... SHELL
shred ..... RAG, RIP, SNIP, STRIP, TAG
shrew ...... SCOLD, VIXEN, XANTIPPE,
                        VIRAGO, KATE, ERD
"   mouse .. SOREX, HYRAX, MIGALE
"   squirrel .... TANA
shrewd CANNY, CUTE, PRACTIC, WILY,
              PAWKY, ASTUTE, SAPIENT, ARCH
shrewdness ... ACUMEN, ARGUTENESS
shrewish .... TERMAGANT
shrill .. SHARP, PIPY, SHIRLY, STRIDENT,
                                    ACUTE
"   noise .... STRIDOR
shrimp ...... NAPEE, CARID, PANDLE,
                                COMARON
shrine ...... ALTAR, ADYTUM, CHASSE,
        CHAITYA, PIR, DARGAH, DURGAH,
                    NAOS, CAABA, STUPA
shrink .... QUAIL, WINCE, RECOIL,
              SHRIVEL, CONTRACT, ANALYST
shrivel . PARCH, WIZEN, PAUCH, CRINE
shriveled .... SERE, THIN
shroud .... COWL, MASK, CEREMENT,
                                    SCREEN
shrouded .... HID, CLOAKED
shrub TOD, BUSH, FRUTEX, BOSCAGE,
          ELDER, HALESIA, LAURUS, YEW,
                        LILAC, OLEASTER
"   ; Adam's needle .... YUCCA
"   ; Arabian leaves, tea KAFTA, KAT
"   , aromatic ... ARALIA, LAVENDER
"   , Asian .... BAGO, DEUTZIA,
                                    WEIGELA
"   ; bean family .. BROOM, ILEX
"   ; botany .... FRUTEX
"   , bushy ..... CADE, SAVIN, TOD
"   , California .... SALAL
"   , cherry .... CERASUS

"   , climbing BIGNONIA, CLEMATIS,
                        LIANA, RUBUS, VITIS
"   , creeping .... PYXIE
"   ; cytisus .... BROOM
"   ; dogwood .... CORNUS
"   , E. Ind. medicinal .... SOMA,
                                    MUDAR
"   , evergreen .. ABELMOSK, BUXUS,
        CAMELLIA, CISTUS, FATSIA, HEATH,
          ILEX, JASMINE, LAUREL, MYRTLE,
          OLEANDER, SALAL, SAVIN, TITI,
                                    PEPINO
"   , evergreen, climbing .. AKEBIA,
                        HEDERA, SMILAX
"   , euphorbiaceous .... ALEM
"   fence .... HEDGEROW
"   , flowering ..... AZALEA, LILAC,
                        OLEASTER, SYRINGA
"   ; genus Rhus .... SUMAC
"   , rosaceous .... SPIREA
"   , hardy ...... ALTHEA, HEATHER
"   ; Hawaii rose .... AKALA
"   , Japan .... AUCUBA
"   ; larch family .... ALDER
"   ; maples, the .... ACER
"   ; mint family .... ROSEMARY
"   , New Zealand ..... RAMARAMA,
                                    TUTU
"   , of silk fiber .... ANABO
"   , Old World; genus ... GENISTA
"   , olive .... OLEA
"   , Oriental .... HENNA
"   , parisitic .... MISTLETOE
"   ; pepper .... KAVA
"   ; periwinkle .... VINCA
"   ; pine family .... SAVIN
"   , prickly .... BRAMBLE
"   , quince; Jap. .... CYDONIA
"   , rutaceous .... JABORANDI
"   , Sambucus .... ELDER
"   , S. Amer. .... CEIBO
"   , spiny .... FURZE, GORSE, ULEX
"   , stunted .... SCRAB
"   , thick-foliage .... TOD
"   , tropical .... ABELIA, ABRUS,
                                    LANTANA
"   used in tanning .... SUMAC
"   , W. Ind. . ANIL, CASSAVA, EBOE
shrubs; genus . ITEA, LANTANA, OLEA,
          RHUS, OLEARIA, RIBES, ROSA, SIDA
shudder ...... GURE, QUAKE, TREMOR
shuffle .... RUSE, SCUFF, MIX, TRICK
"   cards .... RIFFLE
shun ... ESCHEW, EVITE, AVOID, RUN,
                        DODGE, ELUDE
Shunammite, the .... ABISHAG
shunt ...... BYPASS, SWITCH, DEVIATE
shut .... FASTEN, FOLD, STOP
"   out .... OCCLUDE, BAN, EXCLUDE

```
"   up ..... DAM, CAGE, MUTE, END,          sidle . EDGE, CANT, SKEW, CRAB, SKIRT,
                        (S)HUSH                                        DEVIATE
shuttle ........ LOOPER, FLUTE, SLIDE       siècle ....... CENTURY, GENERATION
shy ..... COY, SQUAB, TIMID, MODEST         siege, of a ........... OBSIDIONAL
Shylock ................... USURER          Siegfried's slayer ........... HAGEN
"   , daughter of ........ JESSICA           "     sword ......... BALMUNG
"   , friend of ............ TUBAL          Siegmund's sword ............ GRAM
Siamese and Shans ...... THAIS, TAIS        Siena marble ............ BROCATEL
Siamese capital .......... BANGKOK          Sierra Madre peak ........... LOWE
"   coin ... BAHT, ATT, BAT, TICAL          Sierra Nevada fog ......... POGONIP
"   measure . RAI, SOK, NIU, SEN,           siesta ....... NAP, REST, LULL, MIDDAY
                          SESTI             sieve ...... RIDDLE, BOLT, SILE, TAMIS,
"   river ................. MENAM                    SEARCH, SIFT, LAUN, COLANDER,
"   tongue ............ LAO, TAI                                        PUREE
"   Twins .......... CHANG, ENG             sifaka ..................... LEMUR
"   weight .... PAI, CHANG, TICAL           sift .......BOLT, LUE, SCREEN, RIDDLE
sib ........ KINSMAN, RELATIVE, AKIN        sigh ..... SITHE, SOB, MOAN, SOUGH,
Siberia, river of .... AMUR, LENA, OB                                  GROAN
"   , wild sheep of ........ ARGALI         sight . RAY, VISTA, VIEW, VISION, KEN,
Siberian blizzard ............ BURAN                             SCENE, SHOW
"   city .................. OMSK            "   , per. to .............. OCULAR
"   forest ................ TAIGA           sigmoid ................ CURVE, ESS
"   native ... YUIT, TATAR, YAKUT,          sign .. OMEN, PARAPH, SYMBOL, MARK,
                        YAKOOT                       BADGE, PLUS, MINUS, SYMPTOM
"   squill .................. SCILLA        "   in magic .................. SIGIL
"   squirrel ............ CALABER           "   ; mus. .................. PRESA
"   steppe, people of .... KIRGIZES         "   , per. to a ................ SEMIC
"   swamp .............. URMAN              "   up ............... ENROL, HIRE
"   warehouse ............ ETAPE            signal ... CUE, PST, DOT, DASH, FLAG,
sibilance mark .............. CEDILLA                    FLARE, CURFEW, FAMOUS
sibilate ............. HISH, SISS, HISS     "   flag ................. ENSIGN
sibyl ....... SEERESS, ORACLE, WITCH        "   , railroad ............. FUSEE
Sibyl's cave ................ CUMAE         "   , spirit .................. TAP
Sicilian bull .............. PHALARIS       "   , warning .. ALARM, ALERT, CUE,
"   capital ........... PALERMO                                   SOS, PHAROS
"   evergreen ............ MAQUI            signaling siren ............ HOWLER
"   inhabitants .......... SICANI           signature ........ HAND, SEAL, SIGIL
"   province .. CATANIA, TRAPANI            "   , first word of ........ PRIMA
"   saffron ............. CROCUS            signify ........ DENOTE, BODE, IMPLY
"   secret society ...... MAF(F)IA          Signoret, Miss .............. SIMONE
"   sumac .............. TANNER             silage ................... FODDER
sick a dog on ................ SOOL         "Silas Marner" author ....... ELIOT
sick headache ............ MIGRAINE         silence OYER, OYEZ, CALM, OBLIVION,
sickle .... CROOK, HOOK, FALCATION                  LULL, QUIET, STILL, GAG, PAX, REST,
"   -shaped .............. FALCATE                                 MUFFLE, HUSH
sickness excuse .............. AEGER        silent ...... MUM, MUTE, TACIT, TACET
Siculi ....................... SICEL        Silesian town ................ OELS
Sicyon king ............... EPOPEUS         silex ...................... SILICA
Siddhartha ................ BUDDHA          silica ..................... SILEX
side .... JAMB, LATUS, FLANK, ASPECT,       silicate . MICA, CERITE, OPAL, EPIDOTE,
                          FACET                                        EUCLASE
"   dish ......... ENTREE, ENTREMETS        silk, brown ................. MUGA
"   kick ..................... PAS          "   , corded ............ CRIN, FAILLE
"   of head ......... LORA, LORUM           "   cotton tree ............ CEIBA
"   , per. to ........ COSTAL, LATERAL      "   fabric TASH, SAMITE, SATIN, TULLE,
sides, having unequal ...... SCALENE                            SENDAL, SURAH
sideslip ..................... SKID         "   filling .................. TRAM
sidetrack .... AVERT, SHUNT, DISTRACT       "   , gelatin .............. SERICIN
sidewalk edge ........... CURB, KERB        "   grass ................... ISTLE
sidewise .... ASKANCE, SLYLY, ASLANT        "   , half mask of; Fr. ........ LOUP
```

" hat .... CASTOR, TILE, TOPPER
" , India .... MUGA
" oak .... GREVILLEA
" , plain, glossy .... TAFFETA,
                                LUTESTRING
" , raw .... GREGE
" , reeling .... FILATURE
" , rustle of .... SCROOP
" , source of .... COCOON
" stuff; anc. .... TARSE
" tester .... DENIERER
" , thin .... ALAMODE
" thread ...... BAVE, FLOSS, TRAM
" , twill-woven ..... ALMA, TOBINE
" voile .... NINON
" waste .... NOIL
" , watered .... MOIRE, TABBY
silken .... SERIC
silkweed .... MILKWEED
silkworm .... ERI, ERIA, TUSSAH
" , Chin. ... AILANTHUS, TUSSUR
silkworm disease ...... UJI, PEBRINE
" ; genus .... BOMBYX
" , home of .... ASSAM
" , rel. to .... BOMBIC, FILATOR
silky dress material .... BAREGE
silly .. ASININE, APISH, INANE, DOTED
silver ARGENT(UM), COINS, STERLING,
                                CHANGE
" alloy; Ger. .... ALBATA
" amalgam, cone of .... PINA
" -and-gold alloy .... BILLON
" , ball of .... POME
" citrate .... ITROL
" , gilded .... VERMEIL
" in alchemy .... LUNA
" in ingots .... SYCEE
" lace .... FILIGREE
" , paved space for sorting . PATIO
" , symbol for .... AG
" , uncoined .... BULLION
silver-like alloy .. OCCAMY, NEOGEN
silversides ... SMELT, FRIAR, GRUNION
silversmith, famous .... REVERE
silybum .... MARIANA, THISTLE
simian .... APE, MONKEY
similar AKIN, LIKE, SUCH, HOMOGENE,
                                ANALOGOUS
simile METAPHOR, PARABLE, ANALOGY
simmer .... BOIL, BRAISE, SEETHE
simple .... OAFISH, MERE, NAIVE
simpleton ..... DAW, GUMP, MORON,
    NOODLE, GOWK, NINCOMPOOP,
    OAF, DUPE, BOOBY, ABSERITE
simulate .. FEIGN, APE, MOCK, SHAM,
                        MIMIC, PRETEND
simulation .... FEINT, PRETENSE
simurgh .... ROC
sin CRIME, ERR, EVIL, PECCANCY, VICE,
    TRESPASS, MISDEED, ERROR, LAPSE

since .. SITH, AGO, FOR, HENCE, SYNE
sincere ...... EARNEST, OPEN, INTENT
sinecure .... SNAP
sincerity symbol .... AMETHYST
sing CHIRP, LILT, CAROL, LAUD, CHANT,
                                YODEL
" with trills ... ROULADE, WARBLE
singer ... BARD, CAROLER, DESCANTER,
                MINSTREL, CHANTEUR
" , female ... CANTATRICE, DIVA,
                        CHANTEUSE
single .. SPORADIC, ACE, ALONE, ODD,
        ONE, UNAL, UNWED, SOLO
" ; not one of pair .... AZYGOUS
" thing .... UNIT, UNAL
singly .... SOLO, APART, KITHLESS
sinister ... EVIL, OMINOUS, LEFT, BAD,
                MALIGN, VICIOUS
sink FALL, MERGE, SYE, ENGULF, BOWL,
    GUTTER, BASIN, DOLINA, DROOP,
                                SAG
sinker ...... DIPSY, PLUMMET, WEIGHT
sinning .... PECCANT, ERRANT
sinuous ... WAVY, CROOKED, DEVIOUS
sinus .... BAY, BEND, CURVE
" in a bone ..... ANTRUM, ANTRA
Siouan Indian .... OTOE, IOWA
" tribe .... TETON
sip . LAP, SUCK, SUP, GULP, PEG, DRINK
sipper .... STRAW, TUBE
sippet ..... CROUTON, BIT, FRAGMENT
sire ...... BEGET, MALE, LORD, HORSE
siren .. FOGHORN, CHARMER, LORELEI,
    ALARM, ENTICER, CIRCE, MERMAID
" of the Nile .... CLEO
Sirius .... CANICULA
Sirocco .... KHAMSIN
sisal hemp .... HENEQUIN
Sisera, enemy of .... JAEL, BARAK
siskin .... FINCH, TARIN
sissified .... PRISSY, NICE, PRIM
sister .... SOROR, NUN, NURSE
sit .... MEET, PERCH, HATCH, POSE
site ...... SEAR, SITUS, STANCE, AREA
" of Taj Mahal .... AGRA
" of the pyramids .... GIZEH
Sitsang .... TIBET
sitting .... SEDENT, SEANCE, SESSION
" on .... ASTRIDE
situation .. CASE, SIEGE, POSE, STEAD,
                CRISIS, JOB, STATUS
Siva .... DESTROYER
" , trident of .... TRISULA
" , wife of ...... DEVI, DURGA, UMA
six-footed .... HEXAPOD
" , group of . HEXAD, SEXTET, SESTET
" in dicing .... SICE
" of a kind .... SEXTUPLET

262

```
"  , on basis of ............ SENARY        skirmish ... CLASH, FRAY, TILT, MELEE
"  -pointed figure .............. STAR       skirt PEPLUM, KIRTLE, KILT, MINI, MAXI,
sixth asteroid ................. HEBE                                              MIDI
"   sense ..................... ESP          "   in armor ............... TASSET
sixty sixties ............ SAR, SAROS        "   section ................. PANEL
size .... BULK, CALIBER, MASS, EXTENT,       skit ........ CAPER, JOKE, PLAY, QUIP
                             VOLUME          skittle(s) .... NINEPINS, GAME, PIN
skate ... RAY, GLIDE, SKI, SKIM, MISER       skoal .. SLAINTE, CUP, HEALTH, TOAST
skein ... HANK, RAP, MESH, WEB, COIL         skulk ........... LURK, STEAL, SNEAK
skeleton ... BONES, (F)RAME, ATOMY,          skull .............. CRANIUM, SCAP
                CAGE, CADRE, SPONGE          "  , cavity of .............. FOSSA
"   of ship; adjusted .... RAMED             "   measure ......... CRANIOMETER
skeptic .. DOUBTER, APORETIC, CYNIC,         "  , part of ............ ASTERION
        THOMAS, INFIDEL, AGNOSTIC            "  , per. to ................. INIAL
sketch ...... IDEA, MAP, ANA, DRAFT,         "  , point of junction in ... BREGMA
     DOODLE, DRAW, LIMN, SKIT, CHART         "  , protuberance of ....... INION
skewer ... TRUSS, PIN, SKIVER, STAPLE        skullcap ... YAMILKE, CALOTTE, PILEUS
skid ........ SIDESLIP, TRAVOIS, TRIG        skunk .... POLECAT, HURON, SMELLER,
skiff ................ CAIGUE, SCAPHE                                        CONEPATE
skiing term SLALOM, SCHUSS, WEDELN,          "   -like animal ............ ZORIL
            VORLAGE, SITZMARK                sky .... TIEN, LANGI, WELKIN, VAULT,
skill ... APTITUDE, KNACK, ART, CRAFT,                                    FIRMAMENT
             TECHNIC, FINESSE                "   blue ............ AZURE, CELESTE
skilled mechanical work ...... SLOYD         skylark; genus ............ ALAUDA
skillful DEFT, DEDAL, APT, FIT, HABILE,      slab ... TABLET, STELE, DALLE, PLAQUE
            VERSED, HANDY                    "  -like .................... STELAR
"   operator ........ TACTICIAN              slack .... LAX, LOOSE, REMISS, FRESE,
skim ....... SCUD, RIND, FLIT, SCOON                                         CHAFF
skin .... PARE, BARK, RIND, EPIDERMIS,       slacken ............. RELAX, REPOSE
     PEEL, SUEDE, DERMA, FUR, KIP,           slacker ..................... SPIV
     COAT, FLAY, HIDE, HUSK, EPICARP,        slacks ............ DUFFS, TROUSERS
                             CUTIS           slag .. DROSS, SCORIA, LAVA, CINDERS
"   affection ........ ACNE, PRURITUS        slam ........ RAP, BANG, SHUT, VOLE
"  , beaver ................. PLEW           slander DEFAME, BELIE, ASPERSE, LIBEL
"  ; dark ................. MELANIC          "  , political .. SMEAR, ROORBACK
"   decoration ............. TATTOO          slang ....... DIALECT, ARGOT, LINGO,
"  , destitute of .......... APELLOUS                     JARGON, PATOIS, CANT
"   disease ....... ERYSIPELAS, ACNE,        slant ......... SLOPE, BEVEL, SKEW
                             ECZEMA          slash ...... DAG, JAG, SLISH, REDUCE
"  , dryness of ............ XEROSIS         slat STAVE, TRANSOM, BATTEN, SPLINE
"   eruption .... EXANTHEM, MACULA           slate .. ENROL, RAG, SCHIST, AGENDA,
"   finishing ................. TAW                                       ROLL, TILE
"  ; fold .................... PLICA         "   hammer ................ SAX
"  , layer of ....... TEGUMENT, DERM         slater's tool .............. ZAT, ZAX
"   layers ................. CORIA           slattern MOPSY, CRONE, TROLLOP, SLUT
"  , of .............. DERMIC, DERIC         slaughterer .......... KNACKER
"   of an animal PELLAGE, PELL, PELT         Slav ...... CROAT, SERB, YUGO, POLE
"   of walnut ................. ZEST         slave ESNE, NEIF, SERF, HELOT, THRALL,
"   oil ..................... SEBUM               VASSAL, DRUDGE, DASI, ILOT
"  , redness of .............. RUBOR         "   block ............... CATASTA
skin-diving apparatus ... AQUALUNG           "  , female . ODALISK, BAUBO, IAMBE
skinflint ...... CHEAT, SCREW, PELTER        "  , fighting ............ MAMELUK
skink ................ ADDA, LIZARD          slaver ........ DRIVEL, DROOL, FAWN
Skinner, Cornelia .............. OTIS        slaves, dealer in ........... MANGO
skins, number of fur ........ TIMBER         slaw ................ SALAD, RELISH
"  , rug of .............. CAROSS            slay ............ KILL, LYNCH, BURKE
"  , season .......... SAM, SAMMY            sled ..... TOBOGGAN, TODE, SLEDGE,
skip ... FRISK, DAP, HIP, OMIT, CAPER,                                       SLEIGH
                    JUMP, RICOCHET           sleep ..... NAP, DOSS, WINK, SOPOR,
skipper ............. RAS, SERANG                 SIESTA, FLOP, DROWSE, DOZE
```

" as a deity .... SOMNUS
" , causing .... NARCOSE
" , god of .... HYPNOS
" , inducing .... SOPORIFIC
" , insensibility in .... COMA
" , wander in .... DWALE
sleeper .... CAR, DORMEUSE, SUPPORT,
BEAM, TIE
sleeping .... LATENT, DORMANT
" pill .... GOOFBALL, SOPORIFIC
" place ...... COT, BUNK, BERTH
" -sickness source .... TSETSE
sleepy .... NARCOTIC, OSCITANT
sleeve .... MOGGAN, POKE
sleeveless garment ABA, CADE, MANTLE
sleigh box .... PUNG
" runner .... SHOE
" , sidepiece of a .... RAVE
slender LANK, LEAN, SLIM, REEDY, TRIM,
LITHE, SPARE, PRIN, LISSOME
" woman .... SYLPH
sleuth .. DETECTIVE, TEC, HAWKSHAW,
COP, DICK, GUMSHOE
" hound .... TALBOT
slice .... CUT, SLAB, GASH, LAYER,
COL(LO)P, CANTLE, FLAP, RASHER
slick, post-hole .... LOY
slide SKID, SLEW, SLUE, COAST, CHUTE
" fastener .... ZIPPER
sliding piece .... PISTON, CAM
slight ... CUT, FAINT, NEGLECT, SNUB,
SLUR, IGNORE
slime .... GLEET, ICHOR, OOZE
" deposit .... SILT, MUCK, MUD
slingshot .... PEASHOOTER, CATAPULT,
SHANGHAI
slip ERR, IMP, PEW, SLIVE, BULL, TWIG,
BERTH, BONER, LAPSE, GAFFE
" secretly .... CREEM
slipknot .... NOOSE, SNITTLE
slipper . SANDAL, MULE, PUMP, ROMEO,
BABOUCHE
slippery ... SLY, ELUSIVE, GLIB, FICKLE,
SHIFTY, SHUTTLE, EELY
slither .... SIDLE, SLIDE
sloe .... HAW, PLUM
slogan ..... CRY, MOTTO, SHIBBOLETH
slope ... SCARP, GLACIS, CANT, RAMP,
SPLAY, HADE, RISE
sloping bank .... BRAE
" edge .... BASIL, BEZEL
sloth . INDOLENCE, INERTIA, UNAU, AI
" monkey .... LORIS
sloughing .... ECDYSIS
slovenly SLIPSHOD, FROWZY, SLATTERN
slow DELAY, RELAX, LATE, TRAILY, INERT,
POKY
" ; mus. ... LARGO, LENTO, TARDO,
ADAGIO, ANDANTE
sludge .... MIRE, MUD, SLEET

slug ... DRONE, SNAIL, BULLET, CLUMP,
RATTLE
" , sea .... TREPANG
sluggish .. DRONY, FOUL, INERT, DOPY
slugs; genus .... LIMAX
sluice .... GOUT, CLOW, VENT, FLUME
slur ...... INNUENDO, BLUR, MACKLE,
STIGMA, ELIDE
sly .... ARCH, CAGEY, COVERT, SNAKY,
FELINE, WARY, WILY
smack KISS, TANG, TASTE, BUSS, SNAP,
BLOW, SLOOP
small .. WEE, PETIT, MINUSCULE, PINK,
TOT, LITTLE, LIL, TINY, DINKY,
PALTRY, BANTAM
" amount .... TRACE, MITE, DRAM
" anvil .... TEEST
" area .... AREOLA
" bomb .... PETARD
" bunch .... WISP
" car .... COMPACT
" flag .... FANION
" glass of liquor .... PONY
" group .... SQUAD
" insect .... GNAT
" insect pest .... THRIPS
" loudspeaker .... TWEETER
" person .... MIDGE
" piece ...... MORCEAU, SNIPPET
" rope .... MARLINE
" saddle horse .... NAG
" ; Scot .... SMA
" shield .... ECU
smallage .... CELERY, MARCH
smaller; comb. form .... MIO
smallest component of matter ......
ELECTRON, ATOM
smallness .... EXILITY
smallpox .... VARIOLA
smaragd .... EMERALD
smart . CHIC, TRIM, POSH, TRIG, NATTY,
NIFTY, DAPPER, STING
smash .... STAVE, BASH, RUIN
smatterer .... SCIOLIST, DABBLER
smear ... DAUB, GAUM, GLAIR, GORM
smell .... SCENT, FLAIR, ODOR, REEK
" , offensive .... FEOR, STENCH
smelt .... SCORIFY, FUSE, PRIM
" ; fish .... EPERLAN, INANGA
smelting by-product .... SLAG
" mixture .... MATTE
smile ... FLEER, FAVOR, LAUGH, GRIN,
SIMPER, SMIRK
smiling .... AGRIN, RIDENT, MERRY
smirch SMUDGE, SULLY, TARNISH, BLOT,
STAIN
smirk .... LEER, SIMPER, GRIN
smite .... VISIT, AFFLICT, STRIKE
smith .... FORGER, BOSSER, MIME
smithereen .... CHIP, FLINDER

smitten .... ENAMORED, EPRIS
smock ...... CAMISE, CHEMISE, TUNIC
smoke ...... FLOC, CURE, LUNT, REEK,
                  SMUDGE, SMAZE, SMOG
  "   signaler .... INDIAN
smokeless powder .... FILITE
smoking apparatus ..... NARG(H)ILE
  " , cure by .... REEST
smoky .... FUMID, REEKY
smooth .... LENE, OILY, PAVE, SUANT,
                BLAND, GLIB, URBANE
  " ; comb. form .... LIO
  " ; mus. .... LEGATO
  "   over ... GLOSS, GLOZE, CALM
  " , to .... DUB, EVEN, IRON
smother ..... STIFLE, CHOKE, REPRESS
smudge . SMEAR, SMOKE, SPOT, GRIME
snack .... CANAPE, BITE, MORSEL
snafu .... MUDDLE(D)
snail HELICID, HELIX, PERIWINKLE, SLUG,
       DODMAN, SNAG, DRILL, WHELK
  " ; genus .. NERITA, TRITON, MITRA
snake .... VIPER, REPTILE, SERPENT,
             INGRATE, OPHIDIAN
  " , Asian . DABOIA, JESSUR, BONGA
  " , black .... RACER
  " , bluish .... KRAIT
  " -charmer's flute .... PUNGI
  " , deadly .. COBRA, MAMBA, HABU
  " , deity .... ZOMBI
  " , Egypt .... ASP
  "   eyes .... AMBSACE, ONES
  " , Florida .... MOCCASIN
  " ; python .... ANACONDA
  " , sand .... ERYX
  " , S. Amer. .... ABOMA, BOM
snake-bite aid ...... GUACO, CEDRON
snake-haired woman .... MEDUSA,
       GORGON, STHENO, EURYALE
snake-like .... SERPENTINE, SINUOUS,
                   OPHIOID
snaky .... ANGUINE
snap ...... FILLIP, PHOTO, POP, ELAN
snapper ..... BREAM, PARGO, GUBERA
snare . NET, GIN, GUM, TRAP, NOOSE,
     TRAPAN, WIRE, MESH, PITFALL,
              SPRINGE, DECOY
snark .... BOOJUM
snarl .... TANGLE, GNAR, SNAR, YIRR,
              GROWL, KNOT
snatch .... WRAP, SEIZE, GRAB, FILCH,
              PILFER, EREPT
sneak ...... SPY, LURK, SLINK, SNOOP
snee .... DIRK
sneer .... FLEER, SCORN, GIBE, JIBE
sneeze ..... NEESE, SNUFF, CONTEMPT
sneezing .... ERRHINE, STERNUTATION
sneezewort .... PTARMICA
snell .... SNOOD, TIPPET
snicker ..... SNIGGER, TITTER, LAUGH

sniff .... NOSE, SCENT, SNUFF
snipe .... BLEATER, SCAPE, WADER
  "   eel .... THREAD
  "   hawk .... HARRIER
snob ...... PARVENU, BRAHMIN, PRIG
snobbish . UPPISH, ARROGANT, PROUD
snood .... FILLET, SNELL, HAIRNET
snoop .. LURK, PRY, SLY, PROWL, SKULK
snore .... RALE, RHONCHUS, SNIFF
snoring .... STERTOR(OUS)
snout .... NOSE, NOZZLE, GROIN, NEB
snow .... FIRN, PASH, SLEET, SNA
  " , field of .... NEVE
  "   fly, genus .... BOREUS
  "   grouse .... PTARMIGAN
  "   house .... IGLO(O), IGLOE
  " ; Latin for .... NIX, NIVIS
  "   mouse .... VOLE
snowflake .... CRYSTAL
Snowman, Abominable .... YETI
snow runner .... SLED, SKEE, SKI
snowshoe .... PAC, PATTEN, SKI
snowy .... NIVAL, NIVEOUS
snub .... REBUFF, SLIGHT, SNOOL
snuff .... NOSE, MACCABOY, RAPPEE
snuffbox .... MULL, TABATIERE
  "   bean .... CACOON
snug ...... COZY, COSY, HOMY, TRIG
so ERGO, THUS, SAE, SIC, HENCE, TRUE,
                    VERY
  "   be it .... AMEN
  "   much .... TANTO
soak SATURATE, RET, SOP, SOUSE, DIP,
               IMBRUE, SOG
  "   in brine .... MARINATE
soap ...... SAPO, SUDS, BRIBERY, RUB
  " , convert into .... SAPONIFY
  " -frame bar .... SESS
  "   liniment .... OPODELDOC
  "   plant .... AMOLE
  "   suds ..... FOAM, FROTH, LATHER
  "   vine .... GOGO
soapless soap .... DETERGENT
soap-like compound .... SAPONUL
soapstone .... TALC
soar .... FLIT, SAIL, WING, ARISE
soaring ... FLYING, HIGH, TOWERING
  "   in spirit .... ESSORANT
sob .... SIMPER, YOOP, SAB, SITHE
sober . DOUCE, SEDATE, GRAVE, STAID
sobriquet .... AGNAME, ALIAS
social .... CIVIL, CIVIC, TEA, GENIAL
  "   group CLAN, CASTE, SEPT, TRIBE
  "   insect .... ANT, BEE
  "   outcast .... PARIAH
  "   standing .... ESTATE
  "   system .... REGIME
socialist .... FOURIER, FABIAN, MARX,
                ENGELS, DEBS

society ..... LODGE, ETHNOS, ORDER, GUILD, CLASS, CLUB
" , entrance into .... DEBUT
" , foreign VEREIN, BUND, MAFIA
" swell .... NOB
sock .... VAMP(EY), TABI
" , and _____ .... BUSKIN
sockdolager .... FACER, ONER
socket .. MORTISE, ORBIT, POD, HOSE, SHOE, OUTLET
Socrates, disciple of ... PLATO, CRITO
" , wife of .... XANTHIPPE
sod ..... SWARD, PEAT, TURF, SEETHE, GLEBE
" oil .... DEGRAS
soda .... SALERATUS
" ash, per. to .... ALKALINE
" -ash plant .... BARILLA
" from seaweeds .... VAREC
" niter .... SALTPETRE
sodden ...... SOAK, BOILED, SOGGY
sodium carbonate (A)NATRON, TRONA
" chloride .... SAL, SALT
" oxide .... SODA
" , symbol of .... NA
sofa ..... SETTEE, CANAPE, CAUSEUSE, DIVAN, SETTLE, TETEATETE
soft .... EASY, LOW, MILD, TENDER
" drink .... ADE, POP, COLA, SODA
" hair .... VILLUS
" job .... SNAP, SINECURE
" palate, per. to ... VELAR, UVULAR
" soap .... BLANDISH, BLARNEY
" -spoken .... MEALY
soften ...... MITIGATE, THAW, ALLAY, TEMPER, MACERATE, RELAX
" by kneading .... MALAXATE
" leather .... SAM
" meat fibers .... TENDERIZE
" skins .... TAW
softening, having quality of LENITIVE
softly; It. .... SOAVE
soggy ...... HEAVY, WET, DULL, DAMP
soil .... GLEBE, LAND, LOAM, MARL, HUMUS, DEFILE
" , sub- .... SOLE
solace .... CHEER, CONSOLE, SOOTHE
solan goose .... GANNET
solar disk .... ATEN, ATON
" lamp .... ARGAND
" system, device for showing .... ORRERY
solder .... BRAZE, FUSE, WELD, UNITE
soldier ...... VET, CADET, CHASSEUR, GUFFY, GI, WARRIOR, BUCKSKIN, TOMMY, ANZAC
" bandit .... LADRONE
" , cavalry ..... UHLAN, LANCER
." , French ...... POILU, ZOUAVE
" , Gaelic .... KERN

" , Greek ... MYRMIDON, HOPLITE
" , Indo-British .... SEPOY
" , Moroccan .... ASKAR
soldiers, body of COHORT, MACARONI, LEGION, PLATOON, SQUAD
" , overcoat of .... CAPOTE
" , shelter of ... FOXHOLE, ABRI
sole ...... MERE, FISH, SLADE, ALONE
" of the foot .... PELMA
" of the foot, per. to ... PLANTAR
" , thin inner .... RAND
solemn ...... AUGUST, GRAVE, SOBER
Solenodon .... AGOUTA, ALMIQUE
sol-fa syllables . DO, RE, MI, FA, SOL, LA, SI, TE
solicit .. APPLY, SUE, ASK, BEG, COURT, DRUM, WOO, LOBBY, CANVASS
solicitation ..... INSTANCE, PETITION
solid ...... PRISM, CONE, CUBE, HARD
solidification ..... GELATION, UNION
solidified lava .... COULEE
solidify ...... GEL, SET, HARDEN, JELL
solitary ...... ALONE, SULLEN, SOLE, HERMETICAL, UNIQUE
" ; comb. form .... EREMO
solo .... ALONE, SELF, SPADILLA
Solomon .... JEDIDIAH
Solomon Is. harbor .... KIETA
solon ... LEGISLATOR, SAGE, SENATOR
solution .... KEY, HYPO
" strength .... TITER, TITRE
solve .... DETECT, EXPLAIN, UNDO
solvent ACETONE, ALCOHOL, CUMENE, KETONE, PHENOL
Somaliland capital .... BERBERA
some ... ANY, ONE, SEVERAL, BODY
somersault .... FLIP, LEAP
somewhat .... PART, RATHER
son .... HEIR, MALE, FITZ, MAC, DAUPHIN, SCION, FILS
" , younger .... CADET
son-in-law .... GENER
sonance .... SOUND, TUNE
sonata; closing measure ...... CODA
song(s) .. CAROL, DITTY, MELOS, LIED, LEED, LIEDER, CHANTY, DITE, CHANSON, CANZONE, MELOS, MELIC, NOEL, ANTHEM
" , after- .... EPODE
" composition .... LYRIC
" , depressing .... BLUES
" , merry ...... GLEE, LAY, LILT
" , mystic .... RUNE
" of lamentation ... THRENODY
" of Solomon .... CANTICLE
" of triumph .... PAEAN
" , part .... FALA, MADRIGAL
" , per. to ...... MELIC, ARIOSE, LYRICAL
" , sacred .... MOTET, PSALM

" , short .... ARIETTA, ODE
" twin .... GYMEL
songbird . LARK, VEERIE, VEERY, FINCH,
PIROL, AMSEL, PIPIT, ORIOLE,
THRUSH, WARBLER
songcraft .... POESY
sonnet; last six lines .... SESTET
soon .... BETIMES, ERELONG, PRONTO,
TITE, ANON, IMMEDIATE
sooner .... ERST, ERE(R)
soot .... GRIME, CROCK, SMUT, DIRT
" , particle of .... IZLE
" ; sawdust ...... COOM, COOMB
soothe .... SALVE, CALM, EASE, ALLAY,
COMPOSE, LULL
soothing .... ANODYNE, LENITIVE
soothsayer .. CHALDEAN, AUGUR, SEER,
WEIRD, PALMIST, PYTHON, SPAER,
HARUSPEX, ORACLE
sophism .... ELENCH, FALLACY
sopor .... COMA, LETHARGY
soporific .... ANODYNE, OPIATE
soprano VOICE, CANTO, TREBLE, PONS,
ALDA, BORI, CALLAS, STEBER, PRICE
sora .... CRAKE, RAIL
sorcerer .. CONJURER, WIZARD, MAGUS
sorceress LAMIA, HELIOS, CIRCE, SIREN,
USHA, WITCH
sorcery .... OBEAH, OBI, OBE, MAGIC,
VOODOO, HOODOO
sorghum .... IMPHEE, FETERITA
" , grain . SORGO, CUSH, DURRA,
DARI, MILLET, DOURA(H)
sorrel, wood .... OCA
sorrow ...... BALE, RUE, RUTH, TEEN,
LAMENT, GRIEF, RUING, DOLOR,
WAIL
sorrowful .. DOLENT, SAIRY, BLUE, SAD
sorry .... DICKEY, REGRET, PITY
sort .... BLEND, CULL, ILK, STRAIN
sortie .... RAID, FORAY, SALLY
so so ...... AVERAGE, FAIR, MIDDLING
sot . DRUNKARD, TIPPLER, BIBBER, TOPER
soul ..... EGO, PNEUMA, SPIRIT, AME,
PRANA, JIVATMA, PSYCHE, ANIMA
" , destiny of the .... THEODICY
" devastators .... HARPIES
" , Sanskrit .... ATMAN
sound . BAY, FIRM, GLUB, HALE, PLUMB,
VALID, FATHOM
" , adventitious, in chest . RALE
" , deep .... BONG
" frequencies .... AUDIO
" , harsh ...... GRIDE, SCROOP
" loudly .... BLARE
" : metallic ring .. CLINK, TING,
CLANK
sound of a bullet ... PING, ZIP, PRUT
" of hoof beats .... CLOP
" , per. to ...... SONANT, SONIC

sound-absorbing pane .... GOBO
soup .... PUREE, POTAGE, CONSOMME,
BISQUE, BISK, OKRA, POTTAGE
sour .... WRY, ACERB, ACRID, ACID(IC)
" ; as of the stomach ...... ACOR
" -gum tree .. NYSSA, STINKWOOD
" in aspect . DOUR, HARD, SULLEN
" ; like vinegar .... ACETOSE
" milk .... BLEEZE
" temper, of .... MOROSE
" , turning .... ACESCENT, PRILL
" voice .... GRUM, GRUFF
source ...... FONS, FOUNTAIN, FONT,
ORIGIN, SPRING
" of ipecac .... EVEA
" of veratrin .... SABADILLA
soutane .... CASSOCK
south .. AUSTER, DIXIE, SUR, SUD, MIDI
South African (see also "African") .
BOER
South American (see also "American")
LATIN, ARGENTINE, ARGENTINO,
CHILENO, CHILEAN, BOLIVIAN
South Carolina capital .... COLUMBIA
South Dakota capital .... PIERRE
" " Indian .... BRULE
South Wales, people of ..... SILURES
southern .... AUSTRAL, AUSTRINE,
MERIDIONAL
" constellation ..... DORADO,
PAVO
southwester .... SQUAM
sovereign . PRINCE, LIEGE, SOV, CHIEF,
RULER, IMPERIAL, SUPERIOR, QUID
" decree .... ARRET
" pardon .... AMNESTY
sovereignties .... STATES
sovereignty ... EMPERY, RAJ, SCEPTRE,
DYNASTY, SWAY
Soviet news agency .... TASS
" Union founder .... LENIN
sow .... SCATTER, SEED, PLANT
sow bug ..... SLATER, LOUSE, ISOPOD
" thistle ...... SONCHUS, DINDY,
GUTWEED
sow, young .... YELT, GILT
soybean enzyme .... URASE
spa .... SPRING, BADEN, EMS, BATH
space .. ROOM, OPEN, EXTENT, WHILE,
AREA, AREOLA, PERIOD, INTERVAL,
HIATUS
" between bird's eye and bill ...
LORE
" dog .... STREIKA, LAIKA
" for refueling .. APRON, TARMAC
" monkey .. ENOS, ABLE, BAKER
" traveler .... ASTRONAUT,
COSMONAUT, COSMONETTE
" vehicle SPACECRAFT, SPACESHIP,
MODULE

267

spade SHOVEL, LOY, PICK, SPUD, SLANE,
　　　SLADE, PEEL, DIG, SPITTER, GRUB
spado .... SWORD
Spain, famous palace in ... ESCURIAL
　" , Moorish capital of . CORDOVA
　" , province in .... AVILA, SORIA,
　　　　　　　　　　　　　JAEN
　" , river in ... DUERO, EBRO, ESLA,
　　　　　　　　　　　　　TAGUS
　" , seaport of .... PALOS
　" , ter. division of ...... PARTIDO
spall .... GALLET, CHIP, SPLINTER
span; in inches .... NINE
spangle .... PAILLETTE, SEQUIN
Spaniard .... DIEGO, IBERIAN
Spanish abbot .... ABAD
　" ache .... DOLER
　" after .... TRAS
　" afternoon .... TARDE
　" age .... EDAD
　" all .... TODO
　" Am. biscuit .... PANAL
　" Am. farm HACIENDA, RANCH
　" Am. gruel .... ATOLE
　" apron .... DELANTAL
　" article .. EL, LA, LO, UN, LAS,
　　　　　　LOS, UNA, UNAS, UNOS
　" as .... COMO
　" aunt .... TIA
　" bad .... MALO
　" ball .... BOLA
　" bath .... BANO
　" bay .... BISCAY, BAHIA
　" be .... ESTAR
　" beak .... PICO
　" bean .... HABA
　" bear .... OSO
　" beard .... BARBA
　" beautiful .... BELLO
　" because of .... POR
　" bed .... CAMA
　" behind .... TRAS
　" being .... ENTE, SER
　" belle of lower class ... MAJA
　" black .... NEGRA
　" blanket ..... SERAPE, MANTA
　" blue .... AZUL
　" boat .... BARCA, BARCO
　" bonnet .... GORRA
　" booth or shop ..... TIENDA
　" box .... CAJA
　" boy .... NINO
　" bravo .... OLE
　" brigand .... LADRONE
　" broncho buster ..... GINETE
　" broth .... CALDO
　" brush .... CEPILLO
　" bull .... TORO
　" but .... PERO
　" by .... POR

　" calico .... PERCAL
　" cape .... CAPA
　" card game .... HOMBRE
　" cash .... CAJA
　" castle .... ALCAZAR
　" cat .... GATO
　" cellar .... BODEGA
　" cellist .... CASALS
　" chance .... ACASO
　" change .... CAMBIO
　" chaperone .... DUENNA
　" chief .... ADALID, JEFE
　" child ... NINO, HIJO, CHICO
　" city ... LERIDA, AVILA, CADIZ,
　　　ELCHE, JEREZ, PALMA, GIJON,
　　　　　　　MALAGA, RONDA
　" cloak ..... CAPA, MANTA
　" cloth, woolen .... PANO
　" coffee ...... CAFE, CAFETAL
　" coin ..... DINERO, CENTAVO,
　PESETA, CUARTO, DOBLA, PISTOLE
　" cold .... FRIO
　" collar .... CUELLO
　" commander .... CID
　" composer .... FALLA
　" construction .... OBRA
　" convict .... PRESO
　" cord .... SOGA
　" council .... JUNTA
　" court .... PATIO
　" cow .... VACA
　" cowboy ... RESERO, GAUCHO
　" creek .... ARROYO
　" cupboard .... TROSTERA
　" cut .... TAJO
　" dance ...... JALEO, BOLERO,
　　CARIOCA, DANZA, FANDANGO
　" dance affair .... BAILE
　" daughter .... HIJA
　" dear .... CARO
　" diacritical mark ..... TILDE
　" dinner .... COMIDA
　" direction .... LADO
　" dish .... OLLA
　" dog .... PERRO
　" dollar .. PESO, PIASTER, DURO
　" donkey .... ASNO
　" dove .... PALOMA
　" dress .... TRAJE, FALDA
　" drink .... PULQUE
　" duck .... PATO
　" duty, impost ..... INDULTO
　" dynasty .... OMMIAD
　" each .... CADA
　" ear .... OIDO
　" east .... ESTE
　" egg .... HUEVO
　" elbow .... CODO
　" estuary .... RIA
　" evening ...... NOCHE, TARDE

268

"	event .... ACTO	"	it .... ELLO
"	every .... TODO	"	jack .... GATO
"	evil .... MALO	"	jar .... OLLA, TINAJA
"	eye .... OJO	"	judge .... JUEZ
"	face .... CARA	"	kernel .... HABA
"	fascist .... FALANGIST	"	kettle .... TETERA
"	father .... PADRE	"	kettledrum .... ATABAL
"	feast day .... FIESTA	"	king .... REY
"	few .... POCOS	"	kingdom .... ARAGON
"	finger .... DEDO	"	kiss .... BESO
"	fire .... FUEGO	"	knife .... CUCHILLO
"	flat lowland ...... MARISMA	"	knight .... CABALLERO
"	fleet .... CARAVAL	"	laborer .... PEON
"	float .... NADAR	"	lace .... ENCAJE
"	fly .... MOSCA	"	lady .... DAMA
"	food .... COMIDO	"	lake .... ALBUFERA, LAGO
"	for .... POR	"	landlady .... DUENA
"	fox .... ZORRO	"	landlord .... DUENO
"	friend .... AMIGO	"	landmark .... SENAL
"	gait .... PASO	"	lasso .... RIATA
"	game ..... PELOTA, MONTE	"	legislature .... CORTES
"	garlic .... AJO	"	leisure .... OCIO
"	gentleman .. GRANDE, SENOR	"	light cavalryman .. GERENTE
"	girl .... NINA, CHICA	"	lighthouse .... FARO
"	God .... DIOS	"	linen .... HILO, LIENZO
"	goddess .... DIOSA	"	little . POCO, CHICO, ENANO
"	gold .... ORO	"	located .... SITO
"	good-bye .... ADIOS	"	lookout tower ..... MIRADOR
"	governess .... DUENNA	"	loud .... ALTO
"	government obligation	"	; love, to .... AMAR
	CEDULA	"	low .... BAJO
"	grate, grille .... REJA	"	mackerel ...... CERO, SIERRA
"	grocery store ...... BODEGA	"	man .... HOMBRE
"	guitarist .... SEGOVIA	"	manager .... GERENTE
"	gypsy .... GITANO	"	mantle .... CAPA
"	hair .... PELO	"	mast .... ASTA
"	half-breed .... LADINO	"	master DUENO, AMO, SENOR
"	hall .... SALA	"	mattress .... COLCHON
"	hand .... MANO	"	maybe .... ACASO
"	harbor .... PUERTO	"	mayor .... ALCALDE
"	hat ...... SOMBRERO, BOINA	"	meadow .... VEGA
"	have .... TENER	"	meal .... COMIDA
"	head .... TESTA	"	measure .... DEDO, ESTADAL,
"	herdsman RANCHERO, RESERO		VARA
"	here .... AQUI	"	meat .... CARNE
"	hero .... CID	"	missile .... BOLA
"	high .... ALTO	"	mode of execution GARROTE
"	hill .... LOMA	"	monetary unit ...... PESETA
"	hither .... ACA	"	monkey .... MONO
"	holiday .... FIESTA	"	mother .... MADRE
"	home .... CASA	"	mountain .... GREDOS, GATA
"	horn .... ASTA	"	mountain range .... SIERRA
"	horse .... JENNET	"	mounts, relay of ... REMUDA
"	house .... CASA, CASITA	"	mouse .... RATON
"	how .... COMO	"	mouth .... BOCA
"	husband .... ESPOSO	"	muffler .... EMBOZO
"	hush .... CHITO	"	nap .... PELO
"	inlet .... RIA	"	new .... NUEVO
"	inn . POSADA, VENTA, FONDA	"	night .... NOCHE
"	island .... BALEARIC, CANARY		

269

" north	NORTE	" soprano	BORI
" novelist	MIGUEL	" soul	ALMA, ANIMO
" nun	MONJA	" sound	SANO
" officer	ALCALDE	" south	SUR
" only	SOLO, UNICO	" spear	ASTA
" pace	PASO	" stock farm	RANCHO
" painter	SERT, DALI, MIRO, GOYA, PICASSO	" stream	ARROYO
" past	PASADO	" strong	RECIO
" pastime	OCIO	" summer	ESTIO
" peak	CIMA, PICO	" summit	CIMA
" pianist	ITURBI	" sweetheart	ALMO
" people	GENTE	" swim	NADAR
" perhaps	ACASO	" table	MESA, TABLA
" plain	VEGA	" table cloth	MANTEL
" plainsman	LLANERO	" take	TOMAR
" plantation	FINCA, HACIENDA	" there	ALLA, ALLI, AHI
" play	JUEGO	" thief	LADRON
" police	RURALES	" thimble	DEDAL
" poor	POBRE, ROTO	" thing	COSA
" post office	CORREO	" through	POR
" prairie	PAMPA	" thus	ASI
" press	PRENSA	" time	VEZ
" printed matter	IMPRESOS	" title	DON(A), HIDALGO, SENOR(A), SENORITA
" prisoner	PRESO	" today	HOY
" property	FINCA	" toe	DEDO
" public garden	ALAMEDA	" town	CABRA, TOLEDO, LORCA, IRUN
" purchase	MERCA		
" purse	BOLSA	" treasure ship	GALLEON
" queen	REINA, ENA	" uncle	TIO
" quick	VELOZ	" under	BAJO
" ragged	ROTO	" until	HASTA
" rapier	BILBO	" very	MUY
" red	ROJO	" vessel	CARAVEL, GALLEON
" repairs	OBRA	" village	ALDEA
" ribbon	CINTA	" waistcoat	CHALECO
" rich	RICO	" walking stick	BASTON
" river	EBRO, TAGUS, RIO, MINO, TAJO	" warmth	CALOR
" roast	ASAR	" watch	RELOJ
" room	LADO	" watchtower	ATALAYA
" rope	SOGA	" wave	ONDA
" rum	RON	" wax	CERA
" sailing vessel	ZABRA	" weight	ARROBA, GRANO, TOMIN
" saint	TERESA, DOMINIC, EULALIA	" west	OESTE
" seaport	ADRA, BILBAO, MALAGA, ALMERIA	" where	DONDE
		" white	ALBO
" see	VER	" whole	TODO
" sheep	MERINO	" why	COMO
" sheet	SABANA	" wine	TINTA
" sherry	OLOROSA, XERES	" wine shop	VENTA
" ship	NAVIO	" woman	MUJER, MAJA
" shirt	CAMISA	" work	OBRA
" short	BAJO	" yesterday	AYER
" side	LADO	" young	NINO, NINA
" sign	SENAL	spank	CANE, CHASTISE, PUNISH
" silver	PLATA	spanker	SAIL
" son	HIJO	spanner	WRENCH, TOOL, KEY
" soon	LUEGO	spar	MAST, RUNG, BOOM, YARD
		" , extremity of	YARDARM

" , small .... SPRIT
" , to .... DISPUTE, BOX
" , upper .... TOPMAST, GAFF
spare .. SCANT, LANKY, LENTEN, THIN,
                        EXTRA, GAUNT
spark . FUNK, IZLE, ARC, GLINT, FLASH
sparked .... ARCED
sparkle . CORUSCATE, GLEAM, GLISTEN
sparrow PHILIP, WEAVERBIRD, TOWHEE,
                    SPADGER, CHIPPY
Spartan .... HARDY, STOIC(AL)
   "   bondman .... HELOT
   "   commander ...... LOCHAGE
   "   king .... AGIS, LEONIDAS
   "   lawgiver .... LYCURGUS
   "   magistrate .... EPHOR
   "   parchment .... SCYTALE
   "   slave .... ILOT, HELOT
   "   tyrant .... NABIS
spasm ... GRIP, THROE, CONVULSION,
       CHOREA, CRAMP, ICTUS, FIT, TIC
spat .... GAITER, ROW, TIFF, SLAP
spate .... FLOOD, FRESHET, POND
spatial .... STERIC, SPACE
spatter ...... SLOSH, SPRINKLE, SALLY
spatula .... SLICE, SPADE, THIVEL
   " -shaped .... LYRATE
spawn ...... EGGS, OVA, ROE, BEGET
speak .... LISP, ACCOST, CARP, MOOT,
   SAY, BARK, ORATE, UTTER, DECLAIM
   " , inability to .. APHASIA, ALALIA
   " noisily .... RANT
   " ; to noise abroad .... BRUIT
   " with interruption .... HAW
speaker .. ORATOR, LOCUTOR, RHETOR,
                            AUDIO
spear .. GIG, TREN, ASSAGAI, FIZGIG,
       JAVELIN, GLAIVE, BARTE
   " -shaped .... HASTATE
   " , three-pronged TRIDENT, LEISTER
   " thrower .... WOMERA
specialty .... FORTE, TALENT
specie .... CASH, COIN, MONEY
species KIND, SORT, GENUS, CATEGORY
specimen ..... CAST, COPY, EXAMPLE,
              SWATCH, MODEL, SLIDE
speck .... JOT, WHIT, BIT, MOTE
speckled .... MENALD, MOTTLED
spectacle .. PAGEANT, SCENE, SHOW,
       SIGHT, DISPLAY, VIEW, GOGGLE
specter ..... SHADOW, MANES, MARE,
       WRAITH, GHOST, SHADE, SPIRIT,
                        EIDOLON
spectral .... EERIE, GHOSTLY
speculate .... DOCTRINIZE, THINK
speculum .... DIOPTER, MIRROR
speech .... LIP, SPIEL, VOICE, PATOIS,
       SERMON, LECTURE, ORATION
   " art .... RHETORIC
   " blunder .... SOLECISM

" ; comb. form .... LOGO
" defect ALOGIA, LISP, STAMMER
" , figurative .... RHESIS, TROPE,
                ZEUGMA, LITOTES
" , loss of ..... APHASIA, ALALIA
" , unintelligent ..... CHOCTAW
" , violent .... TIRADE
" with full breathing ASPIRATE
speechless ...... DUMB, MUTE, SILENT,
       APHASIC, APHEMIC, APHONIC
speed .... HIE, FLY, RUSH, PACE, RACE,
                TEMPO, EXPEDITE
speed of sound .... MACH
speedy .... RACING, APACE, RATH
spell .. SPEAK, WORD, WRITE, CHARM,
       JINX, HEX, HOODOO, FIT
spelt ..... FAR, WHEAT, EMMER, FITCH
spend .... COST, EXERT, WISE
spendthrift WASTREL, DAFT, PRODIGAL
Spenserian character .... UNA
spent ... FAGGED, EFFETE, CONSUMED,
                    WEAK, WORN
sphere ..... ORBIT, BALL, GLOBE, ORB
   " , magnetic steel ...... TERELLA
   " of action ... ARENA, THEATER
spherical .... GLOBOSE, ROTUND,
                        ORBICULAR
   " aberration, without ......
                        APLANATIC
sphery .... ROUND, STARLIKE
spice .. MULL, MACE, NUTMEG, STACTE,
       SEASON, CONDIMENT, PEPPER,
              CLOVE, TANG, CASSIA
" , mill for grinding ...... QUERN
Spice is. .... TERNATE
spiced dish .... CURRY, SALMI
spicule ACTINE, ROD, ACTER, SCLERITE
" , sponge .... CYMBA
spicy .... RACY, AROMATIC, SHARP
spider ...... ACERA, ARACHNID, MITE,
       SCORPION, SKILLET, SNARE, COP,
                        GRIDDLE
   " appendage .... PEDIPALPUS
   " fly .... TICK
   " , garden .... ARANEA
   " , leaping ...... SALTIGRADE
   " monkey .... ATELES, COAITA,
                        SAJOU
   " , three-legged .... TRIVET
   " , venomous .... TARANTULA
   " , web-spinning ...... RETIARY,
                        TELARIAN
spigot .... DOSSIL, SPILE, TAP, SPOUT,
                FAUCET, ALETAP
spike . SPADIX, BROB, EAR, GAD, TINE,
                        STAB
"spike" team .... UNICORN
spikelet .... LOCUSTA, SPICULE
spikenard ... ARALIA, NARD, SUMBUL,
                        IVYWORT

spill SHED, SPLASH, TELL, SPILE, SLOP
spin PIRL, BIRL, GYRATE, ROTATE, REEL, TOSS
spinach .... ORACH, SAVOY, POTHERB
spinal .... RACHIDIAN
    " affection .... MYELITIS
    " chord ...... MEDULLA, MYELON
    " membrane .... DURA
spindle HASP, ARBOR, AXLE, MANDREL, TRIBLET, SANDRIL, SPOOL, ROD
    " ; turning beam ...... TRENDLE
    " tree .... GAITER
spine ..... ACICULA, NEEDLE, THORN, CHINE, RACHIS, AXIS, QUILL, BACKBONE, VERTEBRA
spinel, ruby .... BALAS
spinet .... CLAVICHORD, GIRAFFE, VIRGINAL
    " , rel. to .... PLECTRUM
spinetail .... DUCK
spinner .... SPIDER
spinning .... AWHIRL
    " machine .... JENNY, MULE, THROSTLE
    " wheel, part of a .... DISTAFF
    " -wheel rod .... SPINDLE
spiracle .... BLOWHOLE, PORE
spiral COIL, HELICAL, HELIX, SCROLLED
    " canal of cochlea ...... SCALA
    " object .... VOLUTE
spire .... STEEPLE, WHORL, SHAFT, PINNACLE, FLECHE
" , apex of a .... EPI
spirit HEART, METAL, PEP, VERVE, VIM, LIEFE, MORAL, ELIXIR, MORALE, SOUL, GEIST, ELAN
    " , a good ... NORN, EUDAEMON
    " , Arabian AFREET, AFRIT, JINN
    " , Egyptian .... BA, KA
    " , elemental ...... GENIE, GENII
    " , evil AMAIMON, DEVIL, DEMON
    " , female ..... BANSHEE, UNDINE
    " lamp .... ETNA
    " , malignant .... KER
    " of a people .... ETHOS
    " of censure .... MOMUS
    " of fire .... GENIE
    " of nemesis .... ATE
    " of the air .... ARIEL
spirited .. RACY, FELL, FERVENT, GAMY
spiritless .... AMORT, MOPY
spirit-like .... ETHEREAL, GHOSTLY
spirits of dead ancestors ..... MANES
spiritual being .... ENS
    " healing .... PSYCHIASIS
    " meaning of words ANOGOGE
    " nature, depths of .... ADYTA
spite of, in .... MAUGER
spittle insect .... FROGHOPPER, HOMOPTER

spittoon .... PIGDAN, CRACHOIRE
splash .... BLOT, DAUB, LABBER
splashboard .... FLASHBOARD
splay ... BEVEL, CARVE, SPREAD, FLAN
spleen .... MELANCHOLY
    " , per. to .... LIENAL, MILTY
splendid ..... AUREATE, RIAL, SUPERB, GRAND
splendor . ECLAT, GITE, POMP, GLORY, SHEEN
splinter .... SLIVER, SHATTER, FLINDER
split ......CHAP, RIVE, SCHISM, REND, SEVER, TEAR, CLEAVE, BISECT
    " into parts .... BIFID, CLOVEN
    " pulse .... DAL, DHAL
    " , that may be .... FISSILE
splotch .... BLOT, STAIN
Spohr opera .... JESSONDA
spoil .. PELF, MAR, ROT, IMPAIR, SOUR, CODDLE, UNDO, DEFILE, DECAY, WRECK, WASTE, SHEND
spoilsport .... MARPLOT
spoke .... RUNG, BAR, PIN, ROD
spoken .... ORAL, PAROLE, SAID
    " word .... AGRAPH
sponge ERASE, BADAGIA, MUMP, SWAB, MOISTEN, SORN
    " , orifice of OSTIOLE, OSCULUM
    " ; slang .... MOOCH, CADGE
    " spicule TOXA, CYMBA, DESMA, RHAB, TOXON, ACTINE
    " , vegetable ... LOOFAH, LUFFA
sponger .... CADGER, PARASITE, SORN
sponges, group of ASCONES, SYCONES
spongy .... BIBULOUS, PITHY, POROUS
    " substance .... AMADOU
sponsor .... ANGEL, BACKER, PATRON
sponsorship .... AEGIS, EGIS
spooky ...... WEIRD, EERIE, GHOSTLY
spool WHARVE, WHORL, BOBBIN, COP, REEL, WIND
spoon .... LABIS, TROLL, OAR
spoonbill .... AJAJA, POPELER
Spoon River poet .... MASTERS
spore ..... CARPEL, GERM, SEED, SORI
    " case ..... ASCA, ASCUS, THECA
    " fruit ..... AECIA, TELIA, TELIUM
sport .. GAME, RUX, JEST, PLAY, ROMP, PASTIME
    " event ... MEET, RACE, REGATTA, MATCH
sports attendance .... GATE
    " fields ...... GYM, ARENA, RINK, STADIUM, OVAL, GREEN, DIAMOND, GRIDIRON, TRACK, LINKS
sporty .... RORTY, FLASHY
spot MACLE, MACULA, SMIT, SPECKLE, BLOT, FLAW, PLACE

" on a playing card .... PIP
" , small .... FLECK, BLOTCH
spotted .... PIED, PINTO, DAPPLED,
MACULOSE
" fever .... TICK
" with drops .... GUTTATE
spousal .... NUPTIAL
spout .. JET, SPILE, GARGOYLE, EMIT,
RONE
sprang .... AROSE, LEAPT
spray ATOMIZE, TWIG, STOUR, SCUD,
FOAM, LIPPER, BRANCH
spreading out .... RADIAL
spread .. BRUIT, COVER, FEAST, FLARE,
DELATE, SET, WIDEN
" ; as a decree .... EMIT
" ; as plaster .... TEER
" for drying .... THIN, TED
" in front .... DEPLOY
" loosely .... STREW
" over .... SMEAR
spree BENDER, LARK, ORGY, WASSAIL,
BINGE, FROLIC
sprightliness .... LILT
sprightly .. GAY, PERT, BRISK, JAUNTY
spring ... LEAP, SALTATION, AIN, SPA,
FONT, RESILE, DART(LE), RECOIL,
GEYSER, SEEP, FONT
" stay on schooner ..... TRIATIC
springboard .... RAMP, BATULE
spring-like .... VERNAL
springe ... GIN, NOOSE, SNARE, TRAP
springing back .... ELASTIC
" into being ..... RENASCENT
springless bullock wagon .... TONGA
springs FONTS, SPAS, THERMAE, BATHS
sprinkle...... DEG, SPARGE, MOTTLE,
STREW, BEDROP, SAND, SPRAY,
SPRENGE, BAPTIZE
sprinkled .... SEME, BEDEWED
sprite DEMON, BROWNIE, ELVET, HOB,
IMP, ARIEL, ELF, FAIRY, PIXY, PUCK
" , water .... UNDINE, NIX(IE)
sprocket .... TOOTH, CHANTLATE
sprout .... BURGEON, CHIT, (S)CION,
GERMINATE, GROW
" from a root .... TILLER
" or bud .... SPRIT
" , sugar-cane .... RATOON
spruce ..... DAPPER, GIN, SMUG, TRIM
spruce tree ... ALCOCK, PICEA, ABIES,
EPINETTE
sprue .... THRUSH, PILOSIS
spume .... FOAM, FROTH, SCUM
spunk AMADOU, TINDER, SPIRIT, GRIT,
PLUCK
spur .. PRICK, CALCAR, GOAD, ROWEL,
INCITE, HASTEN, URGE
" , having a .... SPICATE
" on a game cock's leg .... GAFF

spurge .... MILKWEED, EUPHORBIA
spurn .... DISDAIN, FLOUT
spurious .... FALSE, IMITATION, SNIDE,
FAKE, PSEUDO, SHAM, BOGUS
spurt ..... BURST, JET, SPOUT, SQUIRT
spy .... PRY, SEE, SCOUT, TOUT, KEEK,
PEEK, CALEB, MOUTON, MATAHARI,
CAVELL
squab .... PIPER
squadron .... SOTNIA, SOTNYA
squall .... MEWL, CRY, GALE, GUST
squander .. SACK, WASTE, (MIS)SPEND
square ..... QUADRATE, AREA, EVEN,
ISAGON, PLAZA, SETTLE, TALLY
squash ..... PEPO, CYMLING, FLATTEN,
SQUELCH, QUELL
squatter .... NESTER, NESTLER
squeak ...... CREAK, CROAK, INFORM
squeeze .. EXTORT, GRIPE, PINCH, JAM,
NIP
squill .... SCILLA
squilla .. SHRIMP, PRAWN, STOMAPOD
squinting .... GOGGLY, STRABISM
squire .... BOW, ESCORT, GALLON
squirming .... EELY, TWISTING
squirrel .. BUN(NY), CHIPPY, MINIVER,
BUNT
" fish .... SERRANO, ALAIHI
" , flying ... ASSAPAN, TAGUAN
" , ground CHIPMUNK, HACKEE,
SUSLIK, XERUS, SISEL
" nest .... DRAY
" , pelt of .... CALABAR
" shrew .... TANA, TUPAIA
" skin .... VAIR
squirrel-like animal(s) ... BANXRING,
DORMICE
stable .. BARN, PADDOCK, BYRE, MEW,
CONSTANT, SOLID
" , make .. FIRM, STEADY, SUPPORT
St. Clare .... EVA
stab .. SPIT, GORE, PAUNCH, WOUND,
IMPALE, PIERCE, TRY
" in fencing ..... PINK, STOCCADO
stabilize .... POISE, SET, BALLAST
stableman (H)OSTLER, GROOM, AVENER
staccato, not .... TENUTO
stack ...... RICK, SCINTLE, PILE, HEAP
stadium ... COURSE, DROMOS, STADE,
STANDS
staff .... BATON, MACE, WAND, ROD,
CROOK, CUDGEL, RETINUE
" , bishop's .... BACULUS, CROSIER
" , bacchantes' .... THYRSUS
" , mountain-climbing .... PITON,
ALPENSTOCK, BALLOW
" , spiked .... ANKUS
stag .... WAPITI, BUCK, MORT, HART,
SPADE, POLLARD

273

stage .... PHASE, STEP, APRON, LEGIT, ARENA, FORUM
" direction . EXIT, MANET, SENNET, SOLI, ASIDE
" extra .... SUPE
" hand ..... FLYMAN, CHIPS, GRIP, JUICER
" , per. to .... SCENICAL
" scenery .... ETS, COULISSE
" , slightly raised .. DAIS, ESTRADE
stagger LURCH, STARTLE, STOT, SWAY, TOTTER
staggers, the .... GID
stagnation .... STASIS
stagy .... ASSUMED, THEATRICAL
staid ... DECOROUS, SEDATE, DEMURE, GRAVE
stain .... IMBUE, BLOT, DYE, SMUDGE, SMUTCH, TINGE, STIGMA
stair .... STEP, STILE, ASCEND
" part .... NEWEL, RISER, NOSING
staircase .... PERRON, CARACOLE
stairway, moving .... ESCALATOR
stake WAGER, ANTE, BET, PALE, PILE, POT, MISE, KITTY
" , swordsman's .... PEL
stale .... BANAL, FUSTY, TRITE, VAPID, EFFETE, PASSE
stalemate .... CHECK, IMPASSE
stalk ...... HALM, CAUL, KEX, PETIOLE, STRAW, CULM, AXIS, PEDICEL, RATOON, STIPE
" for game .... PREY
stall BOOTH, CRIB, NICHE, LOGE, SEAT, PEW, DELAY
stamen, summit of .... ANTHER
stammer .... HEM, MANT, STUT, HAW, FAFFLE
stammering .... PSELLISM
stamp .. BRAND, DIE, PESTLE, EMBOSS, SIGIL, DINK, INCLUSE
" out .... SCOTCH
stamping machine .... DATER
stanch ..... STEM, STOP, LOYAL, TRUE
stand .... BEAR, HALT, EASEL, BASE
" for casks .... STILLION
" it .... BROOK, BEAR, SUFFER
" , ornamental TEAPOY, ETAGERE, EPERGNE, ZARF
" , three-legged .. TRIPOD, TRIVET
standard GONFALON, CANON, FLAG, LABARUM, NORM, TYPE, ENSIGN
" , per. to a .... VEXILLARY
" , Turkish .... ALEM
standing .... STATUS, ERECT, PRESTIGE, STATIC, GRADE
" out SALIENT, AWAY, JUTTING
Standish, Miles; wife of .... ROSE
stands .... BLEACHERS
stand-offish .... ALOOF, RESERVED

stannum .... TIN
Stan, the Man .... MUSIAL
stanza .... STROPHE, VERSE
" , eight-line .... TRIOLET
" , ten-line .... DECALET
staple .... FIBER, LOOP, GOODS, NAIL
star COR, NOVA, ASTER(ISK), STELLA, LUMINARY, BADGE
" , brightest .... SIRIUS
" cluster ...... HYADES, NEBULA(E), GALAXY, MILKYWAY
" ; comb. form .... ASTRO
" , evening .... HESPER
" facet .... PANE
" , feather .... COMATULA
" , fixed .. ADIB, ARCTURUS, VEGA
" followers .... MAGI
" group .... DIPPER
" , heroic .... ESTOILE
" in Aquilae .... DENEB
" in Argo .... NAOS
" in Centauri .... AGENA
" in Cygnus .... DENEB
" in Draconis .. ETAMIN, RASTABAN
" in Lyra .... VEGA
" in Medusa head .... ALGOL
" in Orion .... RIGEL, SAIPH, BELLATRIX
" in Scorpio ..... ANTARES, LESATH
" in Swan .... SADR
" in Taurus .... PLEIAD
" in Ursa Minor .... POLARIS
" , morning .... LUCIFER, PHOSPHOR
" , new .... NOVA, NUVO
" of first magnitude .... ALPHA
" of five or more points ... MULLET
" , path of .... ORBIT
" , relating to .... ASTRAL, SIDEREAL
" -shaped .... ASTROID, STELLATE
" -shaped figure .... ETOILE
" , shooting ...... METEOR, LEONID
" , six-pointed .. ESTOILE, PENTACLE
" thistle .... CALTRAP
" , variable .... MIRA
starch ..... FARINA, SAGO, MANIOC
" grain .... HILUM
" , soluble .... AMIDIN
" -like substance .. ARUM, INULIN
starchy ..... AMYLOID, FORMAL, STIFF
" rootstock .... TARO
stare ..... GAPE, GAZE, LOOK, GLARE, WONDER, OGLE
starfish .... RADIATE
" ; genus .... ASTERIAS
Stark, Admiral; nickname ..... BETTY
starlike PLANETOID, ASTRAL, STELLAR, SIDEREAL, STELLATE
starling .... SALI
stars, covered with .... SEME
" , detached .. SPARSILE, SPORADES

start .. ORIGINATE, SPRING, LOOSEN, JUMP, BEGIN, ENTER, ONSET
starting point ...... DATA, SCRATCH, MARKER
starvation .. FAMINE, INEDIA, PENURY
starwort .... ASTER
state .. ENOUNCE, ESTRE, ETAT, AVER, CANTON, PLIGHT, SPECIFY, MOOD
"State Fair" author .... STONG
state nicknames
Alabama .... COTTON
California .... GOLDEN, GRAPE
Colorado .... CENTENNIAL
Connecticut .... NUTMEG
Delaware .... FIRST
Florida .... SUNSHINE
Hawaii .... ALOHA
Idaho .... GEM
Illinois .... PRAIRIE
Indiana .... HOOSIER
Iowa .... HAWKEYE
Kansas .... SUNFLOWER
Louisiana .... PELICAN, SUGAR
Maine .... PINETREE
Massachusetts .... BAY
Michigan .... WOLVERINE
Minnesota .... GOPHER
Mississippi ...... MAGNOLIA, BAYOU
Missouri .... SHOWME
Montana .... TREASURE
Nebraska .... BEEF
Nevada .... SILVER, SAGEBRUSH
New Hampshire .... GRANITE
New Jersey .... GARDEN
New York .... EMPIRE
North Dakota .... SIOUX
Ohio .... BUCKEYE
Oklahoma .... SOONER
Oregon .... BEAVER
Pennsylvania .... KEYSTONE
South Carolina .... PALMETTO
South Dakota .... COYOTE
Tennessee .... VOLUNTEER
Texas .... LONESTAR
Utah .... BEEHIVE
Washington .... EVERGREEN
Wisconsin .... BADGER
Wyoming .... EQUALITY
stately .... AUGUST, REGAL, TOGATED, MAJESTIC, LOFTY
     " woman .... JUNO
statement .. DICTUM, DIXIT, ACCOUNT, BILL, PRECIS
static, opposed to .... KINETIC
station ..... STOP, DEPOT, RANK, SET, TERMINAL, POST
stationary STATIC, FIXED, STILL, STABLE
     " point .... PINODE
stationery .... PAPETERIE

statue ... ACROLITH, SCULPTURE, BUST, ICON, ORANT, EFFIGY, GALATEA, MAGOG
     " pedestal member ...... SOCLE
     " , primitive .... XOANON
statute ACT, DOOM, TREATY, CANON
stave LAG, STAP, POLE, VERSE, STICK, CASK
staves, bundle of .... SHOOK
stay .... ABIDE, BRACE, PROP, GUY, REMAIN, WAIT, VISIT
staylace .... AGLET
stead .... LIEU, ADVANTAGE, SERVICE, AVAIL, PLACE
steady ...... GUY, REGULAR, STAID
     " , not ...... ASTATIC, UNSTABLE
steal CRIB, PILFER, SNITCH, FILCH, NIM, LOOT, RUSTLE, GLOM, ROB, RATTEN, PURLOIN
     " from a ship's galley MANAVEL
     " game .... POACH, TRESPASS
stealing ...... RAPINE, PIRACY, THEFT
stealthy CATTY, FURTIVE, SLY, SECRET
steam OAM, PUTHER, FUME, REEK, MIST, VAPOR
     " ; comb. form .... ATMO
     " , jet of .... STUFA
     " organ .... CALLIOPE
stearyl .... BENZOYL
steatite .... TALC
steed CHARGER, COB, NAG, PEGASUS
steel ...... HARDEN, ENURE, TOLEDO, DAMASK, IRON, STRONG
     " , armor-plate .... TACE
     " , conversion into ... ACIERATION
     " , process of making .... CEMENTATION
steep SHEER, SOP, CLIFTY, IMBUE, RET, SOAK, BREW, CLIFFY, COSTLY
     " hillside .... BRAE, CLEVE
     " slope .... SCARP
steeper .... TEAPOT
steeple ..... HENNIN, SPIRE, MINARET, FLECHE, EPI
steer BULLOCK, HELM, CON, PLY, STOT, BOVINE, OX, YAW, PILOT, GUIDE
     " into the wind .... LUFF
steeve ...... CRAM, LADE, PACK, SPAR
stein .... FLAGON, MUG
Steller's sea cow .... RYTINA
stem BASE, PROW, BINE, REED, STRAW, ARREST, STANCH
     " joints, per. to .... NODAL
     " of fungus .... STIPE
     " , short, fleshy ... TUBER, TIGELLA, CORM
stemless evergreen herb ...... GALAX
stench .... ODOR, FETOR, STINK
Stengel, Mr. .... CASEY
stenographer of 60 B.C. .... TIRO

stentorian .... CLARION, LOUD
step GAIT, TRAMPLE, PACE, PAS, TREAD,
    STAIR, STRIDE, DEGREE, CHASSE
  " arrangement of troops ECHELON
  " -ladder .... TRAP
  " of ladder .... RIME, RUNG
stepmother, like a ...... NOVERCAL
steps, out-of-door .... PERRON
sterile . BARREN, IMPOTENT, INFERTILE
stern .. GRIM, SEVERE, HARSH, STRICT,
    AUSTERE, AFT, REAR
sternutation .... SNEEZING
sternutative .... ERRHINE
stertor .... SNORE
stevedore UNLOADER, LADER, LOADER,
    STOWER
Stevens; singer .... RISE
Stevenson, Mr. .... ADLAI
Stevenson character .... HYDE
  " , last home of .... SAMOA
stew .. OLLA, HARICOT, POT, RAGOUT,
    SEETHE, SIMMER, WORRY, OLIO
steward ERENACH, SENESCHAL, REEVE,
    ECONOME, DAPIFER, MANCIPLE
stibium .... ANTIMONY
stich .... LINE, VERSE
stick . BAR, BAT, CANE, GLUE, WAND,
    PASTE, FAGOT, CLEAVE, ADHERE,
    STALL, COHERE
  " , as a fishing rod .... GAD
  " , jumping .... POGO
sticky GOOEY, LIMY, TACKY, TREACLY,
    VISCID, GUMMY
stiff . STARCHY, STARK, RIGID, CORPSE,
    DRUNK, POMPOUS
  " joint .... ANCHYLOSIS
stiffen ...... STARK, BRACE, GEL, SET
stigma .... STAIN, BLOT
stigmatize ... BRAND, TAINT, DEFAME,
    MARK
stiletto .... STYLET, PIERCER
still .. COSH, DRIP, MUM, WHIST, YET,
    BUT, EVEN, QUIET
stilt .... POGO, POLE, POST, KAKI
stimulate .. WHET, FAN, PIQUE, URGE,
    AROUSE, INCITE
stimulant ... TEA, THEINE, CAFFEINE,
    SPUR, TONIC, HORMONE
stimulus threshold .... LIMEN
sting ... SMART, GOAD, PRICK, TANG,
    BITE, NETTLE
  " ; as with nettles ..... ACULEUS,
    URTICATE
stinging .... CAUSTIC, SHARP, BITING
stingy NEAR, SCALY, SORDID, MISERLY,
    CLOSE
stint ... DUTY, SCANT, SCRIMP, TASK,
    CHORE
stinted .... LIMITED, SCAMPED
stipe .... PETIOLE, STALK, STEM

stipend ... SALARY, ANNAT, PREBEND,
    WAGE, PENSION
stipulate .... POSTULATE
stir ... AROUSE, RUSTLE, MOVE, ADO,
    FUSS, RILE, TODO
  " about .... ROUST, CAROUSE
  " ; slang .... PRISON
  " , tending to .... AGITATIVE
  " up . BUZZ, INFLAME, ROIL, TEER
stirrup bone .... STAPES
  " ; leather covering .. TAPADERO
  " straps .... CHAPELET
stitch .... ACHE, CRICK, PAIN, SEW,
    SUTURE, BASTE, PUNTO
  " bird .... IHI
  " in knitting PURL, FESTON, CABLE
stoa .... PORTICO, PROMENADE
stoat .... ERMINE, WEASEL, VAIR
stock .... BLOCK, FRAME, PILE, BREED,
    CATTLE, LINEAGE, STIRPS
  " exchange .... BOURSE
stockade . BULWARK, REDOUBT, ETAPE,
    PEN, CORRAL, KRAAL
stocking .... SHINNER, HOSE
stocky ..... PLUMP, STOUT, FAT, STUB
stoker .... TEASER
stole ...... ORARY, PIRATED, LOOTED
stolen goods, rel. to .... FENCE
  " property .. LOOT, PELF, SWAG,
    HAUL
stolidity .... PHLEGM
stoma .... OSTIOLE, PORE
stomach .... RESENT
  " , lower opening of .. PYLORUS
  " of birds .... CROP, MAW
  " of ruminants ..... OMASUM,
    PAUNCH, TRIPE
stomp .... MASH, TREAD, STAMP
stone ... PEBBLE, TALUS, FLINT, LAPIS,
    GEM, PIT, FLAG, SEED, ROSETTA
  " age .... PALEOLITHIC
  " -and-wood figure .... ACROLITH
  " , argillaceous .... SHALE
  " carved in relief ...... CAMEO
  " chip .... SPALL
  " chisel .... CELT
  " , converting into .... LAPIDIFIC
  " crop .... ORPIN, SEDUM,
    ROSEWOOD
  " -cutter's consumption CHALICOSIS
  " cutter's receptacle ... SEBILLA
  " dish .... COMAL
  " : dress roughly ...... SCABBLE
  " engraving .... INTAGLIO
  " face .... ASHLAR
  " for grinding maize .... MANO
  " , fragments of .... BRASH
  " hammer .... KEVEL
  " heap .... AHIL, CAIRN

stone, hollow .... GEODE
" , imitation; Ital. ... SCAGLIOLA
" implement .... NEOLITH
" , lustrous .... OPAL
" made in shape of a pillar....
HERMA
" nodules .... GEODES
" of some fruits .... SEED,
ENDOCARP, PIP
" on which hot glass is rolled ..
MARVER
" , paving .. FLAG, PITCHER, ROCK
" pestle .... MULLER
" , philosopher's ...... CARMOT
" , porous .... LAVA
" , rocking .... LOGAN
" , semi-precious .. SARD, TOPAZ
" , sharpening .... HONE, WHET
" slab .... STELA, STELE
" throwing engine .... ONAGER
" , trim .... NIG
stone, woman turned into ... NIOBE
stonecutter ...... LAPICIDE, MASON
stoneware .... GRES, POTTERY
stoning, kill by .... LAPIDATE
stony ... NIOBEAN, PETROUS, PITILESS
" concretion .... CALCULUS
stool .... CROCK, TABOURET, MORA
" -pigeon .... NARK, DECOY
" support .... TRIVET
stop STANCH, CEASE, FOIL, SURCEASE,
DESIST, ARREST, WHOA, DAM, END,
HALT
" fermenting .... STUM
" ; naut. .... AVAST, BELAY
" up ..... OBTURATE, CLOSE, PLUG
stopgap .... MAKESHIFT
stoppage .... CLOTURE
stopper BUNG, CORK, PLUG, SPILE, WAD
stopwatch .... TIMER
store .. BIN, MART, CACHE, HUSBAND,
CANTEEN
storehouse ...... BARN, ETAPE, SILO,
GRANARY, DEPOT
stork .. ADJUTANT, JABIRU, MARABOU
" , per. to the .... PELARGIC
" , relative of .... HERON, IBIS
" , bill of .... ERODIUM
storm ...... FUME, RAGE, OUTBREAK,
TEMPEST, TORNADO, SQUALL,
BLIZZARD, TYPHOON, (O)RAGE,
RAVE, RAMPAGE
stormy petrel . MITTY, WITCH, SPENCY
story ..... SAGA, FABLE, TALE, LORE,
ANALOGY, JEREMIAD, PARABLE,
LEGEND, EPIC, MYTH, ANALOG,
FLOOR, NOVEL, LEGEND
" , absurd .. YARN, CANARD, HOAX
" -teller ..... RELATER, RACONTEUR
stoss, opposed to .... LEE

stot .... BULL, OX
stout .... BRAVE, BOLD, STURDY, ALE,
BOCK, PORTER
stove .... KILN, ETNA, OVEN, RANGE,
LATROBE, OAST
stow .... LADE, PACK, STEEVE
straggler .... NOMAD, STRAY
straight LINEAL, ARROW, LEVEL, FLAT,
EVEN, CANDID
strain .... STRESS, TRY, HEAVE, RACE,
BEND, BREED, TAX, EXERT
strainer .... SIEVE, TAMIS, SIFTER
strait .... NECK, PHARE, ISTHMUS,
NARROW, PINCH
" near Leyte .... SURIGAO
Straits Settlements port .... PRAI
" " capital SINGAPORE
strand ...... PLY, RIPA, BEACH, FIBER
strange TRAMONTANE, EXOTIC, UNCO,
ODD, NOVEL, RARE
stranger . ALIEN, ODDER, NEWCOMER
strangle ... CHOKE, GARROTE, STIFLE
strap .. LEASH, RIEM, STROP, THONG,
JESS, REIM, BELT, CINCH
straps, arm-shield .... ENARMES
strap-shaped ..... LIGULATE, LORATE
strass .... PASTE
strata, per. to ...... ERIAN, TERRANE
stratagem RUSE, FINESSE, TRAP, TRICK,
COUP, WILE
stratified .... LAMINATED
" deposit .... VARVE
stratum .. BED, LAY, DEPOSIT, SEAM,
FOLIUM, SHEET
Strauss opera . SALOME, ELEKTRA, BAT
Stravinsky, Mr. .... IGOR
straw .... MOTE, CULM, STALK
" coat .... MINO
" color .... FLAXY, ISABEL
" in the wind ..... OMEN, SIGN
" , plaited .... MILAN, SENNIT
" rope .... SIME, TETHER
" to protect plants ..... MULCH
straw-vote man .... GALLUP, ROPER,
HARRIS
strawberry-like fruit ...... ETAERIO
stray ABERR, ERR, GAD, SIN, WANDER
" away .... DIVAGATE, WAIF
streak .. FLECK, ROE, STRIA, GROOVE
streaked .... LINY, LACED
stream . CREEK, SPRUIT, ARROYO, RILL,
BROOK, FLOW, RIO, FLEAM, POUR,
FRESHET, SIKE
" , bed of ... CHANNEL, COULEE
" of forgetfulness ...... LETHE
" , placer .... LAVADERO
streamlet .... RUNNEL, RIVULET
streams, meeting of ...... CONFLUX
street .... ARTERY, CALLE, LANE, VIA,
CORSO, PLATEA, STRADA

277

" -car .... TRAM
" urchin .... ARAB, GAMIN
street show .... RAREE
strength .... SINEW, VIS, MAIN,
        STHENIA, THEW, BEEF, BRAWN,
                                VIGOR
strengthen .... BRACE, FORTIFY
stress .... ARSIS, ICTUS, STRAIN
stretch ... EKE, STENT, SPREAD, REAM,
                            LENGTHEN
" out ...... PROLATE, PORRECT
stretcher ..... LITTER, RACKER, STEND
" , fabric .... STENTER
stretches of interval .... CARSES
strewing .... LITTER, SEME
strict .... RIGOROUS, STERN, RIGID,
        PRECISE, STRAIT, EXACT
stride .... PACE
strife .. BAIT, COMBAT, FEUD, BATTLE,
        CONTEST, WAR, STASIS, RIOT
strike .... BAT, DAB, RAP, BASH, BUMP,
        SOCK, CLOUT, WHACK
" gently .... PUTT, PAT, BUMP
" out ..... DELETE, DELE, EFFACE,
        ERASE, ELIDE
" sharply .... PELTER, SMITE
" to and fro .... BANDY
strikebreaker RAT, FINK, GOON, SCAB
striking, act of .. ELISION, DASHING
string ..... STRAP, CORD, ROPE, RAN
stringed instrument ... LYRA, ROCTA,
        ROTA, MANDOLA, REBEC, BANDORE,
        KIT, GIGA, VINA, GUSLA, FIDDLE
stringent .... TIGHT, STRICT
stripe .... VITTA, BAR, RIDGE, WALE,
        FILLET, PLAGA, CLAVUS
" , thread-like .... STRIA
strip .... DIVEST, FILLET, PARE, WELT,
        RANSACK, FLAY, PEEL, BARE,
        DISROBE, SPLINE
stripteaser .... ECDYSIAST
striped antelope .... BONGO
" lengthwise.. BENDY, VITTATE
stripes, marked with ...... LINEATE
stripling .... BOY, LAD, YOUTH
strobile .... CONE
stroke .. FIT, BAFF, FEAT, WHISK, FLIP,
                                PUTT
" , brilliant .... COUP, MASSE
" , cutting .... CHOP, SLICE
stroll .. PROMENADE, SAUNTER, ROAM
stroller .... FLANEUR
strong .... FIRM, FERE, VIRILE, HALE,
        STOUT, ROBUST, SINEWY, TOUGH
" drink .... SPIRITS
" flavor . RACY, ACRID, PUNGENT
" muscles ..... THEWY, BRAWNY
" point .... FORTE
" pressure of a violin bow......
                                SACCADE

strongbox ..... SAFE, COFFER, VAULT
stronghold CITADEL, MUNIMENT, FORT,
        KEEP, FORTRESS, DONJON
strong-smelling ..... FETID, FROWZY
struck .... SMOTE, SMIT, SHUTDOWN
structural order .... TEXTURE
" unit .... ID, IDANT, FRAME
struggle ...... COPE, VIE, CONTEST,
        WRESTLE, EFFORT, PENIEL
Stuarts, last of the .... ANNE
stubble ...... EDDISH, BEARD, STUMP,
                                ARRISH
" field, unplowed ..... ROWEN
stubborn .... ORNERY, MULISH, SOT
student ..... DISCIPLE, PLEBE, PORER,
        PUPIL, TOSHER, ELEVE, CADET,
        COED, SIZAR, SOFTA
" group ...... CLASS, SEMINAR
studio .... ATELIER, WORKSHOP
study ... CON, EYE, PORE, CONSIDER,
                                WEIGH
" by lamplight ...... LUCUBRATE
" ; mus. .... ETUDE
" of mountains ...... OROLOGY
" of sacred edifices .. NAOLOGY
stuff ...... STODGE, CRAM, FILL, RAM,
        SATIATE, FABRIC, PAD, STOW
" up .... BOSS, WAD, STIVE
stuffing . FORCEMEAT, FARCE, PANADA,
                                KAPOK
stumble .... STOT
stump ..... BUTT, SKEG, SNAG, STUB,
        PUZZLE, TORTILLON
stun BRUISE, DAUNT, DOZEN, STUPEFY,
                            ASTOUND
stunning .... DAZING, FINE
stunt .... ATROPHY, CROWL, DWARF,
                                CHECK
stunted tree .... SCRUB
stupefy BEMUSE, BESOT, DAZE, DRUG,
        DOPE, PALL, STUN
stupid .... BOEOTIAN, CRASS, INEPT,
        DENSE, EMPTY, VOID, DUMB,
        ASININE, DULL
" person .... LOON, STIRK, ASS,
        FATHEAD, CLOD, GOOSE, DOLT,
                                OAF
stupor ...... SOPOR, COMA, TORPOR,
        LETHARGY, TRANCE, NARCOMA
sturgeon .. BELUGA, HAUSEN, STERLET
" roe .... CAVIAR
sty .... PEN, QUAT, BOIL, PIMPLE
style ... DUB, TECHNIC, TON, VOGUE,
        WAY, ENTITLE, FASHION, VOGUE
" ; brief reflection ...... GNOME
" of painting .... GENRE
" of type .. RUNIC, IONIC, ITALIC
styled .... YCLEPT, CALLED, NAMED
stylet .... STILETTO, DAGGER
" , surgical ..... TROCAR, PROBE

278

stylish .. DRESSY, CHIC, TOPPY, NIFTY,
POSH, ALAMODE
styptic .... ALUM, ASTRINGENT
Styx ferryman .... CHARON
subdue .. AWE, QUASH, QUELL, CALM,
CENSOR, SOBER, TAME
subjoin .... APPEND
subject ...... PRONE, THEME, TOPIC,
ENTHRALL, SERVANT, LIEGE,
CITIZEN, TEXT
    "   to analysis .... TITRATE
    "   to change .... AMENABLE,
MUTABLE
    "   to vassalage .... ENFEOFF
sublime .... EMPYREAL, GLORY, HIGH
submarine mountain .... GUYOT
submerged .... AWASH, SANK
submit .... OBEY, BOS, STAND, YIELD,
DEFER, CEDE
subside .. SETTLE, RELAPSE, SINK, EBB,
FALL, LANGUISH, WANE, ABATE
subsist .... LIVE, FARE, BE, EXIST
substance .... ELEMENT, BASIS, GIST,
MATTER, HEART
substantive ..... FIRM, NOUN, SOLID
substitute .. VICE, COMMUTE, ERSATZ,
SUPPLANT, DEPUTY, PROXY, STANDIN
subterfuge .. BLIND, EVASION, SHIFT,
EXCUSE
subterranean ...... HIDDEN, SECRET,
PLUTONIC, ABYSMAL, SUNK
subtle . ARTFUL, TENUOUS, RARE, AIRY,
SLY, WISE, ASTATIC, DELICATE
    "   emanation . AURA, ATMOSPHERE
    "   variation .. NUANCE, MUANCE
subtlety .... FINESSE, GUILE, QUILLET
suburb .... PURLIEU, TOWN
subvert ... RUINATE, CORRUPT, RUIN,
UPSET
subway .... TUBE, METRO
succeed . GET, ENSUE, PROVE, ATTAIN
success .... HIT, FAME, LUCK, ARTHA
successive ... AROW, SERIATE, SERIAL
successor ...... HEIR, HEIRESS, HERE
succinct .... SHORT, BRIEF, TERSE,
LACONIC, PITHY
succor ... AID, ASSIST, RELIEF, NURSE
succulent .... PULPY, LUSH, PAPPY
succumb .... DIE, YIELD, FAIL
suction .... INTAKE
Sudan, native of ..... MOSSI, FULAH
    "   , region in .... SEGU
sudarium .. GRAVECLOTH, VERONICA
Sudra caste .... PALLI
sue ...... BEG, WOO, COURT, APPEAL
suffer .... DREE, LET, SMART, STARVE
suffice .. CONTENT, SERVE, AVAIL, DO
sufficient . BASTANT, ENOW, FIT, FULL,
AMPLE
suffix .... POSTFIX, ATION, INE, OUS

    "   abounding in .... ULENT
    "   denoting action .... ENCE
    "   denoting equality .... ENT
    "   denoting foot .... PED
    "   denoting full of .... OSE
    "   denoting geological period....
CENE
    "   from adjective ..... ENT, ICAL
    "   used in medical terms .. ITIS,
OSIS
suffocate ...... BURKE, STIFLE, CHOKE
suffocation, partial APNOEA, SWOON,
ASPHYXIA
suffrage .. BALLOT, VOTE, FRANCHISE
Sufi disciple .... MURID
sugar .... CANE, RAW, SWEETEN,
SACCHARINE
    "   and molasses .... MELADA
    "   , artificial.. MANNOSE, ALLOSE,
GULOSE, GLUCOSE
    "   , burnt .... CARAMEL
    "   cane .... SUCROSE
    "   -cane refuse .... BAGASSE
    "   -cane stalk .... RATOON
    "   cleaning .... ELUTION
    "   compound .. TRIOSE, ACROSE,
OSAMINE
    "   , crude .... GUR, MAPLE
    "   , crystalline .... MALTOSE
    "   foundation for candy FONDANT
    "   , fruit .... LEVULOSE
    "   , grape ... MALTOSE, DEXTROSE
    "   , lump .... LOAF
    "   , milk .... LACTOSE
    "   , muscle .... INOSITE
    "   : picked up lump .... TONGED
    "   , raw CASSONADE, MUSCOVADO
    "   -refining box .... ELUTOR, TIGER
    "   sack .... BAYON
    "   solution .... SYRUP
    "   works; W. Ind. .... USINE
    "   -yielding plant XYLOSE, SORGHUM
sugars, simple OSES, IDOSES, KETOSES
suggestion .... CLUE, HINT, WRINKLE,
TRACE, INKLING, TIP
suicide .. HARAKIRI, HARIKIRI, SUTTEE,
SEPPUKU
suid(ae) .... HOG, BOAR, SWINE
suit ...... HIT, WOOING, AGREE, FIT,
ADAPT, PLEASE, SERIES, TRIAL
suitable ... MEET, IDONEOUS, APT,
PROPER
suitcase .... VALISE, BAG, GRIP
suite .... RETINUE, STAFF, TRAIN,
CORTEGE, SERIES
suitor .. AMOROSO, SWAIN, WOOER,
BEAU
sulk .... MOPE, POUT, SCOWL
sulky .... GLUM, SNUFFY, GIG, SURLY

279

sullen MOODY, GRIM, MOROSE, RUSTY,
        SATURNINE, MOPY, POUTY
sulpharsenate of copper .. ENARGITE
sulphate, double .... ALUM
    " of barium .. BARYTA, HEPAR
    " of calcium .... GYPSUM
sulphide compound ...... ALASKAITE
    " of antimony ...... STIBNITE
    " of arsenic ...... ORPIMENT,
        REALGAR
    " of iron .... TROILITE
    " of lead .... GALENA
    " of zinc .... BLENDE
    " to darken eyelids ... SURMA
sulphite, lead-copper ...... LINARITE
sulphur alloy .... NIELLO
    " , containing .... THIONIC
sulphuric acid .... VITRIOL
sultan .... MURAD, SELIM
Sultanate ... OMAN, KUWEIT, MAHRA
sultry TORPID, HUMID, MOIST, MUGGY,
        SENSUAL
Sulu Archipelago, is. in JOLO, PANAI,
        NEGROS, BASILAN, BORNEO
Sulu Moslem .... MORO
sum .. RECAP, ADD, POT, TOTAL, FUND
sumac; genus .... RHUS
Sumatra, island near .... NIAS
Sumatran .... MALAYAN, LAMPONG,
        REJANG, BATTAK, BATA(K)
    " kingdom .... ACHIN
Sumerian deity .... ANU, ABU
summary .. COMPEND, PRECIS, BRIEF,
        DIGEST, RESUME, EPITOME
summer .... ESTIVATE
    " flounder .... PLAICE
    " ; French for .... ETE
    " house .. BELVEDERE, GAZEBO,
        DACHA
    " , of the .... ESTIVAL
    " -theater circuit .... STRAWHAT
summit .... ACME, KNAP, APEX, TOP,
        VERTEX, SPIRE, ZENITH, APICES
summon .. EVOCATE, ACCITE, EVOKE,
        PAGE, INVITE, (RE)CALL, CONVENE
    " to court .... CITE, SIST
summoner APPARITOR, CRIER, SERVANT
summons ...... CALL, SIGNAL, CITAL
sump .... BOG, PIT, POOL, WELL
sun .... PHOEBUS, HELIOS, SOL
" bow .... IRIS
" -burn .... HELIOSIS, TAN
" , circle of light around .... HALO,
        CORONA
" ; comb. form .... HELIO
" crossing equator ..... EQUINOX
" disk .... CHAKRA, ATEN
" -fish . FLYER, OPAH, ROACH, RUFF,
        MOLA
" fleck .... LUCULE, GRANULE

" god, Assyr. .... NINIB
" " , Babyl. .... BABBAR, NERGAL,
        SHAMASH, UTU(G)
" " , Celtic .. BELENUS, BELI, LIEU
" " , Egyptian .... AMEN, AMON,
    ATUM, ATMU, HORUS, KHEPERI,
    RA, RE, SHU, OSIRIS, TEM,
        TUM, CHEPERA
" " , Greek .. HELIOS, HYPERION,
        PHOEBUS
" " , Hindu ..... ADITYAS, AGNI,
        VARUNA
" " , Latin .... JANUS, SOL
" " , Norse .... BALDER
" " , Persian .... MITHRAS
" " , Scand. .... FREY, ING
" " , Syrian .... HADAD
" , greatest distance from ... APSIS
" , luminous envelope around......
        CORONA
" , mock .... PARHELION
" , personified .... TITAN
" , per. to .... SOLAR
" room(s) .... SOLARIUM, SOLARIA
" spot(s) .... FACULA, LUCULE,
        MACULA
" , standing still of ..... SOLSTICE
" worship .... HELIOLATRY
sunburnt .... ADUST
Sunda island .... TIMOR, BALI
Sunday ...... DOMINICAL, SABBATH
sunder .. CLEAVE, PART, SEVER, REND
sundial index .... GNOMON
sundog .... PARHELION
sunken fence .... (H)AHA
sunn hemp DAGGA, SAN(A), JANAPA
sunrise .. DAWN, DAYBREAK, AURORA
sun's path .... ECLIPTIC
sunset, toward .... WESTER
sunstroke .... CALENTURE, ICTUS,
        INSOLATION, SIRIASIS
sup .. DINE, SOPE, DRINK, SIP, SNACK
superabundance .... PLETHORA
superannuated ... ANILE, AGED, OLD,
        SENILE, DECREPIT
superfine .... LUXE, EXTRA, NICE
superfluous REDUNDANT, LUXUS, FUTILE
superhighway . FREEWAY, AUTOBAHN
superintend .... BOSS, OVERSEE, RUN
superior ... MISTRESS, PALMARY, BEST,
        OVER, TOPS
superiority ... MASTERY, ODDS, EDGE
superlative, the absolute ELATIVE, EST
superman .... NIETZSCHE
supernatural .... EERIE, ABNORMAL,
    MAGIC, OCCULT, UNEARTHLY
    " being ...... GOD, ATUA,
    BANSHEE, ANGE, ADARO,
        ANGEL

" power ... MANA, NGAI, ORENDA, WAKAN, MAGIC
supersede .. OMIT, SUPPLANT, REPLACE
superstition, object of ...... FETISH, TALISMAN
superstitious, rel. to GOETIC, LEGEND
supervisor .... PROCTOR
supine INERT, LISTLESS, PRONE, ABED, LAZE
supple ...... LITHE, LISSOME, PLIANT
supplement ...... ADD, EKE, SEQUEL
supplicate BESIEGE, CONJURE, OBTEST, PRAY
supplication ...... PETITION, PRAYER, LITANY, AVE
supplies .... ESTOVERS, STORES, ORDNANCE
" by aircraft .... AIRLIFT
" issued to troops ..... ETAPE
supply food .... FEED, GRIST, CATER
support .... TENON, LEG, LIMB, PEG, BASE, STELL
" for a statue SOCLE, PEDESTAL
" , slab .... PLANCH, TRAY
" , to . AID, ABET, BUOY, SHORE, BUTTRESS, PROP
supported ...... ABETTED, SECONDED
" by two threads ... BIFILAR
suppose ... DEEM, OPINE, WEEN, WIS
supposed .... PUTATIVE, SURMISED
supposition .... THEORY, SURMISE
suppress ..... CHECK, QUASH, QUELL, STIFLE
suppurate .... FESTER, MATURATE
supreme .. PARAMOUNT, LAST, CHIEF, ABSOLUTE, CAPITAL, PRIME
" being ... IHVH, JHVH, JHWH
surcoat .... CYCLAS, JUPON
surd .... DISC, VOICELESS
" mutes, one of the ...... TENUIS
surety .. SPONSOR, ENGAGER, BOND, HOSTAGE
surf .... FOAM, SPRAY
" shiner .... SPARADA
surface NAP(PE), PLAT, MEROS, ORLO, RYME, AREOLA, FACET
" , growing above .... EPIGEAN
" , per. to .... ACROTIC
surfeit . CLOY, JADE, SATIETY, GORGE
surfeited with pleasure ...... BLASE
surfeiter .... SATER, GLUTTON
surge .. BILLOW, TIDE, WAVE, GUSH, SWELL, SOAR
surgeon .... LEECH, SAWBONER
surgeon's hammer .... PLESSOR
" instrument .... SCALPEL, XYSTER, MANDRIN, TROCAR
" " case ..... TWEEZE
" " : knife .... CATLIN, LANCET

" " : probe .... ARCUS, STYLET, TENT
" " : saw ..... TREPAN, TREPHINE
surgery .... ACIURGY
" , father of modern .... PARE
surgical compress .... STUPE
" counterirritant ...... SETON
" hook, sharp ..... TENACULA
" instrument ...... BISTOURY, LEVATOR
" machine .... SCALA
" operation .... RESECT
" plug ...... TAMPON, SPLINT
" puncture .... CENTESIS
suricate .... ZENICK, MEERCAT
Surinam capital ...... PARAMARIBO
" toad .... PIPA
" tree, wood of .... QUASSIA
surly .... CRUSTY, GRUM, ARROGANT, DOUR, SULLEN
surmise ...... OPINE, GUESS, INFER, ASSUME, SUPPOSE
surname ...... AGNOMEN, EPONYM, PATRONYMIC, DOE
surpass .... CAP, OUTDO, OUTSHINE, BEAT, BEST, EXCEL
surpassed .... ABOVE, BETTERED
surplice .... COTTA, PELISSE
surplus .. EPACT, REST, EXCESS, OVER, SPARE
surrealist .... DALI
surrender ..... CESSION, CEDE, REMIT, YIELD, DEDITION, RESIGN
surreptitious ... OCCULT, SLY, SECRET, FURTIVE, STEALTH
surround ...... BESET, HEM, ENCASE, HEDGE, INARM, GIRD
surroundings ENTOURAGE, ENVIRONS
surtax .... AGIO, EXTRA, LEVY
survey .. POLL, SEEING, VISTA, PLAN, MAP, REVIEW
surveying .... GEODESY
" instrument ...... ALIDADE, TRANSIT, STADIA, ROD
surveyor .... LINEMAN, OVERSEER, RODMAN
survival .... RELIC, OUTLIVING
suslik ..... SISEL, SQUIRREL, MARMOT
suspend .. HANG, STAY, DEBAR, DELAY
suspended .... PENSILE, HELD, HUNG
suspenders .... BRACES, GALLOWS
suspension .... DELAY, RESPITE
" of proceedings ...... SIST
suspicion ..... HINT, FEAR, MISTRUST, SOUPCON
suspicious .... LEERY, SCEPTICAL
sustained; mus. .... TENUTO
susu-like cetacean .... DOLPHIN, PLATANIST

281

susurrous .... SOUGHING
sutler's shop .... CANTEEN
suttee .... IMMOLATE
suture .. PTERION, RAPHE, SEAM, SEW,
JUNCTION
swab................. MOP, MALKIN
swage .... DOLLY, JUMPER, UPSET
swagger .... BLUSTER, PRANCE, SWELL
swain BEAU, FLAME, DAMON, GALLANT,
LAD, LOVER
swallow SWIFT, BOLT, GULP, ABSORB,
ENGORGE, TERN
swamp .. BOG, FEN, MARSH, MORASS,
SLUE
    " : boggy .... QUEACHY
    " grass .... SEDGE
    " in Maryland ...... POCOSON
    " , muddy .... SLOUGH
    " , relative of ...... MIASMA
swampland in India .... TERAI
swampy .. PALUDAL, ULIGINOSE, UVID
    " lands .... SLASH
    " region .... MUSKEG, TUNDRA,
TAIGA
swan, female .... PEN
    " , male .... COB
    " , whistling HOOPER, OLOR, ELK
    " , young .... CYGNET
"Swan of Eternity"; Hindu ... HANSA
"Swan of the Meander" .... HOMER
swanky .... POSH
"Swann's Way" author ...... PROUST
swap ..... TRADE, EXCHANGE, BANDY,
BARTER
sward ..... SOD, GRASS, LAWN, TURF,
SPINE
swarm .. NEST, FRY, HERD, BEVY, HIVE,
SNEE, THRONG, FLOCK, PACK,
SNY, TEEM, HORDE
swarming .... ALIVE, TEEMING
swarthy .... DUN, DUSTY, BISTERED
swastika .... FYLFOT, GAMMADION
swathe .... WRAP, BANDAGE, BIND
sway . RULE, VEER, WAVER, YAW, REEL,
ROCK
swear ... VOW, AVER, CURSE, DEPOSE
sweat EXUDE, PERSPIRE, OOZE, SUDOR
Swedish admin. province ..... LAN
    " battle .... LUND
    " bodyguard ...... BRABANTER
    " coin .... KRONA, ORE
    " ell measure .... ALN
    " explorer .... HEDIN
    " king ... ERIC, WASA, GUSTAV
    " lake .... MALAR
    " manual training .... SLOYD
    " measure ... AM, STANG, REF
    " Nightingale .... LIND
    " soprano .... NILSSON

    " terr. division .... LAN, LAEN
    " weight ..... PUND, STEN, ORT
sweep ...... DUST, RANGE, SWATH
sweepstakes .... LOTTERY, RACE
sweet DOUCE, HONEY, DULCET, SUGARY,
CANDY
    " cicely .... MYRRH
    " flag .... CALAMUS
    " liqueur .... RATAFIA
    " potato YAM, PATATA, OCARINA
sweetbread .... RIS, RUSK
sweetbriar, fruit of .. EGLANTINE, HIP
sweetheart .... LADYLOVE, LEMAN,
VALENTINE, AMARYLLIS, FLAME, SIS,
BEAU, INAMORATE, SPARK, FLAME,
JO
sweetmeat .... DRAGEE, CARAMEL
sweetsop .... ATTA, ATES
swell BULB, FOP, NOB, STRUT, BULGE,
DISTEND, DILATE
    " of sea ...... SURF, RISE, WAVE
swelled .... TUMID, TURGID
swelling .. BLAIN, EDEMA, STYE, LUMP,
BUBO, DROPSY, NODE, STROMA,
WEN
    " , per. to .... NODAL
swerve SHIFT, VEER, DEVIATE, CAREEN,
DEFLECT, SHY
swift .. FLEET, FAST, FLIT, BIRD, CRAN,
MARLET
swift-footed one ...... ALIPED, ARIEL,
MERCURY
Swift; pen name .... DRAPIER
swim .... CRAWL, DIP, FLOAT
swimmer .... LEANDER
swimming .... NATANT, VERTIGO
Swinburne; poet .... ALGERNON
swindle .. TREPAN, BAM, BUNCO, GYP,
CON, DUPE, CHOUSE
swindler BITER, GREEK, SHARK, CHEAT,
COZENER, APOSTATE
swindling; Sp. .... ESTAFA
swine ESSEX, DUROC, TAMWORTH, PIG,
SHOAT, BOAR, HOG
    " butcher's shop .... PORKERY
    " feeding .... PANNAGE
    " fever .... ROUGET
    " ; genus .... SUS
swineherd in Odyssey ..... EUMAEUS
    " , per. to .... SYBOTIC
swine-like .... PORCINE
swing .... DANGLE, GLIDER, PLY, SLUE
    " music ...... JAZZ, JIVE, BEBOP
    " musician .... HEPCAT
swirl .... GURGE, WHIRL, CURL, EDDY
Swiss .... HELVETIC, SUISSE
    " canton .... URI, GLARUS, VAUD,
BASEL, TICINO
    " capital .... BERN(E)

" chemist .... GLASER
" coin ... ANGSTER, BATZ, RAPPE
" cottage .... CHALET
" lake .... BIENNE, LUCERNE
" mathematician .... EULER
" measure .... ELLE, IMMI
" mountain .... RIGI, SENTIS,
    MATTERHORN, EIGER, BLANC,
    MONCH
" mountain pass .... GEMMI
" official ...... AMMAN, AVOYER
" patriot .... TELL
" poet .... AMIEL, USTERI
" psychiatrist ...... RORSCHACH
" regular army ..... LANDWEHR
" river .. AAR(E), REUSS, SAANE,
    RHONE
" scientist .... HALLER
" theologian .... VINET
" town ... CHUR, ZUG, LOCARNO,
    GENEVA, BASEL, ASCONA,
    LUGANO, DAVOS
" tunnel ... SIMPLON, GOTTHARD
switch .... TWIG, SHIFT, TOGGLE
switchman .... SHUNTER
Switzerland .... HELVETIA, SUISSE
swivel PIVOT, TURN, SWING, TRAVERSE
swollen ....BOLLEN, TUMID, BLOATED,
    BLOBBER, TURGID
swoon .... SWEB, FAINT
swoop .... POUNCE, DESCEND
sword ...... BILBO, BADELAIRE, KUKRI,
    ANDREW, DEGEN, ESTOC, BALDRIC,
    SPADA, PATA, SAX, TURK, STEEL,
    SNICKER, SPIT, GRAM
" , a kind of ... ANDREW, DEGEN,
    ESTOC, BALDRIC, SPADA, PATA,
    SAX, TUCK
" -blade heel .... TALON
" blade, weakest part of FOIBLE
" , broad cutting .... CUTLASS
" , fencing .... EPEE
" having a curved blade SABER
" handle .... HAFT, HILT
" , Highland .... CLAYMORE
" lily .... GLADIOLUS
" , long thin .... RAPIER
" , Malayan .... CREESE
" of death ....MORGLAY
" of finest temper ...... TOLEDO
" of mercy .... CURTANA
" of St. George .... ASKELON
" of Siegfried .... BALMUNG
" , oriental .... SCIMITAR
" pole .... GLAIVE
" , seamen's .... HANGER
" -shaped ..... ENSATE, ENSIFORM,
    XIPHOID, GLADIATE
" : stronger part of blade FORTE

" , two-edged .... PATA
swordfish .. ESPADON, ESPADA, XIPHIA
sworn to secrecy .... TILED
sybarite .... EPICURE
sycamore .... MULBERRY, DAROO,
    PLANTAIN
sycophant .... FLUNKY, SPANIEL,
    TOADEATER, PARASITE, TOADY,
    LEECH, SPONGE
sycosis .... MENTAGRA
syllable, accented .... THESIS
" added to a word .... PREFIX
" : last but one of a word ....
    PENULT
" , lengthening of a ... ESTASIS
" , metrical stress on ... ICTUS
" of three morae .... TRISEME
" , omission of last .. APOCOPE
" , per. to a .... DACTYLIC
" , short .... MORA
" , shortening of a ... SYSTOLE
" used in music .... TRA
syllables, unaccented ARSES, ATONIC
syllogism ..... BARBARA, EPICHEIREMA
syllogisms, series of .... SORITES
sylph .... ELF, FAY, PIXY, FAIRY
sylvan deity .... FAUN, SATYR
symbol TOKEN, PALM, EMBLEM, SIGN,
    TOTEM, PENTACLE
" of authority .. MACE, BADGE,
    STAR, FASCES
symbolic .... IMAGERIAL
symmetrical .... SPHERAL
" , anti- .... ANTIMERE
sympathy .. CONSENT, PITY, CONDOLE
" , lack of .... DYSPATHY
symptom NOTE, SIGN, TOKEN, MARK,
    ALARM, WARNING
synagogue .... SHUL, TEMPLE
" founder .... EZRA
syncope .... ELISION, FAINT
synopsis ABSTRACT, DIGEST, EPITOME,
    CONSPECTUS
synthetic RAYON, NYLON, ARTIFICIAL,
    POLYESTER, SARAN, DYNEL
" rubber .... BUNA
Syracuse, master of .... DION
Syria .... ARAM
" , buried city of .... CAPITAL
" , city of ....DAMASCUS, ALEPPO,
    HOMS
" , tribesman of .... ANSARIE
Syriac script .... SERTA, PESHITO
syrup .... SORGHUM, MAPLE, TREACLE
system ..... ISM, METHOD, REGIMEN,
    ORDER, SCHEME, CODE, CULT
" , geological .... TRIAS
" of Gaelic landholding ....
    RUNDALE

283

    "   of symbols for pitch . NEUME
    "   of writing for blind .. BRAILLE
systematics .... TAXONOMY
syzygy .... DIPODY

T

T, letter .... TEE
T.N.T. .... TROTOL
    "   component .... TOLUENE
T-shaped .... TAU
taa .... PAGODA
tab ..... FLAP, PAN, STRIP, LABEL, TAG
  ", shoe ..... LATCHET, LACE, STRAP
tabard .... CAPE, MANTLE
tabernacle ..... KIRK, TEMPLE, HOVEL
table ... FARE, ABACUS, LIST, PROJECT,
    DEFER, SHELVE, CREDENCE, TRIVET,
                      ROSTER
  "   centerpiece .... EPERGNE
  ", communion .... ALTAR
  "   linen .... NAPERY
  ", three-legged .. TEAPOY, TRIVET
  ", workman's .... SIEGE
tableau ... PICTURE, SCENE, PORTRAIT
tableland ...... MESA, PLATEAU, PUNA
  "   , Central Asia .... PAMIR
  "   of S. Africa .... KAROO
tablet ...... BRED, FACIA, PAD, SLATE,
                      PLAQUE
  ", medicinal TROCHEE, LOZENGE,
                      PILL
  "   of stone .... STELE, SLAB
  ", symbol .... PAX
taboo ...... BAN, INTERDICT, FORBID
  ", opposed to .... NOA
tabor .... ATABAL
taciturn .... SILENT, RETICENT
tack, glazier's .... BRAD
  ", to ... GIBE, BEAT, LAVEER, STAY
  "   with long stitches .... BASTE
tackle .... CAT, GARNET, GEAR, YOKE,
          GUN, RUNNER, OUTFIT
tael, one tenth of .... MACE
taffeta .... SAMITE
tag LABEL, FLAP, STUB, APPEND, AGLET
Tagalog .... MALAYAN
  "   deity ..... BATALA, BATHALA
  "   peasant .... TAO
Tahiti capital .... PAPEETE
  "   native .... OTAHEITE
  "   ; supreme god .... TAAROA
Tahitian canoe .... PAHI
  "   woman ... VAHINE, WAHINE
Tai race, one of .... TAO
tail ESCAPE, FLEE, CAUDA, CODA, FUD,
          TRAIL, TAG, VERSO

  ", boar's .... WREATH
  ", having a .... CAUDATE
  ", kind of short .... SCUT, BUNT
  "   of aerial vehicle .... EMPENNAGE
  "   race .... CHANNEL, FLUME
tailless .... ACAUDAL, ACAUDATE,
                     ANUROUS
  "   amphibian family .. RANIDAE
  "   animal of Madagascar TENREC
  "   coat .... TUX(EDO)
tailor .... SARTOR, CLOTHIER, FIT
  ", iron of ..... GOOSE, SADIRON
  ", lapboard of .... PANEL
tainted .... BAD, IMBUED, PINDY
Taiwan .... FORMOSA
  "   capital .... TAIPEI
Taj Mahal .... SHRINE
  "   ", site of .... AGRA
take .... OCCUPY, TAE, USURP, CATCH,
             SEIZE, NAB, GRAB
  "   away ... HEAVE, WREST, ADEEM,
           TOL, DEROGATE, REMOVE
  "   off .. DOFF, FLIGHT, FLEE, MIMIC,
                  PARODY
  "   possession of ... ESCHEAT, SEISE
  "   ; slang .... GRAB, HOG
taking advantage of ...... ABUSING,
                  MISUSING
  ", act of .... RECEIPT
  "   back .... RECANTING
talc .... AGALITE, STEATITE
tale ..... GESTE, CONTE, LEED, MYTH,
    FALSEHOOD, LIE, NOVEL, YARN
  " -bearer .... QUIDNUNC, BLABBER
  "   of adventure .... GEST
  "   of sorrow .... JEREMIAD
  ", short medieval .... LAI
  ", traditional .... SAGA
talent .... FORTE, KNACK, GENIUS
talent, one sixtieth of .... MINA
Tales, slayer of .... DAEDALUS
talipes .... CLUBFOOT
talipod .... PALM
talisman ... AMULET, CHARM, KARMA,
                FETISH, GRIGRI
talk .. BLAB(BER), GAB, CRACK, HARP,
    PALABRA, KNAP, PALAVER, SPEAK,
           GAS, HARANGUE
  "   foolishly ...... BLATHER, DROOL,
              DRIVEL, PRATTLE
  "   in loud tone .... RANT
  ", rapid .... PATTER
  " ; slang .... SPIEL
  " ; back- ; slang .... SASS
talker ..... PROSER, MAGPIE, ORATOR,
                STENTOR
tall .... HIGH, PROCERE, TAUNT
Tallchief; ballerina .... MARIA
tallest race .... PATAGONIAN
tallow .... SUET, STEARIN, LARD

" tree .... CERA
tally .... SCORE, SQUARE, NOTCH
Talmud, part of the .... GEMARA,
MISHNAH
Talmudic title .... ABBA
Tamara's domain .... IMERITIA
talon .... CLAW, FANG, NAIL
tam .... CAP
tamarisk salt tree ...... ATLE, HEATH
tambourine .... TAAR, DAIRA, TABOR,
TIMBREL
" vibrant effect ... TRAVALE
Tamiroff; actor .... AKIM
tamper ...... TINKER, ALTER, MEDDLE,
MOLEST
tan ..... TAW, BUFF, BEIGE, CHASTISE
tanager .... LINDO, YENI
tangle .. SHAG, MAT, SLEAVE, WEAVE,
FOUL, KNOT, EMBROIL
" of shrubs .... CHAPARRAL
tank .... VAT, POND, POOL
" stopper .... BAZOOKA
tankard ...... HANAP, FACER, GOBLET
tanker .... OILER
tanner's solution .... AMALTAS, BATE
Tanoan Indian .... ISLETA
tantalize .... PLAGUE, VEX, TEASE
Tantalus' daughter .... NIOBE
" parent .... ZEUS
" son .... PELOPS
tantrum ... ANGER, RAGE, HUFF, MIFF,
FIT, SPELL
tap ..... PLUG, SPILE, SOUND, FAUCET,
DANCE, BROACH, BAR, COCK
tape needle .... BODKIN
taper ship's timber .... SNAPE
tapered ..... TERETE, SPIRED, CONOID
tapering .... CONICAL, FUSIFORM
tapestry ...... DOSSER, ARRAS, TAPIS,
GOBELIN, BRUGES
" -making comb .... REED
" warp threads .... LISSES
tapeworm ..... CESTODE, ENTOZOAN,
TAENIA
tapioca source .... CASSAVA
" -like food .... SALEP
tapir................. ANTA, DANTA
tappet .... LEVER, CAM
Tapuyan tribe . APINAGE, BOTOCUDO,
GES
tar ..... GOB, JACKY, MARINER, SALT,
SAILOR, PITCH, PINE, RETENE
" mineral .... MALTHA, BREA
Taraf, subdivision of ...... DHER(I)
Taranaki volcano .... EGMONT
tarboosh .... TURBAN, FEZ
tardy .... LATE, BUSTARD, LAG
tare .... VETCH, WEED
target . BIRD, MARK, AIM, BUTT, GOAL,
BULLSEYE, OBJECTIVE, SIGHT

taro dish .... POI
" plant...... GABE, KOKO, COCCO
" roots .... EDDOES
" ; W. Ind. .... TANIA
tarpon .... MILKFISH, SABALO
tarsus .... ANKLE, HOCK, SHANK
Tarsus governor; Shak. ...... CLEON
tart .... SOUR, SUBACID, ACERB
tartan .... PLAID, SET
Tartar .... TATAR, TURK
" horseman .... COSSACK
" militia, one of .... UHLAN
" nobleman .... MURZA
tartar, crude .... ARGOL, ARGAL
Tartarus .... HADES
"Tartufe" maid .... DORINE
task ... CHORE, PENSUM, STINT, DUTY,
CHARE
" , take to .... LECTURE
Tasmania capital .... HOBART
taste .. PALATE, DEGUST, FREE, SAPOR,
SIP, SAVOR, SMACK, TANG
" , delighting .... FRIAND
" , French for .... SOUPCON
tasteful ...... NEAT, SAPID, ELEGANT,
DAINTY, ARTISTIC
tasteless WATERY, CRUDE, FLAT, VAPID,
GAUCHE, VULGAR
tasty ..... SAPOROUS, SAVORY, NEAT
Tatar (see "Tartar")
tatter .... RAG, PATCH, SHRED
tattle .... DIVULGE, TELL, BLAB, PEACH
tattler . QUIDNUNC, GOSSIP, TELLTALE
tattoo .... PINK
tattooing .... MOKO
tau cross .... ANKH, CRUX
taunt SNEER, JIBE, QUIP, QUIRK, TWIT,
JEER, NEEDLE
taurine .... BULL, TAURUS
taut .. FIRM, TENSE, TIDY, EDGY, SNUG,
RIGID, STIFF, NERVOUS
tautog .... CHUB, LABROID
tavern . CABARET, INN, PUB, TABERNA,
HOTEL, SALOON, BAR, TAP, TAMBO,
BISTRO, KABAK
taw .... MARBLE
tawny .... TAN, DUSKY, RUBIATE, HUE,
SWART, OLIVE, TENNE
tax .... LEVY, SCAT, CESS, SCOT, TAIL,
TOLL, TRIBUTE, EXCISE, ANNATES,
ANNALE, SCUTAGE
" assessment on default DOOMAGE
" , Chinese provincial .... LIKIN
" , English .... HIDAGE
" from a monopoly .... REGIE
" on commodities .. OCTROI, DUTY
" or impost ...... TAILLE, TAILAGE,
CUSTOM
" , Scottish .... STENT, CRO, GALNES
taxed a tenth .... TITHED

285

Taylor, Miss .... LIZ
tea .... CAMBRIC, CHA, YERBA, TISANE,
                    KEEMUN, LAPSANG
" , bitter principle of ..... THEINE
" box .... CADDY
" , Braz. holly .... MATE
" , China, third picking .. CONGOU
" , Chinese .... HYSON
" extract .... ADENINE
" , finely flavored .... PEKOE
" , Formosa .... OOLONG
" , found in .... TANNIN
" , kind of black ... BOHEA, OOPAK
" , Labrador .... LEDUM
" plant .... KAT, THEA
" pot .... TRACK, URN
" table .... TEAPOY
" urn; Rus. .... SAMOVAR
teacake .... LUNN, SCONE
teach EDIFY, COACH, ENDUE, SCHOOL,
        CRAM, PRIME, TUTOR, DRILL,
        MONITOR, TRAIN, EDUCATE
teacher .... PEDAGOG(UE), PUNDIT,
        SCRIBE, MULLAH, ALIM, GURU,
        IMAM, DOCENT, RABBI
teachers' fee .... MINERVAL
    " group .... NEA
teaching .. .. DOCENT, PRECEPT
teak tree .... TECA, SAJ
teal ...... DUCK, CRICK, GREENWING,
                    SARCELLE
team JOIN, PAIR, SPAN, CREW, STRING,
                    YOKE, SCRUB
teamster .. TOTER, BEARER, ACCRIER,
                    CARTER
teapot .... SAMOVAR, STEEPER
tear ... REND, RIP, RIVE, SPLIT, TATTER,
                    BINGE, LARME
" in pieces .... LACREATE, LANIATE
" up, as trees ..... ASSART, ESSART
" up by the roots ... ARACE, PLUCK
teardrop-like figure .... LARME
tearful .... MAUDLIN, WEEPING, SAD,
                    MOIST
tear gas .... LACRIMATOR
tears, of .... LACRIMAL
tease .... BANTER, HECTOR, NAG, RIB,
                    BOTHER, TWIT
teasel ..... BONESET, HERB, MANWEED
teaser .... STOKER
Tebaldi; singer .... RENATA
tedious DREARY, NOXIOUS, DRY, DULL,
                    PROSY, ELENGE
ted .... SPREAD, SCATTER
tedium .... BOREDOM, ENNUI
teehee .... TITTER, SNICKER
teem .... ABOUND, POUR, RAIN
teeter .... ROCK, SEESAW, JIGGLE

teeth ..... BITERS, INCISORS, MOLARS,
                    BICUSPIDS
" cavity, tissue in .... PULP
" , concretion on .... TARTAR
" , double ..... GRINDERS, MOLARS
" , false .... PLATE, DENTURE
" , hard tissue of .... DENTINE
" , long pointed .... TUSHES
" of certain mammals .... TUSKS
" , set of .... DENTURE
" , sharp .... FANGS
" : sockets .... ALVEOLI
" : upper molars' surface CORONA
" , without .... EDENTATE, MORNE
teetotaler ..... RECHABITE, NEPHALIST
teetotum .... TOY
tegument .... CORTEX, SKIN, ARIL
tela .... MEMBRANE, TISSUE
telamon .... MAN, ATLAS
Telamon, brother of .... PELEUS
    " , companion of ... HERCULES
    " , son of .... AJAX
telegram .... DESPATCH, WIRE, CABLE
telegraph code .... MORSE
    " instrument, part of..ANVIL,
                    KEY, TAPPER
    " recorder .... SIPHON
    " speed unit .... BAUD
telephone .... BUZZ, DIAL, RING
    " inventor .... BELL
telescope ..... FOLD, LENS, COLLAPSE
    " site .... PALOMAR
television .... VIDEO
    " cable .... COAXIAL
    " interference SNOW, GHOSTS
tell ..... RECITE, SAY, IMPART, RELATE,
                    NARRATE, RECOUNT, OWN
" against an accomplice ... PEACH
Tell .... WILLIAM
" , home of .... URI
telling .... COGENT, POTENT
    " blow .... COUP, ONER
telluride .... HESSITE
telopea .... WARATAH
telson .... PLEON
temblor ...... EARTHQUAKE, TREMOR
temper MOOD, METTLE, TONE, DANDER,
        TANTRUM, SOFTEN, MIX, PET,
        HUMOR, (AN)NEAL
temperament MOOD, GEMUT, CRASIS,
                    ACTION
tempest BLAST, ORAGE, SAMIEL, GALE,
        TUMULT, BAYAMO
temple HUACA, COVIL, FANE, PAGODA,
        HEIAU, TEOCALLI, MOSQUE, TAA,
        SAA, VAT, WAT
    " builder, earliest ...... MICAH
    " chamber .... CELLA, NAOS
    " gateway .... TORII
    " , relative of a .... HIERON

" portico .... NARTHEX	Tent Maker .... OMAR, KHAYYAM
" vestibule .... PRONAOS	tenuous ...... GASEOUS, RARE, THIN,
Templeton; pianist .... ALEC	SLENDER, DELICATE
tempo .... BEAT, PULSE, RHYTHM, TACT	tenure .... FEU, SOCAGE
" , rapid .... PRESTO	" clauses .... TENENDA
" , very slow .... GRAVE	tequila .... MESCAL
temporal .... CIVIL, LAY, WORLDLY	terebinth ..... TEIL, TREE, TURPENTINE
temporarily .... INTERIM, NONCE	teredo .... BORER, SHIPWORM
tempt ... DECOY, ENTICE, BAIT, LURE,	terella .... EARTHKIN
PROVOKE	tergal .... BACK, DORSAL
ten .... DECA(D), DENARY	tergiversate .... EQUIVOCATE, LIE
Ten Commandments .. DECALOG(UE)	term ...... PERIOD, AGE, ERA, EPOCH,
ten decibels .... BEL	SEMESTER, NAME, LIMIT, RHEMA,
" -gallon hat .... SOMBRERO	SESSION
" million ergs .... JOULE	termagant ... SHREW, VIRAGO, VIXEN
" thousand .... MYRIAD	terminal .... DEPOT, END, YARD
" -year period .... DECENNIUM	" , negative .... CATHODE
tenacity . GRIT, METTLE, PLUCK, LENTOR	" of a leaf .... APICULUS
tenant ..... VILLEIN, RENTER, LESSEE,	" , positive .... ANODE
LEUD(E), SOCMAN, VASSAL,	terminate . CLOSE, END, ABATE, CEASE
COTTER, SAER	termination .... END, AMEN, BOUND,
tenant's neglect to pay ...... CESSER	FINIAL
" tribute .... CENS	termite ..... ANAI, ANAY, ANT, KING
tench-like fish .... CARP, DACE	tern .... PIRR, PIRL, LARID, THREEFOLD
tend ...... CARE, LEAN, MIND, NURSE,	ternary .... TRIAD
SERVE, FOSTER	terns; genus .... ANOUS, STERNA
tendency .... BENT, DRIFT, TREND	terpene .... NOPINENE
tender ... PRESENT, OFFER, SORE, TID,	terrace .. BERM(E), GALLERY, PLATEAU,
PROFFER, MONEY	PORTICO, DAIS, PATIO
tender style; mus. .... AMOROSO	" in series .... PARTERRE
tendon ...... SINEW, MUSCLE, NERVE	terrapin .. TORTOISE, EMYD, COODLE
tendril .. STIPULE, CURL, SPRIG, ROOT,	" order .... CHELONIA
CAPREOL	" , red-billed .... SLIDER
tendrils .... CIRRI, SHOOTS	terrestrial .. EARTHLY, GEAL, TERRENE,
tenfold .... DECUPLE, DENARY	MUNDANE
Tennessee city ...... ALCOA, ERWIN,	terret ..... EYELET, GROMMET, WITHE
MEMPHIS	terrible .... DIRE, GHAST, FEARFUL
" , first governor of . SEVIER	"Terrible, The" .... IVAN
tennis term .... ACE, CUT, LOB, LOVE,	terrier DANDIE, FOX, SEALYHAM, SKYE,
DEUCE, FAULT, SERVICE, SMASH	RATTER, MANCHESTER
Tennyson heroine .... MAUD, ENID	terrify . APPALL, ABAST, DAUNT, COW,
tenon .. COG, TOOTH, TUSK, MORTISE	PANIC
" -like piece .... COAK, LEWIS	terrorist GOON, ALARMIST, SKYJACKER
tenor .. DRIFT, INTENT, PURPORT, GIST,	terse ..... CRISP, SUCCINCT, LACONIC,
TREND, CARUSO, LANZA	PITHY, BRIEF
" violin .... ALTO	tertiary period .. PLIOCENE, NEOCENE
tenrec-like animal ...... HEDGEHOG	Tesla; inventor .... NIKOLA
tense RAPT, TAUT, RIGID, STIFF, PAST,	"Tess and Jude" by _____ HARDY
PRESENT, FUTURE, PERFECT, AORIST	tesselated .... MOSAIC
tensile .... DUCTILE	tessera .... TILE
tent .... CAMP, TELD, PROBE, CANOPY,	test .... TRIAL, TRYOUT, PROVE, TENT,
WIGWAM, TEPEE, TEEPEE, PAWL	DRYRUN, TRY, ASSAY, EXAMINE,
" covering .... TILT	TEMPT, REFINE, QUIZ
" dweller . NOMAD, ARAB, SCENITE,	" pot .... CRUCIBLE
KEDAR	testament .... WILL, COVENANT
" , large field .... MARQUEE	testator .... LEGATOR
tentacle . FEELER, HAIR, PALP, TENDRIL	tester .... CIEL, TRIER, SARAF, SHROFF
tentacles, without .... ACEROSE	testify ..... AVOW, DEPONE, DEPOSE,
tenterhook .... AGOF, STRAIN	SWEAR
tenth part .... DECI, TITHE	testimonial .... TRIBUTE, COMPLIMENT

testy .... CRANKY, PEEVISH
tete-a-tete .... FACING, OPPOSITE,
TWOSOME
tether BIND, LEASH, TIE, ROPE, LONGE,
PASTERN
Tethys .... TITANESS
" , brother of .... CRONUS
" , father of .... URANUS
" , husband of .... OCEANUS
tetrachord .... TA, MESON, NETE
tetrad .... FOUR
Teutonic divinity .... NORN
" dwarf god .... TROLL
" god of chase .... ULL
" god of justice ...... FORSETI
" god of peace .... BALDER
" god of the sea .... AEGIR
" god of the sky .... TYR
" god of thunder DONAR, THOR
" god of war . TIU, TIWAZ, TYR
" goddess of death ...... RAN
" goddess of healing ...... EIR
" goddess of peace .. NERTHUS
" gods .. ODIN, WODEN, AESIR
Texas city .. ABILENE, ENNIS, AUSTIN,
SPUR, ALICE, CUERO, DALLAS, MART,
CRANE
" county ... SABINE, FRIO, KNOX
" flowering shrub ...... BARETTA
" shrine .... ALAMO
text .... THEME, TOPIC, LIBRETTO
textile .... CLOTH, FIBER, FABRIC
" dealer .... MERCER
" worker .... REEDMAN, WEAVER
texture .. WALE, WEB, WOOF, WEAVE,
NAP, GRAIN
Thai .... SIAMESE, LAO
" town .... NAN
Thalia's sister .... ERATO
Thames estuary .... NORE
Thanatos personified .... DEATH
thanks, great . GRAMERCY, GRATITUDE
thankless person .... INGRATE
that is .... IDEST
thatched .... HELED, REEDED
" -roof dwelling .... ISBA
theater ..... ODEON, STAGE, ARENA,
DRAMA, GLOBE, LEGIT, MOVIE,
OPERA, CINEMA, LYCEUM, RIALTO
" curtain .... TEASER
" district .... RIALTO
" group . ASCAP, ANTA, HABIMA
" , part of BALCONY, BOX, CAVEA,
CIRCLE, FRONT, LOGE, PIT, STALL
theatrical .... STAGY, ARTIFICIAL,
POMPOUS
" extra .... SUPER
" representation, art of ......
HISTRIONIC

" role ..... BIT, HEAVY, LEAD,
WALKON, PART
" tour .... ROAD
Thebes, deity of .... AMON
" , one of seven against TYDEUS
" , soothsayer of ...... TIRESIAS
theft-like .... PIRACY, LARCENY
theme .... TEXT, THESIS, TOPIC, MOTIF
then ALORS, POI, ANON, NEXT, SOON
theodolite .... ALIDADE
theologian .... CALVIN, HUSS, LUTHER,
DIVINE
theorbo .... (ARCH)LUTE
theoretical .... ACADEMIC, PLATONIC,
ABSTRACT
" power .... ODYL(E)
theory .. DOCTRINE, HYPOTHESIS, ISM,
SCHEME, NOTION
" , proving of a ..... APAGOGE
therapy .... CURE
there .... YON, IBI
therefore THEN, ERGO, HENCE, SINCE,
THUS
thesaurus .... LEXICON
Theseus' father .... AEGEUS
thesis .... ESSAY, PAPER, THEME
Thespian .... ACTOR, MIME, TRAGIC
Thetis' husband .... PELEUS
" son .... ACHILLES
thick ...... CRASS, GRUMOUS, ROILY,
TURBID, DENSE, HEAVY, CLOSE,
DULL
" ; as of the lip .... BLOBBER,
LABROSE
" place in yarns .... SLUB
" ; Spanish for .... ESPESO
thicken ... INSPISSATE, CLOT, CURDLE,
LYE, CAKE, SOLIDIFY
thicket COPSE, BOSK, COVERT, HEDGE,
RONE, BRUSH, COPPICE, JUNGLE
thickness .... LAYER, PLY
thief .. FAGIN, FILCHER, PIKER, PIRATE,
GANEF, GANOF, BURGLAR, YEGG,
CHOR
Thieves' Latin .... SLANG
thigh, animal's .... HAM
" bone .... FEMUR, MEROS
" , of the .... FEMORAL
thill .... SHAFT, LIMBER
thimblerigger ..... CHEAT, SWINDLER
thin .. LATHY, LANK, SCRAGGY, SHEER,
BONY, MEAGRE, ARANEOUS,
SLEAZY, SUBTILE, TENUOUS, RARE,
SPARSE
" leather .... DOLE
" muslin .... MULL
" out .... DISBUD, DELETE
" plate .... SHIM, TAGGER, TILE
" scale .... LAMELLA
thing........ ENTITY, BEING, MATTER

" found, a .... TROVE
" of little value STIVER, TRINKET
" to be done .... AGENDUM
things .... TRAPS, ITS
" done .... ACTA
" , exaggerated .... HOWLERS
thing(s) in law .... REM, RES
thingumajig .... GADGET
think OPINE, DEEM, MUSE, TROW, WIS,
    BROOD, MULL, IDEATE, COGITATE
thinly scattered .... RARE, SPARSE
thinness .... TENUITY
third degree of scale ...... MEDIANT
" , every .... TERTIAN
" in music .... TIERCE
" power, raise to .... CUBE
thirsty .... DRY, ARID, PARCHED
this; Lat. .... HAEC, HOC
Thisbe's friend .... PYRAMUS
thistle ...... TEASEL, HOYLE, CALTROP,
    ARNICA, COSMOS, CARLINA
thistledown .... PAPPUS
thither ..... YON(D), THERE, TOWARD
thole............ FULCRUM, OARLOCK
Thomas opera .... MIGNON
Thompson .... (ERNEST)SETON
thong .. KNOUT, STRAP, WHIP, ROMAL,
    LORATE, RIEM, QUIRT
thorax .... CHEST, TRUNK
thorn .... STUG, SPINE, STOB, PRICKLE,
    BRIAR, BRIER, BARB, SETA
" apple .... DATURA, METEL
" -back .... RAY, SKATE
" , having a .... SPINATE
thornless .... INERM
thoroughwort .... BONESET
thorp ...... HAMLET, VILLAGE, TOWN
Thor's father .... ODIN
" magic hammer ..... MJOLLNIR
" wife...................... SIF
those in office .... INS
thought IDEA, VIEW, NOESIS, CONCEPT
" , doctrine of laws of . NOETICS
thousand years . MILLENNIUM, CHILIAD
thousandth .... MILLESIMAL
Thrace, town in .... SESTOS
Thracian musician .... ORPHEUS
thrall ..... ESNE, SERF, SLAVE, PEON,
    VASSAL
thralldom .... BONDAGE, SERVITUDE
thrash .... TROUNCE, BLESS, BELABOR,
    CANE, FLAIL, TAN, FLOG, LAM,
    URTICATE, DRUB, WHALE
thread .. LISLE, REEVE, STAMEN, LINE,
    BAVE, CLEW, CLUE, CORD, TRAM,
    WARP, WEFT, FIBER
" ; comb. form .... NEMA
" fish .... COBBLER, CUTLASS
" , shoemaker's .... LINGEL
" , surgical .... SETON

" testing device ...... SERIMETER
" worm .... FILARIA, NEMATODE
threadbare .... TRITE, CORNY, SHABBY
threads, fine; comb. form ...... BYSS
" , of .. FILAR, FILOSE, NEMALINE
" of linen tape .... INKLES
" , separate .... SLEAVE
threaten ..... DARE, IMPEND, MENACE
three .. TER, THRIN, DREI, TRIO, TROIS,
    TRIAD
" , group of .... TERN, TRIAD
" herrings .... WARP
" in one .... TRIUNE
" -knotted .... TRINODAL
" of a kind .... LEASH
threefold .... TERNAL, TREBLE, TRINE,
    TERNARY, TERNATE
three-leaved clover .... TREFOIL
three-legged stand ... TEAPOY, TRIVET
three-mast schooner .... TERN
three-penny piece .... THRIP
threnody CORONACH, REQUIEM, DIRGE
threshold ..... GATE, SILL, EVE, LIMEN
threw .... TOSSED, CAST
thrice; prefix .... TER, TRI
thrifty .... FRUGAL, SAVING
thrill . DINDLE, FLUSH, TIRL, KICK, STIR
thrilling .... ELECTRIC, SHOCKING
thrive .... ADDLE, BATTEN, BOOM,
    SUCCEED, WAX, PROSPER
throat .... MAW, GULA
" , per. to .... (JU)GULAR
throb .... ACHE, BEAT, PULSATE, QUOP
throbbing .... PALPITANT, PITAPAT
throe ..... ACHE, PAIN, PANG, RACK,
    AGONY, SPASM
throne ... SOVEREIGNTY, ASANA, SEAT
throng .. HOST, CREW, SWARM, PRESS,
    HORDE, MOB
throstle .... THRUSH
through ... DONE, VIA, PER, FINISHED
throw CAST, HEAVE, KEST, HURL, WRAP,
    FLING, FITCH
" carelessly .... SLAP, SHY
" obliquely ... DEAL, TOSS, SKEW
" out ...... BOUNCE, LADE, EJECT
thrush . OUSEL, ROBIN, SPREW, SPRUE,
    THROSTLE
" disease .... APHTHA
" , ground .... PITTA
" , Hawaii .... OLAMAO
" , song .... MAVIS, VEERY
thrust .. DIG, RETRUDE, DART(LE), BUTT,
    ONSET, ALLONGE, LUNGE, SHOVE,
    POSS
" aside .... SHOVE, DAFF
" by pushing ..... ENTER, PIERCE
thud .... BUMP, BEAT, BLOW
thug ..... GUNMAN, RUFFIAN, CUTTLE,
    YEGG, GOON, ROUGHNECK

thumb .... POLLEX, THENAR, THROOM
thump .... PUMMEL, YERK, POLT
thunderfish .... LOACH, RAAD
thurible .... CENSER
thus DYCE, HENCE, ITA, SIC, YET, ERGO
thwack .... CLUB, MAUL, RAP, POMMEL
thwart .... BAFFLE, BALK, FOIL, SPITE
thymus .... GLAND, SWEETBREAD
tiara ... CROWN, FRONTLET, CORONET
Tibet .... SITSANG
" , capital of .... LHASA, LASSA
" , ruler of .... DALAILAMA
Tibetan antelope .... GOA
"   beer .... CHANG
"   ox .... YAK
"   priest .... LAMA
"   wild ass .... KIANG
"   wild cat .... MANUL
tibia .... CNEMIS, SHINBONE
Tibur .... TIVOLI
tic .... LATA, LATAH
tick .... ACARID, KED, GARAPATO
" ; genus .... IXODE, ARGAS
ticket SLATE, NOTE, SLIP, PASS, LABEL,
BALLOT
" , sell, illegally .... SCALP
tickle .... TITILLATE, EXCITE
tidal flow .... ESTUARY, SURGE, BORE,
EAGRE, EBB, NEAP
tidbit .... CATE
tidings ..... ADVISE, NEWS, SLOGAN,
REPORT, WORD, GOSPEL, EVANGEL
tidy . SPRUCE, TED, NEAT, TRIM, SNOD,
KEMPT, PRIM
tie ... BEAM, BIND, BOND, LASH, LINK,
MOOR, MARRY, RIVET, TRICE,
HOBBLE, TETHER, SLEEPER, NEXUS,
YERK
" up .... PACK, TRUSS
tied .... EVEN
tier RANK, ROW, SERIES, BANK, LAYER,
GRADIN, CHESS
tiff .... HUFF, PET, SPAT
tiffin .... LUNCHEON, REPAST, TEA
tiger .... SHER, SHIR
" family .... FELIDAE
tight .... SNUG, TAUT, DRUNK, TENSE,
STINGY
tighten LACE, STRAITEN, TAUTEN, FRAP,
DRAW
tightwad FIST, MISER, PIKER, SKINFLINT
til......................... SESAME
tiles(s) FAVUS, PANTILE, TESSERA, FAVI,
SLATER, QUARRY, SLAB, IMBREX
" pattern .... MOSAIC
" , per. to a .... TEGULAR
" , to .... TESSELATE
tiler ...... HELLIER, DOORKEEPER
tilery .... KILN
tillage, fit for .... ARABLE

tilled land .... ARADA, ARATA
tiller . FARMER, HARROWER, PLOWMAN,
HUSBAND, STERN
tilly-vally .... BOSH
tilt ..... HEEL, LIST, TIP, JOUST, CAVE,
CAREEN, ASLANT
timber ..... CAMBER, STUMPAGE, BIBB,
LOG(S), LUMBER
" , decay in .... DOAT, DOTE
" , down bend in .... SNY
" , heartwood of ...... DURAMEN
" , Norway .... DRAM
" of a ship, upright .... BITT
" , squared .... CANT
" support .... CORBEL
" , to taper a ship's ...... SNAPE
timbre, per. to .... TONAL
timbrel .... TABOR, SISTRUM
time . DATE, SPELL, EPOCH, ERA, TENSE,
BEAT, SPELL, TEMPO, EON, AGE
" fixed for bill payment USANCE
" of day .... NOON, MORN
" , per. to a .... ERAL
" , space of .... WHILE
timely .. EARLY, PAT, PROMPT, TOPICAL
timepiece HOROLOGE, VERGE, GHURRY,
HOURGLASS
" , per. to a .. GNOMON, DIAL
" , water .... CLEPSYDRA
times past .... ONST, AGO, ONCE
timid .... SCARY, MOUSY, SHY, TREPID,
FAINT, HENNY
Timor coin .... AVO
timpano .... (KETTLE)DRUM
tin .... STANNUM, CAN, COAT
" box .... TRUMMEL
" dinner pail .... BLICKEY
" -foil for mirrors .... TAIN
" mine .... STANNARY
" mine, workman in ..... SPADIARD
" plate, thin .... FOIL, TAGGER
" roofing .... TERNE
" sheet .... LATTEN
tinamou .... YUTU, TATAUPA, MACUCA
tincture . DASH, TRACE, TOUCH, IMBUE
tinder .... AMADOU, PUNK
tine .... BIT, PRONG, FANG, SNAG
tinea .... RINGWORM
tined, three- .... TRIDENTATE
tinge COLOR, DYE, IMBUE, TINT, TAINT,
TRACE, DASH, TOUCH
tint ..... HUE, NUANCE, TONE, STAIN
tiny ..... MINUTE, PETITE, TEENY, WEE
" creature .... ATOMY, MINIMUS
tip LIST, CANT, HEEL, POINT, TILT, TOE,
COCK, POURBOIRE, BONUS, FEE,
CUE, END
tipping .... ALIST, ATILT
tippet ...... ALMUCE, SCARF, MUFFLER
tipple ... NIB, BIB, GILL, LIQUOR, POT

tippler TOPER, TUMBLER, WINO, WINER,
SOT
tipster ... TOUT, SPECULATOR, INSIDER
tipsy ... REE, DRUNK, GROGGY, MERRY
tirade ..... DIATRIBE, SCREED, SPEECH,
JEREMIAD
tire ... BORE, TUCKER, FAG, IRK, JADE,
WEARY
" part .... RIM, TREAD, SHOE
" saver .... RECAP, RETREAD
tissue . BAST, FAT, FABRIC, FIBER, WEB,
PLEXUS, FASCIA
" , connecting .. TENDON, STROMA
" decay .... CARIES
" , hardening of .... SCLEROSIS
" , nerve .... ALBA
" , web-like .... TELA
Titan ... OCEANUS, ATLAS, HYPERION,
IAPETUS, CRONOS, BANA
" , female .... DIONE, RHEA
" , parents of ..... GAEA, URANUS
titanic .... ENORMOUS, GIGANTIC
titanite .... LEDERITE, SPHENE
Titania's husband .... OBERON
titanic iron-ore sand .... ISERINE
tithe .... TEIND, TENTH, TAX, DECIMAL
tithing .... DIME, TEN, DENARY
titlark .... PIPIT
title .... MUNIMENT, NAME, CAPTION,
HEADING, RANK, RIGHT, TERM
title of dignity, rank, or respect ....
AG(H)A, BABA, ESQUIRE, SIR, DOM,
DON, PANI, EARL, EMIR, GRAF,
KHAN, LORD, MAAM, MADAM,
MULLA, PASHA, PRINZ, SAHIB,
SENOR, PRIMATE, BARON, DUKE,
REIS
titled member of Brit. stock exch. ..
ORCHID
titmice, family ... BLUECAPS, PARIDAE
titmouse .. GOOSANDER, MAG, PARUS,
JACKSAW, OXEYE, BLUECAP,
TOMTIT, NUN
Tito .... BROZ
titter .... TEHEE, GIGGLE, LAUGH
tittle ...... GOSSIP, IOTA, JOT, WHIT
titular .... NOMINAL
"Titus Andronicus" queen .. TAMORA
Tivoli; anc. Roman name .... TIBUR
to . AT, FORWARD, ON, THITHER, NEAR,
CLOE, FOR, TAE
" wit NAMELY, SCILICET, VIDELICET, VIZ
toad . AGUA, PIPA, ANURAN, CRAPON,
PADDO, PODE, PAD
toadfish .... SLIMER, SARPO, SAPO
toadflax ...... RAMSTEAD, GALLWORT
toady .... COWER, FAWN, LEECH
toast ..... BREDE, LEEP, SOAKER, TAN,
SKOAL, SIPPET, SALUT, PROSIT
toastmaster .... MC, EMCEE

tobacco CAPORAL, UPPOWOC, LATAKIA,
CAPA, KNASTER, VUELTA, CUBAN,
QUID, SHAG, BRIAR, DUDEEN
" ash .... DOTTLE, DOTTEL
" juice .... AMBASH
" pipe .... CHIBOUK
" plant: heart leaf .... RATOON
toby .... CIGAR, MUG
toe .... DACTYL, DIGIT, TAE
toga .... TRABEA
together .... SAMEN, UNION
" ; prefix .... COM
toggle .... COTTER, KEY, BOLT, ROD
togs .... CLOTHES, GARB, DUDS
toil ...... DRAG, DRUDGE(RY), GRIND,
TRAVAIL, PLOD
toilet case .... ETUI, ETWEE
Tojo; Jap. general .... HIDEKI
token SCRIP, AMULET, BADGE, EARNEST,
INDEX, SIGN(AL), MARK, SYMBOL
" of respect .... ACCOLADE
tolerate . STAND, ABIDE, BEAR, BROOK,
CONDONE, ENDURE
toll RING, KNELL, PAGE, TAILAGE, FEE,
TAX, CESS
Tolstoy .... LEO
Toltecs, anc. capital of .... TULA
Tom Tulliver's river .... FLOSS
tomb . MASTABA, CRYPT, VAULT, TABUT,
OSSUARY, CATACOMB, TUMULUS,
MOLE, CYST, BARROW
" , empty .... CENOTAPH
tomboy ..... ROMP, HOYDEN, TOMRIG
tommy ...... FOOL, PODGER, ATKINS
Tom o' Bedlam .... MADMAN
Tom of Lincoln .... BELL
tomorrow; Sp. .... MANANA
tone ENERGY, VIGOR, TIMBRE, CADENCE,
NUANCE, PITCH, STYLE
" , without .... ATONIC
Tonga isl. district .... VAVAU
tongs .... GRAMPUS, SERVER
tongue .... LORRIKER, DIALECT, PRATE,
IDIOM, GLOSSA, LINGUA
" bird .... WRYNECK
" bone .... HYOID
" fish .... SOLE
" , projections on ...... PAPILLAE
" , tip of the .... CORONA
" , using .... APICAL
tongueless toads; genus .... AGLOSSA
tongue-like processes ...... LIGULAE
tonic .... BRACER, PEP, ELIXIR
tonsil .. AMYGDALA, ALMOND, KERNEL
too .... ALSO, AND, ELSE, OVER
" much .. EXTREMELY, TROP, NIMIETY
tool . PUPPET, DUPE, RAT, GEAR, PAWN,
GADGET, DEVICE
" , bookbinder's .... GOUGE
" , cutting .... ADZE

" , engraver's .... BURIN
" , flat spreading .... SPATULA
" for cames .... LADKIN
" for cleaving shingles ..... FROW
" , garden ..... SEEDER, DIBBLE, HOE,
RAKE, SPADE
" , marble workers'......... FRAISE
" , metal workers' .. DOLLY, SWAGE
" , steel, for loosening ore .... GAD
" , trimming .... ZAX
tools . DOLLY, KIT, MATTOCKS, GIBBLES,
TEW
tooth .... GAM, INCISOR, FANG, TINE,
TUSK, TUSH, MOLAR, CANINE,
(BI)CUSPID
" , comb. form .... ODONTO
" decay .... CARIES
" , gear-wheel .... COG
" grinding surface .... MENSA
" , having but one ... MONODONT
" , lower part of .... FANG
" , molar .... WANG
" or spike .... TINE
" , part of .... DENTINE
" , projecting .... SNAG
" sockets .... ALVEOLI
" sprocket wheel .... GUB
toothache ..... WORM, ODONTALGIA,
DENTALGIA
toothed .... DENTATE, SERRATED
" formation .... SERRA
toothless .... EDENTATE
top ..... APEX, CAP, COP, VERTEX, LID,
CREST, SUMMIT, ACME, FINIAL, BEST
" , a child's .... GIG
" of a stand for tiles .... CRISS
" , "put-or-take" .... TEETOTUM
tope .... STUPA, SHARK
toper ..... BOOZER, DRUNK, TOSSPOT,
SWILLER, SOT, SOUSE, SOAK
Topi Indian .... TIANG
topic . THEME, TEXT, ITEM, ISSUE, HEAD
topical ..... THEMATIC, TIMELY, LOCAL
" heading .... TROPE
topics .... THEMATA
topknot ONKOS, PANACHE, CREST, TUFT
topmast square crossbar .... FID
topnotch .... TOPS, BEST, ACE, AONE
topsail .... RAFFE
topsy-turvy .... ASKEW, INVERTED
tora .... TETEL
torbernite .... URANITE
torch .. LANTERN, CRESSET, FLAMBEAU,
FLARE
torchman .... LINKMAN
torero .... BULLFIGHTER
torment ... RACK, TEASE, BAIT, DEVIL,
PLAGUE, BADGER, BANE, HARRY,
AGONY
tormenter .... BAITER

torn .... RIVEN, RENT, SPLIT, REFT
torpedo .... MISSILE, SQUIB
" fish .... RAY
" , front end of .... NOSE
" , inventor of ..... WHITEHEAD
torpor .... COMA, STUPOR
torque .... STRAIN, TWIST, BEE, SARPE
torrent FLOOD, FLOW, STREAM, SPATE,
DOWNPOUR
torrid ..... TROPICAL, HOT, PARCHING
tortoise .... EMYD, HICATEE, EMYS,
MATAMATA
" ; order .... CHELONIA
" , species of.......... GOPHER
torture ... MARTYR, PAIN, RACK, FLAY,
IMPALE
Tosca villain .... SCARPIA
toss BANDY, TAVE, FLING, HURL, PITCH,
FLIP
tosspot ...... DRUNKARD, SOT, TOPER
tot .... ADD, CHILD, COUNT, DRINK
total .... UTTER, ENTIRE, WHOLE, SUM
totem post .... XAT, POLE
totter .... BRANDLE, ROCK, SHAKE
toucan .... ARACARI, TOCO
touch ... SHAVE, PALP, IMPINGE, MEET,
TIG, TWIDDLE, TACT, CONTACT,
DASH, ABUT
" ; as a medium . TRIAL, TENT, TEST
" ; comb. form .... TAC
" , examine by ...... TRY, PALPATE
" ; Fr. .... SOUPCON
" , perceptible by .... TACTILE
" up; as a motor .... REV
touchdown .... GOAL
touchhole .... VENT
touch me not; Lat. . NOLIMETANGERE
touching ...... ATTINGENT, TANGENT,
PATHETIC
touchstone .... TEST, BASANITE
touchwood .. AMADOU, PUNK, SPUNK,
TINDER, LYDITE
tough WIRY, WITHY, LEATHERY, CHEWY,
BULLY, ROWDY, STURDY
" pitch .... COPPER
toughen .... TAW, TOR, INURE, TRAIN
tourists' lodge .... MOTEL, INN
tourmaline ...... SCHORL, ACHROITE,
RUBELLITE
tournament . CONTEST, JOUST, MATCH,
TILT, MEET
tourniquet .... GARROT, BANDAGE,
STANCH(ER)
tow ... HALE, PULL, DRAG, DRAW, TUG
toward .... GAIN, TO, AD
" the center .... ENTAD
" the exterior .... ECTAD
" the mouth .... ORAD
" the red corpuscle side HEMAD
" the side .... LATERAD

292

```
"    the stern .... (AB)AFT, ABAFF
towel ...... CLEAN, DRY, WIPER, HUCK
"   fabric ................. TERRY
tower .. MINARET, TURRET, TOR(RION),
                SPIRE, BABEL, ZIGGURAT
"   ; as a marker .......... PYLON
"   , Buddhist .............. TOPE
"   , circular .............. DOME
"   , circular fort ....... MARTELLO
"   , Indian .............. MINAR
"   , medieval ........... DONJON
"   of glacial ice ......... SERAC
"   , pyramidal ..... SIKHRA, SIKRA
"   , small .............. TOURELLE
"   , small round ........ RONDEL
"   , Spanish ............ ATALAYA
"   , spirical ..... STEEPLE, CUPOLA
towhee ..... CHEWINK, FINCH, JOREE
town ..... STADT, URBS, MACHI, VILLE,
                                    BAYAN
"   , per. to a CIVIC, URBAN, OPPIDAN
townsman ....... RESIDENT, CIT, CAD,
                              SELECTMAN
toxic in snake poison ...... VENOM
toxine ...... VENIN, POISON, VENENE
toy .. DALLY, TOP, BAUBLE, TEETOTUM,
                    DOLL, FONDLE, TRIFLE
"   bear .................... TEDDY
trace ... CLEW, VESTIGE, TRACK, TRAIL,
                    TINGE, HINT, COPY
track .... RUT, FOOTPRINT, PUG, RUN,
              SKETCH, SOUPCON, MARK, SPUR,
                                    SCENT
"   of an animal .... SPOOR, SLOT
"   , put on another SHUNT, SWITCH
"   , put off ................ DERAIL
tract .... SWEEP, LOT, AREA, SECTOR
tractate ................... TREATISE
tractor .............. BULLDOZER
Tracy (Dick), Mrs. ........... TESS
trade ..... DEAL, SELL, CRAFT, BANDY,
              METIER, SWAP, SWOP, BARTER
tradesman . MONGER, AGENT, DEALER,
              BROKER, SUTLER, JOBBER
trading ........... MONGERY, VENAL
"   post ... MART, STATION, FORT,
                              CANTEEN, PIT
tradition ........... FOLKLORE, MYTH
trafficking ....... BROKING, TRADING
tragopan ....... PHEASANT, MONAL
trail ... SPOOR, ABATURE, DRAG, FOIL,
              SLOT, FOLLOW, HEEL, HOUND,
                              SHADOW, DOG, LAG
"   , per. to a .. VENT, ODOR, SCENT
"   ; Sp. ............... COMINO
train .... CORTEGE, RETINUE, BREED,
              CHAIN, NURTURE, LIMITED, COACH,
                    LOCAL, EXPRESS, SUITE
traitor ....... JUDAS, RAT, QUISLING

tramp ... HOBO, LANDLOPER, NOMAD,
              BUM, PAD, SUNDOWNER, VAGRANT
"   , to . HIKE, TRAPE, VAMP, TRAIPSE
tranquil . SERENE, EASY, LOWN, STILL,
                              MILD, QUIET
tranquilizer ...... MILTOWN, LIBRIUM
transact .......... DEAL, DO, TREAT
transaction ...... TRAFFIC, SALE, DEAL
transcend ........ EXCEL, OUTDO, CAP
transfer . CEDE, DEPUTE, GRANT, LET,
              CONVEY, PASS, REMOVE, SHIFT
"   design ............. DECAL
"   legally ... ALIENATE, ATTORN
transfix ..... NAIL, IMPALE, PIN, STAB
transform ......... TURN, CONVERT
transgress VIOLATE, INFRACT, SIN, ERR,
                                    OFFEND
transition ... CHANGE, FLUX, PASSAGE
translate .......... RENDER, DECODE
translation ....... PONY, PARAPHRASE
transmit ......... SEND, WIRE, CARRY
transparent .... DIAPHANOUS, LUCID,
                                    CLEAR
"   mineral ......... MICA
"   plastic .......... LUCITE
transport ...... SHIP, RAPTURE, CARRY
transported ................... RAPT
transportation RAILAGE, DAK, LATION
transposition of sounds SPOONERISM
Transvaal gold region ......... RAND
"   legislature .......... RAAD
trap ... NAIL, NET, PIT, GIN, SPRINGE,
                                    TOIL
trapper ..... SNARER, DECOYER, LURER
trapdoor .................... DROP
trapshooting ................ SKEET
trash .. JADE, JUNK, WASTE, RUBBISH,
                    TRUMPERY, TOSHY
travel .... TOUR, MUSH, TREK, WEND
traveler . VIATOR, WAYFARER, NOMAD,
                    PILGRIM, TOURIST
"   , commercial BAGMAN, AGENT
travelers, company of ..... CARAVAN
traveling ................ VIATORIAL
"   ; German ......... REISEND
"   , of ................ VIATIC
traverse CROSS, DENY, FORD, PATROL,
                                    PARADOS
travesty ........ PARODY, LAMPOON
trawl ................ DRAGNET, FISH
tray ........... SALVER, SERVER, HOD
treacle ........ MOLASSES, THERIAC
tread ... STEP, VOLT, WALK, TRAMPLE,
                              PAD, STAMP
treasure STORE, CHERISH, PRIZE, VALUE,
              WEALTH, HOARD, TROVE, CACHE
treasurer PURSER, BOUCHER, HAMILTON
treasury .. EXCHEQUER, BURSE, CHEST,
                    FISC, BURSARY
"   agent ............. TMAN
```

treat ..... REGALE, MANIPULATE, DOSE
" against shrinkage ... SANFORIZE
" badly .... FRAME, ILLUSE
" with malice .... SPITE
treatise THESIS, TRACT, ESSAY, SUMMA,
DONET
" on fruit trees ...... POMONA
" on trees .... SILVA
" , preface to a ...... ISAGOGE
treatment ...... USE, USAGE, REMEDY,
THERAPY
" of water ... FLUORIDATION
treaty MISE, PROTOCOL, PACT, CARTEL
treble .... LATTEN, SOPRANO
tree .... TRAP, WOOD, SILVA, CORNER,
FOREST, TIMBER, BOSCAGE,
PEDIGREE
" , acacia, Austral. .... MYALL
" ; acacia family ... BABUL, SIRIS
" , Afr. . AKEE, BAOBAB, COLA, BITO,
SAMANDURA
" , Afr. prickly ash .... ARTAR
" , alder .... ARN
" , allspice .... PIMENTO
" ; antidote for snake bite CEDRON
" , apple .... SHEA
" , apple; genus .... MALUS
" , ash, mountain ... ROWAN, SORB
" , Asian ..... OLAX, TI, ACLE, DITA,
MEDLAR
" , Asian (scrubby) .... ASAK, BITO
" , Austral. .... TODART, BOREE,
GMELINA, MARARA
" , balsam .... WILGA, TOLU
tree, balsam poplar .... LIAR
" , baobab .... SOURGOURD
" bark .... TAN, ROSS
" , beech .... MYRTLE
" , beech, Chile .... ROBLE
" , betel-nut .... ARECA
" , birch; genus .... BETULA
" , birch, small .... ANSU, TI
" branches .... RAMAGE
" , Brazilian .... ANDA
" , buckwheat .... TITI
" , bully .... BALATA
" , carica ...... PAWPAW, PAPAYA
" , Cen. Amer. .... AMATE
" , Cen. Amer. oil ...... EBO, EBOE
" , chicory .... BUNK
" , Chilean timber MUERMO, ULMO
" , coffee .... CHICOT
" , cottonwood .... ALAMO
" , custard-apple .... SWEETSOP
" , cyrillaceous .... TITI
" , dead .... RAMPIKE
" , devil; Ind. .... DITA
" , devil's-cotton .... ABROMA
" , dogbane (species) .. APOCYNUM
" , dogwood .... NYSSA, TUPELO

" , dogwood; genus .... CORNUS
" , drupe-bearing .... BITO
" , dwarf .... ARBUSCLE
" , dyewood; Phil. Is. .... TUA
" , E. Ind. ... ACH, ASOKA, BANYAN,
DEODAR, PINEY, POON, SAJ,
SAL, TEAK, TOON, SIRIS, NEEM,
PRESS, ACANA, FIG
" , E. Ind.; genus .... ABROMA
" ; emblem of Hawaii ...... LEHUA
" , eucalyptus .... GUM, YATE
" , evergreen .... FIR, HOLM, OLIVE,
YEW
" , evergreen; N.Z. .... TARATA
" exudation .... RESIN, SAP
" , fabaceous .... AGATI
" , fir .... BALSAM
" , fir; genus .... ABIES
" , flowering; U.S. .... TITI
" , forest .... DITA, TUA
" ; fraxinus .... ASH
" , fustic .... MORA
" ; gamboge family .... CALABA
" , genip, wood from .... LANA
" genus .... ACER
" , glasswort .... JUME
" ; Guiana .... MORA
" , gum .... BABUL, ICICA, XYLAN
" , Hawaiian ... KOA, LEHUA, OHIA
" , hickory, species of ..... PECAN
" , holly .... HOLM
" , holly, species of .... YAPON
" , honeyberry .... GENIP
" ; India ...... AMRA, BANYAN, SAL
tree, Indian silk-cotton ...... SIMAL
" , iron .... ACLE, IXORA
" , Japanese .... HINOKI, SUGI
" , Javanese .... UPAS
" , juneberry .... SERVICE
" , lacebark .... LAGETTA
" , large, madder-family ... BANCAL
" , laurel .... BAY
" , linden ...... LIN, LINN, TEIL, TILE
" , locust .... ACACIA
" , locust, pod of .... CAROB
" , lotus .... SADR
" , low evergreen .... ABROMA
" , Malay apple .... OHIA
" , margosa .... NEEM, NIM
" , marmalade ..... MAMEY, CHICO,
MAMMEE, SAPOTE
" , Mediterranean .... CAROB
" , Mexican rubber .... ULE
" , Mexican, wood of .... FUSTIC
" , mimosaceous .... SIRIS
" mosses .... USNEA
" moth .... EGGER
" , mulberry; Ind. ... AAL, ACH, AL
" , myrtaceous .... EUGENIA
" , ngalo .... KIO

294

    " , oak, Cal. live .... ENCINA
    " , oak, Cal. white .... ROBLE
    " , oak, holm .... HOLLY
    " , oak, Jerusalem .... AMBROSE
    " , olive; genus .... OLEA
    " , palm; (see "palm")
    " , Palmyra; Ind. .... TAL
    " , papaya .... CARICA, PAPAW
    " , pea .... AGATI
    " , pear .... PERRY, PYRUS
    " , pear, prickly .... NOPAL
    " , pepperidge .... TUPELO
    " ; Philippines . ANAGAP, BETIS, TUA,
                                YATE
    " , pinaceous ..... KAURI, SEQUOIA
    " , pine .... OCOTE, SABINE
    " , pine, China and Japan .. MATSU
    " ; pine family .... CEDAR, CONIFER
    " , plum; genus .... PRUNUS
    " , plum, wild .... SLOE
    " , poisonous ... SASSY, BUNK, UPAS
    " ; Polynesia .... IPIL, TI
    " , poon .... KEENA
    " , poplar .. ABELE, ALAMO, ASPEN
    " ; genus Quercus .... OAK
    " , quillai .... SOAPBARK
    " , rose-family; Eur. .... MEDLAR
    " , rowan .... ASH, SERVICE, SORB
    " , rubber .... CAUCHO, ULE
    " , salt .... ATLE, ATLEE
    " , sandalwood; N.Z. .... MAIRE
    " , sandarac .... ALERSE, ARAR
    " , sapodilla .... SAPOTA
    " , sassafras .... AGUE
    " , shade .... ASH
    " , soapbark .... QUILLAI
    " , sourgourd .... BAOBAB
tree, S. American ...... EBO, CACAO
    " , S. Am. evergreen ...... PAPAYA
    " , spruce; white ... EPINETTE, LARCH
    " , strawberry .... ARBUTUS
    " , tamarack; Am. .... LARCH
    " , tamarisk; Ind. .... ATLE
    " ; genus Taxus .... YEW
    " , tecoma, species of ...... ROBLE
    " , terebinth .... LIME, LINDEN, TEIL
    " , thorn, Jerusalem ...... RETAMA
    " , thorny .... BEL
    " , timber; Asia .... RASAMALA
    " , timber, forest .... ASH, RATA
    " , timber; Hawaii .... KOA
    " , timber; India .... OAK, DAR, SAL
    " , timber, inferior .... ANAM
    " , timber; N.Z. RIMU, KAURI, RATA
    " , timber, of Pacific .... IPIL
    " , timber, Phil. Is. LANETE, AMAGA
    " , timber; S. Am. .... TALA
    " , timber; W. Ind. .... ACANA
    " , traveler's .... RAVENALA

    " , tropical .... ANUBING, COLA,
                  DAGAME, INGA, NEPAL
    " , trop. Am. ... BALSA, DALI, OLAX,
                  PAWPAW, SAPOTA
    " trunk .... BOLE, CABER
    " , tupelo .... NYSSA
    " varnish; Jap. .... RHUS
    " , wattle; Austral. . BOREE, COOBA,
                              COOBAH
    " , W. African .... AKEE, BUMBO
    " , W. Ind. . ACANA, BALATA, GENIP,
                          LOBLOLLY
    " , W. Ind. cabbage ...... ANGELIN
    " , willow .... OSIER
    " , willow; genus .... ITEA
    " yielding cocoa bean ..... CACAO
    " yielding gum .... ICICA
    " yielding oil .... TUNG
    " yielding quinine ..... CINCHONA
treeless plain ..... PAMPAS, LLANOS,
                      TUNDRA, STEPPE
treenail .... NOG, PIN, SPIKE
trees .... FOREST
    " , genus . OWENIA, CITRUS, ULMUS,
                              ACER
    " , grove of .... DENDRITE, TOPE
    " , maple; genus .... ACER
    " , mulberry; genus .... MORUS
    " , olive; genus .... OLEA
    " , per. to ... ARBOREAL, CACUMINAL
    " , pine, grove of .... PINETUM
    " , rain .... GENISARO, SAMAN
    " , science of life of ...... SILVICS
tree toad; genus ...... HYLA, ANURA
trefoil .... CLOVER, ARCH
trellis .... ARBOR, ESPALIER, PERGOLA,
                         TRAIL, LATTICE
tremble . DODDER, JAR, QUAKE, SHAKE,
                       THRILL, DIDDER
tremulous ASPEN, QUAKY, TREMANDO,
                   TREPID, NERVOUS
trench . GAW, FOSS, LEAT, MOAT, SAP
trencher .. PLATTER, SAPPER, ROUNDEL
trend .... SWING, TENDENCY, TENOR,
                   DRIFT, COURSE, BENT
trespass . ENCROACH, POACH, INVADE,
                   INFRINGE, SIN
tress .... LOCK, RINGLET, BRAID, PLAIT
trews; Scot. .... TROUSERS
triad .... TRINARY, TRINITY, TRIO
trial .... DOOM, ESSAY, TEST, ASSIZE,
                 AGONY, CROSS, ORDEAL
    " performance .... PROLUSION
    " , per. to .... EMPIRIC
    " , scene of a famous ...... RIOM
triangle .... TRIGON, DELTA, SCALENE,
                 OBTUSE, GUSSET
    " , draw circle within . ESCRIBE
    " , side of a .... LEG

triangular .... DELTOID, SCALENE
    "   decoration ..... PEDIMENT
    "   piece of a sail ..... GORE
    "   sail ... LATEEN, SPINNAKER
tribe .... CLAN, RACE, FAMILY, HORDE,
            GROUP, FOLK, SIB, SIOL
    " division .... SEPT, CURIA(E)
tribunal .. FORUM, BAR, COURT, ROTA
tribute .... OVATION, TAX, HOMAGE,
              CAIN, CARATCH
trick ..... GULL, FLAM, JAPE, TREPAN,
   WILE, GAG, RUSE, GIMMICK, DIDO,
   PRANK, DECEIVE, HOAX, FRAUD,
               GLEEK
    " , game .... SLAM, CAPOT, NULLO
tricked, one easily DUPE, GULL, CULLY
trickery .... LEGERDEMAIN, ART
trickle ..... DRILL, SEEP, DROP, OOZE,
              PERCOLATE
tricks, play mean .... SHAB
tricky .... QUIRKY, CRAFTY, SNIDE
trident .... SPEAR, LEISTER, FORK, GIG
tried ...... RELIABLE, CHOICE, ETTLED
Trieste measure .... ORNA
trifle DALLY, MONKEY, DOIT, PINHEAD,
   TOY, FRIVOL, POTTER, DAWDLE,
              DALLY
    " , insignificant .... ACE, FICO
trifles .... STIVERS, AMBSACES, NUGAE
trifling .... PALTRY, PIFFLE, TRIVIAL
trifoliate .... TERNATE
    " plant .... SHAMROCK
trig .... NEAT, SMART, TRIM
triglyphs, space between ... METOCHE
trigon .... TRINE, HARP, LYRE
trigonometric function ..... COSINE,
               SINE
trill .. ROLL, TWIRL, WARBLE, TIRALEE,
              SHAKE
trilling, by .... UVULAR
trillion; comb. form .... TREGA
trim . PREEN, CLIP, LOP, NEAT, SHRAG,
   SNED, NIFTY, PERK, ADORN, TINSEL
    " a coin .... NIG
trimming of lace .... JABOT
trine .... TRIPLE, TRIO
trinity .... THREE, TRIAD
trinket .... BIJOU, BIBELOT, GAUD,
       GEWGAW, TAHLI, BAUBLE
triple .... THREEFOLD
    " crown .... TIARA
triplet .... TERCET, TRINE
    " lily; genus .... HOOKERA
tripod .... EASEL, SPIDER, TRIVET
    " , double .... CAT
Tripoli ruler .... DEY
triptych .... TABLET, VOLET
trisaccharide .... TRIOSE
trismus .... LOCKJAW, TETANUS
tristful .... SAD

Tristram's beloved ... ISEULT, ISOLDE,
              ISOLT
trite . BANAL, PERCOCT, JEJUNE, STALE,
           DULL, CORNY
    " expression .... CLICHE
triton .... EFT, NEWT
triturate .... BRAY, GRIND, PULVERIZE
triumph .... EXULT, VICTORY
trivet .... TRIPOD, BRANDISE, SPIDER
trivial .. DOGGEREL, NOMINAL, PALTRY
    " action .... FRIBBLE
troche .... LOZENGE, TABLET, PASTILLE
trochee .... CHOREUS
trogon .... QUETZAL
Troilus' father .... PRIAM
Trojan .... ILIAN, DARDAN
    " hero .. HECTOR, PARIS, AGENOR
    " horse, builder of .... EPEUS
    " slave .... SINON
troll .... GNOME
trolley ....TRAM
trombone .... SACKBUT, SAMBUKE
    " mouthpiece .... BOCAL
trona .... URAO, NATRON
troop; Anglo-Ind. .... RESSALA
troops .... ARMY, BATTERY, SQUAD,
       BRIGADE, REGIMENT, MEN
    " in reserve .... ECHELON
    " , quarters for .... ETAPE
    " , spread .... DEPLOY
trop .... MANY, TOO
trope, any .... EUOUAE
trophy AWARD, OSCAR, LAUREL, PRIZE,
        SPOILS, SCALP, CUP
tropic .... CIRCLE, SOLAR
tropical .... FIGURATIVE
    " bird .... MOTMOT, MANAKIN,
              TODY
    " cetacean .... INIA
    " clay .... LATERITE
    " cuckoo .... ANI
    " disease .... SPRUE
    " dolphin .... INIA
    " fish; family ...... SCARIDAE
    " fruit ...... MANGO, PAPAYA
    " monkey .... ARABA
    " palm .... ASSAI, CYCAD
    " plant .... AGAVE, TRIURID
    " root stock .... TARO
    " tree (see also "tree"), silk ..
              SIRIS
    " wild cat .... EYRA
Tros, son of .... ILUS
trot ...... JOG, PACE, AMBLE, DANCE
Trotsky .... LEON
trouble ADO, AIL, WOE, ILLS, WORRY,
       ANNOY, GRIEF, MOLEST
trough . HOD, MANGER, STRAKE, TOM,
             GUTTER
    " between waves .... VALLEY

" , inclined .... CHUTE
trousers ...... PEGTOP, JEANS, SLOPS,
　　　　　　　　　　TONGS, LEVIS
trout .. CHARR, SEWEN, KELT, TOGUE,
　　　　　　　　　　LONGE
" parasite .... NAMAYCUSH
trowel .... DARBY, FLOAT, TAPER
Troy .... ILION, ILIUM, WEIGHT
" , defender of .... AENEAS, ENEAS
" , founder of .... ILUS
" , last king of .... PRIAM
" , mountain of .... IDA
" , queen of .... HECUBA
" , per. to .... ILIAC
" , region of .... TROAD
truant . TRIVANT, VAGRANT, LAGGARD,
　　　　　　　　　　TRAMP, TRONE
truce .... LULL, RESPITE, TREVE
truck .. VAN, LORRY, WYNN, RUBBISH,
　　　　　　　　CAMION, GUNK, DILLY
truckle ..... CRINGE, KNUCKLE, YIELD
trudge ..... PLOD, PACE, WALK, SLOG
true .. LEAL, VERY, GERMANE, STANCH,
　　　　　　ALINE, FACT, LITERAL, REAL
" copy .... ESTREAT
truffle ..... EARTHNUT, MISY, FUNGUS
truism . PLATITUDE, POSTULATE, AXIOM
truly ..... AMEN, YEA, DULY, RIGHTLY,
　　　　　　　　　AWAT, VERILY
Truman, Harry, birthplace of LAMAR
" , wife of .... BESS
Truman; playwright .... CAPOTE
trumpet ..... BUCINA, LURE, CLARION,
　　　　　　　TUBA, CLARIN, BEMA
" , blare of .... TANTARA
" blast ..... BLARE, DIAN, LEVIT
" creeper .... TECOMA
" shell .... TRITON
trumpeter .... AGAMI, TROUT
" perch .... MADO
truncheon ...... CLUB, STAFF, BATON,
　　　　　　　　　　WARDER
trundle .... WHEEL, ROLL, TRUCK
trunk .... BOLE, COFFER, STOCK, BOX,
　　　　　　　　CHEST, CABER
" of an animal ... TORSO, SOMA
trust ...... REPOSE, RELY, FIE, HOPE,
　　　　　CUSTODY, CARTEL, MONOPOLY
trusty .... LOYAL, STAUNCH, TRIED
truth .... UNA, DEED, FEALTY, TAO
" drug .... PENTOTHAL
try .. ESSAY, TRIAL, ETTLE, SAY, CRACK,
　　　　　　　SHOT, HEAR, TAX
" again .... RETEST, RETASTE
" for luck .... HANDSEL
tsetse fly .... KIVU, ZIMB, GLOSSINA
" " disease .... NAGANA
Tse-tung .... MAO
tsine .... BANTENG

tub ... HOD, TUN, PIGGIN, VAT, KNAP,
　　　　　　　　KID, FIRKIN, KEEVE
tuba's mouthpiece .... BOCAL
tube ...... DUCT, BOUCH, PIPE, HOSE,
　　　　　　　SIPPER, PIPET(TE)
" for concrete .... TREMIE
" , mus. .... SALPINX
" on which silk is wound ... COP
" , tapering .... BURETTE
tuber .. EDDOE, JALAP, OCA, POTATO,
　　　SALEP, TARO, YAM, BEET, TRUFFLE
tubiform .... TUBATE
Tuchin's house .... YAMEN
tuck ... FOLD, RAPIER, PLEAT, RUCHE
" up .... KILT, COVER
tuckehoe .... PORIA
tucker .... BORE, FAG, IRK, TIRE
Tuesday; Fr. .... MARDI
tuft . CREST, GOATEE, TUSSOCK, STUPA,
　　　　　　　FAG, ALULA, COP
tufted .... COMOSE, CRESTED
tufts .... SCOPULAS, COMAE
tug .... EFFORT, PULL, TRACE, TOIL
tule .... BULRUSH, SCIRPUS
tulle .... LACE, NET
tumble .. DROP, FLOP, SAULT, WALTER
tumbleweed ....AMARANTH
tumbler .... ACROBAT, DOVE, TIPPLER,
　　　　　　　　　　ROLLER
tumbrel .... DUMPCART
tumeric .... REA
tumor ... EDEMA, YAW, CYST, LIPOMA,
　　　　　　　　　　PHYMA
" , fleshy .... SARCOMA
" , glandular .... ADENOMA
" , small .... WEN, MORO, PAP
tumult ...... BABEL, DIN, FRAY, RIOT,
　　　　　　　　　　UPROAR
" ; Fr. .... EMEUTE
tumulus .... BARROW, MOUND
tun, half a .... PIPE
tuna-like fish .... ALBACORE
tune ... SONANCE, LIED, LILT, SPRING,
　　　　TOY, MELODY, AIR, SONG, ARIA
tung oil, product of ...... VARNISH
tungsten, source of .... WOLFRAM
tunic . ACTON, CHITON, STOLA, TOGA,
　　　BLOUSE, JUPON, GIPPO, KIRTLE
tuning of strings to lower pitch .....
　　　　　　　　　　ANESIS
Tunis ruler .... BEY, DEY
Tunisian town BIZERTA, SFAX, SOUSSE,
　　　　　　　　　　SUSA
tunnel ... ADIT, TUBE, CENIS, SIMPLON,
　　　　　　　　　　BRENNER
tunny roes, relish of ...... BOTARGO
tup .... RAM, TOOP
tupelo gums .... NYSSA
Tupian tribesman ...... ANTA, MURA

turban PATTA, MUNDIL, MANDIL, TUFFE,
　　　　　SEERBAND, MOAB
turbid .... PECULANT, ROILED, MUDDY,
　　　　　MURKY, ROILY
turbot .... FLATFISH, BRET
turbulent .... VIOLENT, WILD
turdine-like bird .... THRUSH
turf . SOD, PEAT, CESS, DIVOT, SWARD,
　　　　　VAG, GRASS
turgent .... SWELLING
Turk .... OSMANLI, OTTOMAN, TATAR
　" , the Grand .... SULTAN
Turkestan district .... PAMIR
　" 　　Moslem .... SALAR
　" 　　mountain .... ALAI
　" 　　native .... SART
　" 　　river ILI
　" 　　tribe ..... KIRGHIZ, UZBEGS
turkey ..... TOM, BUSTARD, ALDERMAN,
　　　　　GOBBLER, POULT
　" 　buzzard .... VULTURE
　" 　oak .... CERRIS
Turkey capital .... ANKARA, ANGORA
　" , city of .... ADANA, EDESSA,
　SCUTARI, KONYA, BURSA, ISTANBUL
　" 　in Asia .... ANATOLIA
　" , river in TIGRIS, CORUH, MURAT
Turkish army corps .... ORDU
　" 　army officer .... AGA
　" 　caliph .... ALI
　" 　cap .... FEZ, CALPAC
　" 　cavalryman .... SPAHI
　" 　coin, copper .... PARA
　" 　coin, gold .... LIRA
　" 　coin, old silver .... ALTILIK
　" 　coin, silver .... PIASTER
　" 　college .... ULEMA
　" 　commander .... AGA, SIRDAR
　" 　court .... PORTE
　" 　decree .... IRADE
　" 　district .... ORDU, CILICIA
　" 　dollar .... PIASTER
　" 　fermented drink BOZA, MASTIC
　" 　flag .... ALEM
　" 　garment .... CAFTAN
　" 　government ..... GATE, PORTE
　" 　governor .... BEY, DEY, MUDIR
　" 　grandee .... BASHAW
　" 　high official .. PACHA, PASHA
　" 　hospice .... IMARET
　" 　imperial harem, lady of .....
　　　　　KADEIN
　" 　imperial standard ALEM, TOUG
　" 　infidel .... GIAOUR
　" 　inn .... IMARET, SERAI
　" 　javelin .... JEREED, JERRID
　" 　judge .... CADI
　" 　leader .... AGA, KEMAL
　" 　linear measure .... PIC
　" 　magistrate .... CADI, AGA

　" 　man-of-war .... CARVEL
　" 　measure . ALMUD, DJERIB, DRA,
　　　　　DRAH, KILE, OKA, PIK
　" 　measure (new) .... KHAT
　" 　minister .... VIZIER
　" 　money of account ..... ASPER
　" 　mountain .... ARARAT
　" 　mountain ranger .... ALAI
　" 　name .... ALI, AALI
　" 　officer . ATABEG, ATABEK, AGA
　" 　official ..... EMEER, EMIR, MIR,
　　　　　PASHA
　" 　open pavilion .... KIOSK
　" 　palace .... SERAI
　" 　patent .... BERAT
　" 　people .... OSMANLIS
　" 　pipe .... CHIBOUK
　" 　prayer rug .... MELAS
　" 　prefect .... WALI
　" 　president ..... INONU, KEMAL
　" 　province .... VILAYET
　" 　regiment .... ALAI
　" 　religious war ... CRESCENTADE
　" 　reservist .... REDIF
　" 　royal grant .... FIRMAN
　" 　saber .... YATAGHAN
　" 　sailing vessel .. CARAVEL, SAIC
　" 　seaport .... IZMIR, ADALIA
　" 　Simoon .... SAMIEL
　" 　soldier .... NIZAM, REDIF
　" 　standard .... ALEM
　" 　standard, former ...... TOUG
　" 　subject (non-Moslem) .. RAIA
　" 　summer house ... KIOSK, YALI
　" 　sultan .... CALIF
　" 　sword .... YATAGHAN
　" 　tambourine .... DAIRA
　" 　tax .... AVANIA
　" .. title of honor .. GHAZI, AGHA
　" 　title of respect BABA, BEY, AGA
　" 　veil (women's) .... YASHMAK
　" 　village .... ADANA
　" 　weight BATMAN, CHEKE, KERAT,
　　　　　ROTL, OKA, OKE
　" 　zither ..... KANOON, CANUN
Turk's-cap lily .... MARTAGON
Turks of India .... AFRIDI
Turku .... ABO, ALAND
turmeric CURCUMA, OLENA, REA, HALDI
turmoil .... HURLY, WELTER
turn (RE)VERT, GYRATE, ROTATE, SKEW,
　　　　　SPIN, SLUE, SOUR, DEVIATE
　" , act in .... ALTERN(ATE)
　" aside ... SWERVE, DETOUR, SHUNT,
　　　　　WRY
　" ; comb. form .... TROPO
　" frontward .... OBVERT
　" out to others .... FARM
　" outward .... EVERT
　" rapidly .... TIRL

298

" , revolving .... GYRE, REV
" right .... GEE, STARBOARD
" to left .... HAW, PORT
turncoat ..RENEGADE, DESERTER, RAT,
                              RUNAGATE
turned back .... EVOLUTE
" outward ... EVERTED, EXTRORSE
" over .... KEELED
" the one side .... SPLAYED
" up .... ACOCK
Turner, Miss .... LANA
turning point .... CRISIS, CRISES
" spirally .... SINISTRORSE
turnip .... NAVE, NEEP, RUTABAGA
" -formed .... NAPIFORM
" ; order .... CRUCIFERAE
" , wild .... NAVEW, RAPE
turnkey .... JAILOR
turnsole .... HELIOTROPE
turnstone REDLEG, PLOVER, WHALEBIRD
turntable, gun .... RACER
turpentine derivative . ROSIN, PINENE
" resin .... ALK, GAL(L)IPOT
" tree ... TARATA, TEREBINTH
turret .... TOWER, GARRET, LATHE,
                MINARET, CUPOLA, TOURELLE
turtle .... COOTER, JURARA, TERRAPIN,
                CRAWLER, TORTUGA, MATAMATA
" , fresh-water .... EMYD
" , giant .... ARRAU
" , part of a ... CALIPASH, CALIPEE
" , per. to a .... CHELONIAN
" shell .... CARAPACE
" , snapping ..... SNAPPER, TORUP
turtles; genus .... CHELONE, TESTUDO
Tuscan wine .... CHIANTI
tusk .... RAZOR, FANG, IVORY, HORN,
                              TUSH
tussah .... SHANTUNG
tussis .... COUGH
tutelary deities .... LARES, GENII,
                DAEMONS, PENATES
tutor .. DOCENT, GOVERNOR, MENTOR,
                COACH, GRINDER
tutto; mus. .... ALL, WHOLE
tuyere .... NOZZLE, TEW(EL)
TV .... VIDEO, TUBE, TELLY
" broadcast .... TELECAST
" camera tube .... ORTHICON
" screen coating .... PHOSPHOR
twaddle FLAPDOODLE, DRIVEL, FUSTIAN,
                              ROT
tweak .... TWITCH, PINCH
tweezers .... TWITCH
"Twelfth Night" char. ORSINO, VIOLA
twelfth part .... UNCIA
twelve and a half cents .... BIT
twenty .... CORGE, SCORE
" , per. to .... ICQSIAN
" quires .... REAM

" years .... VICENNIAL
twenty-one pounds; Bengal ...... SER
twenty-fourth part .... CARAT, KARAT
twibill .... MATTOCK
twice ... AGAIN, BIS, ENCORE, REPEAT
twig ... ROD, SWITCH, WITHE, WITHY,
                SLIP, SHOOT, GREAVE
" , flexible .... OSIER
" used for grafting .... SCION
twigs, full of .... RODDY
" , made of .... VIRGAL, WATTLED
twilight .. CREPUSCLE, DUSK, GLOAM,
                              EVE(NTIDE)
" ; Norse myth ..... RAGNAROK
twill .... RIB
twin ..... COUPLE, TOW, GEMEL, ENG,
                CHANG, SIAMESE
" crystal .... MACLE
twine HEMP, COIL, CORD, WIND, TWIST
" , hank of .... RAN
twinge .. PAIN, PANG, QUALM, THROE
twink .... NICTITATE
twinkle .... BLINK, WINK, GLINT
twin(s) .... GEMINI, CASTOR, POLLUX
twirl .... SPIN, WHIRL
twist QUIRK, SNAKE, COIL, TIRL, TURN,
                SQUIRM, TWEAK, OLIVER, KINK,
                SKEW, CONTORT, GNARL
" around . CURL, ENLACE, GAUCHE,
                              SLUE
" inward .... INTORT
" of horsehairs .... SETON
" to and fro .. WRIGGLE, WRENCH
twisted .. TORC, AWRY, TORTILE, WRY
" cord .... TORSADE
" roll of cotton .... SLUB
twisting .... SPIRAL, WRESTING
twit .... JOSH, TAUNT, BANTER
twitch .. JERK, TWEAK, VELLICATE, TIC,
                TUG, YANK
twitter .... GARRE, GIGGLE, TITTER
two .. DUO, PAIR, TEAM, BRACE, TWINS
" and one half inches ...... NAIL
" colors, of .... DICHROMIC
" , consisting of .... DYAD
" ears, affecting the .... DIOTIC
" -edged and sharp ..... ANCIPITAL
" -forked .... BIFURCATE
" -handed .... BIMANUAL
" -handed animals .... BIMANA
" -headed .... ANCIPITAL
" -toed sloth .... UNAU
" -wheeled carriage ...... VOLANTE
" -wheeled chariot .... ESSED(A)
twofold ....DUPLE(X), BINAL, BINARY,
                DOUBLE, TWIN, DUAL
tyche .... FORTUNE
tycoon . BARON, SHOGUN, MOGUL, VIP
Tyndareus' stepchild .... HELEN
" wife .... LEDA

type ..... TOKEN, GENRE, ILK, NORM, BRAND, NATURE, STRIPE, SPECIES
" , assortment of .... FONT
" , blank .... QUAD, QUAT
" collection .... FONT
" frame .... CHASER
" measure .... EM, EN
" mold .... MATRIX
" , part of a .... NICK
" , size of BRILLIANT, GEM, DIAMOND, AGATE, MINION, BREVIER, ELITE, PICA, PRIMER
" , style of ...... CASLON, CURSIVE, ELZEVIR, GOTHIC, IONIC, ITALIC, ROMAN, SCRIPT
" term .... CASE, PI
" tray .... GALLEY
typewriter part ...... PLATEN, SPACER
" type .... ELITE
Tyr .... ER, SAXNOT, TIU
tyrant .... DESPOT, DICTATOR, HIERO, GELO(N)
Tyre, destroyers of .... MOSLEMS
" ; modern name .... SUR
" , royalty of .... HIRAM, DIDO
tyro .. NOVICE, AMATEUR, NEOPHYTE, ABECEDARIAN
Tyrol district .... TRENTINO
" mountains .... DOLOMITES

U

UN agency .... UNESCO, ILO
ubiquitous .... OMNIPRESENT
Uchean Indian .... YUCHI
ugliness symbol .... TOAD
ugly .. SURLY, VICIOUS, EVIL, HOMELY, HIDEOUS
uhlan .... LANCER, SOLDIER, ULAN
Ukraine, money of .... GRIVNA
" , Holy City of .... KIEV
" legislature .... RADA
ulcer in cow's foot .... FOUL
ule .... CAUCHO, RUBBER, LATEX
ulema, leader of .... IMAM
ulex .... FURZE, LING
Ulmaceae; one of .... ELM
ulna .... CUBITUS
Ulrica in "Ivanhoe" .... CRONE
Ultima Thule .... ICELAND
ultimate ...... LAST, FINAL, MAXIMUM
" atom .... MONAD
ultimatum .... DEMAND, ORDER
ultimo, opposed to .... PROXIMO
ultra RADICAL, EXTREME, GROSS, AONE, BEST, TOP
ululant .... HOWLING, WAILING

"Ulysses" author .... JOYCE
Ulysses, father of .... LAERTES
" , wife of .... PENELOPE
umbellifer-like plant ... CELERY, YAMP
umbo .... BEAK, BOSS, KNOB
umbrage .... OFFENSE, PIQUE, SHADE
umbrella ... GAMP, CHATTA, PARASOL
" grass .... MILLET
" tree .. ELKWOOD, MAGNOLIA, GINSENG
umbrette .... UMBER, HAMMERHEAD
umpire ... ARBITER, JUDGE, REF(EREE)
unaccented .... ATONIC
" part of a bar ..... ARSIS
unadorned ...... STARK, BALD, NAKED
unadulterated .. FRANK, NEAT, PURE, GENUINE
unadvised .... INDISCREET, RASH
unaffected .. SIMPLE, NAIVE, GENUINE, SINCERE, ARTLESS
Unalaskan .... ALEUT
unaspirated .... LENE
unau .... SLOTH
unbeliever .. HERETIC, SCEPTIC, KAFFIR, INFIDEL, PAGAN, ATHEIST, AGNOSTIC, HEATHEN
unbend .... FRESE, REST
unbleached .... ECRU, BEIGE
unbranched antler .... DAG
unbroken .... CONTINUED, INTACT
unburden .... DISLOAD, EASE, REVEAL
unbury .... EXHUME
uncanny .. WEIRD, EERIE, UNCO, ODD
unceasing .... ENDLESS, ETERNAL
uncertain .... WAUGH, WAW, VAGUE
unchecked .... RAMPANT, FIFE
uncle . NUNKS, EAM, EME, YEME, OOM, PAWNBROKER, SAM
" , per. to .... AVUNCULAR
unclean .... IMMUND, TREF, VILE
unclose .... OPE(N), SPREAD
unclothe .... TIRL, DIVEST, STRIP
unco .... UNCANNY, STRANGE
uncommon ...... SPECIAL, NICE, RARE
uncompromising .... ULTRA
unconcerned ..... FREE, CALM, OPEN, SERENE
unconscious .... NAIVE, OUT
unconsciousness ... NARCOSIS, FAINT, SWOON, SYNCOPE, COMA
uncouth ..... RUDE, GAUCHE, VULGAR
" person . LOUT, BOOR, YAHOO
uncritical .... NAIVE
unction .... BALM, UNGUENT
" , administer .... ANELE
unctuous .... GREASY, OILY, PINGUID, SALVY, SUAVE
" mixture ... LANOLIN, CERATE
uncultivated .... FALLOW, WILD, ARID
uncultured .... BRUTE, PHILISTINE

300

under . INFERIOR, NEATH, SUB, NETHER, SOUS, SOTTO
underbrush beaten by a stag ABATURE
underdone ...... RARE, REAR, PARTIAL
undergo DREE, STAND, ENDURE, SUFFER
     "   cell destruction .... LYSE
underground stem .... TUBER
underhand COVERT, SECRET, DERN, SLY
     "   throw .... LOB
underlined in red .... RUBRIC
undermine .... THWART, SAP
understanding . BRAIN, ENTENTE, DIG, INWIT, SENSE, ACCORD
understatement .... LITOTES
understood .... AGREED, TACIT
undertake .... FANG, POSTULATE, TRY, ENGAGE, EMBARK, BEGIN
undertaker .... MORTICIAN, CERER
undertaking .... ACT, AVAL
     "   , zealous .... CRUSADE
undertow .... RIPTIDE
underwater breathing apparatus ..... SCUBA
     "   mass of cement .... PAAR
     "   swimmer ..... FROGMAN
underwear ...... LINGERIE, BVD, SLIP, DESSOUS
underworld ... EREBUS, SHEOL, DUAT, HELL, ABYSS, ARALU, HADES, ORCUS
underwrite .. BACK, ENSURE, FINANCE
undeserving ..... INDIGN, UNWORTHY
undeveloped LATENT, EMBRYO, BARREN, RUDIMENTARY
undine ...... NYMOH, GNOME, SYLPH
undo .... COOK, LOOSE, RUIN, DESTROY
undomesticated .... FERAL, WILD
undone ...... DISHED, RARE, RUINED
undraped .... NUDE, BARE
undressed fur .... PELT
undulating .. RIPPLING, WAVY, ARIPPLE
undulation . HEAVE, SURGE, TREMOLO
undyed .... CORAH, PLAIN
undying ... AMARANTHINE, IMMORTAL
unearth ...... DETECT, ROOT, EXPOSE, EXHUME
unearthly .... EERIE, WEIRD
uneasiness . MALAISE, UNREST, QUALM
uneducated .... BENIGHTED
unemployed ..... IDLE, OTIOSE, LAZY
unending ..... TERMLESS, BOUNDLESS
unequal ..... ODD, SCALENE, UNFAIR
uneven EROSE, ODD, ROUGH, RAGGED
unfadable .... FAST
unfading flower .... AMARANTH
unfair .... PARTIAL, FOUL, BIASED
unfeeling ..... NUMB, BRUTAL, STOIC, CALLOUS, HARD, HARSH
unfilled lode cavity .... VUGG
unfit .... INEPT, DISQUALIFIED
unfold .... EVOLVE, DEPLOY, DEVELOP,

    UNROLL, UNFURL, EVOLUTE
unfrequented .... SOLITARY
unfurl .... SLACK, UNFOLD
ungainly .... CLUMSY, GAWKY
ungrateful person .... INGRATE
unguent ...... NARD, CHRISM, SALVE, OINTMENT, POMADE
ungula ... CLAW, HOOF, NAIL, TALON
unhappiness .... WOE, GRIEF
unheard .... SURD, UNKNOWN
unicorn .... MONOCEROS, REEM
     "   fish .... NARWHAL, UNIE
uniform . EQUAL, EVEN, LEVEL, LIVERY, FLAT
uninflected .... APTOTIC
union ..... FUSION, LEAGUE, MERGER, LIAISON, AMALGAM, BLOC, LINK
     " , trade GUILD, ARTEL, HANSE, AFL, CIO, ILA, ITA, TWU, ILGWU
uniplanar point .... UNODE
unique .... ALONE, SINGLE, SOLE
     "   person .... ONER, LONER
unit .... ACE, ONE, SYLLABLE
     " , caloric .... THERM
     " , electric AMPERE, COULOMB, MHO, OHM, PROTON, VOLT, WATT
     " , heat .... CALORIE
     " , hypothetical .... ID, IDIC
     " , magnetic GAUSS, KAPP, OERSTED, WEBER
     " , mathematical .... RADIX
     " of acceleration .... GAL
     " of circuit power .... VAR
     " of conductance ABHENRY, ABMHO
     " of electrical capacity ..... FARAD
     " of electrical pressure ...... BARAD
     " of energy .... QUANTUM, ERG
     " of flux density .... GAUSS
     " of force .... NEWTON
     " of illumination .... PHOT
     " of inductance .... HENRY
     " of kinetic energy .... ERG
     " of light ...... LUMEN, LUX, PYR
     " of magnetic flux ...... MAXWELL
     " of magnetic potential ... GILBERT
     " of mass .... GEEPOUND, SLUG
     " of measure ... PARSEC, REL, CRITH
     " of meter .... MORA, STERE
     " of power .... WATT
     " of radiation .... RAD, REP
     " of saturation .... SATRON
     " of sound absorption ..... SABIN
     " of speed .... VELO
     " of telegraphic speed ...... BAUD
     " of TNT power .... KILOTON
     " of weight CRITH, MAUND, CARAT
     " of work .... ERG, KILERG, ERGON
     " of work energy .... JOULE
     " , ultimate .... MONAD
     " , wire .... MIL

unite ..... FAY, LINK, CONJOIN, FUSE,
    YOKE, ALLY, MIX, WED, KNIT, WELD,
        BLEND, SOLDER
united with FEDERATED, ONED, IMPED
universal .... COMMON, COSMIC,
        CATHOLIC
    " language .... ESPERANTO
    " successor of deceased .....
        HERES
    " writing .... PASIGRAPHY
universe .... LOKA, WORLD, COSMOS
university .. OXFORD, HARVARD, YALE,
        CAMBRIDGE, SORBONNE
    " group .... SEMINAR
    " governor .... REGENT
    " , growing body of a ......
        SENATUS
unjust ...... PARTIAL, UNFAIR, BIASED
unkeeled .... RATITE
unkempt .. ROUGH, SHAGGY, UNTIDY
unkind ...... BRUTAL, CRUEL, HARSH
unknown person .. INCONNU, IGNOTE
    " quantity .... COSS
unlawful .... ILLEGAL, ILLICIT,
        CONTRABAND
unlearn .... FORGET
unleavened .... AZYMOUS
    " bread .... AZYM,
        MATZOS
unless .... NISI, BUT, EXCEPT
unlike .... DIVERSE, SUNDRY
unlooked for .... CHANCE, HAP(PEN)
unlucky .... FEY, ILL, INFAUST
unmarried ... UNWED, CELIBATE, SOLE
    " state .... AGAMY
unmixed .... PURE
unmoved ...... DEAD, INERT, SERENE
unplowed .. UNTILLED, FALLOW, HADE
unqualified .... SHEER, PLENARY
unravel .... FEAZE, SOLVE, SLEAVE
unreal .... ARTIFICIAL, CHAOTIC
unrefined CRUDE, CRASS, GROSS, RAW,
        RIBALD
unruffled ...... SERENE, STILL, SEDATE
unruly .... LAWLESS, TURBULENT
unseasoned .... UNTIMELY, GREEN
unshorn sheep .... TEG
unskillful .... MALADROIT, AWKWARD
unskilled .... INEPT, CLUMSY, PUISINE
unsorted wheaten meal .. ATA, ATTA
unspoken ... TACIT, SECRET, INEFFABLE
unstable ..... LABILE, SHAKY, ERRATIC
unsuitable .... INEPT, INAPT, UNFIT
untamed .. FERINE, FERAL, RAW, WILD
untanned skin ...... KIP, SHAGREEN
untidy ...... MESSY, DOWDY, SLOPPY
    " one .... SLOB, SLUT
untie .... LOOSE, UNKNOT
until .... HENT, TO, TILL

untold .... VAST, COUNTLESS
untouched .... PURE, PRISTINE
untwine .... FRESE
untwist .... FAG, FEAZE
unusual ...... RARE, EPIGENE, OUTRE,
        EXOTIC, STRANGE
unvoiced .... SURD
unwilling .... LO(A)TH, AVERSE
    " , be .... NILL
unwise .... INSIPIENT, IMPOLITIC
unwonted .... RARE, UNUSED
unworthy ..... INDIGN, VILE, UNFIT
unwrinkled .... BRENT, SMOOTH
unyielding .... ADAMANT, FAST, FIRM,
        STANCH, STIFF
up to .... TILL, UNTIL
Upanishad .... ISHA
upas-tree poison .... ANTIAR
upholstery fabric .... TOURNAY
    " silk .... TABARET
upbraid ..... CHIDE, SCOLD, REPROVE
upon .... ABOVE, ATOP, OVER
    " ; prefix .... EPI, SUR
upper .... VAMP, BUNK, OBER
uppish .... PROUD
upright ...... ERECT, MORAL, HONEST
uprising ...... MUTINY, PUTSCH, COUP
uproar ... DIN, HUBBUB, NOISE, RIOT,
        RACKET, CLAMOR, BABEL
upsilon-shaped .... HYOID
upstart .... PARVENU, SNOB
upward bend in lumber .... SNY
    " ; prefix .... ANA, ANO
uraeus .... ASP
uranium .... CARNOTITE
Uranus, daughter of .... RHEA
    " , wife of .... GAEA, GE
urban division .... WARD
    " inhabitant .... CIT
urbane .... BLAND, POLITE, SUAVE
urchin ..... HEDGEHOG, IMP, ELFIN,
        GAMIN, MUDLARK, ARAB, BRAT
uredo .... HIVES, URTICARIA
urge .. INCITE, PLY, EGG, GOAD, HIE,
        ABET, DUN, SPUR, PRESS, PROD
urgent .... EXIGENT
urial .... OORIAL, SHA
Uriel .... ARCHANGEL
urn .. KIST, DEINOS, SAMOVAR, PELIKE
    " -shaped .... URCEOLATE
uroxanthin .... INDICAN
Ursa .... BEAR, MAJOR, MINOR
ursine howler .... ARAGUATO
Urth .... NORN
urticaria .... HIVES, UREDO
urus .... TUR, AUROCHS
us .... WEUNS, WE
usage .... WONT, HABIT, MANNER
usance .... USAGE, USE

use . AVAIL, EMPLOY, EXHAUST, TREAT,
　　　WONT, CONSUME, PLY
useful .... UTILE, PRACTICAL
useless .. IDLE, INUTILE, NULL, OTIOSE,
　　　FUTILE, VOID
usher .... SEAT, DOORKEEPER, SHOW,
　　　TILER, ESCORT
Usnech, son of .... NOISE
USSR news agency .... TASS
usurp .... ASSUME, GRAB, SEIZE, TAKE
Utah, appellation of .... BEEHIVE
　" 　mountain .... UNITA, PEALE
　" 　state flower .... SEGO
utmost .... EXTREME, MAXIMUM, LAST,
　　　FINAL, LIMIT
"Utopia" author .... MORE
utopian ...... IDEALISTIC, VISIONARY
utter SHEER, BRAY, EMIT, MOOT, STARK,
　　　DRAWL, INTONATE, SPEAK, TOTAL
　　　BID, PERFECT
　" 　; poet. .... SYLLABLE
　" 　publicly . ENOUNCE, VOICE, TELL

V

V, letter .... VEE
V-shaped piece .... WEDGE
vacancy ...... BLANK, GAP, OPENING
vacant .... INANE, VOID, EMPTY, IDLE,
　　　BLANK
vacation ...... RECESS, SPELL, RESPITE
vaccine, per. to .... LYMPH, VIRUS
vaccinia .... COWPOX
vacillate .... SEESWA, WAVER, TEETER
vacuum ...... VOID, CAVITY, HOLLOW
　" 　, opposite of .... PLENUM
　" 　tube ...... DIODE, TETRODE,
　　　HEPTODE, ELECTRODE, KLYSTRON,
　　　MAGNETRON, MEGATRON
vague ... DIM, HAZY, OBSCURE, LOOSE
vagabond ..... BUM, WASTREL, LOREL,
　　　HOBO, RODNEY, VAGRANT, TRAMP,
　　　RAPPAREE
vagrant ...... TRAMP, NOMAD, PIKER,
　　　PROWLER, PICARO, EUCHITE
vain ...... EMPTY, IDLE, FUTILE, SMUG
　" 　fellow; Bib. .... RACA
vainglory POMP, SHOW, GASCONADE,
　　　VANITY, CONCEIT, PRIDE
vale ...... DELL, DINGLE, DALE, GLEN
valediction .... ADIEU, FAREWELL
valet ..... ANDREW, CRISPIN, SQUIRE,
　　　FLUNKY, LACKEY
Valetta, native of .... MALTESE
valiant .... BRAVE, WIGHT, STALWART
valid .... LICIT, SOLID, SOUND
　" 　mode of third figure .. FERISON

　" 　, not .... NULL, VOID
validate .... ATTEST, RATIFY, SEAL
validity .... FORCE, COGENCY
valise .... ETUI, ETWEE, SATCHEL, MAIL
valley .... DALE, VALE, COMBE, GLEN,
　　　SWALE, DINGLE, DELL, RILL, RAVINE,
　　　DENE
　" 　between volcanic cones ATRIO
　" 　in Argolis .... NEMEA
　" 　in the Levant ... WADI, WADY
　" 　, Indian .... DHOON
　" 　of Hinnom .... GEHENNA
　" 　of misery .... BACA
　" 　of S. Africa .... VAAL
　" 　of the moon .... RILLE
　" 　of the Sahara .... SAMEN
　" 　stream .... CREEK, COULEE
value ...... ADMIRE, ESTEEM, CARAT,
　　　STERLING, PAR, WORTH, COST,
　　　ASSESS, ESTIMATE
　" 　, assay .... LEY
　" 　, of least possible .... PLACK
　" 　, without .... BAFF, THREEPENNY,
　　　TRASHY
valve ..... TAP, COCK, RAPHE, FAUCET
vamoose .. GO, LAM, SCRAM, DECAMP
vamp .... RECOCT, SOCK, UPPER
vampire .... BAT, GHOUL, LAMIA
van .... TRUCK, FORE, FRONT
vandal .... HUN, GOTH, TEUTON
Van Gogh town .... ARLES
vane .... FAN, TAIL, FLOAT
vanish ...... FADE, PASS, EVANESCE,
　　　RECEDE, SINK
vanity .... AIRS, EGOISM, VAINGLORY
　" 　box ...... ETUI, ETWEE
"Vanity Fair" char. .... SHARP
vantage place .... COIGN(E)
vapid ...... POINTLESS, STALE, FLAT,
　　　INSIPID, JEJUNE
vapor ..... REEK, FOG, MIST, BRUME
　" 　; comb. form .... ATMO
　" 　pressure indicator . TONOMETER
vaporous .... STEAMY
Varangian .... ROS
variable . PROTEAN, MOBILE, MUTABLE,
　　　FICKLE, FITFUL, SHIFTY
variation .. SHADE, NUANCE, LECTION
variegate .... ENAMEL, FRET
variegated...... PAINTED, PIED, PINTO,
　　　SHOT, DIVERSE, CALICO, MOTLEY
variola .... SMALLPOX
variety .... CLASS, MEDLEY, MIXTURE
various .... DIVERSE, SEVERAL
varnish ..... JAPAN, ADORN, EXCUSE,
　　　GLOSS, SHELLAC(K)
　" 　-and-oil mixture ...... MEGILP
　" 　ingredient . LAC, COPAL, ELEMI
　" 　oleoresin ... DAMAR, DAMMAR
vas .... DUCT, VESSEL

vase ...... DIOTA, JAR, URN, SITULA, TAZZA, OLLA, DRUM, TAMBOUR, ETUI, EPERGNE, ECHEA
" , Egyptian .... CANOPIC
" , Greek .... DEINOS, DINOS
" handle .... ANSA
" , jasper .... MURRINE
" used as an oil vessel .... ASKOS
" with separate cover ... POTICHE
vassal ..... SLAVE, LIEGE, MAN, SERF, HELOT, THRALL
vassalage, subject to .... ENFEOFF
vat . BAC, GYLE, KEEL, TANK, TUB, TUN, KEEVE, KIEVE, KIER, GAAL, GYLE, CISTERN
Vatican chapel .... SISTINE
vaticanism .... CURIALISM
vaticinator .... ORACLE
vault .... FORNIX, CRYPT, LEAP, TOMB, SAFE, ARCH, CURVET, CATACOMB
vaulted .. CONCAVE, DOMED, CUPOLAR
" roof .... CAMERA
vaunt .. CROW, BOAST, VAPOR, BRAG
vector, opposite of .... SCABAR
Vedas, divinity of the .... DYAUS
Vedic dialect .... PALI
" god .... SAVITAR, AGNI
veer .. YAW, SWAY, SLUE, SKEW, SHIFT
Vega's constellation .... LYRA
vegetable .... LEGUME, LOMENT
" bath sponge LOOFAH, LUFFA
" mold .... HUMUS
" , onion-like .. LEEK, SHALLOT
" rubbish .... WRACK
vegetables .... TRUCK
vegetate .... HIBERNATE, GROW
vegetation ..... SADD, SUDD, FLORA, HERBAGE
vehemence . HEAT, ZEAL, ARDOR, FIRE
vehement ... ARDENT, EAGER, INTENSE
vehemently .... AMAIN
vehicle ...... AGENT, MEANS, DEVICE
" , automotive . BUS, JEEP, TAXI, SEDAN, TRUCK, OMNIBUS, COUPE
" , horse-drawn . FIACRE, ESSED, CALASH, TONGA, CALECHE, DROSKY, TROIKA
" , railroad .... COACH, DINER, BOXCAR, ENGINE, SMOKER, TENDER
Veidt, Mr. .... CONRAD
veil .. CLOAK, MASK, PRETENSE, VOLET, CAUL, SCREEN, HIDE
" in fungi .... VELUM
" in mosses .... CALYPTRA
" , papal .... ORALE
veiled VELATE, INCOGNITO, CURTAINED
vein .... TENOR, RENAL, VEULA, VENA, CAVA, LODE, ROKE, STRIA

veinstone .... GANGUE
veinless .... AVENOUS
veiny .... VENOSE
Velez, Miss .... LUPE
vellum .... PARCHMENT
velvetleaf .... PAREIRA, DAGGA
venal .. HIRELING, CORRUPT, SALEABLE
vend .... HAWK, SELL, PEDDLE
vender .... ALIENOR
vendetta .... FEUD
veneer ... ENAMEL, FACE, LAC, LAYER, SHELL, POLISH
venerable ... OLDEN, AUGUST, SAGE, WISE
venerate ..... REVERE, LOVE, RESPECT
veneration ...... AWE, DULIA, LATRIA, RESPECT, ESTEEM
Venetian church .... STMARK
" district .... RIALTO
" formal barge .. BUCENTAUR
" medal ...... OSELLA, OSELA
" pleasure boat ... GONDOLA
" ruler ...... DOGE, PODESTA
" traveler .... POLO
" water street .... RIO
" watering place ...... LIDO
"Veni, vidi, _____" VICI
Venice, island near .... BURANO
venom . GALL, MALICE, RANCOR, BANE
Venezuela capital .... CARACAS
" grassy plains ..... LLANOS
" Indian .... CARIB, TIMOTE
" river .. ORINOCO, CACERA, META
" state .... LARA
" town .... AROA
" tree .... BALATA
vent . OUTLET, SAY, (AIR)HOLE, FLUE, EGRESS, SPRACLE
ventilated .... AIRY, WINDY, AIRED
ventral .... STERNAL, HEMAD, HEMAL
ventriloquism, practice ... HARIOLATE
ventriloquist .... (EDGAR)BERGEN
venture . DARE, WAGE, FLING, FLYER, BRAVE, GAMBLE, HAZARD, STAKE, RISK
Venus .. VESPER, APHRODITE, ASTARTE
" , boy beloved by ..... ADONIS
" , epithet of .... CYTHEREA
" , island of .... MELOS
" , planet .... LUCIFER, PHOSPHOR
" , son of .... CUPID
Venus's-flytrap .... DIONAEA
" girdle .... CESTUS
veranda .. LANAI, PYAL, STOA, STOOP, PATIO, PORCH, LOGGIA
verb .... RHEMA, VOCABLE
verbal . ORAL, PAROL, VOCAL, SPOKEN
" noun .... GERUND
" suffix .... ESCE

304

verbenaceae ..... LANTANA, TECTONA
verbiage .... PROLIXITY
verbose ..... PROLIX, WINDY, WORDY
verbs, derived from ...... RHEMATIC
Verdi opera . AIDA, OTHELLO, OBERTO
" " char. AMNERIS, RADAMES
verdigris RUST, FILM, PATINA, AERUGO
verge ..... BRINK, EDGE, MARGE, TOP
" of authority .... WAND
Vergil's Aeneid queen .... DIDO
" family name .... MARO
verify .... ATTEST, PROVE, AUDIT
verily .... AMEN, YEA, INDEED
verity .... TRUTH, REALITY
vermilion .... RED, PIGMENT
Vermont city .... BARRE, LYNDON
versatile .... MOBILE
versation .... WINDING
verse .... ALBA, POEM, STICH, METER,
RHYME, POEM, RONDEL, STROPHE,
STAVE
" form ..... TROCHEE, SPONDEE,
SESTINA, IAMB, IONIC, DACTYL,
PANTUM, TERGIT
" having three feet ..... TRIPODY
" , musical .... STAFF
" , nonsensical ...... DOGGEREL,
LIMERICK
" of four feet ...... TETRAMETER
" of three feet .... TRIMETER
" of two measures .... DIMETER
" , pause in .... CESURA
" stress, per. to .... ICTIC
" with hidden motto ... ACROSTIC
versed .... ADEPT, SKILLED
versifier .... POETASTER, RIMESTER
version ...... EDITION, TRANSLATION
" of Bible .... ITALA, VULGATE
verso .... BACK, REVERSE
vertebra . LUMBAR, CENTRUM, SPONDYL
vertebrate axis .... AXON, RAY
vertical ...... PLUMB, ERECT, UPRIGHT
vertigoes .... DINI
Vertumnus' beloved .... POMONA
verve .... ELAN, PEP, SPIRIT, ZIP, ZEST
" , act with .... EMOTE
very . REAL, TRUE, TOO, MUCH, SAME,
WELL, GENUINE, TRES
vesicle ..... SAC, BLEB, CYST, BLISTER
vespa .... WASP
Vespucci; discoverer ...... AMERIGO
vessel .... DIOTA, CASK, DUBBER, VAS,
VAT, MUG, BOWL, CRAFT, SHIP,
BOAT, POT, CASK, BOTTLE, VASE
" , amount lacking of full in a ..
ULLAGE
" , any round sailing .. CORACLE
" , assaying .... CUPEL
" , beer .... POURIE
" , broad shallow .... PAN

" , Chinese .... JUNK
" , coaling .... COLLIER
" , coasting .... BILANDER, DONI,
HOY, LUGGER, PATAMAR,
TARTAN, DHONI
" ; comb. form .... VASO
" , cylindrical glass ...... BOCAL
" , deep table .... TUREEN
" , drinking GOURD, JORUM, STEIN,
TANKARD, AMPULLA, STOUP
" , Dutch ... GALIOT, KOFF, YANKY
" , earthen ...... CROCK, PANKIN
" , ecclesiastical .... AMA, PYX
" , filter, glass .... ALUDEL
" , fishing, sailing SEALER, SMACK
" for ale or wine .... JUBBE
" for holding illuminant ......
CRESSET
" for napkins, salt, etc. .... NEF
" for oil .... CUP, CRUSE, DUBBA,
FONT
" for refining .... CUPEL
" for separating liquids ....
TRITORIUM
" for sugar refining ..... ELUTOR
" (house boat) of the Nile ....
DAHABEAH
" , Indian coasting .... SHIBAR
" , large rowing; Scot. ... BIRLINN
" , lateen-rigged; Medit. . FELUCCA
" , Levantine . SETEE, KETCH, SAIC
" , (log) raft .... BRAIL
" , Malay .... PRAU, PROA
" , merchant .... ARGOSY
" , narrow-sterned .... PINK
vessel, one-masted oriental ... DHOW
" , part of . SKEG, PROW, DECK,
KEEL
" , per. to a .... VASAL
" , sailing . BARK, DONI, PINNACE,
BUGEYE
" , saucer-like .... PATERA
" , single-masted .... SLOOP, HOY
" , small drinking NOG, NOGGIN
" , small wooden COGUE, PIGGIN,
SKEEL
" , square-rigged . BRIG, SNOW
" , steer .... COND
" , stern of a .... STEERAGE
" , stone or clay ... STEAN, STEEN
" , Thames; Eng. .... BAWLEY
" , three-masted ..... BARK, TERN,
XEBEC, ZEBEC
" , toward stern of .... AFT
" , trading .... BAGGALA
" , twin-hull .... CATAMARAN
" , war .... FRIGATE, BOYER
" , wicker .... POT
" , wine-service .... AMA

305

" with three banks of oars ..... TRIREME
" with two banks of oars BIREME
" , Venetian state .... BUCENTAUR
vessel, part of SKEG, BOW, SNY, GAFF, HELM, KEEL, PROW, SPAR, HAWSE, KEVEL, HATCH, SNAPE
vessels fitted into each other ALUDEL
vest ...... GILET, WAISTCOAT, LINDER
" ; as a right .... ACCRUE
" , stuffed .... ACTON
Vesta; Gr. ....HESTIA
vestal . PURE, CHASTE, VIRGINAL, NUN
" virgin .... TUCCIA
vestige ... RELIC, SIGN, TRACE, TRACK, REMNANT, SHRED
vestment CHASUBLE, EPHOD, SCAPULAR
" , alb-like .... SACCOS
" , Arabian .... ABA
" , clerical .... ALB, AMICE, CASSOCK
" , eucharistic ...... MANIPLE
" , liturgical .... COPE
" , priest's ... SURPLICE, STOLE
vestry .... SACRISTY, CHAPEL
vesuvianite ..... IDOCRASE, XANTHITE
vetch AKRA, FITCH, ERS, TARE, SATIVA, TINEWEED
veterinarian .... FARRIER, LEECH
veto .... DENY, PROHIBIT, QUASH
vex .. HARASS, CARK, FRET, RILE, ROIL, IRK, NETTLE, FASH
vexation .... CHAFE, CHAGRIN, TEEN, THORN, IRRITATION
vial .... CRUET, AMPUL, PHIAL, BOTTLE
viand CATE, FARE, CHOW, GRUB, EATS
Viaud's pseudonym .... LOTI
vibrant .... TRAVALE, VOICED
vibrate . JAR, DINDLE, RESONATE, TIRL, QUAVER, THROB, JIGGLE, THRILL
vibration .... FREMITUS, TREMOLO
vicar .... PASTOR, CURATE, DEPUTY
vice ...... SIN, STEAD, VALI, FAILING
" cap .... CHUCK
" jaw .... CHAP
" king .... VICEROY
" president .... VEEP
victim ...... GULL, DUPE, PREY, CULLY
victory .. NIKE, PALM, CRECY, TRIUMPH
" , celebrating .... EPINICIAN
" cry .... ABOO, ABU
" , hymn of .... EPINICION
" , memorial of .... TROPHY
victual(s) . EAT, FEED, CHOW, VIANDS, KAI
vie COMPETE, EMULATE, FEY, CONTEND, LIFE, STRIVE
Vienna .... WIEN
" park .... PRATER
" river .... DANUBE

Viet Nam president ... THIEU, DIEM, KHAN
" " city ..... SAIGON, HANOI DANANG, HUE
view .. VISTA, SEE, EYE, KEN, GLIMPSE, SCENE, OGLE, SURVEY
vigil .... PATROL, WATCH, ARGUS, EYE
vigilant .... ALERT, AWAKE, WARY
vigilantes .... POSSE
vigor . FORCE, STAMINA, STHENIA, VIR, VIS, VIM, ENERGY, LIFE, ESPRIT, ZIP
vigorous .... COGENT
Viking ... PIRATE, ROVER, ERIC, OLAF, ROLLO
" poet .... SKALD
vile .... ABJECT, MEAN, ODIOUS, BASE
vilify ...... MALIGN, REVILE, TRADUCE
village . BURG, DORP, TOWN, HAMLET, KAIK, STAD, KRAAL, ALDEA, PUEBLO, DESSA
villain ...... BADDIE, HEAVY, ROGUE, RUFFIAN, BEZONIAN, CAITIFF
" of Othello .... IAGO
villein CORL, CHURL, CARL, ESNE, SERF
Villon; poet .... FRANCOIS
vim .... PEP, ZIP, ELAN, ESPRIT, GIMP, FORCE, SPIRIT
vindicate ... ASSERT, JUSTIFY, AVENGE
vine . HOP, IVY, GRAPE, LIANA, LIANE, CUPSEED, BINE
" parasite .... APHIS
" , part of a .... CIRRUS, TENDRIL
vinegar ..... ACETATE, ACETUM, EISEL
" ; comb. form .... ACETO
" , dregs of .... MOTHER
" made of ale .... ALEGAR
" , preserve in .... MARINATE
vinous .... WINY
viol . RUANA, SARINDA, GIGUE, VOYAL
viola .... ALTO, TENOR
Viola's brother .... SEBASTIAN
violate ..... ABUSE, RAVISH, PROFANE
violent Norse people; myth. .... BERSERKERS
violently .... AMAIN
violet .... MAUVE, BLAVER
" dye .... ARCHIL
" -root glucoside .... IRIDIN
" leaves, oil in .... IRONE
violin bow .... ARCO
" , famous . AMATI, ROCTA, STRAD, CREMONA
" , first .... REBEC, REBAB
" , part of a .... NECK
" , per. to .... KIT
violinist . YSAYE, ELMAN, STERN, BULL, MORINI, AUER, HEIFETZ, MENUHIN, OISTRAKH
viper .. ADDER, ASP, CERASTES, KUPPER

virago ... FURY, RULLION, TERMAGANT, VIXEN
vireo .... GREENLET
Virgil's hero .... AENEAS
" patron .... MAECENAS
virgin .... VESTAL, PURE, CHASTE
" warrior in the "Aeneid" .... CAMILLA
Virgin Is. discoverer ..... COLUMBUS
Virgin Mary's flower .... MARIGOLD
Virginia ————— .... DARE
Virginia capital .... RICHMOND
" county . BLAND, CRAIG, FLOYD
" creeper ..... BINEWOOD, IVY
" juniper .... CEDAR
" poke .... HELLEBORE
" wake-robin .... ARUM
" willow .... ITEA
" woodcock .... PEWEE
virgularian .... SEAROD
virtu, article of .... CURIO
virulence .... MALIGNITY, HATE
virulent .... RABID, BITTER
virus ailment .... FLUE
visage .... FACE, ASPECT, PUSS
viscous (S)LIMY, ROPY, STICKY, GLUEY, SIZY
Vishnu, incarnation of ..... KRISHNA, RAMA, AVATAR
visible ..... PATENT, OBVIOUS, OPEN
" to naked eye ... MACROSCOPIC
Visigoth king .... ALARIC, ALARIK
vision .... DREAM, FANCY, PHANTOM, SIGHT
" ; comb. form .... OPTO
" , double .... DIPLOPIA
" , science of .... OPTOMETRY
visionary ...... FEY, IDEAL, DREAMER, UTOPIAN, AIRY, UNREAL, ROMANTIC
visit ... GAM, SEE, CALL, STAY, HAUNT
visiting, a .... SOKEN
Vistula tributary .... SAN
visual disorder .... STRABISMUS
vita .... LIFE
"Vita Nuova" author .... DANTE
vital .... INHERENT, ORGANIC
" force .... HORME, NEURISM
" growth force .... BATHMISM
" juice .... SAP
" strength .... STAMINA
" thought force .... PHRENISM
vitality ....LIFE, PEP, ZIP, SAP, VIGOR
vitamin ANEURIN, THIAMIN(E), NIACIN, RIBOFLAVIN, BIOTIN, CITRIN, CHOLIN, ADERMIN
vitiate DEBASE, SPOIL, POLLUTE, TAINT, DEFILE
vitrine .... SHOWCASE
vitriol .... CAUSTIC, SORY

vivacity .... DASH, ELAN, VERVE
vivandier .... SUTLER
vivarium .... PARK, STEW
vixen .... SHREW, VIRAGO
vocal TONAL, ORAL, SONANT, VERBAL, PHONETIC
" composition .... MOTET
" flourish .... ROULADE
voiceless . SPIRATE, SURD, DUMB, MUTE
" sound .... TENUIS
voices, for all .... TUTTI
void .. ABOLISH, NULL, ANNUL, EGEST, ABYSS, VACATE, CANCEL
volatile .. FITFUL, FLIGHTY, MERCURIAL
volcanic ejection ..... BELCH, LATITE, LAPILLI, MOYA, SLAG, LAVA, SCORIA
" glass ...... PERLITE, OBSIDIAN
" glass froth .... PUMICE
" rock .... RHYOLITE
" saucer .... CRATER
" tufa .... TRASS, TERRAS
volcano .... SPITFIRE, FURNACE
" in Iceland ...... ASKJA
" goddess; Hawai. .... PELE
" in Japan . ASAMA, ASO, FUJI
" in Mindanao, P.I. ...... APO
" in United States .... SHASTA
" ; Italy ...... ETNA, VESUVIUS
" ; Martinique .... PELEE
" , mouth of .... FUMAROLE
" of Guatemala ..... ATITLAN, FUEGO
" of Java .... GEDE
" of the Andes ......COTOPAXI
" of the United States . LASSEN
" , slaggy eruption of .. SCORIA
" ; Sumatra .... MERAPI
Volga, anc. name .... RHA
" , city on .... SAMARA
volley PLATOON, SALVO, DRIFT, FLIGHT
"Volpone" char. .... MOSCA
Volsunga Saga, king in .... ATLI
volt or demivolt .... REPOLON
Voltaire, name of .... AROUET
" , novel by .... CANDIDE
voluble .... FLUENT, GLIB, OILY
volume .... BULK, CUBAGE, TOME, LOUDNESS, BOOK, SIZE
" in ten parts ..... DECAMERON
Volund's brother .... EGIL
volute .... CILERY, SCROLL
voodooism .... OBEAH
voracious .... EDACIOUS
voracity .... EDACITY, RAPACITY
vortex ...... EDDY, GYRE, MAELSTROM
Vosges mountain pass ...... BELFORT
votary .. DEVOTEE, BUFF, FAN, ZEALOT
vote .... STRAW, LOGROLL, BALLOT
" of assent ..... AYE, NOD, PLACET
votes, receptacle for .... SITULA

vouch for .... ATTEST, SPONSOR
voucher .... CHIT, NOTE
vouchsafe . BESTOW, CONCEDE, DEIGN
vow .. PLEDGE, PROMISE, SWEAR, VUM
vowel change in German ... UMLAUT
   "   gradation .... ABLAUT
   " , mark placed over ...... TILDE,
                                MACRON
   "   point .... TSERE
   " , short .... BREVE
   "   sign .... DIERESIS
   "   sound, per. to .... VOCALIC
   "   suppression .... ELISION
vowels, contraction of two .. CRASIS
   " , group of two DIGRAM, DIGRAPH
Vulcan .... HEPHAESTUS
   " , son of .... CACUS
   " , wife of .... VENUS
vulcanite .... EBONITE
vulgar LEWD, RIBALD, DOWDY, FRUMPY,
        RANDY, COARSE, BOORISH
vulgate .... ITALA
vulture .. CONDOR, PAPA, SCAVENGER,
      URUBU, AASVOGEL, CORBIE,
      DIRTBIRD, RAPTOR, GEIR

W

wad ... MASS, BAT, LUMP, PAD, STUFF,
                         PLUG
waddle .... PODDLE, WAMBLE
wade .... FORD, PLODGE, SLOG
wadi .... CHANNEL, STREAM
wading bird .... FLAMINGO, JACANA,
      HERON, STORK, STILT, EGRET,
           PEWIT, GRALLAE
wafer .... OBLEY, TROCHE, DISK, HOST
waffle .... GAUFRE, GOFER, CAKE
wag .. FARCEUR, ROGUE, WIT, MOMUS,
             WAVE, JOKER
wage ...... HIRE, PAY, STIPEND, UTU
wager .. BET, PLEDGE, STAKE, HAZARD,
                     RISK
waggish ... ARCH, JOCULAR, ROGUISH
Wagner; composer .... RICHARD
   "   opera PARSIFAL, LOHENGRIN,
                     RIENZI
Wagnerian role .. ELSA, ERDA, SENTA,
                   ISOLDE
wagon ... TRAM, TONGA, VAN, WAIN,
      CART, CAR, CAISSON, CHARIOT,
      COACH, ARABA, TELEGA
   "   part CLEVIS, THILL, NEAP, POLE,
                   BLADE
wahoo fishes .... PETOS
waif GAMIN, STRAFE, STRAY, WASTREL,
                  CASTAWAY

wail ..... SOB, WOW, ULULATE, KEEN
waist ... BODICE, BASQUE, GARIBALDI
   "   in dressmaking CARPEL, TAILLE
waistband .... SASH, BELT
waistcoat ..... DOUBLET, VEST, BENDY,
             GILET, SINGLET
wait .... LINGER, STAY, TARRY, PAUSE
waiter .. GARCON, SALVER, STEWARD,
            DRAWER, CARHOP
waive ... FORGO, RELINQUISH, CEDE,
            DEFER, RESIGN
wake-robin ..... TRILLIUM, SNAKEBITE
Waldensian .... LEONIST
wale ...... BLOW, RIB, WELT, WHEAL
Wales .... CAMBRIA, CYMRY
   " , floral emblem of ...... LEEK
   " , legendary prince of .. MADOC
   " , people of .... WELSH
walk .. STRAM, DADDLE, GAD, TRAMP,
      TREAD, MUSH, PLOD, GAIT, HIKE,
      LIMP, PACE, STEP, AMBLE
   "   aimlessly . MINCE, LURCH, PAUP
   " , shaded .... MALL, ALAMEDA
walked softly .... STOLE
walking about . PASSANT, PERIPATETIC
   "   like a bear ... PLANTIGRADE
   "   meter .... PEDOMETER
wall ... MUR(E), BAIL, DIKE, ESCARP,
      SEPTA, SEPTUM, PARAPET
   "   lizard .... GECKO
   " , of a ...... MURAL, PARIETAL
   " , outer face of a ..... PARAMENT
   "   piece .... DADO, PANEL, TEMPLET
wallaba .... APA
wallaroo .... KANGAROO
Waller; pianist .... FATS
walls of cavity .... PARIES
walnut .... NOGAL, TRYMA
walrus ... BRUT, MORSE, ROS, MARINE
   "   herd .... POD
walruses .... PINNIPEDIA
Walter; actor .... ABEL
wampum BEADS, SE(A)WAN, PEAG(E)
wan ... FADE, HAW, PALLID, WAXEN,
             ASHEN, ASHY
wand . CADUCEUS, ROD, VERGE, MACE,
      BATON, SCEPTER, CUDGEL,
      TRUNCHEON, WATTLE
wander ... GAD, MOON, RANGE, ERR,
      ROVE, TRAPE, RAMBLE
   "   aimlessly .. DIVAGATE, STRAY
   "   in a winding course.........
         MEANDER, SCAMANDER
   "   widely . PEREGRINATE, ROAM
wanderer ... ARAB, NOMAD, TRUANT,
      WAG, SCENITE, VIATOR,
      VAGABOND, BEDOUIN, GYPSY,
             MIGRANT
wandering ...... ODYSSEY, ERRANT,
     NOMADIC, BOHEMIAN, ASTRAY

        "   votary .... PALMER
wane ...... ABATE, EBB, FADE, PETER
   " , opposed to .... WAX
wangle .... FINAGLE, WAG
wanigan .... ARK
want .. ABSENCE, LACK, MISS, DESIRE,
               COVET, PENURY
   " of appetite .... ASITIA
wantage .... ULLAGE
wapiti .... DEER, ELK
war .... WEER, FIGHT, CRUSADE
   " agency .... OPA, OSS, OWI
   " bird .... ACE
   " cry .... ALALA
   " machine .... TANK
   " scare .... FLAP
   " trophy .... SCALP
   " vessel CORVETTE, PTBOAT, UBOAT,
          LST, CARACK, MONITOR,
          IRONCLAD, FLATTOP,
          GALLEASS, CRUISER
warble ... SING, CAROL, TRILL, YODEL
warbler .... TITIEN, BUCKPOLE
warbling .... CHIRM, CHIRP
ward ... FEND, FENCE, PARRY, STAVE,
           MINOR, CUSTODY
warden GUARDIAN, RANGER, CURATOR
wardrobe . ALMIRAH, AMBRY, CABINET
warehouse .... MART, DEPOT, ETAPE,
         STORE, GODOWN, ENTREPOT
warfare ... CRUSADE, STRIFE, POLEMY
   " , non-aggressive .. SITZKRIEG
warlike .... MARTIAL, MILITANT
warm ..... BALMY, (RE)HEAT, CALID,
         HUMID, MUGGY, GENIAL
   " , growing .... CALESCENT
   " , keep .... STOVE
   " , make moderately ..... TEPIFY
   " room .... TEPIDARIUM
   " , Spanish for .... CALIENTE
warmed over .... RECHAUFFEE
warmth .. ARDOR, ELAN, ZEAL, TEPOR
   " , per. to .... THERMAL
warn . ADVISE, FLAG, SIGNAL, PREVISE
warning .... ALERT, OMEN, SEMATIC,
        ALARM, CAVEAT, TOCSIN
   " signal .... ALARUM, BEACON,
          BLINKER, SIREN
warp .... BIAS, DISTORT, SWAY
   " in weaving .... CRAM
   " thread .... STAMEN
   " , to .... DEFLECT, CAST
   " yarn .... ABB
warrant ..... ENSURE, PLEVIN, BERAT
warren .... RABBITRY
warrior . TOA, VET, IMPI, KEMP, SPAHI,
     FIGHTER, HESSIAN, GLADIATOR
   " , female .... AMAZON
wars; ancient .... PUNIC

   " ; medieval .... ROSES
warship .... RAZEE, TRIREME, BIREME,
        GALLEON, SULTANA
wart .. PAPILLOMA, TUMOR, ECPHYMA
   " -hog .... SWINE, EMGALLA
wary ... CANNY, CHARY, WISE, ALERT
wash . RENCH, LEACH, TYE, LAUNDER,
        LOSH, LOTION
   " lightly .... RINSE, LAVE
   " out, to ...... ELUTE, ELUTRIATE
washing ..... BATH, LAVAGE, SLUICE
washings .... ELUATE
Washington capital .... OLYMPIA
   " city ... SEATTLE, YAKIMA,
        TACOMA
wasp ...... HORNET, WAMP, DAUBER,
        DIGGER, STINGER, VESPID
wasp nests .... VESPIARIES
waste . IDLE, FRITTER, BANGLE, CHAFF,
      SPILL, RAVAGE, DECAY, DREGS,
   DROSS, CONSUME, REFUSE, ATROPHY
   " fiber .... NOIL
   " , lay .... HAVOC, SACK
wasted .... GAUNT, POOR
wasteful .... PRODIGAL, LAVISH
wasting away ...... TABETIC, TABID,
      MARASMUS, EMACIATION
   " time .... IDLING
wastrel .... ARAB, VAGABOND, WAIF,
      LOSEL, SPENDTHRIFT
watch . EYE, TEND, SPY, GAZE, GLOM,
      STARE, MIND, VIGIL
   " ; as a soldier .... SENTRY
   " chain .... ALBERT
   " , mounted .... VEDETTE
   " pin .... STUD
   " tower .... BEACON, MIRADOR,
      ATALAYA, MIZPAH
watchful ..... ALERT, VIGILANT, WARY
   " guardian .. ARGUS, CERBERUS
watchman SENTINEL, SENTRY, GUARD,
     MINA, SERENO, CHOKIDAR,
     HEIMDAL
watch pocket .... FOB, VEDETTE
watchword ..... SHIBBOLETH, SIGNAL
watchwork, device in .. ESCAPEMENT,
      VERGE, DETENT
water ..... RAIN, SEA, BROO, DILUTE,
      IRRIGATE, SPRINKLE
   " bag .... MUSSUK, MATARA
   " boatman ..... SKIPPER, CORIXA
   " bottle .... CARAFE, CANTEEN
   " channel ..... FLUME, TAILRACE
   " clock .... CLEPSYDRA
   " cocks .... KORAS
   " color .... AQUARELLE
   " course .... FLUX, RACE, WADI,
      CANAL
   " cress .... BILDERS, EKER
   " exhibition .... AQUACADE

" , French for .... EAU
" gauge .... UDOMETER
" hen .... COOT
" jar .... BANGA, LOTA(H)
" -lifting engine ..... NORIA, RAM,
SHADOOF, SAKIETH, TABUT,
TABOOT
" lily ...... NYMPHAEA, LOTUS,
BOBBIN, WOCAS, WOKAS
" mill .... CLOW
" nymph ...... NAIAD, UNDINE
" opening .... GAT
" opossum .... YAPOK
" ousel .... DIPPER
" passage .... SLUICE
" -plant genus .... TRAPA
" rat .... VOLE
" receptacle, eccl. .... FONT
" sapphire .... IOLITE
" , seek .... DOUSE
" , sheet of .... NAPPE
" spirit .... ARIEL, NIX, UNDINE
" , Spanish for .... AGUA
" spout ...... SPATE, GARGOYLE
" sprite ...... KELPIE, NIS, NIXIE
" thrush ..... OUZEL, WAGTAIL
" trench .... LEAT
" wheel ...... DANAIDE, NORIA,
TURBINE, TYMPANUM, SAKIA,
SAKIEH
Water Bearer .... AQUARIUS
waterfall ... LIN(N), LYN, CASCADE,
FOSS, NIAGARA, CATARACT
waterfowl .... PELICAN
wateriness .... AQUOSITY
watering place . OASIS, SPRING, WELL,
EMS, SPA, LIDO, BADEN
waterless .... ANHYDROUS
water-like culture .... LYMPH
watered; Fr. .... MOIRE
watershed .... DIVIDE
waterskin .... MATARA
waterwort .... ELATINE
waterway .... BAYOU, CANAL, RIVER,
SLUICE, CHANNEL, STRAIT
watery AQUEOUS, TEARFUL, SERO(US),
SOGGY, VAPID
" eye ...... EPIPHORA, RHEUM
" portion of animal fluid SERUM
wattle .... DEWLAP, LAPPET, GILL,
CARUNCLE
" tree .... BOREE
wave .. RIPPLE, FLY, SEA, BORE, ONDE,
BILLOW, ROLLER, SIGNAL
" ; comb. form .... ONDO
" , ship a .... POOP
" , tidal .... EAGRE
" , top of a .... CREST
waver .... TEETER, VEER, SWAY
waves' lift .... SCEND

wavy UNDE, ONDY, UNDATE, REPAND,
NEBULE
wax .... CERE, GROW, PELA
" bees, fatty acid of .... CEROTIC
" , candle .... CIERGE
" , cobbler's .... CODE
" , cover with .... CERE
" figure .... CEROPLAST
" match .... VESTA
" ointment .... CERATE
" unguent .... CEROMA
" , yellow .... CERESIN
waxy .... CERAL
" substance; basis of cork......
SUBERIN
way .... VIA, MODE, ROUTE, PATH
" , on the .... AGATE
" out .... EXIT, EGRESS
wayfarer . VIATOR, TRAVELER, PALMER,
PILGRIM, TOURIST
waylay .. AMBUSH, ROB, SEIZE, BESET
we; Lat. .... NOS
weak .. DEBILE, PECCABLE, WAN, FLAT,
PUNY, FAINT, ANEMIC
weaken . PETER, CRAZE, SAP, UNMAN,
WATER, DILUTE, VITIATE
weakfish TOTUAVA, DRUMMER, TROUT
weakling .... PULER, SISSY
weakness .. ASTHENIA, FAULT, FOIBLE
" of an organ ...... ATONY
weal .... SUCCESS, WELFARE, STATE,
STRIPE, WALE, WELT
wealth .... CAPITAL, RICHES
" , mad pursuit of PLUTOMANIA
" , person of .... MAGNATE
" , worship of .... PLUTOLATRY
wealthy ...... FLUSH, HEELED, RICH,
MONIED
weapon ..... ARM(E), CLUB, SWORD,
TOMAHAWK, DAGGER, SPEAR,
LANCE, GUN, GAT, RIFLE
" , long-handled .... VOUGE,
HALBERD
" , medieval ...... CROSSBOW,
GISARME
" , prehistoric .... CELT
" , single-edged .... BOLO
" , wooden .... BOW, MACANA
wear away ...... CHAFE, FRET, FRAY,
ABRADE, ERODE, CORRODE, USE,
RUB
weariness .. ENNUI, FATIGUE, TEDIUM
wearisome .... TEDIOUS, DREE
weary ...... TIRE, BORE, JADE, SPENT
weasel ...... MUSTELA, STOAT, VARE,
OTTER, HURON, VAIR, VISON
" , white .... ERMINE
" -like animal .... MINK, FERRET,
TAYRA, MUSTELINE

weather cock .... FANE, VANE,
        GIROUETTE
   " -map line .... ISOBAR
   " -resisting plywood .... IMPREG
weathers .... SKIES, BRAVES
weave .. ENTWINE, MAT, PLAIT, KNIT,
        SPIN, LOOM
   " together .... PLEXURE
   " twigs .... WATTLE
weaverbird ..... BAYA, TAHA, MAYA,
        OXBIRD
weaving term .. LOOM, SLEY, LEASE,
   LISSE, BOBBIN, COP, LAPPET,
   WOOF, SHUTTLE, LATHE, BEAM,
        RAFFIA
web .. CAUL, TELA, TISSUE, GOSSAMER
web, per. to a ...... RETIARY, TELARY
webbed .... PALMATE
webbing on bird's foot .... PALAMA
wed ESPOUSE, MARRY, MATED, MERGE,
        WIVE
wedding snow .... RICE
wedge .. CAM, COTTER, GIB, SCOTCH,
   QUOIN, JAM, CHOCK, GLUT, GORE,
        GUSSET, SPRAG
   " -like contrivance .... CLEAT
   " -like piece .... EMBOLUS
   " -shaped .... CUNEATE, SPHENOID
Wednesday name source .. WODEN
wee .... LITTLE, SMALL, TINY
weed .... DOCK, TARE, KNAWEL, HOE
   " killer .... HERBICIDE
   " , poisonous .... LOCO
   " , prickly .... BUR
   " , to .... EXTIRPATE
   " , wiry grass .... DARNEL
week SENNET, SENNIGHT, HEBDOMAD
   " day, per. to a .... FERIAL
   " , having intervals of a .. OCTAN
weep ... LAMENT, SOB, ORP, BLUBBER,
        CRY, WAIL, BOOHOO
weeping woman .... NIOBE
weft .... WOOF, WOFT
weigh .... POISE, STUDY
weighing .... TARING
   " machine .... TRONE, SCALE
weight ..... ROTL, HEFT, TON, POISE,
        TROY, LOAD, VALUE
   " allowance .... TRET
   " , Anglo-Ind. ...... SER, TOLA
   " , apothecaries; anc. ... OBOLE
   " , as a load .... CLOG
   " , balance .... RIDER
   " , Burmese .... KYAT
   " , Chinese .. CATTY, HAO, KIN,
      LI, PICUL, TAN, TAEL
   " , clock .... PEISE
   " deducting tare ...... SUTTLE
   " , Denmark .... LOD, ORT
   " down .... BALLAST

   " , Egyptian: anc. .... KAT
   " , English; obs. .... MAST
   " , equal .... ISOBARIC
   " , estimated in terms of.....
        PONDERAL
   " , Hindu .... SER, TAEL
   " , hundred.; Eur. .... CENTAL,
        CENTNER
   " , Madras .... POLLAM
   " measure MINIM, TON, METAGE
   " , metric unit of ...... KILO
   " nightmare .... INCUBUS
   " of Arabia .... DIRHEM
   " of France ... GRAMME, KILO,
        LIVRE, ONCE, SOL
   " of gold in Br. Ind. .... TOLA
   " of Great Britain for coal KEEL
   " of Greece .... MINA
   " of India .... PICE, SER
   " of Japan ...... MO, FUN, RIN
   " of Java .... AMAT
   " of Mongolia .... LAN
   " of one hundred pounds CENTAL
   " of Persia .... SIR
   " of Russia .... DOLA, LOT
   " of Siam .... BAT, CATTY, KATI
   " of Spain .... ARROBA, MARCO
   " of Syria .... COLA
   " , pharmaceutical OBOL, OBOLE
   " ; precious stones ...... CARAT
   " , relating to .... BARIC
   " , Roman; anc. ...... AS, BES
   " , sash-cord .... MOUSE
   " , Straits Settlements .... CHEE
   " , system of .... TROY
   " , Turkish .... OKA, OKE
   " ; wool, cheese, etc. .. CLOVE,
        NAIL, TOD
weighty .... ONEROUS, SOLID
weir ...... DAM, HATCH, LEAP, STOP
weird .. ELDRITCH, EERY, EERIE, UNCO,
        ODD, UNCANNY
weka .... RAIL
weld .... FUSE, SOLDER, UNITE
welfare .... SUCCESS, SELE, WEAL
   " organization .... CARE
welkin .... HEAVEN, SKY
well .... HALE, TRIG, AIN, BIEN,
      FOUNT(AIN), FLOW, SHAFT
   " -boring drill .... JAR
   " -born .... EUGENIC
   " done .... BRAVO, GOOD
   " , feeling .... EUPHORIA
   " , lining of a ...... STEAN, STEEN
   " pit .... SUMP
Welland .... CANAL
Welles; actor .... ORSON
Welsh .. CYMRIC, CYMBRIAN, TAFFY
   " dialect .... CYMRY

311

      "   dog .... CORGI
      "   hamlet .... TREF
welt .... LASH, WALE, STRIP
Welty; novelist .... EUDORA
wen ...... CYST, MOLE, CLYER, TALPA
wend .... GO, PASS, SHIFT, PROCEED
Wend .... SORB
wergild .... ERIC, FINE, CRO
West African .. ASHANTEE, NIGERIAN
W. Indian coral is. .. CAICOS, TURKS
  "   "   fish . BACALAO, CERO, SESI,
                         TANG, BOGA
  "   "   flea ...... CHIGOE, CHIGRE
  "   "   island(s) ...... LEEWARD,
             ANTILLES, BAHAMA, ARUBA,
                 TOBAGO, NEVIS
  "   "   liquor .... MOBBY
  "   "   native .... CARIB
  "   "   remora .... PEGA
  "   "   rodent .... HUTIA
  "   "   shark .... GATA
  "   "   sorcery .... OBE(AH), OBI
  "   "   tree .... CALABA, BONACE,
                          ARALIE
West Indies, music of .... CALYPSO
  "   "   , sugar works of ... USINE
West, Miss .... MAE, REBECCA
West Pointer YEARLING, CADET, PLEB(E)
West Saxon noble .... GODWIN, INE
western .... HESPERIAN, OATER
"Westward Ho" char. .... LEIGH
wet ... SOPPING, DANK, SOAK, MOIST
  " ; as flax .... RET
wether .... CALF, SHEEP
whacky .... MADCAP, WILD
whale .. CETE, CALF, NARWHAL, ORC,
    COW, GRAMPUS, ORCA, BELUGA,
                    RORQUAL
  "   , carcass of .... KRENG
  "   , famous .... MOBY(DICK)
  "   fat .... CETIN
  "   hunter .... AHAB
  "   , morbid secretion in..........
                      AMBERGRIS
  "   -oil cask .... RIER
  "   , strip blubber from ... FLENSE
whalebone .... BALEEN
whales' food .. BRIT, HERRING, SPRAT
  "   , school of ...... GAM, POD
  "   , skin of .... SCULP
wharf ...... DOCK, JETTY, KEY, QUAY
  "   space .... QUAYAGE
  "   , staging upon a ..... STAITH
Wharton, Edith; hero .... FROME
whatnot .. CABINET, ETAGERE, STAND,
                       ANAN
whaup .... CURLEW
wheal .... WALE, STRIPE, WELT
wheat ... DURUM, SUJI, SPELT, EMMER,
                      GRAIN

  "   , beards of .... AWNS
  "   , disease of BUNT, SMUT, ERGOT
  "   , gritty part of ..... SEMOLINA
  "   , head of .... EAR
  "   , outer coat of .... BRAN
  "   , repository for ... MATTAMORE
  "   , substance of .... GLUTEN
wheatear ..... CHACK(ER), ORTOLAN
wheedle .. BAM, BLANDISH, INVEIGLE,
                      COAX
wheel ... DISK, HELM, ROLL, ROTATE,
      SPIN, TIRE, ROWEL, CASTER,
        PULLEY, SHEAVE, COG
  "   check .... SPRAG
  "   , iron tire of .... STRAKE
  "   part .... HUB(CAP), CAM, AXLE,
      NAVE, HOB, RIM, ARBOR,
                    SPOKE
  "   rim, part of .... FELLY
  "   -shaped .... ROTATE, ROTIFORM
  "   , turbine ...... ROTOR, NORIA
whelk .... GASTROPOD, BUCKLE
whelp .... PUPPY
when .... (WHERE)AS, WHILE, THO
where; Fr. .... OU
  "   ; Ger. .... WO
  "   ; Lat. .... UBI
wherefore ...... WHY, BECAUSE
whereness .... UBIETY
wherry .... ROWBOAT
whet .. GRIND, HONE, SHARPEN, EGG
whether .... IF, EITHER
whey of milk .... SERUM
whiff .... GUST, PUFF, WAFT
while ...... WHEN, SPEND, DURING,
             ALBEIT, DAWDLE
whim CAPRICE, FREAK, MAGGOT, TOY,
      CHIMERA, FANCY, QUIRK
whimper .. MEWL, PULE, SNIFF, KEEN
whimsy .. CROTCHET, HUMOR, FANCY
whin ...... FURZE, GORSE, ULEX
whine .. PULE, SNIVEL, YAUP, GROWL
whinny .... HINNY, NEIGH
whip . LASH, CAT, FLAGELLATE, WALE,
    FROTH, KNOUT, QUIRT, DEFEAT,
       PLET, WHISK, CHICOTE
  "   ; Afr. .... KURBASH
  "   mark .... WEAL, WALE
whirl .... REEL, SPIN, GYRATE
whirling .... PIROUETTE, GYRALLY
whirlpool .... GORGE, EDDY, VORTEX,
           SWIRL, MAELSTROM
whisk .... CHOWRY, FLISK, COWTAIL
whiskers ..... BEAR, BARBEL, GOATEE,
                  VIBRISSA
whiskey ... MOONSHINE, FIREWATER,
      HOOCH, ROTGUT, POTEEN
whist term ... MORT, MISERE, TENACE
whit .... DOIT, ATOM, BIT, IOTA, JOT

white ... HOAR, ALABASTER, CHALKY,
    WAN, PALE, SNOWY
   "   ant .... TERMITE, ANAY
   "   filmy clouds .... CIRRI
   "   fish .... ATINGA
   "   , growing .... CANESCENT
   "   lead .... CERUSE
   "   man ... CACHILA, PALEFACE
   "   of egg .... GLAIR
   "   substance .... LININ, DEXTRIN
white-collar girls .... STENOS
whitefish . LAVARET, CISCO, VENDACE
White Friars in London .... ALSATIA
White House designer ...... HOBAN
whiten ... ETIOLATE, ALBIFY, BLANCH
whitish .... ALBESCENT, HOARY
whitlow .... AGNAIL, FELON
Whitman; poet .... WALT
Whitsunday .... PENTECOST
Whittier heroine ...... MAUD, MOLL
whittle .... PARE, CUT, TRIM
whiz .... HUM, WHIRR, PIRR, PURR
whoa; Scot. .... PRUH
whole ...... PURE, UNCUT, ALL, SUM
   " ; comb. form .... TOTI
   "   note .... SEMIBREVE
wholeness ..... ENTIRETY, INTEGRITY
wholly .... ALL, QUITE, SOLELY
whorl .... RAY, VERTICIL, VOLUTE
   " , having a .... SPIRED
wicked ...... EVIL, SINFUL, HEINOUS
wickedness .... BELIAL
wicker basket .... KISH
   "   cradle .... BASSINET
wicket ... ARCH, GATE, HOOP, HATCH
widen .... SPREAD, FLUE, DILATE
widgeon ...... GOOSE, SMEE, WHIM,
    BALDPATE, BLUEBILL, WHISTLER,
    MARECA, POACHER, ZUISIN
widow ...... SKAT, RELICT, SUTTEE
   " , dower right of .. TERCE, MITE
widowhood .... VIDUAGE
wield .... PLY, USE, RULE, SWAY
wife ...... FRAU, RIB, BRIDE, SPOUSE,
    FEMME, MATE, UXOR, CONSORT
   " , bequest to .... DOS, DOT
   " -killer .... UXORICIDE
   " , one .... MONOGAMY
   "   sacrifice .... SUTTEE
wig PERUKE, TOP, TUFT, DIVOT, DOILY,
    TETE, TOUPEE, JASEY, SPENCER,
    SERVAL
wigwam .... TEPEE, HOGAN, TIPI
wild .... UNEXPLORED, FERAL, FERINE,
    REE, FIERCE, SAVAGE
   "   beasts .... ZIM
   "   beasts, collection of.........
    MENAGERIE, ZOO
   "   buffalo .... ARNEE, ARNI
   "   cat .... EYRA, BALU

   "   desolate region .... WASTE
   "   goat .... TAHR, TUR
   " , growing .... AGRARIAN
   "   hog .. BOAR, BABIROUSSA, BENE
   "   honey bee .... DINGAR
   "   horse .... TARTAN, BRUMBY
   "   sheep ... ARGALI, OORIAL, SHA
   "   swan .... ELK
wildebeest .... GNU
wilderness .... FOREST, WASTE, ZIN,
    WILDS
wile ... ART, RUSE, TOY, TRICK, GUILE
will ...... BEHEST, MUN, VOLITION
   "   addition .... CODICIL
   " , convey by .... DEMISE
   " , having made .... TESTATE
William .... LIAM
willing . FAIN, PRONE, BAIN, MINDED
willingly .... GLADLY, LIEF, LIEVE
willow ... SALEX, ITEA, OSIER, TEASER
   "   basket .... PRICKLE
   "   catkin .... RAG
   "   hat .... SALACOT
   " , plaited .... WICKER
   "   twig .... WITHE, SALLOW
willows .... HOLT, SALICETUM
willowy .... SVELTE, SLENDER, SUPPLE
wily ..... ASTUTE, CRAFTY, FOXY, SLY
wince ..... RECOIL, REEL, FLINCH, SHY
wind .... GALE, GUST, BLAST, STORM,
    TRADE, BREEZE, SQUALL
   " , Afr. SIMOOM, SIMOON, SAMIEL
   " , Alpine .... BORA, FOEHN
   " , any .... NOSER, NOTUS
   "   cloud .... SCUD
   " , coastal, of Chile and Peru.....
    SURES
   " , cold .... MISTRAL, PUNA
   " , cold (myth.) . SANSAR, SARSAR
   " , desert .... SIROCCO
   " , dry; northeast ..... BISE, BORA
   " , dry, of Madeira Is. ..... LESTE
   " , east .... EURUS
   " , Egyptian ... KAMSIN, KHAMSIN
   " , equatorial .... TRADE
   "   gauge .... ANEMOMETER
   " , gentle ....AURA, ZEPHYR
   "   instrument .... HORN, BUGLE,
    HELICON, OCARINA
   " , Medit. .... MISTRAL, LEVANTER,
    SOLANO
   " , north .... BOREAS
   " , northeast ...... CAECIAS, GALE
   " , northwest .... ETESIAN
   " , per. to ... ANEMONAL, VENTAL
   " , Peruvian .... PUNA, SURES
   "   rope .... COIL, WOOLD
   " , science of the ... ANEMOLOGY
   " , shelter from the .... LEE
   " , soughing of the .... SOB

    " , south .... AUSTER
" , south; Eur. .... BISE
" , southeast .... EURUS
" , southwest .... AFER, NOTUS
" , southwest, strong ... PAMPERO
" storm, Asiatic .... MONSOON,
                           BURAN
" , strong ... TEMPEST, BIRR, PUNA
" , summer .... AESTAS
" , to .... SINUATE
" , warm, moist ...... CHINOOK
" , west .... FAVONIUS, ZEPHYRUS
" yarn .... WINDLE
windfall ..... BOON, VAIL, FORTUNE
windflower .... ANEMONE
winding . SNAKY, SINUOUS, AMBAGE,
                           SPIRAL
windlass ..... CRAB, CAPSTAN, REEL,
                          WINCH
windmill part ...... GIN, FAN, AWE
window ... FENESTRA, ORIEL, OXEYE,
      DORMER, SKYLIGHT, ROUNDEL,
                     TRANSOM
" part ...... CANE, SASH, SILL
" setter .... GLAZIER
windpipe ...... THROPPLE, WEASAND
" , subdiv. of .... BRONCHUS,
             GUGGLE, STROUP
windrow .... SWATH, TRENCH
winds, father of .... ASTRAEUS
" , god of ...... ADAD, AEOLUS,
      BOREAS, RAMMAN, VAYU,
            EURUS, ADDU
" ; myth. .... SASARS, VENTI
windshake .... ANEMOSIS
Windward is. .... GRENADA, STLUCIA,
                DOMINICA
wine ...... VIN, ASTI, VINO, NEGUS,
    MEDOC, MOSELLE, MUST, TYRE,
          MASSIC, TOKAY
" , bordeaux-type ..... MARGAUX,
                  COSNE
" bottle .... MAGNUM
" , burgundy, white .... CHABLIS
" cask .... BOSS, BUTT, LEAGUER
" , deposit from new ..... GRIFFE
" dipper .... OLPE
" dregs .... MARC, SALIN
" : dry .... SEC
" , ecclesiastical .... TENT
" , Eur. .... MUSCAT
" evaporation .... ULLAGE
" , flavoring of .... DOSAGE
" , French ..... MADEIRA, MEDOC,
                HERMITAGE
" glass .... RUMMER
" , Hungarian .... RUSTER, TOKAY
" , India .... SHRAB
" jug .... OLPE
" , light .... CANARY

" , Madeira .... TINTA
" -making, per. to .. OENOPOETIC
" measure .... PIPE
" measure, Rus. ...... BOUTYLKA
" merchant .... VINTNER
" pitcher .... OLLA, OLLE
" receptacle .... AMA
" , red .... CLARET
" , renews .... STUMS
" sampler .... TASTER
" , sherry ...... OLOROSO, XERES
" shop .... BODEGA, ESTAMINET
" -skin .... ASKOS
" , Sp. .... CHARNECO
" , spiced ..... NECTAR, SANGAREE
" , strength of .... SEVE
" , to make .... VINT
" , unfermented .... MUST
" vessel .. AMA, CRATER, AMPHORE
" , white ... SACK, HOCK, MALAGA
" with honey .... MULSE
wines, study of .... (O)ENOLOGY
wineshop; Sp. .... BODEGA
wing ALULA, ALA, PENNA, PINION, ELL,
    ALETTE, ANNEX, TEGUMEN
" , a; Gr. .... PTERON
" cover .... ELYTRUM
" cover of a beetle .... SHARD
" , equip with .... IMP
" , part of a ..... AILERON, FLANK
winged .... FLEW, AILE, ALATE, ALAR,
                PENNATE
" boots .... TALARIA
" cap of Mercury ..... PETASUS
" elm .... WAHOO
" fruit .... SAMARA
" horse .... PEGASUS
" , two- .... DIPTERAL, VOL
" warrior .... ZETES
wing-footed .... ALIPED
wingless APTERAL, DEALATE, EXALATE
" bird .... APTERYX
wing-like ..... ALAR, PTEROID, PTERIC
wink ...... BAT, NICT(IT)ATE, FLICKER
winner .... ACE, EARNER
" of the Golden Fleece JASON
"Winnie the Pooh" author .... MILNE
winnow .. SIFT, WIM, FAN, CULL, BOLT
Winslow ————— .... HOMER
winter .... HIVER
" , of HIEMAL, HYEMAL, BRUMAL,
                HIBERNAL
" , to .... HIBERNATE
wintergreen PYROLA, TEABERRY, JINKS,
                DRUNKER
"Winter's Tale" char. PERDITA, EMILIA
wipe .... EFFACE, RUB, ERASE, SWAB,
               TAUNT, GIBE
" out ...... ELIMINATE, LIQUIDATE

wire ...... CARD, CABLE, CORD, LEAD,
LINE, CIRCUIT, LAMETTA
" measure .... MIL
" worm .... ELATER, MYRIAPOD
wireless .... RADIO
Wisconsin capital .... MADISON
" county .. DUNN, OCONTO,
PEPIN
" Indian .... SAC
wisdom WIT, LORE, GNOSIS, SAPIENCE
" tooth .... MOLAR
wise .. SAPIENT, SANE, ERUDITE, SAGE,
SAGACIOUS
" man .. SOLON, NESTOR, ORACLE,
SAVANT, SOLOMON, WITAN,
MENTOR
" men of the East MAGI: GASPAR,
MELCHIOR, BALTHASAR
" saying .... ADAGE, REDE
wiseacre .... GOTHAM, SCIOLIST
wish .... YEN, YEARN, ASPIRE, INVOKE
" , tense expressing ..... OPTATIVE
wishbone .... FURCULUM
wisp .... TAIT, WASE
witticism .... MOT, SALLY, SLENT, PUN
wit .... HUMOR, SENSE, TID, WAG
witch ...... HAG, LAMIA, SIREN, HEX,
LILITH, CIRCE, WARLOCK, CRONE,
HECATE, SIBYL, BRUJA
" city .... ENDOR, SALEM
" doctor ..... GOOFER, SHAMAN,
BRUJO
witch-hazel .. PISTACHIO, HAMAMELIS
with speed .... TIVY
withdraw ... AVOID, DISAVOW, QUIT,
RETRACT, SECEDE, RETIRE
wither .. FADE, SERE, DECAY, ATROPHY,
WILT, SHRIVEL
withhold ..... CHECK, ABSTAIN, DENY
within .... INNER, INTO, ON
" ; comb. form END, ENDO, ESO
without .... EXEMPT, EXTERNAL, OHNE,
SANS, SINE, MINUS
" ; comb. form .... ECTO
" fluid .... ANEROID
" polarity .... ASTATIC
" purpose .... IDLY, MINUS
withstand .... LAST, OPPOSE, BIDE
witness .. TESTIFY, ATTEST, RECORDER,
DEPONENT
Witt's planetoid .... EROS
witty .... DROLL, GASH, SHARP
wizard ...SHAMAN, FIEND, SORCERER,
PELLAR, DIVINER, MAGE
wizen .... DRY, WITHER, SHRIVEL
woad .... DYE, INDIGO, ANILE, PASTEL
woe .. BANE, DOLE, MISERY, ANGUISH
wolf COYOTE, LOBO, ISEGRIM, CANID
" , head of a .... HURE
" , Odin's .... GERE, GERI

Wolfe, Thomas; hero .... GANT
wolfhound .... BORZOI, ALAN
wolfish .... LUPINE, RAVENOUS
wolf-like .... THOOID
wolframite .... CAL
wolfsbane ... ACONITE, MONKSHOOD
Wolsey's birthplace .... IPSWICH
wolverine .... CARCAJOU, GLUTTON
woman BURD, DISTAFF, MULIER, FRAU,
FROW, FEMME, CAT, SHE, FEMALE,
MISTRESS, GYNE
" adviser .... EGERIA
" , beautiful BELLE, HOURI, PERI,
VENUS
" , beloved .... INAMORATA
" ; comb. form .... GYN
" , frenzied .... MAENAD
" -hater .... MISOGYNIST
" , killing........... FEMICIDE
" , noble ...... DUCHESS, LADY
" , old CRONE, GAMMER, VECKE,
HAG
" ruler .... MATRIARCH
woman's club .... SOROSIS
" garment .. BODICE, NEGLIGEE
wombat BADGER, MARSUPIAL, DIDELPH
women's apartments; Gr. ... THALAMI
wonder .. AWE, RARITY, MUSE, MARVEL
" , world .... PHAROS
wonderful .. MIRIFIC, UNIQUE, DANDY
wont ..... HABIT, HAUNT, USE, DESIRE
woo .... COURT, SPARK, SUE
wood . BOIS, FOREST, ALERCE, LUMBER,
TIMBER, HOLT
" , a large collection of ... TREES
" , billet of .... SPRAG
" block, small ..... DOOK, NOG
" ; comb. form .... LIGN(O)
" demon .... NAT
" drug, bitter .... QUASSIA
" dust .... COOM, COOMB
" , East Indian KOKRA, ENG, SAL,
SATIN
" , flexible; obs. .... EDDER
" gum .... XYLAN
" , hard ..... NARRA, COCOBOLO,
EBONY
" hen .... WEKA
" hoopoe ..... PICARIAN, IRRISOR
" horse .... TRESTLE
" hyacinth .... SCILLA, HAREBELL,
SQUILL
" , Ind. .... SISSOO
" : ironwood of Pegu ...... ACLE
" louse .... PALMER, SLATER
" , mottled streak in .... ROE
" or grove; per. to ... NEMORAL
" overlaying .... VENEER
" peg in boat .... THOLE
" pin .... NOG, FID, SPILE

315

"	pores, one of the cortical ..... LENTICEL	
"	sage .... AMBROSE	
"	screen .... BLINDAGE	
"	shoe .... PATTEN	
"	sorrel ... LUJULA, OXALIS, OCA	
"	stand, top of .... CRISS	
"	stork .... IBIS	
"	, strip of .. BATTEN, LATH, LATT, SPLINE	
"	support, in a mine COG, NOG	
"	tar oil .... CREOSOTE	
"	used for cabinet work ... YEW	
"	wheel brake .... SPRAG	

woodbine .... CREEPER, HONEYSUCKLE
woodchat .... SHRIKE
woodchuck .. MARMOT, MONA, SUSLIK
woodcock-like bird .... SNIPE
wooded landscape .... BOSCAGE
wooden .... TREEN

"	brick .... NOG	
"	bowl .... KITTY, MAZER	
"	hanger .... STANG	
"	shoe .... CLOG, SABOT	
"	vessel .... PIGGIN	

woodland deity PAN, SATYR, SILENUS, FAUN, SILVANUS
woodpecker ..... YAFFLE, AWL, CHAB, FLICKER

"	-like .... JACAMAR	

woodpeckers; genus .... PICUS
woods ...... GROVE, SYLVA, MOTT(E)
woodwind .... OBOE, BASSOON
woody .... LIGNEOUS, XYLOID

"	tissue .... XYLEM, LIGNUM	
"	vines; genus .... HEDERA	

woof ....ABB, WEFT, FABRIC
wool ..... DOWN, GARE, YARN, HAIR, FLEECE

"	blemish .... MOTE	
"	, comb .... CARD	
"	, combing of .... NOIL	
"	fabric ... SERGE, TRICOT, BEIGE, DELAINE, HERNANI	
"	fat .... LANOLIN	
"	, fatty substance from sheep .... SUINT	
"	, inferior .... CLEAMER	
"	, knot of .... NEP, NOIL	
"	measure .... HEER	
"	, old weight for .... TOD	
"	on sheep's leg .... GARE	
"	package .... FADGE	
"	, remove foreign substance from GARNETT	
"	, short .... BROKE	
"	, twisted roll of .... BLUB	
"	, unravel .... TEASE	

woolen cloth .. (E)TAMINE, DOESKIN, SARCILIS, KERSEY

"	blanket, coarse .... COTTA	
"	" strainer ... TAMIS, TAMMY	
"	fabric..... ARMURE, TARTAN, CASHA	
"	goods MOREEN, YERGA, SATARA	
"	goods remade ...... SHODDY	
"	twilled stuff .. RATINE, SERGE	
"	vest .... LINDER	

wooly .. LANOSE, LANATE, FLOCCOSE, SOFT

"	covering.............. FLEECE	

word ..... NEWS, TERM, VERB, IDIOM, LOGOS, PAROL, RHEMA, PLEDGE

"	book .... LEXICON	
"	: deletion of last letter APOCOPE	
"	derived from another PARONYM	
"	, figurative use of a...... TROPE	
"	-for-word .... LITERAL	
"	having same sound but other meaning ..... HOMOMORPH, HOMOPHONE	
"	, imitative .... ONOMATOPE	
"	, last syllable of .... ULTIMA	
"	, magical .... SESAME, PRESTO	
"	, misuse of .... MALAPROP	
"	of honor ...... PLEDGE, PAROLE	
"	of sanction .... YEA, AMEN	
"	, omission of middle letter of a SYNCOPE	
"	opposite in meaning . ANTONYM	
"	put for another ..... METONYM	
"	puzzle .. CHARADE, ANAGRAM, REBUS, ACROSTIC	
"	, repetition of a .... PLOCE	
"	, root form of a ...... ETYMON	
"	sign .... LOGOGRAM	
"	square .... PALINDROME	
"	that unites .... COPULA	
"	, unknown-meaning ..... SELAH	
"	, vowel omission in .... APHESIS	

wordiness ..... PLEONASM, PROLIXITY, VERBIAGE
words, doctrine of .... NEOLOGY

"	, loss of appropriate .. APHASIA	
"	, per. to shortening of APHETIC	
"	, play upon .... PUN	
"	spelled alike but pronounced differently .... HETERONYMS	
"	, spiritual meaning of ANAGOGE	

wordy ..... WINDY, PROLIX, VERBOSE
work .. EFFORT, ERGON, JOB, (CO)ACT, RUN, STINT, TRAVAIL, FAG, MOIL, OPUS, LABOR, OEUVRE

"	, disposition toward.... ERGASIA	
"	hard MINE, MUG, TOIL, PEG, PLY, MUCK, OPERATE	
"	shift .... SWING, GRAVEYARD	

″ , unit of .... ERG, KILERG
″ unskillfully .... PINGLE
″ with black inlay .... NIELLO
workbag .... RETICULE
worker(s) CREW, HAND, PEON, VOLK,
                            OPERATOR, CAGER
workhorse .... CAPO
workman ARTISAN, LABORER, NAVVY,
                                 ROTO
″ replacing a striker .... RAT
workshop ...... LAB, ATELIER, PLANT,
                      STUDIO, MILL, FACTORY
world ...... COSMOS, EARTH, GLOBE,
            UNIVERSE, LOKA, MONDE, WARL
″ , the great .... MACROCOSM
″ -wide .... ECUMENIC, PANDEMIC,
                         PLANETARY
World War I group ...... AEF, AMEX
″   ″ II area .... ETO
worldly . MUNDANE, TERRENE, CARNAL,
         LAIC, MORTAL, LAY, SECULAR
World's Fair site ... OSAKA, SEATTLE,
        PARIS, GHENT, CHICAGO,
        MONTREAL, VIENNA
world's largest land mass .. EURASIA
worm ...... SINUATE, ANNELID, NAID,
        LURG, ESS, LEECH, NEMATODE,
                  INCH, TERMITE
″ , earth- .... MAD
″ , edible .... PALOLO
″ , fluke .... PLAICE
″ , mud .... LOA
″ , round .... ASCARID
″ , ship .... BORER TEREDO
″ , silk- .... ERIA
″ , snail-like .... SLUG
″ that infects eye .... LOA
″ , thread .... FILARIA
″ track .... NEREITE
worm-eating mammal .... MOLE
worms, class of .... NEMERTINEA
″ ; larval stage .... CERCARIA
wormwood ...... MOXA, SANTONICA
worn .... SERE, ATTERED, TRITE
″ away ABRADED, ATTRITE, EATEN,
                          EROSE
″ out ...... JADED, SPENT, EFFETE,
                    PASSE, SEEDY
worry BAIT, FRET, CADDLE, HARRY, VEX,
           STEW, CARE, FAZE, RUX
worrying .... CARKING
worship ..... SERVE, HONOR, REVERE,
        ADORE, DULIA, HOMAGE
″ , place of .... ALTAR
″ , system of .... CULT, FETISH,
                      RITUAL
worst .... BEAT, BEST, ROUT
worth .... MERIT, VALUE, VALOR
″ , thing of little .... STIVER

worthless .. PUTID, RACA, RAP, FUTILE,
                   PALTRY, SCURVY
″ fellow .. BUM, JAVEL, LOSEL
″ leaving .... TRASH
″ rock .... SLAG, GANGUE
wound LESION, RIST, SCATHE, TRAUMA,
           VULN, OFFEND, INJURE
″ , discharge from a .... ICHOR,
                        SANIES
″ , lint roll to dilate a .... TENT
woven with variegated color DAMASSE
wrack ..... SEAWARE, SEAWEED, KELP
wraith .... APPARITION, SPECTRE
wrap . CAPE, CERE, SWATHE, FURL, LAP,
                      SWADDLE
″ fishing line with wire .. GANGE
″ , long loose .... PELISSE, FARDEL
″ up .... ENROL, MOS
wrapper TILLOT, PEIGNOIR, ENVELOPE
wrapping machine .... BALER
wrasse ... CUNNER, SEAWIFE, BALLAN
wrath .... ANGER, RAGE, IRE, CHOLER
wreath ANADEM, CROWN, LEI, TORSE,
        CHAPLET, CIRCLET, GARLAND,
                FESTOON, INFULA
″ of laurel .... IRESINE
wreck .... RUIN, SMASH, RAZE, UNDO
wreckage .... FLOTSAM, JETSAM
wrench ... SPRAIN, WRAMP, SPANNER,
                 TWIST, JERK, YANK
wrest .. ELICIT, REND, GARBLE, WRING
wrestle .... TUSSLE
wrestling hold .... (HALF)NELSON
″ , place for .... PALESTRA
″ , throw in ...... HIPE, HYPE
″ trick .... CHIP
wretch ... PARIAH, CULLION, CAITIFF,
                    RONION
wretched .... PALTRY, SAD, YEMER
wriggling .... EELY
wrinkle .. RIMPLE, RUCK, SEAM, RUGA,
                CREASE, PUCKER
wrinkled RUGATE, RUGOUS, RUGOSE,
                CORRUGATED
wrinkles, free from .... ERUGATE
wrist ...... CARPUS, SHACKLE(BONE)
″ -bone .... CARPAL
″ guard .... BRACER
writ .. PONE, TESTE, PROCESS, VENIRE,
                  MANDAMUS
″ , judicial ..... CAPE, ELICIT, TALES
″ of execution .... ELEGIT
″ , order for .... BREVE, PRECIPE
″ to bring to court ..... SUBPOENA
write .. TOOTLE, INDIE, PEN, SCRAWL,
                  SCRIVE, TYPE
writer ...... POET, AUTHOR, PENMAN,
                PROSER, SCRIBE

writing BOOK, HAND, OPUS, LEGEND, POEM, STORY, TEXT
" instrument STYLUS, PEN(CIL), QUILL, PLUME
" on the wall .... MENE, TEKEL, UPHARSIN
" used in ancient mss. UNCIAL
writing desk .... ESCRITOIRE
written, not .... ORAL
" , under- .... SUBSCRIPT
wrong ... EVIL, SIN, WRY, VICE, HURT, MALA, TORT, AMISS, FAULTY
wroth .... IRED, IREFUL
wryneck .. LOXIA, TORTICOLLIS, WEET, SNAKEBIRD
" ; genus .... IYNX
Wyclif, disciple of ... HUSS, LOLLARD
Wyoming city ..... LARAMIE, LANDER, CASPER
" Rockies .... TETONS

X

X .... TEN
xanthic acid, salt of ...... XANTHATE
Xanthippe's husband ..... SOCRATES
xanthous ..... YELLOW, MONGOLIAN
Xavier; Span. Jesuit .... FRANCIS
xenos .... ALIEN, STRANGE
xerotic .... DRY
xylem .... HADROME
xylonite .... CELLULOID
xylophone ...... MARIMBA, GIGELIRA, SARON, GAMELANG, BALAFO, VIBRAHARP

Y

Y, letter .... WYE
y-clept .... CALLED, NAMED
yacare CROCODILE, CAIMAN, CAYMAN
yacht pennant .... BURGER
yaffle .... WOODPECKER
yak .... SARLAK, SARLYK
Yalta palace .... LIVADIA
" , sea near MARMARA, MARMORA, BLACK
Yale .... ELI
yam HOI, UBE, UBI, UVE, UVI, INAMIA, TUGUI, IGNAME
" bean .... KAMAS, WAYAKA
yang, opposite of .... YIN
Yangtse River .... KIANG

yap .... BARK, YELP
yard GARTH, HOPPET, TYE, CURTILEGE, CURTAIN
" measure .... VERGE
yards .... SPARS
" , 1¼ .... ELL
yarn .... STORY, TALE, THREAD
" ball .... CLEW
" , bleached .... SPINEL
" , conical roll of .... COP
" for the warp .... ABB
" measure ...... CLUE, CLEW, LEA
" , skein of .... HANK, RAP
" spindle .... HASP
" , to wind .... WARP
" , twisted .... CREWEL, FOX
" waste .... THRUM
" winder .... PIRNER
yarrow .... MILFOIL, SNEEZEWORT, ALLHEAL
yaupon .. CASSINE, HOLLY, CASSENA, CASINA
yaw .... DEVIATE, TUMOR
yawl .... DRANE, DANDY, MIZZEN
yawn GAPE, OSCITATE, CHASM, GANE, GANT
yawning .... OSCITANT, AGAPE
yaws .... FRAMBESIA
ye .... THEE, THOU, YOU
yea .... PRO, AFFIRM, FOR
year; Fr. .... ANNEE
" ; Ger. .... JAHR
" ; Mayan .... HAAB
yearly ANNUAL, ETESIAN, PERANNUM
" excess .... EPACT
" payment .... CENS
yearn .. HANKER, WISH, CRAVE, FLAG, PINE, LONG, ACHE
years, one thousand .... CHILIAD
" ; Latin .... ANNI
yeast .. BARM, LEAVEN, FERMENT, KOJI, LOB, ANAMITE
yell .... CHEER, GOWL
yellow .. CHROME, ECRU, GULL, JAUNE
" alloy .. AICH, BRASS, SEMILOR
" ; as butter .... BLAKE
" bugle .... EVE, IVA
" calla .... AROID
" , canary .... MELINE
" color, of a pale BUFF, FLAXEN
" , deep .... SAFFRON
" dyestuff .... MORIN, MARTIUS
" iris .... DAGGERS, SEDGE
" , king's .... ORPIMENT
" ochre .... SIL
" , pale-, pigment ..... ETIOLIN
" pome-like fruit ..... AZAROLE
" pond lily .... KELP
" race .... MONGOL

Yellow River .... HWANGHO
yellowbird ...... GOLDFINCH, GOLDY
yellowhammer .. SKITE, YITE, FLICKER,
FINCH, GLADDY
Yellowhammer State ...... ALABAMA
yellowish .... SANDY, SALLOW
    "   brown .... TAN
    "   catechu .... GAMBIER
    "   crystal substance ... MORIN
    "   green .... OLIVE
    "   -green mineral .... EPIDOTE
    "   powder .... TANNOGEN
yelp BARK, YIP, YAP, YAUP, CRY, YAWP,
KIYI
Yemen capital........ SANA, SANAA
    "   city DHAMAR, MOCHA, DAMAR
    "   ruler .... IMAM
yen .... DESIRE, HANKER, YEARN
yercum, bark yielding .... MUDAR
yes; Fr. .... OUI
 " ; Ger. .... JA
 " ; Russ. .... DA
 " ; Span. .... SI
yet .... AGAIN, BUT, STILL, EEN
yew CONIFER, HEMLOCK, CHINWOOD
yield (CON)CEDE, LOSE, RELENT, CROP,
VAIL, SOFTEN, DEFER
    "   gold .... PAN
yoga BHAKTI, HATHA, INANA, KARMA
yogi .... SWAMI
yoke GANGUE, PILLORY, BANGY, BOND,
TEAM, COUPLE
yokel   BOOR, BUMPKIN, HICK, RUSTIC,
OAF, RUBE
yolk of egg .... YELLOW
yore .... AGO, ELD, ERST
young .... FRESH, GREEN
    "   animal .. CUB, PUP, COLT, GILT,
JOEY, STOT, WELP, FILLY, SHOAT
    "   hare .... LEVERET
    "   herring .... BRIT
    "   oyster .... SPAT
    "   squab .... PIPER
younger son .... CADET
youngster BABY, LAD, TAD, TOT, KID,
BOY, GIRL, YOUTH, SHAVER,
YONKER, GOSSOON
youth .... LAD, TEEN, ALADDIN
youthful .. BOYISH, MAIDEN, NEANIC
Yuan .... TAEL
Yucatán Indian .... MAYA
yucca ...... SOTOL, PALMA, PALMITO,
LILIUM
Yugoslav .... CROAT, SERB, SLOVENE
    "   capital BELGRADE, BEOGRAD
    "   seaport .... POLA
    "   silver coin .... DINAR
    "   town .... PIROT
Yugoslavia is. .... PAGO

    "   , leader of .... TITO
    "   , province in .... BANAT
    "   , river in ..... UNA, DRINA
Yum-Yum's friend KOKO, NANKIPOO
Yutang .... LIN

Z

Z, letter .... ZEE, ZED, IZZARD
Zagreus .... DIONYSUS
Zambal .... MALAY
    "   , language of the ...... TINO
Zambales, capital of .... IBA
zany ..... FOOL, BUFFOON, CLOWN,
SAWNEY, BADAUD, GABY, POOP,
COMIC, ANTIC, JESTER
Zanzibar sultan .... SAYID
zarf .... CUP, HOLDER
zeal ... ARDOR, FERVOR, ELAN, ZEST,
GUSTO, RELISH
zealot .... DEVOTEE, PARTISAN, FAN,
BUFF, BIGOT, FANATIC, VOTARY
zealous .... AVID
zebra ...... QUAGGA, EQUID, DAUW
    "   wood .... ARAROBA
zenana .... HAREM, SERAGLIO
zenith .. ACME, APEX, PEAK, APOGEE,
HEYDEY, PRIME
    "   , opposite of .... NADIR
Zeno's daughter .... PROSERPINA
    "   follower .... STOIC
zero CIPHER, NAUGHT, NIL, NOTHING,
BLANK, NUL(L)
    "   _____ .... HOUR
Zerulah's son .... ABISHAI
zest . FLAVOR, RELISH, TASTE, GUSTO,
GLEE, RAPTURE, KICK, TANG
zestful .... SAVORY, SAPID
Zeus, attendant of .... NIKE
    "   , attribute of .... AEGIS
    "   , brother of .... HADES
    "   , consort of .... HERA
    "   , epithet of .... AMMON, SOTER,
TELEIOS
    "   , festival for .... NEMEAN
    "   , messenger of .... IRIS
    "   , mother of .... RHEA
    "   , oracle seat of ...... DODONA
    "   , princess beloved by .. EUROPA
    "   , sister of .... HERA
    "   , son of . AEACUS, APOLLO, ARES,
PERSEUS, HERMES
    "   , surname of .... ALASTOR
    "   , wife of .. DIONE, HERA, LETO,
MAIA, METIS, THEMIS
zigzag .. CHEVRON, CRANKLE, AWRY,
TRAVERSE

zinc .... TUTENAG, SPELTER
   " alloy .... BIDRI, PAKTONG
   " -and-copper alloy .... OROIDE
   " silicate .... CALAMINE
zingel .... PERCH, PERCID
Zionist clergyman .... VOLIVO
zip .... HISS, SIBILATE, PEP, SNAP
zipper .... TALON
zither ..... ROTA, CANUN, KANOON,
                      GALEMPONG
zizany .... COCKLE, TARES
Zobeide, half-sister of ...... AMINA
zodiac .... BALDRIC, BALDRICK
   " sign .... PISCES, LEO, LIBRA,
       SCORPIO, GEMINI, RAM, CANCER,
       TAURUS, ARCHER, BULL, TWINS,
       FISHES, VIRGIN, SCALES
   " , 10° degree division of......
                      DECAN
Zola; author .... EMILE
   " novel ... NANA, TERRE, VERITE,
                      DEBACLE
zone . ISLE, BELT, CLIME, GIRTH, TRACT

zoogeographic division .... EOGAEA
zoographies .... BESTIARIES
zooid of a coral growth ... POLYPITE
zoological vessel .... ARK
zoril .... POLECAT, ZORILLA, MARIPUT
Zoroaster commentator ...... ZEND
Zoroastrian .... PARSEE, PARSI, YEMA,
                     MAZDAIST
zounds .... OONS
zuche .... STUMP
Zuider _____ .... ZEE
zuisin .... WIDGEON
zule; her. .... ROOK
Zulu army .... IMPI
   " king .... CETEWAYO
   " marauder .... VITI
   " meeting .... INDABA
   " spear .... ASSAGAI
Zululand capital .... ESHOWE
zymogen, substance actuating a.....
                     KINASE
zymome .... GLUTENIN